No Time to Quit

by

Janelle Wootton McQuitty

No Time to Quit

Pioneer America
Seen through the Life of Rocky Mountain Man
Richens Lacy "Uncle Dick" Wootton

© 2017, 2018 Janelle Wootton McQuitty

All Rights Reserved

Published by Janelle Wootton McQuitty LLC

New Mexico, United States of America

Printed by Createspace

Second Edition, 2018

ISBN: 978-0-9988385-1-9

Dedicated to Jack McQuitty, Sr.

Researched and written for my children, grandchildren,
and the generations following—and for yours—
that the story of our heritage not be lost

With Gratitude

Jack McQuitty, Sr., for miles driven, for pouring through indexes and microfilm, for encouragement and support during years of research and writing, for all the times you came when I called, "Do you have a minute?"

My parents, Johnnie and Eileen Wootton—my source of interest in history, precision, learning, and communication

Lin Harris, Barb Lukow, and Don Snell for critiques

Research librarians—especially those at New Mexico State Library; Denver Public Library; and Pueblo, Colorado's Rawlins Library

Those who taught me, instilling diligence and integrity in their areas of expertise: Philomae Rago, Verna Walker, Elizabeth Wilson, Cone J. Munsey, Mrs. Viles, Dave Richert, Mrs. Scott, Dorothy McGuire, Vic Malone, Mrs. Milligan, Mrs. Johnson, Dora Robertson, Ruth K. Stark, Helen Lancaster, Betty Vivian, and Verl DeSpain

Bill Dorris III, Robert Wootton, Margaret Wilson, and Glenna Lawrence, who shared photos of their "long-ago" grandparents

Many, now deceased, whose conversations or correspondence aided research. This story is richer, more alive, because of them.

Grandpa Wootton—Uncle Dick Wootton's son John, who carried his father's legacy to his children. Although he, like his son Johnnie, Jr., was primarily an oral historian, he left a little paper trail of photographs and clippings.

Contents

Preface   i

Prologue   iii

Story

Independence	1
Wagons West	3
A New World	7
Working for the Company	10
Land of Opportunity	15
Five Thousand Miles	19
1840-1841	23
New Mexico and the Republic of Texas	26
El Pueblo Days	31
Hunting, Trading, and Trapping	36
Manifest Destiny and the Mexican-American War	41
Revolt	50
Battle of Taos	57
Important Matters	61
Navajo Country	63
Growing Pains	66
What Are Friends For?	69
Close Call	71
Peace Loving Grizzlies?	75
White Massacre	76
Trading with the Comanche	79
Old Spanish Mines	80
Missouri by Horseback	82
California	83
Huerfano Village	88
Rustlers, Thieves, and Frontier Justice	92
El Pueblo Massacre 1854	94
Change of Plans	99
Ft. Barclay and Ft. Union	101
Cross-Country Freighting	103
Freighting into Mormon Country	110
Headed Home	112
On the Banks of Cherry Creek	114

Christmas	116
Growth, Organization, and Politics	118
Pike's Peak or Bust	121
Frontier Newspaper	123
It'll Be Okay After All	125
New Year 1860	131
Exit States, Enter Territory	134
Civil War Rides West	139
Battle of Glorieta	141
Loyalty Costs	144
The Southwest Has Troubles of Its Own	148
Grit	150
Sand Creek	156
No Time to Quit	160
Raton Pass	163
Trinidad, Colorado	166
The Trinidad War	169
Battle of Beecher Island	171
Goodbye, Old Friends	175
A New Road and a New Home	177
Battle of Summit Springs	179
This 'n That, 1869-1871	180
Back at the Ranch	183
Last Buffalo Hunt	186
Ute Rebellion and Meeker Massacre 1878	188
Not All Is Strife in the Midst of Wars	190
Maxwell Land Grant and the Colfax County War	191
Iron Horse Race	198
Changes	203
Family	205
Better Write It Down	207
Hoodlums in the House	208
End of the Frontier	210

Sketches

Biographical Sketches	215

   (Albert, Autobees, Baca, Baker, Barclay, Beard, Beaubien, Beckwourth, Bent, Bridger, Brown, Carson, Chalifoux, Claymore, Doyle, Fisher, Fitzpatrick, Guerrier, Hatcher, Hicklin, Kinkead, Kroenig, LeDuc, LeFevre, Leroux, L'Esperance, Maxwell, Metcalf, New, Owens, Ryder, Sabille, St. Vrain, Silva, Simpson, Tharp, Tobin, Towne, Turley, Waters, Watrous, Williams; Canby, Doniphan, Johnston, Price Sibley; Morley, Robinson, Strong; Beshoar, Byers)

Bent St Vrain & Company	272

The Westward Movement: Exploration	274
Trails: El Camino Real; Old Spanish Trail; Goodnight Trail	279
Santa Fe Trail	281
Western Indians	300
Indians and Newcomers	306
Indian Wars	311
Mail and the Pony Express	317
Railroads	319
Raton Pass	327
Dick Wootton's Family	329
Simple List of Uncle Dick's Ancestors	340
Raton Pass House in Later Years	342

Album (See Illustrations, Maps, and Photos below)   343

Timeline   389

1816-1893 events pertaining to Dick Wootton, the Southwest, the United States, a few major world events and later dates relevant to Raton Pass or Dick's family

Illustrations, Photos

Printed sources from the author's collection are noted in parenthesis; date is listed once. Further information may be found in the bibliography.

Federal Hall, New York (McMaster, 1897)	iv
Charles Bent; Ceran St. Vrain (Conard, 1890)	2
Wagon Circle (Conard)	3
Buffalo, small herd	6
Bent's Fort	9
Bent's Fort, store	14
Old Customs House on the Santa Fe Trail	30
Kit Carson (Conard)	41
Commanders in the Mexican War (Jameson, 1899)	49
Statesmen of the Middle Period (Jameson)	67
Lucien Maxwell (Conard)	69
Ute Village (Conard)	74
Wagon Mound	78
Joseph Doyle; William Kroenig (Conard)	89
George Simpson (Conard)	100
Denver's First Cabin (Conard)	116
Denver 1859 (Conard)	130
Jim Baker (Conard)	132
Confederate Generals (Jameson)	136

Generals of the Civil War (Jameson)	137
Stagecoach (Hurd, 1921)	138
Emigrants Attacked (Conard)	154
Portion of Wootton's Raton Pass Road (early 1900's postcard)	162
Father Munnecom	167
Chief Conniach (Conard)	169
Buffalo Soldiers	174
House where Kit Carson died (Bradley, September 1912)	175
Trinidad Youth	185
Buffalo	186
Chief Ouray (Conard)	189
A.T. & S. F. Tunnel through the Raton Mountains	202
Ida Wootton and a friend	206
Uncle Dick's book	207
Funeral Card	211
Auguste "Gus" Claymore (Conard)	237
W. B. Strong, Lewis Kingman, W. R. Morley (Bradley, 1914, 1915)	269
Bent's Fort	273
Adobe House	289
End of the Santa Fe Trail (Hurd)	299
Albuquerque Depot 1880 (Ernest Hall, 1921)	299
Chipeta (Conard)	305
Uncle Dick's Raton Pass Road	328
Uncle Dick at home (Conard)	345
Mary Pauline Lujan Wootton c 1871	346
Uncle Dick wearing trapper garb	347
Mary Pauline Wootton	348
Wootton homes on Raton Pass	349
Wootton Ranch	350
Uncle Dick Wootton, from a tintype	351
Mary Pauline Wootton, widow	352
Uncle Dick "Cuthand" Wootton with granddaughter	353
Eliza Wootton Walker	354
Hon. R. L. Wootton, Jr.	355
Uncle Dick Wootton; Mrs. Wootton and her mother	356
Young; funeral card; R.L. Wootton, Jr.; M. P. and Fidelis Wootton	357
Lucy, John, and Mary Wootton	358
John, Fidelis, Frank, and Jesse Wootton	359
Ida, John, Frank, and Jesse Wootton	360
Mrs. (Ida) Felix Baca	361
Alec and Lucy Wootton Meiklejohn	362
Ida Wootton Baca; Lucy Wootton Meiklejohn and son	363
Elizabeth Fuss Wootton	364

Wootton, Baca, Meiklejohn	365
May Tynes Wootton	366
Ida and Felix Baca and daughters; Felix and Bert Baca	367
May, Frank, Richens Wootton; Under-sheriff John Wootton, Sr.	368
John Wootton, Sr.; John Wootton, Sr. and granddaughter	369
Fannie Brame Wootton	370
David Christopher Wootton, Jr. and family	372
Alexander James Wootton	373
Jesus Maria Lujan; Sheriff Teodoro Abeyta; Dr. Michael Beshoar	374
Mrs. Frank Sivyer and children	375
Mrs. George McBride and daughters	376
Mr. and Mrs. Rocco Motto	377
Baldwin Locomotive: "Uncle Dick"; Mrs. Wootton's home	378
Jesse Wootton, linotype operator	379
Deaf Reunion, Colorado School for the Deaf and Blind	380
Wootton Family fishing picnic c1909	381
Chicago 1833 (Montgomery, 1910)	405
Howe's first sewing machine (McMaster)	417
Port of Entry on Raton Pass	477

Maps

US 1789 (McMaster)	iv
US 1792 (Montgomery)	v
1820 Missouri Compromise (Montgomery)	vii
Erie Canal (Montgomery)	viii
Independent Trappers 5,000 Mile Expedition (adapted)	19
The First Pacific (Transcontinental) Railroad (Montgomery)	178
Santa Fe Trail (Hurd; Inman, 1914)	382
Routes of Early Explorers (McMaster)	383
US 1826 (McMaster)	384
US 1851 (McMaster)	385
US 1860 (McMaster)	386
US July 1861 (McMaster)	387
US 1893 (McMaster adapted)	388
Cumberland/National Road (Montgomery)	393

Bibliography 479

Index 489

Preface

Day-by-day we write with the ink of the present on the annals of time. Some will not understand the choices we make, the thoughts we think, the lives we live. Sometimes we don't understand ourselves. But when we hand the pen of life to others, it will be, not to rewrite our history, but to write their own—to write a better history, if they can. It is up to each individual to profit from the past, whether by enjoying the benefits or by not repeating the undesirable. Each life writes its own page.

"A hundred times a day, I remind myself that my inner and outer life are based on the labors of other men, living and dead, and that I must exert myself in order to give in the same measure as I have received." (Albert Einstein)

Sands of time obliterate the record of most individual lives, but a few survive. Stories of Richens Lacy Wootton, later dubbed Uncle Dick, represent a slice of life during the pioneering years of the United States of America. "The varied roles he played during his active career involved him in so many different activities that his life story constitutes a fair approach to an encyclopaedia of life on the Southwestern American frontier."[1]

The first time I was asked about the man, I explained, "He's my Daddy's Daddy's Daddy."

For years I listened. When I saw that many accounts blurred fact and fiction pertaining to my great-grandfather—Dick Wootton, I began to collect facts for my children. Others asked for information. I searched deeper and found not only more of Dick's story, but also that of his generation of pioneers. Research spanned a twenty-five year period. The past ten years taught me to set aside "my" that I might present the man, his place and time—"wart freckles, and all"—a peephole view of those who paved paths before us when our nation was young. I have included not only well-known, but also little-known lives and have attempted to present these people according to their places and times—their outlook, whether I or anyone else agrees with their times and perspective or not. It is not my purpose to take sides, but to present America's pioneers as recorded in history or as remembered by those who knew them. It is the story of a man, people of his era, and of their young nation, the United States of America.

There were fewer state lines as the story begins. Names of approximate present-day state, county, or town locations may be included in parenthesis.

Janelle Wootton McQuitty

---

[1] Conard, *Uncle Dick Wootton*, 1980, back cover.

Inscription

Prologue

On a spring day in Southern Virginia, David and Fannie Wootton placed their firstborn in his cradle. They'd married in Mecklenburg County, Virginia, February 28, 1815. There, on Monday, May 6, 1816, their broad-faced, blue-eyed son was born. He was the first grandchild on Fannie's side. As was Southern custom, they named him Richens Lacy for Fannie's father, Richens. The name came into the family more than 125 years earlier, after Fannie's great-great-great-grandfather John Brim (Brame) and his neighbor John Richens fought side-by-side in Bacon's Rebellion.

David and Fannie's families were Scotch-English—a sturdy stock. Seldom, if ever, did their generational mothers or their babies die as a result of childbirth. The fathers weren't men of particular renown, but men from both families had aided the patriot cause during the American Revolution. David and Fannie were the first generation in their family lines to be born in the independent infant nation, the United States of America. Their families sowed opportunity, whether in the field as planters, in the House of Burgesses as representatives, in the church as people of faith and action, or on the sea as transporters. For the most part, they were people of the soil, but not bound to one piece of land.

David's Wootton ancestors—stalwart Scotsmen with strong convictions—had sailed to Virginia from Scotland soon after David's grandfather Samuel was born in 1726.[2] Fannie's people had been in Virginia since 1638. Though some were prominent in Jamestown, hers were a people who did whatever became necessary to settle a new land. One ancestor came with money, another as a 12-year-old orphan who worked his way across the Atlantic Ocean.

When David Christopher Wootton was born in Boydton Parish, Mecklenburg County, Virginia, in 1789, only five U. S. cities boasted a population of 8,000 or more: Baltimore, Boston, Charleston, Philadelphia, and New York. There were only a few dirt roads for horse and buggy travel. There was no unified national currency.

Two years before David's birth, the nation's founding fathers met in Philadelphia, put their heads together, dipped their quills in ink, and drafted the U. S. Constitution. They hoped to replace the Articles of Confederation and bolster the nation as a Union of states.

Most states had ratified the Constitution by the time David was born. In April 1789 they chose George Washington as president. People gathered to celebrate and greet him as he rode through their small communities on his way to New York City. He was aware of the gravity of his position, of the importance of laying the foundation of the nation. Standing on the Senate chamber balcony in New York on April 30th, he took the presidential oath with his left hand on an open Bible and his right hand raised toward Heaven. With solemnity, he added, "So help me, God!" and kissed the Bible. He was serving his second term when Fannie was born in Mecklenburg County, June 14, 1795.

---

[2] After James Edward Steward, "the Old Pretender," fled and before his son Bonnie Prince Charlie rose to lead the Scots against English rule.

Federal Hall, New York

THE UNITED STATES March 4, 1789

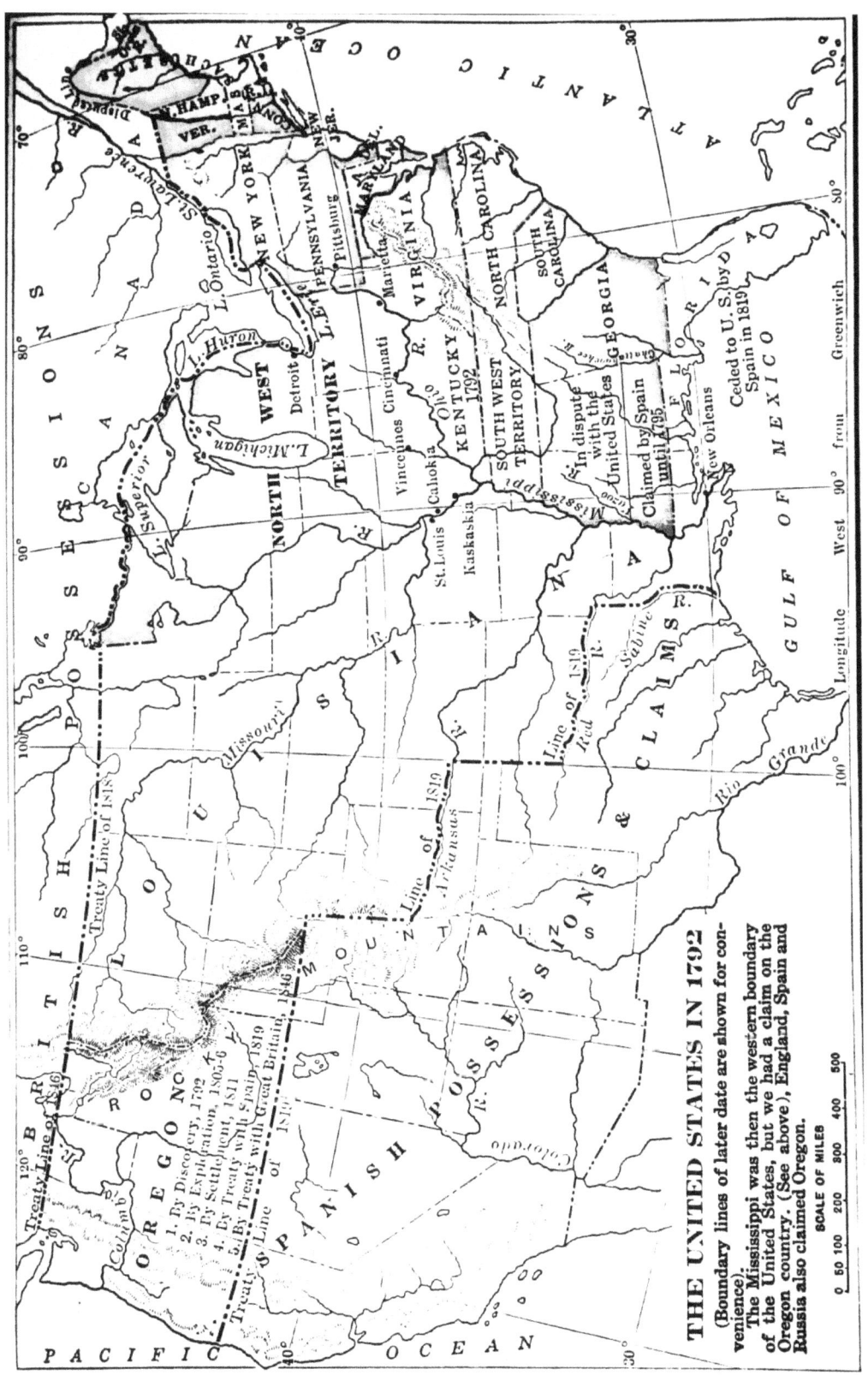

David was third of nine children, Fannie the oldest of ten. They were blessed with an abundance of kin. In Mecklenburg County a family of five to twelve children was common.

Throughout the young United States in 1816, children were growing up. Among them were: Marcus Whitman, Ceran St. Vrain (age, 14); Robert E. Lee, Asa Packer (11); Henry W. Longfellow (9); Salmon P. Chase, Jefferson Davis, Andrew Johnson (8); Abe Lincoln, William Bent, Kit Carson, Cyrus McCormick, Edgar Allen Poe (7); Phineas Taylor Barnum (6); Horace Greeley, Harriet E. Beecher (5); Samuel Colt (2).

What would become of their generation? Of the young nation? What would each child add to or subtract from his nation, from his fellow man?

The United States showed signs of progress. Eli Whitney had already invented the cotton gin. Daniel Boone had forged west to Missouri. Robert Fulton's "Clermont" had shown the capability of a steam-powered ship. Opportunity abounded in education, science, religion, industry, medicine, transportation, politics, the arts, and on the frontier.

In June 1816 two large snowstorms killed people and livestock in New England and Canada. 1816 became known as the "Year with No Summer." In the U. S. some called it "Eighteen Hundred and Froze to Death"; others called it "Poverty Year."[3]

Although David Wootton was a tobacco planter, the weather didn't affect him as much in Virginia as it did farmers in New England, where temperatures often rose to a normal summer high during the day, then dropped to near freezing at night. New York and Connecticut recorded frosts every month in 1816. Some lakes and rivers as far south as Pennsylvania had ice in midsummer. A few crops were harvested, but nights weren't warm enough to ripen corn. Shortages hiked prices. The past few years hadn't been easy for New England farmers, but this blow sent them packing. Primary farming focus shifted to the Midwest. New England focused on industry.

James Monroe won the U. S. Presidential election in December 1816. The White House was under reconstruction because of the British attack during the War of 1812, which some referred to as the second war for independence. Many northerners opposed the war, which hurt, even ruined some New England merchants. It had been two years since the Treaty of Ghent (December 24, 1814) ended the war. Sections of the nation were still bitter; so, in the summer of 1817, President Monroe donned his Revolutionary soldier garb and toured the northern states. Seeing him reminded patriots of times they fought side-by-side for freedom. They remembered Monroe's unblemished record, his honest purpose, and welcomed him. He encouraged them to value the Union over sectional interests.

Richens Wootton's brother John Christopher was born in 1817, his sister Mary Catherine in 1818. She was named for both grandmothers. The month after her birth, Illinois became a state. Ohio, Vermont, Kentucky, Tennessee, Louisiana, Indiana, and Mississippi had already been added to the original thirteen.

U. S. Major Stephen H. Long explored the U. S.'s western land in 1819-1820 and concluded that people depending on agriculture could not survive in the West. He labeled the land "The Great American Desert." His opinion was printed as fact in textbooks, taught to schoolchildren, and believed by the general public for years. But there have always been a

---

[3] The volcanic eruption of Mount Tabora in 1815 was the main influence on weather patterns in 1816.

few intrepid souls, adventurous spirits who choose to find out for themselves.

Near the end of 1819 Congress admitted Alabama as a state, but couldn't decide about Maine and Missouri. They were embroiled in the discussion when Richens' brother Thomas was born on David and Fannie's fifth wedding anniversary in 1820. Fannie now had four children, who were four years of age and under.

A little over two weeks later Congress agreed on the Missouri Compromise, quieting sectional rivalry for the time being. The same year, 1820, the federal government imposed the death penalty for importing African slaves. The first black slaves arrived in the U. S. in 1619. At that time and for decades afterward the colonies had more indentured servants than slaves. However, Southern farmers began to rely on African slave labor. In the early 1800's the use of slave labor increased with the invention of the cotton gin and the need for cotton in Northern manufacturing.

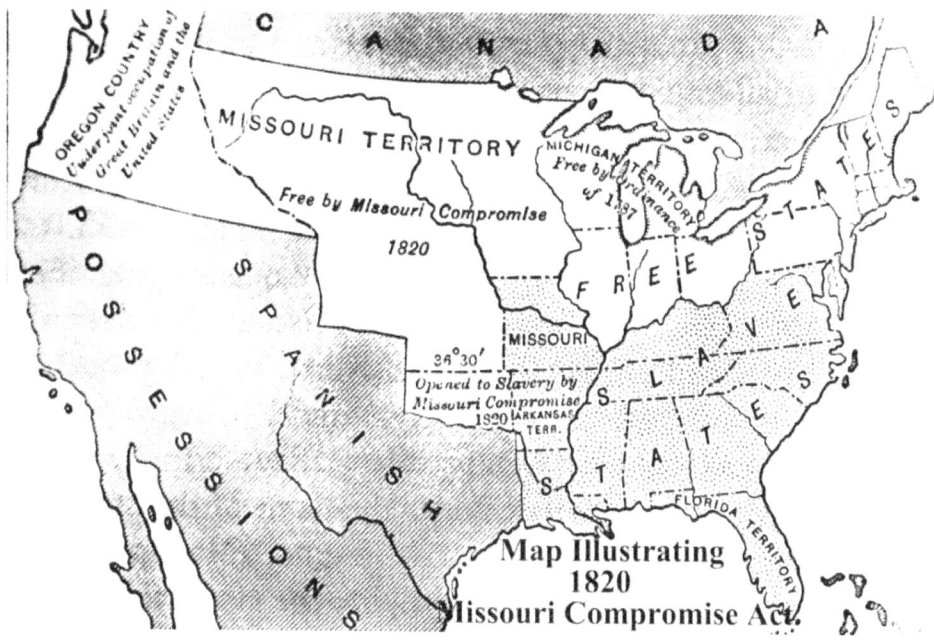

Mexico wrested independence from Spain in 1821 and took Spain's Southwestern lands. Mexico welcomed the daring or desperate men who opened Santa Fe Trail trade between the U. S. and Santa Fe, the capital of Mexico's New Mexico borderland settlement. Santa Fe Trail trade bolstered hope and began to nourish the young U. S., which had been hit hard by the War of 1812-14, "Poverty Year" (1816), and then a financial panic in 1819.

Richens was five-and-a-half when Santa Fe welcomed traders. He was six when his brother David Christopher, Jr. was born, eight when brother William arrived on Christmas Day 1824, ten at the birth of brother Alexander James, and twelve when brother Samuel was born.

Growing up on the family's small plantation, Richens obtained a good education, in books and—except for the time he chopped off half of two fingers on his left hand—in everyday know-how. Once healed, Richens never allowed the loss of his fingers to interfere with his riding, shooting, or life. At an early age, he and his siblings were taught to ride and manage a team. Boys who grew up in Virginia at that time were taught to shoot a rifle well enough to shoot a squirrel in the eye; thus, there was no waste of meat, fur, or ammunition.

Whether through personality or childhood training, Richens would never be one to pity his losses. He seemed to figure the closing of one door allowed him opportunity to open another. He grew up familiar with the concept of Providence and the sovereignty of God. Many of Fannie's forefathers were Christ Church folk. David and she raised their family in the Scottish Presbyterian faith and lived with faith in God and in Jesus Christ as their personal Savior.

Congress passed the Tariff of Abominations in early 1828; President Adams signed his approval in May. Northern industrialists appreciated the tariff help; but Southern farmers were angry they had to pay higher prices on manufactured goods without any help on their farm prices. The pots of sectional rivalry heated once again.

In January 1830 Congressmen Daniel Webster and Robert Hayne spent the better part of two weeks debating the issue of states' rights. Richens' brother Powell was born that year.

In the West the Santa Fe Trail trade prospered. In the Northeast the Erie Canal opened travel and shipping to some interior areas of the country. While the canal was under construction (1818-1825), folks shook their heads and complained about Governor De Witt Clinton's "Big Ditch"—such a waste of hard earned money.[4] Once the use of the canal began to save travel time and draw commerce into New York City and pay for itself, folks began singing a different tune. It had cost ten dollars to ship a barrel of flour from Albany to Buffalo (New York); it cost thirty cents via the canal. A trip that had taken three weeks was reduced to one week. Towns began springing up along the Canal.

The Erie Canal

Every now and then an individual or family from Virginia moved to a less settled area. Friends or family often followed. Other times a group moved en masse to an unsettled area and built a new community. Brame-Wootton relatives pioneered in Mississippi, Georgia, Alabama, Kentucky, Missouri, and Texas. David and Fannie Wootton chose Christian County, Kentucky. David's brother-in-law and sister James and Nancy Coleman and a few other kinfolk were already there. In the summer of 1830 they sold their Virginia land and moved to Christian County, where they again joined a group of Presbyterians. Richens was

---

[4] It cost $7,143,789—almost half as much as the whole Louisiana Purchase (about $15,000,000).

fourteen.

David raised tobacco as he'd done in Virginia.

Less than 100 miles from where the Woottons had lived in Virginia, Nat Turner, a literate slave, led a rebellion in August of 1831. Slaves killed about 56 "whites," including Nat's owner, Joseph Travis, and family. The Virginia Militia quelled the uprising and captured and hung about twenty slaves. The public—some out of fear, others out of anger—killed about a hundred more. Turner was found a few weeks later and hung. As a result of the rebellion, the Virginia legislature tightened slave laws. The laws stopped united rebellion, but not individual acts.

Congress approved another tariff in mid-1832. On November 18, South Carolina declared the tariff null and void and threatened to secede from the Union on February 1, 1833, if the government tried to collect that tariff or the tariff of 1828. In early 1833 Henry Clay, Kentucky's Virginia-born representative, helped negotiate the Compromise Tariff of 1833. It provided a reduction in tariffs over the next nine years. By the end of that time the maximum tariff allowed would not exceed twenty percent. Known as the Great Compromiser or Great Pacificator, Clay, time and again, negotiated between differing sectional interest groups, and helped preserve the Union from being ripped apart on his watch.

Meanwhile, the Woottons added daughter Eliza Ann and welcomed relatives. Fannie's father and mother, Richens and Catherine Brame, and all of Fannie's siblings—except John T.—moved with their families from Mecklenburg County, Virginia, to Christian County, Kentucky.[5] Fannie's Uncle Joseph and Aunt Jane Brame, their children, and their families came along with Fannie's parents. Her Uncle James Dabney Brame, whom the family called Dabney, had moved to Mississippi.[6]

Soon after the extended family arrived, seventeen-year-old Richens agreed to work for Uncle Dabney and said goodbye to the folks at home. Dabney's Mississippi plantation was about 250-270 miles southwest of the Wootton home. There Richens had opportunity to expand his business understanding. While he was there, his brother Joseph Edward was born. His youngest sibling, Frances, was born two years later.

In early 1835 news arrived that Richard Lawrence had attempted to assassinate President Jackson on January 30, 1835. Fortunately, his gun misfired.

As spring approached, Richens considered life on his own, finished his business in Mississippi, and traveled northwest—about 475 miles—to Boone County, Missouri. There news of the West abounded.

Richens listened.

He not only heard that trappers and traders were multiplying profits, but also, if a man was willing to work, he could exchange labor for a ticket West. In May 1836 Richens headed for Independence, Missouri,[7] the eastern terminus of the Santa Fe Trail.

---

[5] Fannie's brother William later established a plantation in present-day Paris, Texas.
[6] Dabney, the same age as David Wootton, established a cotton plantation. In time he owned about 100,000 acres of cotton in Pontotoc County, Mississippi.
[7] Franklin, Missouri had been the Trail's eastern terminus. By 1836 the terminus moved about 100 miles west to Independence, Missouri.

Richens Lacy "Uncle Dick" Wootton
His Story

Independence

Six-foot-six, just turned twenty, Richens Wootton stepped into Independence in May 1836. The bustling little Missouri settlement was the new gateway to the West. Richens knew some called western country the Great American Desert, but he'd also heard of the land's opportunity.

He had decided. He was going across "The Desert." If he could find a Santa Fe Trail wagon train that could use a hand, he'd work his way west. A fifty-seven-wagon train with a crew of about 150 had left for Santa Fe the day before.

Though he didn't weigh quite 200 pounds, Richens had meat and muscle enough on his bones for a young man ready to work. While he wasn't enamored with work, he was always one to pitch in and do at least his fair share. His large hands had long—not thick, not thin—fingers, except for those last two accident-stubbed fingers on his left hand. His hands and head were accustomed to work; he preferred work that incorporated both.

Quick-witted, he enjoyed the humorous side of things. His deep-set blue eyes were accustomed to seeing, observing. His full, thin-lipped mouth generally waited for his eyes to give understanding before he spoke. Once he knew what he wanted to say, he spoke his mind and convictions and stood by them.

Richens knew what he wanted; so he'd come to Independence. The way he had it figured, he'd work hard. In five years or less he should have enough capital to return home to Kentucky and begin a comfortable life. In the meantime, he'd see some new sights and enjoy what adventures came his way.

He saw a dark-haired man preparing a seven-wagon train for the Trail going West. When he met Charles Bent—a man almost a foot shorter than he and seventeen years his senior, Richens Wootton had no idea of the impact Charles, his brother William, and their partner, Ceran St. Vrain, would have on his life. Many men who wrote their names in the sands of the nineteenth century Southwest began their careers with Bent-St. Vrain & Company.

Charles and William and Ceran settled in the Southwest in the 1820's. In recent years, they'd formed a partnership to work the Santa Fe and Indian trades. By 1836 they owned stores in Santa Fe and Taos, New Mexico,[8] and Bent's Fort on the U. S.-Mexican border, near

---

[8] Taos/San Fernandez de Taos is in a valley about seventy miles northeast of Santa Fe. To survive Indian attacks, most New Mexicans lived in towns or villages and farmed surrounding fields. Women carried water from a stream near town. Men cut firewood in the foothills and stacked it precariously wide and high on the backs of burros and led them into town. Loose animals were common in Taos and Santa Fe.

Taos structures were built of adobe. Some had varying degrees of gypsum coating, from freshly coated to done at one time. Home sizes ranged from a single room to a walled home with central courtyard and gated entry, wide enough to admit a carriage. Windows were small. Some were covered with mica. Others were open and covered, as needed, with what the residents had on hand. There was no window glass.

present-day La Junta, Colorado. Its locale facilitated trade with Indians, trappers, and traders.

Charles Bent **Ceran St. Vrain**

William traded at the fort, traveled to Indian encampments, and sent company traders to Indian camps.[9] Charles, in charge of company supply trains and the Taos store,[10] made at least one trip to the States and back each year.[11] He often visited the fort, but made few trips among the Indians. Ceran sometimes accompanied a company supply train to and from Missouri, but his primary sphere was the Santa Fe trade. He operated the Santa Fe store and sometimes took goods further south into Mexico proper. To facilitate business, he'd become a Mexican citizen in 1831.[12]

As Richens Wootton and Charles Bent talked, Bent told him that he planned to catch up with the fifty-seven wagon train before he reached the most troublesome area of Indian country. When Richens asked if he could use a hand, Mr. Bent allowed he could use a young greenhorn muleskinner.

Richens signed on for the trip of a lifetime.

---

[9] They traded primarily with Arapaho, Comanche, Kiowa, Ute, Pawnee, Sioux, and Cheyenne, but also with Nez Perce, Blackfoot, Flathead, and Crow in Colorado, Kansas, Wyoming, Nebraska, South Dakota, and Texas.

[10] Bent's store was on the south side of Taos Plaza. In the late 1700's and early 1800's, Taos was the hub of southwestern trapping. There trappers outfitted and left to work rivers and streams—the Pecos, Gila, Colorado, and others. They returned to sell furs and enjoy community life.

[11] Bent-St. Vrain purchased goods from Missouri to the Atlantic, from England, and mainland Europe.

[12] When Mexico gained independence from Spain in 1821, it took Spain's New Mexico Territory, which included present-day Arizona and parts of other states. New Mexico was a territory of Mexico, never a state.

Wagons West

At dawn the following morning, Richens and the other muleskinners hitched the mules to the wagons and waited. At Bent's call, "Stretch out!" each muleskinner climbed up onto a wagon seat and geed the mules. Wheels creaked as heavy-laden wagons rolled westward.

Travelers on the Santa Fe Trail followed signs left by previous wagons and kept a sharp watch for landmarks: hills, mountains, creeks, rocks, river crossings. Some distant landmarks could be seen a day or more in advance. But the Santa Fe Trail was just a trail, not an improved road.

Richens hadn't traveled far before men of the train decided "Richens" wasn't much of a name to carry West. They shortened it to Dick, and the name stuck.

It took about ten days for the train to reach Neosho River Crossing at Council Grove (eastern Kansas).[13] With good grass, good water, and places to rest, the miles between Independence and Council Grove were the easiest part of the trip though they were sometimes muddy in spring.

Bent's small train soon caught up with the fifty-seven-wagon Santa Fe train, which had left earlier.

Each time the train stopped for the night, wagons were pulled together in a close circle.

If camped in a particularly troublesome area, the men brought animals inside the wagon circle. Otherwise, they picketed them outside the circle to graze. At bedtime the crew

---

[13] Trains stopped at Council Grove to make needed repairs, get any needed parts or supplies, and rest before heading across Indian territory.

stretched out on the ground inside the circle and slept, rifles by their sides. A few men stood guard beyond the wagon circle. Each man took his turn. Dick said the mules themselves were pretty good guards. They slept lightly and snorted when an Indian or wild animal came near.

The train hadn't had any Indian trouble before Dick's name came up for guard duty. The train was camped on the banks of Little Cow Creek (Kansas). Freighting was new business to him, but day-by-day he'd paid attention and stood in pretty good stead with the travel-seasoned men. Their simple instruction to him when it came his turn to guard was: shoot anything—any moving thing—beyond the furthest line of the mules. Dick lay down on the ground at his post, but he wasn't about to sleep. He said he couldn't have slept if he'd tried. An occasional animal sound or pesky mosquito quashed the great alone sound of silence in the vast open country. Only the moon and a few stars delineated shapes in the blackness.

It was after midnight—somewhere between one and two—when Dick heard something. He watched. Something out there, about seventy yards off, was stealing toward camp. His first thought was Indians. But he didn't jump the gun. In the darkness he couldn't tell for sure. Was it a savage? Maybe a wild animal. He thought it over. Whatever it was didn't belong there. He was guard. He wouldn't take a chance. He blasted gun powder into the darkness. The form dropped. At the sound of Dick's shot, the camp came alive. Men jumped out of their blankets, grabbed their guns, and came running. Dick told them he thought he'd killed an Indian. There seemed to be no others, but guards remained in place while men cautiously stepped to examine the quiet form. From his post Dick heard someone exclaim, "I'll be cussed if he haint killed Old Jack [a lead mule]."[14]

Oh! How the men razzed him. He took it good-naturedly and laughed at his own expense. He said he didn't allow the incident to disturb him because, after all, that mule had disobeyed orders wandering off like it did.

Miles later, Dick encountered his first real Indian attack when the train was camped across Pawnee Fork Crossing in Comanche country. Comanche were superb horsemen and, at this time, always fought on horseback. They seldom fought at night, but it was an exceptionally bright moonlit night. Like other Indians, they commonly yelled or let out war whoops, skillfully using sight and sound to instill fear, when they attacked. About 250-300 yelling, whooping Comanche descended on the train, shooting in rapid fire, attempting to break through the train's corral and stampede the animals. Some braves shot muskets, firing slugs or copper balls. Others wielded pole spears with long steel butcher-knife-like blades. The rest masterfully aimed and shot whizzing arrows—some of flint, some of steel. After three or four attempts to break through the train circle barricade, the Comanche retreated under heavy fire. Dick lived to see many Indians in many places, in various circumstances, but he never forgot the fierce faces of his first encounter.

Next morning at the call, "Stretch out!" all men, mules, and horses were accounted for, none lost in the night's attack.

A few days later, near Coon Creek, they met a large party of travelers enroute to Missouri. They camped, enjoyed the company, and continued on their journey. Rolling along at about fifteen miles per day, the wagons arrived at The Caches about four days later. The men had

---

[14] Conard, *Uncle Dick Wootton*, 1980: 26.

begun to notice sign of Indians in the sand hills south of the Arkansas River. Every now and then a wisp of smoke caught their attention.

As they traveled next day, seventeen-year-old Jim Hobbs, another greenhorn muleskinner traveling with Bent's train, saw a buffalo cow and shot at it with his pistol. The animal just moseyed along and swam across the river. The crew enjoyed that about as much as they would have enjoyed biting into a piece of the meat. Riled by their laughter and razzing, Jim determined to bring that cow back for supper. He grabbed his rifle, and called out for John Baptiste, a young mule packer, to bring his mule along to help haul the meat. The boys hurried after the buffalo.

Bent hollered for Hobbs and Baptiste to let the buffalo be. He knew the smoke in the sand hills meant Indians and had seen the cow heading that direction. He ordered the boys, "Come back!" But the boys either didn't hear or didn't heed. Darkness set in. When Hobbs and Baptiste hadn't returned by daylight, Bent and a search party went looking for them. No corpses. But tracks told the story: the boys got their buffalo, but the Comanche got Jim Hobbs and John Baptiste. By the tracks, the men knew the boys were long gone, knew the Indians would have traveled far with them by now. Even if they could make up the time and close in on the Indians, their party would be no match for that large Indian band. The somber searchers reluctantly returned to the wagons, disturbed when the call came to stretch out and roll.[15]

A short distance later, at the Cimarron Crossing, the fifty-seven-wagon train turned to travel toward Santa Fe on the Cimarron Cut-Off.

There were two main branches of the Santa Fe Trail: the Mountain Branch and the Cimarron Cut-Off (Dry Branch). Although the Cimarron Cut-Off was shorter than the Mountain Branch, the route offered more Indian trouble and less water than the Mountain Branch. Evading those two problems would have made it worth traveling the extra miles on the Mountain Branch, except for Raton Pass. The tedious crossing over the Raton Mountains could cost days or weeks, depending on the weather. Raton Pass had a reputation for wrecking wagons that got away and ran down an incline or rolled off a precipice. Although individuals, and occasionally wagons, did cross Raton Pass, the Dry Branch was the common route of choice for wagon trains.

Those who traveled the Cimarron Route had a few Arkansas River crossings from which to choose; choice depended on the depth of water at the time. Although part of the riverbed might be dry or shallow, there were also deep channels and beds of quicksand, which sometimes swallowed a stranded animal or wagon. If a wagon stuck solid in midstream, traders transferred the wagon's load to pack animals or another wagon in order to free the stranded wagon. Sometimes men had to dismantle a wagon and carry it out of the river piece by piece.

Because some channels required draft animals to swim part of the way, traders often repacked their wagons before crossing. They put items on the bottom that could survive a soaking. Then they yoked up extra oxen or mules—ten, twenty, on occasion up to fifty yoke

---

[15] Hobbs and Baptiste survived. Hobbs lived among the Comanche until released to a company of hunters and trappers in 1839.

per wagon, as many as they figured necessary to pull each wagon, considering the load and conditions. With extra animals, some would always be pulling, while others swam.

Those who traveled the Cimarron Cut-Off learned to fill enough barrels with water to last at least two days after crossing the Arkansas River. George E. Vanderwalker, a Santa Fe Trail bullwhacker, said the group he traveled with carried ten-gallon kegs of water on the reach poles at the rear of their wagons.

If wagons traveled a long dry spell, drivers stopped a good way off from known water sources to unhitch their draft animals. If they didn't, the thirsty animals would sense water, rush off, and pull the wagon toward the water—often bogging wagons in mud.

Charles Bent and his seven-wagon train continued on the Mountain Route, which followed the Arkansas River all the way to Bent's Fort. Along this stretch Dick killed his first buffalo—didn't do anything for his financial goal, but it was a new venture and one that provided meat for the train.

A few buffalo in Colorado

A New World

Dick sighted Bent's Fort. From opposite corners of the massive fortress two circular bastions stood watch over the vast prairie. They afforded a 360 degree view of the surrounding plain at all times. The fort's brown adobe walls stood seventeen or eighteen feet high. When mountain men, trappers, and traders first caught sight of Southwestern settlements, some thought they looked like mud settlements. They were correct. Most Southwestern buildings were made of adobe. Homes were made of adobe mud blocks, top to bottom. Dick had never seen adobe.

As the train neared the fort, a party of mounted men, with Ceran St. Vrain in the lead, rode out to meet them. They'd been expecting Charles' return and, accustomed to vigilance, had seen his train in the distance.

The men exchanged news from the States, from Santa Fe, Taos, and the fort: News from the States: It looks like Congress is going to make a state out of Arkansas, may have already. In New Mexico, Navajo are raiding settlements again. Governor Perez is going to get after them.

The train passed an Indian camp. The fort was located in an area frequented by several tribes; so it was common for hundreds of tepees to dot the surrounding area for days. Small groups or whole bands with thousands of tepees would camp outside the wall while they traded or had conferences. Indians lived where they were and moved on when they were done.

It was a new sight for Dick. He took it all in as the train rolled toward the fort. This would be his country until he gathered enough to return home. He'd arranged to stay on at the fort and work as a hunter to help supply the daily fare.

The population of Bent's Fort fluctuated. At times there were up to 150 working in and out of the fort; but the usual number was sixty to a hundred. In addition, there were itinerant folk—travelers, trappers, traders. It was common to need daily provisions for 200; the main fare was wild game.

Mules pulled the seven-wagon train through the fort's open gates and stopped.

Dick stepped into a new world.

From Independence to the Pacific there was no place like Bent's Fort for planning, precision, and supply. The whole place, except for timber posts, beams, and gates, was made of adobe bricks. The heavy outer gates were iron-sheathed wood. St. Vrain and the Bents had brought men from Taos, New Mexico, to make the adobe on site. They'd mixed mud with grass and cheap wool for stability, formed the mud into bricks, and cured them in the sun.

Adobe blocks were made in various sizes. Those at the fort were four to six inches thick, about nine inches wide, and eighteen inches long. The workmen mortared them together with clay. The outer walls were about six feet thick at the base. No pitched roofs. The flat roofs were graveled on top. It was something, this mud castle on the Plains.[16]

Dick noticed a variety of people without knowing their distinct nationalities. The laughter and play of children and the clank and buzz of work being done in the fort joined the sounds of the prairie's grasses, bugs, and birds. Sure seemed to be enough animals around—dogs, chickens, turkeys, magpies, peacocks, mockingbirds, pigeons, sheep, goats, cows, oxen, and plenty of mules. Women dressed different here; some wore hides—tanned leather of sorts. Others wore cloth skirts, all right, but not long enough to cover their ankles. Many employees had Spanish, Mexican, or Indian wives who lived at the fort. Dick couldn't understand what everyone was saying. He heard the nasal French, the musical Spanish, the short, guttural Indian language; maybe there was more than one Indian dialect. He couldn't tell. All he knew was English and a few words he'd picked up on the Trail.

In the center of the fort was a plaza courtyard, about ninety to a hundred feet square. Except for necessary passageways, the plaza was surrounded by a veranda supported by log post columns. Behind the veranda were about twenty-five rooms whose doors opened toward the plaza. Walls were plastered. The hard packed dirt floors were sprinkled with water several times a day to keep them from becoming dusty. It made them almost as hard as brick. Large vigas/logs spanned the space between walls to support the mud roofs. On the average, the rooms were about 300 square feet.

Adobe buildings remain cooler in summer and require less heat in winter than frame or brick structures, but most rooms had a fireplace. People cooked in their quarters unless they ate from the common mess. Charlotte Green, the Bents' black slave from St. Louis, cooked for the owners' dining room.[17] Her husband, Dick, and brother-in-law Andrew also worked at the fort.

There seemed to be rooms for everything—quarters for the carpenter, blacksmith, other workers, and boarders; the tailor's room; carpentry and blacksmith shops; a kitchen and a room for the cook; a council room; warehouses; a store; a barbershop; an ice house; and quarters for the owners. St. Vrain's was upstairs, the Bents' downstairs.

The room for the new billiard table brought in this year was upstairs, as were quarters for guests, trappers, traders, and hunters—that's where Dick would sleep. Across from that common sleeping room was the office for company clerks.

Upstairs, the bastions rose about thirty feet in the sky. Each bastion was manned and equipped with a small cannon. Armed guards walked along the battlements, constantly patrolling. To William Bent vigilance was part of the price of peace. It nipped trouble in the bud and allowed the peaceful flow of life enjoyed at Bent's Fort.

Downstairs, near the entrance, was a nine foot interior passage, wide enough for wagons to drive through to the wagon house and yard in the rear. Twelve to fifteen large wagons could be sheltered in the wagon house to await repair or to be kept safe. Animals could be housed there in case of attack though large animals were generally kept in the large corral,

---

[16] Estimations of the size of Bent's Fort vary. Thomas J. Farnham's, who visited in 1839 estimated it to be about 100'x150'. Three years later Matthew Field estimated that 200 men and 300-400 animals could live within the fort walls. Ceran St. Vrain said the fort and corral were each 180' square.

[17] The owners' dining room was set with linen cloths.

which shared the back wall of the wagon house. The corral fence was only six to eight feet high, but cacti planted thickly along the top of the adobe fence discouraged intruders. Each spring the walls seemed to burst into color when the cacti bloomed white and brilliant red.

The well was in the center of the plaza. The water was good. A buffalo hide press stood nearby. Each evening the brass cannon Dick had seen outside the main gate was pulled inside the plaza. Each morning it was taken back out—just another safety measure.

The floor of the small, short—almost square—watchtower upstairs formed the roof over the fort's vestibule-type entrance. It had a window on each side. The powerful telescope mounted inside could be turned to view any direction. A belfry stood atop the watchtower. Towering above the belfry, an American flag flew freely. The partners were Americans and the fort was within the bounds of U. S. territory on land that was part of the 1803 Louisiana Purchase.

Top: Entry; Bottom: Interior, of the restored Bent's Fort, near La Junta, Colorado

Working for the Company

A few days after his arrival, Dick began to hunt. He supplied buffalo, venison, or bear, as requested, but primarily buffalo. The Plains were so full of buffalo that, at times, it looked "as though the prairies themselves were on the move."[18] Dick hunted by day; by night he schooled himself in the ways of mountain men.

Bent's Fort, which reflected the southern hospitality of its owners, was an oasis to travelers. Trappers and traders stopped for supplies, stayed a few days, a few weeks, or a season. To many, Bent's Fort became a home away from home—a place where frontiersmen were bound with a common bond. In the evenings men sat around playing checkers, cards, or billiards, swapping stories, chewing the fat, forming friendships that bonded closer than many families. At the fort they heard news from the States, made repairs, and restocked before heading back out to work. It was an ideal place for one who wanted to learn.

Dick listened.

Many men worked their way West on Bent-St. Vrain wagon trains or worked for the company when they arrived and at various times thereafter when a well of life ran dry or low. Some remained company men for years. There was work to fit 'most anyone's liking. Company employees traveled back and forth to the States with company trains, taking pelts and returning with supplies. They hunted, raised livestock, did day-to-day maintenance—repaired wagons, pressed hides, cooked, cleaned, sewed, barbered, did carpentry or blacksmith work, gathered fuel. One old fellow kept busy just hauling extra water from the river and hauling trash out of the fort. Others tended store or kept the books, while others went out to barter in Indian camps.

Only chiefs were allowed into the interior of the fort. Other Indians, only a few at a time, were permitted entrance through the front gate into the large vestibule-type passage, which led to the plaza. Purchases were made through a shuttered window that opened to the company store.

Interests didn't vary much from tribe to tribe. They wanted manufactured goods—axes, guns, knives, and kettles. They liked vermilion and lead pigments, in addition to or in place of native dyes. They preferred beads to the porcupine quills they used for adornment, warm wool blankets to hides, and awls rather than bones. They enjoyed rings, bracelets, ribbons, and mirrors.

Some traders and companies pandered to Indians' love of alcohol to woo trade. That wasn't acceptable to Bent-St. Vrain. Though the company did trade alcohol and tobacco, both were trade items like blankets and axes, not tools to cheat. Bent-St. Vrain valued the respect of all they dealt with—Indians, trappers, and employees. Among the tribes, they and their men had a reputation for fair trade.

---

[18] Conard, *Uncle Dick Wootton*, 1890, 87.

Furs and buffalo robes were the Indians' primary trade items. Braves hunted and killed animals; their women tanned the hides and prepared them for use. They kept some hides for their needs, killed more animals and prepared those hides to trade.

Each side traded commodities they had for commodities they desired—the backbone of merchandising. Traders wanted pelts and hides for the Eastern market. Indians wanted merchandise that made life easier or more pleasurable. Dick picked up on exchange values and began to make inroads of understanding trade methods and communication.

Each year William Bent sent several trading teams from the fort to trade among Indians in their encampments. He expected his traders to keep up the Company's good reputation for fair trading, whether at the fort or in the field.

They'd been trading in the South Platte region at least three years when Dick arrived. Others were now moving into that area. Louis Vasquez and Andrew Sublette had built a fort. Lancaster Lupton was building one a little south of Vasquez. Bent-St. Vrain must keep up or lose out. Until they could build a fort, William continued to send traders. Three or four weeks after Dick arrived at Bent's Fort, William placed him in charge of a thirteen man, ten-wagon trading expedition.

Dick welcomed the opportunity and the extra wage. At a dollar a day he'd earn twice what he earned as a hunter. He was to trade northward beyond Ft. Laramie (Wyoming) into land dominated by the American Fur Company. He was to focus primarily on the Sioux, who roamed in present-day Colorado, Wyoming, Nebraska, and the Dakotas.

William Bent, Ceran St. Vrain, or the company clerk gave each trader a proposed route and a list of goods allotted for the expedition. A clerk prepared the merchandise and charged them to the trader's account. Each trader was responsible for all the goods he left with. Traders earned a wage; the rest of the profit went to the Company.

Trade goods taken often included: butcher knives; kettles; awls; small axes; brass wire; hoop iron used to make arrowheads; lead; black gun powder; vermilion; coffee; sugar; tobacco; red cloth; beads—primarily red, white, blue; cloth; ribbon; blankets—white, blue, blue-black; mirrors; abalone shells—used to make earrings for warriors and accents on clothing for women and children; and sometimes Navajo wool blankets, which were prized by other tribes.

Dick's small trading party with its ox-pulled wagons headed north toward the south fork of the Platte (below present-day Denver, Colorado), past Ft. Laramie, and on to Rawhide—a stream which emptied into the north fork of the Platte (Wyoming). There were no roads. They spent three to four weeks there trading with the Sioux. At each Indian encampment Dick set up camp near the village. He rode into the village with one or two men to determine if the Indians were ready to trade. If they were, Dick smoked a peace pipe with the Indian leaders. They exchanged goodwill gifts. Indians always expected an exchange of gifts and a time of formalities before trading began. Dick generally traded in the tepee of the Indian he deemed the friendliest.

Tepees varied in size. At this time, they were generally made of white buffalo skins, that is, skins squaws had tanned on both sides. Teepees were squaw work. The women tied three twelve-foot to fifteen-foot long poles together at the top and spread them out at the bottom. They braced the space between the poles with shorter poles. When they spread the skins over the pole frame, they formed a perfectly round tent. Squaws left an opening at the top of the teepee to allow smoke to escape. They crafted their teepees with a couple of wings at the top, near the hole; so they could adjust the flaps to keep wind from blowing into their home or to keep smoke from blowing back inside.

By the time Dick arrived, an ordinary teepee could sleep up to twelve people, lying with their feet to the central fire and head to the outer wall, like spokes on a wheel.[19]

Traders often appointed young warriors as soldiers to guard merchandise. They were called "Dog Soldiers" (not to be confused with later Dog Soldier warriors). The position was one of prestige, honor, and trust. No trader is known to have ever reported lost goods while those diligent young men protected them. It became Dick's habit when trading to uniform the warriors he chose. He provided brass-buttoned militia coats complete with epaulets, top hats accented with red feathers, and gilt-handled swords. Each coat cost Dick more than a week's wage at his present salary.

After exchanging goodwill gifts, trade began. Squaws traded first. They put the most work into the hides; so they had robes to trade. There was quite a bit of haggling at first because first exchanges influenced value for the rest of the trading. Once the squaws had the price they wanted, they took their time shopping. Traders became used to it and often played games while women made up their minds. When a squaw was done, she'd take a few puffs on the trader's pipe, and that was that. When the women finished, the men brought their robes to trade.

Buffalo robes and pelts were thickest in winter; so that was the best time to trade. Indians were no fools, nor were the traders. They each did a certain amount of haggling to obtain what they felt was a fair or advantageous trade. As Joseph Millard said, "They [Indians] were cheated, but not in trades like these or men like Dick Wooton [*sic*]. Privately, the Indians thought white men were the fools to trade such vital necessities as knives and guns and powder for beaver skins…As for beads, they were intrinsically as useless as the quarters and half dollars in the white man's pocket. But like the coins, they were the symbol of wealth and a medium of exchange."[20]

Dick's reputation as an honest, shrewd trader spread by word of mouth. As Cheyenne were known for their horsemanship, Sioux were renowned as the best barterers. They held themselves in high esteem for their skillful trading. Some rode in from distant villages to match wits with Dick—as if bartering were a competitive sport. It seemed that trading, like storytelling, was in Dick's blood, a part of his nature.

Miguel Otero, a New Mexico governor (1897-1906) and longtime friend of Dick's, said:

Dick was probably more successful as an Indian trader than at any other vocation. He knew to a T the trick of taking beads, trinkets, bullets, guns, pistols, knives, blankets, hats …tin pans…and the like to the villages… and exchanging them for buffalo robes, hides, buckskin, furs and ponies, at the same time satisfying the Indians and enriching his own pocket. During the many years that he was engaged in this business, he travelled over

---

[19] Tepees were sized according to the number of hides required: five, ten, or more. A ten-skin tepee was about fifteen feet high at the center pole.
[20] Joseph Miller, "Blazers of Trails West," (McQuitty Clipping Collection), 94.

practically all the western country.[21]

Dick and his men looked for as much natural shelter for themselves and their animals as they could find. They sometimes built a little shack—nothing fancy, nothing airtight. They were just passing through, just there to trade. They gathered fuel—wood, animal chips, or what they could find. In wet or freezing weather they had to have enough dry fuel to get a fire going.

They gathered or killed for the bulk of their diet. On occasion they'd be invited to share Indians' fare. In the evening they'd build a small campfire; someone would put on a pot of coffee. They preferred to make coffee over a greasewood fire, wouldn't use anything else if greasewood was available. To their notion it just made good coffee.

In cold weather they warmed their hands around the fire, let the moisture melt off their whiskers and wiped their noses as the hairs thawed. As darkness deepened, they drank coffee, ate, and talked, sometimes sang. Each one positioned himself close to the fire with one buffalo robe folded under him and one over—and went to sleep, serenaded by the area's wildlife. Travel in other seasons had some of the same amenities, just varied weather conditions—snow, wind, heat. For the most part the men enjoyed their travels, enjoyed trading with most Indians. Most had favorite tribes. Few, if any, enjoyed trading with the Comanche.

After trading north of Fort Laramie a good while, Dick led the outfit back toward Bent's Fort. They followed the South Platte and then traveled east along the Arkansas River. As they neared the fort, they met Ceran St. Vrain and eighteen or nineteen men headed for Taos. The Mexican government had become suspicious of foreigners, decided Americans in Taos were spies, and imprisoned many. St. Vrain was gathering all the help he could muster to help free his partner Charles Bent and other friends. Dick joined him. When they were about twenty-six miles from Taos, Charles Bent came riding along. Fearing retribution or razing of the town, Taos authorities had freed the Americans. Dick returned to Bent's Fort with St. Vrain and his volunteers.

By the time he returned to the fort, Dick figured that, at current market prices, his party had brought in about $25,000 worth of peltry for the company. Dick wasn't prepared to tan hides, but perhaps trapping…He'd heard stories around campfires. A mature beaver weighed about thirty to forty pounds. Pelts weighed about two pounds each and were selling for about seven dollars a pound. If a trapper set out eight traps a day, he could hope for four or five pelts on a good day. The math wasn't hard. Dick could bring in his own pelts and rake in the profit for himself.

As he planned and waited for spring, he made a trip to Taos—in New Mexico, Mexico's territory—for Bent-St. Vrain. Because of the location, it was relatively easy to smuggle goods across the Mexican border, in and out of Taos.

In southwestern New Mexico that spring (1837) James Johnson killed Apache Chief Juan Campo and set off so much trouble the Santa Rita copper mine closed.[22]

---

[21] Otero, *My Life on the Frontier*, 143.
[22] Some sources say Johnson's name was John. The mine was in southern New Mexico.

Back East, the States had its own trouble. A financial panic skyrocketed prices of staple goods. When the price of flour reached ten dollars a barrel in February and March 1837, Bread Riots erupted. The militia was called into New York City to suppress hungry, angry mobs who were breaking into warehouses and helping themselves.

And in the West, Bent-St. Vrain and Company was building Ft. St. Vrain about a mile below St. Vrain Creek on the South Platte, near Vasquez's and Lupton's places. It was approximately halfway between Ft. Laramie and Bent's Fort.

Interior of the store at the restored Bent's Fort, near La Junta, Colorado
(On the left is the trading window that opens to the entry passageway.)

Land of Opportunity

In the spring of 1837 Dick organized a party of seventeen trappers who would travel together for safety, yet trap independently. Two of the men, Briggs and Burris, were married to sisters, who accompanied them, cooked for them, and cared for their clothes. Being Snake Indians, the wives were accustomed to living a nomadic lifestyle.

The expedition left Bent's Fort in June 1837. They trapped along principal streams and watercourses as they crossed the mountains into South Park (Colorado). They found plenty of beaver along the sources of the Rio Grande, trekked to the headwaters of the San Juan River and on to the Wasatch Range on the western edge of the Rocky Mountains and the eastern edge of the Great Basin. It was on this trip—in October—Dick Wootton and Kit Carson met and began a lifetime friendship.

Some Southwestern trappers trapped for Bent-St. Vrain or for William H. Ashley, but most trapped independently. The majority banded together with an individual or group. Because independent trappers trapped with different groups and often met other trapping parties, they became a well-acquainted, close-knit community. In an odd sort of way they were somewhat like an extended family—isolated by day, a campfire community by night. They were knit together in availability to one another when needed.

Traversing mountain streams, passes, and plains months on end, independent trappers became well-acquainted with the Southwest. Some trapped as far west as California and as far north as Canada; but most of their trapping was in present-day New Mexico, Colorado, and southern Wyoming. Independent trappers were primarily French from Canada or Missouri, Hispanic, or American—chiefly from southern states, especially Virginia, Kentucky, and Missouri.

The French were daring. They never seemed to draw back from taking the long chance, but they tended to placate Indians more than Americans did. Americans were sure shots, hardy men, yet more brusque. They preferred aggression to stalemate.

Trappers had unwritten codes of methods and behavior. One principle was: "Let no Indian depredation go unpunished." Early on trappers understood Indian mentality and adapted to those they lived among, so much so that trappers were sometimes referred to as "White Indians."

They became well-acquainted with individual Indian tribes, knew what to expect from each. They learned to recognize each tribe's footprints, arrowheads, and manner of travel. Tribes used different shaft markings and feathers on their arrows.

Indians were just as savvy as trappers. When warring, warriors sometimes collected enemy arrows. They used them to conceal their presence from trappers or Indian bands and shift blame for their actions onto their enemies. Trappers seldom had trouble with the Arapaho.

It was Indian custom not to harm anyone who came into their camp, but to give a hospitable welcome. They may kill the person as he left, but not while he was a willing guest within their camp. Following Indian tradition, Dick Wootton and trappers he traveled with extended hospitality to any Indian who visited their camp.

Indians and trappers ranged far. When Indians came into a trapper camp having visited another trapping camp, they exchanged news. When encamped near other trappers or on the move to another site, Dick and those with him stopped to visit any trappers along the way. A visit could last a matter of hours, overnight, or longer if they had to hole up because of weather.

Another trapping principle Dick observed was to set traps as he ascended a stream. That way, beaver couldn't whiff his scent; but he could see beaver cuttings floating downstream, which indicated beaver at work. Signs of Indians on a river bank also floated downstream.

Dick liked to set his traps in the evening, check them in the morning. He carried sixty to sixty-five pounds worth of traps and chains as he started upstream. Traps cost about $12-$16 each. There were less expensive traps, but lesser grades often burst in icy water. Once in a while a trap caught another animal. Dick said once in a while a bear would put a paw in a trap, rip the trap out of the water, and haul it off, crying as he went. Dick said there wasn't anything to do but follow the tracks until he found the bear and killed it. There was no way the bear could shake off the trap, and no one he knew fancied removing a trap from a live bear.

Beavers' main diet desire was the buds and bark of certain green twigs. Desires are the best bait; so that's what trappers used to bait them. They set a trap inconspicuously under the water, bent the tasty twig in such a position the beaver had to cross the trap to reach the tempting twig. The trap was set to quickly draw the beaver under the water to minimize suffering and ensure a catch.

In order to persuade the beaver it was okay to taste the branch, a trapper rubbed a bit of castoreum on it—only a few drops per twig.[23] It made the twig smell like other beaver had been there, tasted, and okayed the morsel.

Traveling within eight to ten miles of camp, a trapper had a full day's work skinning his catch, harvesting the castor glands, saving meat—especially the tasty beaver tails—resetting traps, and hiking back to camp. After setting traps in the afternoon, trappers gathered at camp, built a campfire, cooked, and ate. They brought along coffee, sugar, and tobacco; but depended on their catch and game. Night after night, they sat by the campfire, smoked and swapped stories and dried out a bit.

In company camps, like those in the Pacific Northwest, companies hired men to stretch and dry pelts. Independent trappers each worked their own. They fashioned withe willow frames on which they daily stretched beaver pelts to dry. About half the weight of a beaver skin was fat. They fleshed out beaver and otter before stretching the pelt. Mink didn't require fleshing.

Dick considered four to five pelts a good days' catch, a good season about 400 pounds.

---

[23] Trappers made castoreum by mixing beavers' urine and castor gland secretion to the consistency of mustard. The secretion was a musky, butter-like yellow substance found at the base of the beaver tail in the groin glands of both male and female beavers. Trappers kept it fresh for weeks in a stoppered container.

When it was time to move camp, Dick packed pelts in hundred pound sacks and loaded them onto pack animals. He preferred Indian ponies for pack animals.

When trappers lacked grass for their pack animals, they fed them bark. There were two types of cottonwood bark—sweet, which animals enjoyed, and bitter, which was poisonous. Animals also ate willow and other barks, as well as some leaves; oak leaves were especially nutritious.

The men wore buckskin moccasins and carried extra buckskin to mend clothes or to make another pair of shoes. They wore three-piece outfits made of wool or buckskin. Wool was warmer and wouldn't draw up like buckskin, but it wore out sooner. The outfit consisted of pants or leggings; a pullover type jacket, held in place by a belt at the waist; and a hat or hood.

Seams on buckskins were sometimes made with fringes to shed water. Men often wiped their greasy campfire utensils across the buckskin to help waterproof the leather. Each trapper wore a belt of tools. Dick hung two 6"-7" knives, two pistols, and a tomahawk on his belt and kept his twelve pound rifle and plenty of ammunition handy. With a tomahawk he could chop wood, meat, or anything that needed chopping. Like Indians, trappers handled tomahawks skillfully.

Each trapper in Dick's group brought his own supplies: rope, whetstone, meat saw, awl, flints, knives, sewing supplies, scent sack, tools to repair traps, and gun—with gunpowder, lead, and extra springs. The tools were used for a variety of tasks, including medical procedures. A sharp knife and meat saw could amputate limbs wounded beyond repair. The same knife could remove bullets or arrows. When possible, a trapper pulled an arrow shaft through for his fellow trapper. If the shaft couldn't be pulled through, it was cut off. The sinew holding the arrowhead to the shaft would eventually loosen its hold and allow the remaining shaft to work loose; so it could be cut off. If a bullet couldn't be removed in camp, the men plugged the hole with tobacco.

If an accident happened in icy weather, the men numbed the wound with ice. To cut off circulation, they'd wrap a handkerchief around the wounded area, tie the ends to a tree limb, and twist the hankie until blood stopped flowing. A red hot iron cauterized wounds.

When they needed a poultice, they made one of plants and applied it to a wound—unless a plug of tobacco was more applicable to a particular wound. They always tried to cleanse a wound with running water before dressing it. They covered the dressed wound with a piece of fur, if available, and tied it on with a strip of hide or cloth. If a trapper's wound disabled him, his comrades made a litter for him by wrapping a buffalo hide over two poles. When it was time to move, they'd balance his litter on two horses and take him along from camp to camp until he was able to move about or until they finished trapping and returned to a settlement.

Some trappers depended on building makeshift thatched roof type shelters if they didn't find a natural shelter. Others carried along a small Indian-style buffalo hide teepee. Each man slept on and under buffalo robes. During the day he sometimes wrapped a buffalo robe around himself Indian style—though not when stepping into a stream.

Other than the elements and accidents, there was the danger of Indian or animal attack, as well as the possibility of theft. Two trappers who set out with Dick went out one morning to check traps, just like the others, but disappeared, never came back. Having searched and finding no sign of them or their remains, the trappers figured Indians must have killed them; and animals must have finished what was left. They never heard tell anything of the two after that.

The remaining men wintered in Wyoming and trapped along most of Wyoming's streams. On their return they followed the Green River to the Grand (Colorado) River. Along the Grand a band of Snake Indians spied them and their packed horses. Rather than being surprised, the alert trappers surprised the Snake. During the Snake's two attack attempts, trappers killed about twenty. They lost no men, nor did the Snake trouble them again when they trapped in that area.

The brigade covered more than 2,000 miles and trapped most of the waterways in present-day Colorado, Wyoming and northeastern Utah. After almost nine months out, they returned to Bent's Fort, pleased with their take. Dick had a few hundred pounds of beaver pelts.

At Bent's Fort, Bill Williams talked to Dick about trapping down on the Chicorica and the Una de Gato (northeastern New Mexico). Bill, Dick, Rock (Mexican), Anos (French-Canadian Indian), and James Waters (from New York) planned their trip, gathered supplies, and headed south to trap beaver on the Picketwire and the Chicorica. For close to three months they trapped from the source of the Chicorica to its juncture with Red River. This was Dick's first time in the Raton Mountains.

To maximize his profits, Dick returned to the States to sell his peltry. He stayed in Westport a few weeks, sold his pelts for seven dollars a pound, and netted about $4,000. In retrospect, Dick said he was like the early gold-seekers: he figured just a little more time and he'd be rich. If he could have just two more good years like this, he could accumulate enough to return to Kentucky and live the comfortable life he'd figured on when he'd first crossed the Plains. He didn't go home to visit, but wrote to tell his mother his plans. At the time he didn't know that his youngest sibling, Frances, was born that summer and his thirteen-year-old brother, William, died.

Since Dick left the States in 1836, John Deere had invented a plow sturdy enough to turn prairie sod, and the financially strapped U. S. had changed banks. Gold and silver from Santa Fe Trail trade flowed into and circulated in the Missouri Valley. That made the Bank of Missouri one of the soundest banks in the nation; so the U. S. government chose the Bank of Missouri as its bank of deposit.

On his return to Bent's Fort that summer of 1838, Dick went over to Taos with Charles Bent. While camped along the way at Iron Spring, Bent pointed out mountains near and far, called them by name. He pointed out the various ways a person could get across the mountains. They discussed whether to cross the mountains through Sangre de Cristo Pass or Raton Gap. Up until this time and the time trapping with Williams, Dick had known little of this side of the Arkansas. None of the paths across the mountains were wagon roads, just trail paths worn by game, Indians, and trappers over the years.

Five Thousand Miles

After he returned from Taos to Bent's Fort, Dick planned a trapping expedition with nineteen other trappers, including Auguste Claymore, Jean Baptiste Chalifoux, and six or seven Arapaho and Shawnee. Chalifoux was fairly fresh in from his 1837 horse-thieving raid to California.

The trapper brigade left Bent's Fort in September 1838 and followed the Arkansas River to its source in the Rocky Mountains. They followed rivers as they flowed, winding in and out of the United States, Mexican territory, and jointly claimed U. S.-British territory. There were no state boundaries—no western states.

Using state names, Dick said they first trapped most of northern Colorado's streams and then followed the Green River into Utah. From there they trapped north into Wyoming,

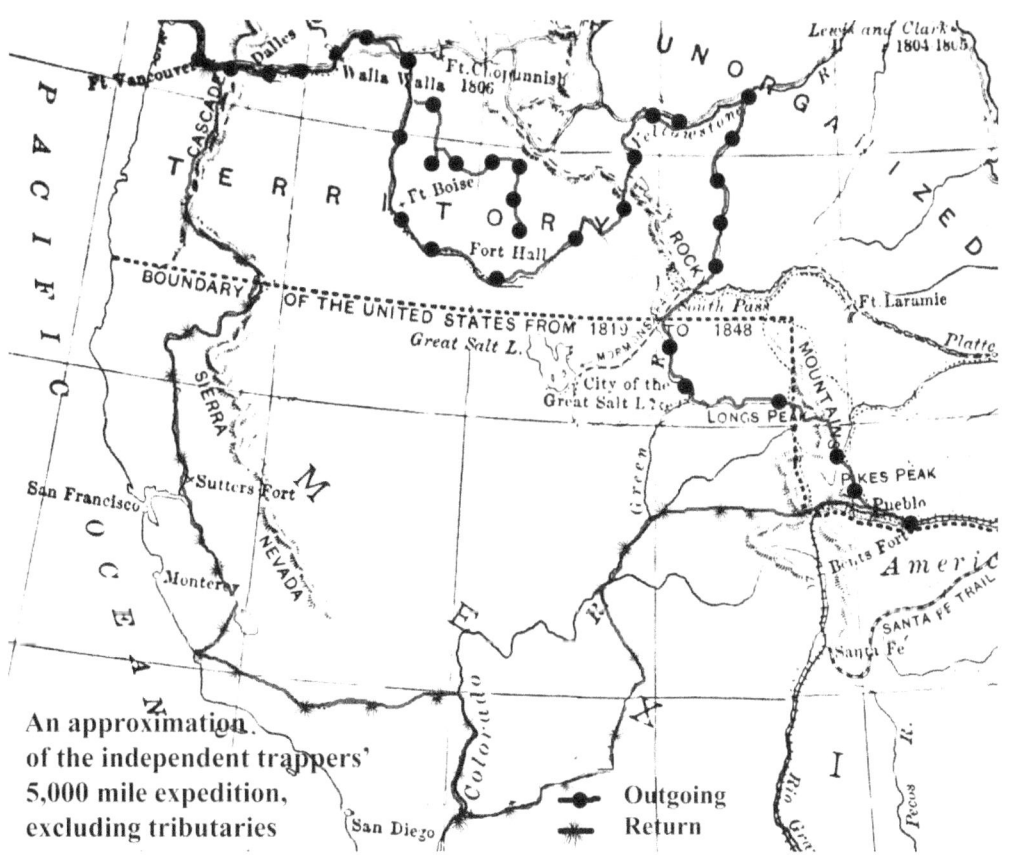

An approximation of the independent trappers' 5,000 mile expedition, excluding tributaries

trapping along tributaries of each main stream. While they trapped along the Green River (Utah, Wyoming), Auguste Claymore crossed paths with a group of Snake Indians. They clubbed old Gus' head so severely they crushed his skull, tore his brain and smashed some of his brain matter before his compadres came on the scene. They arrived soon enough to interfere and spare Claymore from losing his scalp. They took him back to camp and waited to bury him before they moved on. One man donated a suit of his own clothes for Claymore's burial. But Claymore regained strength and was mighty pleased to have a new suit of clothes. He wore his burial suit with pride and loved to tell about wearing out his funeral suit.

They continued north to the Yellowstone River (Montana) and followed its lead to the Snake River, which seemed to slither down the side of Wyoming into Idaho. From the Snake, the brigade followed the Salmon River northwest across Idaho. Leaving the Salmon, they trapped along the Columbia River and its tributaries in Washington. Trapping had been good and continued to be bountiful in Oregon and Washington. While they trapped in the winter of 1838-39, the eastern Cherokee were walking the Trail of Tears to Indian Territory.

While camped in eastern Washington, Baptiste Chalifoux was a ways off from camp when a band of Blackfoot Indians began to chase him. His good Nez Percé horse stayed ahead of the arrows. Chalifoux outran his pursuers until he came upon a wide deep chasm. Like Moses, the only way for Chalifoux was across. To stop would mean certain death; so he spurred his horse forward. But he and the horse landed at the bottom of the chasm. The horse died instantly. Chalifoux lay there with both legs broken. The Indians stood on the rim peering down into the gorge. Either they thought he was dead or not worth the effort to climb down after. They left. He knew his friends would look for him, but what to do? If he signaled, who would find him—friend or enemy?

By the time Chalifoux decided to take a chance and fire a few shots, his friends were searching for him. With determined effort, they reached him and transported him back to camp. They set his legs—it was up to them or no one—and fixed a litter between two pack animals; so he could lie down and ride in what ease they could provide. Before that episode Chalifoux thought the men should be kinder in their considerations of Indians; but after his narrow escape and two-month litter ride, his opinion was narrower than theirs.

Each trapper started with as many pack ponies as he thought he'd need. When Dick needed more, he traded with Indians: pelts for ponies. The trappers' pack animals were heavy laden as they neared Vancouver; they decided to go on into Vancouver and lighten their loads. It would be easier on them and the animals, and wouldn't be such a temptation to Indians along the way.

Before illness struck in the early 1800's, thousands of Indians lived in the Vancouver area. The first European settlement in the Pacific Northwest was established in 1824 when Hudson's Bay Company established a trading post for its fur trade. Since that time Americans and British had moved into the Oregon territory. When Dick Wootton arrived, Oregon included present-day Oregon, Washington, Idaho, and bits of Canada, Montana, and Wyoming. England and the U. S. held the territory jointly. Ownership had become a dispute between the two and wouldn't be settled until the Oregon Treaty was accepted on June 15, 1846.[24]

After selling enough pelts to lighten their load, Dick and the others decided they'd gone

---

[24] President Polk's 1844 campaign slogan was "54-40 or fight"; the 1846 agreement between the U. S. and Britain set the boundary at the 49th parallel.

far enough from home and turned south. They trapped along Oregon's western rivers and streams.

The Monarch Indians killed three of the trappers while they were in the Oregon country.[25] While the men were camped about a mile from a Monarch village, the Indians stole three horses that belonged to one of the Shawnee trappers. The trappers went to the village—a migratory camp, which was the Monarch manner. They found the Shawnee's horses picketed among the Monarchs' and retrieved them. The men figured they'd have to fight the band sooner or later and may as well stand up for their property from the beginning. A small number of Monarch trailed them to camp. About midafternoon they attempted to rush the camp and drive off more animals; but the trappers were ready. They'd remained in camp, waiting for them. They stood together as one. No one depended on another for defense; each did his part. Each one knew it was kill or be killed. They took turns loading and firing; so the Monarch had to contend with constant gunfire.

When the Monarch retreated toward their village, Dick and the others followed, firing. The battle continued at the Monarch encampment until the Monarch fled. Trappers tore down the lodges and returned to camp. They'd killed many Indians and lost three of their own in the day's three-to-four hour battle. The next day Lone Wolf, an 80- or 90-year-old Monarch, came into the trappers' camp to ask for peace. He explained some foolish young men started the trouble; they were wrong. He said now that the trappers had punished the tribe, his people wanted peace. The trappers explained that's what they'd wanted all along and invited his chief to come talk. Chief Sitting Buffalo came with a white flag of truce. He, a few of his warriors, and three men chosen from among the trappers sat in a circle and smoked the peace pipe. As the pipe was passed around the circle, each man took a puff and passed it to the next man. As long as they were in that country, the trappers and Monarch had no further problems.

The brigade trapped down into Mexico's California Territory and south to the Pacific Ocean at San Luis Obispo. They followed the Colorado River across California and trapped on the Gila River and its tributaries, as they had on each main river so far. They were disappointed with pelt quality in southern California and Arizona. Pelts weren't as thick and rich in the warm climates.

Leaving the Gila River region, they followed the Colorado River north into Utah. While trapping in Pah-Ute country (Utah), they met a group of Mexican slave traders. (Both Mexicans and Indians practiced slavery. It was common for Indians to sell or trade captives taken in raids.) Dick knew some of the men and sent a load of peltry to Taos with them.

In Utah, Pah-Ute/Piute Indians killed two more of the brigade. Le Bonte/La Bonte, a seasoned trapper who was traveling behind his fellows, was killed quietly. When the men turned back to find him, they found little of Le Bonte. Being cannibals, the Pah-Ute had cut and carried off most of Le Bonte's meat, leaving his bones.

The next to go was a Frenchman Dick called Le Duc, not to be confused with Maurice LeDuc. As the men sat around their campfire one evening, a small group of warriors crept

---

[25] There is a Monache Indian tribe in present-day California. It's uncertain if there was another group old-timers called Monarch or if Dick called the Monache, Monarch.

around the camp. From their flurry of arrows, one found a mark in Le Duc. His wound was slight, but the arrow's poison insured his death. Dick said he died in great pain about twenty-four hours later.

Dick explained how Indians prepared poisoned arrows:

They would take a piece of fresh liver from an animal recently killed, and place it on the end of a long stick. Then, having located a rattlesnake, they would keep poking it at the snake which would of course become very angry and would bite the liver several times. After this had been done, the liver would be placed in the sun and allowed to decompose. Then the arrow points would be dipped into this mass of poison until they were entirely coated with the vile stuff.

A very slight wound from such an arrow meant certain death and but few of the Indian tribes would use them, because of their fear that some of the poison might get into their system through a cut finger or hand, and this they well knew would mean death to them.[26]

As far as Dick knew, the only tribes who used poisoned arrows were the Digger, the Pah-Ute, and the Mescalero Apache.

From Utah the trappers crossed into western Colorado. They'd been in Mexican territory since entering California. Crossing the American border, they continued southeast and returned to Bent's Fort. Not counting the miles following tributaries, they'd traveled approximately 5,000 miles, traversing land little traveled—or untraveled—by Americans at that time.

They had little idea of calendar time. Early on, they realized they'd forgotten to carry along an almanac; but Chalifoux agreed to be their timekeeper. He simply cut a notch on a stick each day. However, on Chalifoux's horse-ride descent into the abyss, his calendar stick had flown who-knows-where. The expedition's sense of time literally flew. Indians measured time by snows (years), suns (days), moons (months), and half-moons (half months). That's the best the trappers had for the remainder of their journey. The exact date was anybody's guess.

They could have asked the date at some settlement in Oregon or California, but they preferred to make it a matter of wager among themselves. Because the climate was so much warmer in California and Arizona than climates they'd been accustomed to, they thought perhaps it was later in the season than it was. All their wild hare guesses were off.

Five men had been killed. Two had been wounded severely: Baptiste Chalifoux in his flying leap and Auguste Claymore, the oldest member of the party. The fourteen surviving men arrived at Bent's Fort in 1840, almost two years after their departure.

Beaver prices had begun to fall by the mid-1830's. (Men's hat styles, which required beaver pelts, changed in Europe and the U. S.) By the 1840's the golden age of southwestern trapping had come to an end, and buffalo robes became the marketable pelts. By that time trappers had learned the Southwestern country and named mountains and streams.

---

[26] Otero, 143, 144.

1840-1841

After Dick Wootton settled back at Bent's Fort, he crossed the plain and over the mountains to Taos to pick up the peltry he'd sent ahead with the Mexican slave traders. From season to season a trapper never quite knew what to expect from the Mexican government; but, when Dick arrived, things were relatively calm.

About thirteen years before, New Mexico Governor Narbona attempted to increase revenue by regulating trapping in his territory. When he cracked down on foreign trappers, American trapper Ewing Young hid his thirteen packs of pelts at Luis Maria Cabeza de Vaca's house in Pena Blanca (New Mexico). But word got out—word always gets out—and reached Governor Narbona. He sent a corporal and eight soldiers up from Santa Fe to visit Cabeza de Vaca and pick up Young's estimated $20,000 worth of pelts. Cabeza de Vaca refused to deliver. The soldiers killed him, seized the pelts, and filed their report: Cabeza de Vaca died "defending a violation of the… rights of the nation."[27]

A couple months later, Governor Manuel Armijo gave Young and a couple other Americans permission to help the Santa Fe alcalde shake moths out of pelts, which the government had confiscated and kept in storage. As the pelts aired on the Plaza near the Palace of the Governor, Young's partner Milton Sublette asked him which pelts were his. Young pointed.

Quick as a flash, Sublette dashed over, grabbed a bundle, and darted off, to the startled surprise of the guards. As interesting as he now was to the Mexican government, Sublette laid low until the next trapping season, when he headed into the Rockies with Sylvestre Pratte's group.

Now, thirteen years later, some of those trappers were gone. Pratte had died on a trapping expedition. Sublette was dead. Young had been in Oregon more than five years.

A man had time to remember, to think, to plan, as he traveled along on horseback. As Dick returned from Taos to Bent's Fort that autumn of 1840, he made his way slowly through the mountains during a heavy snowstorm. Something moved in a snowdrift. Instinctively, he silently lifted his rifle. Observing closely, he realized the moving object was an Indian—a female.

Dick knew enough of the Arapaho language to know the young lady was an Arapaho. As was common practice, she and many other Arapaho women and children had been captured by the Ute when they defeated her people in battle. She'd escaped, barefoot and scantily clad, was hungry and near freezing.

Dick helped her onto one of his ponies. They rode along until it was time to make camp. He made a place for her near the campfire and fixed her something to eat. They traveled a couple days then, near her tribe, she went on alone. In her village she told what had happened. Dick was surprised when the Arapaho came out to meet and thank him; he'd never

---

[27] Horgan, *Great River*, 467.

seen such behavior among Indians. They offered him two Indian ponies and refused to take no for an answer. From that time on the Arapaho considered Dick Wootton a friend of the Arapaho. There was never any trouble between them. Because of Dick's two stub fingers, they nicknamed him "Cuthand."

The winter of 1840-41 was relatively mild along the Arkansas River and in much of Colorado and New Mexico. Dick went with a group on a trading expedition into Mexico in early spring.

During that time, U. S. President William Henry Harrison caught cold at his March 4th inauguration. Never did get over it. The cold turned into pneumonia, and he died on April 4, 1841. Vice-president John Tyler succeeded him. (Dick and Tyler were very distant relatives. Walter Chiles II, their common ancestor, died in Jamestown in 1671.)

Harrison and Tyler were Whigs, but Tyler wasn't a strong one. When Whigs put him on the ticket as vice-president, they thought he'd balance out the voting ticket to help carry Southern states. Before Tyler's term was done, the Whigs kicked him out of the party. Of Tyler's cabinet only Daniel Webster hung on.

On his return from Mexico, Dick arranged to herd sheep across the Plains to Westport, Missouri, for Mathew Kincaid in the summer of 1841. He gathered what goods he had to sell and took them along. As he was herding sheep across the Plains, the Sioux and Cheyenne started kicking up their heels in northern Colorado. They went on the warpath and killed several trappers in the process. In August they killed Jim Bridger's partner, Henry Fraeb.

The end of October 1841, Comanche killed and scalped Charles and William Bent's youngest brother, twenty-five-year-old Robert, right outside Bent's Fort. The Bents buried their brother outside the fort and covered his grave with rocks and cactus to discourage wolves. Years later William took him home to be buried in St. Louis. William was that way, always a family man.

Back from Missouri, Dick again supplied meat for Bent's Fort. He said the Plains were sometimes black with buffalo as far as an eye could see—to count them would be like counting ants. He enjoyed watching Indians hunt buffalo. They'd circle a herd, close in on the animals, race in with bows aimed, but wait to shoot until they were alongside their target. They left buffalo calves for their boys to practice on.

When he hunted, Dick felt it was only fair to give the buffalo a sporting chance—an opportunity to escape. He saved his saddle horse fresh for the chase. When hunting to supply the fort, Dick took another man or two along to butcher and load the meat onto pack animals or into wagons to transport back to the fort.

Like the Indians, mountain men knew the ways of buffalo. Buffalo could be counted on to be cantankerous in rutting season and calving time (April to early May). It didn't take much figuring: if a buffalo had his tail arched or pointed up and started heading your direction, it was your turn to get in the first lick or high-tail it. There were days Dick took twenty to thirty buffalo for meat at the fort. Indians, also, generally killed only as many buffalo as they needed to eat.

Dick said that as long as Indians and settlers hunted buffalo for meat, there was no noticeable change in the size of the herds. He said grey wolves did take a toll on calves, would even attack and kill adult buffalo. While wolves attacked from the front, other wolves sprang from behind and tore into the buffalo's hamstring. Without a leg to stand on, the animal would tumble down and be ripped apart. In later years skin hunters came onto the Plains for buffalo robes and almost wiped out the buffalo population in the western United States—unimaginable to the mountain men and Indians in the 1840's.

While Dick was in Westport selling sheep in the summer of 1841, an expedition from the struggling young Republic of Texas had arrived in New Mexico. New Mexicans considered the Texas-New Mexico Expedition an annexation attempt. Retired General Andrew Jackson called it "the wild goose campaign against Santa Fe."[28]

---

[28] Horgan, 585.

New Mexico and the Republic of Texas

New Mexico and Texas belonged to Spain until Mexico gained independence in 1821 and took Spain's Southwestern territories. Mexico granted a group of Americans permission to form a colony in Mexican-held Texas. In 1836 the Texans/Texians fought and won independence from Mexico and established the Republic of Texas.

Aware of the stable Santa Fe Trail trade, the impoverished young republic cast its eyes toward Santa Fe and figured a good bit of New Mexico belonged to them as territory gained in its war for independence. An 1836 congressional act of the Republic of Texas claimed all the land encompassed by the Rio Grande from its source to its mouth—approximately 98,000 square miles, which Mexico also claimed. It included all of eastern New Mexico as far west as the Rio Grande, including Santa Fe and its lucrative Santa Fe Trail trade. Texas even had names picked out for places in New Mexico, but Mexican officials in charge of New Mexico didn't tally with Texas' figures. During the Republic of Texas' first years, it was so busy with business at hand it didn't have time or resources to cross the hundreds of miles to enforce its claim.

In spring 1841, however, solicitations appeared in the Austin, Texas, newspaper for volunteers to cross the plains to Santa Fe. Texas President Mirabeau Bonaparte Lamar sought men who'd provide their own arms, mount, and equipment to accompany ten wagons the government was supplying to merchants who wanted to take or send goods to Santa Fe. Commissioners would travel with the train to represent Texas to the people of Santa Fe.

The Mexican government thought the ads for escorts sounded like a military expedition. Thinking Texas was attempting to put feet to its claim, Mexico City authorities warned New Mexico Governor Armijo and informed him Mexico would send him military reinforcement.

Two hundred seventy men, formed into six companies, signed up to accompany the Texas train. Calling themselves "Santa Fe Pioneers," the group included ten San Antonio merchants and their employees, commissioners, and a few tourists. Brigadier General Hugh McLeod was the leader in charge. President Lamar included three joint-commissioners from New Mexico to work with his Texas commissioners. By the time the oxen-pulled train rolled toward New Mexico more merchandise wagons were added to the train, plus a medical wagon, a baggage wagon, and a couple wagons for the commander. Mules pulled a howitzer.

Someone—supposedly from Santa Fe—had circulated a letter that said many Mexicans and all Pueblo Indians and Americans would welcome Texans' arrival. The merchants and mounted volunteer guard thought Santa Fe was waiting for them. Come to find out, they were.

President Lamar printed a letter in English and Spanish and sent it along:

We tender to you,…a full participation in all our blessings. The great River of the North, which you inhabit, is the natural and convenient boundary of our territory, and we shall take great pleasure in hailing you as fellow-citizens, members of our young Republic, and co-aspirants with us for all the glory of establishing a new and happy and free nation....This communication I trust will be received by you and by your public authorities, in the same spirit of kindness and sincerity in which it is dictated,[29]

If New Mexicans accepted this first communication, President Lamar promised to send commissioners later in the summer to explain the conditions for unifying Santa Fe and Texas.

Santa Fe Pioneers left on June 6, 1841. On June 22, the U. S. representative in Texas wrote U. S. Secretary of State Daniel Webster: "An expedition...under the controul [sic] of three commissioners, left Austin, on the 6th instant for Santa Fe. The object of the Republic is to open a trade with the people of that country, and induce them, if possible, to become an integral part of Texas."[30]

In Santa Fe, Governor Armijo continued to hear rumors. Maybe the Texans would try to assassinate him. He continued to prepare. He waited. He scrutinized Americans, jailed suspects. Stories circulated around town inciting fear and stirring up loyalty to Mexico.

En route to New Mexico one of the Texans' two Mexican guides deserted. Indians killed five Texans—took the heart out of one of them—and harassed the train along the way. Supplies were low by the time they crossed the parched plains of their Republic and entered New Mexico's summer-arid eastern plains. They ate whatever bugs or critters they could catch and any edible plants they found. Adding to the misery, many men were left afoot when Indians stole eighty-three horses in the dead of night. Sickening in the August heat, men began to discard weapons and ammo.

New Mexico Governor Armijo sent Captain Damasio Salazar to scout for the Texans. In September he found them: sick, hot, and hungry, wandering across New Mexico's eastern plains. The first ones Salazar found were Commissioners Baker, Howland, and Rosenbury, who were traveling ahead of the party with President Lamar's letter. Salazar jailed them in Santa Fe. They escaped. Pursuers killed Rosenbury, recaptured Baker and Howland and locked them up at San Miguel del Vado. Mexican soldiers found the remaining Texans.

Governor Armijo warned all foreigners in New Mexico, including the American consul, to stay put. Concerned for their lives and property, Americans sent word to U. S. Secretary Daniel Webster in Washington.

Armijo and his armed recruits—about a thousand Mexicans and Indians—met Captain Salazar marching the Texans near Pecos Pueblo. When the Governor asked the Texans who they were, Captain Lewis said they were Santa Fe Trail merchants from the United States.

That spurred Governor Armijo into a tirade: What! Did the man think he couldn't read the word on his uniform buttons, "Texas"? Did Lewis think he couldn't see the Lone Star of Texas on his uniform? No. Armijo lived in Santa Fe; he knew the look of merchants. These men were not merchants! Armijo asked more questions. Mr. Kendall, traveling with, but not a member of the group, showed Armijo his legitimate Mexican passport. Armijo examined the paper, told Kendall that would be figured out later. For now Kendall was to be kept with the rest.

Armijo marched them to Las Vegas (New Mexico). On Las Vegas Plaza, September 23, 1841, rural and regular New Mexico troops stood armed in columns, as soldiers escorted

---

[29] Horgan, 571.
[30] *Ibid.*, 571.

Texans to the Plaza and paraded them for all to see. By order of Governor Armijo, Justice of the Peace Hilario Gonzales set fire to a large stack of firewood in the middle of the plaza. A trumpet sounded, heralding Governor Armijo's arrival with his officials and honor guard. Armijo announced the reason for gathering, then threw all of the Texans' papers—constitution, bylaws, proclamations and invitations to New Mexicans—into the blazing fire. As the papers turned to smoke and ash, Armijo signaled: Troops fired in unison. Flutes, drums, and trumpets sounded; citizens shouted.

After parading the men, Mexican officials took them back to San Miguel del Vado and jailed them in a house on the plaza. The women of San Miguel prepared food for the Texans and treated them kindly. Mexican guards did not. They murdered Howland in front of the other prisoners to give them an idea how Mexicans treated escapees.

By October 17th Mexican authorities had rounded up almost 200 Texan prisoners. Captain Salazar marched them from San Miguel to Pecos, toward Santa Fe. He gave the hungry men nothing to eat, but Pueblo Indian women who lived along the way came out and gave what food they could.

After displaying the Texans in Santa Fe, Governor Armijo charged Captain Damasio Salazar to march them to Mexican headquarters in Mexico City, 2,000 miles away. Salazar roped the men together and marched them southward. Most of the men no longer had shoes, but Salazar allowed no one to ride the extra mules. On the third day they arrived at the Indian settlements of Santo Domingo and San Felipe. Again, Indian women pitied them and brought them food.

Famished and exhausted, the group straggled down the long, dry Camino Real toward Mexico City. Not wanting authorities to think he allowed any to escape, Salazar collected the ears of those who died or those he shot because they couldn't keep up. When he reached El Paso, Salazar had the exact number of men assigned him, including five sets of ears. News of Salazar's cruelty had preceded him; orders for his replacement awaited when he arrived in El Paso.

Don Jose Maria Elias Gonzales, commanding general of Chihuahua (Mexico), took charge of the prisoners. He divided the Texas men into small groups and placed them in El Paso homes, where they received food and wine. As for Salazar, he was held and later court-martialed for cruelty, for murdering three Texans, and for stealing Texans' property. When the United States and Britain heard of the cruelty, both countries interceded.

Texans rested in El Paso three days before resuming the march. When they arrived in Mexico City they were put in several prisons, where they remained. In celebration of his birthday in June 1842, President Santa Ana released most of them—with their hard earned grudges. One severely punished prisoner remained in prison until he escaped in January 1845.

By the end of summer 1842 neither Texas nor Mexico was happy. Texas wanted New Mexico commerce and was riled at the treatment of its soldiers. Mexico, indignant that Texas invaded its territory, invaded San Antonio. In an effort to retaliate and gain much-needed cash, a group of Texans planned to waylay travelers on the Santa Fe Trail and interrupt Trail travel.

On February 16, 1843, as per Colonel Jacob Snively's request of January 28, Texas President Sam Houston commissioned Snively to recruit volunteers to intercept Mexican caravans on the Santa Fe Trail and to take their goods. Snively and his soldiers could keep half the profits; the other half would belong to the Republic of Texas. The next Mexican train on the Trail got wind of the plans, bypassed the Texians, and arrived safely in Independence.

In February 1843 Texas Colonel Charles Warfield's recruit John McDaniel from Missouri led a band of men, who attacked New Mexico trader Don Antonio Jose Chavez on American soil (near Little Cow Creek, Kansas). Chavez, of the wealthy and politically influential Chavez family,[31] was traveling ahead of the spring train from New Mexico. Dick Wootton said he traveled in what was called "the old Spanish style"—in a carriage with outriders.

The band held Chavez prisoner three days, hoping he'd cough up more revenue.[32] Seven of the band disagreed with McDaniel and insisted they should take the loot they had and leave. They took their share and left. McDaniel and eight men held out. They murdered Chavez.[33] Because he was a prominent man, all involved in his murder were brought to justice in St Louis. McDaniel and his brother were hung; the others were sent to the penitentiary.

In early June 1843 Texas Colonel Warfield attempted to drum up recruits from among the free traders and men at Bent's Fort and the nearby area. Neither the Bents nor St. Vrain wanted anything to do with him or his plans. St. Vrain considered him and his recruits outlaws and warned American traders to be cautious. Aware of Texas' plans to raid Trail travelers and of Warfield's illegal recruiting on American soil, the U. S. government sent Philip St. George Cooke and 300 dragoons to escort trains on the Santa Fe Trail as far as the Arkansas River Crossing.

Mexican officials in Taos became suspicious of Charles Bent and other Americans. They arrested Bent and imprisoned him until his family and friends came up with $800 to buy his release. Once out of jail, Charles hopped on a horse and headed to Bent's Fort on American soil. When he arrived at the fort, he found Texas' recruiter still hanging around. After Charles talked to would-be recruits, they decided not to aid Texas.

Colonel Warfield had few men, but Texas Colonel Jacob Snively was on the way with more. Warfield sent a ten-man observation unit into New Mexico. Then he and his twenty-one-man troop headed toward Mora, New Mexico. On the way he gave his men the choice to stay or leave. Three left. The remaining men came upon the camp of Captain Ventura Lobato's Mexican cavalry. The Texans killed five Taos Pueblo Indians whom Governor Armijo had impressed into service. They wounded and captured others and confiscated all the cavalry's horses and military equipment. Though they released the captives, the skirmish added fuel to anti-white sentiment in Taos. Taos locals ransacked property, including Charles Beaubien's store. On their way to Missouri, Kit Carson and Manuel Alvarez stopped at Bent's Fort and reported the incident.

---

[31] Antonio, fifty-five, was born at Chavez' Los Padillos home. He married the niece of a governor. His father was Mexico's first New Mexico governor. One of Antonio's brothers also became governor. The family raised sheep, farmed, and mined. They became Santa Fe Trail traders soon after the Trail's inception. They traveled East in spring to sell their merchandise and purchase goods to trade in Santa Fe and Chihuahua (Mexico).

[32] Dick Wootton heard they stole $60,000. R. L. Duffus wrote of the incident almost ninety years later. He said Chavez had $10,000 in specie and bullion. Stories of his mode of transportation vary.

[33] After Chavez' murder, Little Cow Creek was named Chavez Creek, later called Jarvis Creek.

Texans retraced their steps and camped near Wagon Mound, New Mexico. Mexicans caught up to them and drove off most of their horses. Warfield and his men walked north to Raton Pass, then east to Bent's Fort—more than 150 miles. About the same time Texas Colonel Snively and about 180 recruits arrived near the crossing of the Arkansas River.

Governor Armijo made plans for 600 soldiers to meet incoming wagon trains on the Cimarron Branch of the Santa Fe Trail; Philip St. George Cooke and his dragoons escorted the Santa Fe Trail caravan as far as the U. S.-Mexican border. After Cooke's dragoons delivered the trade caravan to the border, they met Snively and his troop on American soil about ten miles from present-day Dodge City, Kansas. Snively insisted they were on Texas soil; Cooke maintained it was American. Cooke explained that soldiers of another country were not allowed to be armed on American soil and confiscated their weapons to divert trouble. Not wanting to leave the men unprotected, Cooke allowed them to choose: return to Texas or return to Missouri with him. The U. S. Government later paid Texas for the weapons.

Because of Texan interference in Santa Fe Trail trade, Mexico President Santa Ana closed customs houses at Taos, El Paso, and Presidio del Norte on August 7, 1843, and halted trade via the Santa Fe Trail. On March 31, 1844, after he heard of Philip St. George Cooke's stand against Snively and heard that the murderers of Don Antonio Chavez were brought to justice, Santa Ana reopened the customs houses.

Said to be the customs house at San Miguel del Vado (Bado) along the Santa Fe Trail (seen on the right) in New Mexico
Wagons crossed the nearby Pecos River, which skirts the trail on the right.

El Pueblo Days

While Texas was concentrating on New Mexico and New Mexico was concentrating on Texans, George Simpson, Joseph Mantz, Robert Fisher, Mathew Kinkead and Francisco Conn—all from Mora, New Mexico—built a trading fort in the Arkansas Valley near the juncture of Fountain Creek and the Arkansas River (Colorado). The site was near water and grazing. What the men lacked in capital, George Simpson's doctor father in St. Louis supplied. Hired hands from Taos and Mora made adobe on site and helped construct the fort west of the river.[34]

The fort's original name when built in 1842 was Plaza del Rio de Penasco Amarilla. It was shortened to Fort el Pueblo, but was usually called El Pueblo or Pueblo. It was close enough to the mountains for trade with trappers, yet handy for Indian trade. Cheyenne, Arapaho, and Ute frequented the area. The enterprise outfitted traders who headquartered in or near the fort and went out to trade in Indian villages.

El Pueblo's large wooden gate opened to the east. Inside, rooms surrounded the central plaza on the north, west, and south sides. Rooms were not interconnected; each opened onto the plaza. Beyond the walls were outbuildings. Within the walls were sleeping quarters, kitchen and dining rooms, trade rooms, blacksmith shop, and space to shelter stock.

At the time, area Indians were peaceful, even friendly; however, they did practice the adage "finders keepers, losers weepers" and were good finders. In fact, something need not be lost for them to find it. Dick Wootton, who headquartered nearby, said area Indians were a thieving lot, and added that if it didn't require too much effort to take something, they took it.

One day, when hunting game for Bent's Fort a couple years before (1840), Dick had killed about twenty buffalo. While he waited for the butchers to finish their task, he noticed orphaned twin buffalo calves. He wasn't sure what he'd do with them, but drove them back with him to Bent's Fort. He credited a good-natured cow for helping him raise them.

As he supplied meat for Bent, Dick noticed that after every kill there were calves milling about, lost without their mothers. He figured he may as well capture some of the orphans and try domesticating a herd.

He put his hand to it and established his buffalo farm near El Pueblo. He built corrals and purchased forty-four milk cows. When their calves neared maturity, Dick captured forty-four buffalo calves and replaced the cows' calves with buffalo calves. He said that "at first the cows were not inclined to look with much favor on the hump backed, ugly looking little animals, but by and by they began to think better of it, and in a short time they were getting along as well together as if they had belonged to the same family."[35] The Plains were so full of roaming buffalo that Dick's idea of domesticating them seemed about as smart as domesticating Jackrabbits. He took a good bit of razzing, but he didn't mind being the brunt

---

[34] In 1858 the fort was about 70-80 feet from the river.
[35] Conard, 1980, 73.

of good-natured banter. He wasn't the first to domesticate buffalo. Unknown to Dick, George Washington tried the same thing at Mt. Vernon.

In the early to mid-forties Dick continued independent trading and trapping while domesticating his little buffalo herd and riding for Bent and others. He often crossed the Mexican border carrying peltry into Taos for himself or for hire. The Arkansas River was the border at that time.

With ever changing Mexican regulations, Dick smuggled goods into Taos, primarily for Charles Bent, Ceran St. Vrain, and for merchant Charles Beaubien, who'd been established in Taos since the mid-twenties. To lower overhead levied by the Mexican government, some New Mexico traders and merchants resorted to bribery, others to smuggling—whether they did it themselves or hired it done. Smugglers sometimes cached goods by day and hauled them in on pack mules by night. Dick knew the country well.

In the years Spain possessed New Mexico, it jealously guarded its New Mexico territory from outside trade, if from nothing else, because New Mexico provided a borderland buffer zone. Every three years the crown, or its representatives, sent a train north from Mexico to supply New Mexicans with goods at exorbitant prices. When Mexico gained independence from Spain, it widely opened the gate to outside trade.

When Mexican officials saw the influx of goods and the number of traders arriving in New Mexico, they realized they could profit. The Mexican-controlled government continued to allow traders to bring in their wares, but began to tax traders and to charge a per diem tax to foreigners who kept shops. The tax was so high that traders found ways to get around the charges. When the government charged tax on goods in traders' wagons at the customs houses, traders built deeper wagon beds with false bottoms; so there was less merchandise to be seen and taxed. To circumvent that, Mexicans levied a $10 duty per wagon, regardless of contents. In 1839 New Mexico's Governor Manuel Armijo raised the levy to $500 per wagon. In turn, Eastern wagon makers began manufacturing larger wagons. Traders began driving their wagons close to the New Mexico border, transferring more goods onto one wagon, filling each wagon to the hilt. They'd double up the teams to pull the tottering wagons to the customs houses.

At one time Governor Armijo taxed foreigners—naturalized or not—and exempted native-born New Mexicans. He encouraged informers to report any importing or selling of contraband items such as iron, gunpowder, candle wicking, and lead. Iron was so scarce in New Mexico that some traders, having sold their goods, burned their wagons, sold the iron, and garnered enough profit to pay for their trouble. Any suspicion of dealing in contraband gave Mexican authorities the right to pilfer through any merchant's wagon or store. Merchants bore the cost of damage.

When Mexican officials tore through Beaubien's and Bent-St.Vrain's stores (Taos, 1841) looking for contraband, foreign businessmen throughout New Mexico concluded it was another proof Governor Armijo was bent on eradicating competition. American consul Alvarez reported the matter to U. S. Secretary of State Daniel Webster.

There were times Mexican officials tightly taxed native New Mexicans, also. Back in 1837 when Albino Perez was governor, New Mexicans grumbled because new regulations cut into their rights and lifestyle. Shepherds were required to pay twenty-five cents per head for each animal driven through Santa Fe on the way to market. Each month woodcutters were charged a five dollar license. Why work at that rate? If a person took fees as encouragement to be lazy, the Mexican government had that figured out. They had a new edict which required the arrest of anyone without a regular lawful occupation. When New Mexicans faced Perez with the situation, he explained he was only carrying out orders from headquarters. He could honor Mexican orders if he wanted, but New Mexicans had had it! They killed "El Chico," Perez' Secretary of State. Then they caught Governor Perez himself right there in Santa Fe, killed him—cut his head right off and used it like a ball, tossing it and kicking it around! They even went after former Governor Abreu, didn't make it easy or fast for him. The devils—or whoever controlled the mob that day—made it slow going for him—pulled out his eyes, his tongue, and cut off his hands, all the while accusing him of whatever came to mind. He probably didn't hear much of it.

That Rebellion of 1837 caught Americans betwixt and between. Governors Perez and Armijo both required supplies of the Americans; so Pueblo Indians thought Americans sided with the Mexicans. Mexican loyalists, in turn, thought the Americans supplied arms for the rebellion.

Traders didn't know what changing tariff or regulation awaited them from season to season. Governor Armijo's successor, Mariano Martinez (1844-45), raised the levy per wagon to $750, then to $1000. Empty wagons were charged $50 each. During Martinez' term, the Mexican government monopolized tobacco sales in New Mexico. Even New Mexicans weren't allowed to sell their own homegrown tobacco.

During the years Dick Wootton smuggled goods into New Mexico and raised cattle and buffalo near El Pueblo, he became well-acquainted with many people who would travel in and out of his life over the years, people who etched their influence, large or small, in the history of Southwestern settlement. Among those who lived in El Pueblo area in the 1840's were:

Joe and Cruz Doyle
George and Juanita Simpson
Charlie Autobees
Charlie's half-brother Tom Tobin
John and Luisa Brown
Bill Tharp with Antonia Luna
Bill's brother Ed Tharp
Jim and Candelaria Waters
Calvin Briggs
Maurice LeDuc
Robert and Romualda Fisher
LaFontaine
Colorado Mitchell
Valentine "Rube" Herring with Nicolassa
Richard "Dick" Owens
Bill Guerrier/Garey and his Indian wife
Whittlesey (killed LaFontaine)

Archibald Metcalf and his young wife, Luz
Charlie Williams
Alexander Barclay
John Burris/Burroughs
Tuscon (a dark complexioned man, looked like an Indian)
Jim Beckwith living with Magdalena Martinez
Marcelino and Tomasa Baca and young sons, Jose and Luis (arrived 1846)
Mathew Kinkead living with Teresita Suaso[36]
Bob/Asa Estes (Istuss/Istess/Iskus)[37]
Joe Richard/Jo Rashaw/Reshaw.[38]

Bent-St.Vrain established a weekly express service between Bent's Fort (southeastern Colorado) and Ft. St.Vrain (northern Colorado). They expanded it to include El Pueblo and Taos. Dick Wootton, Asa Estes, and other mountain men rode as couriers. On some trips Dick carried up to $60,000 in silver. He felt fortunate to never lose a dollar entrusted to him.

U. S. government pathfinder John C. Fremont stopped at El Pueblo on his second venture and noticed Bent's couriers. It was said that, on his return to Washington, he reported the system to his father-in-law, Senator Thomas Hart Benton, and other politicians and spoke of the possibility of a courier system from the States to the Pacific. Years later the Pony Express was born.

In December 1842 Dick made a trip into Taos with goods for Ceran St. Vrain and Charles Bent, who were both in Taos at the time. A few days before Christmas they sent John Hawkins and Dick back to Bent's Fort with ten pack mules loaded with about a thousand pounds of beaver skins and $60,000 of silver. They started out close to midnight with a promise that Charles or Ceran would send men to help pack the goods through the deep snow. Help hadn't arrived by the time they reached the Trinchera (northwestern New Mexico); so they stopped and waited until the men caught up with them before traveling across the plain to Bent's Fort.

By early 1843 St. Vrain was back at Bent's Fort and had another little pack train of goods for Wootton and Hawkins to take to Taos. New Mexico citizens Charles Beaubien and

---

[36] Mother of Mrs. Simpson, Mrs. Doyle, Mrs. Kroenig, and Andres Kinkead.
[37] Asa Estes was with Bent-St. Vrain in July 1846. For a time he kept a saloon in Taos.
[38] Joe (Joseph) Richard had two brothers—John Baptiste and Peter. They pronounced their name with such a French accent that they are often known as Rashaw or Reshaw.

In 1849 the California Gold Rush increased, traffic on the Oregon Trail (cut-offs to the Mormon and California Trails). Travelers forded the North Platte east of present-day Casper, Wyoming. Although others had tried to bridge the river, John Richard, Charles Bordeaux, Louis Guinard, Joseph Bissonette, and William Kenceleur built the first solid, lasting bridge (15' x 18' wide, about 1,000' long). About 150 miles up from Ft. Laramie, it was known as The Bridge, Reshaw's Bridge, Platte Bridge, Lower Platte Bridge. Toll charges rose and diminished according to the river's swell. Some paid as much as $8.00 per wagon during high water. The Richard brothers had a trading post near the bridge, traded strong cattle for emigrants' weak cattle, and traded in general with emigrants and Indians. John was about 100 miles south near Rock River on the Overland Trail. The bridge was dismantled in the winter of 1865-66. Like the Western frontiersmen they were, they had already moved on to the next opportunity. The brothers worked from New Mexico to the North Platte.

Guadalupe Miranda had recently obtained the Mexican land grant they'd applied for—a large tract of land in northeastern New Mexico. Charles Bent, who hadn't taken New Mexican citizenship, was a silent partner. Early in February, Beaubien and Bent sent a letter with a man named Tate to Ceran St. Vrain at Bent's Fort. The letter stated that Beaubien was setting out with a party from Taos to set landmarks at the grant boundaries. Tate arrived with the news before Hawkins and Wootton left with the pack train; so they expected to meet the party somewhere between the Raton Mountains and Rayado (New Mexico).

About five days out from Bent's Fort—near the Raton Mountains and still a good way north of Rayado, Wootton and Hawkins saw a small party on horses and mules. They presumed they were Indians. It was Charles Beaubien and Alcalde Cornelio Vigil with a party of about ten men, including Jesus Silva, Pablo Jaramillo, Jose Maria Valdez, Joaquin Leroux, and Pedro, a brother of Miranda's. Because the Mexican government had set the prescribed boundaries, Alcalde Vigil had come along to help establish the bounds.

By the time Wootton and Hawkins reached them, it was late. They set up camp together—a common practice.

About sunrise Dick accompanied Beaubien's party. Riding along on horseback between Judge Beaubien, as Dick called him, and Cornelio Vigil, Dick heard all about the grant. They reached the north edge of Chicorica Mesa and set up a mound to mark the grant's northeast corner. They returned to camp after sundown. Next morning Wootton and Hawkins traveled with the party awhile and then parted ways to continue on to Taos.

In late March 1843 Dick returned to Bent's Fort and took sixty-eighty yoke of Mexican oxen and fifteen to eighteen Taos men to work at the fort. They arrived in early April. Dick stayed long enough to gear up for a trapping expedition with a small group of independent trappers. They trapped along the Arkansas in late April, continued to South Park on the Platte River, and circled back to Bent's Fort. They arrived in late June or early July—two months and ten days after their departure. Dick sent his robes and skins to Westport with Bill Tharp of El Pueblo and furnished ten or twelve mules for the trip. Shortly after that, Dick rode up into northern Colorado and traded with Yellow Hair's band of Cheyenne.

That summer, 1843, pioneer missionary Dr. Marcus Whitman led about 1,000 emigrants across the Plains and mountains to settle in Oregon country. By the end of the 1840's more than 10,000 settlers would live in the Columbia River Valley.

At the same time Whitman was leading emigrants across the Plains, George Simpson and Robert Fisher, two of El Pueblo's founders, tried their hand at agriculture in the Hardscrabble Valley about thirty miles from El Pueblo. Over the years many had said land west of the Mississippi, especially land near the Rockies, wasn't fit for agriculture. Simpson and Fisher's fields grew fine. Mountain man John Brown had settled nearby at Greenhorn and opened a little store. In the spring (1843) he'd hewn local granite into burrstones to use as millstones and built himself a gristmill housed in a log cabin. Nothing fancy, but it served his purpose, ground his grain and that of any neighbor who needed some ground.

Hunting, Trading, and Trapping

Dick Wootton enjoyed telling the story of his friends Dick Owens and trapper John Burris. One day, while Burris and Owens were hunting in the 1840's, they met up with a huge grizzly bear. Each man fired. Both men missed. Each eyed a lone cedar and ran for it. Owens, ahead of Burris, grabbed onto that cedar and clambered to the only available safety. Burris wasn't far behind. No time to figure if one lone tree can hold two birds. He'd just gotten off the ground when the bear grabbed him from his low perch and mauled him. Burris fell to the ground and, with wisdom that probably saved his life, lay perfectly still as the grizzly clawed his body. Seeming content he had Burris under control, the grizzly left him and went after Owens—climbed up the tree for him. Owens stabbed at the bear with his hunting knife. As the two fought up in the tree—about ten or twelve feet above ground, Burris crawled to his gun, loaded it, and found an angle from which to shoot the bear and not Owens. He shot just as the bear snatched Owens' left hand in its mouth. As the bear fell to the ground, he bit off some of Owens' fingers. Wounded, the grizzly regained his footing and took off. Wootton and other hunters were in camp nearby when the bear came charging through. Dick said grizzlies don't appreciate being shot at, and the big fellow wasn't in good humor. Between them, it took several shots for the hunters to quiet him. Owens and Burris survived; but each had scars to prove their story. Neither completely recovered. The last time Dick saw him, Burris was a successful rancher in California.

Tending his herd, trading, riding for Bent, Dick was often in and out of El Pueblo—a trapper and mountain man resort. There, Dick said,

> I have passed some of the happiest days of my life, telling and listening to talks of wild and desperate adventures that thrilled my blood; tales of hand to hand encounters with savages when the odds were ten to one against the white man; of ambuscades and tragic deaths; of wrestling with black and grizzly bears; of wild racing after buffaloes, with a thousand incidents of their lives in hunting and trapping on the plains and in the mountains.[39]

Dick made three trips into Taos the winter of 1843-44. Before going to Taos in November, he acquired a license to trade with the Ute. They were usually in New Mexico, but they sometimes camped on the U. S. side of the border. The U S. government required anyone who traded with an Indian tribe within the U. S. border to obtain a license from the U. S. Indian Agent in charge of that tribe. To obtain a license a trader must agree to government laws pertaining to conduct while trading and pay a required bond. In this case, Dick put up $2,000.

The Ute were at peace; the Apache were not. Dick had to pass Apache camps along the way; so he traveled lightly with only one Delaware Indian as a companion. Their pack mules were loaded with guns, ammunition, beads, knives, and paints. The two headed south across

---

[39] Hall, *History of Colorado*, 236, 237.

Raton Pass into New Mexico in search of the Ute.

A few miles into New Mexico, they found an Indian village near Sugarite Creek. There were thirty-forty lodges, but they saw no Indians. Toward evening, Dick and the Delaware stopped under some cottonwood trees and prepared to set up camp before going to the Indian camp. When they did enter the camp, they saw a few old men. Squaws peeked out at them. Oh. These were Apache, not Ute.

The warrior band was hunting; only women and old men were in camp. Knowing there was little chance the women or old men would attack, Dick and the Delaware kept their composure. They mounted their horses and put many miles between themselves and the Apache camp before dark. They camped in a thickly wooded area in case defense should be necessary. Dick had about fifty rifles among his trade goods. He unpacked and loaded each one and set each in order. He could fire in succession, if necessary. The Delaware and he stood guard all night.

In the morning a few Apache came to their camp, wanted to enter; but Dick and the Delaware knew better and did not allow them. After a good bit of discussion, the Apache left. Dick and the Delaware packed up and continued to put miles between them and the Apache as they searched for the Ute. The Apache didn't pursue. Dick figured they were a little too close to Ute country for Apache comfort. They found the Ute in the Texas Panhandle near the Canadian River.

Their timing was poor. The Ute chief lay on his deathbed; and Dick knew their custom: they must kill the first stranger in their midst after the death of a chief. Dick was anxious to get the Indians in a trading mood, trade, and be gone. The Ute asked for medicine for the chief, but Dick knew he had nothing that would help the old fellow. If he gave them anything now, they'd blame him for the chief's death.

While the chief lay dying, warriors didn't go outside camp to hunt. Neither did Dick, nor the Delaware. Determined to make their stay short, they remained in camp and ate what the Ute ate. The meat didn't taste like anything Dick had ever eaten, but he asked no questions. He had his idea, but he didn't ask. When he saw them butcher a scrawny dog, his suspicions were confirmed.

As Dick saw the chief declining, he kept thinking maybe he should high-tail it out; but on the third day the Indians started to trade. Dick made quick work of it, traded for some ponies, mules, furs, and robes. The Delaware and he loaded the peltry on their horses and headed to El Pueblo. He heard that the chief died two days after they left.

For decades the trapping industry flourished. At the height of the beaver market, $200,000 worth of beaver pelts were shipped from Taos to the eastern market in one year. Trapping was still worthwhile in the mid-1840's, but the demand for beaver had reached its climax by the early 1840's. Fur seal, hare, and silk replaced beaver in the men's hat fashion market in the States and abroad. This impacted both trappers and Indians, who'd begun to depend upon the exchange of pelts and hides to obtain commodities that enriched their lives. Most trappers didn't immediately give up trapping entirely, but began to diversify, if that was not already their lifestyle.

In the spring of 1844 Dick and four friends trapped along the tributaries of the Grand Canyon of the Arkansas, crossed over the mountains to the Grand (Colorado) River in Middle

Park, and on to the Laramie plains (Wyoming), from there to the Green River. When they reached the headwaters of the Bear, they turned west and trapped to the Big Snake River and to the headwaters of the Wind River.

They had trouble with Indians all along the way. Finally, the five banded together with other trappers—about fifty, all total—and took a stand against the main band, killed many, and destroyed the belongings the Indians had brought along.

While Dick and his trapping compadres were watching out for their necks, Samuel F. B. Morse set up his new telegraph contraption in Washington, D. C. On Friday, May 24, 1844, he sent the first wireless message to his assistant Alfred Vail in Baltimore, Maryland. The message: "What hath God wrought?"

The U. S. government was busy at home and abroad. To encourage settlement of western lands, Congress passed the Townsite Act of 1844, which allowed the government to sell 320 acres of available land at $1.25 per acre to anyone who wanted to establish a townsite. Abroad, the government was negotiating its first trade treaty with China to open trade between the two.

In Hartford, Connecticut, Dr. Horace Wells impressed townsfolk when he introduced the use of nitrous oxide gas as an anesthetic while extracting teeth.[40]

1844 was a rough year weather-wise for Santa Fe Trail travelers. Heavy rains began in Kansas in March and continued on the Plains well into June. Bent-St. Vrain's eastward train bogged down near Pawnee Fork (Kansas) on April 23rd and was stranded almost a month. When they were able to cross Pawnee Fork, the wagons traveled to Walnut Creek and bogged down again on May 21st. They remained stranded almost another month. Mosquitoes multiplied. The rains of 1844 caused unusual flooding—so much that the course of the Missouri River changed in places.

On October 12, 1844, a snowstorm near the Arkansas River overtook Santa Fe Trail traders Albert Speyers and Dr. Henry Connelly (future New Mexico governor) and killed some of their mules. A few days later another snowstorm hit their caravan near Willow Bar on the Cimarron. That storm killed more than 300 mules during the night, forcing the traders to camp until more draft stock could be brought from Santa Fe. There was less traffic on the Santa Fe Trail in 1844: about $200,000 worth of goods crossed the Plains in less than a hundred wagons.

In the fall and winter (1844-45) Dick traded with Indians around Bent's Fort and with Ute in New Mexico. He spent some time at Ft. St. Vrain and other forts and continued to smuggle goods into New Mexico.

By 1845 Dick had kept his buffalo almost three years, domesticated them, and broken a few to work as teams. He was satisfied with his experiment, but there was no market for them in the area. He drove his herd like cattle across the Plains to Kansas City in the spring of 1845. There he sold them to an agent who represented New York City's Central Park. The agent, in turn, sold them in New York. Some were used in shows; others were kept in zoos.

Dick did not return home to Kentucky before he returned.

---

[40]Earlier, in March 1842, Dr. Crawford Long of Georgia used anesthetic (ether) when he removed a tumor from James Venable's neck. Ether protected Venable from surgical pain. Before publishing his find in 1846, Dr. Long used anesthesia on other patients: childbirth; amputation.

As usual, Charles Bent was on the Trail in spring 1845; but this year he preceded the annual train. Some suspected he went ahead to confer with Colonel Stephen Watts Kearny, who was preparing a western expedition. Bent's knowledge and experience would certainly have been beneficial. Western Indians had little respect for "white men." They'd seen the numbers of Americans trappers and traders and scorned the white tribe as being sparse and weak, easy to rob and overcome. One Indian chief boasted it was easier to kill a white man than a buffalo and much more profitable. In order to dispel that opinion, the U. S. government was sending Colonel Kearny and 280 dragoons on a Rocky Mountain expedition to give Indians a better perspective. Kearny left Ft. Leavenworth on May 18, 1845.

Fewer steamers floated down the Missouri River with supplies for Santa Fe traders in the spring of '45. Last year's flooding had created sandbars in places and changed the course of the river. Plus, most of the rain was used up last year. With this year's low rainfall and last year's flooding, the river was difficult for steamers to navigate between St. Louis and Independence.

After Dick sold his buffalo in the summer of 1845, he returned to the Arkansas Valley and built a cabin on the banks of the St. Charles (San Carlos)—about twelve miles south of El Pueblo.

In October Alexander Barclay and he loaded pack mules with goods and rode up the Rio Grande del Norte to trade with the Ute in their villages. Except for the common problem of thievery, 1845 was a time of relative peace between Indians and citizens in the El Pueblo vicinity. The men accomplished their trading and returned in a month. With no buffalo to care for, Dick headed back out to spend the winter of 1845-1846 hunting and trapping.

On one trip to an Arapaho village his horse gave out in deep snow about thirty miles short of his destination. Dick set the horse loose, buried his saddle in the snow, and set out on foot. In the afternoon he began to sprint in order to reach the village before dark. He noticed movement about 400-500 yards away—antelope? No. Pawnee. He'd been watching for them.

They caught sight of him about the time he caught sight of them. They took off after him. All were on foot. Two Pawnee outstripped their fellows and gained on Dick. He had to run over a little rise and took advantage of the opportunity to get a bead on one of the runners. He stopped him in his tracks. Dick jumped back up and reloaded his rifle as he ran. He turned to shoot the other lead runner, but he'd dropped back and was running with the band. They were gaining. Dick saw the Arapaho village, and they saw him. About forty Arapaho rode out.

Dick was too exhausted to mount the horse they brought him; so they pursued the Pawnee without him. He went on into the village. When the warriors returned, they were elated that they'd not only been able to aid Cuthand; they'd also killed all but one of Pawnee—as was their custom. They had seventeen fresh scalps of their hated enemies.

Colonel Henry Inman wrote of Dick and the Arapaho, "The tribe had the utmost veneration for the old trapper, and he was perfectly safe at any time in their villages or camps; it had been the request of a dying chief, who was once greatly favored by Wooton [sic], that his warriors should never injure him although the nation might be at war with all the rest of the whites in the world."[41]

---

[41] Inman, *Old Santa Fe Trail*, 354.

In early 1846 Dick went out with Joe Doyle, Bill New, Bill Tharp, and Levin Mitchell, all from the Pueblo settlement, to trade with Indians. By the first of February, a series of snowstorms piled up enough snow to stop them in their tracks. They holed up in Goshen's Hole, a steep-walled canyon on the Spring Branch of Horse Creek (Wyoming), until the first of March. Before long, traders Alexander Barclay and Benito Sandoval, also from Pueblo, joined them.

In 1846 Barclay, Doyle and other El Pueblo families moved to New Mexico to build Ft. Barclay.[42] The climate was better for farming than it was at El Pueblo. Dick remained near El Pueblo (1846), but rode southeast to trade with the Ute at Sierra Grande in northeastern New Mexico (eastern Colfax County).

As 1846 Santa Fe Trail spring traders began arriving from the States, they brought news of impending war. It was marching across the Plains to New Mexico. The first news arrived in Santa Fe on June 26, 1846, and grew with the telling.

---

[42] Later it was sometimes called Kroenig's fort.

Manifest Destiny and the Mexican-American War

The westward movement seemed a part of the American way before the United States became an independent nation. When times were hard for individuals or when there was a national panic, there was always hope that a person could "make it" somewhere else.

The United States considered it an opportunity, if not an obligation, to spread freedom and democracy across the American continent as it expanded its boundaries. Americans believed democracy and freedom would better all mankind. They called the civilizing movement "Manifest Destiny."

John L. O'Sullivan had coined the phrase in the New York *Morning News* in 1845: "Our manifest destiny is to overspread and possess the whole continent which providence has given us for the…great experiment of liberty." He wrote in the *Democratic Review*, "Nothing must interfere with the fulfillment of our manifest destiny to overspread the continent allotted by Providence for the free development of our yearly multiplying millions."

At the time O'Sullivan referred to the annexation of Texas, but his phrase defined the sights of many Americans: one nation from the Atlantic to the Pacific. Some had a wider vision: one nation from Alaska to Panama. Others, like U. S. Congressman John Wentworth, editor of the Chicago *Democrat*, thought it wasn't too much to aim for one North and South American nation. After Congress voted to allow the Republic of Texas admittance to the Union as a state, the U. S. government, following the course of Manifest Destiny, decided to push further west to Santa Fe and on to California. Concerned that Great Britain might take California, the United States sent John C. Fremont on a third western expedition.

Haled as America's Pathfinder, John Fremont left Missouri for California with Kit Carson as guide. Some found Fremont difficult to work with, but Carson had the temperament and skill to guide wise choices and dispel differences. His manner kept rifts from becoming insurmountable.

Dick wasn't gifted with ability for such long term service as guide. He guided at times and met some fine people. But, overall, he kept his guiding trips short term because he had little respect for people who had a higher perception of themselves, their position, or their opinions than he considered practical. Those with knowledge or authority in one area who thought they knew it all in all areas rubbed him.

Kit Carson

In the unfolding Manifest Destiny drama, Mexico and Texas had an ongoing land dispute over parts of New Mexico. Now that Texas was part of the U. S., President Polk sent John Slidell to Mexico in November 1845. He offered $25,000,000 and the assumption of debts owed American citizens in exchange for the New Mexico land and California. The land was not for sale.

Fremont arrived in California in December 1845 and began encouraging Americans living there to revolt against Mexican rule.

Provoked by Mexico's refusal of Slidell's offer, President Polk ordered General Zachary Taylor not to allow any Mexicans north of the Rio Grande in Texas. That provoked Mexico. The Mexican Army crossed the Rio Grande anyway in April 1846 and captured a unit of Taylor's men near Matamoras.

Congress declared war on May 13, 1846. New England abolitionists opposed the war; they thought Texas aimed to expand slavery. Whigs opposed, but only sixteen Congressmen voted against the war. The federal Army consisted of about 7,365 soldiers. The government approved the call for 50,000 volunteers. Congress authorized ten million dollars to cover costs.[43]

Volunteers from the original thirteen states averaged about 1,000 per state; Texas and the Mississippi Valley added about 50,000, many from Missouri. Dubbed Missouri Volunteers, the Army of the West gathered at Ft. Leavenworth to prepare under the command of Stephen Watts Kearny. "Ho! for New Mexico!" became their watchword.

Kearny was fifty-two, a small man with large eyes. He brushed his graying hair forward as he'd done since his early military days when he fought in Florida. Trained and skilled in warfare, he was reserved and militarily strict, but kind to his men. Whether by gift or accomplishment, he communicated skillfully and candidly, yet mannerly. Kearny accepted compliments, but wasn't vain; he commended others, also. He seemed at ease whether in command or in social situations.

Kearny had his orders: hold northern Mexican provinces until peace is established; establish temporary civil governments (Keep as many present officials in charge as feasible.); see that Santa Fe Trail trade continues uninterrupted.

Ready to move beyond the confines of the U. S. government, a Mormon battalion of about 500 under their leader Brigham Young joined Kearny's volunteers. After a difficult time in Illinois and Missouri, the Mormons had set their sights on the Salt Lake Basin (Utah). As soldiers, they could be paid as they moved. Perhaps their service would make a better name for them. Loosely interpreting the War Department's allowances for laundresses and service people, the battalion took along Mormons' wives (about thirty), children, and other relatives.[44] Kearny and his Army of the West left Ft. Leavenworth on June 30th, accompanied by a group of seasoned Santa Fe Trail traders.

At times officers found it difficult to rein in some raw recruits, who looked upon their western venture as an opportunity to shoot at buffalo and Indians. Both were new sights to many recruits.

---

[43] Horgan, 692.
[44] Some of the Mormons joined a Mormon group near El Pueblo; others went to Santa Fe. Kearny ordered Philip St. George Cooke to lead them to find a wagon road to California. They left Santa Fe in mid-October.

When spring traders arrived in Santa Fe with news of the coming war, buzzing rumors metamorphosed into inflammatory speeches on the plaza: Americans must be stopped, beginning now with Americans in Santa Fe and Taos—in the territory. Governor Armijo called his troops.

Tom Boggs, John Hatcher, and Charles Bent's brother George felt the atmosphere in Taos merited them moving their families to Bent's Fort. They took Josefa Carson and Ignacia Bent and her three children along. (Carson was in California with Fremont; Bent was getting supplies in the States.) They arrived at Bent's Fort on July 3, 1846.

The first of the Army—Moore's dragoons and Dave Waldo's two companies guided by Tom Fitzpatrick—arrived at Bent's Fort on July 27, 1846, and camped outside the walls. Glad to see signs of civilization after miles across the Plains, soldiers bought tobacco and liquor and enjoyed life. They drank and fought. One drunken soldier swam and then lay naked in the shade where he died of sunstroke. G. F. Ruxton, visiting the West, said the troops were "the dirtiest, rowdiest crew I have ever seen collected together."[45] They disgusted traders at the fort.

William Bent tried to operate business as usual and keep his traders supplied and commissioned. The market was especially good with emigrants to the north. But added guests—hundreds of soldiers and officers and traders traveling with them—kept William and his brother George hopping. They entertained the officers, answered all kinds of questions, and helped the sick. (Twenty-one had dysentery or scurvy.)

The military had come and acted like it owned the place. The Bents found supplies and storage for the Army's needs and put up with the military riffraff. In addition, many traders were concerned about the market during the war and hoped Bent would help them, too. After all, many of them were longtime friends.

At the same time Bent's Indian friends had a poor hunting season and camped near the fort. They were amazed at the number of white men; they had no idea there were so many. William's brother Charles and Ceran St. Vrain were still in the States. Charles didn't return until August 17th; Ceran came later with the fall wagon train.

Three Mexicans showed up at the fort claiming to have letters for Kearny, but William and his brother sized them up as spies. They tried to get past the guards. William didn't care: let them see the number of soldiers, the weapons. He turned them over to the Army.

Before Kearny and his officers left, William and George Bent held a fandango in their honor. Among the ladies who attended were: Mrs. Archibald Metcalf, Mrs. Tom Boggs, Mrs. Charles Bent, Mrs. Kit Carson, Mrs. George Bent, and several Indian women.[46]

Kearny summoned William Bent, said he planned to begin invasion of New Mexico on August 2nd, asked William to scout the Raton Mountains, see if he could pick up any information to be certain there wasn't a Mexican ambush. Kearny said he knew no man could do the job like William. He offered a paltry remuneration. Worn to a frazzle with his freeloading guests, William cursed and said if Kearny wanted help, he could pay what it was worth. Kearny sent a mediator and reached a compromise with William the next day.

---

[45] Moody, *Stagecoach West*, 61.

[46] When inflammatory fires stilled to a smolder in Santa Fe, Boggs took his family, Charles' family, and Kit's wife back to Taos.

Marcellin St. Vrain took command of the fort while William and a handful of trusted men, including Asa Estes, headed toward the Raton mountains. Scouts captured five Mexican spies and others carrying the Taos prefect's proclamation to draft all males between the ages of fifteen and fifty. William took the spies to Kearny. They informed him that 600 soldiers were preparing to repel them at Las Vegas, New Mexico. William found no opposition awaiting Kearny between the fort and the Raton Mountain, nor in the mountains.

Tom Fitzpatrick guided Kearny's Army of the West as it marched out of Bent's Fort toward New Mexico. They left, but Army supplies continued to arrive at the fort to be held in store. By October 31, 1846, there were 140 tons of Army stuff lying around William Bent's fort.

The Army of the West had a rough go crossing Raton Pass. The altitude made breathing difficult for soldiers from the lowlands, but the terrain was the main problem. Brothers James and Samuel Magoffin were among the Santa Fe Trail traders traveling with the army. Samuel's wife Susan, who accompanied him, described one of the days crossing Raton Pass: "They are even taking the mules from the carriages this P.M. and a half dozen men by bodily exertions are pulling them down the hills. It takes a dozen men to steady a wagon with all its wheels locked.... we came to camp about half an hour after dusk, having accomplished the great travel of six or eight hundred yards during the day."[47] A month later Marcellin St. Vrain attempted to haul freight over the Pass and lost his wagons. His 5,700 pounds of freight veered off the mountain, crashing and smashing, before it came to a stop against a pine tree.

Kearny's Army crossed the Pass and entered New Mexico. In little settlements along the way people came out to meet them and offer what food they had available to sell. All along the way Kearny received rumors: thousands of Indians would come …Governor Armijo's army would stop them here or there, but definitely at Cañoncito, less than twenty-five miles from Santa Fe.

On August 14, 1846, the army camped about a mile outside of Las Vegas. While in camp, Kearny received a dispatch commissioning him Brigadier General.

On August 15th, the Army entered the Las Vegas Plaza and raised the American flag without any noticeable trouble. At noon Kearny climbed atop a single story, flat roofed building, which faced the Plaza. He proclaimed: "My government will keep off the Indians, protect you in your life and property and…will protect you in your religion."[48] Right then and there two Las Vegas alcaldes took the oath of allegiance to the United States and accepted American citizenship. The people of Las Vegas cheered. They were experienced in conquests and had found courtesy their best policy. At least, it was best to start out that way. Navajo had raided the town a few days before. Maybe the Americans could protect them better than the Mexicans had.

The Army of the West marched on toward Santa Fe. Seasoned trader James Magoffin was familiar with Santa Fe and its ways. Kearny sent him and Colonel Philip St. George Cooke ahead to meet with New Mexico's Governor Manuel Armijo and his military commander, Colonel Diego Archuleta. Some viewed Archuleta as the stronger of the two, the man to be

---

[47] Lee, *Colorado, A Literary Chronicle*, 120.
[48] Dr. James Beatson, "Kearny's bloodless conquest makes Vegans Citizens," *Daily Optic*, 27 July 1979, 3.

dealt with.

Cooke and Magoffin arrived in Santa Fe on August 12, 1846. Governor Armijo received them in the Palace of the Governors on Santa Fe Plaza. Cooke remained in the palace; Magoffin went out to do business. What the men accomplished above board or under the table remains a matter of conjecture. There are always conjectures. The general consensus of the rumors: Armijo was paid; Archuleta was promised. The supposition is Magoffin gave Archuleta to understand the U. S. was only interested in New Mexico as far west as the Rio Grande. Archuleta would be free to lead New Mexico territory beyond that. That included present-day Arizona. Not knowing Kearny's plans had changed to go on to California, Magoffin may have offered Archuleta something that was no longer available.[49]

As the Army marched toward Santa Fe, Santa Fe citizens were terrified. There'd been rumors since spring. Now the Americans were close. Priests warned that when the Americans came, it'd be worse than an all-out Indian attack. Americans would kill, take their women, desecrate their churches, and steal their property. The spies who'd been captured at Bent's Fort added to the hype: There were thousands of American soldiers! Some New Mexicans who lived in outlying areas fled into town and the safety of numbers. Some who lived in town packed up and left to hide in the mountains.

Earlier in the summer, Governor Armijo attempted to raise defense support to no avail. He'd now drafted every male between the ages of thirteen and fifty-nine, confiscated horses and mules for government service, and opened a war chest for loyal citizens who wanted to contribute. Those who could paid $20-$100 to be excused from military service. Four thousand others marched or rode to Cañoncito to build ramparts and wait. On August 16, 1846, Governor Armijo joined them. New Mexico Legislators and the remainder of Armijo's soldiers accompanied him.

Armijo strategically positioned the artillery and zealously ordered men into posts behind earthen works. He told the men and boy soldiers that Vegas had fallen. With the passion of an orator, he warned them the Americans were upon them. He told them what that would mean and what they would do to the Americans. Were they ready? No. He knew they were not; they were all cowards! He consulted his officers and then ordered all recruits—the cowards!—to leave. How could he be expected to repulse invaders with such cowardly, undisciplined men! Armijo and his regular Mexican soldiers would do what needed to be done: attack or cross the river and guard. Armijo wrote a letter to Kearny to be delivered by Colonel Diego Archuleta.

Armijo and his soldiers rode back to Santa Fe. There Armijo loaded up all the goods he could take and, with his personal body guards—the regular soldiers, escaped, herding confiscated livestock downriver.

---

[49] From Santa Fe, Magoffin went to Chihuahua, where he'd traded since 1825. He'd married a Mexican in 1830 and made Chihuahua his home until 1844. On this trip his business was to prepare a way for General Wool. Apparently news of his mission preceded him. On arrival, Magoffin was arrested and jailed in Chihuahua and Durango for nine months. Well-liked, he was allowed to destroy the papers he carried. It's said he procured his jailors' favor with champagne and gifts. After all was done, Magoffin submitted expenditure claims to Congress. Congress agreed to pay $50,000. By the time he received payment, the amount changed to $30,000.

Kearny expected a skirmish at Cañoncito—the narrow defile between Vegas and Santa Fe; but, when his army arrived, they found only deserted earthen works. Kearny received Armijo's letter. Armijo wasn't giving New Mexico to him; but because Mexico was so far away, he hadn't yet received reinforcements and was retreating with his military until he received further orders from Mexico City.

In Santa Fe, Lt. Governor Juan Bautista Vigil y Alarid acted as provisional governor after Armijo fled. He posted copies of the letter Kearny sent Armijo, in which Kearny promised to deal kindly. Vigil sent Kearny word that Armijo was gone; Kearny was welcome.

August 18, 1846, was a rainy day in Santa Fe until about 5 p. m. Then the New Mexico sun broke through the just-finished-raining, deep-blue sky. Bright, deep red chile peppers hung in ristras from vigas protruding from the rich-brown adobe homes. Red geraniums bloomed in the windows. Dogs made their way out of hornos behind adobe homes.[50]

Kearny's force had marched since 5 a.m. and covered twenty-nine miles by the time they caught sight of Santa Fe. They weren't the only ones watching. As the army neared town, many Americans went out to meet them. Provisional Governor Vigil and his officers greeted Kearny. Vigil relinquished his office. The American flag was raised above the Palace of the Governors. New Mexico was conquered without shot or bloodshed—for the time being.

The next day, from Santa Fe Plaza, Kearny announced "Kearny's Code." Any who wanted could leave New Mexico. To those who chose to remain, he offered U. S. citizenship with full protection of life, property, and religion. Some left. Most stayed. Ex-provisional Governor Vigil accepted the proffered American citizenship. He pledged allegiance and added, "To us, the power of the Mexican Republic is dead."[51]

Dressed in their finery on August 20, 1846, Pueblo chiefs from along the Rio Grande met Kearny in Santa Fe and promised allegiance to his government. They had a belief passed down that white men would come from the east and relieve them from the injustices of the Spaniards.

In an effort to make good his promise of protection, Kearny ordered construction of an Army post in Santa Fe—the first U. S. military post in the Southwest. The Post of Santa Fe, later renamed Ft. Marcy in honor of Secretary of War William L. Marcy, was built less than a half mile from Santa Fe Plaza.[52]

The Army District of New Mexico was headquartered in Santa Fe's Palace of the Governors. The first officer quarters were nearby at 116 Lincoln Avenue.

When merchant James Magoffin left for Chihuahua, he reminded Kearny to remember Colonel Archuleta; but on August 22nd Kearny defined the original boundaries of New Mexico as the boundaries. That left no door for any private domain west of the Rio Grande, nor any Texas claim to New Mexico land east of the Rio Grande.

---

[50] Shaped similar to a miniature igloo, an horno was built of adobe and plastered smooth with a mud mixture. It was constructed to maintain heat for baking purposes when preheated with wood. An horno could double as shelter for the family dog. [Author never saw one used for that purpose.]
[51] Horgan, 731.
[52] Begun August 23, 1846, completed spring 1847. Built to garrison 280 soldiers, it could shelter 700 or more. The 9' high walls were constructed of 24" x 20" x 6" adobe.

Kearny took half of his troop south into New Mexico settlements and met with Indian delegations and priests before he left the area. Colonel Sterling Price was on his way from the States with reinforcement troops. Things in New Mexico seemed settled enough. Price could handle New Mexico and free Kearny to march to California. On September 22nd, Kearny appointed civil officials to govern New Mexico: First U. S. Governor of New Mexico Territory: Charles Bent; Lt. Governor: Donaciano Vigil; Commander in charge of Santa Fe until Price's arrival: Colonel Alexander Doniphan; Auditor: Eugene Leitensdorfer. Twenty-five-year-old Frank Blair was appointed Attorney General. Charles Beaubien and Joab Houghton were two of three superior court judges.

New Mexico's lone printing press printed new laws for New Mexico according to the U. S. government regulations Kearny set in place.

Governor Bent knew the no-shot-fired idea of conquest wasn't all it was cracked up to be. Some Spanish families came to New Mexico before the founding of Jamestown and settled before ships sailed in to Plymouth. This wasn't going to be a simple transition. The day Kearny appointed him governor, Charles wrote U. S. Secretary of State James Buchanan. He outlined needs: law books—New Mexico courts had none; business forms or blank business books; translators—Spanish was New Mexico's primary language, but Indian dialects, French, and English were also spoken in the territory; mail service at least once a month to connect New Mexico to the States; primary schools. Charles advised that, with all the changes taking place, taxing wasn't wise. On September 24th, he wrote a similar letter to Missouri Senator Thomas Benton, advocate of the West. He cited New Mexico needed an Indian agent, a surveyor general, and land commissioners.

That evening (September 24, 1846) New Mexico's new civil officials honored Kearny and his officers with a ball at the Governor's Palace. With everything in such good shape in Santa Fe, Kearny and most of his army left for California the next morning.

Colonel Sterling Price and his occupation troops arrived October 3, 1846—arrived and behaved like occupation troops. Governor Bent reported the lack of discipline to Kearny and spoke to Colonel Doniphan. He pressed each to require troops to respect the rights of New Mexicans. He knew the people well enough to know they wouldn't long put up with that sort of behavior.

A week later New Mexicans called for Kearny's promised protection. Navajo were raiding, and General Kearny had promised he wouldn't let that happen. New Mexicans hadn't resisted the Americans and had accepted the offer of American citizenship. Now they called for him to honor his word. Tom Boggs took the word to Doniphan, who wasn't yet organized. Raids continued. Governor Bent continued correspondence with Washington. On November 10th he wrote to request permanent military protection and presence in the territory and permanent military forts.

Once he was situated, Colonel Doniphan did address the problem of Navajo raids. Navajo chiefs and U. S. Colonels Doniphan and Gilpin signed the first U. S.-Navajo treaty at Ojo del Oso (New Mexico) on November 22, 1846. Though the inexperienced considered it an accomplishment, Governor Bent didn't set stock by it. He wrote U. S. Secretary of State James Buchanan that he had little grounds to hope the treaty would be permanent.

Bent heard nothing from Washington in answer to his requests. He wrote Thomas Benton again on November 30th. He re-emphasized the need of permanent military to secure against rebellion in the territory and to protect enterprise; so New Mexico could be an asset to the nation.

Kearny conquered New Mexico without firing a shot; but after he left, the fireworks began. Dissatisfied New Mexicans planned a revolt for mid-December 1846, but they weren't quite ready. They postponed action to finish preparation.

La Tulles—Gertrudis Barceló, madam at the center of Santa Fe gambling activity, got wind of the uprising, rescheduled for Christmas Eve. She secretly got word to Governor Bent through Lt. Governor Donaciano Vigil. With the leak, the insurrection lost its spark. Some plotters were arrested. The revolt was averted; but ringleaders Augustin Duran and Tomas Ortiz escaped.

On Christmas Day 1846 Governor Bent requested Colonel Sterling Price allow the artillery battalion to remain in Santa Fe, rather than moving it to the battle in Mexico. American merchants in Santa Fe petitioned Price for guns and soldiers. Guards patrolled Santa Fe streets and interrogated anyone who looked suspicious.

At the same time the Comanche blamed American soldiers for disease that hit their tribe and went on the warpath. Pawnee and Comanche attacked government supply wagons driven by inexperienced teamsters. That cut down supplies in Santa Fe.

In late December rumors circulated in Santa Fe that Mexicans had defeated American troops further south. In the first week of January, war reports arrived which told of American victory, not defeat at the Battle Brazito (New Mexico). Governor Bent announced the victory and encouraged New Mexicans not to pay attention to rumors that incite rebellion.

With the storm clouds of rebellion apparently dissipating, Governor Bent considered it safe to allow U. S. artillery in Santa Fe to join forces fighting in Mexico.

COMMANDERS IN THE MEXICAN WAR.

R. F Stockton.   Winfield Scott.   Philip Kearney.
John C. Fremont.   Santa Anna.   Zachary Taylor.

Revolt

After reports of American victories, calm seemed to settle in Santa Fe; but rumbles of discontent stirred in Taos. Governor Charles Bent continued to hear rumors of smoldering resentment. On Thursday, January 14, 1847, he left Santa Fe for Taos with his brother-in-law Pablo Jaramillo, Taos Prefect Cornelio Vigil, Sheriff Stephen "Steve" Louis Lee, Circuit Attorney James White Leal, and Narciso Beaubien, who had recently returned from college in Cape Girardeau, Missouri. With preliminaries of the new government in place, Bent could bring his family from Taos to live with him in Santa Fe.

Charles Bent was related by marriage to many in Taos, had long lived there, and considered most residents his friends. He didn't think he needed a military escort; he'd be able to handle the situation. If Taos residents saw a military escort, they may think he didn't trust them.

The party made its way to Taos through deep snow. As they neared town, a number of Pueblo Indians approached them and demanded release of some friends jailed for theft. Bent explained the matter would be handled in the course of the law. They warned him to flee.

Charles arrived in Taos, welcome in his warm adobe home. The house was full—Ignacia and the children, her sister Josefa Carson, whose husband, Kit was in California with Fremont, and Ignacia's daughter, Rumalda. Rumalda's husband, Tom Boggs, at work on the newly established mail route between New Mexico and the States, was on his way home.

That cold winter night, as Charles and his family prepared for bed, they heard noise in the street.[53] The noise grew loud in the still night air and heightened as a clamoring mob came closer to their home. Sounds of gunshots pierced the tumult. Charles calmly quietened the children.

Fists beat on the front door. The women, wise concerning Indian and Mexican ways and accustomed to being alone at night, told Charles not to open the door. He didn't have their same Spanish inner sensing, that gut knowledge. Even though he knew of the 1837 Revolt and of the time his store was rifled and Beaubien's was looted, he continued to see himself as home among friends. Surely, any differences could be settled. He relied on mutual respect and friendship built over many years.

He walked to the door and called, "What do you want?"

Many voices answered, blending into a blob of sound. Ignacia had lived in Taos all her life, knew the people better than Charles. She brought his guns.

No, Charles wouldn't shoot; that could cost the lives of the women and children. Confident he could quell the unrest, he stalled the mob, talked to them through the door. He offered money. The boastful, self-assured mob responded with the noise of individuals' hoots rippling through the raucous rumble of the mass. They had the taste of blood. Money they did not want.

---

[53] Some say they were in bed; others say it was almost morning.

In the next room, Ignacia, Josefa, Rumalda, and an Indian slave frantically dug with a spoon and stove poker into the adobe wall that separated them from their neighbor. Ten-year-old Alfredo stood strong by Charles' side, "Let's fight them, Papa."

No. Charles knew that wasn't an option; he motioned Alfredo to go over by the women and children. To the mob, Charles suggested a meeting to discuss issues. The mob responded by pounding on the door.

The children heard the sounds of footsteps on the roof. The events of the night wrote indelibly on the memory of Bent's children, especially his five-year-old daughter, Teresina. A rifle stock shattered the window. Chards scattered about the room. The women continued digging.

Buying time for the women and children—and Americans in the area, Charles offered to go with the mob if they'd leave everyone else in town alone. Mob mentality had already taken over. They saw the governor as an American, not as Charles Bent. In answer to his offer, shots shattered through the door, grazed Charles' chin, then a straight shot into his stomach. Arrows preceded the mob pressing through the door and struck Charles in the face and chest.

Many feet ran across the courtyard roof. Many hands tore at the roof and removed its protecting cover. The hole in the wall was big enough now; the women had bored through, right into their neighbor's home. The women shoved the children through. As they crawled through, they kept calling Charles. He ignored their pleas to escape. The room swarmed with Indians, pressing through the broken door, springing through the roof.

Finally, Charles attempted to follow his family. Indians overtook him and scalped him with a bowstring. Holding his bleeding head, Charles tugged at the arrows in his body, pulled out three. He was near the hole. As the women began to pull him through the hole, he tried to speak. "I want—" Realizing no one understood him, he futilely made a sign he wanted to write.

Then he raised his hands to deflect blows. Knives slashed both hands.

"'We want your gringo head,' yelled Tomasito Romero, Pueblo Indian Alcalde,…"[54]

Charles died in Ignacia's arms.

Ignacia pleaded; the children cried.

Who was it with knives and axes slashing Charles' wrists and chopping his hands, mutilating his body? There were too many to tell who was doing what. Buenaventura Lobato and others in the mob shouted angrily to the butchers: what were they doing? They should not have killed the governor; they should have taken him captive!

Ignacia and Josefa implored the mob to spare Rumalda and the children.

Horrified, their neighbors tried to help and hid Rumalda under blankets. The mob decided not to take the women and children, but warned them, ordered them not to leave the house. Terrified, the children wondered if the mob would return and what would happen if they did. The murderers tacked Charles' scalp to a board and left to parade the governor's scalp through the streets of Taos.

Dick Wootton said they didn't just take Charles Bent's scalp, but beheaded him and carried

---

[54] C.W.A. Workers, "LaPlata Huerfano and Mesa …," 163.

his bodiless scalped head around town to frighten women and children and those who were not in sympathy with them. Charles' head was never recovered.

Thus began the Taos Massacre and Revolt, January 19, 1847.

With the taste of blood, the mob thirsted for more. Reinforced with liquor, leader Pablo Montoya sent for reinforcements from nearby Taos Pueblo. The mob dragged Sheriff Steve Lee out of bed into the cold winter night. Lee broke away, ran across the snow covered ground, up onto a roof. They tailed him, killed him, mutilated him.[55]

Taos Prefect Cornelio Vigil, who was one of the party Dick Wootton had accompanied to mark the northeast corner of the Beaubien-Miranda Land Grant, was on the mob's list—or came to someone's mind. Accustomed to old Spanish manners and rule, Vigil ordered the unruly mob to break up. Hoodlums like these were below his station. In response, they attacked him, killed him, chopped him into pieces.

Somebody in the mob knew where Attorney James Leal was staying after his arrival with Governor Bent. They woke Leal, stripped him, forced him to march nude through the streets of Taos on that freezing January night. The mob followed behind him, singing as they went, prodding him with lances, piercing him with arrows. Ready to move on, they used his body like a pin cushion, piercing it with arrows—piercing, but not killing. They shot arrows into his eyes, his nose, his mouth. He begged them to kill him. They scalped him, kicked him in a ditch, and left him to blindly wander the streets. Enough entertainment with Leal; they went to find others.

They were looking for the young men who came with the governor: Pablo Jaramillo[56] and Narciso Beaubien.[57] Where could they be? A woman informed them. A friend had hidden them in a pile of straw, but Narciso's head wasn't completely covered. The mob found them, lanced them to death. Stabbed until you couldn't really tell who they'd been. Narciso had a nice ring. They cut off his finger and took it. Dick Wootton said that day's victims were horribly mutilated and every one of them scalped.

What happened to Leal? Several hours later a young boy shot Leal, put him out of his misery. Roaming hogs took over. In the afternoon Mrs. Beaubien, whose son Narciso had been killed, rescued Leal's body from the feasting, snorting hogs and saw to it the attorney had a burial.

Fearing to leave, Bent's family remained in the home of their neighbor Mrs. Juana Catalina Valdez-Lobato. What was left of Charles' dead body in its drying pool of blood lay nearby. Very early the next morning, under the cover of darkness, friendly Mexicans—for mobs only appear to be everyone—kindly, bravely came to the Bent home, took Charles' headless body and buried it. They brought food and clothing for the family. A few days later the women and children were able to move to the safety of other friends' home. An old Mexican protected them. Disguising them as squaws, he put them to work grinding corn on metates.

Whooping it up, the mob looted American homes and businesses and paraded that day and

---

[55] Lee and his wife, Maria de la Luz, had at least one daughter—Maria Benigna Lee, born in 1830.
[56] Pablo was the brother-in-law of both Charles Bent and Kit Carson.
[57] Narciso was the son of Judge Carlos Beaubien and brother-in-law of Lucien Maxwell.

the next. They weren't only after Americans, but after anyone connected in any way with the new government. They murdered twelve on January 19th. Bolstered by their accomplishments, the reactionaries sent emissaries to encourage revolt in outlying areas. They began to make plans for their own government.

Fortunately, many Americans were out of town. Lucien Maxwell, Manuel LeFevre, and George Bent were on the Arkansas. Dick Wootton, who'd frequently been in and out of Taos in late 1846 and early 1847, was at El Pueblo.

Mothers of light-skinned children tried to darken their children with coffee…so many children in town were mixtures of Indian or Spanish and American or French.[58] Remembering children whose mothers tried to disguise them, Dick Wootton said, "A majority of the half-breeds were dispatched as summarily as Governor Bent and his friends had been."[59]

While rioters were looting, Charley Towne and Charlie Autobees slipped out of Taos. Towne headed to Santa Fe. He arrived on January 20th and went to Jim Beckwourth's Santa Fe hotel. Beckwourth relayed Towne's message to Colonel Sterling Price. Price soon received word that revolutionaries' emissaries had been intercepted carrying a message that Jesus Tafoya was marching toward Santa Fe with 1,500 men. They were to invite Santa Feans to join the revolt.

Colonel Price was hard pressed to come up with 300 soldiers. He contacted Ceran St. Vrain, in Santa Fe, and asked him to recruit volunteers. That was right down St. Vrain's alley. It wasn't hard for him to gather men; individual men counted him their individual friend. In no time, he mustered sixty-five volunteers from among mountain men, traders, merchants, Mexicans and native New Mexicans in Santa Fe. Each man was determined to avenge Charles Bent's death. Among the volunteers Ceran mustered, Charles Beaubien had a score to settle: the murder and mutilation of his only son. Price commissioned St. Vrain captain and Archibald Metcalf lieutenant.

In the meantime, Charlie Autobees rode like a madman. He rode past Simeon Turley's distillery at Arroyo Hondo, New Mexico, warned them the mob was coming, and turned his steed toward Bent's Fort.

Come they did. When Simeon Turley saw about 500 rebels approaching his mill and distillery stockade, he shut the gates. For more than fifteen years he'd offered the most continuous employment for area Hispanics and Indians. Like Bent, he found warning words incredulous. Turley thought he belonged here by now.

There were about ten men with Turley inside the gates. During the uproar of the siege, John Albert and the others at Turley's Mill barricaded themselves within the compound. Rebels shot arrows and balls, but Turley and his men held off the mob. They held out long; but the angry assailants stormed through into Turley's corrals, killed his sheep and hogs, and managed to torch the stockade's main buildings. On the second day some of Turley's men died. As the siege worsened, those within the compound gave up hope that the mob would

---

[58] Maria de la Luz Dillette, Dick Wootton's future mother-in-law—half-French, half-Spanish—lived in Taos at the time and remembered those days vividly.
[59] Conard, 1890, 177.

fall back. Their only thread of hope was escape. The men clung to that, repeating the word to themselves throughout the day. Their ammunition was giving out. Now the fire was burning. Crackling, smoldering. Now bursting flames. Tongues of fire licking up the fresh crisp winter air, belched out choking smoke. The sky darkened.

As the second day drew to a close, John Albert called the men together: if they were ever going to escape, the time was now. At what stage of readiness each man stood when he heard John's words is one of the questions of unwritten history. John flung open the stockade door and darted out, shooting into the mob as he ran. The others followed suit. Grasping his two-pound knife, John began slashing his way to freedom before the angry mob recovered from the surprise. But they did recover, killed some of the escapees on the spot and chased down others who had escaped the assailants' line. John cleared the line and escaped, but lost his hat in the fray. He hadn't even thought to grab his coat; but there was no going back.

Among those killed at Turley's were Simeon Turley, William Hatfield, Joseph Marshall, William Austin, Peter Robert, Louis Tolque, and Albert Turbush.

In the darkness John Albert and Tom Tobin escaped. Tom headed to Santa Fe and lost no time reporting to Colonel Sterling Price. John Albert headed toward El Pueblo; he knew mountain men would be there.

Spurred by fresh memories of fire and attack and the slaughter of animals and friends replaying in his mind, John traveled on foot through the freezing night without adequate protection.

As morning began to dawn, John set a straight course for the Arkansas River. He felt the stinging cold, but kept moving across the deep, heavy snow covering his course. Crossing the Sangre de Cristo Range, he killed a large deer, ate the gut meat, only to vomit it back up.

How can one's system handle great tragedy and simple digestion at the same time? He skinned the deer in such a way that he was able to use the body hide and head for a coat and cap. The hide soon cooled and froze stiff on his body, but it kept off some of the wind. Perhaps he could build just a little fire—cook the meat a little—without being found. He did.

When John reached Greenhorn, he rested a day before he continued toward El Pueblo. He saw a man riding a mule and hailed him. If the man was a Mexican like those who'd besieged Turley's Mill, he'd just kill him and take his clothes. The thought came instantly without deliberation. The man saw John dressed in the deer hide coat and deer head cap. He turned his mule and took off like he'd seen a demon. (John learned the man was part of a Mormon hunting party.)

It was dark by the time John passed the Mormon settlement near El Pueblo. The village slept, except for a large black dog. It wasn't content to bark, but ran to attack him. John shot the dog.

It'd been five or six days since Charles Bent's massacre when John Albert reached El Pueblo. When he arrived—covered with hide—in the dark of night, he was a sight to behold. His bare feet were scratched and torn from the terrain; his clothing was torn. He was cold and starving.

It was his report, not his appearance, which propelled Dick Wootton and the mountain men at El Pueblo to join the Mexican-American War Battle of Taos. Rage burned in the mountain men as they heard of the massacre of their compadres. Immediately, some concluded they should round up all twenty Mexican employees at the fort and kill them for a start. Wiser council prevailed; sound reasoning quelled initial impulses.

The mountain men held a council of war and discussed the wisest way to handle the situation. Ties of friendship in the mountains were as thick as family ties back home. They knew their number wasn't enough to quell a large rebellion. They considered what they could do to avenge their friends' deaths and see to it their families would have the property entitled to them. They had no idea when troops would be sent, but they knew the U. S. would send troops. Not knowing Autobees had ridden to Bent's Fort, they sent a messenger to William Bent. Then five mountain men, including Dick Wootton and red-headed Levin Mitchell, left for Taos to help where they could. They'd be there. They rode over the mountains, 165 miles south to Taos.

Charlie Autobees had ridden hard to carry his message to William Bent, but William wasn't at Bent's Fort. Louey Simonds found him trading with the Cheyenne. When the southern Cheyenne heard Who-pi-ve-heo (their name for Charles) had been scalped, chiefs held a war council and readied to march to Taos as one man to avenge Charles' death. They came to William to let him know they were sending their young braves to scalp every Mexican in Taos. William couldn't allow such a ride; who knew what vengeance that would wreak? –Untaken turns in history.

Grief stricken, William was deeply touched by his people—they were his people by marriage. William assured his family of his deep gratitude, but said it was the responsibility of the soldiers and of the men from Bent's Fort to take care of the uprising. The Army had set the stage for the situation; it was up to the Army to handle it. William returned to Bent's Fort. He'd go to Taos. No. William's friends persuaded him to remain at the fort with a few men: who knew if the mob would attempt to reach the fort?

Seventeen men at Bent's Fort volunteered to go, among them Bill Bransford, Manuel LeFevre, François Lajeunesse, and Lucien Maxwell. Maxwell and LeFevre had family in Taos. They were raring to go; but Captain Jackson, at the fort, wouldn't leave until he had better understanding. He sent a messenger to the Mormon brigade near El Pueblo. The rider reported that Captain Brown and the Mormon battalion were drilling in case they were needed. The troop from Bent's Fort set off. All but five of the men were walking. When they reached the Purgatory ranch, they appropriated U. S. government stock. From there all the men rode to Taos.

Meanwhile, revolutionaries spread south, east, and north from Taos into villages along the Rio Grande, to Mora, New Mexico, and to the Bent-St. Vrain ranches. Along the Rio Colorado they surrounded Americans Mark Head and William Harwood, who were transporting furs to trade in Taos. The rebels shot them in the back and left them dead.

The revolutionaries were in Mora on January 20th. They attacked a wagon train and killed eight Americans, including thirty-three- year-old Lawrence Ludlow Waldo, William and David Waldo's younger brother. Lawrence had been well-respected by New Mexicans and Indians.

The garrison from the Vegas (New Mexico) post descended on Mora like a summer cloudburst. They broke into every house from which anyone was firing. They shot or bayoneted twenty-five on the spot. After seventeen more were captured, rebels took refuge in an old fort and fought the troop from there. On January 24th Captain Israel Hendley died in the Battle of Mora. Until the garrison brought in artillery, they were no match for the guerrillas. Then they did their best to level the rebels and the town. The rebels yielded.

On January 24, 1847, along about evening, a band of rebels rustled hundreds of oxen, hundreds of horses and mules, and a thousand head of government cattle from Bent-St. Vrain's Ponil and Vermejo ranches (New Mexico). Ranch hands escaped to the upper Purgatory ranch and reported the incident to Frank DeLisle, camped there tending a large herd of company stock. DeLisle packed up to head to Bent's Fort. Louey Simonds raced ahead to report to Bent. The officer of a government party prepared breastworks on top of a hill near Ponil Creek.

Rumors striking fear were the only thing that loomed as large as the revolt.

Before he left Santa Fe, Colonel Sterling Price enforced martial law and jailed any suspicious characters. His soldiers destroyed the residence and provisions of Don Diego Archuleta, an influential leader in the rebellion.[60]

Price sent word to the Albuquerque garrison to come protect the capital. Lieutenant Colonel Willock arrived and took command.

Colonel Price and Captain St. Vrain left on January 23, 1847. Only St. Vrain's volunteers had mounts. The next day they met advancing rebels—at least 1,500 Mexicans and Indians—at La Cañada, about twenty miles north of Santa Fe. Price's only hope was that his men were better trained. He ordered St. Vrain's volunteers to guard the baggage train while soldiers attacked.

St. Vrain and his recruits were chomping at the bit for a piece of the action. When rebels neared the baggage, that was all St. Vrain's men needed. Whooping, they chased rebels up into the hills. The day's cost to the military: six or seven wounded, two dead—a teamster named Mussersmith and a private named Graham. Cost to rebels: forty-five wounded, thirty-six dead—including General Tafoya.

The troops searched for a trail through the snow and forged on toward Taos. They cut a path for the baggage wagon. On the 28th (January 1847) Captain John H. K. Burgwin, Lt. Wilson, and their cavalry company caught up with Price's unit. That brought the total men to 480. To help even the score, they added a six-pound howitzer to those Colonel Price had. The reinforced troop met the rebels again and fought at Embudo. Private Papin was killed. Dick Green, the Bent's black servant, was injured. Pushing the insurrectionists back to their village, the troops marched into Taos on February 3rd. Resistance was concentrated at Taos Pueblo, about three miles further.

---

[60] Archuleta was the man with whom James Magoffin had presumably made a deal prior to Kearny's arrival in Santa Fe. Augustin Duran, Tomas Ortiz, and Archuleta had plotted insurrection.

Battle of Taos

Built for fortification, Taos Pueblo withstood attack for centuries. An adobe-walled church had been added to the compound; but, like the Pueblo itself, it had no opening facing the outside world. To enter the pueblo, an Indian climbed a ladder and drew it up behind him.

Not all insurgents were at the Pueblo. Only about six or seven hundred men and their families took refuge behind the formidable walls. That was where they lived, where they were well-stocked for winter months or for enemy attack. A creek ran under the frozen ground into the pueblo and provided fresh water. They were set.

Dick Wootton and the mountain men from El Pueblo arrived and waited in the hills, watching for troops. The troops arrived the same day. The mountain men made their way down the mountain into the soldier camp and joined St. Vrain's volunteer company. Though it was already midday, Colonel Price decided to attack.

Troops made no headway before the winter sun set.

Attack resumed early the next morning, February 4th, and lasted until sundown. Inside the pueblo, men fortified themselves in the church, La Iglesia de Taos, and shot down on their assailants through holes in the parapet. One shot hit Captain John Burgwin.

The adobe walls of the old church were thick; howitzer shells couldn't penetrate them. There was only one thing to do: someone must ax through the thick adobe by hand. Volunteers were called for. Dick Wootton and thirty-four others responded. They dug into the walls, chopping until there were holes large enough for howitzer shells to pass through. Indians fired on the men as they worked and killed three or four. Fighting was heavy until about 3:30 in the afternoon.

Soldiers brought their little howitzer close to the ax holes and started firing. To be sure shells exploded where they wanted them to, volunteers lit some and threw them through the holes by hand and created a tumult in the church. By the time the howitzer shot ten times, it had carved a little "soldier door" into the church. Bents' slave Dick Green jumped in first to get his hands on the murderers.[61] As soldiers began streaming in the howitzer hole, rebels began exiting. Following pueblo custom, a few soldiers climbed ladders up the wall. They set the roof on fire.

With the bright New Mexico sun shining down on the frozen landscape, St. Vrain's volunteers covered the rear of the pueblo. The enemy fled in all directions. Some attempted to escape to the nearby mountains—a delight to the many mountain men of St. Vrain's company.

All their years in the mountains, living in the rough and among Indian ways, prepared them for this day. Those rebels had killed more than one of their own. Mountain men shot;

---

[61] Bents gave Dick Green and his wife their freedom for his gallantry. In May 1847 they returned to the States.

they clubbed; they chased; they tomahawked. "No quarter," Indians had long taught them. They were well-schooled and remembered their education. Some called trappers and mountain men "White Indians." Now they had a score to settle and would play on Indian terms whether they pursued a group or an individual. Only two or three attempting escape escaped them. They killed fifty-one. When St. Vrain spotted Jesus de Tafoya wearing Governor Bent's coat, he shot him.

Colonel St. Vrain had two close calls. While aiming at two Indians, another jumped him from behind. A man named Chavez struck the assailant with his rifle and split his head. Later, St. Vrain was riding with Wootton and two or three others when he saw a rebel leader lying on the ground, apparently dead. When he stopped to examine the man, the leader came to life and grabbed St. Vrain's throat. He swung St. Vrain as a shield from the others and raised his arm to stab him with a steel-pointed arrow. Wootton jumped off his horse:

> I sprang to his assistance as soon as I saw the struggle commence, but the Indian managed to keep the colonel between him and me, and was so active in his movements that I found it difficult to strike a lick which would be sure to hit the right head. I managed after a little, however, to deal him a blow with my tomahawk, which had the effect of causing him to relax his hold upon the colonel, and when he stretched out on the ground again, there was no doubt about his being a dead Indian.[62]

Darkness set in before Colonel Price's battle was done. He waited for morning. At the pueblo, death wails pierced the winter night.

Soldiers had killed 100 or more, in addition to the fifty-one killed by St. Vrain's recruits. Dick estimated close to 200 Indians and Mexicans had fallen. There was no exact count.

Americans lost thirty-five, including Captain Burgwin. Dick thought Burgwin was as brave as they come. Not all died on the battleground; some of the wounded died later. Burgwin was buried in a grave of his own; the others were buried in a long trench.

Surrounded by death and dying, pueblo leaders realized their inability to continue resistance. Before daylight pueblo women carrying white flags and children carrying crosses and religious relics approached Colonel Price and asked for peace.[63]

Price said if they wanted peace, they had to surrender leaders of the rebellion. He jailed Pablo Montoya and Tomas/Tomasito Romero (two principle ringleaders) in the small jail on the north edge of Fernandez de Taos. Jesus Maria de Tafoya (dead), Pablo Chaves (dead), and Manuel Cortes (Mora Valley ringleader escaped.) had also led in the revolt. Padre Antonio Jose Martinez seemed to favor the rebellion; but Colonel Don Diego Archuleta was reportedly at the root of the whole plot.[64] Archuleta and another ringleader or two escaped.

Dick Wootton was appointed as a temporary marshal under military authority. In the next few days, he kept busy helping round up ringleaders. Not all involved in the revolt would be tried in Taos; some would be tried in Santa Fe. Attorney Frank Blair prepared for trials.

While arrests were being made, St. Vrain heard about an attack on the Bent-St. Vrain ranches and sent men to assess the situation on the Vermejo and Ponil. When they arrived,

---

[62] Conard, 1890, 183,184.
[63] Reports vary: either Pueblo leaders sent them or went with them.
[64] Archuleta supposedly planned to oust Americans as the Indians had the Spanish in 1680.

they found William Bransford had already arrived from Bent's Fort.

Ringleader Tomasito Romero was in hold, slated for trial, when a soldier named John Fitzgerald shot him in the head. Killed him instantly. Fitzgerald's brother had been killed years before in the Texas-Santa Fe Expedition. Strange, some folks think history's dead.

After he killed Tomasito, Fitzgerald high-tailed it out of the country to avoid punishment for taking the law into his own hands. He could have waited. As Dick Wootton said, "the Indian deserved to be killed and would have been hanged anyhow, but we objected to the informal manner of his taking off."[65] The remaining ringleaders would be tried by martial law.

The jury was chosen and judges appointed. Some have intimated the jury may have been partial—actually, downright partial. They represented Americans, Mexicans, and French Canadians; but it was a close community: who had not heard? In Taos, in Santa Fe—in fact, in New Mexico Territory—it would have been difficult, if not impossible, to find a juror not associated with or related to—by blood or marriage—one side or the other or both. Had not every thinking person within riding distance formed an opinion at that time and place of lifeblood loyalty to family, friend, and cause? However, names stand out.

Charles Beaubien and Joab Houghton were judges. Both had been Charles Bent's friends. Beaubien was the father of slain Narciso Beaubien. Bent's brother George was foreman of the grand jury. Ceran St. Vrain interpreted for the court. Robert Fisher, oft employed by Bent, was foreman of a petit jury. Elliott Lee, related to Sheriff Lee, was a grand jury venire man.

There was more than one trial. Among the jurors were Lucien Maxwell, Antoine LeRoux, Charlie Autobees, Charley Towne, Manuel Laforet, Asa Estes, William LeBlanc, Charles Robidoux, Baptiste Chalifoux, trapper Joseph Paulding, and several Mexicans.

The first trial opened at 9 a.m., Monday, April 5, 1847, Judge Beaubien, presided. The courtroom was a long, narrow adobe building. There was standing room only. Dick Wootton attended.

Ignacia Bent, Rumalda Boggs, and Josefa Carson sat on a wooden bench to the side, waiting their time to witness. The prisoners on trial faced Judge Beaubien. As Ignacia Bent testified of her husband's massacre, the prisoners' faces were motionless and unresponsive.

Having heard all prosecution and defense, the jury deliberated less than fifteen minutes before returning its verdict: five men guilty of murder in the first degree, one guilty of treason in the first degree. Judge Beaubien pronounced sentence: "Muerte, muerte, muerte." He added that because of crowded jail conditions, they'd be executed before further trial proceedings. The condemned appeared impassive.

The first hangings were set for Friday, April 9, 1847, in Taos; but there was a problem. Newly appointed Sheriff Archibald Metcalf had no rope. St. Vrain's men found out that Louey Simonds, John Hatcher, and Lewis Garrard had lariats. A government teamster had some hemp picket cords. They borrowed those. A couple mountain men helped Metcalf tie the nooses.

The scaffold stood in a field 150 feet from the jail. Soldiers positioned their howitzer within four feet of the jail and aimed the muzzle at the door. Another howitzer stood guard on

---

[65] Conard, 1890, 185.

the flat roof of the jail, its muzzle pointed toward the gallows.

Spectators clambered atop the flat roofs of nearby homes to gain a better view. Soldiers on three sides and mountain men on one side formed a square to receive the condemned as they left confinement. The remaining soldiers stood at attention.

At 9 a.m. a priest administered last rites to those who wanted them. Jose Manuel Garcia, Juan Ramon Trujillo, Pedro Lucero, Hipolito "Polo" Salazar, Ysidro Antonio Romero and his sixteen-year-old brother Manuel Antonio Romero filed toward the government wagon under the scaffold. Each stepped up onto the single plank, which spanned the rear of the wagon. The narrow scaffold left no elbow room between them. When nooses and white covering caps were in place, the wagon driver motioned to the two mules. The mules pulled the wagon forward.

When the ropes were taken off the convicted, the government teamster stood by to make sure no one cut his picket cords. Those picket cords cost him a dollar each; he had to have them to tie up his mules.

All trials were over by the end of April. On April 30, 1847, five Indians and four Mexicans were hanged for their parts in the Taos Massacre and Revolt. All total, court held session fifteen days and sentenced fifteen men to death.

Some rebels were flogged, rather than sentenced to death. In other areas of New Mexico about twenty more who'd murdered were executed. Some of the men executed were fathers of young children.

Don Diego Archuleta's father-in-law, Antonio Maria Trujillo, who'd led the attack against Colonel Price and the troops on their way to Taos, was among those tried in Santa Fe. He was convicted and pardoned. According to historian Ralph Twitchell, none convicted in the civil court at Santa Fe were punished.

Charles Bent's body was disinterred and reburied in Santa Fe. During his short time in office Governor Bent set in motion the beginnings of the territorial government that served New Mexico until it attained statehood in 1912.

Important Matters

Colonel Doniphan left Santa Fe for another phase of the Mexican War. He planned to take Chihuahua, Mexico, and to join forces with General Wool. On his way, Doniphan sent a message, requesting Dick Wootton to join as a guide and scout into Mexico. Dick had met Doniphan in Santa Fe and agreed to accompany him if he needed help. Before the middle of February, Dick rode hard for four days to catch up to Doniphan and his troop.

Whenever Dick worked as a guide, he rode ahead of the man in command to keep him informed. Dick assessed the lay of the land for the easiest practical route and searched for water and good places for noon stops and evening campgrounds. He seemed to have an instinct for finding water, but it was sometimes difficult to find water for hundreds of men and animals. He lived alert for any sign of enemy activity. When he scouted for the military, he traveled with ten to fifteen men in case he came upon enemy and needed assistance. In camp each evening he presented an overview of the next day's ride to the man in command.

Dick sighted no enemy until they reached Rio Sacramento, which intersected the Chihuahua road. Mexicans had gathered to fortify Sacramento River Pass. Mexican General Heredia had transformed Chihuahua Governor Angel Trias' nearby hacienda into a stronghold, which housed about 4,000 Mexican soldiers.

Renowned Indian fighter James Kirker offered Doniphan a strategic plan. With a few men he prepared the way for American forces to capture Trias' hacienda about eighteen miles from Chihuahua. After battling about three hours, Doniphan's troop drove out the Mexicans and controlled the hacienda. The brief Battle of Sacramento was over: February 28, 1847.

Dick hoped to see Chihuahua; but, at Trias' hacienda, Doniphan ordered him back to Santa Fe with a sealed dispatch. Doniphan offered to send men with him, but Dick thought it best to go alone. He knew the troop hadn't marched without notice. Those hostile to them would be aware of returning travelers. A few men would be too many to pass through unnoticed and a few wouldn't be enough if he met enemy forces. One man alone might be able to outrun or outsmart pursuers. Dick accepted the sealed dispatch, packed needed provisions, and rode.

Dick knew he must travel north with caution. Where possible, he traveled through mountains. He often saw Mexicans and Indians in the valleys below. He crossed plains only after careful observation and consideration. Sometimes he traveled after dark. Every now and then he'd sleep a couple hours or a few minutes and then be on his way. In the nine days of travel, he never lit a campfire or his pipe, never shot his gun or did anything to draw attention to himself.

When he neared Albuquerque Post, the Rio Grande was overflowing its banks. Dick started to ford it, but the sentry stopped him midstream and demanded Dick to give the countersign. He knew no countersign. Cold in the icy river and tired to boot, Dick lost his patience. That made no difference to the sentry. Dick remained in the middle of the river until an officer came and gave him permission to cross. After he ate and slept at the post, Dick continued north to Santa Fe, where he delivered Doniphan's dispatch. He never knew what the dispatch contained.

He needed to go into Taos to retrieve some mules that had been taken from him. Like many mountain men, Dick had often been in and out of Taos. While riding north with Doniphan's dispatch, he decided to move to Taos. He'd travel back and forth to his cattle near El Pueblo.

In Santa Fe, Dick heard that Ute and Apache were on the warpath between Santa Fe and Taos. He rode a few miles out of town, then traveled through the mountains to avoid the established trail. About twelve miles out of Taos he swam across the Rio Grande and edged his way around a large Ute camp. The next day Indians murdered several travelers on the established trail.

In Taos, Dick went into business as a sutler for the First Dragoons. Able to raise beef on his place near El Pueblo, he contracted to furnish beef for area troops. Several mountain men contracted to furnish meat or other provisions for the Army.

Taos wasn't a large town, but it had become a trade center for people of diverse nationalities and backgrounds. Originally an Indian community, Taos was near Santa Cruz de la Cañada, the birthplace of Spanish colonization in New Mexico. From La Cañada many colonists moved to Abiquiu; some from both places lived in Taos. Others—especially trappers, traders, and entrepreneurs—came to Taos from Canada, Mexico, France, and the United States.

In Taos, Dick became acquainted with the family of Ramon and Maria de la Luz Lopez. This long-established New Mexican family had seven daughters, some a little older, some younger than Dick; six were spoken for. Three had married Frenchmen (Manuel LeFevre, Alarid Blanco, Antoine Dillette) who came to Taos in a trapping brigade in the 1820's. One married Dick's friend Robert Fisher, who'd come on a wagon train years ago. Two married local men.

Ramon and Luz Lopez did have one granddaughter who turned nineteen in June 1847. Pretty Dolores LeFevre was Manuel and Teodora LeFevre's firstborn. Many girls in Taos married in their early teens, but Manuel and Teodora were particular about their firstborn.

Dolores may or may not have been the reason Dick returned to Taos, but she certainly was worth staying for. Lewis Garrard, who visited the LeFevre home, described her: "Senorita Le Fevre was one of those beauties, fair to gaze upon—impressive in her simple, quiet manner of conducting herself. Though we could not converse, eloquence was in her silence, persuasion in her eye. A look at her frank, intelligent countenance made me wish for her a better home and more refined company than that of San Fernandez [Taos]."[66] Fortunately for Dick, he'd been in the Southwest long enough to understand and speak Spanish fluently.

Dick and Dolores soon decided to marry; but, to please her parents, they waited. They married on March 6, 1848. The same day Dick was appointed Sheriff of Taos—a temporary position.

---

[66] Garrard, *Wah-to-yah*, 179.

Navajo Country

Because Kearny's 1846 code promised protection to all who chose to remain in New Mexico as American citizens, New Mexicans who lived in outlying places appealed for protection from Indians who were stealing their people, their livestock, and other goods.

In March 1848 Colonel Newby and Major Reynolds left Santa Fe with six companies of soldiers to try to persuade the Navajo to be better neighbors. Dick Wootton and Antoine Leroux went along as guides.

They crossed the Rio Grande at San Felipe, rode to Jemez, crossed the Rio Puerco, and continued to Navajo country.[67] When Wootton saw four Navajo, he reported to Colonel Newby and suggested they halt until evening in order to make a surprise attack. When mountain men were hired to find Indians, they didn't think it improper to offer advice.

Colonel Newby ordered an immediate forward march. The Indians sighted the soldiers and, with skillful smoke signaling, warned the entire area of the Army's arrival. By the time the Army reached the Indian camp, there wasn't an Indian in sight. Newby ordered Major Reynolds to pursue, but to return at nightfall if he hadn't caught up to them.

After Dick directed Newby to a camp site near a spring, Colonel Newby instructed him to go along with Reynolds' detachment. Knowing Indians' cunning and knowledge of the land, Dick knew pursuit was an effort in futility; but he followed orders.

Near midnight they turned back toward camp. As they approached, they heard gunfire from the ridge above camp. Dick and the soldiers ran in yelling and shooting. Indians scattered. After the detachment reached camp and bedded down, Indians returned to the overhead bluffs and shot down into the camp again. The troops were well-protected by overhanging rocks, but the noise was annoying. The situation made Newby nervous. He sent a company of soldiers to return the volley. The Indians retreated. The soldiers followed.

The next morning Newby received a message that fourteen Navajo wanted a peace powwow. Dick rode with the troops; Colonel Newby rode ahead. When Newby met the Indians, he ordered his soldiers to take the Indians' weapons, rather than asking them to voluntarily set down their weapons for a powwow. The Indians assumed they were being taken hostage and began to fight. By the time Dick arrived, the Navajo weren't interested in peace. All but two got away: one was taken prisoner; the other was killed. That reinforced the Indians' assumption.

Reynolds, Wootton, and a party of five pursued the twelve escaped Indians. Dick noticed two riding behind the others. One appeared wounded. The other seemed to be helping the wounded man, but soon left him. The wounded man dropped out of sight. Dick had an idea where he'd be. He saw the Indian lying motionless with a bow and several arrows in his hand. Dick warned Reynolds. Reynolds thought the man was dead and rode forward without

---

[67] Each of these locations is in New Mexico.

caution.

Dick threw his feet out of the stirrups and watched the Indian closely. When he saw the slightest movement of the Indian's hand on the bow, Dick jumped off his horse in the opposite direction of the Indian. The rest of the party, traveling single file, followed suit. The Indian noted Dick's action, assumed he was the leader, and started shooting. By the time Dick quieted his horse and took aim to fire, fourteen arrows whizzed past his head. The Indian didn't stop shooting until Dick stopped him with a shot to the head.

The next day Dick saw two Indians and asked Newby's permission to approach them alone. When he came near, Dick dismounted, held up his gun and arms and dropped them to the ground. The Indians understood he wanted a peace powwow and set down their guns. Dick and the Indians met halfway and smoked the peace pipe. Dick explained that the Great Father in Washington was displeased with their depredations and stealing and had sent messengers to punish them, but he was willing to make peace if they would mend their ways.

They reluctantly agreed to talk with Colonel Newby. As a result of the powwow, they agreed to bring 3,000 sheep to replace those they'd stolen and to return all the Mexicans they'd stolen.

The soldiers camped at Cow Springs and waited. Every day or two an Indian came into camp to report they couldn't quite meet the Great Father's demands and ask for a little more time or a little change in requirements. Soldiers' rations were running out. Near the end of their stay each man was allotted two ounces of pork and three ounces of flour daily. They waited.

On the twenty-seventh day, the Navajo brought in five Mexican children and a little less than a hundred old rams.

Soldiers broke camp the next day and traveled along the San Juan River toward Taos. They followed the river a good way, crossed it, and headed east and south. Soldiers could have half of the returned sheep. They soon ate those. The day after they left the San Juan River (New Mexico), Dick rode ahead to hunt game. He shot a couple deer and was preparing to go after another when he heard a grizzly growl behind him. He said he hadn't signed on to hunt deer for grizzlies to eat; so he shot the bear and added that to his pack. The next morning he shot another bear; the troop had meat enough for a couple more days of marching.

Near Abiquiu (New Mexico) Reynolds sent Wootton ahead to find someone who'd sell supplies to the Army. The only one there with provisions enough to help was a padre who had no use for the United States or the needs of any American. He had no interest in anything Dick had to say. Dick didn't force the issue. He knew when the Army came through they'd get what they needed. When Major Reynolds arrived, Dick explained he knew where there were provisions; but he'd need some soldiers to help get them. It seems the padre didn't mind doing business with soldiers.

By the time the soldiers ate breakfast next morning, they'd eaten about all the food the town had to offer. They left town early in the morning and hoped to arrive in Taos before dark. They marched to Cienega and swam across the Rio Grande. Those who couldn't swim tied knots in the horses' tails and hung on for the crossing. They were a few miles shy of Taos when night fell.

With nothing to eat since breakfast, the soldiers were a pretty unhappy lot until Dick spotted a herd of goats and suggested to the Major that they use as many as necessary to feed the ragged men. They killed about eighty goats and had started eating when an old Mexican man approached camp. He explained to the Major that those goats had been his only means of supporting himself and his family. Reynolds assured him that if he would bring in a claim to the post in Taos he'd be repaid. Early next morning the troops arrived in Taos and heard that the Mexican War was over.

    A day or two later the old Mexican came to town with his claim and left satisfied with his rightful money in his pocket.

Growing Pains

In the Mexican-American War, the United States fought Mexico on land and from the sea. It won battles in Texas and Mexico and Mexico's territories of New Mexico and California. The victory stretched the U. S. border to the Pacific Ocean. Whether the new territories would allow slavery aroused concern.

The Mexican-American War began in 1846 and ended with the signing of the Treaty of Guadalupe Hidalgo (February 2, 1848). The U. S. Senate ratified the treaty March 10th; Mexico ratified it May 25th. President Polk announced treaty ratification on July 4, 1848. Among the treaty's provisions were:

--U. S. assumption of approximately $3.25 million of debt Mexico owed American citizens

--Recognition of the Rio Grande and the Gila River as international boundaries. Mexico agreed to give clear title to all disputed area in Texas and cede land that included all or part of the future states of New Mexico, Arizona, Utah, Nevada, California, Wyoming, and Colorado.[68]

--U. S. payment of $15,000,000 to Mexico: $3,000,000 paid immediately. The remainder was paid at the rate of $3,000,000 per year plus six percent per annum until paid in full.

People in the ceded land had the right to choose American citizenship or to retain Mexican citizenship. If they hadn't chosen within one year, they automatically became American citizens. Citizenship was granted immediately to those who chose it.

The U. S. promised to honor land grants, water rights, and to protect new citizens under the U. S. laws. About ten-fifteen percent of the people relocated.

The U. S. gained citizens living in the annexed areas and added more. Wagon trains rolled into the annexed areas, carrying settlers with their own legal, political, and educational ideals.

Even after New Mexico became a U. S. territory, Texas maintained its claim to a portion of New Mexico. After an 1848 Texas state legislative act confirmed the claim, Texas sent Spruce M. Baird to hold court in New Mexico. Baird found a friend in, of all people, former Governor Armijo, who'd paraded and imprisoned Texas' expedition soldiers. Confident in their status of American citizenship, New Mexicans ignored the Texans and chose a territorial delegate to Congress.

The Governor of Texas threatened to seize the territory claimed. The U. S. Government informed Texas that if they sent troops to New Mexico, the U. S. government would deal with them as aggressors. Southern states sided with Texas, said the central government had no right to step in, said it was overreaching its power.

There was growing division in the States concerning states' rights, slavery, and tariffs. In Washington, for a quarter of a century, Daniel Webster spoke for the North, John Calhoun for the South. Henry Clay, "the Great Compromiser," of Kentucky repeatedly bridged the gap.

---

[68] Through the Louisiana Purchase the U. S. already owned parts of some of these future states.

STATESMEN OF THE MIDDLE PERIOD.

Thomas H. Benton.   Robert Winthrop.
Stephen A. Douglas.   Edward Everett.
Silas Wright.
John C. Calhoun.   Daniel Webster.
Henry Clay.   W. L. Marcy.

Pro-slavery Texas was given the right to divide into five states when it joined the Union. New Mexico was large enough for division. The South noticed; the North noticed.

At the same time Texas eyed New Mexico's material resources and commerce. In 1850 a joint resolution of Texas' legislature reasserted its claim.

In September 1850 the U. S. Congress included the matter in the Compromise of 1850. Among other issues, the compromise granted New Mexico the disputed land and divided New Mexico into two territories: New Mexico and Arizona. (Each could decide on the slavery issue when it became a state. New Mexico had asked to be a state.[69]) The Compromise allowed California to be admitted as a free state, and it awarded Texas ten million dollars for permanent relinquishment of its New Mexico claim. (Half of the money would be paid at the time conditions were accepted. The other half would be paid when Texas paid debts owed the U. S. from the time it entered the Union.) Texas was given until December 1, 1850, to accept or reject. Texas accepted on November 25, 1850.

Although the Mexican-American War officially ended with the Treaty of Guadalupe Hidalgo in 1848, boundary disputes weren't settled until 1853. The Treaty of Guadalupe Hidalgo relied upon maps by Philadelphia mapmaker James Disturnell, who didn't accurately describe the area. The United States and Mexico continued negotiations until the Gadsen Purchase of 1853 when the U. S. purchased the disputed territory from Mexico.

With land acquired in the Gadsen Purchase, the United States was free to build forts in strategic locations and attempt to enforce law and order in the borderland strip where Apache, Comanche, and Lipan Indians raided and terrorized. Borderland tribes were accustomed to going back and forth; the Mexican-American border meant little to them. The United States' attitude toward Indians at that time was to assimilate them: teach them a trade or profitable methods of agriculture, help them build homes, and educate their children.

---

[69]It would be over 60 years before New Mexico and Arizona became states. Slavery would be a moot point by the time New Mexico and Arizona became states in 1912.

What Are Friends For?

In June Lucien Maxwell left Taos with a party of twelve and rode up the northern Rio Grande to gather horses for government service. After they gathered about a hundred horses, they picked up two children in an upper Rio Grande settlement to take to relatives in Taos.

Lucien Maxwell

As they rode, they realized they were near a band of Ute.

Two companies of U. S. soldiers, with the help of James Kirker, Bill Williams and other mountain men, had recently (May) gone out to stop the Ute who'd been causing trouble in the Raton hills (New Mexico). To avoid trouble, Maxwell and his party rode along the Arkansas River and planned to return to Taos from the east, rather than from the north—a detour of about 150 miles.

As they ate breakfast on Manco de Burro Pass on June 19th, a band of Ute ambushed them. Ute stampeded their mules—worth $7,200—and horses, drove off all of them. Thirty to forty warriors began shooting into camp. Maxwell's party scurried for the cover of nearby trees. Warriors shot Maxwell first—in back of his head. Maxwell fainted. Indian George filled a hat with water and brought it to Maxwell to revive him.[70] When Indian George was wounded in his arms and several other places, Maxwell returned the favor. For four hours Maxwell's party and the Ute exchanged fire. The Ute killed Charley Towne; Black Hawk, a Delaware Indian; Jose Cortez; and Maxwell's partner, Joseph H. Quinn. They wounded every one of the surviving men, except Peter Joseph. They kidnapped the children and carted off the deerskins Maxwell's party was transporting. Many of the party were seriously wounded, but there was no nearby settlement where they could obtain help. They had no horses. They couldn't remain where they were; so they started toward Taos on foot. Traveling by night and hiding by day, the starving men walked cautiously across the mountains, alert for Ute trackers. Thick underbrush tattered their clothes.

When friendly Arapaho reported the fight in Taos, Dick Wootton organized a search party. By the time the search party found them, about thirty miles east of Taos, Maxwell and his party were near the end of hope. Though Dick knew they'd been attacked, he didn't expect to find the men in such pitiful shape. Some were so hungry from starvation and weak from

---

[70] Indian George was Jorge Gallabis, a Mexican captive William Bent purchased from the Delaware.

wounds that they could barely stand. Some had lost most of their clothes to rough terrain. Dick and those with him field dressed the wounds as best they could before transporting them to Taos. Maxwell had been gone two to three weeks.

The bullet was still lodged in Maxwell's head when they returned in Taos. He was immediately taken to Santa Fe, where a doctor removed the lead ball. Maxwell spent the rest of the year recuperating and working for his father-in-law, Charles Beaubien, in Taos.

Each wounded man eventually recovered.

Scouts Bill Williams and Robert Fisher, led a troop of soldiers to track down the Ute. When they found them, they purchased the kidnapped children from the chief for $250. Dick said it was the old custom of Indians when they raided settlements to take along as many small children as was convenient; so they could receive ransom for them. If their relatives were unable to pay, the children would be brought up as Indians. He said it was easier for young children than for adults to forget and to adapt to Indian ways of life. There were times, especially if a child was inconsolable, the captors traded the child off to another tribe.

Close Call

Dick and Dolores Wootton lived in Taos in 1848, but Dick continued to keep cattle near El Pueblo. Though it was late in the year for Dick to travel back and forth between El Pueblo and Taos, one of John C. Fremont's journalists said Dick was at El Pueblo when Fremont arrived on his fourth western path finding expedition. The purpose of the expedition was to find a central route for a cross-country railway. Fremont reasoned it would be best to see the route at its worst and was determined to cross the San Juan Mountains (Colorado) in the dead of winter. Mountain men at Bent's Fort refused to accompany him. John Hatcher told Fremont those mountains couldn't be crossed in winter; Tom Boggs agreed. Kit Carson, Fremont's favorite, was in Taos; so Fremont headed to El Pueblo to find a guide.

Snowfall had delayed the expedition a day by the time they reached El Pueblo. Seasoned men warned Fremont his plan was foolhardy, sheer folly. They knew those passes, and snow was already flying. Fremont was determined to engage a guide, insistent. A chronicler of the expedition said Dick Wootton was at El Pueblo at the time and refused to guide him across the San Juans. Bill Williams finally agreed to accompany the expedition. Dick said any pathfinder would want to have Bill along. He knew every known pass in the Southwest. The expedition left Hardscrabble (Colorado) on November 23, 1848.

They trudged over the Sangre de Cristo Mountains through snow, across the San Luis Valley, and up into the San Juan Mountains. Snow continued falling. Indians had accurately predicted more snow than usual. Wind whipped the wet snow and blasted it against the men as it fell. The heavy snow piled up.

They needed a railway pass through the mountains. Fremont chose one direction; Williams advised another. John Scott, a mountain man with the party, said that Williams pointed out Cochetopa Pass. Williams told Fremont they might be able to cross that pass. Fremont said it was too far and pointed out the more direct route he wanted. Williams was firm: not in winter. He explained it was questionable if they'd be able to cross Cochetopa in this weather, but there was no possibility of crossing the way Fremont wanted.

By the time the discussion was over, Alex Godey, a less experienced young man, was in the lead. Williams was in the rear. They headed Fremont's direction. Antoine Leroux, a well-traveled mountain man, was surprised when he heard the story; for there was no mountain man, nor Indian who knew of a path the way they traveled. He thought no one would be insensible enough to even think of trying it in winter. He'd crossed Cochetopa Pass in Williams' company several times and knew Williams had perfect knowledge of the country.

Following Fremont's direction, the men were soon surprised by another heavy snowstorm. They decided to turn back. The storm stopped them. The expedition spent Christmas Day in the snow-packed mountains and ate some of their mules for Christmas dinner.

It was common for snow to cover the mountains about three-fourths of the year, but this season the canyons were filling with snow. The men lost all their animals. For a time, the men were lost. Had they realized their fate, they could've jerked the mule meat before they broke camp and wandered from the site. In time, the men were grateful to eat leather from their belts and boots.

If there was a possibility of getting out of the mountains, the men would have to leave their gear and attempt to find a way out the best way they could. They divided into groups. If one group reached a settlement, they could send back help. They cached their gear and wandered in the mountains several days before they arrived in Taos.

Dick Wootton, who had returned home to Taos on the well-traveled route, happened across some of the straggling men as they neared town. He took Fremont to Carson's home. He and others helped find homes for the remaining men. Taos homes opened to them, warmed them, fed them, and nurtured them back to strength. Carson and his family cared for Fremont until he was able to travel. Three of the party of eighteen had frozen to death along the way.

Soon after Fremont arrived in Taos, he sent men to recover the papers, instruments, and bags; but the snow was too deep. They returned without the gear. That trip cost them at least ten mules.

Fremont laid the blame of the disaster on Bill Williams. The Kern brothers, who traveled with the expedition laid responsibility solely at Fremont's door. When Fremont blamed Old Bill, they came to his defense. Dick Wootton, who was well-acquainted with Williams and knew the route they traveled, said Bill knew every traversable mountain pa-ss. Mincing words, as he was prone to do, Dick said if Fremont had heeded Williams, he wouldn't have taken his men into a death trap.

While recuperating, Fremont wrote his wife, Jessie, on January 27, 1849: "At the Pueblo, I had engaged as a guide an old trapper well known as 'Bill Williams,' and who had spent some twenty-five years of his life in trapping various parts of the Rocky Mountains. The error of our journey committed in engaging this man. He proved never to have in the least known, or entirely to have forgotten, the whole region of country through which we were to Pass."[71]

He spoke of his men: "The courage of the men failed fast; in fact, I have never seen men so soon discouraged by misfortune as we were on this occasion; but, as you know, the party was not constituted like the former ones."[72]

Yet before this Jessie had written in her account:
Many of the men had been with Colonel Fremont before, and he knew the power of the party, numerically so small. While expense had been minimized, the animals, arms, and all the essentials were excellent, and the intention of many of the party to settle in California, gave a united determination and solidity of purpose that promised well for the outcome of the Expedition should it be attacked.[73]

On February 6th Fremont wrote Jessie of the men who died:
I say briefly, my dear Jessie, because now I am unwilling to force myself to dwell upon particulars. I wish for a time to shut out these things from my mind, to leave this country, and all thoughts and all things connected with recent events, which have been so signally disastrous as absolutely to astonish me with a persistence of misfortune, which no

---
[71] Hafen and Hafen, *Fremont's Fourth Expedition,* 200, 201.
[72] *Ibid.*, 203.
[73] Hafen and Hafen, *Fremont's Fourth* Expedition, 301.

precaution has been adequate on my part to avert.[74]

When Fremont's expedition left the States, the Kern brothers—Edward M., Richard H., and Benjamin J.—highly respected him. Edward joined the expedition just to return to California. Richard, artist and topographer, documented the expedition trail and sketched birds and other wildlife along the way. Benjamin, a medical doctor, served as the expedition physician. All three accompanied Fremont without pay. By the time they arrived in Taos each changed his opinion and parted company with Fremont.

When Fremont recuperated, others of the expedition refused to accompany him further. He found replacements and regrouped. He persuaded Lucien Maxwell, Dick Owens, and possibly Kit Carson to guide him to California. Before he left town, Fremont arranged for Dick Wootton to go back up on the Del Norte when weather permitted and retrieve the instruments and papers he'd left behind. He promised Dick could have all the other valuables for going after the items he wanted. Dick and Dolores' first child, Eliza Ann, was almost two weeks old by the time Fremont left; so Dick would be free to go as soon as the weather permitted.

On February 13, 1849, Fremont resumed his expedition. He chose a southerly route: south to Albuquerque, to the Gila River, west to Tuscon and on to California. He didn't find a practical central railroad route.

After Fremont left town, Dick learned that Bill Williams and Dr. Kern planned to go back into the mountains to recover the goods cached on the Del Norte. Many items were their personal belongings, including instruments, drawings, and information pertaining to the natural history of the area traversed. Fremont hadn't consulted them before making arrangements with Dick and hadn't mentioned them to him. Understanding the situation, Dick deemed it best to step back and let the men recover and reclaim their goods.

The end of February Bill Williams and Dr. Kern employed local Mexicans to accompany them up the mountains. They progressed slowly in the deep snow, but found and retrieved the goods in early March. They turned back toward Taos.

At nightfall they set up camp within about a half mile of the Ute village they'd passed. Bill and the Ute went back a long way. He knew their language, favored them among southwestern tribes and had been a favorite of theirs for years. What Bill and Dr. Kern didn't know was this particular band was on the warpath. Major Beall and his Taos Dragoons had just whipped them.

A band of Ute had joined Apache and clashed with Major Reynolds near Raton Pass last year (1848). It hadn't been a good summer for the Ute. After they fought the Army, they'd been whipped by their longtime foes, the Arapaho. The Ute had been on the warpath ever since—looting and fighting against settlers and other Indians—and getting away with it. Raids continued until Major B. L. Beall, commander of the 1st Dragoons at Taos, ordered Lt. J. H. Whittlesey to make the Ute understand peace was not an option. The Army required peace.

---

[74] *Ibid.*, 208, 209.

A UTE INDIAN VILLAGE.

On March 11, with Antoine Leroux, Lucien Maxwell, Charlie Autobees and his brother Tom Tobin as scouts, Lt. Whittlesey had led his thirty-seven dragoons up the Del Norte Valley of the San Juan Mountains to deliver the message. On March 13 the Army sighted smoke from a Ute village nestled among piñon trees about fifteen miles north of Rio Colorado. Soldiers approached the village. Chief men came out and asked Lt. Whittlesey what the soldiers wanted.

"I came to fight."

"It is well," the Indians replied; and the fight was on. Bested, the Ute fled and left behind most of their belongings, except their animals.

The Ute were still pretty sore about the fight the night Williams and Kern camped. The next morning at daybreak Bill and Dr. Kern were sitting by the campfire when about a dozen Ute walked into their camp. Bill thought nothing of it. Without fanfare or warning, two braves lifted their rifles and shot. One ball blasted through Bill's forehead and burrowed in his brain. The other sunk into the doctor's heart. Wide-eyed, the Mexicans near Williams and Kern jumped to flee. The Ute stopped them. They weren't after them; their war was with the white man. The Ute gathered all the mules, packs, instruments, and goods and ordered the Mexicans to stay in camp until the next morning. The Mexicans returned to Taos and reported the Indians had taken everything.

Captain John Chapman searched for the culprits. In homes in the Mora River Valley he found Dr. Kern's pick and some clothing from the packs, in addition to a dragoon saddle and pistol taken from soldiers who'd been killed. Over time various expedition items were found in a Mexican settlement near Abiquiu, New Mexico.

Peace Loving Grizzlies?

In 1849 Dick hunted in the Cimarron Mountains (New Mexico) with two companions. For thirteen years he'd listened to seasoned mountain men and trappers around countless campfires and had come to the conclusion bears were peace lovers. "My experience has been that the bear will always sacrifice his reputation for courage to avoid a conflict with the hunter, provided the hunter makes no hostile demonstration when they come in contact with each other."[75]

One morning Dick got the notion to bring in bear meat for breakfast and left camp alone. Bears were plentiful. It wasn't long before he saw grizzly sign. He tracked the bear through about a hundred yards of scrub oak before he sighted his bear. But, instead of one bear in the clearing, there were four mature bears standing around his bear. He said he would have left them to their discussion, but they sighted him about the same time.

Dick stood stalk still. To advance would be to challenge; yet the bears would view retreat as cowardly. They hated cowards. They stared at Dick a few seconds, then growled. They stepped toward him, growled furiously, and stepped back. They'd growl, dare him, and eye him to see if he'd meet them halfway. Dick didn't like being bullied, but his judgment overrode his emotions. After he stood still about five minutes, "the bears seemed to reach the conclusion that they had no quarrel with me, and…they started off on a run in different directions."[76]

All seemed pleased to part company. Dick's companions told him one of the grizzlies was in such a hurry it tore through camp and ran right through their campfire. Dick figured if the bears could get by without human meat that morning, he could get by without bear meat.

---

[75] Conard, 1980, 138.
[76] *Ibid.*, 139.

White Massacre

Dick said that, after Ute in northern New Mexico and southern Colorado got crossways with the Mexicans in 1847, they were pretty much out-of-snuff for several years. They warred here and there, robbed, killed. At times Dick made peace with them and traded among them. But they stole from him, as well as from anyone else.

Under contract to supply beef to U. S. troops at Taos, Dick often traveled from Taos to his place on the Arkansas (Colorado) to supply his meat contract. On each trip he had to guard the cattle carefully. On one occasion, some of Dick's men were driving 100 head of steers from the Arkansas to Taos when the Ute met them at Clifton (northern New Mexico) and saved them the trouble of driving the cattle any further. Not long after that the Ute executed one of their most chronicled massacres—remembered and retold in a variety of versions:

According to Dick, Mr. White, a wealthy farmer from Jackson County, Missouri, was traveling by stage to Santa Fe with his wife and daughter and the daughter's black nurse. Other passengers included two prominent businessmen—both named McCoy—from western Missouri. A baggage wagon followed. Counting passengers and men in charge, there were fifteen travelers.

The coach crossed the Arkansas River and followed the Cimarron Branch of the Santa Fe Trail. When they neared Wagon Mound (New Mexico), Mr. White assumed they were beyond the point of danger from Indian attack. He and a few men rode ahead to Santa Fe.

The stage kept on the Trail and passed Whetstone Springs. It lumbered through a narrow stone-walled passage. In places, stones jutted beyond the walls. There the Ute waited, biding their time with the forte of Indian patience.

Except for the occasional chirping of a bird, there was little to interrupt the monotonous sound of wagon wheels rolling across the wide expanse of the northeastern New Mexico prairie. Until the sudden crack of rifles, the whiz of arrows, the thud of horses. There is no measure of mind speed at such a time, no predictable measure of thoughts…shock, fear…hours in an instant. The mules stopped, shot dead in their tracks. The coach jolted to a halt.

When time passed and the stage didn't arrive, a search party set out and found the wagons. They found enough mutilated bodies to account for all except Mrs. White, her daughter, and the child's nurse. They sent all available information post haste to Major William Grier, commander of the first dragoons in Taos. Because of bad weather, the news didn't arrive until October 29th, about two weeks after the massacre. Tom Tobin, Antoine Leroux, Robert Fisher, Dick Wootton, and others who'd long been in the mountains volunteered to accompany Major Grier and five companies of cavalry in an effort to rescue the women. When they reached Kit Carson's home in Rayado, he joined them.[77]

---

[77] Another version said James White and his family left Missouri in September with Francis Aubrey's wagon train: Aubrey's wagons, White's thirteen wagons, and ten others. One account said White

Not knowing where the Indians had gone, the rescue party rode to Whetstone Springs, where the massacre occurred, and began their search. Tracks were about three weeks old, but mountain men were accustomed to tracking.

Like Indians, mountain men knew if a footprint was made by a white man or an Indian. If the track was made by an Indian, they knew from which tribe, just as they knew a tribe by its arrowheads.[78] Whether tracking man or animal, they could tell about how long it'd been since the track was made if they followed the track for a distance. In places where there was no discernible footprint, they looked for marks of change in vegetation, rock positions, or landscape.

Colonel Henry Inman wrote of the incident:

Carson, Wooton [sic], and Lerous [sic], after scanning the ground carefully at every point, though the snow was ten inches deep, in a way of which only men versed in savage lore are capable, were rewarded by discovering certain signs, unintelligible to the ordinary individual,—that the murderers had gone south out of the canyon immediately after completing their bloody work,…Carson, Wooton, and all other expert mountaineers, when following a trail, could always tell just what time had elapsed since it was made. This may seem strange to the uninitiated, but it was part of their necessary education. They could tell what kind of a track it was, which way the person or animal had walked, and even the tribe to which the savage belonged, either by the shape of the moccasin or the arrows which were occasionally dropped.[79]

Regarding tracking, U. S. Army Captain Randolph Marcy said:

I know of nothing in the woodman's education of so much importance, or so difficult to acquire, as the art of trailing or tracking men and animals. To become adept in this art requires the constant practice of years, and with some men a lifetime does not suffice to learn it. Almost all the Indians whom I have met…are proficient in this…, the faculty for acquiring which appears to be innate with them…I have seen very few white men who were good trailers.[80]

At Whetstone Springs, the mountain men determined the direction the Ute had traveled. Beyond the springs snow had fallen up to a foot deep in places and complicated the search. Dick said the country was intensely cold at the time.

The party searched through the Canadian River canyon and followed the stream about 400 miles. The mountain men knew they were nearing a camp when they noticed ravens circling. Taking into account the timing of the birds' flight, the men figured how far they were from the Ute village. Early in the morning, a day and a half later, they knew they were very near.

---

established businesses in Santa Fe and El Paso in 1847; another said he was a Santa Fe Trail trader. One version said that about seven days from Santa Fe, White left his wagons with Aubrey and went ahead. Dick Wootton, a member of the search party, said the Indians were Ute. Another says they were Jicarilla Apache. That version says Jicarilla Apache killed the men and abducted the females. Some say the White child was ten, an infant, or give no age.

[78] Indians claimed arrows were so distinct an individual could identify his own arrow.
[79] Inman, 164.
[80] Marcy, *Prairie Traveler*, 173.

The rescue party stopped, took off their heavy overcoats, and prepared to fight. Major Grier gave the charge, and the men rushed toward the village. The sudden surprise caused confusion in the Ute village. Abruptly, Major Grier ordered the men to halt. He'd decided he should parley with the Ute. Soldiers and mountain men—all under his command—were so riled it appeared Grier might have to deal with mutiny, as well as Indian trouble. Carson cursed. Leroux, his French blood boiling, upbraided Grier rapidly in an admixture of broken English and French.

While Grier tried to persuade his troop that parlay was an appropriate course of action, a bullet struck him. Fortunately, metal on his suspenders deflected the bullet. His wound wasn't serious. Once the Ute opened fire, everyone forgot parlay. The troop charged the village. They found Mrs. White's warm body; her heart closed around three arrows. In the battle that ensued, eighty to eighty-five Indians were killed. Some fled on horseback. The troop pursued for six miles, captured Ute baggage, some horses, and a couple of children.

All involved realized delay cost Mrs. White her life, but Carson thought death was a mercy considering the treatment she'd endured. Colonel Bell hired William Kroenig and a companion to go to the Ute and find out what happened to Mrs. White's child. She was never found. Two years later the Comanche were seen with a girl whom some thought matched the girl's description. But the child wasn't returned; so there was only speculation. No sight or sign, living or dead ever confirmed the whereabouts of the child or her nurse.

The rescue party battled a blizzard as they returned. Robert Fisher and a few others were the first to reach Ft. Barclay. Wind drove some of the others off course. One man froze to death. Grier, Carson, and Leroux arrived at Fort Barclay two days after Fisher's group. The men forged on to Taos through a heavy snowstorm with blizzard conditions in places.

Wagon Mound (New Mexico), noted landmark on the Santa Fe Trail

Trading with the Comanche

In the winter of 1849-50, the Comanche had buffalo robes and buckskins to trade and requested a trader come to their area. Bent's Adobe Walls in the Texas Panhandle was out-of-business.

Dick and a dozen men went to trade with them near the Canadian River. Dick usually traded in the Indians' villages, but not with the Comanche. He said they "never had even that small sense of honor which characterized the average western Indian. They never made a pledge or promise of any kind for which they had any regard whatever. When they made peace it was always for a purpose. It was either to save their own lives, when whipped and cornered, or to obtain something which they stood in need of, and every such peace was made to be broken at the very first opportunity that presented itself."[81] Dick considered the Comanche a quarreling, treacherous lot, with no sense of humor like other southwestern Indians possessed.

The traders made Bent's deserted Adobe Walls trading headquarters. The first order of business was a powwow. Traders smoked a peace pipe with the Comanche and exchanged gifts. The Comanche required $700-$800 worth of gifts before they'd begin trading. In exchange, they gave the traders a few ponies worth maybe $40.

It took a few weeks to finish trading. Though they went home with twelve Pennsylvania Conestoga wagons loaded with pelts and buckskins, Dick and the traders with him were glad to be done. They enjoyed adventure, but they didn't care for the kind they found in Comanche country; and none cared to become a fulltime trader among them.

That was the only time Dick traded with the Comanche.

He returned to Taos where he and his soon-to-be brother-in-law, Charles D. Williams, had established a general merchandise store on the south side of Taos plaza.[82]

Both men worked the store. When Dick tended cattle, hunted, or went out-of-town, Williams minded the store. They hired teenager Juan Delos Reyes Santistevan to help. He worked for them until the fall of 1852.

---

[81] Conard, 1890, 241.
[82] Charles, born about 1821, had come to New Mexico from New York as a soldier with Kearny's Army.

Old Spanish Mines

Taos was a money hub for years—not the kind of riches that builds empires, but the kind that is earned and spent. In the 1830's and early 1840's trappers made money quickly. They worked long weeks far from family and surrounded by few companions. When they returned to town, many spent freely, liberally. Some liked to toss handfuls of coins into the street to see children scramble for them. Spending continued with the arrival of American soldiers, but their resources were limited.

Then word of gold discovery in California's Sacramento Valley (1848) trickled into Taos. Prospectors who crossed the Plains chose various routes to California. Some went north through present-day Colorado and Fort Laramie (Wyoming). Others passed through New Mexico. One year, during that time, a man living on the Plains counted 10,000 wagons heading West. Indians were amazed there were so many white men. But trouble rolled westward in many wagons in 1849.

Cholera broke out in St. Louis and ravaged the area three to four months. At the height of the epidemic scores died daily. St. Louis attempted to quarantine the sick, but cholera spread to Westport (Missouri), where wagons were outfitting. It traveled in wagons with emigrants and gold seekers and killed many along the Trail.

Plains Indians weren't exempt. Cholera, which Indians called the Big Cramps, infected some Kiowa and killed about half of the southern Cheyenne. The disease didn't hit Taos.

By the time Dick heard news of the great gold successes in California, his daughter Eliza Ann was almost one; and Dick and Dolores were waiting the birth of their second child. (Richens Lacy Wootton, Jr. was born on March 21, 1850.) Dick hated to miss the gold prospecting adventure, but he needed to care for his family.

Rather than go to California, Dick decided to search for the famous old Spanish mines in Colorado and New Mexico—close to home. Stories of the old mines abounded, but few folks knew where they were.

Men pointed out a mine to Dick in the Sandia Mountains (near Albuquerque, New Mexico), but wouldn't go in—said it was haunted. Not concerned with ghosts, Dick went in with a couple of companions. They found a place where quite a bit of lead had been mined. There were bones of three or four men, who Dick thought had probably died in a rock slide.

In Taos there was a lot of talk about an old Eldorado mine. Indians claimed they knew exactly where it was. One Indian agreed that for $300 he'd show Dick where it was. Dick outfitted a party and prepared to leave, but the man was killed the night before they were to leave. After that, those who'd claimed to know the mine location forgot.

Dick searched. As he traveled, he kept a sharp eye, especially in passages that could easily be used for ambush. If a place looked like a good hiding place for Indians, Dick examined the area carefully before riding through. It saved his life and the lives of others more than once. Before entering the Sangre de Cristo Pass with a small party of prospectors, Dick noticed an Apache, disguised as a rock, lying on a flat rock overhead. Dick had no idea how many more

Apache might be around; but he knew there'd be more. He knew when he shot the one, more would show up.

His shot rang out, killing the man disguised as a rock. Rocks seemed to come to life, as Indians sprang out of hiding. When prospectors joined Dick in the volley of fire, the Apache ran out of bullet range. Dick and his party traveled on through the Pass without mishap.

When they prospected in the mountains near the San Luis Valley (southern Colorado) along the northern Rio Grande, Dick and his party noticed a herd of elk in the valley across the river.

Low on meat, another prospector and he decided to ride down and get a couple elk. After they crossed the river and traveled about half the distance to the game, they got a better look. Those were strange elk. When they crossed a ravine and saw a band of Indian ponies, they rechecked the elk and turned around. Those were no elk. They were Ute in elk hides. When the men turned and rode off, the Indians threw off the hides, ran to their horses, and pursued them. The Ute followed them as far as the river, watched them, and turned back. Dick and the prospectors waited until nightfall and left the area.

The main thing Dick found in the old mines was wild animals. He decided that what may have been a rich mine in other times probably wasn't worth mining and transporting in his day. All in all, Dick concluded that looking for the old mines was about like chasing the rainbow and much more expensive.

In New Mexico and Colorado Dick had opportunity to dabble in mining, but he preferred trading and found it more profitable.

Missouri by Horseback

In the spring of 1851 Dick went to St. Louis to buy merchandise for his Taos store. He started from Taos on horseback with a small group of men, including Major (Colonel) William Grier. Along the way Dick and the Major wagered on who'd arrive in Missouri first. Grier was a hardened Army officer and used to riding, but Dick figured he had more stamina. He made the trip in a little over seven days. Grier got laid up along the way and arrived in Westport (Kansas City) almost two weeks later.

Dick left his horses in Westport and boarded a steamer to St. Louis. He made his purchases quickly, but couldn't get them shipped immediately because of low water in the Missouri River. He made arrangements to have the merchandise shipped to Westport. He'd go on back to Westport and look around for a few days and wait for the merchandise. When the goods arrived, he'd be on hand to unload them, reload them onto wagons, and head back to Taos. He didn't go home to Kentucky.

When he arrived in Westport, Dick's plan changed. A cholera epidemic broke out about the time he arrived. He figured it'd be useless to have survived the dangers of the elements, the frontier, and Indian attacks only to die in an epidemic within the borders of civilization. He settled his accounts and contracted to have his merchandise freighted to Taos.

He hopped on his horse pronto and put miles between cholera and himself. Decades later cholera would catch up and rob him.

That winter, in December of 1851, his thirty-one-year-old brother, Thomas, died back home in Christian County, Kentucky. Dick was thirty-five.

Dick and Dolores's daughter Frances Dolores was born in April 1852.

California

When reports of California's gold fields had reached Taos, Dolores Wootton's Uncle Bob (Robert) Fisher had gone to California with his friend George Simpson. Her Aunt Romualda stayed home with the children. They had a baby and another on the way; the oldest child was 9. Uncle Bob never returned. Simpson brought Romualda word that he died in California.

In California beef and mutton were in such demand that prospectors were paying amazingly high prices for cattle and sheep. According to reports in Taos, sheep were selling for ten times the New Mexico price. Dick wasn't about to leave his family as a long term prospector; but, ever the trader and entrepreneur, he planned to make the most of the situation.

Dick had been in California on his trapping expedition. Having been on the 5,000 mile expedition, he knew something of the risk of a trip across 1,600 miles of mountains, plains, and desert.

Charles Williams and he purchased 9,000 sheep near Ft. Barclay (New Mexico) and fattened them up before having them brought to Taos. Dick would take the sheep to California; Charles would remain at Wootton and Williams' general store in Taos.

On trapping and trading expeditions Dick was accustomed to traveling with men whose character and ability he knew. This trip he had to take the men he could get and take his chances of them causing trouble or backing out at a point of danger. He hired fourteen Mexican sheepherders and eight discharged American soldiers. He armed each with a knife, a pistol, and a rifle. He also counted on the help of eight trained goats and one good shepherd dog.

Dick purchased about a thousand dollars' worth of supplies, including food staples and ammunition, and loaded them on pack mules. On Thursday, June 24, 1852, Dick and his twenty-two men rode out of Taos on mules, driving the sheep toward California's Sacramento Valley gold field. Knowing the general terrain, he took no horses.

They followed the Rio Grande, north into present-day Colorado. Each day, by turn, Dick positioned two of the trained goats in front of the flock to lead the sheep. The dog took up the rear, to round up stragglers.

Progress slowed after they turned west along the Continental Divide, near the source of the Rio Grande. Melting snow caused streams to rise, making travel difficult the next 200-300 miles.

As Dick led the sheep along the Uncompahgre River, nine thousand sheep proved to be too much temptation for the Ute. One evening the Indians attempted to stampede Dick's mules in order to drive off the sheep, but watchmen scared them off. The next day Chief Uncotash and his braves met Dick and insisted Dick pay for traveling through their country. Dick told him that, when he reached the river, he was going to make camp for the night and would be able to have a powwow and make things right. The chief, his braves, and a couple of Dick's men went ahead to a campsite.

Afraid, Dick's men returned. The Ute assumed Dick was going to renege; so Chief Uncotash and at least a hundred men returned. The chief rode alongside Dick. Dick noticed the braves had divided into small bands. Each little band seemed assigned to surround one of Dick's men so that each man had his own escort. Dick had never had such a scare in his life, but he knew better than to let on. He explained to Uncotash, but the chief wouldn't settle down. He kept belching out accusations until he made Dick mad.

Forgetting the danger, Dick jumped off his horse. He intended to use the chief as a breastwork and, from that vantage point, persuade the Indians he would not be bullied. When Dick jumped off his horse, Uncotash followed suit. In the jump Dick dropped his rifle. He knew there wasn't time to retrieve it. Being larger and stronger than the chief, Dick locked arms with him and held him down. Instantly, Dick grabbed his knife and held it to Uncotash's throat to persuade him to consider peace. Dick knew his life wasn't worth a plug nickel if he killed the Chief.

While still guarding Dick's men, braves had already begun shooting sheep.

Chief Uncotash knew he was in such a position that his warriors couldn't reach him before Dick would be able to slit his throat or plunge a knife into him. He ordered his warriors to fall back and quit killing the sheep. He would allow Dick to drive the sheep. Dick and Uncotash got up and rode along together until they arrived at the arranged campsite a couple miles away.

Dick set up camp as usual and then sat down for a powwow with Uncotash. Grateful for his life and the lives of his men, Dick felt generous that evening. The powwow went smoothly. He gave the Chief several hundred dollars' worth of staples, ammunition, and other things the Chief wanted in exchange for his kindness in allowing Dick's outfit to pass through his land. To be certain they didn't attack again, Dick required them to leave one man hostage for the night. He made sure they understood he would kill the captive immediately if there was any trouble.

Dick guarded the hostage; so he would have no opportunity to escape. After they crossed the river and left Ute country, he freed the man. They had trouble with other Indians, but they had no further trouble with the Ute. Decades later Dick met a man he recognized, but he couldn't place where he'd seen him. The man, a Ute, said he'd been with Uncotash that day. He told Dick that about fifteen years after the incident Uncotash spoke of Dick as "'heap brave' and 'heap fool'."[83]

Dick and the herders had to make rafts to get the sheep and themselves across the Uncompahgre, Grand, Gunnison and Green Rivers—took almost two days to cross the Grand. The trained goats were especially helpful for stream crossings. Dick would lead a couple into a stream. As they crossed, the sheep followed.

After they crossed the Green, they traveled north across the Wasatch Mountains at the head of Spanish Fork and on to Salt Lake City (Utah). Because mountain snowcaps were melting, rivers ran full. The men were able to get the sheep—almost 9,000—to swim across

---

[83] Conard, 1980, 431.

some rivers. They built rafts to get them across others.

When Dick and his outfit neared Salt Lake City, they set up camp outside the city. Because of the Ute toll, Dick needed supplies. He went into town to purchase supplies for the remainder of the trip. He met Ben Holladay for the first time and purchased supplies in his general store.

As Dick worked with his sheep the next day, a man walked out of a fine house and asked who he was, where he was from, where he was going. Dick told him. Brigham Young said he'd heard of Dick and invited him into his home.

Having been raised a gentleman, Dick considered his buckskin britches. When he crossed mountain rivers and streams, his buckskin britches had stretched. That wasn't a problem; it was easy enough to trim them off—nice thing about buckskin. But traveling for days in the heat across the desert, his buckskins had dried and drawn up so much they resembled knee britches. They were okay for traveling, but were hardly suited for entering the home of a man of distinction, especially a home where there were so many women.

But Dick's curiosity got the best of him. He followed Young into his home.

Dick and Brigham visited for about a half hour and drank wine together. When Dick left, Young invited him back for the evening; so he called again. Dick said he was received courteously "and when I left him, I felt that I could commend his wine if I couldn't his religion."[84]

Several men who hired on in Taos remained in Salt Lake. Dick hired others, but left Salt Lake with four less men than when he arrived three days before. From Utah they followed the Emigrant Trail. As Dick crossed Nevada, Digger Indians killed a few sheep.

Dick almost lost a bundle to six employees, who'd made arrangements with a nearby emigrant train. The plan was that, when the emigrant train would drop back, the six men would leave pockets of sheep for the emigrants to pick up to help pay for their trip to California. Dick kept finding and gathering those sheep. When he understood what was happening, he approached the six in the evening after all the men laid aside their weapons. He unloaded the six men's packs and, at gunpoint, ordered them to take their belongings and leave. He followed them a way to be sure they were far from camp before he returned. He figured the emigrant train would pick them up, but felt no responsibility to make reservations for them.

Dick and the remaining men crossed the Sierra Nevadas at Donner Pass, just ahead of a heavy snowstorm. They followed the American River to the Sacramento Valley and arrived October 9, 1852, after 107 days on the trail. Percentagewise, the sheep fared better than employees. Dick left Taos with twenty-two men and arrived with twelve. None of the employees were lost to injury. Of the 9,000 sheep that left Taos, 8,100 arrived in California.

Dick quartered in Elk Grove—twelve miles from Sacramento on the Stockton road—until he disposed of all his sheep, goats and mules.

He was in California when Californians first voted in a presidential election. (Franklin Pierce was elected President.) Citizens were in a festive mood, elated at being able to vote.

---

[84] Conard, 1890, 255, 256.

The night after the election Dick saw the fire that almost wiped out the little city of Sacramento. It broke out in a section known for ill-repute.

Flames jumped from building to building, lapping up one wooden structure after another. By daybreak it looked almost like a city of embers. But, by the time the embers cooled, men were busy rebuilding. Sacramento had begun to look like a city again by the time the city flooded in January 1853. Until flood water receded in the Sacramento Valley people took refuge in second stories of buildings.

Early in 1853 Lucien Maxwell, John Hatcher, Kit Carson, and others drove more sheep from New Mexico to California.

Once Dick sold the last of his stock, he prepared to head home. He packed money in green hides, which dried around the money and made it less conspicuous. He carried his profits—$14,000 in gold and more than $28,000 in drafts on St. Louis—in a pair of saddle bags.

In the Southwest people generally kept their assets in a safe place. Banks were few. Dick didn't think folks were necessarily more honest then. Rather, he thought the way justice was administered deterred crime and had a good deal to do with the lack of fear people had about having things stolen from home. Stealing was a high risk career in the early days of western settlement. Because there were no jails, justice had to be administered immediately. If thievery was the profession a man chose, it was best for him to get out of the country when he finished his job. Killing a person unprepared for defense, or killing in order to rob, was considered murder; swift trial and swift punishment followed.

There were times men were killed in brawls when they'd been after one another. Folks let them settle their own differences. For other infractions there were three degrees of punishment:

--Minor offenses: thirty-nine lashes to the back.

--Major offenses: death.

--An offender whose crime appeared to merit punishment, but whose guilt couldn't be clearly proven, was encouraged to leave the country. It was clear to the accused that was his ticket to safety, not a suggestion.

With profits packed, Dick decided to see some new county and save a few miles to boot. He stopped and visited San Francisco. Four-and-a-half years earlier the population had been 820. Now it was teeming with prospectors and transients, with riches and crime. From San Francisco Dick took a steamer to Los Angeles,[85] where he purchased pack mules and riding mules for himself and the three men traveling with him to New Mexico.

Dick and the three rode to San Bernardino, California, where they met six Mexicans and two Americans on their way to Taos. They traveled together. They could've ridden relatively straight across Arizona into New Mexico, but Apache were on the warpath. Dick chose to sidetrack. The men, who'd joined in San Bernardino, didn't want to go the same route. They parted company.

Dick and the remaining three men filled their canteens. They carried a generous water supply and used water sparingly as they crossed the desert, south to Yuma. They made good

---

[85] Los Angeles population in 1850: 1,610; in 1860: 4,385.

time to Yuma; but traveling to Sonora, Mexico, and back up toward Tucson was time consuming. They ran out of water for man and beast two days short of Tucson. Dick said if a person's food supply runs out in the desert, there are always roots or seeds or lizards or beetles to eat, but water is a different matter. Many a person crossing the southwestern desert left his skull to dry in the sun.

A few miles from Tucson the men were tickled to see the most memorable sight of their whole trip: a large spring. They hadn't seen water for a hundred miles. They slowly drank their fill before filling their canteens and setting up camp. The next day they rode in to Tucson and purchased supplies. From Tuscon they traveled northeast to the Rio Grande del Norte above the Jornada del Muerto in New Mexico and followed the Rio Grande, north to Taos. The trip from Los Angeles to Taos took thirty-three days.

Dick saw Indians on the trip home, but had no run-ins with any. The Pima went out of their way to help direct the men on their journey. Dick was impressed by Yuma, Pima, and Maricopa hospitality. He'd camped near the Mojave and Yuma. Those tribes lived off the land, ate lizards and ants and such things. Dick said they lived naked and dirty.

One evening when he and the men were camped near a Yuma village, some of the men went to the village and bought bread, like biscuits. As they sat by the campfire eating, they noticed the bread had an unusual taste. They examined it in better light and found the bread was made of red ants crushed together and sun dried. How many ants does it take to make a biscuit?

Dick was impressed with the industry, thrift, and intelligence of the Maricopa. He said the Maricopa's efforts at farming and raising stock became more successful once the government gave them more protection from Apache and Navajo—the worst enemies of that peaceable tribe.

Dick and Dolores' daughter Lorett was born shortly before Dick arrived home.

When Dick left for California, he'd left several thousand dollars of silver coin at home. On his return, he learned the money had been loaned to a friend who squandered it. Soon after, misplaced trust on his own part cost most of what he'd earned on his California venture.

Dick began to turn the focus of his ventures back toward present-day Colorado. With Ceran St. Vrain's permission to settle on his Vigil-St. Vrain land grant, Dick began to divide his time between Taos and southeastern Colorado.

In August or September (1853) Dick, Charlie Autobees, Levin Mitchell and William Kroenig began establishing Huerfano Village on St. Vrain's grant. Many emigrants passed that way, some to prospect in California, others to establish a religious refuge and home in Utah. Others were attempting to establish a Central Route to the Pacific. In summer 1853 John W. Gunnison and his Congressional authorized expedition had begun to search for a central railroad route. Gunnison was killed in the process.

Huerfano Village

Because of Huerfano's strategic location, Dick planned to build a trading post for cross-country travelers and for those traveling locally or into New Mexico.[86]

He chose a defensive site for his fortress on the south side of the Arkansas River. It was about a mile from the mouth of the Huerfano—where the Huerfano empties into the Arkansas—and about twenty miles southwest of El Pueblo.

Dick built high sharp-pointed-picket walls with two bulletproof circular bastions at opposite corners of the stockade. He hired several Taos men to help. The bastions, like those at Bent's Fort, provided a vantage view of all the surrounding countryside. The gate was on the southwest side. Outside the walls were corrals and a fenced area, where the Taos men built an horno for baking purposes.

Log buildings, with logs laid horizontally, lined the inner walls, leaving an open plaza in the center. Structures included: Dick's family home (large living room, kitchen, and two bedrooms); trading post; blacksmith shop (with forge and bellows); rooms for employees; a shed (in the rear of the fort). The puncheon-floored shed was used for husking and storing corn, but also provided storage space for wagons and heavy equipment. The shed's roof, covered with a few inches of dirt, provided a place for women—Dolores and the women who worked at the fort or whose husbands worked there—to plant household gardens.

Because Indians were on the warpath, Dick didn't think it safe to move his family from Taos until he prepared a secure place and until the Indians settled down a bit. He frequently visited his family. Riding hard and steering clear of established paths to avoid Indian attack, he could ride the 165 miles between his homes in just under twenty-four hours. On one trip he saw Indians in several places. He kept riding, but they saw him. As bullets whizzed past his head, he decided to ride straight through without sleep.

On October 15, 1853, Dick's friend Joe Doyle and his family left Ft. Barclay to relocate at Huerfano. A group came with them.[87]

---

[86] The Mountain Branch of the Santa Fe Trail turned southward near Bent's Fort. The Taos Trail or Western Branch, a less common cut-off, continued west from Bent's, across the St. Charles and Greenhorn Rivers, to Ft. Massachusetts, through the Sangre de Cristo Mountains, across Sangre de Cristo Pass, to Santa Fe by way of Taos. The Central Route to the Pacific followed the Taos Trail as far as Ft. Massachusetts, turned to Little Salt Lake, through the Sierra Nevada Mountains, and down the San Joaquin Valley (California), to Stockton or San Francisco.

[87] Those who came from Ft. Barclay with Doyle: His mother-in-law, Teresita, her son Tomas Sandoval, her brother Jose Benito Sandoval and family; Maurice LeDuc, wife, Elena, and their two children; Charlie Pray and wife, Lena Gomez; Ben and Josie "Chipeta" Ryder and family; Juan Ignacio Valencia and his Mexican wife; Tanislado de Luna and family; Bob Rice and son Tom; an American named MacIntosh, his Mexican wife, Amiceta, and their daughter, Mary; Taos-born Juan Chiquito Trujillo; Mrs. Doyle's brother-in-law George Simpson. George left his wife, Juana and children in Mora for a time because Juana was expecting their fifth baby in about three weeks. Mrs. Doyle and Mrs. Simpson were Mrs. Kroenig's half-sisters.

In spring 1854 another cholera epidemic broke out, but it didn't reach Huerfano Village. Smallpox came a little closer. A Cheyenne visited a Kiowa camp and carried smallpox back to his clan encamped near William Bent's new Stone Fort. Always caring for the Cheyenne, Bent persuaded them to stay put; so the disease wouldn't spread. They allowed him to quarantine ten affected lodges. He took care of the sick and burned everything they used. One person died. The disease spread no further.

In preparation for his family, Dick built a roughhewn ferry.

By early summer 1854 Dick and Dolores Wootton had five children: Eliza Ann, Richens Jr., Dolores, Lorett, and baby George. In July Dick arranged to bring them home to Huerfano. They traveled to Fort Massachusetts (Fort Garland, Colorado) on their own and with a military escort from Fort Massachusetts to Huerfano Village.

At the time, Huerfano Village was one of the largest settlements in the area which would later be the state of Colorado. There were five placitas in the area: Charlie Autobees', Dick Wootton's, Joe Doyle's, Juan (Guerro) Pais', and William Kroenig's.

Joseph Doyle   **William Kroenig**

Doyle's place was about a hundred yards east of Dick's on the south side of the Arkansas River.[88] Tom and Maria Whittlesey had a cabin between Wootton and Doyle.[89] Northeast of Doyle, several Frenchmen and Mexicans lived in dugouts. Dick's longtime friend Charlie Autobees lived about two miles upriver in a well-protected spot. Jean Baptiste Chalifoux and John Smith and Smith's Cheyenne wife lived downstream. Colorado (Levin) Mitchell, Alexander Barclay, and others settled about a mile from the mouth of Huerfano Creek, also

---

[88] Doyle built his in the spring of 1854. When he first arrived, he settled at El Pueblo for the winter. It had been inhabited and abandoned over the years. Doyle hired his wife's Uncle Benito Sandoval to help repair some of the fort's rooms. Afterward Sandoval helped prepare planks for building Doyle's home. Doyle built his home about six miles east of the mouth of the St. Charles, but decided he didn't like the location. A few months later he moved east to a location about .2 mile from Dick's placita.

[89] Tom's nickname was "Tomas el Matador"; people counted him a bad man.

on the south bank of the Arkansas. A few traders temporarily headquartered eight miles upriver at the mouth of the St. Charles; they were the last settlers between Huerfano Village and El Pueblo.

Doyle and Wootton built the first irrigation ditch on the Huerfano. The main ditch provided enough water to meet the needs of the settlement. Laterals supplied individual needs.

Dick used local rocks for millstones and built a crude gristmill. He concocted a will-do contraption for the water wheel. Come harvest time, he filled the hopper with grain at night, went to bed, and let the mill do its work while he slept. In the morning he sacked the meal or flour.

He farmed and ranched—raised stock and grew vegetables, wheat, corn, and other grains. Residents trapped and raised livestock to trade with locals, Indians, and travelers. They fully intended to establish a permanent settlement.

The sight of Huerfano Village, with its fields of grain and cattle, encouraged many emigrants, who had traveled across the Plains for weeks. They knew then that their dreams were possible: one really could thrive in a place so far removed from the life they'd known.

Wootton's home gave them a safe place to rest as long as needed. His stockade provided a place to mend their wagons and gear. If their provisions had run low, they could restock from his. If they'd lost livestock or if their animals had worn out and couldn't travel further, they could trade them to Doyle or Wootton for strong healthy ones, generally two worn out animals for one strong, healthy one. Dick and Doyle pastured and nourished worn animals back to strength.

One Saturday a wagon train arrived in Huerfano Village with a young mother, weakened by the rigors of the journey across the Plains. Both of her children—a boy and a girl—had become sick and died along the trail. Then Comanche attacked the train and killed her husband. Train members carried her—Mrs. Shaw—into the Wootton home. She relaxed, grateful to have a "civilized" place to rest, but died within a few hours. The next day a Methodist minister held Mrs. Shaw's funeral service; she was buried by the Arkansas River. Her poor old mother didn't know what to do. There was no way to return to East. The emigrants promised to take care of her as best they could and took her with them.

Emigrants followed the Arkansas River and often camped in the cottonwood grove on the north side of the river, across from the east end of Huerfano Village. They could cross the ford behind Kroenig's place or use a ferry about thirty feet below the ford.

Dick always kept a few hired hands. The men helped with farming and ranching and were available in case of attack. Ben and Chipeta Ryder had a cabin in a corner of the placita. Chipeta helped Dolores; Ben farmed for Dick. Juan Chiquito Trujillo baked for the Woottons for a time, but came to be better known for stealing livestock from Wootton, Doyle, and Autobees. It wasn't a personal thing toward them.[90] That's who he was.

A French Canadian named Murray and his Mexican wife lived in one of Dick's cabins.[91] She was a hardworking woman, who made grain sacks and did housework for the Woottons.

---

[90] Juan Chiquito robbed Mexicans traveling from Ft. Laramie to New Mexico, killed some.
[91] Dick said Murray was French. LeRoy Hafen said he was Irish out of Canada.

Her husband seemed to enjoy alcohol more than work. Actually, flat-nosed Lucas Murray was known to be just plain lazy and had a reputation as a short-fused, irascible man.[92]

Dick always paid wages to the person who earned them; but Mrs. Murray had a hard row to hoe. She'd work hard, but her husband would take her money. Poof! It was gone. She asked Dick if she could leave her wages at his house; so she could use her money when needed. Dick agreed, but Lucas resented the setup. He threatened to kill Dick if Dick wouldn't give him his wife's money. Dick didn't pay attention to the threats, figured Murray was just carrying on.

One day as Dick was doing chores around the place, he heard the click of Murray's rifle. Looking up, he saw the barrel of Murray's cocked rifle about ten feet from him. Murray repeated his threat: if Dick didn't give him the money, he'd shoot. Dick began to discuss the situation with him. As he talked, he edged his way toward Murray. When he'd cut the distance in half, he sprang toward Murray, grabbed the rifle, and turned it on him. He ordered Murray to get on his knees and ask him not to kill him. He did. Dick took what ammo Murray had on him, fired the rifle, handed the gun back to the man, and told him to get back to work.

Murray kept control of himself for quite a while—until one day about corn shelling time. He was on hand when his wife received her pay. When she left it with the Woottons for safekeeping, Murray stormed out of the house. Dick, whose guns were always loaded, picked up his gun and walked out onto his porch. Murray came out of his house, saw Dick, and raised his gun to shoot; but his right arm went limp. Dick's first impulse had been to kill Murray without giving him another chance to kill someone, but he decided he could accomplish the same purpose and save the man's life by just shooting Murray in the right elbow. Murray never bothered Dick about his wife's wages after that.

---

[92] He'd almost stirred up war when he was a head trader for Bent. When a Shoshone war party was denied entrance to Bent's Fort, they shot arrows over the wall. Murray shot into the crowd and killed a warrior. Fortunately, the small war party was far from allies. Murray retrieved the dead warrior's scalp and presented it to a Cheyenne and Arapaho war party, who were delighted and celebrated with a scalp dance.

Rustlers, Thieves, and Frontier Justice

In 1853 and '54, cattle and horse thieves harassed Dick and his neighbors. The small group of cattlemen organized a group of regulators and appointed Dick captain. They discovered a band of Mexican thieves headquartered on the Fountain River near El Pueblo. The band ran the rustled cattle into New Mexico. Dick said it didn't take long to break up the gang: "Sometimes we brought back the robbers and sometimes we left them where we found them, but in either case they never stole any more of our stock."[93]

The regulators often convened their frontier court in a cottonwood grove, where Pueblo's Union depot was later built. Frontier courts in which Dick was involved always required a judge and jury, as well as counsel for the prosecution and defense. Questioning and cross-examination seldom took more than an hour or two. The number of jurors varied: three, six, twelve. The jury's deliberation and decision was prompt, as was the judgment.

If punishment was in order, it was administered on the spot. If the punishment was a lashing, the men tied the offender to a tree—or something stationary—and brought out a rawhide whip. They delegated the job to someone who had enough muscle to mete out the punishment. If the culprit was judged worthy of death, two men were chosen to act as executioners. Both men were handed a rifle; only one rifle was loaded with ammunition. The matter was discharged quickly.

In that manner, Dick said, they were able to keep pretty good law and order in the early days; but, when immigration began in earnest, lawlessness marked the country. Dick considered that disgraceful. Later, when governmental justice was organized, Dick and his compadres willingly set aside their methods of justice, as long as they were sure justice would be done without delay.

Once cattle rustling was under control in the Arkansas Valley, life quieted down. Settlers knew Indian attack was always a possibility; but, after living a few months without problems, they began to relax and enjoy the feeling of safety.

In December Joe Doyle and Bob Rice went up the Arkansas to trade some of Doyle's and Dick's goods with the Arapaho. As was his habit when Doyle was gone, Dick stayed close enough to watch over his family and Doyle's. Dick and Doyle did that for one another—looked out for the other's family and place when the other was absent.

Having carefully checked for sign of Indians and finding none nearby, Dick figured it was safe to go hunting. He took five men up the Arkansas with him. One named McDougall wanted large game. Dick promised to kill a couple of deer for him. They found wild turkeys and small game, but no deer. Early in the morning Dick went out of camp to fulfill his promise. He found day-old elk tracks near Coal Creek, but noticed horse tracks among them. He dismounted to examine the tracks, recognized them, and returned to camp.

He told the men Ute were in the area, and he was leaving. The men laughed and hurrahed

---

[93] Conard, 1890, 283.

him. Dick gave them the edge, said maybe they were right. Maybe he was overly concerned, but the fact remained: he was leaving with or without them. McDougall reminded him of the promised deer. Okay, Dick said, he'd go for the deer; but the men must be prepared to leave next morning. Dick rode out of camp, keeping a sharp eye for deer and Indians. He spotted an Indian's head first. He turned back toward camp and saw two deer standing together. He shot them for McDougall and returned to camp.

Dick stood night guard. They broke camp 3 a.m. On the way home Dick stopped to warn folks at El Pueblo. A Mexican man came out to meet them, said a large band of horses crossed the river last night. People from El Pueblo had seen the tracks. Dick told the old fellow it was a band of Ute and warned him of danger. The hospitable old Mexican insisted Dick and his party come into El Pueblo for the night for safety. Dick refused. Though he had employees who could help at home, it was his responsibility to get home to his family and Doyle's.

The day was Christmas Eve. Dick knew it was a day of great celebration for Mexicans; so again he warned the man to be extremely careful. He advised him not to allow any Indians inside, even on their feast day. Knowing the hospitable Hispanic nature, Dick warned them their safety depended on remaining inside the Fort and keeping the Ute out. On his way down the river, he stopped some traders camped at the mouth of the St. Charles to give them the word. He hurried home to garrison his household and guests and prepare for possible attack. The traders he'd warned came by to see if Dick and his people wanted to go down river with them to a more secure place. Dick invited them to remain with him; but they wanted to move on.

The Woottons, Doyles, and Dick's employees and their families remained. Four men helped Dick garrison the stockade. He looked out the bastions from time to time, keeping an eye on things.

In the middle of the next afternoon Dick saw a man galloping toward him from the direction of El Pueblo. He was sure trouble had started. The breathless man rode in and told his story: he'd been on his way to El Pueblo when he saw the Ute enter. He rode up a hill to see what would happen. From what he saw, he couldn't see how anyone would be left alive. He felt sure everyone at El Pueblo must be dead by now.

Dick stationed two men at each bastion with plenty of arms and ammunition. He wanted to give the Ute a warm reception. He didn't think he'd lose his fort or the lives in it, but he fully expected to lose his herd of cattle down by the river. Nothing happened.

El Pueblo Massacre 1854

Men at El Pueblo enjoyed an all-night card game on Christmas Eve. On Christmas morning before dawn, Guerro Pais—some called him Benito—rode out of El Pueblo on horseback to go for milk over at Marcelino Baca's. As he rode, he heard a Ute whistle on a nearby hill. Pais sped to Bacas'.

The Bacas had come from Greenhorn to Fountain Creek two summers ago. Marcelino Baca was well-off, had about fifty horses, four hundred-five hundred head of cattle, his log cabin near the river bank, and two or three other cabins for his employees. The Ute stopped at Baca's place first. Ninety-year-old Jose "Viejito" Barela was there.[94] He warned Baca not to let the Ute step foot in the door.

With rifles aimed at the Indians, the two men went out to meet them. Baca's young daughter started to follow her father; but Tomasa, her Pawnee mother, grabbed her, whipped her, and told her she'd kill her before she let the Ute get hold of her.

Ute Chief Tierra Blanca led the band. The stocky chief, about 5'9", carried himself tall and straight. Chief Blanca (called both Blanca and Blanco) wanted to talk, "amigo/friend". Baca could see the Ute had his horses; Chief Blanca was riding his prized white stallion. Baca told Blanca if he came any closer, he'd blow his head off.

The Ute turned toward El Pueblo. As they left, they appropriated all of Baca's horses and cattle that weren't in the corral.

After the war party left, Viejito Barela took a horse from the corral and rode to notify those living at Huerfano and on the St. Charles River that the Ute had arrived.

At El Pueblo, Felipe Cisneros went outside the fort for horses. He saw no horses; he did see an Indian. He leaped into a ditch and lay there breathing quietly for the next five hours. While he waited, he heard shots in the direction of the fort. He hid until Viejito Barela returned.

Meantime, Chief Blanca and approximately sixty Ute and a few Apache rode to El Pueblo.[95]

Right outside the fort were cribs full of Benito Sandoval's corn, which he'd contracted to sell to Colorado (Levin) Mitchell of San Carlos. Ignoring the full cribs, a lone Ute approached El Pueblo. At the gate, he told the men he was hungry. They told him he couldn't come in; he returned to Chief Blanca.

In a few minutes, Chief Blanca appeared at the gate and dismounted. He challenged Benito Sandoval to a shooting match. Indians enjoyed competition. Sandoval told Rumaldo Cordova, chief man at the fort, to shoot Blanca. Blanca looked around to see who would shoot; but when Rumaldo looked up, he recognized Blanca. "This is a friend of mine," Rumaldo told the others. Chief Blanca and Rumaldo went into a room to talk.

---

[94] Jose was the uncle of Terasita Suaso and Benito Sandoval.
[95] Accounts of warrior numbers range from 60-150. General Garland, commander of the Department of New Mexico, reported the number of Ute/"Utahs" and Jicarilla Apache to have been over 100.

Some say a shooting competition followed during which time more and more Ute meandered in to watch. Others mention no competition, just say warriors began to arrive one-by-one.

Being a polite people, the Mexicans (called both Mexican and Hispanic) invited the Ute to join their feasting. Blanca and his warriors bode their time. Not drinking as freely as their hosts, the Ute waited for their hosts to begin to become intoxicated.

Blanca claimed Rumaldo's gun.

Rumaldo didn't object. "All right."

With that, Blanca shot Rumaldo in the mouth with Rumaldo's own gun. It didn't kill him.

Twelve-year-old Felix Sandoval was out gathering firewood when the fighting began. An Indian came along and whisked Felix up behind him onto his horse. Felix managed to slide off once; but the Indian grabbed him up again and threatened Felix to stay on.

As they rode away, Felix looked back and saw an Indian shoot his father, Benito, through the chest. The Indian lanced Benito in the chest twice. Benito grabbed his gun and his seven-year-old son, Juan Isidro (sometimes referred to as Juan Ignacio), and ran into a small corner room. He locked the door, fortifying his son and himself against the enemy. Some said his bastion was a room he used for a kitchen/sleeping quarter. The Ute tore off the roof and jumped into the room. Benito let go of Juan Isidro, grabbed his gun, and shot two Indians. One warrior snatched Juan Isidro, while another killed Benito. Dying, Benito grasped the ridgepole. His bloody handprints could be seen on the pole for years afterward. He was forty-one.

Benito's wife was away, visiting their daughter, Mrs. Cecilia Adamson, in Mora, New Mexico. Benito Sandoval and his family had a cabin at Marcelino Baca's in the summer, but were planning to move to the Wootton-Doyle settlement. They'd come to the fort after harvest and planned to stay only long enough to finish selling their corn. The Indians carried off all the corn.

Chipeta Miera, a pretty Mexican woman who'd been living at El Pueblo, was moving to Juan Chiquito's place. She had her wagon loaded and was ready to leave with her brother-in-law Rumaldo Cordova. After the Indians arrived, she climbed up into the wagon. They jerked her arm to pull her down off the wagon. When Rumaldo heard her scream, he ran to help. The Ute shot him many times, stabbed him several times in the chest, shot him through the neck with an arrow, and tossed his limp—but living—body aside. They rode off with Chipeta and seven-year-old Juan Isidro Sandoval, leaving no one to tell how everyone died.

Less than an hour after the Indians left Baca's place, those living at Baca's heard crying, shooting, and then silence. When "Viejito" Barela returned, Marcelino Baca and his men went to see what happened. They found Jose Ignacio Valencia dead along the way at the ford of Rio del Almagre.

The next body they found was Guadalupe Vigil. The Ute had found him on the road between El Pueblo and Bacas. They killed him at Puertecito, a gap in the hill west of Fountain Creek.

Baca found Juan Rafael Medina trying unsuccessfully to hold his guts from spilling out of the slashed gash in his abdomen. He asked for a drink, which Baca gave him.

Standing by El Pueblo and covered in blood, Rumaldo Cordova saw Baca and Barela coming and tried to make his way toward them. With his mouth shot, he couldn't talk; but he could and did use Indian sign language to tell them the story.

Baca took Medina and Rumaldo home with him, but both died. Rumaldo had too many wounds and died of infection.

Early the next morning, the trappers whom Dick had warned to move downstream sent nine Cherokee teamsters with wagons to recover the gear they'd left behind. The teamsters passed Wootton's place. They hadn't gone far before Ute ambushed them. Dick heard the shots and saw smoke rising from their burning wagons. From the position in which the teamsters were found, it appeared they put up a valiant fight; but not one escaped. Dick and others buried them.

After their kill at El Pueblo, the Ute continued downstream to Charlie Autobees' place, about two miles from Dick's. All but one of Autobees' men were behind his fortress walls. That one poor man was outside the wall digging a grave for an old trapper comrade. When the grave digger saw the Ute approach, he jumped into the unfinished grave and stayed put until the band left. They didn't attack Autobees' place, but drove off his stock. They also stole forty head of cattle from Levin Mitchell down on the San Carlos.

When it appeared to be safe, Huerfano men rode to El Pueblo to see what had happened and what could be done. They learned that the people in El Pueblo had been celebrating their Christmas feast when the Indians arrived, asking for food, feigning friendship. The Ute killed a few others in the valley, besides the teamsters. The total number killed was between thirty and forty.

To help bury the dead, three men came from Baca's, three from Wootton's and Doyle's, and twelve from San Carlos. Among them were Marcelino Baca, Dolores Padilla, Tom Grass, Jose Barela, Francis Yara, Levin "Colorado" Mitchell, California Charlie, and Coxo Dolores. They buried five in front of the fort and about ten in the southeast corner of the fort. They tossed the five or six Indian bodies out onto the plain for the wolves.

Charlie Autobees and Jesus Vialpando searched for Joaquin Pacheco. They found him dead about a half mile up from El Pueblo. They never found Juan "Shoco" Aragon or Tanislado Luna.

On December 27th the Ute swept into the valley on a second raid. Between Napesta and the mouth of the St. Charles River, they killed two Americans, who'd come from Bent's Fort to buy corn from Marcelino Baca. At the same time the Ute killed an Indian and shot a Mexican herder. With three arrows in his back, the herder feigned death until they left, then walked to the St. Charles settlement.

Marcelino Baca, J. W. Atwood, and John Jurnegan reported the massacre at Camp Burgwin (near Taos). They arrived January 7, 1855. Baca reported seventeen Mexicans killed and $6,000 worth of livestock stolen. Atwood went on to report the raid in Santa Fe and at Ft. Union.

Soldiers began preparations for a campaign against the Ute and their allies. Meanwhile, the Ute divided into two bands in an effort to fan out and sweep through the Arkansas and Huerfano Valleys.

At the time of the massacre, those living at El Pueblo had been planning to move down near Wootton's place at Huerfano Village because they were concerned about rising Indian trouble. Marcelino Baca abandoned his place after the massacre and went down to Wootton's. Ten or twelve other men and their families moved into Dick's fortress. Doyle was still out trading; his family was still with the Woottons.

Dick piled sacks of corn all around the edge of the fortress roof. With the advantage of added manpower, he stationed men behind the sacks of grain.

When Ute Chief Blanca and Jicarilla Apache Chief Guero led their warriors across the plain on January 19, 1855, guards in the bastions quickly spotted them. Dick and the men in his fortress mounted horses, rushed out of the stockade, and charged the Indians. The Indians ran. They didn't know the men were being certain to remain near enough not to leave the women and children unprotected. The Indians attempted to rustle cattle as they left, but Dick didn't lose one animal in the encounter.

The Ute, who were also at war with the Arapaho, were getting too close to Arapaho country; so they turned back. The next morning, Arapaho pursued them and beat them soundly. They killed some Ute, took some of their horses, destroyed their village, and carried off whatever booty appealed to them. Unfortunately, the Ute had had an outbreak of smallpox. The Arapaho carried off smallpox in blankets infected with the disease. Many Arapaho died of smallpox.

During the Ute-Arapaho battle, Ute women hastily packed up as much of their camp as they could and hid in the forest with their El Pueblo captives until the battle was over.

By the end of February, the U. S. military organized a campaign against the Ute. The campaign involved five companies of volunteers under Lt. Col. Ceran St. Vrain—always a good man to enlist volunteers. Captains Charles Williams and Francisco Gonzales also led units in the campaign, which lasted five months. The military pursued the warriors so relentlessly that the Ute couldn't even hunt game. By the end of June 1855, the Ute were interested in talking peace.

It was some time before relatives knew what became of captives Chipeta Miera and Felix and Juan Isidro (Ignacio) Sandoval. Captain Williams' unit found Chipeta's scalp with ribbons on it. After his release, Felix Sandoval told Chipeta's story:

Twelve days after the massacre the Ute and their captives stopped for water at Arroyo Salado (Salt Creek) south of Pueblo. They allowed the captives to dismount and drink. As Chipeta washed her face, she heard two Indians talking angrily and riding around behind her. She ran, but they shot her in the back at such an angle that the tip of the arrow came out her breast. She pulled at it, yanked at it, but couldn't pull it through. She fell down trying. Indian children, watching the incident, picked up rocks and stoned her to death. Felix said Chipeta had been discouraged, just couldn't seem to get her spirits up. Indians weren't noted for putting up with any drag, especially crying babies or fussy or downhearted folks.

The Ute returned Felix as part of the negotiation when they made a treaty with the military at Abiquiu (New Mexico) in September 1855. He was released to Joe Doyle, his cousin by marriage. (Twenty-three years later, 1878, Felix died of smallpox in Trinidad, Colorado.)

The Ute traded Felix's brother, Juan Isidro, to the Navajo. He remained a Navajo slave until a Mexican speculator bought him at Canyon de Chelly and traded him to his mother for a Hawken rifle, some silver, and other merchandise amounting to about $300. He was in captivity five years and ten months.

Among El Pueblo casualties (unless listed in parenthesis, the person had no known weapon):

Juan "Shoco" Aragon (musket) His body was never found.

Rumaldo Cordova, (rifle) Multiple wounds. Died after telling of the massacre.

Juan de Dios Encinas, a dragoon

Guadalupe, a Navajo

Manuel "Trujeque" Lucero from Taos grabbed a flat iron and used it as a weapon until he drew his last breath. When found, he had the flat iron clenched in his dead fist.

Estanislado de Luna's body was never found.

Juan Blas Martin, found dead inside the fort.

Juan Rafael Medina (bow and arrows) was lanced in the abdomen. Taken to Bacas' where he lived about twenty-four hours.

Francisco Mestes died inside the fort.

Chipeta Miera, (younger sister of Rumaldo Cordova's wife, Albina) kidnapped, killed later

Guadalupe Miranda, a dragoon

Joaquin Pacheco (rifle) from Arroyo Hondo, New Mexico; wasn't over twenty years old. He was found dead in the willows about a half mile from the fort.

Jose Benito Sandoval (rifle) was shot and lanced to death.[96]

Cristobal Sena, a very black Mexican, was a dragoon.

Jose Ignacio Valencia, from Taos, played cards at the fort all night before the massacre. When he arrived home (near Baca's), he realized he'd forgotten his knife and went back for it. The Ute met him on the way and killed him. His wife, Andrea, was the sister of Maurice LeDuc's wife, Elena, and was at Baca's at the time of the massacre.

Guadalupe Vigil was found with an arrow in his back and one through his fingers.

An Indian lady named Rosa may have escaped. Charlie Autobees' son Tom, who was a little boy at the time, said there were eighteen killed at El Pueblo, not counting Chipeta

The Ute-Apache raid in January 1855 was the only direct trouble Dick had with Indians while living with his family at Huerfano Village. At the time, he was on good terms with the Plains Indians, especially the Cheyenne and Arapaho—he was always on good terms with those two tribes. What trading he did with Indians while he was at Huerfano Village he generally did with those two tribes. Many of them often stopped by his place to visit. Even when the Cheyenne went on the warpath in later years, Dick never had any problem with them, never had any difficulty making peace with them himself. Other mountain men, like Carson and Bent, had the same experience with those tribes.

---

[96]Before moving to El Pueblo, he lived in Mora and Loma Parda (New Mexico) and helped build Ft. Barclay. He and his sister, Teresita Suaso, (only children of Gervasio Sandoval and Ramona Barela [sister of Jose 'Viejito' Barela]) were born in Taos.

Change of Plans

Dick had entertained the thought that perhaps he wasn't meant to die at the hand of an Indian. He'd often been shot at and attacked by Indians of various tribes. Though many would have enjoyed dancing around his dangling scalp, none had harmed him. Escaping death during the Ute raid reinforced his thought.

His parents had taught him of the providence and sovereignty of God. He came to believe he was destined to die some other way—a manner of thinking resulting from the influence of his upbringing. Dick concluded he was lucky. He said that belief often made him more daring than he would have been otherwise.

Afraid of further attack, most settlers and families abandoned Huerfano Village in early 1855. Levin Mitchell, Joe and Cruz Doyle and family, and Dick's employees Ben and Chipeta Ryder moved to New Mexico. That made it more difficult for Dick to go on trading trips. He wouldn't make a change immediately, though, because Dolores was expecting their sixth child in the spring. He didn't want her to endure the rigors of travel during pregnancy. Chipeta Ryder was an excellent midwife; Dolores had hoped she would stay until after the baby was born.

Farming and ranching was profitable, and Dick enjoyed it okay; but it was a quieter lifestyle than he was accustomed to and definitely a slow way to make a living. When Dick lost money in 1853, he didn't mind so much because money was easier to come by then. In the back of his mind, though, he hadn't given up his plan to return home to Kentucky. He'd hoped to replace the finances he'd lost on his return from California more quickly than he was able to do in his present situation.

From New Mexico Joe Doyle wrote Dick and proposed that they form a freighting partnership. They'd have to buy wagons, teams, food and supplies, hire workers, and pay for maintenance. They'd be responsible for lost or damaged goods, except those lost to Indians or acts of God because a wagon master was his own insurance man for the merchandise he freighted.

The U. S. government hired freighters by contract. It awarded transportation contracts to "the lowest responsible bidder, after due public notice." The Army was paying eight dollars per hundred pounds for goods hauled from Kansas City to Ft. Union, the military's southwestern supply depot along the Santa Fe Trail. An average wagon train could carry about 200,000 pounds. Supplies were stored at Ft. Union until needed at other posts. Freighters also contracted for distribution from Ft. Union to outlying forts and posts.

Dick knew there was a demand for such a service. Southwestern military supplied few of their own needs. Most supplies must be transported to them. Moving freight by wagon was the only way to get supplies to the interior of the American continent.

Dick and Joe made plans to haul freight from Kansas City to Ft. Union—about a four month round trip—and from Ft. Union to outlying posts, especially south to the Albuquerque (New Mexico) Post. They'd operate out of Doyle's Ft. Barclay, a few miles from Ft. Union.

After the baby was born and Dolores was able to travel, Dick would move his family down to Ft. Barclay. They'd begin freighting in the spring of 1856.

Jose Manuel Wootton was born April 29, 1855. Eight days after his birth Dolores died. The little family buried Dolores at the base of Rumaldo Cordova's grave hill.

Dick needed help, especially with the youngest children. Like Dick's family in Virginia and Kentucky, Dolores had far-reaching family ties in Taos. He would take the children to Taos. On the way, Dick and the six children—Eliza, Richens, Dolores, Lorett, George, and baby Jose Manuel—stopped at El Pueblo for several days. Six-year-old Eliza always seemed to love being near her Daddy and took in everything. She noticed the graves from the Christmas Massacre and stared at the blood stains on the fort's whitewashed walls. She remembered other people living at the fort. George Simpson and his brother-in-law Tom Suaso were there.

Dolores had nine siblings. They welcomed the children, but on July 14 baby Jose Manuel died. They were Catholic; so the baby was buried in Our Lady of Guadalupe Parish Cemetery. Taos' Padre Antonio Martinez, whom Santa Fe Bishop J. B. Lamy unfrocked the year before, officiated.

Dick returned to Huerfano Village. John Brown and his family had left Greenhorn and moved to California. Simpson and Suaso moved south to Mora (New Mexico). Only Charlie Autobees, his family, and a few hands remained in Huerfano Village.

Dick thought maybe he should give up the idea of freighting with Doyle, but the LeFevres were willing to care for the children if Dick freighted. In the meantime, he traded with Indians and with emigrants. He was often in and out of Bent's Fort in the fall of 1855.

An emigrant train traveling from Pike County, Missouri, to California stopped to winter at the fort. Dick met Mary Ann Manning, a widow traveling with the train. They married at Bent's Fort.

Ft. Barclay and Ft. Union

After General Kearny claimed New Mexico in 1846, Alexander Barclay and Joseph Doyle thought it would be advantageous for the U. S. to man a fort in New Mexico along the Santa Fe Trail. They found an ideal location near the junction of the Mountain and Cimarron branches of the Trail, near the juncture of the Mora and Sapello Rivers (near Watrous, New Mexico). There was water for military needs and plenty of grazing for livestock. The area needed protection from Indian raids.

George Simpson

In addition, Indian Agent Tom Fitzpatrick wrote Barclay on December 18, 1847, that the government would want to establish military posts. He agreed the Mora River would be a good location. Barclay and Doyle speculated that, if they built a fort there, they'd be able to sell to the government. Barclay rode south to Santa Fe and purchased several hundred acres of the Scolly Grant (1843), for their proposed site.

At that time, Doyle and Barclay lived at El Pueblo. They packed up their families and left on Sunday, April 23, 1848. Among those who accompanied them were George Simpson, Maurice LeDuc, Doyle's brother-in-law Tom Suaso, Barclay's foreman William Adamson, George Lewis, and their families. Some had relatives in Mora, New Mexico, about twenty-five miles from their destination. They left the women and children in Mora and picked up some hired hands. They arrived at the building site in mid-May 1848.

Barclay and Doyle built Ft. Barclay, a forty room fort. El Pueblo could have fit inside. Other than the main building and outbuildings, the fort included an ice house, corrals, stables, and a mill that could grind forty-five bushels of grain daily. The men raised horses, cows, and hogs and planted an orchard. They dug two large acequias/irrigation ditches to power the mill and irrigate their trees and 200 acres of vegetables and grain.

In August 1846, General Kearny's volunteers had begun building the Post of Santa Fe near Santa Fe's Plaza. The post commanded a strategic view of the town. It was so close to the town's hub of activity that soldiers didn't have far to walk for entertainment. That put a kink in military discipline. Officials contemplated moving the post. Alexander Barclay offered Ft. Barclay to the U. S. government for $20,000 in 1850. No, thank you. The government wanted its own site.

In 1851 Colonel E. V. Sumner, commander of the U. S. Ninth Military District in charge of New Mexico,[97] moved most soldiers from Santa Fe to construct a fort the base of the Turkey Mountains, west of Coyote Creek, about six miles from Ft. Barclay and the Santa Fe Trail. Colonel E. B. Alexander was in charge of the soldiers who constructed Ft. Union on a piece of land eight miles square. They cut building logs in the Turkey Mountains.

Ft. Union soldiers fought many campaigns against Apache, Arapaho, Cheyenne, Kiowa, and Ute on the Santa Fe Trail and in the Rocky Mountains. In 1853 or '54 the Jicarilla Apache almost wiped out a company. The fort was in a poor location for defense, often needed repair, and was in an area also known for its dust storms.

When the Civil War began, soldiers quickly constructed an earthen works fort for better defense. The second Ft. Union was built in the shape of an eight point star and provided underground quarters for 500 men. It was a stopgap measure. The well-planned, well-built Ft. Barclay, which Barclay and Doyle offered the government, outclassed the first two forts.

In 1863 Brigadier General James H. Carleton began construction of a third Ft. Union in the same general locale. The finest of all three Fort Unions, the third Ft. Union was a six-company post. It included a five-warehouse supply depot and a sutler's store, which did $3,000 worth of business per day soon after it was completed. More than 1,000 carpenters, wagon builders, smiths, harness makers, and laborers were constantly employed at Ft. Union. Civilians worked there, fulfilling ordinary tasks at the large facility. At its peak, the population at Ft. Union was about 3,000.

The post hospital was set off from the post, within easy walking distance from the parade ground. A surgeon, assistant surgeon, and a staff of eight cared for patients in the thirty-six bed hospital. Medical care was free to military personnel; civilians paid board.

A primary reason for moving soldiers out of Santa Fe was to minimize distracting attractions. The little settlement of Loma Parda sprung up not far from the fort and offered the soldiers about as much diversion as they had in Santa Fe. In addition, Ft. Barclay was close and open for business. The Ft. Union commander and Alexander Barclay had their run-ins.

In 1853 the commander found Barclay selling whiskey to his soldiers and destroyed a large quantity of Barclay's merchandise. Barclay told the commander he'd sell to whom he wanted on his own place. Disagreements escalated to the point that Colonel Sumner ordered Barclay to get off the land. They wound up in court. The Army was ordered to pay Barclay $1,200 rent per year for encroaching upon Barclay's land, which he purchased and owned fair and square.

Unable to sell the fort, Doyle had moved to the Arkansas Valley when Wootton and others established Huerfano Village. Alexander Barclay remained at Ft. Barclay. Doyle returned in early 1855. When Barclay died at the fort in December 1855, his brother in London claimed the fort; but the courts recognized Joseph Doyle as Barclay's legal partner.

When Doyle and Wootton discussed freighting, Doyle proposed they headquarter at Ft. Barclay. Dick moved to Ft. Barclay in time to prepare for the 1856 freighting season. His young brother Joseph came out from Kentucky to join him.

---

[97] Later the Department of New Mexico. Administration center was at the corner of Lincoln and Palace.

Cross-Country Freighting

By daybreak March 1, 1856, Dick's thirty-six-wagon freight train was lumbering out of Ft. Barclay eastward on the Santa Fe Trail. A thirty-six-wagon train stretched out about a mile long. Ten oxen pulled each wagon. Dick took 400 animals and rotated them in and out of the lineup to keep teams from wearing out. Extra cattle were called the cavey yard.

In addition to freight wagons, Dick always took an ambulance wagon. It was an all-purpose wagon. He used it to carry provisions, paying passengers, and anyone who became sick or injured along the way. Dick's passengers were usually soldiers who'd fulfilled their duty and wanted a cheaper ride home than the mail and stage line offered. Travel eastward was easier, lighter, than return trips; so Dick took passengers and a few wagons with pelts—some of his own, some he'd purchased. He tried to take enough peltry to pay his trip expenses.

His wagon trains required at least forty employees: men responsible for the stock, one driver/teamster per wagon, and two assistant wagon masters. Stock handlers could replace a man who deserted or became ill. Dick was major domo, a Mexican term for wagon master in charge of the train. To insure safety as they traveled through Indian country, he armed his employees and himself with the best weapons available.

There were about thirty Mexicans and about the same number of Americans on Dick's first trip. Most of the Americans were passengers. The Mexicans were hired teamsters and bullwhackers. A muleskinner drove mules; a bullwhacker drove oxen.

Dick charged passengers $30. Dick relied heavily on wild game along the way. He, his crew, and passengers ate buffalo, rabbits, deer, and occasionally elk or antelope. Passengers did guard and camp duty along with the others. The number of night watches varied among wagon masters. Some outfits had as many as eight watches per night to allow each man some rest. A man didn't stand guard every night. Passengers were helpful to have along in case of attack. The very presence of more men sometimes discouraged attack.

Dick divided the men into messes of ten and provided each with a cooking outfit—utensils and food basics for each mess. Each mess elected a cook for the entire trip from among their group. It put extra work on the teamster chosen, but he received extra pay and was excused from guard duty and other duties. Usually there were plenty of dried buffalo chips or cow chips left by previous trains to use as fuel for campfires. The major domo supplied the men with gunny sacks; so they could collect and carry along a few chips in case there weren't any at the next campsite.

Dick always liked to start his trains about sunup. He'd learned long ago on the Bent-St. Vrain train that wagon trains had to be organized and move with military precision. An order given had to be obeyed promptly, precisely for facility and safety. That's the way Dick ordered his train.

When wagons lined up in the morning, Dick rotated the order; so the same teamster didn't always travel at the back, eating and breathing dust stirred up by the others.[98] When they hitched the wagons first thing in the morning, each teamster stood by his wagon and waited for orders to roll. At the order: "Stretch Out!" the wagons rolled. Each wagon kept within a certain distance of the next wagon. Such precision enabled teamsters to circle wagons quickly in case of attack. It also kept wagons from lagging behind and becoming a prey. It'd be easy for one lagging wagon to be attacked without the need to attack the whole train.

They drove until about midmorning, stopped, ate, drank, and refilled their water supply, if good water was available. They rested a little and let the cattle graze. This was the time they gathered wood or cow chips and cooked the main meal of the day. About midafternoon—after a four or five hour break—they traveled on. In that manner, Dick was able to travel fifteen to twenty miles a day; he averaged sixteen. Terrain, grass, availability of water, the wagon master's skill, and weather influenced the number of miles traveled.

Few wagon trains traveled on Sunday, the Sabbath they called it, unless they'd had a lot of trouble and felt the necessity to make up time. Wagon masters found that both man and beast did better if they had a day to rest. Marian Russell, who traveled with Francis X. Aubrey's wagon train, said, "Religion occupied the mind of folks more in those days and God's Sabbath was not lightly violated."[99] Those she traveled with often sang hymns together in the evenings and closed the day with silent prayer around the campfire.

Each midmorning and evening stop was a time for the crew to check animals, to doctor any that needed care, to make repairs, and to grease wagon parts. Wooden wagon wheels had a tendency to dry out and shrink as they rolled across the dry Plains. They frequently needed repair. Sometimes the problem could be remedied by tightening the hoop iron, which surrounded the wheel, or by inserting wood wedges on opposite sides of the wheel. At other times, wheels were soaked in water overnight to swell the wood for a snug fit in the iron rim.

In the evening Dick rode ahead of the train and selected a campsite. He looked for a strategic location in case of attack, a site with good water, yet safe from flashflood.

For two reasons experienced wagon masters crossed streams before camping for the night: First, teams pulled better in the evening. In the morning their muscles had to limber up from the previous day's pull. Second, an overnight rain could swell a stream and delay crossing.

At the campsite teamsters drove the wagons to form a circular wagon-corral. The front wheel of one wagon stopped against the back wheel of the wagon in front of it. Wagon tongues pointed outward. Teamsters unyoked the oxen and left them in the care of herders who watched over them as they grazed and rested. If the train was in an area where attack was likely, teamsters drove the wagons to form a circle called a fighting corral. In that case, wagon tongues faced inward; and the animals were kept inside the wagon corral. Wagons were used as breastworks during an attack.

After the evening meal, men gathered around the campfire, relaxed, played cards, swapped stories. If someone could play a musical instrument or come close to carrying a tune in a bucket, others sang along.

Dick's wagon train rolled along pretty good as it traveled through New Mexico. But as the

---

[98] Those who made the transition from wagon travel to motor vehicle noted the relief from dust.
[99] Russell, *Memoirs Along the Santa Fe Trail*, 78.

days wore on and Dick's strict military-style discipline continued to be a way of life, some men began to resent it. Added to that were remnants of resentment between Mexicans and Americans leftover from the Mexican War eight years ago.

Occasionally, Dick heard men complain. Some of the Americans came to him and reported grumbling among employees. Dick watched, but the outburst caught him by surprise.

He was about to break camp at Ash Creek near Pawnee Rock when a Mexican came up to him and asked for something from the supply wagon. Dick promised to help him as soon as he finished the task at hand; the man went back to his friends. When Dick finished, he found the man, said he was ready to get what he needed. The man didn't acknowledge his presence, but turned on him with a butcher knife. With only a Navy Colt and four bullets, Dick wasn't prepared for trouble of this scope. The man advanced toward Dick, cursing in a mixture of Spanish and English. Dick pointed his pistol at the man's head and ordered him to drop the knife. His words fell to the ground. Dick didn't want to kill him; so he backed up. The man continued to advance. Dick retreated until he backed up to a wagon. He knew it had to be the Mexican's life or his. In an instant it was the Mexican's. The man's friends began shooting at Dick. With three shots left, Dick knew he didn't have one for each. To use up what he had would be suicide. This was time for his Scottish Presbyterian upbringing to come forefront. As he said, he "could do little more than stand there to be shot at, hoping at the same time that my good luck and a kind Providence would let me through with a whole skin…while I stood there, thirteen bullets pierced my clothing, but only one of them grazed the skin."[100]

The rest of the teamsters and passengers stood transfixed. Dick managed to get behind a small tree (6"-7" trunk); so it could share in being the target. Dick shot and wounded a man in the hip. The men fired about twenty more shots at Dick, then stopped. Whether the men ran out of ammo or stopped for another reason, it didn't matter to Dick. What mattered was that it gave his brother time to bring Dick his knife, rifle, pistol, and ammo.

Something had to be done immediately. Dick could have mustered teamsters from among the passengers to replace the mutinous teamsters; but to leave men on the Plains would have meant almost certain death from starvation or attack. On the other hand, this episode made it clear Dick couldn't count on help from teamsters or travelers in another mutiny.

He allowed mutineers to remain with the train and ordered the train to line up and roll. He gave directions for the train to proceed to Bill Allison's Fort, twenty-eight miles ahead, near the Big Bend of the Arkansas River. Dick rode ahead to enlist Allison's help.

Although Allison had only one arm, he was known for his marksmanship and courage. Dick explained the situation and asked his help to disarm the train. When the wagon train arrived the next day, Dick and Bill were waiting. They each had four loaded pistols in their belts and a rifle in hand. Dick ordered Mexicans and Americans alike to surrender all their guns, knives, and pistols, and to place them in one pile. They were Dick's property. He'd intended them to be used for the protection of all; but he had no thought whatsoever of furnishing a weapon to anyone as an enemy. He allowed his brother and a very few

---

[100] Conard, 1890, 344.

employees, whom he trusted explicitly, to have a weapon. He knew there might be Indian trouble further along, but he preferred to defend himself from trouble without than to travel continually on guard from trouble within.

From Allison's Fort they traveled to Council Grove. There were a few businesses in Council Grove, mostly housed in log cabins.

The Kaw Indians there were ready to go on the warpath because Seth Hayes, the government sutler, had killed a Kaw. Dick decided to stay a few days to give the Indians a chance to cool down before he traveled on. In the meantime, he thought he may be of help in the situation.

He explained to Hayes that the Indians expected some kind of payment, wouldn't be satisfied until something was done to clear the situation. Hayes asked Dick to talk to them. The chief and Dick talked long. The chief decided if the sutler would give them a pony and a hundred dollars' worth of goods from his store, his tribe would accept that. Hayes agreed. The chief and he smoked the peace pipe.

Dick and his wagon train lumbered on eastward. Without further incident the train arrived in Westport before the 1856 U. S. presidential campaign began. Dick paid the teamsters and stock handlers and dismissed the troublemakers.

During the third week of June 1856, "the great Pathfinder," as Dick called John C. Fremont, was nominated Republican presidential candidate. Among skeletons raised to life was Fremont's fourth expedition guided by Bill Williams. The *New York Evening Post* published a letter in answer to claims against Fremont. Signed by Alex Godey of the expedition, the letter exonerated Fremont and condemned Williams. Some, who remembered Alex Godey as a man who could sign his name and little more, found the vocabulary and style of writing impressive. Errors in geographic explanations added to doubts of the authenticity of the letter.

Even though the Compromise of 1850 had held the nation together, it hadn't killed sectional rivalry, nor silenced the issues of tariffs and slavery. Abolitionists considered Westport proslavery and sometimes attacked wagons leaving town. Dick had no problem with them.

When he was loaded and ready to return, Dick hired teamsters to replace those he fired.

The return trip was uneventful until the train reached the swollen Arkansas River in early June. It took eighteen teams of oxen to pull a loaded wagon through the river's sand. Dick spent most of the day standing waist deep midstream overseeing the crossing of the train. In some places they had to build bridges.

After the train crossed the river, Dick rode ahead to find a campsite. After a bone-tiring day, it was relaxing to be out of the water and riding alone. He allowed his usual vigilant eyes and mind to relax and focus on a good campsite. When he looked up, he saw an entire band of Indians. They weren't just a scouting party. There were four or five hundred of them. He quickly assessed the situation: the river on one side, the Indians on the other, him in-between. If he played it right, he could cross the river, ride along the other side, re-cross the river, and meet the wagon train. He was about to follow through with his quickly laid plan when he noticed the Indians waving at him and realized they were Arapaho. He was among friends. They rode toward one another and exchanged greetings. The Arapaho were pretty happy;

they'd just been victorious over the Pawnee and were on their way home with many ponies and a slew of fresh scalps. And now, as if frosting on their celebration cake, they'd pulled a good joke on Cuthand, as they called Dick. They'd recognized him as soon as they saw him and thought it would be great fun to surround him and see how he'd react.

He chose his campsite. The Indians picked one nearby. Knowing they'd be having a night of celebration, Dick gave them sacks of sugar and flour and a barrel of hard tack when the wagons arrived. The chief had known Dick a long time and appointed four of his braves to guard Dick's stock during the night. Dick told the young braves what time he needed the animals.

Throughout the night those in Dick's train who were new on the Santa Fe Trail were aware of eerie celebration sounds of the scalp dances nearby. Long before other nationalities set foot on the North American continent, Indian tribes marked their victories with their opponents' scalps. One old timer said there was nothing that set a person in good standing with an Indian tribe like showing them scalps from an enemy tribe. He added that all were glad to see a Comanche scalp.

In the morning the four braves had Dick's animals ready for him at the precise time.

Comanche attacked the train a few days later. The wagons formed a fighting corral. The Comanche only attacked once. Arrows stuck in the wagons, but none of the men were wounded.

As they neared the New Mexico line, they met up with William Bent and his wagon train. They traveled along, relatively close together until Dick found a stick in the ground with a piece of paper on it, which read, "Good-bye." Dick realized William planned to beat him to Ft. Union and be waiting when he arrived. They'd known one another twenty years. There was little a mountain man enjoyed more than competition or wagering on his competence and judgment. Dick folded the paper and put it in his pocket. He looked over his cattle. They were in pretty good shape, even after all the miles. A little hard driving wouldn't harm them.

Dick instructed his men.

When Bent's train went into camp a couple miles ahead, Dick rode over, just as one old friend would make a social call on another. William and Dick played a few hands of cards and had a few drinks while Dick's men drove his wagons beyond William's. They circled far enough around not to arouse attention. By morning light, Dick's train was a couple miles ahead. It was his turn to leave a note. Dick and his train had been at Ft. Union a day and a half when William arrived.

As soon as Dick's wagons were unloaded at Ft. Union, a few of the wagons were reloaded with goods for the Albuquerque Post. Dick seldom had more than a couple days at home between freight runs. He kept this pace as long as the weather held.

For years the distance from Ft. Union to the Albuquerque Post was reckoned to be 160 miles. Teamsters were paid by the weight of goods and the distance traveled. Over years of working with cattle and measuring distances of various terrains, Dick had a pretty accurate idea of mileage. After making round trips from Ft. Union to Albuquerque, he felt certain the distance was off. When it was time to settle with the government for 800,000 pounds of freight hauled to Albuquerque, Dick asked for a mileage survey. He agreed to personally pay the survey cost if the distance didn't prove to be more than 160 miles. Dick said the survey added two and a half miles to the distance and several hundred dollars to his pay and to the pay of every other freighter thereafter.

Dick gathered his family and moved them to Ft. Barclay. Dick and Mary Ann's first son was born in December. They named him for Dick's twenty-one-year-old brother Joseph, who was with them at Ft. Barclay.

The winter of 1856-57 was hard on pastured herds in the West—especially those involved in freighting to Utah. When winter storms slowed travel, Dick turned his cattle onto the prairie and let them roam for the winter until he rounded them up in the spring. He did some trading in winter months. On February 23, 1857, Ft. Union commander, Colonel William W. Loring, wrote Joe Doyle, accusing him of sending Dick Wootton to trade gunpowder with the Plains Indians.

While freighting between posts, Dick became acquainted with many soldiers and officers. Some became prominent a few years later during the American Civil War, some as Yankees, some as Confederates. Most of the people he met wrote their stories only in the lives of people who knew them—forgotten names, whose influence trickles on down without a name attached.

Doyle and Wootton were concerned about an education for their children. A couple of private schools had opened in Santa Fe a few years ago, but there were no public schools in New Mexico Territory. In the States, Massachusetts had set a precedent in 1852 by requiring children to attend school. Between them Doyle and Dick had three school age children by the spring of 1857, but there were other families at Barclay. The Simpsons had four school-aged children. Eliza Wootton was eight; R. L., Jr. was seven.

Even as a grandmother, Eliza remembered the school room—the little lookout over Ft. Barclay's entrance in the southeast side of the fort. Mexicans called it La Charita, the little cage. There was a window on each side of the little square room and one or two on the front side. Sometimes Eliza sat in the window on the southeast side as she worked on her lessons; but the bright, warm sunshine often made her so sleepy it was hard to do her afternoon schoolwork. R. L. and she were glad when the teacher, Mr. James Mayberry, boarded at their house.

The first couple years of freighting, Dick had about as much trouble from thieves near Ft. Union as he did with Indians on the Santa Fe Trail. 1856 and 1857 were relatively calm as far as Indian attack on trains across the Plains.

Dick had learned courtesy with Indians from Bent. Dick had visited the Cheyenne and come to an understanding with them. They didn't want it known that they showed partiality, letting some white men go and not others. With government regulations what they were, traders couldn't stop along the trail and offer Indians goods without permission. But Indians watched for traders they knew. When a small party, or even a brave or two, made their presence known, it was polite to drop a little gift off the wagon for the band. Once he'd seen the men, Dick would drop off large sacks of flour, sugar, and coffee as tokens of his friendship. After the train passed by, the Indians came along and picked up the gifts. Even in relatively peaceful times, Dick didn't let his manners slip.

The gang of thieves holed up at La Plazarota, about three miles from Ft. Union were another thing. They were about as slick as Ali Baba and his forty thieves. Size made absolutely no difference to them. They'd steal anything from tack to a complete wagon. Dick was on the road much of the year and was only home between freight runs or during snowy weather. Ft. Union and his home at Ft. Barclay were a few miles apart from one another and from La Plazarota.

Each time Dick came home it seemed something was stolen. This was happening to everyone who spent time at Ft. Union, but none of the authorities would go over to La Plazarota and take care of the situation. The gang of about thirty men stood united as one. When one of Dick's wagons was stolen, he'd had enough.

He found out who stole his wagon. Next, he gathered seven men, including William Kroenig, to go with him to La Plazarota in the dark dead of night. Quietly, the eight men rode. Six stopped a safe distance from the settlement and stood guard. Dick and another man dismounted and entered the house where the thief and several others lay sleeping in the same room. They knew any sound from the thief would rouse the entire gang. They stepped to the thief's bed. No one had noticed. The thief caught sight of them as they laid hands on him. A cold gun barrel on each side of his body encouraged him to remain silent, to get up, and go outside with them. The three walked to the waiting guards. All nine men mounted horses, rode a couple miles or so to a place suited for a hanging, and dismounted.

Dick appointed jurors and called court in session. The charge: theft. The verdict: guilty. The sentence: death.

In quiet solemnity the men knotted a rope and began preparations to carry out the sentence. Very aware of his predicament, the thief began impassioned pleadings for mercy, promised to return the stolen wagon, promised he'd never ever steal again—not as long as he lived. William Kroenig was so sure Dick and the other men meant business, that he pled for the thief's life.

When Dick and the other six were sure the thief believed them as much as Kroenig did, they let him go. He walked back home. The next day he returned Dick's wagon. As far as Dick and the others knew, the man kept his word and never stole anything the rest of his life. Less than a week later the thief went to a dance, got in a fight, and was killed.

Dick made four freighting trips across the Santa Fe Trail in 1856 and 1857. A snowstorm overtook him and his train on one trip through Kansas. Needing to find shelter for his animals, he circled the wagons and drove the cattle to the sand hills for shelter. When he returned to his wagon circle, he found a stagecoach inside the wagon corral. The stage passengers were sitting around a campfire made from the yokes he'd just taken off his oxen.

Freighting into Mormon Country

After they were driven from Illinois and encouraged to leave Missouri, many Mormons emigrated into Mexican territory. They settled primarily in the area now known as Utah. At the end of the Mexican War, however, Mexico ceded that territory to the United States.

In an attempt to maintain their own rule, Mormons organized a state, named it Deseret, and sought admittance to the Union. The statehood attempt was unsuccessful, but they seemed satisfied when President Fillmore appointed their leader, Brigham Young as Utah Territorial Governor.

Young appointed officials in sympathy with Mormon interests. That didn't seem to be a problem until he sent U. S. appointed district judges packing. Young was removed from office. The gubernatorial appointment was offered to non-Mormon Colonel Edward Steptoe in 1854, but the situation in Utah was too volatile to accept outside leadership.

Alfred Cumming, former Georgia politician and one of General Scott's staff in the Mexican War, was appointed governor in 1857. When Cumming asked Washington for 2,500 soldiers to help enforce law and order in Utah, Brigham Young called Mormons to arm and fight for their liberties.

A state of rebellion was declared. With all the divisiveness between North and South, Congress was familiar with fomentations of impending rebellion—especially since the deaths of spokesmen Daniel Webster (1852), John Calhoun (1850), and the great compromiser Henry Clay (1852). For the time being, Congress was managing to keep a lid on things in the Union of States. They would see what they could do about this Utah situation.

On September 11, 1857, Mormon elder John D. Lee led Indians and a band of Mormons, including Isaac C. Haight, and William H. Dame to attack an emigrant train on its way from Arkansas and Missouri to California. They met the train in southern Utah's Mountain Meadows and confiscated the emigrants' weapons before they killed 120 men, women, and children—all except seventeen of the children. Lee was later convicted and executed at the scene of the massacre.

General Albert Sydney Johnston led U. S. troops toward Salt Lake City, Utah. Mormon troops cut him off, burned his wagons, and drove off 800 head of cattle. Johnston retreated to Black Forks near Ft. Bridger and spent the winter of 1857-58 with few provisions. After that, war picked up.

In 1858 Dick Wootton and Joe Doyle freighted supplies to General Johnston and his troops. Because of the extra distance, teamsters could only make one round trip to Utah per season. Utah freighters preferred the large Chicago wagon because they could pack 2500-3500 pounds of freight into its long bed (3 ½' wide, 12' long, 1 ½' deep).

The return trip was seldom a problem because wagons became trade items. Salt Lake Valley settlers wanted farm wagons and were willing to pay about $500 for a wagon that cost about $120 in the States. Of course, a freighter took a great loss if he sold his trail-worn draft animals.

Wootton and Doyle left New Mexico early in 1858, picked up supplies in the States, and traveled the Salt Lake Trail from Atchison, Kansas, to Omaha (Nebraska), Ft. Laramie, Pacific Springs, Ft. Bridger (Wyoming), and on to Salt Lake. They traveled the 1,225 miles in ninety-seven days.

The Kansas Plains enjoyed a good season of rain in 1858, but the rain muddied up the trail, obstructed travel in some places, and in other places caked mud on wagon wheels.

Many freighters didn't make it to Utah that season because of Spanish fever. Once they passed the mud plains of Kansas, Dick and Joe passed through an area where Spanish fever killed hundreds of oxen. Some watering holes along the way were so littered with carcasses that it was difficult to find safe water for their own animals. They came across scores of abandoned wagons. With no draft animals, teamsters had been forced to abandon their wares.

When they arrived in Salt Lake City, Dick found Mormon hospitality had changed since his visit in 1852. It wasn't a personal thing toward him—he was well-treated—but toward non-Mormons, in general. Because of the war, Mormons watched incoming travelers closely. They welcomed Mormon immigrants to stay and encouraged others to travel on.[101]

Because Salt Lake City was their freighting destination, Dick and Doyle were in town longer than when Dick passed through with his sheep. Always a son of the South, Dick enjoyed meeting people. On this trip Dick became acquainted with several well-known Mormon leaders. When Brigham Young heard Dick was back in town, he sent him an invitation to visit in his home. Dick went over one afternoon and enjoyed visiting with Brigham and dining with him in the evening. Dick was more comfortable this time—wearing proper attire, rather than the weather-shrunken britches he had when he passed through in 1852. Recalling the visit years later, Dick said, "My opinion of Brigham Young then, was that he was a shrewd, in fact a very able man, who among other things was making his religion very profitable; and when he died, and I learned that he had left a fortune of more than two million dollars, I flattered myself that I had judged him correctly."[102]

---

[101] The U. S. Government and Mormons reached a compromise. Soldiers remained stationed near Utah Lake, about forty miles from Salt Lake, until 1860. With the outbreak of Civil War, soldiers were needed in the States.
[102] Conard, 1890, 363.

Headed Home

In September 1858, when all their wagons were unloaded and their Salt Lake City business was done, Dick Wootton and Joe Doyle started back home to their families at Fort Barclay. As the wagons rolled, they talked. Dick hadn't forgotten about going back home to Kentucky. He hadn't amassed the fortune he'd set his sights on when he crossed the Plains as a greenhorn muleskinner back in 1836. Fortunes had come and gone, but he had enough to get a good start at an easier lifestyle than he'd lived the past twenty-two years. The kids were growing. It'd be easier on Mary Ann. Dick was looking forward to making a home for his growing family where they might enjoy a little more society and less hardship. Having his brother Joseph nearby refreshed his thoughts of home. Dick hadn't seen his parents in over twenty-four years; he hadn't even met his youngest sister.

Life in the mountains had been an adventure, and friends here had become like family. Of course, there were still the family ties with Dolores' family in Taos and Mora. But he'd been thinking it would be good to see his family and friends and places of long ago.

Several old timers from his early days in the Rocky Mountain region had already gone. Brown, Kinkead, and Waters had gone to California in the 1840's. Robert Fisher'd gone to California, went out to the Sacramento Valley with Simpson after gold was discovered, died out there. Marcellin St. Vrain had been back in Missouri ten years—left after he killed that Indian in a wrestling match at Bent's Fort. Tom Fitzpatrick, Bill New, Barclay, and the Tharp brothers, all dead. Indians and Mexicans had massacred Turley and Bent (Charles) back in '47. Only William was left of the Bents. Indians'd got Charley Towne up on Manco de Burro Pass not long after that (1848). Fremont had come close to being the end of Old Bill Williams, but it was Ute that got him after all. Then last winter old Bill Guerrier dropped ash in a powder keg and blew himself to thunder.

Dick did want to see the Arapaho. He'd make one more trip north to trade with them—that was it; then he'd head back to Kentucky when weather permitted. Not far out of town, Dick sold Joe his interest in their freighting outfit and returned to Salt Lake City. He hoped to find a stage. There was no stage. Four other men were in the same strait; so they formed a party and rode horseback across the mountains. Included in the party were Dr. Cavanaugh of Taos, mountain man Zan Hicklin and a little Mexican boy in their charge. Dick had a great time traveling with those two old friends; he always enjoyed Zan's sense of humor. With no wagons to pull, they made good time. They ran short of food along the way, but there was wild game. They enjoyed the bear roast Dick served until they found out it was a badger he'd killed, dressed, cooked, and served as "bear." On the spot, each decided he'd had his fill, didn't have room for another bite.

By the time Dick arrived at Ft. Barclay, he'd been gone from home a little over seven months. Son William, "Willie," was born about the time he arrived. They'd leave when Mary Ann and the children were up to traveling. He'd take them along on the trading trip and leave from there.

Dick began winding up his affairs at Ft. Union and Ft. Barclay. He transferred most of his money to drafts on St. Louis where he had his investments. In early October 1858 he loaded four wagons with trade goods and a few family belongings. He helped Mary Ann and the seven children into the wagon, and said good-bye to Ft. Barclay. His brother Joseph traveled with them.

Snow fell early that autumn; so travel was slow as they rolled north toward Kansas Territory (Colorado). They stopped at Cimarron City (New Mexico) to visit Lucien Maxwell and his family. They stayed several days—such visiting and hospitality was common among mountain men. They bid the Maxwells adios and set their course north through Raton Pass. Because of the combination of weather and terrain, it took them almost a month to travel fifty miles in that area. They had a couple hundred more miles to travel before reaching the Platte River (Colorado), where they were headed. After they left Maxwell's place, they didn't see another person or dwelling until they reached the Greenhorn, about seventy-five miles north of present-day Trinidad, Colorado. Charlie Autobees and his family still lived near the Huerfano.

The Woottons traveled to El Pueblo and from there toward the Platte. Cherry Creek, where traders often traded with Indians, was along the well-used route. The Woottons arrived at Cherry Creek on Christmas Eve.

There they found two little settlements of treasure seekers of various nationalities and walks of life. A few had heard about the old Spanish mines, but most of them had followed recent reports of more substantial gold near Cherry Creek.

On the way to the California gold fields in 1850, Louis Ralston, John Beck, and a group of Cherokee—all experienced gold miners from northern Georgia—had traveled through present-day Colorado. While camped along Ralston Creek (northwest of Denver), they found color, but not enough to lure them from the bright promise of California's Sacramento Valley.

After they returned to Georgia, they had talked about the color they'd found on Ralston Creek. Maybe it'd be worthwhile to head back to the Rockies and check out the foothills near the South Platte. They mentioned it to William Greeneberry "Green" Russell, who'd also mined in Georgia and California. Green had pulled up stakes in Dahlonega, Georgia, and was farming in Kansas in 1857.

By the time the Woottons arrived in December 1858, Green Russell's Party, as well as a party from Lawrence, Kansas, had arrived and begun the two little settlements. Auraria camp had sprung up on Cherry Creek's west bank and Denver City on the east bank.

On the Banks of Cherry Creek

In the winter of 1857-58 Green Russell and John Beck had contacted relatives and friends to ask if anyone else was interested in giving South Platte prospecting a try. About sixty Cherokee and about twenty others—seventy-eight in all—were interested. Among Green Russell's Party were P. H. Clark, G. W. Kiker, A. T. Lloyd, and Green's brothers John and Oliver Russell. The men traveled from their respective homes in Georgia, Missouri, Arkansas, and Kansas to meet at Great Bend, Kansas on April 25, 1858. Most men brought ox teams and six months' worth of provisions.

The Green Russell Party arrived at William Bent's Stone Fort on June 12, 1858. They were impressed by Bent's spacious, well-kept facility. More men arrived, bringing the party to 104.

From Bent's, the party traveled northwest more than 200 miles to the mouth of Cherry Creek on the Platte River, then camped a day or two. Except for Sundays and their stay at Bent's Fort, the men had traveled daily since they left Great Bend.

They didn't find much color on Cherry Creek. They moved on to Ralston Creek, where they'd first found gold flecks, and spread out from there. Arapaho in the area were friendly to them.

After searching about ten days, most of the party decided the trip was an effort in futility. Green called the men together, told them if at least two wanted to stay, he'd stay. Green and thirteen others (six from Kansas, seven from Georgia) remained. All the Cherokee went home.

The remaining prospectors broke camp and followed the South Platte. They set up camp twelve to fifteen miles from the mouth of Cherry Creek. Near the mouth of Dry Creek (south of Denver) they found enough gold to pay for their time. John Cantrell drove by in his wagon on his way to Missouri and stopped to talk. He agreed to take a bag of their gold dirt to be assayed in Missouri.

About the time Green Russell's party thinned out, a party from Lawrence, Kansas, arrived in the region. After he scouted for Colonel Sumners' expedition in 1857, Fall Leaf, a Delaware Indian, arrived in eastern Kansas with a quill of gold dust from the Rocky Mountain region and stirred up interest. Talk turned to action over the winter of 1857-58. The Lawrence Party organized in the spring and set out for the Rocky Mountains. They arrived near present-day Pueblo, Colorado, in time to celebrate the Fourth of July.

They worked the Pike's Peak region (Colorado Springs area), hence, the name Pike's Peak gold fields. At summer's end they had nothing to show for their effort. They heard of Russell's success on the Platte, loaded their gear, and moved about sixty-five miles north.

September found them pitching their tents on the banks of the Platte. Still, they found nothing. They set up a working camp in a grove of cottonwood on the east bank of Cherry Creek. With the help of traders John Smith and William McGaa—both married to Indian women—the Lawrence Party established the St. Charles Town Association and named their site St. Charles.

Mormon Samuel M. Rooker and his family had arrived near Cherry Creek on August 30th and were living in a tent. About the second or third week of October 1858, A. H. Barker, John Smith, and Rosswell C. Hutchins each began building a log cabin along a little dirt street called Indian Row. Rooker began construction of his cabin on October 26th.

In the autumn Elbridge Gerry at Ft. Laramie (Wyoming) sent John Smith to Cherry Creek with a load of goods. On October 29th, Andrew J. Williams and Charles H. Blake arrived from Iowa with four wagons loaded with supplies, which they soon sold to the prospectors.

The Green Russell Party anticipated that others would be attracted to Cherry Creek once John Cantrell showed their gold in Missouri. They set up winter camp on the west bank of Cherry Creek across from the St. Charles camp. On November 1st they named their camp Auraria Town Company. Both camps planned streets and building lots. Auraria offered shares of stock to anyone who would build a house in the prescribed city limits by July 1, 1859. The house had to be at least 16' x 16' and be approved by the board of directors.

On the other side of the bank Charles Nichols was unable to interest anyone in building a log structure—even when he offered one hundred lots to any person who would build. In early November he left a partially finished cabin to hold the St. Charles townsite and returned to the States for the winter.

On November 16, just days after Nichols left, General William Larimer, his adult son, and Richard E. Whitsitt arrived in Auraria with a party of men from Kansas—the Kansas Party. They brought a wagon loaded with building tools, nails, pine planks, and other provisions for their own use. There was no place of regular supply anywhere near. When they stopped at Bent's Big Timbers (Stone Fort) enroute, they'd purchased a dozen apples for a dollar and a buffalo robe for four dollars.

General Larimer was a tall man with a military bearing—from his days in the Pennsylvania militia—and was a firm believer in temperance. More interested in town-company development than in gold, Larimer's Kansas Party surveyed the vacant St. Charles site on November 17, 1858. Some of the party thought the townsite was too far from water, but Mr. Whitsitt persuaded the men to give it a try. He offered to haul buckets of water to them until they could dig wells of their own. After that, the Larimer-Whitsitt Company built cabins on the St. Charles site. They called it Denver City Town Company in honor of Kansas Territorial Governor James W. Denver.

Moving right along with their jumped townsite, the Larimer Company adopted a constitution on November 22 and appointed officers, including William McGaa of the original St. Charles Company. John Smith, also associated with the St. Charles Company, relinquished his right to his St. Charles Company claim for a small amount. Each of the original forty-one Denver City Town Company shareholders was required to build at least one building within ninety days. Anyone who built a cabin at least sixteen feet square received two lots. From the beginning, Denver and Auraria competed like two hometown teams.

Christmas

When the Woottons arrived at Cherry Creek on Christmas Eve, they found a few teepees here and there and a smattering of tents and cabins—built and being built—on both sides of the creek. Many cabins had canvas roofs. General Larimer had brought some window glass with him, but no cabin had window glass installed yet.

DENVER'S FIRST CABIN; BUILT IN 1858.

Dick said there were a few hundred living in the two camps.[103] Prospectors had holed in for the winter, waiting for spring; so they could prospect in earnest. There were four women in the settlements: Mrs. David Smoke, Mrs. Henri ("Countess" Katrina) Murat, and Mrs. S. M. (Rebecca) Rooker and her daughter. Mary Ann Wootton made five.

One thing the two camps had in common was low rations. Fortunately, game was plentiful. Although Dick intended his goods for the Arapaho and Cheyenne—he preferred to trade for furs, which he could sell on the Eastern market—here was a need, a ready market. He rolled a couple barrels of Taos Lightning out of a wagon and invited everyone from both sides of the creek to celebrate Christmas Eve free of charge. Residents could bring their own cups or drink out of his cups dipper style; he didn't have cups for everyone.

Celebration started up again Christmas morning. With no rooms large enough for everyone, the community celebrated outdoors. It was a sunny day, but it was present-day

---

[103] Between 200-500 by various estimates.

Colorado. Men gathered brush and wood and kindled a bonfire. Some danced. Several, including Larimer, made speeches. Residents raised their tin cups and toasted the future.

The Woottons ate Christmas dinner on the banks of Cherry Creek. On the Denver side of Cherry Creek, General Larimer's son cooked dinner for his father and about two dozen guests. He cooked dried corn, beans, rice, game, and dried apple pie, served with coffee. Most residents ate wild game for their Christmas entree.

In the afternoon F. C. "Con" Orem set up a wrestling match for a purse:[104] two oxen and a wagon. Charlie "Chuck-a-luck" Gilmore, the area's first professional gambler, spread blankets on his cabin's dirt floor and invited men in for games of chance.

Christmas was a welcome rest for the Woottons after weeks of travel. But, after the holiday, Dick pitched a large tent in Auraria, at 12th and Wazee (3rd) and began selling fabric, salt, New Mexico flour, and other goods from his loaded wagons.

He soon moved his family and business into a little log cabin. He rolled some barrels out of his wagons and set them up as counters. With no stores nearby, it wasn't long before Auraria-Denver townsfolk purchased all his goods. He'd done well enough to reconsider his immediate return to Kentucky. Some of the men who owned land offered Dick land if he'd stay. Land was plentiful and relatively cheap; but merchants and merchandise were hard to come by.[105]

Dick and Mary Ann decided to settle in the area for the time being.

In the first four months of 1859 land in Auraria-Denver was given to Dick Wootton and several other citizens.[106] In January 1860 directors of Auraria rescinded some of the allotted land.

---

[104] Orem was later a champion prizefighter.
[105] Land offer reports vary from a few to several town lots to 160 acres. Some say the promise didn't materialize.
[106] Those given land: Mr. Boughton; Heifman and Brauner; W. H. Bassett; S. W. Beall; J. W. Cooper; Mr. Foster, the surveyor; Messrs. Gilman, Edwards, Thompson, and Putnam; Dr. Griffith; G. F. Griffith; Jessey Heisman; R. H. Lusby; Mr. Ming; William Hilliard; Henri Murat; James Knight; William Parkinson; James Knight; Thomas Pollack; Jarvis Richardson; H. P. A. Smith; R. Smith; R. L. Wootton; and N. G. Wyatt.

Growth, Organization, and Politics

Business bustled in the infant Cherry Creek settlement in January 1859. Dick Wootton began Auraria-Denver's first business block when he built a hewn log store on the east side of Ferry (11th) Street between Market (4th) and Wazee (3rd) in Auraria. His 20' x 32' building was the first built in either settlement solely for business purposes. It was also the first two-story structure in Denver-Auraria. An outside stairway led to the second story; the floor was made of whip-sawn boards. Folks thought the clapboard roof and glazed windows gave an uptown look to the settlement—especially the windows. Dick later built an addition to the original structure.

In his enterprise Dick incorporated a general store, saloon, loan business, and a ten-pin alley—the first bowling alley in the community. Folks gathered in his store to visit and catch up on news. In that era a general store merchant pretty well knew any news available.

News of Cherry Creek spread. Beans, onions, and flour arrived from New Mexico in January. There'd been a few cases of scurvy in the settlement; so the onions were especially welcome.

In January, Rice and Heffner opened a saloon on the northwest corner of Market (4th) and Ferry (11th) in Auraria. Thomas Pollock, arrived from New Mexico on December 29, 1858, opened the community's first smithery on January 10, 1859. He set up shop on the southwest corner of Market (4th) and Ferry (11th), across the street from Rice and Heffner's saloon.

Early the same month Henry Reitze opened a bakery on the east side of Ferry (1426 11th) between Market (4th) and Wazee (3rd)—on the same side of the street as Dick Wootton's store. Reitze's sign read: "Gold dust, flour, dried apples, etc., taken in exchange for bread and pies."[107]

Frenchman Henri Murat and his wife did their part to help the community along. She charged $3 to launder a half-dozen pieces of linen. Murat shaved beards for a dollar. He said he was a nephew of Murat, Bonaparte's King of Naples—and who else would know better than he? They remained in Auraria until they moved across the creek to Denver in the spring of 1860.

On February 1, 1859, Henri Murat and David Smoke opened "El Dorado,"[108] a hewn log hotel located on the southeast corner of 10th and Larimer in Auraria. It had a dirt floor. Mrs. Murat, Mrs. Wootton, and Mrs. Rooker made a silk flag from old dresses. It flew atop the building on a pine mast until someone took a liking to the flag and stole it.

Thomas Warren from Kentucky began operating a ferry between Auraria and Denver at the base of Ferry Street in February. He charged a dollar to ferry a wagon and team.

Denver McGaa, son of William "Jack Jones" McGaa and his Indian wife, was the first child born in the Cherry Creek settlement. He was born March 3, 1859. The first "white

---

[107] Hall, 233.
[108] El Dorado burnt down in March 1877.

child" was born to Mr. and Mrs. Henry Humbell in a place at the corner of 10th and Larimer in the autumn of 1859. The community presented Mrs. Humbell with several corner lots. She didn't think the lots of much account and left for Oklahoma in 1863.

Joseph Merrival's son was the first known death in the community; he died in March 1859. Jack O'Neil soon joined him.

Jack O'Neil and Johnnie Rooker (Samuel and Rebecca Rooker's son) got crosswise during a poker game. It wasn't their first altercation; but this time O'Neil insulted the Rooker women. Johnnie Rooker, originally from Arkansas, was of a mind to kill him for talking that way—not to mention O'Neil once called Johnnie a yellow coward. Johnnie told him that the next time they met it was going to be the end for one of them. The two left. Johnnie had a friend bring a fast horse to his house. Jack went home and kept his guns handy. Men wagered on the showdown.

Johnnie Rooker hid near the front door of Wootton's store (about 1413-1415 11th Street). About 10 a.m. Jack O'Neil passed by on his way to the hardware store. The street cleared. Johnnie got a bead on O'Neil and cursed as he shot. Jack cried out and crumpled to the street.

Johnnie jumped on the waiting horse and took off. The doctor went to Jack, but it was no use. Johnnie'd hit him with thirteen buckshot. Jack smiled when his sweetheart, Kate, came to him. He died with the smile on his face. He was buried next day at Mount Pleasant, the new cemetery southeast of town. After that, locals called it O'Neil's Ranch.

By early April 1859 two steam-powered sawmills arrived from the Missouri River region. One belonged to Hiram P. Bennet and N. S. Wyatt,[109] the other to D. C. Oakes and William Street.[110] Oakes and Street's mill arrived a few days after Bennet and Wyatt's. Both mills were installed south of the mouth of Cherry Creek: Oakes and Street on Plum Creek, Bennet and Wyatt on Running Creek. There was plenty of timber in the area for both mills.

With all the building going on, Kasserman and Willoughby opened a carpentry shop.

On April 21, 1859, Bennet and Wyatt had the first batch of milled lumber ready for sale. They sold it to Thomas Pollock and Dick Wootton. Pollock built a hotel (corner of Market and Ferry). Dick built a two-story home for his family on the north side of 10th Street (St. Louis) between Market (4th) and Larimer (5th). He was pleased it had a shingled roof for his family—a touch of class in a frontier town. It was the first frame house in Auraria.

Dick's brother Joseph E. Wootton and D. D. Cook partnered in an action and commission business next door to him. Joseph left for the States in the spring of 1859 to pick up a supply of goods. He took R. L., Jr. along to be educated in Kentucky.

In March those interested in the future of the Cherry Creek settlements gathered upstairs at Wootton's store—Wootton Hall, they called it. It wasn't large; but, small as it was, it was the largest room in town. It was a sheltered place where men could gather to voice their opinions and vote their choice.

Cherry Creek was in Arapahoe County, Kansas Territory. Arapahoe County held its first election for county officers on March 28, 1859. Seven hundred and seventy-four votes were

---

[109] Cooper operated Wyatt's mill; the mill was sometimes referred to as Cooper's mill.
[110] D. C. Oakes came to Cherry Creek the previous autumn and returned to his Iowa home for the winter.

cast: Auraria cast 231; Denver, 144; the remainder of the county, 399.[111]

Denver-Auraria residents began talk of breaking away from Kansas Territory. On Monday, April 11, 1859, delegates from Arapahoe County's various precincts met in Wootton Hall to discuss preparation of a state constitution.[112] The convention agreed on a series of resolutions in support of adopting a state government. They proposed the state be named Jefferson and presented a resolution asking residents to elect delegates to a constitutional convention to be held in Denver on the first Monday of June 1859. On May 14th the Auraria precinct elected Uncle Dick to serve on the Denver City Constitutional Convention. On June 6th delegates met at Blake and William's Denver Hall and appointed a committee to write a state constitution. Uncle Dick was appointed one of three tellers for balloting of officers of the convention.

The county sent B. D. Williams to Washington, D. C. and Captain Richard Sopris to Kansas. Williams sought Congressional approval for a territory independent of Kansas. Sopris went to get the okay for establishment of Arapahoe County.[113]

---

[111] Elected: D. D. Cook, Sheriff; John L. Hiffner, Treasurer; J. S. Lowrie, Register of Deeds; Levi Ferguson, Clerk Board Supervisor; S. W. Wagoner, Probate Judge; Marshall Cook, Prosecuting Attorney; Ross Hutchins, Assessor; C. M. Steinberger, Coroner W. W. Hooper, Auditor; L. J. Winchester, R. L. Wootton, Hickory Rogers, Supervisors.
[112] Auraria delegates: Allen, Slaughter, McLain, Pollock, Russell, Cook. Denver's: Blake, Clancey, Smith, Lowry, Larimer, Merrick.
[113] Arapahoe County, Kansas Territory, was created August 30, 1855. In 1859 it was divided into six: Arapahoe, El Paso, Fremont, Oro, Broderick, and Montana.

Pike's Peak or Bust

After John Cantrell arrived in Westport (Kansas City) with Cherry Creek gold, he stopped by the newspaper office and mentioned where it came from. The *Kansas City Journal of Commerce* headlined the report in journalistic style: "The New Eldorado!!! Gold in Kansas Territory!!" The story grew like a watered weed. While men discussed the news and planned their trips, Auraria-Denver prepared for them.

"Pike's Peak or Bust" became the slogan of thousands who grasped onto hope of something more, something better. It's estimated that 100,000 "fifty-niners" left Missouri for the Rocky Mountain gold field in 1859 and that more than a third of those returned home before they finished the trek across the Plains.

Though most of the people flooding into the mining district were the law-abiding type, there were enough shiftless scoundrels thieving around and causing trouble to merit the organization of a vigilance committee. One April day (1859) a Hungarian named Stoefel came into Dick's store and sold him a little sack of gold dust. As it turned out, there was one little problem. The gold dust wasn't his, or at least it hadn't been when he and his German brother-in-law Thomas Biencroff left home. Somewhere between town and their place near the mouth of Clear Creek, Stoefel shot Biencroff in the head, took his gold, and went on to town. According to Dick's firsthand account, a couple Mexicans found the body and told about it in town while Stoefel was still there. Confronted, Stoefel confessed and was taken to vigilance court.

Twelve jurors were chosen. Stoefel was represented by a lawyer, but he admitted his guilt. He said he'd followed Biencroff from the East to kill him. The jury quickly reached the verdict of guilty, the sentence: hanging at two o'clock that afternoon. A minister from the East and the executioner—a frontiersman called "Noisy Tom"—rode along with Stoefel in a two-horse wagon. Their destination was a cottonwood tree near the intersection of 10th (St. Louis) and 3rd (Wazee)—near Dick's home. Someone threw the rope over a cottonwood limb and slipped it over Stoefel's head and down around his neck. The minister reminded Stoefel to kneel for prayer like the others were doing. The minister prayed. The wagon drove off. This execution and others like it in the coming months encouraged a more law abiding start for Denver's infant stage of development. Some, who didn't care for law and order or for a noose, chose to move on.

Dick said, "'Stealing is the only occupation of a considerable proportion of the population, who take anything from a pet calf or a counterfeit dollar to a sawmill.'"[114] (One of the area's steam sawmills had been stolen in transit.)

Augustus Wildman wrote from the Cherry Creek settlement to his father in the States:
Our laws, or rather, the laws of the miners, are so framed as to protect the innocent and punish the guilty, and that is more than you can say of those as now executed and in vogue

---

[114] Zamonski and Keller, *The Fifty-Niners*, 73.

in the States. Take them as a whole, we have as good and wholesome a code of laws as ever were enacted. They are founded on justice and right, and executed with vigor and dispatch. They are not written upon parchment, nor printed in books, but they are impressed upon the mind of the miner by their daily observance, and regarded by him in all his transactions… The morals of the people are generally good, in fact much better than the generality of the cities and towns in other parts of the country. We have no Sunday laws, and yet the Sabbath is more generally respected than in St. Louis. We have no laws against selling liquor on Sunday, but the shops that sell the ardent generally close their doors on that day. We have no license laws to prevent the sale of ardent liquors, and yet there is not one quarter the amount drank to the man here that there is in St. Louis. During the two months that I have resided here I have never seen a drunken man, that I recollect of.[115]

---

[115] Hafen and Hafen, *Wildman Letters*, 139.

Frontier Newspaper

John L. Merrick arrived in Denver with the first newspaper printing outfit brought to Cherry Creek. His printing press was small, but big enough to put out a little newspaper. He started preparation for the *Cherry Creek Pioneer*.

William N. Byers and Thomas Gibson also had plans for a newspaper in the Rockies. On March 8, 1859, they left Omaha with a few men, including printers John L. Dailey and Charlie Semper. Byers wasn't sure where he'd locate—somewhere in the Rockies; so he named his paper the *Rocky Mountain News*. That would fit any locale in the area. On the way Byers set up camp at St. Vrain; so his men could prospect. He went ahead to Cherry Creek to assess the Cherry Creek settlements. He arrived on April 17th and chose to set up shop in Auraria. On the way to the Rockies, when he was at Ft. Kearny, he'd heard of Merrick and knew of his presence now. But Byers, an energetic and industrious man, was not easily deterred. On the 18th he sent a messenger to instruct his party to hurry to Auraria with equipment and supplies.

Dick Wootton offered Byers space in the upper floor of his store. Byers accepted the offer and rented a portion of the upstairs for his newspaper office. He called it a little office in Wootton's attic. Little as it was, it became the first office building in Denver-Auraria, an infant forerunner of the Denver skyline.

While waiting for his party to arrive with the press and supplies, Byers scoured the town for local news to add to his preset copy. He'd obtained ads from Omaha merchants before he left and had already compiled and set copy for those and some general news.

Byers' crew arrived on April 20th. They carried the press up the outside stairs and began typesetting the local news Byers had gathered. They worked by candlelight, far into the night and again through the next day. The heavy, wet snow, which had piled up on roofs, began to melt. Rivulets of melting snow trickled through Dick's clapboard roof and dripped onto the editor and his staff. They rigged up a sort of indoor tent to protect the press and paper and kept working.

The first editions of Merrick's *Cherry Creek Pioneer* and Byers' *Rocky Mountain News* hit the streets within a half hour of each other on the evening of April 23, 1859. The general consensus of townsfolk was that the *Rocky Mountain News* came out twenty minutes ahead of the *Pioneer*. The next day Merrick sold his outfit to Gibson and Byers for some flour and bacon.

Printers' supplies were scarce; everything had to be hauled in. Sometimes supplies were lost to an Indian raid enroute. At such times Byers did what he could to publish as regularly as possible. Sometimes he printed his paper on wrapping paper from Dick's store.[116] Conditions in a small western settlement weren't ideal for publishing a newspaper.

Day-by-day the prospect of gold faded. Disillusioned men cleared out of town. When

---

[116] Purchases were wrapped with paper or paper and twine.

Editor Byers lacked other news, he bragged on the area and its possibilities. To some body-weary and very impoverished immigrants, that seemed more like a lie than sheer optimistic filler. Hundreds of men were beyond disappointment; they were hungry.

Dick Wootton and a partner had opened a boarding house. When hungry men came around to his store, Dick sent them over to the boarding house for a meal. Although Dick had an eye for opportunity and had no problem selling or dickering, feeding a hungry man was a horse of a different color. It wasn't in him to deny a hungry man food just because the man had no money. It wasn't long before Dick and his partner's boarding house venture went belly up.

Cherry Creek men called Dick, "Uncle Dick." Some say it was because of his supplies: the Taos Lightning on Christmas Eve 1858, the boarding house meals, his store and loans. Others say it was because he was an old-timer in the area when they arrived. For whatever reason, that's what they called him. "Uncle Dick" stuck the rest of his life.

Hungry, worn, and destitute, hundreds headed back to the States. Some starved to death before they got home. Editor Byers coined the byword "Gobacks" for those who returned. He was confident many Gobacks would want to return within six months.

Those who returned to the States met gold seekers on their way to the Rockies: "Pike's Peak or Bust." Anxious to get rich, hundreds arrived in Auraria-Denver at all hours of the day and set up tents. Merchants continued to build. As in many boom towns, men gambled their resources and strength on boom, rather than bust. Some towns materialized; others emptied, leaving framed or brick structures for the wind to whistle through—testimonies to hopes, dreams, and efforts.

It'll Be Okay After All

On Sunday, May 8, 1859, a short, thin prospector, with a full beard, walked into the Express Office. Waiting his turn, he began talking about the area's wealth. He was hesitant at first; but, as he warmed up, he told about finding gold-bearing dirt, a dollar's worth of gold to the pan. He pulled out some pieces he called gold-bearing quartz and a container with about $40 worth of gold. Listeners gazed. Those who'd been to California estimated it was as fine as any quartz they'd seen. Others came in and examined it. It was the first gold-bearing quartz reported in the area. Next day several men from Auraria went back up the gulch with the prospector to see his new "Gregory Mine." John Gregory's find and that of George Jackson earlier in the year established the fact there was gold worth mining in the Rocky Mountains.

Traders arrived at Cherry Creek with supplies. Uncle Dick had gone down to New Mexico in March and hauled up a load of flour. In April, Ceran St. Vrain had sent six wagons loaded with flour, furniture, and other goods; they arrived from New Mexico on the 13th. On June 1, 1859, butter sold for a dollar a pound, lettuce for ten cents a bunch, and peas for ten cents per quart. In August, Ceran St. Vrain made the trip from New Mexico himself. He brought shoes, tools, bacon, coffee, tobacco, whiskey, and his San Luis Valley flour. Louis Vasquez and Jim Beckwourth hauled in a wagon load of dry goods, crockery, window glass, nails, dried fruit, and, to top it off, wine and champagne. All summer supply wagons lumbered into town, stopped in front of stores and unloaded—every wagon of interest to townsfolk.

Captain Edwin Scudder, who opened one of Denver's first grocery stores, started his store in the tent in which he lived. A cheerful man, Scudder loaded items in his wheelbarrow and made grocery deliveries, whistling or singing as he went. It wasn't long before he had enough business and capital to move his business into a building. He became a prominent man among businessmen and politicians. He also supported the Vigilance Committee.

Auraria already had a couple of hotels. Andrew J. Williams and Charles H. Blake, who'd brought supplies to the area in October 1858, owned the first Denver City hotel. Carpenters Willoughby and Avery built the 32' x 110' building of cottonwood logs on the north side of Blake Street. It was the largest building in Denver or Auraria. Not having supplies for such a large roof, the top was covered with canvas for the summer. Blake and Williams lived in part, kept part for their stock, and used the remainder for a hotel. They opened for business on May 11, 1859. Inner rooms were partitioned with canvas covered frames, seven feet high. The place was called by various names: Blake and Williams' Hall, Denver Hall, Elephant Corral. Outside the hotel was a campground and stables for the convenience of traders and wagon masters.

The saloon and dining area were next to one another at the front of the building. The saloon boasted a dozen gambling tables. Hotel rooms were at the back; they had cottonwood framed beds. For personal hygiene, each room had a tin washbasin. When guests needed water, they could fill their basin from the barrels of water in the hallway. Finished with the water, they could simply toss it out—outside or on the floor. If on the floor, it could serve to harden the dirt floor.

Before winter, Blake replaced the canvas roof with a shingled roof and later added plank floors. By that time Williams had sold out[117] to Blake and returned to freighting.

A stage line began passenger and mail service into Denver in May 1859. Stages were due to arrive on Mondays and Wednesdays; but weather played into the schedule equation. John S. Jones of Missouri and William Hepburn Russell had organized the line when they heard rumors of gold in the Pike's Peak region. Russell's freighting partner Alexander Majors wouldn't join the venture. He knew the distance required too much outgo without enough inflow unless the government subsidized the line.

On 90-day credit Jones and Russell purchased enough Kentucky mules and Concord coaches to make the line a reality. They hired men to build stage stations every fifteen-twenty miles from Leavenworth (Kansas), up the Kansas River, through Kansas, across to Denver. They planned daily runs between Denver and Leavenworth. The trip cost a passenger $75.

When Jones and Russell couldn't meet their note, Alexander Majors covered their bacon. They continued stage service into Denver. A few months later they purchased Hockaday and Liggett's line from St. Joseph, Missouri, to Salt Lake City, Utah. They added stage stations to that portion.[118] The firm sold out to Ben Holladay in March 1862.

On June 6, 1859, Horace Greeley, editor of the *New York Tribune*, correspondent Albert D. Richardson of the *Boston Journal*, and Henry Villard of the *Cincinnati Commercial* rode in on the stage to provide their readers a firsthand report of the Rocky Mountain gold fields.

Later in the month (late June), M. Slaughter came into Auraria telling about his escape from a Ute attack on miners in the mountains. He said Ute killed and scalped Dr. Shunk of Niobrara, Nebraska Territory, right before his eyes. He also saw them shoot and kill Burt Kennedy from Plattsmouth.

Indian Agent Kit Carson looked into the matter and found Mr. Slaughter's report accurate.

Even with the new transportation service, Cherry Creek residents paid postage both on incoming and outgoing mail. When the U. S. Post Office opened in August, residents hoped they'd be able to send letters for the standard three-cent rate; but, for some reason, they still had to receive mail at the Express Office and pay twenty-five cents tariff per letter.

Wages in the Pikes Peak gold district ranged from fifty cents to $2.50 per day. The most common mediums of exchange were town lots and gold dust. Varying purity of gold dust and a lack of scales created an iffy exchange system. By September it was generally agreed that a pinch of gold dust would be accepted as exchange for twenty-five cents.

Building continued. In the summer of 1859 the area boasted three sawmills. Lumber was selling for $30 per hundred feet. With the availability of milled lumber at prices so much less than in the spring, some hastily-built cabins were remodeled. Others were built. Canvas was removed from many window openings and replaced with glazed glass. Some cabins had no windows to start with. Windows were cut, sashes built, and glazed glass installed. By early August there were about a hundred framed houses finished or in the process of construction.

---

[117] Williams sold out July 30, 1859.
[118] Stations were manned and supplied for riders and teams. Teams were changed at each station. Those stations also serviced Russell, Majors, and Waddell's Pony Express.

By the end of the month, lumber sold for $75 per thousand feet, delivered.

On July 4th a group of men from Omaha arrived with brass instruments and hosted a concert in celebration of Independence Day.

On July 10th Rocky Mountain News editor, William Byers wrote the Western Press to affirm there was plenty of gold in the Pikes Peak district, but advised men not to rush to Pikes Peak that fall, with winter about to begin. He warned men not to trust luck, but to be prepared with determination and enough provisions for six to eight months.

July rains came to the Rockies—rained every single day of the month. Prospectors kept working. Many caught cold. Those with rheumatism felt the weather in their stiffened, swollen joints. Many miners came down with Mountain Fever. The fever often hit a person in the morning and killed him by nightfall. In some diggings the fever was rare; but one week five to six miners died every day at the Gregory Diggings.

On August 1, 1859, Uncle Dick served on Arapahoe County's Constitutional Committee, which met at Kasserman and Co. (corner of 6th and St. Louis) in Auraria. During the weeklong meeting, one hundred sixty-six delegates from thirty-seven districts debated whether they should draft a state or territorial constitution. Most delegates preferred statehood. They put the matter on the September ballot. Voters chose territory.

By the third week of August, the effects of Mountain Fever and the work slowdown in the mines were felt in Denver. Money became so scarce there was little activity in town. Some wondered if the place would survive the coming winter.

Rumor of an Indian raid riffled through the community on the morning of August 27, 1859. Word was that 2,000 Cheyenne and Arapaho were on the warpath, had raided along the Platte, and were on their way to raid and burn Auraria-Denver that night.

About noon J. D. Rice came into town from his ranch twenty miles up Cherry Creek. He brought word from an Arapaho that the Kiowa were killing prairie settlers far and wide, but that they wouldn't attack Auraria-Denver. There were too many fighting men.

Auraria-Denver citizens weren't taking chances. They wanted to know why there was a large Indian camp nearby and sent two old-timers to find out. Jim Beckwourth and Uncle Dick Wootton rode out to the camp and came back with the facts. Other than their usual bent to beg or steal, the Indians camped near town meant no harm. U. S. troops had driven out the Kiowa who'd been killing and warring. Soldiers were pursuing them. Renegade parties attacked wagon trains, but whole tribes had not. Another large party of Apache, Arapaho, and Cheyenne had indeed gathered to the south; but that was in preparation for a treaty meeting at Bent's Stone Fort.

Strong rivalry continued between Auraria and Denver. Auraria had the larger population and the major business district. Some Denver men attempted to induce Auraria residents to move across the creek to Denver City. Many citizens saw the need of a unified government. On September 24th, town meetings were held in both settlements to promote a unified community.

In September, Buddee and Jacobs opened a two-story store building (1361 Eleventh) in Denver City. In off hours their building housed the Denver Masonic Order and the area's first Sunday School, led by Owen J. Goldrick.

Dick's friend and former freighting partner, Joe Doyle, had established a ranch in the

Pueblo (Colorado) area. In spring 1859 he'd gone to St. Louis and employed educator O. J. Goldrick to come to his ranch to tutor his children.[119] Goldrick came, but in the fall he moved to Denver and established the first public school in present-day Colorado. He advertised in the *Rocky Mountain News* on September 29, 1859:

> UNION DAY-SCHOOL. The subscriber would respectfully announce to the citizens of Auraria and Denver city that the above school will be open for the reception of pupils on Monday next, October 3, in the room lately occupied by Col. Inslee, Auraria, until a more commodious and comfortable school room and school furniture is made ready. From many years' experience as Principal and Superintendent of Schools and Academies in the East, and a familiarity with the latest approved modes of teaching and successful governing he trusts to be able to secure the speedy and substantial improvement of all grades of pupils that may be committed to his care, and to build up a first class school, wherein the young will be thoroughly grounded in the elementary and practical studies, and the more advanced prepared for college or the counting-room. Pupils may enter by the month, and continue while convenient, as each scholar shall receive a due share of individual attention, adapted to his or her peculiar wants and capacity. For particulars, inquire at the school room, or refer to R. L. Wootton, Esq., Auraria, and Joseph Richard, Esq., Denver City. Terms moderate. O. GOLDRICK, Principal.[120]

He charged three dollars per student per month.[121] On Monday, October 3, Mr. Goldrick opened Union School in a log cabin on Cherry Street, a couple blocks from the Wootton house. The roof served to stop rain and snow from immediately landing upon the students, but moisture did trickle through and drip down on them. A wagon cover tacked to the lintel served as a door. The roof had enough of a gable that an opening at the end of the gable served as a window.

Dick's daughters Eliza Ann, ten, Dolores, seven, and Lorett, six, were among the school-age children. Within three weeks the school boasted twenty students with an average attendance of fifteen or sixteen students during October. Mr. Goldrick advertised again in the *Rocky Mountain News* on October 20th:

> Special attention is paid to correct spelling, good reading and elegant and expeditious penmanship, and a thorough readiness in arithmetical calculation. Instructions in elocution, book-keeping, letter-writing, business forms and correspondence, will be given throughout the course…The discipline is just what it ought to be; not too harsh, nor yet too indulgent:…instruction is simple enough for the smallest, while it is scientific enough for the largest…The grades range from the little ones, just learning abcs, to those in reading, writing and the useful branches of Arithmetic, Eng Grammar, Geog, &c[122]

The day before Goldrick placed his ad, W. P. McClure challenged R. E. Whitsitt to a duel to settle their differences. The terms: Colt revolvers at ten paces. The place: about a mile up

---

[119] Born in Ireland in 1833 (died 1886), Owen J. Goldrick received his education at the University of Dublin and at Columbia College in New York. After college, he taught school and worked in book publishing in Cincinnati, Ohio.
[120] Flynn and Hafen, "Early Education in Colorado," 16.
[121] To supplement his income, Mr. Goldrick wrote articles for Eastern newspapers and local news articles for the *Rocky Mountain News* for more than five years.
[122] Flynn and Hafen, "Early Education in Colorado," 19.

from town on Cherry Creek. About 200 spectators gathered at the designated site. Whitsitt wounded McClure, but both survived.

On October 10th, delegates met, adopted a constitution, and called for an election of territorial officers. Among provisions adopted were mining districts and provision for a legislature. Citizens accepted the Constitutional Committee's proposed constitution for the Territory of Jefferson. On October 24, 1859, they voted on provisional territorial governor and officers.

Robert William "R. W." Steele was elected governor. Near the top of his agenda was to organize a militia. He appointed Dick Wootton brigadier general, but there were no resources and no militia to command. He was only to be prepared to lead should the need arise.

The new government held a legislative session November 8-December 7, 1859. The U. S. Congress hadn't yet officially recognized the territory.

Indians continued to raid outlying areas. The almost daily attacks on or killing of an immigrant, settler, or miner within a few miles of town often frightened Cherry Creek citizens. Indians came into town, but they never made a stand in town, never did attack Auraria-Denver.

One old Comanche chief came to town and terrorized women, children, and some men who weren't used to taking a stand. One day about five or six hundred Comanche came to town. Drunk, their old chief came into Uncle Dick's house. Dick wasn't used to tolerating abusive behavior in the mountains; he sure wasn't going to put up with it in his own home. He reached for his gun; the chief reached for the door. As the muzzle of Dick's gun pressed against the chief's body, he sobered by the second. The gun misfired. The chief dashed out onto his horse and rode off. And Dick realized it was a good thing the gun misfired.

About the first of November Professor Goldrick rented a larger cabin (corner of Blake and 10th) and relocated Union School. That cabin had a real door and a glazed window.

On November 3, 1859, Methodist ministers George W. Fisher and Jacob Adriance—known to be hard working, self-sacrificing men—announced in the *Rocky Mountain News* the Union Sunday School would meet in their home near Cherry Creek each Sunday afternoon at three o'clock. They invited all Cherry Creek children, but asked parents to keep their children's attendance punctual and regular. D. C. Collier, Lewis N. Tappan, and Professor O. J. Goldrick helped. The community had had regular Sunday preaching services since June.

To facilitate travel between Denver and Auraria, a bridge was constructed over Cherry Creek in mid-November. It was an extension of Larimer Street.

Jack Templeton arrived at the end of 1859 and, like many prospectors, wasn't finding color. It was so cold and snowy in the mountains the first week of December that miners couldn't get much done. Templeton said men were about ready to hang anyone who told them there was gold in the country. But then, he said, Dick Wootton encouraged him when he told him men were finding a little color at Russell's Gulch (Central City). Men took courage at the news.

By Christmas Eve 1859 the Cherry Creek community had seen many changes since Dick and Mary Ann Wootton arrived with their seven children and four wagons on Christmas Eve 1858.

As 1859 drew to a close, things were going well for Uncle Dick's business and family.

The children were settled in school; their home was built; business was good. If men didn't have cash for purchases, they usually had something to trade. Most of the news from back home in Kentucky was good—marriages and new nieces and nephews. His brother Powell had become a doctor and was practicing back home in Christian County (Kentucky). His brother Joseph hadn't returned to Cherry Creek, but remained in Kentucky; he and his wife, Mollie, were expecting their first child. Dick and Mary Ann were also expecting a baby in March.

Denver 1859

New Year 1860

In January 1860 ladies of Auraria-Denver met at the home of Mrs. William N. Byers to form the Denver Ladies Union Aid. Their goal was to help destitute families. Many in their community who'd hoped to find gold had not, and their resources had dwindled to the point that some were on the verge of starvation. With a common goal to help others, the women began to form a sense of community among themselves.

On January 30th a little claim jump war livened up the winter scene in Denver for several days. Mr. Mickie, Mr. Parkinson, and Mr. Thompson took possession of some lots claimed by the Denver Company on the northern outskirts of Denver. The three fortified themselves in a small cabin. After several days of negotiations, they settled the matter under a flag of truce. They gave up their claim in exchange for reimbursement of what they'd invested in the effort.

The twin towns settled down to ordinary life until the night of March 5th. At a fancy dinner at the Broadway House in Denver, the toast alluded to the Provisional Government question. That set Lucien W. Bliss, Jefferson Territory Secretary of State, and Dr. J. S. Stone, judge of Central City area's Miners' Court, at odds. At that time and for many years afterward, ideals, patriotism, convictions, and honor were no small matter. The variance was enough that Bliss and Stone determined to settle the matter with a duel. They met the next afternoon with their double barrel shotguns. Bliss mortally wounded Stone, but Stone didn't die for five more months.

Dick and Mary Ann's son Frank arrived almost three weeks later (March 25), but Mary Ann died. Their little Willie was one and a half; Joseph wasn't yet three. Eliza Ann—Dick's oldest, who was six when her own mama died—was now eleven. She pitched in to help; but Dick hired women to help care for the small children. On the frontier emotions often bowed to survival.

Politics, organization, and growth continued to interest the little settlement. On April 5, 1860, Auraria and Denver incorporated into one community: Denver City.[123] John C. Moore was chosen first mayor of the combined city.[124] There was no salary connected with the position.

At noon the next day (April 6), John O'Farrell was filling his coffee pot in the river at California Gulch and noticed flakes of gold in the sand. That began the Leadville gold boom about a hundred miles southwest of Denver. The first mines staked were the A. Y. and Minnie mines.

South of Denver, Mr. Fraser and Mr. Scoville began an iron foundry.

In May 1860 L. L. Todd constructed a brick building for Clark, Gruber, and Company at G and McGaa (16th and Market) in Denver. The solid, secure building housed Clark and

---

[123] The law to consolidate had been approved the previous December 3rd.
[124] When Moore resigned to join the Confederate army in 1861, Charles A. Cook (1861-63) became mayor.

Gruber's new bank and private mint. There was plenty of area gold to coin.

Jim Baker

Trappers and traders were accustomed to western manners, customs, places, and to each other. This was not a strange country or experience to them. They were a community within the Cherry Creek community. Trappers and traders John Poisal, Jim Baker, Joseph Richeau (earlier of Ft. Laramie), and Daniel Boone's grandson Colonel Albert G. Boone were among the early citizens.

Denver's first business directory, published in 1860, listed several mountaineers as local merchants. On Ferry Street were H. Z. Solomon, J. B. Doyle, and William Dunn of J. B. Doyle and Co.; R. L. Wootton; and Samuel Hawken, a gunsmith.[125] On the Denver side: Charles Beaubien, F. Muller, and G. Denver owned Beaubien & Muller; Tom Boggs and L. B. St. James were proprietors of St. James & Boggs; A. Pike Vasquez managed A. P. Vasquez & Co.

Doyle and Wootton each placed advertisements in the directory. Doyle, on Ferry near Fourth, advertised groceries, hardware, and miscellaneous merchandise. Wootton advertised his saloon and ten-pin alley.

Miss Sopris opened a school in west Denver on May 7, 1860.[126] Goldrick's Union School had grown enough that he needed another teacher. In May he hired Miss Miller from Iowa. Denver was about half the size of Auraria when Goldrick began his school in the fall of 1859. Since the consolidation, east Denver was growing so rapidly that a third school opened. Miss Ring from Kansas opened the school in east Denver for the school year of 1860-61.

In May 1860, Goldrick moved Union School to 14th and Holladay in east Denver.[127] His new school building even had desks. In the evening it was used as a reading room and on Sundays for Rev. John H. Kehler's Episcopal Church services.

In his first two years of business, *Rocky Mountain News* editor William Byers reported duels, murders (15), and fights. Sometimes he reported the loss of part of a nose or ear. On May 30, 1860, he reported that tents were filling every available space in the city and along Cherry Creek and the Platte.

---

[125] The Hawken rifle, made by Jacob and Samuel Hawken of St. Louis, was dependable and allowed one to shoot three half-ounce balls per minute. It weighed about twelve pounds. A Hawken cost $40 in St. Louis, $60 in Independence, about $90 in New Mexico. Hawken's son Samuel had a shop in east Denver. Rifles were available locally for $80-$90.

[126] Later Mrs. Cushman of Deadwood, S. D.

[127] After Colorado Territorial legislature set up a free public school system in Denver, Principal Abner Roe Brown and two lady teachers opened the first public school for all Denver children (December 1, 1862). They held school upstairs in Asa Middaugh's large frame building near the corner of Larimer and 10th, near Wootton's home. December 10th, a public school opened at 16th and Blake in east Denver. O. J. Goldrick was county school superintendent.

On June 27th, Byers reported that hundreds who came to the Pikes Peak region in hopes of establishing mines were returning to their homes in the east. Some thought the mines would all be played out in three or four weeks.

Byers set standards for his newspaper and used his journalistic influence to do what he could to set standards for the community. He spoke forthrightly against lawless folks and exposed what some considered trivial infractions. Not everyone took kindly to publicity. One morning a couple men had had enough, went to his printing office, and shot out all the windows. The armed printing crew returned fire and killed one of the men.

In the early days all Byers employees carried guns. Uncle Dick said, "About the first question Byers asked of an employee in those days was whether he could handle a gun to good advantage, and a printer who was handy in this respect stood well with the proprietors of the paper, even though he had a multitude of shortcomings as a compositor."[128]

Some of Byers' employees regularly slept on the floor of the printing office. They had enough to do to defend Byers' printed word without trouble from any rowdy men downstairs in Uncle Dick's saloon. When he was able, Byers moved his printing office.

Gold on Cherry Creek didn't pan out; but, because Denver prepared and established itself early on, it became the supply center for mining camps. Freight wagons bringing supplies were a common sight on Denver streets in the summer of 1860. Wagons pulled up in front of the intended store and stopped to unload. In October 1860, forty-five wagons arrived from Salt Lake City loaded with produce, including, eggs, flour, butter, oats, barley, and onions.

In the summer of 1860 prospectors discovered gold near Silverton in the San Juan Mountains of Utah (Colorado). Many miners left the Pike's Peak fields for the San Juans. Though he continued to live in Denver and operate his store, Uncle Dick began to keep a herd of cattle at his Pueblo area ranch.

Charles Goodnight and Oliver Loving made their first cattle drive to the Pike's Peak gold field market. They exchanged longhorn cattle for gold, but lost a chunk of their income when one of their pack mules ran off with a pouch containing $6,000 worth of gold.

On November 6, 1860, Abraham Lincoln, of the new Republican Party, won the Presidential election. The States were trying not to come apart at the seams, but the presidential election strained the fabric of unity. Denver knew sectional rivalry had been fomenting for decades. But, for the time being, national problems had not eclipsed daily life lived in one's own locale.

On December 2nd Charles Harrison killed James Hill in the Denver area, but was acquitted when he pled self-defense. Twelve days later, on the 14th, Patrick Kelly killed Richard Doyle. When Kelly went to trial, he was released.

National news began to demand attention. On December 20, 1860, South Carolina seceded from the Union. The day after Christmas Union troops moved to Ft. Sumter, South Carolina. South Carolina sent President Buchanan word to remove the troops.

Troops remained.

---

[128] Conard, 1890, 378.

Exit States, Enter Territory

Five more states—Mississippi, Alabama, Florida, Louisiana, and Georgia—seceded from the Union in January 1861. Together with South Carolina they organized the Confederate States of America in Montgomery, Alabama, on February 4th and named Jefferson Davis Provisional President of the Confederacy. As Mississippi's senator, Davis had immediately resigned from the U. S. Senate when Mississippi seceded.

The Territory of Kansas became a state on January 29, 1861, and opened the door for Arapahoe County citizens to become a territory. On February 28th Congress created the Territory of Colorado. Arapahoe County residents didn't seem to mind too much that the fathers in Washington named the territory Colorado, rather than Jefferson—their choice. Congress carved the territory out of Kansas and a little of Utah, Nebraska, and New Mexico.[129]

Daily life went on. In Denver, Thomas Evans and "Buckskin" got into a disagreement at the St. Charles Saloon. Evans ran; but, as he ran out the door toward the street, "Buckskin" shot. The ball whizzed past Evans and hit hard-working Edwin Morris and killed him. Morris, a slave from St. Louis, had been allowed to come to the Pike's Peak region to earn his freedom. He was close—he'd worked off about $600 and only owed about $200 more for his freedom.

Abraham Lincoln was inaugurated U. S. President on March 4, 1861. On the 22nd he appointed William Gilpin Governor of Colorado Territory. Gilpin was acquainted with the Southwest.[130]

In April 1861 Indians burned ranch buildings and rustled cattle near Denver.

War had been brewing for years before it broke out at Ft. Sumter, South Carolina, on April 12, 1861. Three days later the United States declared war on states which seceded from the Union. President Lincoln called for troops.

The Confederate States of America—the seceded states—declared war against the Union on May 6, 1861 (Uncle Dick's forty-fifth birthday). It wasn't long before every American knew.

Telegraph lines had reached Denver. That, plus the fact Texas had become part of the Confederacy, brought the Civil War a little closer. Though Colorado was far from the East, the clouds of war began to cast shadows on the mountains. Even in the mountains, men felt loyalty toward the home they'd left behind. Lines were drawn in Denver. It wasn't like it used to be three, even two years ago in the Rocky Mountains. There were so many newcomers—from all parts of the States. Each man came from somewhere, and each

---

[129] New Mexico Territory was divided at the 37th parallel. Land north of that line became Colorado; it included Ft. Garland and the San Luis Valley.

[130] Gilpin marched with Kearny's Army of the West in 1846 and led a force in the Mexican War in 1847. In the summer of 1848 he defended Pike's Peak area residents from Indian attacks and helped reopen trails that had closed because of Indian attacks.

American seemed to feel a loyalty to one side or the other. Though sentiment in Denver was strongly Northern, Uncle Dick figured a man wasn't much if he had no feeling of loyalty for his native home and birthplace. Dick, like generations of his family before him, was born in Virginia. His parents, brothers, sisters, and their families lived in Kentucky.

Virginia had hoped to remain neutral, but seceded on April 17th after war was declared. Kentucky maintained neutrality at the beginning. When Confederates invaded, Kentucky chose to remain with the Union.

Western mines promised to be a great asset to the side that controlled them. Western gold and silver could pay for European munitions and goods. There were mines in Colorado, California, Montana, Nevada, New Mexico, and Arizona. The southwest also offered the blockaded Confederate states a possible path to the Pacific Ocean and a route for a transcontinental railroad.

In Denver, Wallingford and Murphy showed their colors. They raised a Secession flag above their Larimer Street store on April 24, 1861. Angered patriots ripped the flag down. The next day a mass meeting congregated to declare loyalty to the Union. A band played patriotic songs. There were speeches, cheers, and resolutions of loyalty. They concluded with a bonfire. Southerners were in the minority, but there were enough to have their own parade and music. Both sides realized their folks back home were in the thick of trouble.

Talk increased. The Colorado Territorial Legislature voted to remain in the Union.

On May 20th, Colorado Territory residents turned out en masse to welcome their new governor, William Gilpin.

In May, 190 Denver businessmen agreed on a standard gold exchange value per ounce. Gold from Blue River: $20; Clear Creek, Fairplay, French, Humbug, Nigger, and McNulty Gulches: $17; California Gulch: $16; Russell Gulch: $15. Nearby towns followed Denver's lead.

Cherry Creek residents were ready to plant. They'd been encouraged by last year's yield of up to 400 bushels of potatoes per acre. They bought seed potatoes for nine dollars a bushel. (With more food raised locally, prices would be down by the end of August. Potatoes would cost three dollars per bushel; flour, twelve dollars per barrel; meat, eight to fifteen cents per pound.) A house that cost $1,000 was renting for twenty-five dollars per month.

Military officers, soldiers, and civilians left the Southwest to join the Union or Confederacy. Many men returned to the States to join the war. Men in the States were too busy fighting to emigrate. By the middle of June times became a bit dull in Denver, and it was hot—104 degrees in the shade on June 16, 1861.

Times weren't dull in New Mexico. In July, John Baylor led a Confederate unit of Texas militia into southern New Mexico and occupied Mesilla. On August 1st he claimed all of New Mexico south of the 34th parallel for the Confederacy and named it Arizona Territory of the Confederacy. Later in the month Union Major Isaac Lynde abandoned Ft. Fillmore near Las Cruces, New Mexico. Baylor's Confederate forces took control.

The toehold in New Mexico was a step in the Confederacy's plan to secure New Mexico—especially the Ft. Union supply depot—incorporate lands between Colorado and California and parts of northern Mexico, gain western minerals, and open access to the ocean.

CONFEDERATE GENERALS.

Braxton Bragg.
P. G. T. Beauregard.
James Longstreet.
Joseph E. Johnston.

David H. Hill.
J. E. B. Stuart.
Robert E. Lee.
Leonidas Polk.
John B. Hood.

Thomas Jonathan Jackson.
A. S. Johnston.
A. P. Hill.
Jubal A. Early.

GENERALS OF CIVIL WAR.

George Gordon Meade. D. C. Buell. James B. McPherson. Joseph Hooker.
A. E. Burnside. George B. McClellan. Nathaniel P. Banks. W. S. Rosecranz.
Philip H. Sheridan. Ulysses S. Grant. William T. Sherman.
Benjamin F. Butler. Irvin McDowell. John A. Logan. Winfield S. Hancock.
David Hunter. Henry W. Halleck. George H. Thomas. John Pope.

Though the Union was shaky, Colorado was pleased to be its territory. Colorado held its first Territorial election in August 1861 and its first Territorial Legislature meeting in

September. Among other business, representatives and councilmen divided Colorado into seventeen counties.

Auraria and Denver had become one city in April 1860, but incorporation papers weren't signed until November 1861. Richens L. "Uncle Dick" Wootton was one of the men who signed Denver City's incorporation papers. By this time, Dick was involved both in Denver and the new settlement of Pueblo. He maintained his primary residence in Denver; but, by the summer of 1861, he'd built two cabins on his Pueblo ranch.

Colorado City was chosen capital of Colorado Territory on November 5, 1861. The honor was brief. Uncle Dick was appointed marshal of Colorado City briefly during a "reign of terror" in its very short life as capital. The capital was soon moved to Golden.

In the winter of 1861 there had been little snow in Denver by Christmastime. On December 23rd Denver resident Augustus Wildman wrote his father that the weather had been so favorable cattle still grazed on native grasses without any need of hay. He said there were about 1,500 military men in the area, but everything was quiet. He figured the men would soon be called to join the war. He was a little put out with Horace Greeley, who'd come to report on the Pikes' Peak field. Augustus thought Greeley didn't care for publishing the truth, but published anything anyone in the area wrote.

In December rumors of possible war between England and the U. S. spread around the community. Unfortunate timing for the Union—such a war would guarantee independence for the Southern states. In spite of the war in the States, most Denver homes welcomed callers on New Year's Day 1862, as they'd done the previous New Year's Day.

This stagecoach, which had three inside seats that could seat three per seat, is the stagecoach in which Horace Greeley made his trip to Denver. It was ordinarily pulled by six horses.

Civil War Rides West

Before he joined the Confederacy, General Henry Hopkins Sibley commanded Ft. Union and knew the area's resources, strengths, and weaknesses. He was aware of the strategic importance of that military supply post, which could outfit a troop for a trek to and conquest of California. He'd garner minerals along the way and gain an open seaway on the Pacific.[131]

He presented a strategy to Confederate President Jefferson Davis. Davis liked Sibley's idea, but he had no troops to offer. He authorized Sibley to enlist and train volunteers in Texas.

In February 1862 Sibley and his Texas volunteers invaded southern New Mexico. Through sleet and snow, they marched north along the Rio Grande and camped within sight of Ft. Craig. Snow gave way to gusting wind, blowing sand. Union Colonel Edward Canby of Ft. Craig ordered Colonel Ben Roberts to attack. Confederates killed many Union soldiers as they crossed the Rio Grande to fight. In the afternoon more Union soldiers crossed; more died.

Canby relieved Colonel Roberts; Colonel Tom Green relieved Sibley. Colonel Green ordered a sudden, daring charge, killing many Union soldiers. Survivors ran for their lives—to the river and across. Confederates prepared to pursue; but under a flag of truce, representatives of Canby's Union troop asked permission to bury their dead. Sibley granted their request.

Although Sibley's volunteers bested Canby's Union dragoons in that battle, known as the Battle of Valverde, they didn't wipe them out. As the Confederates marched north, they left their wounded in Socorro. Canby's courier raced to notify the Albuquerque Post. Union troops in Albuquerque burned military supplies and evacuated to Santa Fe. When Sibley arrived in Albuquerque, he had no opposition and found few supplies. Confederates occupied Albuquerque Post on March 2, 1862.

Confederate troops garnered some supplies from nearby stores. Sibley led a troop west to Cubero Post—he knew the country. It was miles off the trail to Santa Fe, but there they found a well-filled twenty-five-wagon train loaded with supplies intended for Indian use. The troop added those to their lot and marched on toward Santa Fe—New Mexico's capital.

Because he'd served in New Mexico, Sibley expected public sentiment and military support. He'd also been promised a thousand-man reinforcement when he reached Colorado.

When Canby's message of invasion was relayed to Santa Fe, New Mexico Territorial Governor Henry Connelly, his territorial staff, and a few soldiers loaded up 120 wagons with as much as they could of their governmental supplies. They left Santa Fe on March 4, 1862, intending to relocate the territorial government at Ft. Union; but they stopped in Las Vegas (New Mexico) and set up temporary headquarters in the hotel on the Plaza.

Realizing war was imminent, Ft. Union commander Colonel Gabriel Paul wired Colorado

---

[131] In 1860 mines in Colorado alone produced $7 million in gold.

Governor William Gilpin for help. Washington had given Gilpin permission to organize a Union regiment of volunteers. However, the Union told Colorado what Jefferson Davis told Sibley: no money to arm or support a regiment. Colorado volunteers—the Pike's Peakers—organized.

In August 1861, Governor Gilpin had utilized wartime measures and issued $375,000 in drafts on the national treasury. With the drafts he paid merchants for supplies needed by the volunteers.

The day after Sibley's forces clashed with Canby's at Ft. Craig, Major John Milton Chivington and Denver attorney Colonel John P. Slough led the Pike's Peakers south toward New Mexico.[132] They arrived at Ft. Union by March 10, 1862. Ft. Union soldiers and New Mexico Union Volunteers, led by Lt. Colonel Manuel Chavez, joined them.

On March 10th an advance unit of Confederate soldiers occupied Santa Fe without conflict. They lowered the Stars and Stripes and raised the flag of the Confederate States of America. Once again a new flag flew above the Palace of the Governors.

Another unit of Confederate soldiers arrived March 13th. One detachment, under Colonel William R. Scurry, camped at Galisteo, a village south of Santa Fe.

When General Sibley officially occupied Santa Fe, he offered amnesty to New Mexicans, as Kearny had done in 1846. But he found neither the supplies, nor the support he'd hoped for. When the Confederates arrived in Santa Fe, they expected to use their Confederate currency as a medium of exchange; but locals were hesitant. They entertained their old friends who were among the Confederate Army—entertained them and their soldiers well. They danced and they drank—but the money? They understood gold and American currency better. Besides, Sibley's soldiers were primarily Texans.

Didn't Sibley remember the 1841-42 Texas-New Mexico Expedition? New Mexico settlements were more than 200 years old before Americans established the Republic of Texas. Had Sibley forgotten Texans claimed Santa Fe and parts of New Mexico belonged to them? New Mexicans hadn't forgotten.

Wise Governor Connelly, who'd been in the Southwest since 1824, hadn't forgotten. With military skill, he refreshed New Mexicans' memories before packing off to Las Vegas, New Mexico. He didn't call advancing troops Confederates; he said the "Texans" were coming. New Mexicans may not outwardly resist, but they weren't going to give their lives or meager supplies. The Confederates weren't the first to misjudge the New Mexican spirit. Confederates were not entirely without support in Santa Fe, however.

Texas Volunteers left Santa Fe. Colorado Pike's Peakers left Ft. Union. They met at Apache Canyon near Glorieta, New Mexico.

---

[132] Of the 4, 903 Colorado Volunteers who volunteered in all phases of the Civil War, 1,300 fought in New Mexico. Some later fought guerillas in Missouri. Of the total, about 300 died in the war.

Battle of Glorieta

The Sangre de Cristo Mountains run like a backbone down northcentral New Mexico. There was one narrow defile through which wagons traveled on the Santa Fe Trail between Ft. Union and Santa Fe: Apache Canyon's Glorieta Pass. On Wednesday, March 26, 1862, Confederate and Union soldiers met on the west side of Glorieta Pass and immediately laid into one another.

The first day the battle raged nip and tuck. Many of the Colorado and Texas men had lived in the West long enough to be hardened by elements and tactics. Some used an Indian war whoop. Nothing like a good loud whoop to strike terror. Men of both sides knew what it was to withstand Indian warfare. Texans were used to hard work, taming a land, making it home. Coloradoans were used to the mountains and altitude. Both sides shot skillfully; it was their way of life. No man on either side seemed to care if he lived or died, but only that his side won.

The day ended indecisively. Colonel Slough camped at Bernal Springs with the main unit of Colorado Volunteers. Texas Volunteers camped at Johnson Ranch. Neither Sibley, nor Canby— Confederate and Union leaders—were on hand.

The next day, Thursday, each side waited for the other. The sun set. The Confederate unit, which had camped at Galisteo, New Mexico, marched about sixteen miles through the dark of night to reinforce their comrades at Johnson Ranch.

Friday dawned. Colonel Scurry, in charge of the combined Confederate force, left a few guards at Johnson's Ranch in charge of the supply train and the wounded.

The North and South met at Pigeon's Ranch.[133] Once battle began, Confederates kept the Union on the defensive all day—pushing, pushing them back to Koslowski's ranch. The infantry, cavalry, and artillery charged and countercharged all day. Soldiers of both sides used western honed skills and knowledge of the terrain to advantage. They leaped around, up, and down mountainsides, making the most of their on-the-go marksmanship. The Union recovered lost ground before darkness fell. The armies withdrew for the night.

Away from the heat of battle, New Mexico Lt. Colonel Manuel Chavez guided Major John Chivington and his unit over Glorieta Mesa before sundown. Chavez saw the Confederate supply train at Johnson's Ranch below and told Chivington, "You are on top of them."

Stealthily Chivington's unit moved close to the mesa rim. Sure enough! Sixty to eighty wagons, a Texas howitzer, and a muzzle aimed at Apache Canyon were in plain sight. There were more than a hundred sick or wounded Confederates lying around. There were few guards.

Chivington ordered Captain William Lewis to lead the unit down the mountain with the

---

[133] Alexander Vallé, a Franco-American, operated a stage station-store-saloon-hostelry east of Glorieta Pass. People who knew the man called his place "Pigeon's Ranch" because of his broken English.

command to kill the men and animals and to torch the supply wagons. The Confederates saw them coming, but not soon enough to defend themselves at such odds. Reports vary: All with the wagons were killed; some were taken captive, while others escaped to Santa Fe. Union men torched sixty-four supply wagons. One ammo wagon blew up and injured some. To save ammunition, soldiers bayoneted the animals—600-1,100 horses and mules.

Confederates lost everything from ammunition to blankets to Bibles. The attack left them with less than forty rounds of ammo per soldier. Colonel Scurry had packed enough provisions to reach Ft. Union. Now he must retreat. They buried the dead near Pecos in a field east of Pigeon's Ranch, not far from the old Indian pueblo. More than a fourth of the soldiers involved in the Battle of Glorieta were killed or wounded.[134] Sibley's troops retreated to Santa Fe where they secured about $30,000 worth of government property.

Colonel Slough led Union forces north to Ft. Union.

The Battle of Glorieta was fought after the 1st Battle of Bull Run and was over before the Battle of Shiloh. With this defeat, all hope of Confederate victory in the Southwest, of access to an open seaway, of having land from shore to shore, and access to Western resources—which supported Union war efforts—were gone. Because it was the Southwestern turning point between North and South, the Battle of Glorieta Pass is called Gettysburg of the West.

Confederate forces left Santa Fe on April 8, 1862; Union forces reoccupied Santa Fe on the 11th. As Sibley and his recruits walked the long dry miles from Santa Fe to southern New Mexico, their provisions ran low. They encountered minor skirmishes at Albuquerque and Peralta. By early May they were back in El Paso, Texas. Defeated.

Dick Wootton, who knew the commanding officers on both sides, figured Sibley and his soldiers might've done a sight better if they hadn't spent so much time dancing, dining, and drinking in Santa Fe before they marched toward Ft. Union. With the supplies from Cubero Post, they were supplied for such a march.

Although Colorado Volunteers foiled Confederate plans to secure western resources, the federal government refused to honor drafts Governor Gilpin issued to support the effort. Money was scarce and times hard for Denver merchants who'd accepted government drafts in exchange for goods to supply the militia. Though many Denver merchants were die-hard Union men, they could ill afford such contributions as they'd advanced the government. W. N. Byers led an attack against Governor Gilpin in his *Rocky Mountain News*. Unable to persuade Washington to honor the drafts, Gilpin was removed from office (May 1862). President Lincoln appointed Dr. John Evans, a physician and founder of Northwestern University, to replace him. Gilpin was gone, but Denver merchants still held the bag for goods they'd exchanged for government drafts.

The Civil War continued to take its toll back in the States. On August 29, 1862, the 2nd Battle of Bull Run was fought, followed by the Battle of Antietam on September 17th.

The war feeling became bitter in Denver. The tide and tempest of war loyalties overshadowed loyalties of friendship and comradeship that had been building the past three and a half years. In the fall of 1862, southern sympathizers, including several of Green Russell's party, were encouraged to leave Cherry Creek. The Russell brothers, Green's

---

[134] In the 1990's Kippy Siler found the gravesite. Texas families were contacted.

nephew James H. Pierce, Patterson and other originators of the community left to return home to Georgia to aid the Confederacy. They stopped at Zan Hicklin's place on the Greenhorn. They planned to travel through New Mexico, into Texas, and across to Georgia; but news of their expedition drew military attention.

Soldiers pursued them into New Mexico and captured them as prisoners of war. Some of the party had contracted smallpox; so soldiers waited until the epidemic subsided before imprisoning them at Ft. Union. Carson, Maxwell, St. Vrain, Wootton, Gilpin and others who held Green Russell in high regard used their influence to help free the party in the spring of 1863.

Born and bred in the South, Uncle Dick was secesh.[135] Being a vocal man with more than a liberal sprinkling of Scotch blood, Dick did not hide his loyalties. Regardless of one's former involvement in the community, it became apparent in person and print that those who favored the South were not welcome in Denver. All Southern sympathizers were encouraged to leave. In the heart of the community, Dick was well aware of the polar changes—not that it altered his opinion or his voice. As was his manner, Dick Wootton lived where he was, without hesitation to speak, to stand. He marked himself. He'd pay the price. At the time, he maintained both his Denver store and his Pueblo ranch. If he had to move, it'd be okay.

Denver ebbed and flowed with the mines; it was pretty much at a standstill in 1862. Though population was about twenty times what it was when Dick arrived in 1858, it was questionable whether Denver would grow forward or stagnate. Money was scarce. Dick's business was doing well, but he had to accept more and more business on credit; so he didn't mind the thought of moving. He wouldn't stay out of the community altogether.

He sold his cabin at, and all his claims to, Manitou Springs to Whitsitt and Company for $500.[136]

He prepared for come what may.

---

[135] Secesh was a slang term used for those who favored secession.
[136] Manitou Soda Springs (sometimes called: Medicine Springs, Pike's Peak Springs, Simpson's, Red Rock Springs), near Colorado Springs: When Joe Doyle was still working for Bent-St. Vrain, Doyle, Dick Wootton, George Simpson, and William Kroenig had obtained the natural soda springs and hundreds of acres around them. The springs were reputed to excel Eastern and Southern springs. Speculators expected Manitou to become the Sarasota of the West when a railroad arrived. Dick Wootton had built a cabin there. He sold out in 1862.

Loyalty Costs

After Mary Ann died, Dick established a ranch on the Fountain Qui Bouille about eight to nine miles north of Pueblo and kept a herd of cattle. When Denver no longer cared for his company, he was already well-established. He and his children moved down to the cabins he'd built on his ranch. He had a store in one cabin. He and the children lived in the other.

He began farming his place in 1862. Others whose dreams of prospecting failed realized they could farm the Colorado plains and settled in as farmers and ranchers. Many settled in Pueblo County, but not many lived in town. Pueblo had stores, a small hotel, and a saloon in December 1861. By 1863 there were about ten homes in the actual town.

Before Uncle Dick left Denver, Governor Gilpin had appointed him as one of Pueblo County's first commissioners to serve until the election (July 19, 1862).[137] The earliest commission record was dated February 17, 1862, when Dick was elected chairman. He and the other officers chose the location for the county seat and, at the same meeting, decided county business needed a building. Under the direction of Stephen Smith, the commission took bids for the first Pueblo County courthouse.

At a specially called meeting (March 1, 1862), commissioners awarded a $300.00 contract to Mr. Eastman to build the courthouse. He constructed a sturdy hewn log building (18' x 24') at the corner of Santa Fe Avenue and Third Street. It served as county headquarters until 1871.

Dick's salary would be $40.80. Salaries were approved at the commissioners' regular meeting on June 25th. Didn't do Dick much good—he wasn't elected to office at the county's first election.

One day in 1863 Dick rode up to Denver on business. His friends there told him Union-minded authorities were interested in having him back in town—behind bars. Because of his secesh stand, authorities considered him an enemy of the state and were on the lookout for him. Dick had always been fond of the outdoors. Besides, he had a family to care for back in Pueblo. In the morning he did his business quickly and prepared to head home. As he left town, Dick was told a posse had formed to find and arrest him. He wasted no time. He rode south all day until he reached Kiowa Creek in the evening. Not many old timers went that way because of Fagan's Camp.

One of Captain Marcy's soldiers named Fagan had died while standing guard near Kiowa Creek and was buried in a lone grave out there along the Cherokee Trail. As time passed, stories grew of a soldier who marched in circles around Fagan's grave. Every night he guarded the mound with his musket. Some said the soldier had been buried alive and, at times, his ghost could be seen riding a buffalo or wild horse. One night Arapaho Chief Left

---

[137] Governor Gilpin's temporary appointments: Henry Way, sheriff; Stephen Smith, clerk; William Chapman, O. H. P. Baxter, and Richard [sic] Wootton, commissioners.

Hand saw him wearing a white blanket and shot him. As the bullet passed through the ghost, he laughed at the chief. Sometime after that Zan Hicklin, in his early fifties, and Colorado lawmaker Matt Riddleburger rode home along the Cherokee Trail, sharing a jug of whiskey. Stopped to camp, Riddleburger woke Hicklin to show him Fagan's ghost. Zan tried to ignore him and covered his head to sleep, but Riddleburger was insistent. Hicklin sat up and shot the white object. When the men heard something drop, they hurried to find Riddleburger's dying white mule.

Dick didn't know the exact location of Fagan's grave, but it didn't really matter. Weaknesses he had, but superstition wasn't one. He dismounted, hid his horse in a nearby canyon, made a little campfire, warmed himself, and ate. After that, he lay along a little mound of earth, which gave him a bit of protection from the raw wind. He quickly fell into a sound sleep.

Even in deep sleep, Dick was sensitive to the slightest out-of-the-ordinary sound. He'd slept a few hours when the sound of distant horses awakened him. The embers of his campfire weren't enough to draw attention, but Dick went to his horse in case it was the posse. Not given to alarm, he stood by his horse, ready if need be, but interested to know who was coming.

He heard the men say they'd been on his trail. Dick recognized the voices of friends. With hesitation they walked toward Fagan's grave. Something was glowing on the grave—a campfire!

"'It's Dick Wootton's camp fire, and I'm a natural born liar if he haint been asleep on Fagan's grave.'

"'You're right, partner, as sure as I've got a front and a hind name. That fellow would camp in a sepulcher without having any bad dreams, or risk going to sleep in a powder magazine with his pipe lit. He aint far away from here now either. Let's call him.'"[138]

Dick joined his five friends and found they'd left Denver for the same reason he had. They didn't bother going back to sleep, but added fuel to the fire and sat around the campfire talking until morning. In daylight they traveled on to Pueblo. They didn't run into the posse. As for Fagan's Grave, it lost its reputation. Not long afterwards someone built a cabin near the grave.

Dick built more cabins on his Fountain farm. Farming was more profitable than it'd been on the Arkansas in the 1850's. He had less loss from theft; and he had a good market—miners in Colorado and government troops in New Mexico and Colorado. He raised various grains and produce, but wheat and corn (100 acres of corn) were his main crops.

In 1863, his cornfield was especially productive. One summer evening, when the corn was high, Uncle Dick was sitting in his cabin when his dogs began raising Cain. Dick picked up his gun and stood in the open doorway, listening. Looking out into the darkness, he heard someone calling. He could hear the sound; but the way the dogs were carrying on, he couldn't make out the words. He hushed the dogs and called out to the stranger. Judge Allen A. Bradford, on his way to hold court in Conejos (Colorado), had taken a wrong turn and ended

---

[138] Conard, 1890, 399.

up lost in Uncle Dick's cornfield. Dick went out and found the judge.

"When he got up to where the light shone on him," Dick said, "I think he looked less like a judge than anybody I ever saw, unless it was a Yuma Indian. The cornfield was very muddy and the mule which he was riding, a consumptive-looking animal…, had mired down several times and both man and mule looked like they had been made of adobe and hadn't got dry."[139]

Dick didn't get irritated at Bradford for tearing up part of his cornfield. He brought him into the cabin and gave him a clean trapper's outfit to put on—not quite the right size;[140] but the clothes were clean and dry—a welcome change for the judge. Dick fixed him something to eat and a place to sleep—a bed in the house with the family. In the morning Dick sent the judge off on one of his good horses, instead of the scrawny mule he'd ridden in on. With his new clothes, Bradford looked more like a trapper than a judge. That was mountain man reception. In later years Judge Bradford often had a good laugh about getting lost in Dick's corn patch.[141]

Dick had heard of Judge Bradford before he came to "visit," but hadn't met him. It wasn't long until the two met again. Dick explained it like this:

The question at issue, as the lawyers say, when my presence in Judge Bradford's court was required, was a political one and I didn't agree with the court politically. In the course of the proceedings, which from my standpoint seemed to be a little irregular, I suppose I must have gotten somewhat excited. Anyhow I did some swearing which wasn't of the character that men are called upon to do in court. The Judge called me to order very mildly, but he didn't fine me for contempt of court, as everybody present expected he would, and I always thought the reason he didn't fine me was because he had not forgotten that cornfield scrape.[142]

The issue at hand was that Uncle Dick and a handful of Southern sympathizers, including Samuel B. Watrous, had been rounded up in a widespread secesh net. Summoned to appear before Judge Bradford to pledge allegiance to the Union, Dick promptly obeyed. Judge Bradford ordered all the men gathered in his courtroom to stand and take the oath of allegiance. Each man did as instructed. When Judge Bradford told them they may be seated, Dick remained standing. Judge Bradford asked if there was something he wished to say. Uncle Dick addressed Judge Bradford, swore, and said he'd joined his church, but hadn't swallowed a bit of his religion.

After the Battle of Glorieta, Uncle Dick had made up his mind that the Civil War wasn't going to be fought in the West; so there wasn't much sense being at one another's throats over it. After that he considered it merely a difference of opinion and wasn't out to fight the war with anyone. But he did have his opinion and stood by it. That's who he was. Throughout his life he had no qualms voicing opinion, accepting the consequences, and moving on. By the same token, he thought it natural others would have convictions of their own and stand by

---

[139] Conard, 1890, 404.
[140] Dick was 6'6" and weighed about 200 pounds.
[141] Judge Bradford lived at the place Marcelino Baca began building before the 1854 El Pueblo Christmas Eve Massacre. (After Pueblo grew, the place would be called Catalpa Street.)
[142] Conard, 1890, 405.

them.

According to *Colorado Families: A Territorial Heritage*, Uncle Dick's property was confiscated during the war; but it wasn't in Judge Bradford's court that day.[143]

Dick Wootton and his friend Joe Doyle again lived in the same vicinity. Doyle cultivated 600 acres near Pueblo. With infant cities growing up around him, Joe found a market for farm and ranch products in Pueblo, Denver, Canon City, Ft. Garland (Colorado) and Ft. Union.

Doyle became a Huerfano County commissioner and judge and was later elected to the Territorial Legislature. At times when Doyle was away, Dick acted as overseer of his place, while maintaining his own. Doyle had many employees.

It was on Doyle's Ranch that Dick met Miss Fannie Brown. They married on October 5, 1863.

At the time, Dick's oldest daughter, Eliza Ann, fourteen, was at boarding school in Canon City (Colorado); R. L. Jr., thirteen, was with Dick's family, attending school in Kentucky. Dolores, eleven, was at Mrs. Leslie's private school, a few miles down the Huerfano River from Doyle's. George, nine, and the little boys, Joseph, almost seven, Willie, five, and Frank, three, were at home with Dick and Fannie. His daughter Lorett died sometime between 1860 and 1864.

Dick's father, David, had died in Kentucky on September 18, 1863.[144]

In March 1864, Uncle Dick once again stood for his old friend Joe Doyle, who often stood for him. Joe and his family were living in Denver during the legislative session when Joe suffered a heart attack. He died two or three days later. Dick was asked to escort Joe's family from Denver to Pueblo. Someone had been killed on the same road the day before Dick and the Doyle family returned. Others were killed on it the day after. As Dick and the family rode near present-day Colorado Springs, they saw ravens circling. They turned aside to see what drew the birds. Tied to four trees were the skeletons of four men, each wearing a pair of boots, each man with a bullet hole in his skull, each picked clean to the bone. Later Dick found out the bodies were those of Jim Runnels and his gang of thieves. Dick was grateful to deliver the Doyle family safely home.

---

[143] Frances Cragin (*Far West Notebook XI*) and LeRoy Hafen (*Fur Trappers and Traders*) each wrote that Dick Wootton lost his property at Pueblo during the Civil War—that because of his Southern sympathies, the Colorado Territorial Legislature confiscated his land. However, in December 1865, Dick sold some property to Daniel Hayden and John W. Shaw.

[144] David Wootton, age seventy-four, was buried in Jones Cemetery, Christian County, Kentucky. When Ft. Campbell was constructed, he and other family members buried at Jones were moved to Flatlick Cemetery.

The Southwest Has Troubles of Its Own

Though several new forts were constructed in New Mexico and Colorado, the Southwest was left with minimal military protection during the American Civil War. Plains Indians seized the opportunity to increase raids. When Sioux hostilities fired up in 1862, many Arapaho and Cheyenne lent a helping hand. Trouble raged from Minnesota to Texas.

In February 1863, to quell trouble between whites and western Indians, President Abraham Lincoln sent for a delegation of Ute, Cheyenne, and Arapaho leaders to meet and discuss problems. On March 27th, he greeted fifteen Western chiefs in the East Room of the White House. He told the men that if any of them had anything to say, he would be glad to hear them. Cheyenne Chief Lean Bear and Arapaho Chief Spotted Wolf spoke. Lincoln listened.

Through an interpreter, Lincoln explained the white man's way. He told the chiefs there are various types of pale faces, just as there are various types of red men. His aide held a globe. Lincoln explained where the pale face came from, where the red men live, and where they sat in Washington at the moment. He spoke of the advantage of cultivating land and the disadvantage of war. He told them he didn't presume that way was best for everyone, but it had worked for the white man. It enabled the white man to prosper with more work and less war. He explained to the chiefs that treaties are made with the best intention even though some may violate them.

He spoke as one chief to other chiefs; for chiefs knew one cannot always control how one's children behave. From that point on Ute Chief Ouray attempted to keep his tribe at peace with the "Great White Father."

In spite of the Washington visit, Indian hostilities continued.

Dick Wootton said the most serious Indian trouble in Colorado erupted in 1863-64. In the summer of 1863, Colorado Governor John Evans wired Washington, D. C. for help.

In New Mexico, Apache and Navajo were on the warpath.

After the Battle of Glorieta, the Military Department of New Mexico had turned its attention to Indian warfare. General James Carleton, head of the department, decided it would be best to put Indians on a reserve to teach them farming and the ways of civilization. He chose Bosque Redondo, forty fertile acres near Ft. Sumner on the Pecos River in eastern New Mexico.

When Apache continued to plunder and kill in the winter of 1862-63, Carleton ordered Kit Carson to stop them. In March 1863 Carson took 400 Mescalero Apache to Bosque Redondo.

The U. S. had adopted a policy of total war with the Navajo before the Civil War interrupted. Now that New Mexico was safe in Union hands, the war resumed. In March 1864 the majority of the Navajo were marched to Bosque Redondo, where their hated Apache enemies were living. Soon after the Navajo arrived, the Apache left and continued raids off-and-on until 1880.

The Army planned to train workers and leaders at Bosque Redondo, but they hadn't counted on drought. Disease and hardship reigned.

The Navajo were not required to stay at the reservation at all times. Allowed to hunt, the men ranged as far as Las Vegas, New Mexico. Las Vegas residents asked the Army to return the Navajo to their homeland; they were stealing too much from them. After four years, the Army and the Navajo headmen made a treaty which allowed the Navajo to live on a reservation in their own homeland. They returned home in 1868.

In Colorado, the Cheyenne, who were generally on good terms with mountain men, turned against settlers. This was nothing new for the Comanche, traditional enemies of the Cheyenne. They'd been hostile to whites from the time any came into the Southwest. When Comanche got wind of the Cheyenne's change of mind—especially among young warriors, they incited the Cheyenne further. A group of Prairie Apache had already joined the Comanche force. The Kiowa had joined the Comanche long ago after Cheyenne and Arapaho had almost exterminated them.

Uncle Dick said that once the Comanche drew the Cheyenne into their alliance, it was probably the largest number of Indians that ever went on the warpath at the same time in the Far West. Later, even the Arapaho joined in. They were angry because settlers cut down Big Timber, a grove near Ft. Wallace, Kansas. Because buffalo were plentiful there, it had been one of their favorite wintering sites. Arapaho gathered there to tan buffalo hides to trade with white traders. When they found Big Timber destroyed, the Arapaho vowed to kill one white man for every tree that had been cut down.[145] Uncle Dick reckoned they kept their word.

Murderous, thieving raids plowed the minds and hearts of immigrants, leaving fear of murder and torture in their wake. Travel became not mere transportation and definitely not a leisurely excursion, but a daring venture. Pony Express riders were attacked, some murdered. People in Denver were concerned Indians might soon be bold enough to attack large settlements.

It was a bad time for scant forces, but in 1863-64 American military forces were busy at Chancellorsville, Gettysburg, Vicksburg, Chickamauga, Chattanooga, Spotsylvania, and other Civil War battles of rigor and privation.

In 1864 Indian trouble intensified on the Santa Fe Trail. Indians destroyed all stage stations and stock ranches—except Ft. Larned —between Diamond Springs (Kansas) and Ft. Lyon (Colorado). U. S. military escorted every overland coach between Ft. Lyon and Ft. Larned. In spring several Indian tribes rendezvoused in the Smoky Hill country of western Kansas and agreed to forget past differences and focus on a battle plan against "whites."

---

[145] The grove was cut down by contractors who built Ft. Wallace.

Grit

In spite of Indian trouble, Dick planted his acres of grain and vegetables along the Fountain River. 1864 looked like a good year as little green blades broke through the soil. By the end of May his crop was doing very well. Spring rains were abundant. On Colorado's western slope, rivers and streams began to swell. They began to flood.

In northern Colorado a flood swept through Camp Collins—wrecked it.[146]

About midnight on Friday, May 19th, Cherry Creek began sloshing over its banks. By morning, water roared through Denver streets. It destroyed houses and businesses, including Denver City Hall with its records. A little east of Market Street bridge it sucked the new Rocky Mountain News building and its 3,000 pound steam-powered press into Cherry Creek. John Chivington rowed a boat over to Editor William Byers' house. The Byers family, perched on the rooftop, was glad to see him. On a brighter note, the effects of the flood united the town and helped overcome much of the rivalry leftover from pre-consolidation days.

Further south, the Fountain River and its' surrounding streams swelled. One morning about daybreak, Uncle Dick heard water rushing, pounding down through the valley. The bank of rushing water looked a hundred feet high and a mile or two wide. Dick wasn't off on the width; but actual water mark measurement proved to be only eighteen and a half feet high. His house was built on high ground, but his neighbor Dodson's wasn't. Dick stayed to care for Fannie and the children. He sent his ten-year-old son, George, to warn them. Without taking time for saddle or bridle, George hopped on his horse and rode furiously, keeping his horse on high ground.

Doc Dodson had lived a few years on Colorado's Front Range of the Rocky Mountains, but he'd just begun farming on the Fountain that spring.[147] When George arrived, the Dodsons had time to throw on a few clothes and snatch up a few things—a guitar and their clothing trunks. They threw those into a wagon, hitched up, and fled to higher ground. In his haste, Dodson forgot his bottles of gold dust.

Within two hours the flash flood swept down the valley, uprooted cottonwood trees as large as four-five feet in diameter, and rearranged anything in its path. The front of Dodson's cabin—three cabins formed his house—had been about twenty to thirty yards from the stream. The flood dashed off with the front of his house, entered the main of the house, and lapped the soil out from under the front legs of his stove, leaving a hole fifteen feet deep. Nine people lost their lives in the flood that swept through the valley.

The stream changed course. The main channel now flowed where the front part of Dodson's house had stood.

---

[146] Ft. Collins was built to replace it.
[147] Late in 1861 Dodson started to move to Texas. Because of Civil War trouble, he stayed at Baster's Ranch for the winter. In February 1862 he rented Zan Hicklin's ranch and farmed a year before moving south to Pueblo. He bought a hotel there in 1863 and ran it until he moved up near Wootton. In 1865 he moved twenty-eight miles southwest of Pueblo to ranch on the St. Charles.

Many helped hunt for Dodson's gold, but no one ever found it that Dick or Doc heard of.

When the water receded—as flash floods quickly do, Dick went out to survey the damage on his place and his neighbors'. He found uprooted trees and parts of cabins, wagons and farm equipment, as well as just plain debris, on his corn and wheat fields. The grain was completely beaten down, but it wasn't washed out. Dick set to work clearing the field. He and his son helped their neighbors where they could.

Within a couple weeks Dick's grain seemed to overcome its shock and showed signs of recovery. It looked like he'd have a good crop after all.

Indian trouble persisted. On June 11th, Arapaho Chief Roman Nose killed and scalped a couple and their two children.[148] When the mutilated bodies were displayed in Denver, townsfolk prepared to defend themselves.

On Little Cow Creek (Kansas), Chief Little Turtle and his 150 warriors surprised teamsters at mealtime. The Indians scalped, tortured, and mutilated them. They took what they wanted out of the wagons before torching them and rode off with the trains' goods and mules. Scouts from Ft. Larned arrived two hours later and found two teenagers still alive. Each teen had been scalped, stabbed, and staked to the ground with arrows. Robert McGee, one of the boys, survived to an old age; the other died soon after the rescue.

In July 1864 Indians attacked stage stations and wagon trains between Julesburg and Denver, crippling travel and supply to and from Denver. Roads between Kearney, Nebraska, and Latham, Colorado, were almost deserted. Food became scarce in Denver; the price of flour skyrocketed from $9 to $25 per 100#.

When Ceran St. Vrain, operating his mills down in New Mexico, heard of Denver's dire need, he said to Pat O'Neill, "It isn't right, Pat, that they should starve while there's plenty in the barns…and…, man, they're paying $20 a sack [100 lb. sack]."[149]

St. Vrain hired O'Neill to haul fifteen tons of flour in 100# sacks from the Mora Valley in New Mexico to Denver. When his wagons arrived in Denver, the town stopped. Folks took off work and formed a block-long line to get in on the flour. Telling the story years later Pat remarked, "A charitable old cuss, that St. Vrain. He only got $6,000 for 300 sacks of flour [including $900 he paid O'Neill]."[150]

On Uncle Dick's farm, corn grew; wheat began to head. Then the hail came, knocked the heads off the wheat and beat the rest of the farm ragged. There would be no crop in 1864.

In July, men who claimed to have raided with Quantrill robbed the mail and stole ranch stock in South Park, Colorado. They got by with it until Jack Sparks and his men set out to set things right. On July 30th they paid a surprise visit to the thieves' camp. The raiders tried to disperse; but one was killed, and five were captured and killed soon afterward.

Folks in northern Colorado had had about enough of Indian raids. Colonel John Chivington heard that a large band, camped on Bear Creek (Colorado) near the junction of the South Platte, was preparing to attack settlements in the foothills. He sent a troop from Denver. When the Indians caught wind of the soldiers, they cleared out.

---

[148] Some called Roman Nose a Cheyenne. Uncle Dick, who knew him personally, said he was Arapaho.

[149] Lavender, *Bent's Fort*, 448.

[150] *Ibid.*, 448.

Because of Cheyenne hostilities, settlers along Boulder Creek (Colorado) united and built Ft. Chambers. There, Captain Nichols of Boulder recruited and trained men to protect the Platte River wagon road, the northern Colorado supply artery. The trained men proceeded to Valley Station, fifty miles from Julesburg and joined Captain C. M. Tyler's company from Black Hawk.

The twenty-two soldiers came upon Chief Big Wolf and a small band of warriors heading north for the winter. Soldiers killed eleven warriors. Among the loot the warriors left behind, soldiers found the chief's shield and boxes of goods taken from wagon trains: bedding, women's and children's clothing. On the chief's shield were five scalps; one was a woman's fresh scalp.

In August, bands of Arapaho, Cheyenne, Kiowa, and Sioux terrorized the overland mail route, killed, mutilated, stole, and burned for about 400 miles—from about eighty-five miles out of Denver to about one hundred miles southeast of Ft. Kearny.

The Eubanks family became an example of the atrocities. Indians scalped Mr. Eubanks in front of his wife. When an Indian started to dash her one-and-a half-year-old's head, Mrs. Eubanks ran, grabbed the child, and ran. They caught her. The Chief took her into his tent as his own for the next year and two months, during which time squaws mocked and abused her. Each time she attempted suicide, Chief Two-Face foiled her plan.

In southeastern Colorado, near Ft. Lyon, Kiowa and Comanche attacked a wagon train on August 7, 1864. The week after the attack, Comanche stampeded a wagon train's stock and killed five men near Lower Cimarron Springs (southwest Kansas). Denver residents built up defenses and foiled Indian plans to attack the town on August 12th.

In mid-August Indians killed four men and kidnapped two women about fifteen miles from Colonel A. G. Boone's post office on the Arkansas River (Colorado). By that time all stage traffic from the East stopped. Mail no longer traveled the Plains; it was rerouted from the East by steamer to San Francisco, transferred to rail as far as Placerville, and carried across country. Local wagon travel was a risk. Some settlers from outlying areas moved into Denver; but settlements were under such attack people feared there would be no safety even in Denver.

On August 21st, two male bodies were found scalped about eighteen miles west of Fort Lyon.

In August William Bent wrote to chiefs in the Cheyenne village. His son George and son-in-law Ed Guerrier were there to read his letter to the chiefs. Bent worked with and in behalf of the tribe. Chief Black Kettle seemed to understand the merit of change for the betterment of his people. As a result, the council of chiefs overrode objections of their Dog Soldiers, a league of fierce young warriors.

After Indian hostilities cut off communication between northern Colorado and the States in the latter half of August 1864, John Chivington, commander of the military district of Colorado, instituted martial law in Denver. He allowed grocery stores, supply stores, and those that dispensed medicine to open for business three hours each day. He shut down all other businesses. Every able male, sixteen years old and older, was required to enlist in the militia. No wagons were allowed to leave the Territory.

All of September and into October of 1864 soldiers Joe Connor, Ike Bakeman, Albert

Neiland, Oscar Packard, Alston Knox Shaw, and Ad Williamson headquartered at Dick's ranch, as they escorted stages in charge of the U. S. mail from Pueblo to Colorado City. The trip usually took two days—one day up and one day back, but in heavy snow it took them up to three days one way. They moved on when they were needed elsewhere.

When Army Captain Morgan heard there may be an attack at Latham, Colorado. He led his "Colorado 100-dayers" down from Denver. On Sunday, September 18, 1864, the troop pitched camp west of Latham. With a troop in the area, the road blockade was lifted. Many families returned home to their ranches. Six days after Morgan and his men arrived, a stage pulled into Latham station on its way to Atchison, Kansas. Mail began arriving on September 28th.

One wagon train on the Plains late in the summer of 1864 was so harassed that it was slowed and caught on the Plains by winter weather. The mule skinners ate most of the flour and some of the mules. The contractor was left holding the tab for the flour, the animals, and the payroll; but that was part of the risk of freighting across the Plains. Trouble continued into the winter.

In September 1864 a group representing about 600 Indians of different tribes, approached Major Wynkoop at Ft. Lyon and proposed peace. They arranged for five chiefs to go to Denver for a peace conference and agreed to return captive women and children. They only returned four.

On September 28th, the five chiefs—Cheyenne Chief Black Kettle; his brother White Antelope; Bull Bear, a southern Cheyenne; and Arapahos Neva and Bosse—traveled to Denver. They met Colorado Governor John Evans and his delegation at Camp Weld.

Bull Bear spoke of Indian prowess. Black Kettle said he wanted peace, but said he knew there were factions among the Arapaho and Cheyenne that did not. The chiefs explained that young warriors and the Sioux were the ones causing trouble. Chief Black Kettle was well-intentioned, but he didn't have complete influence over his tribe. Young bucks had minds of their own. Many Cheyenne and Arapaho remained hostile.

Colorado citizens and the military were now as tired of Indians as Indians had been of them. The assessment of many was that Indians were looking for safe lodging and government provision in cold weather; so they could raid and war again in spring when weather would be more favorable.

Governor Evans rebuked the chiefs for ignoring his proclamation to go to the forts. He warned them against further uprising and insisted attacks and atrocities stop. Colonel Chivington promised the chiefs there would be a decisive end to fighting. He told them in no uncertain terms that if the warring didn't stop, they would be "wiped off the face of the earth."

Nothing definite was decided and understood by both sides. In light of Governor Evans' reference to forts, some Indians seemed to think if they moved close to a fort they'd be protected, fed, and maintained through the winter, regardless of their summer behavior. Six hundred fifty-two Indians moved near Bent's Stone Fort. In spite of the fact he'd been ordered not to make peace, Major Anthony returned arms the band had surrendered; so they could hunt to provide for themselves. Except for Chief Left Hand and a few followers, the band moved eastward.

In October 1864, Chief Left Hand, a friendly Arapaho, returned some plunder to Major Wynkoop at Ft. Lyon; but attacks continued. Freighters refused to travel without military escort. No one was allowed to travel along the Arkansas or the Missouri River trails without one. General Samuel R. Curtis, district commander, wrote Chivington that he wanted Indians to reap a little more of what they'd sown. He said they needed to suffer. Until then he wanted no peace.

Arapaho Chief Left Hand and a few of his followers stayed around Ft. Lyon until Wynkoop told him to go to Sand Creek, about forty miles from the fort. Chief Black Kettle and his Cheyenne band were encamped at Sand Creek, a tributary of the Arkansas River. William Bent's son George was home at Big Timbers (Bent's Stone Fort) when he heard that his mother's people—Chief Black Kettle's village—were at Sand Creek. William's son Charles and daughter Julia and her husband, Ed Guerrier, were with them. George went to visit.

On November 8th, Abraham Lincoln was re-elected President. November 15th Union General W. T. Sherman began his 300 mile "March to the Sea."[151]

In New Mexico, General James H. Carleton, commander of the Military Department of New Mexico, had sent Colonel Kit Carson to warn Kiowa and Comanche: "they must not think to stop the commerce of the plains, nor must they imagine that we are going to keep up escorts with the trains. We do this now until we learn whether they will behave or not. If they will not, we will end the matter by a war which will remove any further necessity for escorts."[152]

EMIGRANTS ATTACKED BY INDIANS.

---

[151] As Sherman burned a swath from Atlanta to the Atlantic, he allowed his army of over 60,000 to pillage, as they desired. On December 21st, he captured Savannah, Georgia, and presented it to President Lincoln as a Christmas gift.

[152] Walker, *Wagonmasters*, 265.

When attacks did not stop, Carleton decided to visit Santa Fe Trail raiders on their turf. He sent Kit Carson and the 1st NM Cavalry against Kiowa and Comanche in the Panhandle of Texas near Adobe Walls. On November 26, 1864, a fierce battle raged all day. Late in the day soldiers torched the Kiowa village; it was like torching a hornets' nest. Outnumbered about 10 to 1, soldiers retreated. Thanks to Carson's skill, his unit wasn't wiped out. Casualty count: Army: three killed, twenty-one wounded; Kiowa, Comanche: approximately sixty-one killed, one hundred-two hundred wounded. It would be awhile yet before Kiowa and Comanche warfare ceased.

From Colorado, Governor Evans pled with Washington to send troops or allow him funds and permission to raise a volunteer army. Colorado gold and silver continued to aid Washington's war effort. After waiting and receiving no reply, Coloradans took to their own defense.

Colonel Chivington trained 750 volunteers. Trusting the U. S. Government would come through with funds, Governor Evans borrowed heavily from Denver merchants to equip the volunteers. Rocky Mountain News publisher, William Byers backed the effort with his pen.

The way Dick Wootton assessed it, Indian forces were shrewd; they wouldn't all go on the warpath at once. While one group killed emigrants and attacked settlers, others carried on business as usual with traders. They did the trading for the whole group. "It was some time," Dick said, "before we found out how it was that the Indians who were actually doing the fighting kept themselves supplied all the time with arms of as good pattern as those used by the soldiers, and also with plenty of ammunition."[153] When it finally came to the attention of traders and settlers, they considered any confederated tribes equally at war whether they were fighting or furnishing supplies. "It was the necessity for punishing all the Indians who belonged to the hostile combination, whether they were actually caught scalping their victims or only sharpening the knives for those who did the scalping, which led Col. Chivington to march against the Cheyenne with the Colorado First and fight the first band he came across."[154]

When settlers had enough, Chivington marched to Sand Creek.

---

[153] Conard, 1980, 389.
[154] Ibid., 389.

Sand Creek

Colonel John M. Chivington and Colorado's 1st and 3rd volunteer units were determined to deal a decisive blow against Indian hostilities, as they had against Confederates at the Battle of Glorieta. Like General William T. Sherman, Colonel Chivington wasn't a man to have as an enemy. The troop rode 300 miles—100 through two feet of snow—southeast from Denver.

On November 28, 1864, they arrived at Bent's Big Timbers (Bent's New Stone Fort). Jim Beckwourth had guided the troop from Denver, but gave out at Big Timbers. Knowing William Bent's love for the Cheyenne, Chivington let him know his destination. He appointed men to guard William to be sure he couldn't send a message to the Sand Creek encampment. Three of his children were there.

Chivington compelled Bent's son Robert to lead him to the Sand Creek encampment. He'd enlisted Charlie Autobees' boys as scouts. He added Major Scott Anthony and 125 men to his force and two howitzers to his two pieces of light field artillery.

The troop traveled throughout the night. By daylight, November 29, they arrived at Sand Creek. Smoke curled from the tepees of a few early risers. The early morning artillery and musket fire caught the Indians by surprise, as Chivington intended. He wanted to surprise them as they'd surprised Mexican and American settlers. He'd planned ahead and had run off many of the Indians' horses.

A few early risers hollered and ran to find Chief Black Kettle, others to find John Smith. Some say warriors were there; others say most warriors were gone. Chief Black Kettle raised a white flag and an American flag. Firing didn't stop. Orders were: no quarter. Black Kettle ordered his people to flee.[155] He and about 200 men fled, leaving the women and children behind.

Some Indians fought; some attempted surrender. Soldiers' orders remained: Give no quarter. It was as though Chivington and those of his soldiers seasoned in the West viewed these people through smoldering cabins, bloody scalps, mutilated bodies, and the tears of families who'd had their women and children tortured, killed, or kidnapped. They seemed to see them as those who'd given no mercy, and they were retaliating without mercy. Not all the soldiers approved. Those who'd seen Indian ravages time and again didn't seem to mind copying the actions. Chivington called a halt to hostilities; fighting stopped by noon.

Reports of the number of dead and wounded of both sides vary widely. Nine to fourteen of Chivington's men died; thirty-four to thirty-eight more were wounded. George Bent, half Cheyenne and half white, was there. He said about 163 Cheyenne were killed.[156]

Early in the battle, soldiers captured Jack Smith and Charles Bent, William's son. Jack confessed to an ambush and rape and was killed on the spot. Soldiers targeted their pistols on

---

[155] General George Custer destroyed Black Kettle's village four years later, on November 27, 1868.
[156] Reports vary from 150-500 Indians slain.

Charles' head. Charlie Autobees' sons intervened, and soldiers lowered their pistols.

Chief White Antelope and Chief Left Hand died early in the skirmish. Soldiers shot and killed Chief One-Eye and Yellow Wolf, and shot a ball into George Bent's hip.[157] Julia and Ed Guerrier, William Bent's daughter and son-in-law, escaped.

When news of Sand Creek reached Denver, townsfolk rejoiced. People of Denver and in Colorado settlements considered Chivington a deliverer. They welcomed him and his troops at a public meeting on their return. The consensus among townspeople and soldiers was that the Indians had been broken. This would end molestation. But not everyone was pleased. Some of Chivington's recruits who'd not seen or been affected by atrocities and others who had friends or relatives at Sand Creek were horrified. They testified of the atrocities. Word of Sand Creek traveled east and outraged the American public. Washington listened.

Infuriated by the massacre, Cheyenne, Arapaho, Kiowa, and Comanche went on the warpath with renewed vengeance in Kansas, Nebraska, and Colorado—openly attacking settlers, freighters, and travelers; burning homes and stage stations; killing; seizing people; destroying crops; stealing weapons and animals; holding up mail wagons and stagecoaches. Sioux joined in. Dog Soldier Charles Bent (William's son) organized and fought like a man gone mad with hate.

For the most part, Eastern voices condemned the massacre. For the most part, Western voices approved, saying, you don't live here—he did what he had to do. One media report portrayed Chivington's men celebrating their return to Denver by displaying scalps taken at Sand Creek. Uncle Dick said there were scalps exhibited, but not as the media reported. They weren't Indian scalps, but scalps of victims taken from the Indian encampment at Sand Creek. "They were the scalps of gray-haired men and prattling children, of fair-haired and dark-haired women who had suffered a thousand deaths…"[158] He said Chivington's purpose exhibiting the scalps was to demonstrate why punishment was deserved.

Whether or not Indians camped at Sand Creek were peaceful remains a matter of dispute. One side says that though Black Kettle had been unable to control his young warriors, he and his Cheyenne band were camping as they'd been instructed. They'd recently received rations at Ft. Lyon and felt they should have been under government protection. Others believed they were camped for winter waiting for spring's more favorable weather for further war.

Chivington stood his ground. He argued that such warfare was what Indians understood and that he and his troop had undoubtedly saved Denver and other nearby towns.

Twenty-five years later Uncle Dick spoke of the incident:
I was never on very friendly terms with Colonel Chivington and have censured some of his acts as a military officer as severely as anybody, but my opinion of this particular military campaign and his action in connection with it is, that if it is any part of the business of soldiers stationed in the Indian country to protect the lives and property of settlers, he and his men did their duty and did it well.[159]

Uncle Dick said the people of central and western Kansas and eastern Colorado were glad

---

[157] After a month in the village, George's hip wasn't healing; he returned to his father's fort. Once healed, he returned to the camp with Indians who had been imprisoned at the fort.
[158] Conard, 1980, 390-391.
[159] Conard, 1890, 410-411.

to learn that those who'd killed scores of people in cold blood had been severely punished, whether the Indians were on the warpath right then or not.

George Vanderwalker, who traveled the Santa Fe Trail in 1864, said Indians had been through and destroyed all the stage stations and cattle ranches that had been at Cow Creek, Turkey Creek, Jarvis Creek, Walnut Creek, and Big Bend. Every coach he met had a military escort.

Even as an old man, Irving Howbert, one of Chivington's youthful volunteers, supported him. He said those who testified against Chivington did so because they were political enemies, jealous officers, or men whose business was hindered by Chivington's attack.[160]

For decades people debated the Sand Creek attack. A hundred and fifty years later people were left to read what was written and surmise what was and what was not.

In August 1865 the U. S. sent peace commissioners James R. Doolittle, Lafayette Foster and Lewis W. Ross to Ft. Lyon, Colorado, to investigate the massacre. They summoned William Bent and Kit Carson.

William told the Congressmen, "If the matter were left to me, I guarantee with my life that in three months I could have all the Indians along the Arkansas at peace without the expense of war."[161] The Congressmen turned to Carson and asked his opinion. Kit replied, "His suggestions and opinions…coincide perfectly with my own….I have much more confidence in [his] influence with the Indians than in my own….I believe that if Colonel Bent and myself were authorized, we could make a solid, lasting peace."[162] The council provided apologies and provisions, but included nothing of what Kit and William wanted for the Indians that would allow them to live freely.

The council condemned the massacre, denounced Chivington, and recommended his removal from office. The U. S. government confessed Chivington's action was wrong and paid reparations to families that suffered or lost family members.

George Bent, who fought alongside the Cheyenne, helped gather tribes for another treaty in 1867. His brother Charles remained a fierce Dog Soldier. A price was put on Charles' head. His savageries were so atrocious his own father disowned him. One night, not knowing his father was away, Charles returned home to kill him. Before he could return to kill his dad, he was wounded fighting the Pawnee. He returned to his Indian village and died of malaria.

Near the end of 1864 the Army set fire to the prairie west of Denver. With the help of a northwest wind, fire burned over a 300 mile swath to Ft. Kearny. Within three days tongues of fire lapped up prairie grass as far south as the Arkansas River and on into the Texas panhandle. That reduced winter fodder for game and for Indian horses. To further reduce the threat of Indian attack to Colorado settlers and supply trains, General Mitchell waged a winter campaign and drove Indians out of winter camps on the Republican River.

Incensed, Indians retaliated in early 1865.

Southern and Northern Cheyenne joined forces and, in January and February 1865, burned Julesburg, rustled cattle, took wagons, and attacked here and there in northern Colorado. But the overall effect of the Army's work in the winter of 1864-65 would be felt in Denver and by

---

[160] Chivington left Denver in 1867, returned sixteen years later, and died in 1894.
[161] Lavender, *Bent's Fort*, 388.
[162] *Ibid.*, 388.

travelers and settlers by spring 1865—safety at home, freedom to travel, and availability of goods. When freight wagons again traveled freely, safely, prices of goods dropped.

There would be more violent battles before all was truly quiet on the Western range.

No Time to Quit

It's said there's nothing like a new baby to help overcome the grief of a lost loved one. Dick's brother Samuel had died August 23, 1864, and their mother, aged sixty-nine, on September 15th. Dick and Fannie's first baby was due in about a month.

Twelve days after Dick and Fannie's first anniversary, Frances Virginia was born at Doyle's Ranch. She was named for her mother and grandmother. But Fannie died in childbirth. Dick had her funeral there at Doyle's and buried her on Doyle's ranch. Time has erased or defaced the marks on some of the little cemetery's gravestones, including Fannie's.

Childless Dr. and Mrs. Walter C. Burt cared for baby Fannie.

Dick's older girls were at school. R. L., Jr. was at school in Kentucky. Dick's younger boys—George, Joseph, Willie, and Frank, ages ten and a half to four and a half—were at home.

Dick had helped at Doyle's place after Doyle's death in March 1864. Mrs. Doyle's brother, Tom Suaso, and John Horn were the ranch foremen. After hail finished off Dick's crops in the summer, he worked at Doyle's, primarily as overseer. It wasn't a good situation. A few relations seemed concerned about their part of Doyle's large estate.

With ranch dissention, it was no place to stay.

It was no time to leave, no time to return home—no sense taking the kids into the midst of Civil War. Yet, with present unrest in the West, it was no time to stay. But it was no time to quit.

Dick had reconsidered his career as a farmer. For months he'd mulled over an idea that had been in his mind for the years. Today it is an occasional inconvenience to be stranded in Trinidad, Colorado, or Raton, New Mexico, because of snow on I-25 across Raton Pass. In the mid-1800's the Pass wasn't a one-day crossing even in fair weather.

Dick knew Raton Pass was the natural highway into New Mexico, but it was common knowledge that the Pass was extremely difficult for wheeled vehicles. That's why the Dry Branch/Cimarron Cut-Off of the Santa Fe Trail was the primary freight route.

The Mountain Branch had better landmarks and water supply, but the Dry Branch was shorter and had no mountain range to cross. Other than lack of water, the Cut-Off's main disadvantage was that it crossed through Kiowa and Comanche hunting grounds. It was on that stretch Comanche killed Jedediah Smith back in 1831.

Even Raton Pass, however, wasn't a complete stranger to Indians and thieves. In the current year—1864—Don Antonio Manuel Otero's wagon train was attacked near the summit of Raton Pass. All his money and animals were stolen.

Dick was aware of a growing need for a year-round road from Colorado into New Mexico. Horses and mules could cross the Pass anytime, but winter weather restricted stagecoach and wagon travel. Snow often filled arroyos. Stages and wagons were sometimes stuck in snow for days. Men who knew the Pass carried #50 shovels to clear their way when needed.

Barlow and Sanderson wanted to include Trinidad, Colorado, on its regular stage route, but couldn't safely cross the Pass year round, much less keep any sort of predictable schedule.

Steep grades up and down the Pass challenged the strength of animals and vehicles. Precipices and rocky obstructions—like the Devil's Gate—challenged drivers' skill and stood ready to boost drivers and crew into eternity. "The Devil's Gate'…an overhanging rock forced the stages to the very edge of the precipice. A little careless driving here and neither stage, mules, nor passengers were likely to be of much use thereafter."[163]

Looking beyond seeming impossibilities, Uncle Dick saw opportunity to provide for his children and to open access for others. He figured he could build a toll road across Raton Pass as good as any average turnpike he'd known in his youth or in his travels. He planned to have it done before summer travelers arrived.

In late 1864, Dick rode down from Pueblo, across Raton Pass, to visit his friend Lucien B. Maxwell in Cimarron City, New Mexico. Raton Pass and the surrounding area were part of Maxwell's large Maxwell Land Grant, which included close to 1,714,765 acres—over 2,500 square miles. Dick explained his plan. A toll road across the Raton Mountains would open a gateway into New Mexico and provide easy access to Maxwell's country. Maxwell liked the idea and gave Dick 2,500 acres—almost four sections of land—across Raton Pass and into New Mexico, in exchange for perpetual free use of the road. The gentlemen's agreement wasn't recorded, but in 1867 Maxwell gave Wootton a signed quitclaim deed for the property.

Dick applied to the New Mexico and Colorado legislatures for a charter to construct a toll road across Raton Pass. It would begin near Trinidad, Colorado, and cross over the New Mexico line.

The original New Mexico charter was either lost or not recorded by the territory. Though there is no record of the original charter, a later New Mexico legislative record refers to it.

On February 10, 1865, near the end of the legislative session in Golden, Colorado, the legislature approved the act to incorporate Dick's Trinidad and Raton Mountain Road. The Colorado charter gave Dick permission to build a road from Trinidad through the Raton Mountains. "The road was to lead from Trinidad up the Purgatory to the southern line of Colorado through and over Ratoon [sic] Mountains by way of 'or as near as possible to the old route known as the Santa Fe and Bent's Old Fort Road.'"[164]

In January 1865, before Dick received both charters, his daughter Eliza Ann, married William R. Walker. Though Southern born, William was a Yankee—twenty years her senior. He came to the Southwest as a soldier in the Mexican War and served at Fort Union after the war. Uncle Dick and William each held their opinion of the Civil War, but they got along well enough to live in the same household. Eliza loved both; and, having often been her Daddy's right hand at home, she remained devoted to each as long as they lived.

When the toll road charters arrived, Dick moved to Raton Pass. He made his home in a large tent and began work with half a dozen hired workmen. Some quit or worked for a short time; he hired others. They worked with Dick ten to fourteen hours a day. "There were

---

[163] Duffus, *Santa Fe Trail*, 250, 251.
[164] Willard, "A Raton Pass Mountain Road Toll Book," 77, 78.

hillsides to cut down, rocks to blast and remove, and bridges to build by the score."[165] Original bridges were temporary and improved later.[166] (Al Berg, who later lived at the Wootton Ranch said the road crossed Raton Creek fifty-three times.) Dynamite wasn't available until 1867; but they brought the Devil's Gate and other rocky obstructions to terms. More than one man was killed by falling trees and tumbling rocks.

Scenic Highway, Raton, N. Mexico.
(Card posted October 1916)

A portion of Dick Wootton's road, as seen in the early 1900's (see page 328)

Uncle Dick skirted his road around cliffs, which flirted with precipices, and straightened and smoothed a way over rocky rutted paths. When finished, twenty-seven miles of writhing road snaked up, over, and beyond the Raton Mountains. Dick devised a system of cables to help wagons up in some of the more difficult places.

He'd built his toll road and opened easy access into Maxwell's country, Fort Union, Santa Fe, and on to Mexico, Arizona, and southern California. He kept half a dozen men employed fulltime to help keep the road and bridges in good repair. There was plenty of work for everyone, especially after heavy rains or runoff. He provided a cabin for employees who needed lodging. At times, workers camped on the mountain when doing repair work.

Santa Fe Trail trader Mr. Huning, who first traversed Raton Pass about 1862, said it was about fifteen miles from Red River to Raton Canyon. In two places he and those with him had to let their wagons down with ropes and chains. There was plenty of water; but the twenty-five mile trip across Raton Pass and through its canyons was rugged, rocky, and hard on his wagons. Huning added that the ruggedness of the trip changed once Dick Wootton built his toll road.

---

[165] Conard, 1890, 419.
[166] Berg, "Old Wootton Ranch…," p. 2.

Raton Pass

Uncle Dick opened his Raton Pass toll road in spring of 1865. He built a gate on the Colorado side of Raton Pass and strung a heavy chain across the road. No one passed without his permission, but Colorado and New Mexico territorial governments regulated charges.

Dick's first customers were 150 wagons traveling in a military-escorted train. He had a variety of customers: freight wagons, wagon trains, stagecoaches, miners, soldiers, individual immigrant families, cattlemen with their cattle, and highwaymen. He drew East-West traffic and intermountain and local travel. All freighting between the railhead[167] and New Mexico went over the toll road, as did government supplies and troop travel.

Because cattle rustling was a common means of livelihood, Dick didn't charge posses. One bright day when a group of soldiers stopped at Dick's, a thief stole one of their mules right out from under their noses.

In addition to posses, Dick didn't charge Indians, funeral parties, clergy, or folks who seemed down-and-out. He became known to thousands of travelers as "Uncle Dick."

His toll charges in 1869-70 were:

Wagon with team	$1.50
Smaller vehicles	$1.00
Horseman and pack animal	$ .25
Livestock per head	$ .05
Lodging	$ .50
Meals (each)	$ .75

Dick tossed the coins into a barrel. When he went into Trinidad, he'd load up full barrels and take them to the bank. The barrels contained a variety of coins, but local lore said they were full of silver dollars. How much did the toll road pay? It was told that Dick once said he earned $500-$600 per day. Another source estimated he grossed about $600 a month from the road.[168] If he kept account books, he either didn't keep them long-term, or they may have been destroyed in a fire (1890). Whatever method he used, Dick knew; that was his character.

On June 12, 1865, Major John C. McFerran, chief quartermaster of the Department of New Mexico, recorded his use of the toll road:, "Left camp at 6 ½ a.m.; crossed Red river; marched ten miles, and commenced the ascent of the Raton mountains, four miles to the summit; descended three miles, struck a mountain stream and a good road, with a tollgate on

---

[167] The railhead was in Kansas when he built the road.
[168] From April 1st, 1869, to January 1st, 1870, George McBride kept a ledger account of money he took in at Raton Pass for tolls, taking a team up the mountain, hay, meals, whiskey, and a candle. His recorded total: $6,548.82. It's uncertain whether his account covers all the money taken in during that time period, or whether it is the money taken in by McBride and recorded to give an account to Uncle Dick.

it, thirteen miles further to the town of Trinidad, Colorado Territory…."[169]

In July 1865 Captain Haley led a 150-wagon train across Uncle Dick's toll road. Before the train left Las Vegas, New Mexico, Corporal Juan Cruz Torres had three privates bound and gagged for raising Cain at a dance. All four—the corporal and three privates—were Mexicans. Though Vegas was more than a hundred miles to the south, the privates were still sore by the time their train camped on Raton Pass on July 13th. Every so often some of the soldiers walked down to Uncle Dick's place. The four men were among those who came. They didn't let on that anything was wrong. When they left, however, Dick noticed they headed the opposite direction from camp.

Dick closed up his house for the night. Later, he heard talking in the dark of night. A man cried out—a cry like Dick had heard when a man received a death blow. In the morning light, not more than 300' from his house, he found Corporal Torres' dead body lying across Raton Creek.

In July Dick began construction of a large three-room home near the tollgate —about a thousand feet below the summit of Raton Pass on the Colorado side. He finished it by fall. The home doubled as a place for his family and as a stage stop. One room, which had a large fireplace at one end, was a large public room in which Dick welcomed guests. Guns and animal heads, horns, and skins decorated the walls. His daughter Eliza helped him build a stone garden.

William and Eliza lived with her father and kept house for him and her four brothers. She hired women to help her prepare meals for soldiers, officers, scouts, and stage passengers who stopped when they crossed the Pass. Meals and supplies were available to the public.

Less than three months after Eliza's marriage Confederate General Robert E. Lee surrendered at Appomattox, and John Wilkes Booth assassinated President Abraham Lincoln. With the Civil War over, westward immigration picked up in the spring and summer of 1865.

In August 1865, Dick's daughter Dolores, married Thomas "Brigham" Young. They lived at Iron Springs stage station, where Brigham was in charge.

In spring 1866 sixteen-year-old R. L., Jr. graduated from LaFayette College in Kentucky and returned home. Because of constant Indian threat and no available military escort, a group of Mexican teamsters didn't want to honor their contract. They overcame their boss and returned the twenty-one-wagon train to Trinidad. The train was scheduled to go from Trinidad to Ft. Lyon and to the Kansas railhead. The U. S. government had finally decided to move out of William Bent's fort and build its own Ft. Lyon on the fork of the Arkansas and Purgatory Rivers. The wagons were partially loaded with lumber for the new fort. Hides and furs piled on top of the lumber filled the wagons. Those were to be delivered to the Kansas Pacific Railroad terminus at Sharon, Kansas. Uncle Dick sent R. L. to replace the wagon boss. He advised him to keep Indians in mind every minute and not to give the Mexicans an inch. R. L. quelled the mutiny.[170] Indians attacked once. One man was killed before the goods were safely delivered.

About the time R. L. returned from Kentucky, Charles Goodnight, Oliver Loving, and

---

[169] Simmons, *On the Santa Fe Trail*, 103, 104.
[170] After that, R. L. freighted goods across the Plains two seasons for Beard and Walker of Trinidad.

sixteen cowboys drove 2,000 head of Texas longhorn from Texas to Ft. Sumner, New Mexico. They made a good profit selling most of the cattle to the government for soldiers at Ft. Sumner and Navajo at Bosque Redondo and drove the remaining 700-800 cows, calves, and bulls on to Denver. When they reached Raton Pass in June 1866, Goodnight was incensed he had to pay Uncle Dick five cents per head for his cattle to lumber across Dick's road. When all was said and done, Goodnight paid; but he vowed he'd find another way for next year's drive. He did.

Though Goodnight objected to the fees, Colonel Meline noted in 1866 that freighters didn't seem to mind paying toll on the road Uncle Dick built the year before. He added that after Uncle Dick built his toll road, the Dry Branch of the Santa Fe Trail fell into disuse. After the 1864 season, traders abandoned the Cimarron (Dry Cut-Off) Branch of the Santa Fe Trail.

In the fall (1866) a Ute had shown copper rocks at Ft. Union. William Kroenig and William Moore paid him to show them where he'd found them. He led them to Baldy Mountain near Cimarron. Moore and Kroenig staked out the Mystic Lode copper mine near Willow Creek in the Moreno Valley, near the top of Baldy Mountain. When Ute and Jicarilla Apache sold copper in Cimarron in October 1866, word of their discovery spread.

The same month, three workmen at the Mystic Lode were waiting for supper; one of them panned in the stream and found color. The three agreed to keep news of their gold discovery to themselves, but word got out. Virginia City sprang up. Nearby Elizabethtown, "E-town", boomed. Traffic across Dick's Raton Pass toll road increased as thousands headed to the Moreno Valley on Lucien Maxwell's Land Grant.

To the north of Dick, Trinidad, Colorado, was a small, but growing community. Many old-timers in the mountains were involved in its foundation.

Trinidad, Colorado

Mouche Ute and Jicarilla Apache were the primary tribes living in the Trinidad area when Dick Wootton moved to Raton Pass.[171] Comanche and Kiowa hunting parties visited the nearby Purgatoire and Arkansas River lands. Since about 1820, Cheyenne and Arapaho had often roamed the region, attacked, and raided the Ute. In turn, the Ute visited them on the Plains.

John Hatcher had built a cabin—the first place built in the area—in spring 1846. He raised a good crop, which the Indians took home for the winter. They soon drove him off.

In 1860 Felipe Baca cleared land along the Purgatoire River and farmed profitably. He returned home to Guadalupita, New Mexico, to recruit families to begin a permanent settlement. In 1862 (year of the Battle of Glorieta) twelve families, moved with him to establish Trinidad. Baca opened the first general store and donated land for the Catholic Church.[172] The Lujans and McBrides, related to Wootton's first wife, were among the families who came with him.[173]

More of Uncle Dick's acquaintances moved to the up-and-coming community. Over decades the lives of mountain men intertwined. Each new settlement or endeavor seemed to draw them together, either in the same locale or in supporting roles from a distance. Trailblazing and breaking ground seemed to be in their blood.

Bill and Rel (St. Vrain) Bransford and family moved to Trinidad. Jake Beard and his family arrived from Doyle's ranch in 1865. Beard's father-in-law, George Simpson, and family followed. Jake had milled for Joe Doyle. He went back East in 1868, bought machinery and built a flour mill of his own in Trinidad. Robert Bent, son of the late George Bent lived in Trinidad with his mother, Cruz.

On February 9, 1866, the Colorado Territorial Legislature created Las Animas County out of Huerfano County and named Trinidad the county seat. Uncle Dick's Raton Pass home was in the new county.

Governor Alexander Cummings appointed George McBride sheriff until the first county election. Dick's son-in-law William Walker was the county's first coroner; he became sheriff after McBride. Walker also became Justice of the Peace and was called Judge Walker from then on.

Bishop Jean B. Lamy of Santa Fe appointed a priest for Trinidad: Jesuit Fr. Peter Munnecom from Holland.[174] Munnecom's lifestyle didn't measure up to Trinidad's idea of a

---

[171] Kiowa and Comanche had driven the Apache north to northern New Mexico mountains and to the Trinidad area.
[172] Felipe Baca became Trinidad's first school board president in 1866. In 1870 he was elected to the Colorado Territorial Legislature. His son Felix married Dick Wootton's daughter.
[173] McBride had been a distiller at Guadalupita, New Mexico. He was married to Dolores Wootton's cousin Piedad Dillette.
[174] Lamy became Archbishop in 1875 after Santa Fe became an archdiocese.

man of the cloth. The congregation, primarily Spanish speaking, was displeased that Munnecom (pictured on the left) did not speak Spanish. Nevertheless, he remained Trinidad's priest for ten years and became a good friend of the Wootton family.

William and Eliza Walker established the U. S. Hotel—the only one in town at the time—on the south side of Main Street, near the corner of Maple and Main. It was a six room house with a public room.[175] On November 26, 1866, Barlow & Sanderson stage leased space in the hotel. They'd had a contract to carry mail from Dodge City, across Raton Pass, to Santa Fe since the early 1860's.

Dr. Michael Beshoar opened a combined medical office and drugstore in Trinidad on August 17, 1867. He'd planned to settle in Denver after the Civil War, but *Rocky Mountain News* Editor W. N. Byers made it plain who was and who was not welcome. Galvanized Yankees like Dr. Beshoar were not. Trinidad welcomed him.

In 1867 four of Dick's friends were Las Animas County officers: George McBride, sheriff; Jake Beard, school superintendent and county commissioner; and George S. Simpson, county clerk. William Bransford was appointed Treasurer on July 3rd.

Politics in Trinidad were running much smoother than back in Washington, D. C. Feelings, factions, and administrations just weren't patching together smoothly since the Civil War ended. On November 25, 1867, the House of Representatives began impeachment proceedings against President Johnson. Proceedings continued until late spring 1868. Johnson was acquitted.

Two weeks later Denver became the permanent capital of Colorado.

By summer 1868, Trinidad's population was 500-600. Philo Sherman had added his hotel,

---

[175] They established the U. S. Hotel, 1866. A larger hotel of the same name was later built on the same location.

which became a stage stop for the Denver and Santa Fe stage. In September 1868, William Walker and his brother Thomas Walker opened another hotel, the Templar House, with Thomas as proprietor. William included a stable and corral for guests' convenience.

When twenty-two-year-old Sister Blandina Segale arrived in Trinidad, there were two schools: the public school, taught by Catholic nuns, and a Methodist Academy. By the end of 1872, a few houses lined one side of Commercial Street for a couple blocks. There were a few stores here and there along Main Street and about seventy-five adobe houses in the area of town called "Mexican Hill."

Law enforcement wasn't a big deal in Trinidad. Most prisoners escaped from the adobe jail before the Circuit Court judge arrived from Denver.

The Trinidad War

Early in the fall of 1867, a large band of Ute stopped by Uncle Dick's to visit. They often did.

The Ute loved to wager. Dick said he never knew "any Indians, at least none of the roving tribes, who were not inveterate gamblers."[176] The Ute told Dick they were on their way to race horses with the white men in Trinidad. Their horses were so fast they were sure they were going to "win heap bets."[177] Dick tried to persuade them not to go. He figured they'd win, all right; they had fine horses. But Dick knew how those horse races went. The Ute had a tendency to be hot-tempered. Sooner or later, there'd be trouble. Nah, the Chief promised him they'd be on their best behavior. They wouldn't argue with anyone.

And they didn't—at first. For several days things went well. The Indians did win big. Then there was some argument. Ute reaction scared Trinidad folks. They had no military protection in town, but called for Major Alexander, who came with a company. He talked to the Ute; they weren't interested. Alexander and his soldiers notified settlers in surrounding areas they better come to town for protection. They warned Dick. He thanked them, but said he'd best stay and mind his place.

Chief Conniach

The Ute were camped along the Purgatoire River, near a Mexican settlement a couple miles from town. One morning about ten, the Ute accused the Mexicans of sealing some of their fine horses. The Ute had nothing on the Mexicans when it came to quick tempers. One Mexican shot and killed a Ute. That was it. War. The Ute sent their women and children into the mountains.

Major Alexander and his soldiers rode out to quiet things down. The Ute opened fire, killed some soldiers, wounded others. Soldiers returned fire; the Ute retreated into the mountains.

---

[176] Conard, 1890, 139, 140. Dick added, "Drunkenness was quite as much a besetting sin of the Indians as gambling. I never saw one who didn't drink rum, and some of them had liquors of their own before any were brought into the country by 'Whites.'…Some tribes… drank much more than others,"
[177] *Ibid.*, 454.

Two Ute went to Uncle Dick to tell him how unfairly they'd been treated in Trinidad. They threatened to call in the whole Ute tribe to ride for revenge.

Lucien Maxwell, who'd been especially kind to the Ute in the past, heard of the situation and sent word to Kit Carson, in charge of Ft. Garland. Carson wasted no time. On the way he met Major Alexander in pursuit of the Indians and persuaded him to return to Trinidad. One company of soldiers would be no match for the Ute that had gathered.

Carson went to the Ute, listened intently. He understood their language, spoke it fluently. Chief Conniach and other chiefs among the group agreed to go down to Maxwell's at Cimarron City. They'd talk things over. Maxwell sent for Wootton to join them. Carson and he rode down to Maxwell's to see what could be done. Maxwell "friend of the Ute" had given them horses once before. He gave them ponies again. Communication coupled with the gift helped quell the anger—especially the gift.

Battle of Beecher Island
(Battle of the Arickaree)

In the annals of the Western frontier Uncle Dick was considered second only to Kit Carson as an Indian fighter. On an individual basis, however, each had countless friends among Indians. While both men truly did fight, they were also called upon to settle disputes. And they did, with an aim and preference to settle matters without bloodshed.

Miguel Otero and his father knew Uncle Dick well:

As a frontiersman, Uncle Dick was much on the order of Kit Carson. Both of them stood in the highest esteem with the Indians and were regarded by them always as good friends, but both had their eyes well opened to the Indian character and could not be taken in. They knew how little reliance could be placed upon the word of an Indian, especially when mischief was lurking in the back of his head, and they seemed to know almost intuitively how far to trust their red friend.[178]

Dick and other old-timers said, "The only good Indian is a dead Indian." They referred to good as pertaining to integrity or morality. That opinion developed from narrow escapes and from involvement in others' experiences.[179] Dick saw firsthand the way tribes treated one another and maintained that, at the rate they were going, Indians would've killed each other off if white men hadn't come along.[180]

Mountain men had favorite tribes. Dick especially liked Arapaho and Cheyenne, but he also got along very well with the Ute. Those tribes continued to visit Uncle Dick at his Raton Pass home as long as they were in the country.

One day in 1868 Arapaho Chief Roman Nose stopped by Dick's with a band of warriors. He let Uncle Dick know that he'd traveled out of his way just to see him. The warriors spent the day at the Pass, while Dick and Roman Nose talked over old times. Roman Nose wanted to know what had become of some of their old friends, the trappers and traders of bygone years.

Roman Nose and his warriors left Dick's Raton Pass home and traveled north. It wasn't long before they were involved in the Battle of Beecher Island.

The previous fall—1867, the same fall as the Trinidad War—a band of Cheyenne and Arapaho had gone into eastern Colorado with letters given them at a U. S. peace treaty. Although the letters declared them peaceful, they attacked and killed settlers on Bijou and Kiowa Creeks. From there they rode though Ute Pass to South Park and killed several Ute— their traditional enemy—along the way. They stole livestock in Colorado City and killed

---

[178] Otero, 142.

[179] Some of Dick's experiences: a fellow trapper dying from a poisoned arrow; thievery, massacre, kidnapping in the Pueblo area; mutilated bodies—including Mrs. White's warm, arrow-pierced body; friend Bill Williams' death at the hands of the tribe he'd lived among.

[180] One instance: Indian raids about wiped out the Indians at Pecos, New Mexico; they'd had to abandon their pueblo and join another.

some settlers along Monument Creek.

Because troops weren't available in that area, repeated appeals were sent to General Phil Sheridan at Ft. Leavenworth, Kansas. Sheridan was in charge of the U. S. Military in Missouri, Arkansas, Kansas, Colorado, New Mexico, and Indian Territory.

The U. S. government had granted Indians' request for guns and ammunition for hunting, but the rifles were used to attack settlers and travelers and to fight soldiers sent for protection.

In March 1868 President Johnson had signed orders to close three forts on the Bozeman Trail; the U. S. arranged a peace treaty with area Indians on April 29. Soldiers left Bozeman Trail forts in August. Indians then demolished the facilities and controlled the trail.

Meanwhile, the Cheyenne became infuriated when the Kansas Pacific Railroad laid tracks further and further across buffalo country in western Kansas (summer 1868). They hindered rail progress and attacked Nebraska and Kansas settlements until General Sheridan stepped in. He authorized Colonel George A. Forsythe, a member of his staff, to select fifty scouts for temporary service.

Forsythe chose seasoned men—Civil War veterans, scouts, and trappers—to begin service on August 29, 1868. Forsythe and his scouts left Ft. Hayes and rode to Ft. Wallace, the western terminus of the Kansas Pacific Railroad. At Ft. Wallace, Forsythe received Sheridan's order to pursue raiders who had attacked a freight train about thirteen miles east of Ft. Wallace. He searched six days with no results.

On the evening of September 16, 1868, Forsythe and his scouts camped in a valley on the middle fork of the Republican River. In the middle of the river was a small island with a few trees. Surrounded by low bluffs, the valley was about two miles wide and two miles long. At daybreak, scouts spotted a single warrior. In no time at all, warriors daubed with war paint swarmed the place. Drums beat. Gourds rattled. War whoops broke the morning stillness.

Chief Roman Nose—over 6'3", weighing 230 pounds—rode forefront on a large chestnut horse. His 1,000 warriors outnumbered the scouts twenty to one. In his report, Colonel Forsythe described Roman Nose.

Save for a crimson silk sash knotted around his waist and his moccasins on his feet, [he was] perfectly naked….[His face was:] hideously painted in lines of red and black, and his head crowned with a magnificent war bonnet, from which just above his temples and curving slightly forward, stood up two black buffalo horns, while its ample length of eagle's feathers and heron's plumes trailed wildly on the wind behind him; and as he came swiftly on the head of charging warriors, in all his barbaric strength and grandeur, he proudly rode that day the most perfect type of a savage warrior it has been my lot to see …he drew his body to its full height and shook his clinched fist defiantly at us; then throwing back his head and glancing skyward, he suddenly struck the palm of his hand across his mouth and gave tongue to a war-cry that I have never heard equaled in power and intensity.[181]

Under cover of their best marksmen, the scouts headed for the small island, quickly dug trenches, and killed their pack mules for cover.

Forsythe received three wounds early in the battle, but continued to command. Lt.

---

[181] *Rocky Mountain News*, Centennial Edition 1959, 10E.

Fredrick H. Beecher,[182] second in command, was mortally wounded the first day. While helping the wounded, Surgeon John H. Mooers received his death wound the first day and died the second. There was no other skilled help for the wounded.

Chief Roman Nose reformed his line and attacked again and again and again—five times. During the fifth attack one ball hit and killed him. His warriors became disconcerted. Nearby, squaws began a death wail. Warriors rescued Roman Nose's body from the water, retreated, and changed tactics—wait. In time, soldiers would have to surrender or starve.

Forsythe realized their plight. Their only hope was to get word to Ft. Wallace. Seventeen-year-old Jack Stilwell and trapper Pierre Trudeau made moccasins out of their boot tops. In the darkness that night, they snuck out of camp and slipped away from the Indian encampment. They walked backwards along the riverbed in case an Indian should find their tracks. They did reach help, but Forsythe had no way of knowing. The next night he sent two more men. Four hours later they returned, unable to slip through.

On the third day, soldiers took heart when they noticed the Indian women and children leave; but they soon realized the warriors intended to remain on guard. Trapped on the island, soldiers ate their dead horses and dug in the sand for water.

On the fourth day, suffering with the ball in his thigh, Forsythe asked his men to cut out the ball. They refused. He dug it out himself.

On September 23—the seventh day—one soldier shot a coyote; the scouts enjoyed fresh meat. The next day Forsythe encouraged any of the men who could, to escape. None left. They wouldn't forsake the wounded. Someone found wild plums and shared them.

On the ninth day Forsythe's personal friend Captain Louis H. Carpenter, his seventy Buffalo Soldiers of the Tenth Cavalry, Lt. Banzhaf, and Lt. Orleman arrived with surgeon Dr. Fitzgerald. They brought an ambulance and a supply wagon. When the Indians spotted the rescue party, they packed up and cleared out.

On the tenth day Colonel Bankhead arrived from Ft. Wallace with a one-hundred-man reinforcement troop, a surgeon, and two howitzers. Transporting the wounded in the ambulance, Carpenter's, Bankhead's, and Forsythe's troops made the four-day journey back to Ft. Wallace.

The island on which Forsythe's Scouts took their stand was named Beecher Island in honor of Lt. Fredrick Beecher, who, with five others, was buried on the island.

---

[182] A nephew of Henry Ward Beecher, Fredrick was a veteran of Gettysburg.

Buffalo Soldiers
New Mexico

Goodbye, Old Friends

On May 23, 1868, Dick lost his friend Kit Carson. They'd met in the fall of 1837 and trapped together along many streams. In recent years, they met more often in passing: Kit's work had turned to aiding the military, Dick's to private enterprise. Sister Blandina Segale wrote:

> these men have been intelligent guides to avoid warring with the roving Indian Tribes. Kit Carson was, for a time, General Fremont's 'Power behind the throne' in scouting and guiding over the trails,...Mr. Wooten [sic] is an entirely different character from Mr. Carson.... Mr. Carson is astute and daring Mr. Wooten is kind hearted and depends much on luck as he terms it. I am acquainted with all his children....[183]

WHERE THE FAMOUS KIT CARSON DIED, ON MAY 23, 1868

Kit, not yet fifty-nine, died in Boggsville, Colorado, as a result of an old injury. His wife, Josefa, had died less than a month before. They left their minor children with Tom Boggs and Rumalda, his wife—Josefa's niece.

In his lifetime Carson attempted to help reconcile the U. S. and Indians. Years after his death, some questioned some of his actions while he served the U. S. military. Mistakes were made and the armchair diagnosticians have come forth with many ways that might have worked better. It should not be forgotten, however, that the Army was not the maker of policy, but merely the instrument of its execution. Just as in years previous, and in years later, the military and lawmakers occasionally disagree on policy, the fact remains that the government, and not the military, determines the national policy.[184]

The summer after Kit's death, raids continued. Indians raided settlements near Plum Creek and Cache la Poudre River (Colorado). Comanche and Kiowa attacked Ft. Dodge (Kansas). On June 10th, General Sherman traveled through Trinidad to visit northern Colorado military posts.

On July 11th, the government began a new survey of the Colorado-New Mexico border. It took a little over a month. Rumor was that the upper Las Animas River and Wootton's place on Raton Pass might end up in New Mexico. If that happened, Las Animas County would lose at least 200 residents. On August 27, 1868, the *Pueblo Chieftain* was happy to report that

---

[183] Segale, *End of the Santa Fe Trail*, 100.
[184] Hart, *Old Fort*, 6.

Las Animas County wouldn't lose the land a mile or two south of Uncle Dick's place.

In the same issue the *Chieftain* reported a letter from an individual at Bent's Fort, which told of Indian attacks along the Smoky Hill Route. Indians killed twelve families near Harker and went on up the road killing any small parties with whom they came in contact.

On August 30, 1868, Captain Penrose of Ft. Lyon reported the country is "overrun with hostile Indians" from Ft. Dodge to Ft. Lyon, from there to Denver, and in the Smoky Hill region. He and his soldiers were doing what they could, but he didn't have a cavalry unit.

On October 9th, Indians captured Clara Blinn and her two-year-old son, Willie, east of Ft. Lyon. After that, Cheyenne and their allies moved south to winter near the Washita River. People could then travel between Ft Wallace and Ft. Lyon without fear.

With the influx of settlers, times were changing in the Southwest. Some people came to prospect, others to settle, to homestead, to ranch or farm. All sorts of people came: learned and unlearned, honest and dishonest, settlers and the unsettling. In the midst of the changing populace were Spanish, Mexicans, Indian tribes, and a few traders and mountain men, each with its own way of life. It was a time of unsettling settlement, the infant stage of a new era in the West.

Political folks along the Potomac remembered Manifest Destiny. They made more treaties with Indians: Navajos in New Mexico, survivors of Sand Creek in Colorado, Medicine Lodge Treaty, Ft. Laramie Treaty…Options began to wear out. The U. S. had dealt with Indians in the East long before they attempted to deal with Indians in the West. In the winter of 1868-69, the Army waged a relentless winter campaign, forcing many Plains Indians onto reservations. It didn't snuff out all trouble immediately, but slowed it way down.

While the U. S. worked on peace in the West, it continued to deal with postwar pains. In December 1868 President Johnson pulled the tablecloth down on his head again. On Christmas day he proclaimed amnesty for all Confederates involved in the Civil War. All, of course, included former president of the Confederacy, Jefferson Davis. He'd been arrested May 10, 1865, indicted for treason in 1866, and released on bail in 1867. His trial had begun in early December 1868. As it was, President Johnson and his Congress hadn't seen eye to eye on many occasions. Even public sentiment wasn't completely with Johnson on this one. Some said he didn't have the right to pardon Davis. But Davis was pardoned.[185]

In early May 1869 William Bent came by Dick's. He was heading east with his spring train and had come up across the toll road. He left Dick's and continued on past Bent's Old Fort, on to his Stone Fort on the Purgatory. When he arrived, his daughter Mary realized he was very sick and sent for the doctor from Ft. Lyon. Pneumonia, the doctor said. There was nothing he could do. William died at home on May 19th.

William Bent's obituary in the *Pueblo Chieftain* estimated he left a fortune of $150,000-$200,000. But William and his brother Charles and their partner, Ceran St. Vrain, left a legacy to the Plains and the Mountains and to the United States that cannot be measured in dollars. It cannot be measured. They were honest men in a hard land. They paved paths for individuals, tribes, the nation and civilization, provided refuge, set standards, and gave a foothold of opportunity to countless others in their time.

---

[185] Davis' citizenship would not be restored until 1978.

A New Road and a New Home

Little-by-little railheads moved farther west. A railhead reached Sheridan, Kansas, in May 1868. In June the Southern Overland Mail & Express Company made Pond Creek, Kansas, it headquarters.

Uncle Dick realized the opportunity. "What distinguished him from other brave men of that era was what his contemporaries described as 'a shrewd eye for a swap.' Wootton had a talent for business."[186] Uncle Dick with George McBride formed the Kit Carson & Ft. Union Bridge Company.

From Kit Carson, Colorado, they built a road south to within a few miles north of Big Sandy Station, southwest toward Big (Gageby) Creek, south to Bent's Old Fort. Five miles above the fort, they built the first bridge over the Arkansas River. It was an ordinary wooden bridge at the site of King's Ferry. Across the bridge, the road continued seven miles to the area of present-day La Junta, Colorado. Wootton and McBride intended the road to be used primarily as a freight road to provide freighters easier access to the railhead. Toll charges were:

    $ .75: One wagon and one span of animals; each extra horse
    $ .25: One man and horse
    $ .10: One person on foot; per head of loose stock
    $ .50: Bridge toll in fair weather, $1.00 during high water

Uncle Dick advertised the road as the shortest route between Kit Carson, Colorado, and Ft. Union, New Mexico. It cut sixty-two miles off the distance between the two—about four days' travel time. Wootton and McBride operated the bridge five years—1868-1873.

By December 1869, the railhead reached Kit Carson, Colorado. There, about 300 people lived in tents while eight buildings were being framed. In March 1870, the stage company moved its office to Kit Carson and branched a road south to Ft. Lyon. Freighters continued to drive supply wagons to Ft. Union and Santa Fe.

With his toll roads established, Dick turned his attention to enlarging his home on Raton Pass. From outside appearances, his new home was Southern through and through, complete with a veranda across the front. The walls, however, were 30" thick adobe. The fourteen-room addition to his original house included a public room downstairs and a ballroom upstairs. Dick carried his décor—guns, animal horns, heads, and skins—from his former public room into the new addition and set up a welcome place for all who stopped.

When the home was almost complete, Dick hosted a party. Pleased to have enough space for a large group, he invited folks from all over the surrounding area to a dance in the new ballroom. During intermission, the fiddlers stepped outside. There were few two-story homes in the area. The fiddlers either forgot they were on the second floor or that the veranda hadn't

---

[186] Curtis, "The Exit to Wootton."

been built. They made a swift descent onto a pile of shavings twelve feet below. One landed on the shavings. The other had the added cushion of his fellow musician.

On May 10, 1869, the Union Pacific and Central Pacific railroads linked the nation with the first transcontinental railroad. Crowds gathered at Promontory Point, Utah, to see the gold spike hammered in to mark the junction.

The First Pacific Railway

Military telegraph between Ft. Leavenworth and Santa Fe were completed July 8th.[187] A few days later the Cheyenne Dog Soldiers fought their last united battle.

---

[187] Transcontinental telegraph lines had replaced the need for the Pony Express and put it out of business back in 1861.

Battle of Summit Springs

July 11, 1869, was hot and windy in northeastern Colorado. With the help of Pawnee scouts, General Eugene A. Carr's 300-man cavalry searched for Mrs. Maria Weichell and Mrs. Susanna Alderdice. About three o'clock that Sunday afternoon General Carr's 5th Cavalry surprised Tall Bull and about 500 Cheyenne Dog Soldiers at their camp approximately fourteen miles southeast of Sterling, Colorado. [188]

Mrs. Maria Weichell, a young lady—about twenty—from Germany, and Mrs. Susanna Alderdice, a twenty-eight-year-old mother expecting her fifth child, had been abducted from their homes near Lincoln, Kansas, during a Dog Soldier raid on May 30th. Dog Soldiers killed Maria's husband, but Susanna's husband wasn't home. They forced Susanna to watch them kill her sons, ages five and a half, four, and two.[189] They took Maria and Susanna and her daughter, Alice, captive.

Susannah's husband and brother had been with Forsythe's Scouts at Beecher Island the previous summer. When her husband returned home, he pursued the warriors and found his eight-month-old Alice strangled to death with a bow string. Because of her crying, Dog Soldiers killed her three days after the capture. Mr. Alderdice informed the military; General Carr took immediate action.

When General Carr surprised the Dog Soldier encampment, Susanna and Maria were at opposite ends of the camp. When Indians caught sight of the soldiers, they shot Maria in the back. The bullet deflected off a bone into her breast. She didn't die. Susanna, who'd been required to live in Tall Bull's lodge, was shot above the eye. To be sure she died, one of Tall Bull's squaws tomahawked Susanna's head and crushed her skull.

The battle was fast and furious. The trumpet charged at 3 p.m.; the battle was over about 6 p.m. Soldiers killed at least fifty-two Dog Soldiers, but most of them escaped. The dead included Tall Bull, Black Sun, Heavy Furred Wolf, Powder Face, White Rock, Big Gip, Lone Bear and Pile of Bones. The cavalry captured seventeen women and children and rescued Maria Weichell. An arrow grazed one soldier, but no soldiers died. After the battle, lightning and thunder filled the sky. A thunderstorm drenched everyone and everything.

The next morning soldiers buried Susanna, torched the Indian lodges, and destroyed everything the Dog Soldiers left behind. They took Mrs. Weichell to Fort Sedgwick (about a mile from Julesburg, Colorado), where she received medical treatment for the next three weeks. Through a German-English interpreter, she described what happened to her and to Susanna during the past six weeks. Through tears she detailed the abuse.

Remnants of the Dog Soldier band continued to attack settlers for years to come, but this battle marked the end of the Dog Soldiers as a united military force.

---

[188] Mostly Cheyenne, some Sioux and a few Arapaho, Dog Soldier warriors had become a group unto themselves.
[189] Willis Alderdice, age four, lived awhile after his mother was taken.

This 'n That, 1869-1871

Trinidad, Colorado, was an up and coming town by 1869. Uncle Dick's son-in-law William Walker and a partner built a sawmill six miles from town on the Animas River that summer. Later in the year Dick's son R. L., Jr. opened a general store in town.

Because his business was regulated by Colorado and New Mexico Territories, the government controlled Uncle Dick's toll charges and collected their share from him. In 1869 the Las Animas County Commission reduced toll rates on the Colorado side; so Dick raised the toll on the New Mexico side. If New Mexico interfered with his business, he did business on the Colorado side.

Not everyone appreciated his road. That is, they appreciated the road, but not the toll charge. Toll roads were common in the eastern United States, but people who lived in the West or who traveled westward sometimes took exception to the idea of being charged. "The West" was considered free open space which belonged to no one in particular and to everyone in general. Nevertheless, Dick had built the road and intended to collect for his effort. About a thousand feet below the summit, his chain gated the road; and he collected his fee. Anyone who passed without paying could be fined twenty-five dollars; but a firm word or an upheld club saved travelers—and Dick—the time and expense of going to court.

The behavior of some seemed to imply that Uncle Dick and his employees should stay on the mountain and keep the road ready for them without charge. Dick said patrons always came to an understanding about the toll. Although he allowed Indians to travel without charge, many of them seemed to understand that he'd made passage more convenient. They stopped to thank him for letting them use his road. Occasionally one would give him a gift.

Freighters, stage drivers, and military personnel were glad to have the improved road. Mexicans, however, considered tolls highway robbery. They:

> did not take kindly to the idea, looking upon the tollgate as a scheme for robbery;...the Mexican majority in the territorial [New Mexico] legislature, in response to the popular native demand for the free use of its noted toll road, twice endeavored by enactment to put an end to the collection of toll. On February 1, 1872, the legislature passed an act declaring that 'Any charter may be held by one Richard [sic] Wootton over any portion of the Trinidad and Raton Mountain road, running from Red river to the town of Trinidad in the Territory of Colorado, and passing by the house of said Richard Wootton, was not to be received as evidence of the existence nor as the charter of any corporation or company, and the said charter, or so-called charter, is hereby declared void and of no effect, and the said road is hereby declared to be a public road of this Territory and subject to the statutes concerning territorial or public roads.' In spite of this legislation, Mr. Wootton continued to collect toll[190]

W. R. Thomas writing for the *Rocky Mountain News*, April 12, 1870, described his recent ride across Raton Pass in a Barlow & Sanderson stagecoach: The stage followed a winding

---

[190] *History of New Mexico*, 106.

road before it entered a narrow canyon. After passing the "devil's gate," the stage began a long slow ascent up the mountain. Reaching the crest at sunset, passengers caught a glimpse of Raton Peak, Spanish Peaks, and Greenhorn Mountain to the north. The stage descended rapidly for two miles and arrived at Uncle Dick's stage station, where they traded the tired mule team for a fresh team. Thomas said the road was well-maintained and that in good weather, with a change of teams at Wootton's, a stagecoach could average up to nine miles an hour traveling the toll road over the Pass.

Kid Barton and his gang brought a Barlow & Sanderson stage to a halt on Raton Pass. They shot and killed the express manager and two passengers and carried off about $60,000. A large posse tailed them to eastern New Mexico (Tucumcari area). Rather than surrender, Barton shot it out with the posse. After he killed a sheriff and two deputies, the posse didn't bother to haul in the Kid. They knew where a bridge was; they hung him off of that.

Colorado laws note a Certificate of Incorporation was issued February 1, 1870, to the Ratoun [sic] Wagon Road Company of Wooten [sic] Ranch. Corporate officers were George McBride, Guadalupe Lujan and Jose Louis Dillette. Each man was related to Dick's first wife, Dolores.[191]

Most of New Mexico's Spanish and Mexican Archives were lost in spring 1870. Governor William Anderson Pyle, member of the Santa Fe Ring, said he sold them as waste paper.[192] On April 23, New Mexico Territory Judge Kirby Benedict reported the loss to President Ulysses Grant and recommended the President remove Pyle from office.

Even with a little conflict with the government and a few patrons, it was better that Dick was no longer farming in the Fountain Valley. In 1867 corn prices there had dropped to three cents a pound. Farmers kept their corn, rather than give it away at that price. From 1873-78 grasshoppers hopped into Kansas and Colorado, chewed up crops, and spit out farmers' hopes.

Jay Gould and James Fisk, Jr. attempted to corner the U. S. gold market on Black Friday, September 24, 1869, and thrust the nation into a financial emergency. To steady the price of gold, the U. S. Treasury put $4,000,000 of gold on the market. Gould and Fisk cleared about $11,000,000.

Uncle Dick's youngest brother Joseph, who'd been with him at Ft. Barclay and in Denver, died in Kentucky in 1870.[193] In October Dick's longtime friend Ceran St. Vrain died in Mora, New Mexico. Ceran was sitting on his own porch, smoking a cigar when he suffered a stroke—more than twenty-three years after his close calls during the Taos Revolt.

For many years the U. S. government had spent a lot of manpower and money in unsuccessful attempts to make peace with Indians. On March 3, 1871, the Indian Appropriation Act nullified all previous Indian treaties and declared Indians wards of the government. The government "dictated that the United States Army would clear the way

---

[191] Like McBride, Lujan was married to a cousin (nee Maria de la Luz Dillette) of Dolores, Dick's first wife.
[192] Though Dick had obtained permission under American rule, it is little wonder the original record was not found in Santa Fe.
[193] Joseph was survived by his wife, Mollie Wootton, and little daughters, Mary Elizabeth and Phoebe Eugenia.

westward. Between 1850 and 1890 this was what the Army did, undermanned, underpaid, and under-recognized."[194]

In the Midwest, on October 8, 1871, Chicago, Illinois, burst into flames. It'd been a dry summer. Since the 4th of July, Chicago had only had about a quarter of its usual rainfall. The story passed down through time says Mrs. Patrick O'Leary's cow kicked over a lantern, which ignited a fire in the barn. Wind whipped the flames from southeast to northwest Chicago, destroying the downtown district and many homes. Flames blazed more than twenty-four hours, killed about 300 people, and left 90,000 homeless.

---

[194] Hart, 6.

Back at the Ranch

Meanwhile, back at the Wootton Ranch, Uncle Dick tended the toll road, stage stop, and inn at his Raton Pass home. He employed several on road and grounds maintenance. Among those he employed was Jose Luis Dillette, a cousin of Dick's first wife, Dolores. Dick knew the whole family, including Luis' sister, Luz. Her children were about the age of Dick's oldest children.

Dick's daughter Dolores, her husband, Brigham, and their three children lived nearby. Eliza, her husband, Judge Walker, and their daughters were in Trinidad. R. L., Jr. had a ranch and a little mercantile business just over the state line in Colfax County, New Mexico. The three younger boys, Joseph, fifteen; William, thirteen; and Frank, eleven, lived at home. Seven-year-old Fanny was with Dr. Burt and his wife.

A week before Christmas, on December 18, 1871, Dick married Luis Dillette's niece Mary Pauline Lujan, daughter of Guadalupe and Luz Lujan. Their witnesses were Paula Trujillo and Prudencio Lujan. Mary Pauline was four years older than her mother had been when she married, but she wouldn't be seventeen until January 25.

R. L., Jr. moved back to Trinidad in 1872 and married Florence Walker. Before her death in 1877, they had three children; but each predeceased her. He had no other children.

On September 20, 1872, Dick and Mary Pauline's first child, Fidelis, "Dellie," was born. On the day before her first birthday, "Black Friday" brought America's financial boom to a screeching halt and began the Panic of 1873. But the Woottons had already had their own black day with the death of thirteen-year-old Frank. George had died by 1870.[195] At some time Frank's or George's leg was amputated. The surgery was done on the dining room table in the hall of the Wootton house on the Pass. There was no anesthetic. The family record passed down did not say if the amputation contributed to death or if the surgery had been performed some time before.

As is the case with death, life goes on for others. In their own world, inventors Jacob Haish and Joseph Glidden argued over the patent for barb wire. Glidden eventually won. Hailed by some and resisted by others, his wire contributed to the transformation of the western cattle range, ending open cattle ranges in the West. Some men considered any open range free for their use and resisted fenced farms and ranches that limited grazing rights.

Late in 1873 Alfred Packer led twenty men from Salt Lake into the San Juan Mountains, a good way west of Dick's place. They arrived at Ute Chief Ouray's camp on the Uncompahgre River (Colorado). Ouray told the men the snow at that time would make the journey too dangerous. He knew the mountains. He knew the snow. Ten men understood and remained behind. Ten others divided into two groups of five each and continued on. Packer led one group.

---

[195] George died before the new Catholic cemetery was established in 1872; his sister Eliza had his body moved from the original Catholic cemetery to the new one.

Quite some time later Packer returned to Los Piños Indian Agency, near Chief Ouray's camp. He reported his five men abandoned him. But Chief Ouray knew the country and the conditions. He said Packer was too fat to have endured the hardships he reported. Packer had possessions that belonged to some of the men who "deserted"; plus, his stories contradicted.

Changing his story, Packer claimed the oldest man died of starvation: the others had to eat him. Maintaining innocence, Packer explained how the others died and were eaten. Investigation showed that one of the five was shot; the skulls of the others were crushed. The flesh of four was stripped.

Legend tells that, when Packer was sentenced to forty years in prison, the judge exclaimed, "Packer, you depraved Republican…, there were only five Democrats in Hinsdale County, and you ate them all!"[196]

In February (1874) Dellie's sister Ida Dillon Wootton was born—Dick and Mary Pauline's second child. The girls looked much like their mother's Spanish-French line though Dellie would resemble her father's Scotch-English as she aged.

The Wootton home was a gathering place for young people and old friends. Dick and Mary hosted "grand fiestas" for friends. Dick enjoyed people of all ages and stations of life. His years trading, storekeeping, toll tending, and inn keeping gave him opportunity to be with people. He enjoyed hosting people in his home. Invited or uninvited, extras were always welcome.

Not every encounter was friendly. There were times, at the tollgate, some objected to payment to the point that Uncle Dick would call out, "Ma, bring my toll collector." Mary Pauline would walk out the front door carrying Dick's rifle. The size of rifles in the late 1800's was impressive; he never used the rifle for more than appearance in collecting tolls. Occasionally, near the Colorado-New Mexico border, an individual can still be found, indignant because of the exorbitant tolls the individual believes Dick charged.

Some didn't like Uncle Dick; some did. In his youth, Miguel Otero, who became a New Mexico governor, was well-acquainted with the Woottons. In later years he told of the days when he was often a guest in their home:

> Uncle Dick was a fine old man, always kind and gentle, and as hospitable as a Southern colonel. When dances were given at his home, and the fun was over, which meant either broad daylight or at least sun-up, we would have a good breakfast before starting home, and the last words of Uncle Dick to us would invariably be, 'Now, boys and girls, come out here whenever you like. Just send me word and I'll arrange everything, even the music. All you have to do is to get your conveyance and land right here with me. I'll do the rest.' On these parties we were always careful to observe the conventions, and would have several married couples along to act as chaperons. The atmosphere at Uncle Dick's parties was always wholesome and above criticism, for he was a stickler for the proprieties."[197]

Many people came to camp or have picnics on Dick's place in the scenic Raton Mountains. He often stopped to visit with them.

Most evenings the Woottons had guests in their stage stop inn. In the evenings Uncle Dick

---

[196] Lee, *Colorado, A Literary Chronicle*, 283.
[197] Otero, *My Life on the Frontier*, 141, 142.

visited with them. Sitting cross-legged, smoking his pipe, he listened to their adventures and told of his. A wide variety of guests came—from the Vice President of the United States to men who proved to be ordinary horse thieves. Dick invited some to leave.

One day in August or September 1877, 6'3" Phil Schneider and his partner, "Happy Jack," stopped by Dick's. They'd scared some of the good townsfolk down in Cimarron (New Mexico) with their drinking and shooting. Then they began to argue with one another. They'd been at each other's throat three days by the time they crossed Raton Pass and sat down to dinner at Dick's table. Each man ate with his left hand. Each kept his gun hand free. When each thought the other wasn't watching, they shot each other. "Happy Jack" hit Schneider in the thigh, but Schneider's lead pierced "Happy Jack's" breast. Schneider got a ride into Trinidad. He hung on several weeks, but took a turn for the worse and died. Pretty bad turn.

Another time five men, a lady, and child arrived in an arrow pierced stage. With arrows stuck in all directions, the stage looked like a pincushion. Comanche had waited to attack them in an area beyond military escort. Once attack began, the driver drove hard and didn't stop until he reached Dick's place.

Some Trinidad youth

Last Buffalo Hunt

The U. S. Government had tried to stop Comanche raids, but the Comanche and Kiowa were mighty warriors. The Army had retreated in the initial battle of the Red River War (1874). War continued. The great Comanche Chief Quanah Parker and his Quahadi band held out until June 1875, when they surrendered at Ft. Sill (Oklahoma). (A year later, in June 1876, General Custer and his men were no match for Sioux at the Montana Battle of the Little Bighorn. Sioux killed Custer's entire unit; the Army sent more soldiers to Montana.)

With no Comanche threat in the Texas Panhandle, hide hunters came for the buffalo. In 1874 a community grew up at Adobe Walls to supply hide hunters. By April 1874, two stores, a restaurant, a blacksmith, and a saloon were in business. In early years of western settlement buffalo were plentiful even when natural disasters killed many.[198] But hide hunters, who came in the 1870's, came close to wiping them out. They had found a ready market in the clothing industry. It's estimated that hide hunters killed over one and a half million buffalo for the hides.

When Uncle Dick heard there were buffalo in the Panhandle of Texas, he went down. He still hunted meat for his family and his inn, but he usually hunted nearby.

Times had changed. Dick found the buffalo temperamental from being overhunted. Temperamental? Did Dick think an old bull was temperamental just because, after Dick wounded him, the bull got up and chased him?

Dick shot the bull, set down his rifle, picked up his skinning knife, and walked to within ten feet of the wounded bull before he realized it was still alive. The bull stirred, got up, and chased him to the edge of a ravine. There was no time for Dick to retrieve his rifle, call for help, or run for his horse. He lunged for a tree growing out of the edge of the ravine and hung on. The bull stood at the base of the tree, pawing the ground—not in the best humor. Eventually Dick was able to get down into the ravine, skirt around and out. The boy who came with him brought Dick's horse and rifle; so he could finish the job. The boy and he loaded the wagon with meat and headed home.

---

[198] While hunting at St. Mary's in 1863, Judge Bradford's son Tom Bradford saw a large area near Pueblo strewn with buffalo skeletons. He found no live buffalo. Tabejuache Indians explained that a big storm had killed them many years ago, and there had been none in the area since then.

With miles of time to think, Dick decided this would be his last buffalo hunt. As long as Indians and old-timers hunted buffalo for meat it hadn't seemed to diminish the herds, but Dick realized hide hunters had changed all that. He arrived home a bit nostalgic. His sons Joseph and William teased him, said they thought they saw a tear in his eye when he told of the diminishing buffalo herds.

Roaming Indians were also scarce. More and more were moved to reservations. The Ute were still around and visited Dick often. They were his nearest neighbors in the Raton Mountains until they were placed on a reservation in 1878. They'd sometimes come over to Dick's and challenge him to a marksmanship contest—always for stakes. When little Ida would see them coming, she'd run to her Daddy. Dick would pick her up and put her on his shoulders as he visited with them. Somehow the Indians didn't seem quite as scary when she looked down from her perch on his shoulders.

Chief Conniach tried his marksmanship repeatedly, but those heavy bulky rifles took a lot of handling before firing them became second nature. He'd challenge Uncle Dick. After a few rounds with Dick, he'd sometimes challenge one of Dick's sons. When bested, Conniach was ready to go again for more stakes: five buckskins to five Mexican silver dollars. Dick didn't want to take any payment. He tried to find a way to return the old man's stakes; but Chief Conniach was adamant: it was his Ute honor to pay his debt.

Dick had taught his children to shoot at a young age, as he and many mountain men had learned. They became accustomed to shooting heavy weapons quickly and accurately, even from their mounts. In time, Indians became skilled marksmen. When they first learned to use rifles, some carried a rod or two. They'd set a rod upright on the ground and steady the rifle on it. They'd hold the rod with one hand, aim and fire with the other.

Ute Rebellion and Meeker Massacre 1878

In 1868 the U. S. Senate had ratified a treaty which provided two Ute agencies in Colorado: the southern Ute on Rio de los Piños; the northern Yampa and Uintah bands on White River in northwestern Colorado. The Ute near Uncle Dick's Raton Pass home were southern Ute.

Over the next nine years, agents came and went at White River Agency. None were able to civilize the Ute as they hoped to do and were expected to do. White River Ute enjoyed their own lifestyle—roaming, hunting, stealing, murdering. Some held grudges against one or another of the former agents.

Nathan Cook Meeker, founder of Union Colony at Greeley, Colorado, and former agriculture editor of the *New York Tribune*, was appointed White River agent. An idealist, Meeker was certain he could teach the Ute self-sufficiency. He planned to teach all Ute to speak English and behave in a civilized manner. His wife and daughter Josephine helped; Josephine taught the children to read and write. He taught adults to farm and raise cattle.

As he'd taught easterners to irrigate and farm at Union Colony, he'd teach the Ute. Meeker looked for better terrain and found it twenty miles away. He relocated agency headquarters. Though they protested, the Ute dug two and a half miles of irrigation ditches. Some plowed and planted crops, but that was it. They would tend crops no further; they wanted to fish and hunt and roam. Meeker told them if they didn't take care of the crops, they'd have nothing to eat. Opposition broke out, but Meeker promised he wouldn't force them militarily. Violence wasn't part of his plan or person. As time wore on, Meeker's plan continued to fail. He notified his superiors he must have the help of federal troops or he'd have to resign. His superior told him to bide his time; things would work out.

Meeker persisted. His wife said he never compelled men to work, but offered them extra government goods as per diem wages. Two hundred more acres were plowed for cultivation. Soon afterward, Chief Johnson broke into Meeker's house, took him outside, and beat him.[199]

Because of the unrest, General Sheridan ordered troops for Meeker, but they were slow in coming. On September 12, 1878, warriors began a war dance in front of Meeker's home. Meeker ordered them to disband. They danced.

On September 14, 1878, Major Thomas T. Thornburg and a troop left Ft. Steele (Wyoming) with supply wagons. Indian Jack and his Ute warriors from the White River district ambushed them on September 24. They killed Thornburg and shot every officer, except Lt. Cherry. The surviving soldiers scurried to take cover behind the wagons and dead animals. In an effort to destroy the wagons and use the smoke as a cover, the Ute set fire to the grass and sagebrush. Frantically, soldiers beat at the flames and fought the fire with dirt.

At ten p. m. a scout named Rankin left to obtain help in Rawlins (Wyoming). He traveled

---

[199] Chief Johnson's oldest wife was a sister of southern Ute Chief Ouray.

the 160 miles straight through and arrived in twenty-eight hours; it usually took two days. Rankin sent couriers to various places with news of Thornburg's death. One courier left Rawlins to warn Captain Dodge and his cavalry, who were traveling from Ft. Garland, via Middle Park (Colorado). Troops gathered to form a united force under General Merritt.

Captain Francis Safford Dodge and his fifty black cavalrymen arrived first. They joined Captain Payne, who commanded the trenches.

The Ute resented the fact that "Buffalo soldiers," (black cavalrymen) were the ones who came to withstand them. One of their captives during that time described the Ute in camp: "One of their favorite amusements was to put on a Negro soldier's cap, a short coat and blue pants, and imitate the Negroes in speech and walk."[200]

General Merritt and his troop marched day and night. On their way, they stopped to help soldiers in need and to send the wounded to Rawlins. At the White River Agency, they found Meeker and nine employees, all dead. All buildings were burned. When the troop came in sight of the battlefield on Sunday morning, October 5th, they sounded trumpets and shouted.

The Ute left with captives, including Mrs. Meeker and Josephine, and held them twenty-three days. Southern Ute Chief Ouray and his wife Chipeta are credited with the captives' safe return.

Chief Ouray

Years later Mrs. Meeker said she thought the massacre was caused by misunderstandings. A former agent had purchased flour from Cheyenne speculators. The flour made the Ute sick. When Meeker became agent, he exposed those who cheated the Ute. As a result, articles were written and published that angered the Ute. They thought Meeker wrote the articles.

Another misunderstanding was that they believed that the more land they plowed, the more land they were giving up.

While Mrs. Meeker was held captive, Douglas, one of the captors, repeatedly asked why her husband had written the articles. When he understood Meeker didn't write them, he was sorry.

Mrs. Meeker thought that if Chief Ouray had not been sick with his kidneys at the time, he may have been able to prevent the massacre.

After lengthy inquiry, the U. S. government did not punish any individuals for the Rebellion, but removed the Ute from Colorado to a reservation in Utah and opened Ute lands to settlement.

Conniach and his Ute continued to live in southeastern Colorado—primarily in the Cucharas and Stonewall areas—until they were moved to Los Piños Agency in southwestern Colorado.

---

[200] Craig, *Brief History of Colorado*, 105, 106.

Not All Is Strife in the Midst of Wars

In the Eastern United States, Scotch-born Alexander Graham Bell worked on his new invention. As he prepared to test a transmitter on March 10, 1876, he spilled acid on himself and called out, "Mr. Watson, come here. I want to see you." His assistant, Thomas A. Watson, ran in. "Mr. Bell, I heard every word distinctly!"[201] The invention worked. Graham obtained a patent for the "telephone" and exhibited it at the Philadelphia Centennial Exposition in June.

The U. S. celebrated its Centennial on July 4, 1876. In 100 years it had withstood the War of 1812, fought a Civil War, weathered financial ups and downs, mourned the assassination of a president, purchased land and fought for land, adding enough land to become a nation from the Atlantic to the Pacific.

On August 1, 1876, after years of waiting, Colorado became a state. Colorado would be able to vote as a state in the upcoming presidential election. There was a slight problem with the 1876 election. Florida, Louisiana, South Carolina, and Oregon each submitted two sets of election returns. Democrats submitted returns claiming victory. Republicans submitted returns claiming victory. On December 6, the Electoral College decided: Rutherford B. Hayes would be President.

From New Mexico, miners sent more than 207,500 pounds of copper and copper ore eastward in 1874. Uncle Dick's business grew steadily. It's estimated that more than 6,600 wagons, loaded with 40,000,000 pounds of merchandise, traveled Uncle Dick's toll road in 1876.

As a child, Emma Smith of Trinidad visited the Woottons with her mother. When they arrived, the young Wootton children were entertaining themselves with cigar boxes filled with money.

In December 1876, Dick's son Joseph married, but his daughter Lucy Anne was born the following July; so Dick again had five children at home: William, eighteen, Dellie, four, Ida, three, Johnie, one, and baby Lucy. The winter Johnie was born, Dellie contracted scarlet fever. When the illness was spent, she was deaf and mute—"deaf and dumb" they called it then, with some paralysis on her right side.

In September 1877 Uncle Dick was called to testify in the Maxwell Land Grant Case. After Lucien Maxwell sold his land grant, feuds ensued and erupted into the Colfax County War in northeastern New Mexico, just south of Dick. Trouble also broke out in southern New Mexico in the Lincoln County War. That rivalry warred for years, in spite of government efforts.

---

[201] J. M. Freeman, "Telephone," *World Book Encyclopedia, Vol. 19*, 84.

Maxwell Land Grant and the Colfax County War

Lucien and Luz Maxwell had purchased Miranda's share of the Beaubien-Miranda Land Grant in 1858 for $2,745. They inherited part of her father's (Charles Beaubien) share in 1864 and purchased all remaining shares from relatives of the original owners.

Maxwell's was a dominion people dream of owning: thousands of sheep and cattle on his hills, valleys, and plains; thousands of acres under cultivation, yet utilizing only a portion of his more than one and a half million acres of land; plus gold mines. He knew there was gold on his land and kept nuggets in a pouch for his children to play with. But there were more minerals than one man or even a small group of men could mine.

When others discovered his minerals, thousands flocked to line their pockets with gold and copper in his Moreno Valley. As he leased land and sold supplies, Maxwell's wealth multiplied. Baldy Town, Elizabethtown, and Virginia City prospered and boomed on his land. Some prospectors claimed they made a thousand dollars a day. Emigrants came, saw the wide open space, and moved onto Maxwell's land as if it were their own.

To many, Maxwell's land seemed free for the taking, for whatever purpose: mining, farming, ranching. They thought if they found vacant land they had a right to build homes and create their own little farms or ranches where they chose. They made good use of the land and were apparently hurting no one. Others didn't know where actual boundaries were and had unwittingly settled on a portion of Grant land.

To complicate matters, some did indeed own land within the grant. Lucien Maxwell seldom kept record. Sometimes he recorded transactions, but just as often neither party kept written record. It was common for Maxwell to use land for barter or to pay for services. To Lucien Maxwell, as with many of his time, his word or his handshake sealed a deal. He and the other person remembered; that was enough.

With an influx of people, Maxwell foresaw trouble in trying to manage his vast domain. On January 28, 1870, Lucien Maxwell sold his Maxwell Land Grant to a group of Colorado and New Mexico investors. The new owners were informed of their toll free access over Raton Pass and took advantage of the option.

The Maxwells moved to Ft. Sumner, New Mexico. Lucien established the First National Bank of Santa Fe. He also invested in a railroad company; which didn't succeed.

New Mexico and Colorado investors who purchased the Maxwell Land Grant resold it to British investors the following year. It eventually became a Dutch concern. Though the initial investors were said to have doubled their money, the resale price was less than a dollar per acre. Cimarron in Colfax County was the New Mexico headquarters for the Maxwell Land Grant Company.

Even after the Maxwell Land Grant was sold, it continued to attracted miners and squatters. The new owners began to call on miners and settlers to account for their claims.

Lucien Maxwell died in Ft. Sumner, New Mexico, four years after he sold. He hadn't been in his grave more than six weeks when Grant officials began to investigate. To some the timing appeared advantageous. The fact that the Maxwell Land Grant Company seemed to be abetted by the notorious Santa Fe Ring was a stench in the nostrils of Colfax County residents.[202]

Determined to turn a profit, the company tried to oust all who couldn't prove their claim. Maxwell's word was as good as a legal document, but only as long as he was alive. Dick Wootton had built his road over Raton Pass on Maxwell's word. Although Maxwell had given him a quit claim deed two years later, Dick never saw the need to record it.

Cimarron residents began speaking out against the Maxwell Land Grant operation and the Santa Fe Ring. Reverend Franklin J. Tolby, Cimarron's circuit riding preacher, made no bones about his stand. He planned to do what he could to bust up the Ring. One September day in 1875 he didn't return from his circuit ride. Folks searched. On September 14, 1875, they found him in Cimarron Canyon, dead, shot in the back. It wasn't robbery. Nothing was missing. Folks figured the Santa Fe Ring killed Tolby or had it done to stop his tongue and pen.

Thirty-six-year-old Reverend Oscar Patrick McMains succeeded Tolby and counted it his personal responsibility to find Tolby's assassin.

One murder seemed to call for another. A couple weeks later a masked mob approached Cimarron Town Constable Cruz Vega, and accused him of Tolby's murder. Vega suggested Manuel Cardenas may know something, but that he himself wasn't involved. Nevertheless, that was Vega's last night. The next morning found him dangling from a telegraph pole. Vigilante rule in Colfax County was different than the vigilance committees Dick Wootton had known. This was more rule by the enraged.

Anyone who knew the New Mexican spirit knew Vega's death wouldn't be the end. One of Vega's relatives—Pancho Griego, former Santa Fe Marshall who allegedly had changed sides of the law—put out threats. He thought rancher Clay Allison was at the root of his primo's death.

On November 1, 1875, Griego walked into the St. James Hotel Saloon and began drinking with Allison. Griego decided this would be a good time to accuse Allison of lynching Vega.[203] Actually, this would be a good time to shoot Allison.

No. It wouldn't. Seeing Griego move toward his pistol, Allison drew and fired two bullets

---

[202] Headquartered in Santa Fe, the Santa Fe Ring was a group of men influential in controlling territorial events and politics. Governor Samuel Axtell, Henry Waldo, and attorney partners from Missouri: Stephen Elkins (New Mexico's Congressional delegate) and Thomas Catron (Territorial Attorney General 1869-1872) were considered influential Ring members. The question of land boundaries was at the heart of the turmoil. Spanish and Mexican governments had issued many land grants. General Kearny promised the U. S. would honor land holdings. The Santa Fe Ring stepped into the situation. Many families lost land or held on at great expense.

[203] Tennessee born Robert A. "Clay" Allison (6' 2" tall, blue eyes, wavy brown hair) homesteaded in New Mexico after gun slinging in Texas. He had a bent for alcohol, but won the respect of area ranchers because he sided with the common man or weaker person. His way of taking things into his own hands gained him notoriety in the Colfax County War. As Clay returned home with a wagon load of ranch supplies on July 1, 1887, his bum leg slipped from the brake. The wagon bolted down into an arroyo, threw him from the wagon and under its wheels. He died instantly at age forty-seven.

into Griego. That was the end of Griego.

Manuel Cardenas confessed he killed Vega for implicating him. He confessed connection with Land Grant men. As Cardenas was taken to jail, someone killed him. A couple of Grant men high-tailed it out of town.

Governor Samuel B. Axtell, of the Santa Fe Ring, dispatched cavalry from Ft. Union to insure order in Cimarron. He relocated district court from Cimarron to Taos. If anyone in Cimarron wanted to register a judicial complaint, they'd now have to travel farther to do it.

President Grant sent Lew Wallace to replace Samuel Axtell as governor. He hoped Wallace could end the southern New Mexico Lincoln County War in which the Santa Fe Ring appeared to be involved. Cimarron residents rejoiced at the news.

Two Santa Fe Ring supporters, prominent men in Cimarron, won local elections in 1875: Attorney Melvin Mills, state legislator; Dr. Robert H. Longwell, probate judge.

In 1874 the U. S. Secretary of the Interior had declared the Maxwell Land Grant to be public domain, in spite of the fact that the U. S. had promised to honor Mexican land grants. Maxwell Land Grant owners went to court—eventually, all the way to the U. S. Supreme Court.

On September 24, 1877, Dick Wootton gave his first testimony concerning Maxwell Land Grant boundaries. Other old-timers, including William Brownell, Captain Fisher, Calvin Jones, William Kroenig, Charles Williams, William Bransford, George Simpson, and Maxwell's chief man, Jesus Silva, testified.

The U. S. wanted a survey of the Grant and asked Uncle Dick and Jesus Silva to point out boundary markers to surveyors Elkins and Marmon. The 1879 survey confirmed the grant was indeed 1,714,764.93 acres (2679 sq. miles), and the U. S. Circuit Court confirmed the Maxwell Land Company's title to the entire acreage claimed.

Beyond his determination to find Tolby's assassin, O. P. McMains led a dogged effort to open the Land Grant to public settlement. He traveled to various parts of the Grant to work with settlers and continued his crusade.

In 1883 attorney Frank W. Springer represented the Maxwell Land Grant and Railway Company in Federal Court hearings in Colorado. In September, Uncle Dick again found himself among the pioneers called to testify. R. L., Jr. also testified. Many mountain men who knew the area and could have helped settle the boundary dispute were dead.

In his testimony Wootton established his credentials as one who had been well-acquainted with Maxwell, Carlos Beaubien, Cornelio Vigil, St. Vrain, Jesus Silva, Carson and the Bent brothers. He'd lived in the Raton Mountains almost twenty years, but had been well-acquainted with the country for over forty years.

He testified that in February or March of 1843, shortly after the land had been granted, he was with a group of men when they erected a monument on Chicorica Mesa to mark the border of the Carlos Beaubien-Guadalupe Miranda Grant, later known as the Maxwell Land Grant.

Dick further testified that, when a survey was called for, Maxwell's head man, Jesus Silva, and he had taken surveyors Elkins and Marmon to the place on Chicorica Mesa where the monument had been erected before the railroad came.

Uncle Dick's testimony pertaining to boundaries didn't set well with some people. He greatly enjoyed people, whether individually or in a group. But, when it became a question of speaking to please people or speaking what he was convinced was right, people always came up hindmost. He told what he knew and made enemies with his testimony, generational enemies. More than 135 years later descendants of those enemies could be found still irritated at "Uncle Dick." Some think the Maxwell Land Grant Company had him in pocket. A few still resent the court's decision because, by the time litigation was complete, many people who'd invested years of their lives building up a farm or ranch on Grant land were required to give it up.

Colorado Circuit Judge David J. Brewer accepted Silva's and Wootton's testimonies regarding original boundaries. He ruled in favor of the Maxwell Land Grant Company. The case was appealed.

Attorney Frank Springer took Wootton's and Silva's affidavits with him when the case was argued before the U. S. Supreme Court, March 8-11, 1881. Among other things, the justices discussed the possibility of fraud. The case was not decided at that time.

Rev. O. P. McMains went to Washington D. C. and appealed to the Acting Attorney General. While he waited, McMains published a pamphlet to inform politicians and the public in Washington D. C. of the situation.

In June, McMains returned to New Mexico in high hopes. The public welcomed and honored him with a reception on July 3 at the Raton House in Raton. Governor Edmund Ross[204] wired that he would attend and arrived on the evening train. Decorations adorned the walls and chandeliers. Chinese lanterns lit the room as dinner was served by course. Toasts were made.

The U. S. Supreme Court found no representation of fraud on either side in the history of the Maxwell Grant. In April 1887 the United States Supreme Court ruled in favor of the Maxwell Land Grant boundaries, which had been accepted by Judge Brewer in the U. S. Circuit Court in Colorado.

The Maxwell Land Grant and Railway Company gained clear title to the 1,714,764 acres, which U. S. Land Commissioner James A. Williamson had allowed surveyors to recommend for patent in 1879. The size of the Maxwell land patent had been approved, rather than the limited size allowed in the colonization law.

With judgment and patent in hand, the Maxwell Land Grant and Railway Company renewed its effort to take the land. The company offered to purchase improvements made by those living on the land if they would move. Some sold. Some waited for payment before they packed. Others planned to stay.

Many who planned to stay lived in and around Stonewall, Colorado, about sixty miles from Trinidad. It was good land, and settlers had made it better. The community had its own school house and church. Neighbors met for sings and dances. They even had a literary society.

Richard D. Russell's wife, Marian, said he was given land when he was discharged from the Army. Over the years settlers or squatters had moved into the valley and established

---

[204] As a U. S. Senator from Kansas, Ross cast the deciding vote against removing President Andrew Johnson from office. As New Mexico Governor (June 1885-April 1889), he was against the Santa Fe Ring.

ranches or farms. Homes were built, orchards and gardens planted—without deeds.

By 1888 many weren't interested in leaving home and starting again. They found a champion in O. P. McMains. He believed the Grant had overstepped its bounds and fought fervently in behalf of settlers. He didn't believe the Grant included any Colorado land. The Court be hanged.

In August 1888 Thomas J. O'Neil arrived in Stonewall. He contacted Richard Russell and James Cox, who helped him find a place in an area the Grant Company had already cleared of squatters. O'Neil spent the weekend in Stonewall and returned to Trinidad for his family.

E. J. Randolf was foreman of the Maxwell Land Grant Company herds near Stonewall. Early the same week a group of masked men ordered him and his wife to leave. The men promised to hang them if Randolf remained loyal to the Company. After the Randolfs fled to Trinidad, their home was burned. Squatters/settlers were blamed; they thought it was a setup.

On Friday, O'Neil returned with his family. A six-man posse also arrived from Trinidad to protect Grant employees and to issue more ejections. The posse checked into the Pooler Hotel, also called the Coe Hotel.

Traffic being what it was, Richard Russell thought it strange the O'Neils and the posse arrived close together; but he focused on the posse. Russell called settlers to take a united stand. They didn't know O'Neil was a Pinkerton agent working for the Maxwell Land Grant Company.

On Saturday morning, August 25, 1888, settlers gathered in Stonewall and waited for O. P. McMains to come up from New Mexico. He arrived with a hundred settlers to stand with the Stonewall men.

Twenty-five-men arrived to reinforce the posse. Among the men were Las Animas County Sheriff W. T. Burns and his deputy, William Hunn, Land Grant attorney R. B. Holdsworth, Pinkerton agents, Land Grant employees, and ordinary men who'd been deputized.

After McMains talked with the settlers, he walked to the Pooler. Others walked with him. McMains shouted orders for the posse to leave and then asked if they would. Deputy Hunn came out, talked with McMains, and went back in to confer with the others. Those in the hotel decided they'd done nothing out-of-order and wouldn't leave. McMains turned to the crowd. There was a shot somewhere in the crowd.

McMains ordered his men to surround the hotel; cover all exits. Sheriff Burns saw what was brewing and sent a man out the back door with orders to head to Trinidad to request help from the governor and the state militia.

In the bullet whizzing crossfire, one man and a boy were killed. Richard Russell was mortally wounded. His wife said he was shot as he carried a white flag on his way to discuss the issue.

One account reports that, about noon, someone inside the hotel waved a white flag and asked to talk with leaders of the settlers. Deputy Hunn and McMains met. Hunn asked if some of the men in the hotel might leave. McMains agreed. The two continued negotiations without resolve; fighting resumed.

Sheriff Burns' messenger arrived in Trinidad and reported the situation. Word was wired to M. P. Pels, the Grant man in Denver. The situation was bigger than his ability; Pels hired more Pinkerton agents and notified the governor.

In Trinidad, another posse organized. Las Animas County Commissioners Duane D. Finch and R. L. Wootton told them they were going about it the wrong way. They argued that the situation required diplomacy in order to avert an all-out battle. They pointed out that the settlers were willing, ready, and united to fight to protect their homes. Wootton and Finch offered to ride out to Stonewall alone, check the situation, and see what they could do. They'd seen situations handled both ways.

Deputy Sheriff Alex Taylor thought the two could go as friends and mediate. Maybe they could get the men holed up in the Pooler Hotel released without bloodshed. After discussing the issue back and forth, it was decided. Finch, Wootton, and Dr. Z. E. Funk would be sent. They prepared to ride the 60 miles to Stonewall.

In Stonewall things seemed to settle down that evening until a fire erupted in a barn near the Pooler Hotel. Once the fire was put out, Stonewall men slept in their places near the hotel.

Early the next morning Finch, Wootton, and Funk rode into town and found fifteen to twenty settlers near the Pooler. Settlers allowed the three to pass through to the Chaplin home where McMains was lodging. The three talked with McMains. When they learned that settlers were prepared to ambush any posse sent, they sent Frank Haddon to warn the sheriff in Trinidad.

With the settlers' permission, Wootton, Finch, and Funk entered the Pooler to talk with the posse. They came back out. No one was inside. A few settlers looked in. The men had escaped. Settlers thought the men hadn't returned the occasional gunfire for lack of ammunition. As it turned out, the posse left during the barn fire the night before. In the midst of the confusion and under cover of darkness, they escaped Stonewall and stayed in the mountains overnight. In the morning they traveled to Trinidad and arrived Sunday afternoon.

O'Neil and family left town. Some settlers felt they'd been tricked; others felt they'd accomplished their purpose forcing the posse out of town.

After that, someone set fire to the Pooler. Hundreds of settlers stayed near Stonewall a few days, but the Grant Company didn't react. They'd chosen a different tactic. Over time, the company found quieter ways to evict or settle with those living on their land. O. P. McMains was sentenced to six months in the Pueblo County Jail for his part in the Stonewall War.

Richard Russell's widow wrote her perspective of the events at Stonewall:

…we received notice from the Maxwell Land Grant Company to abandon the domain we had so laboriously wrested from the wildness. Twenty-four hours the company gave us to get off our land and out of the Valley. Twenty-four hours were given us to appear at a hearing in Denver, over two hundred miles away.…we were thirty-five miles from the railroad.…Many men were murdered and unhappiness brought to their families through the loss of their homes on the Maxwell Land Grant.

Many accounts of the Maxwell land steal have been written;…The Maxwell company deputized armed men and sent them into our Stonewall Valley to drive the settlers there from their homes.

…When the notice of evacuation was received the Stonewall settlers buzzed like angry bees. It was soon necessary for the Maxwell deputies to barricade themselves in the Coe Hotel. Richard…became the spokesman for the settlers.…

Richard was shot while carrying a flag of truce and attempting to negotiate with the deputies who barricaded themselves in the Coe Hotel.… settlers had burned the Coe Hotel and the deputies had crawled away like serpents through the tall grass and escaped.… The messenger we had sent for a doctor had been intercepted by the Maxwell minions. Richard died. There was nothing we could do.

Five hundred armed men followed my husband's body to the little cemetery.[205]

The Maxwell Land Grant and Railway Company didn't deal like Lucien Maxwell, nor did they limit their land disputes to those who had small land holdings. Before all was said and done, John B. Dawson, Uncle Dick Wootton, and others like them who had made land transactions with Maxwell would have to prove their ownership, especially those who had land rich in coal. The Maxwell Land Grant & Railway Company wanted to trade coal land to the Santa Fe Railroad for four-five thousand acres near Morley, Colorado. Wootton's and Dawson's land claims, especially, stood in their way.

John Barkley Dawson had purchased 250,000 acres on the Vermijo from Maxwell in January 1869. He ranched, grew an orchard, and sold a little coal off his place. The Grant Company filed against Dawson after the Stonewall incident. He had to end up proving his ownership in court. Represented by Frank Springer, Dawson took his case all the way to the U. S. Supreme Court, which ruled in his favor in 1893.[206]

The Grant Company had been notified of Dick Wootton's land ownership when they purchased. The Company let the issue lie dormant for awhile, but now they wanted proof. Wootton insisted that the purchasers were given full notice of his rights and conceded his title when they used the toll road without paying. In addition, he said that after he built the toll road, he wanted title to the land; so he purchased the land from Maxwell. Maxwell wrote him a quit claim deed, but Dick didn't record it. Maxwell wrote it; he had it. That was good enough for Dick.

In old notes and papers, the Company found references to the deal. Eventually the company searched Maxwell's files back far enough to find record of Wootton's ownership of four sections, 'more or less' on the north side of Raton Mountain. They found the quitclaim deed to Richens L. "Uncle Dick" Wootton from Maxwell and his wife, written by Indian Agent John Henderson and issued on November 7, 1867. It mentioned Maxwell's free use of the mountain road.

The Company offered to issue verification of Maxwell's deed if Wootton would release all coal rights on the property for $1,200. On February 25, 1889, the Maxwell Land Grant & Railway Company issued the confirmation. Dick waited until he received payment. When the company paid the $1,200 on March 9th, Dick signed over the coal rights.

---

[205] Russell, *Memoirs Along the Santa Fe Trail*, 138, 139.
[206] Dawson sold much of his Colfax County land, which included Dawson, New Mexico. The rich coal fields there supplied a livelihood for thousands of people well into the twentieth century.

Iron Horse Race

As railheads moved farther west and south, two railroads set their sights on Raton Pass: the Denver and Rio Grande Western Railroad (General William Jackson Palmers's Rio Grande, D. & R. G.) and the Atchison, Topeka, and Santa Fe Railway (A. T. & S. F., Santa Fe).

In April 1876 the Rio Grande railhead built to El Moro, Colorado. Trinidad, with its well-established businesses and population of 2,500, had hoped for a railroad. General Palmer intended to build across Raton Pass into New Mexico, but he didn't intend to build into Trinidad.[207]

El Moro rails were about five miles from Trinidad—too far in that day of horse travel to adequately serve the young, thriving community on a daily basis. The narrow gauge Rio Grande planned to build its own town and commercial center.[208] Trinidad resented the rejection, took it personally.

Before the Civil War, in 1859, Cyrus K. Holliday began planning a railroad to replace the Santa Fe Trail. Established communities along the way could help support a rail line. In 1863 Holliday's original charter for a rail line in Kansas was changed to give him authority to build toward Santa Fe. He changed the name of his railroad from the Atchison & Topeka to the Atchison, Topeka & Santa Fe Railway.

Finances were hard to come by during the Civil War and during the national depression that followed in the early 1870's. But Holliday definitely planned to enter Colorado, cross Raton Pass into New Mexico, as well as lay track westward to Colorado's silver mines.

There was one route over the Raton Mountains into New Mexico: Raton Pass. On the east of Raton Pass was 9,600' Fisher's Peak. On the west were the 12,000' Spanish Peaks. Since 1862, the Santa Fe Railroad had been eyeing Raton Pass as the one practical route into New Mexico. It was the pivotal gateway for building a railroad empire into New Mexico, Arizona, California, Mexico, and to the Pacific. Water necessary for steam engines was readily available.

Santa Fe Trail trade, gold and silver mines, and Raton Mountain coal beds were prizes to be desired. Coal beds in the Raton Mountains and down into Colfax County, New Mexico, provided the best coal known west of Pennsylvania, and there was plenty of it. Coal was the fuel of the day. It heated homes, cooked meals, fueled trains.

The Santa Fe had especially skilled men in vice president William Barstow Strong, chief engineer Albert Alonzo Robinson, and surveyor William Raymond Morley. Morley made a preliminary survey from La Junta, Colorado, to Isleta, New Mexico, in 1877.

---

[207] Palmer had worked for the president of the Pennsylvania Railroad. In the Civil War, he distinguished himself as a Union man at Antietam, Chickamauga, Atlanta, and Missionary Ridge. After the war he'd worked with the Kansas Pacific and Union Pacific railroads.

[208] Narrow gauge rails are 3' apart.

At Raton Pass, Ray Morley borrowed a band of sheep from Uncle Dick and disguised himself as a Mexican sheepherder. With a black hat shielding his eyes, Morley wrapped himself in a serape and herded sheep around the Raton range, surveying Raton Pass as he went. When needed, he hired other "shepherds" to help survey. He often stopped in at Uncle Dick's for provisions. In the evenings, by his campfire, Morley would pull out his little book and finish his day's sketches and figures, including necessary curves and grades. He finished his Raton Pass survey in October 1877.

The Rio Grande attempted to survey without the Santa Fe's knowledge. General Palmer had a survey plan laid out for his line to cross Raton Pass to Cimarron, New Mexico. Though he'd repeatedly mentioned his aim to build across the Pass, he never mentioned it to Wootton.

Neither railroad filed a plat; neither line had much to spend. Competition became intense. The two lines picked up each other's coded telegraph messages and watched the other's moves.

Although General Palmer and his D. & R. G. had also been slowed by the Panic of 1873, his El Moro station was about twenty miles from Wootton's tollgate. The Santa Fe had only built to Pueblo and La Junta, Colorado.

Once Santa Fe vice president William Strong had Morley's survey, he went to Santa Fe, New Mexico. On February 6, 1878, with the help of Miguel A. Otero,[209] Strong obtained a legislative charter to build the Santa Fe Railroad in New Mexico Territory.

William Strong was a decisive, seize-the-moment type of guy. With the survey and charter in hand, he prepared to move as soon as he obtained the go-ahead from Santa Fe President Nickerson. Keeping up with telegraph messages, the D. & R. G. knew. The Santa Fe was just as alert. Santa Fe engineer A. A. Robinson overheard D. & R. G. men discuss plans to start work on Raton Pass in order to claim first grading. As soon as Santa Fe President Nickerson sent the go-ahead, Strong wired A. A. Robinson to seize the Pass.

On February 26, 1878, D. & R. G. engineers McMurtie and DeRemer boarded their D. & R. G. train at Pueblo enroute to begin grading Raton Pass. Santa Fe's 33-year-old A. A. Robinson and 31-year-old Ray Morley rode the same train. When they realized the situation, Robinson and Morley hid their faces from the D. & R. G. men.

McMurtie and DeRemer left the El Moro depot and checked into a hotel. As far as they knew, the Santa Fe had no work crew in the area. Robinson and Morley left the El Moro train station. They hired a buckboard and the best team they could find and drove to Trinidad. They had no trouble gathering a crew. There were plenty of men ready to help the Santa Fe after the Rio Grande's bypass. Though many folks may not hold out-and-out grudges, they do form opinions. A few do form outright grudges. Regardless, there was no sense fooling around. Morley and Robinson stopped at Joseph Davis' store for supplies. Sore at the Rio Grande, he made sure the Santa Fe men had all the shovels and supplies they needed.

From Trinidad, Robinson and Morley went straight to Uncle Dick's. Late as it was, they knocked. He opened the door and heard their story. Robinson wasn't authorized to offer anything for the right-of-way at the time, but the Santa Fe would make it right. Uncle Dick was well-acquainted with the overall situation. Morley and he had already talked. He liked

---

[209] Otero was an influential New Mexico politician. His son Miguel became a New Mexico governor.

the Santa Fe; he liked Morley. They went back a way and had become better acquainted during the survey.

Uncle Dick had known for some time that railroads were coming. He welcomed progress. As he said, he had "to make way for the locomotive."

Wootton added a few men to the construction crew from among the young folks at his place and from patrons at his inn. About fifty men, including Santa Fe men, Trinidad men, Wootton and his guests, headed up the mountain with shovels and lanterns.

As Robinson neared the pass, he noticed campfires on the mountain. They could be those of travelers or of Uncle Dick's hands. He hoped they were the campfires of Santa Fe engineer Lewis Kingman, who was to meet him with laborers from Cimarron on March 2. Ray Morley sent a young man to see. If those were Kingman's campfires, the young man was to tell Kingman to start grading now! It was. He did.

About 4 a.m. the dark winter morning of February 27, 1878, the Santa Fe crew began shoveling a grade to establish the right of prior construction. They divided into several crews. Robinson said, "One of these forces consisted of 'Uncle Dick' nearly single handed. He began work on the north approach of what is now Raton tunnel by lantern light. Uncle Dick always was friendly to the Santa Fe."[210]

Before daybreak—twenty to thirty minutes after crews began work in their respective places, the D. & R. G. crew arrived to take the Pass. Angry, McMurtie told Robinson the Pass belonged to the D. & R. G. They'd surveyed it while the Santa Fe was still in Kansas. Robinson talked to DeRemer and McMurtie while Wootton and his volunteers held them off. Tempers were hot and high, but there was no bloodshed. Words wouldn't be enough to take the Pass.

The Santa Fe crew continued work. The Rio Grande crew retreated. Neither Palmer, nor any of his representatives ever tried to obtain any type of right-of-way from Uncle Dick.

The next time the two roads wanted the same route the Rio Grande wouldn't give up. But the line over Raton Pass gave the Santa Fe the opportunity to build a railroad empire.

Laying track across 7,863' Raton Pass was a challenge.[211] The Santa Fe constructed a switchback, with some grades at 6%, to enable engines to climb Raton Pass. Normally engineers built a grade so that tracks wound around and ascended a steep mountain gradually. On Raton Pass there was no space for rails to wind around and ascend gradually. The switchback was completed December 1, 1878.

New Mexico politician Miguel Antonio Otero, who helped Strong obtain the New Mexico charter drove a golden spike at the line's dedication.

On December 7, 1878, the first Santa Fe engine chuffed up and over Raton Pass into New Mexico. Even with the switchback, the climb required such a pull that a tunnel was necessary. With the help of others, civil engineer William Engle designed a 200' tunnel under the summit of Raton Pass. Drillers tunneled through from both sides of the mountain. At 3:35 p.m., on Tuesday, July 6, 1879, the crew working the north side and the crew working the south side broke through and met. The workmen shook hands, and a locomotive whistled in

---

[210] Bradley, "Uncle Dick Wootton," 36.
[211] Google Earth, Raton Pass, New Mexico, April 2014.

celebration. Trains no longer needed the switchback over the mountain. Later a second tunnel was added.

Even with the tunnel, the grade was too difficult for standard ooOO engines of the time to pull loads across Raton Pass. The Santa Fe wired the Baldwin Locomotive Works for a more powerful engine to be built and sent as soon as possible. A thirty-ton engine was about the maximum size built at the time. Baldwin engineered and manufactured a sixty-five-ton engine and shipped it West in parts. The weight of the assembled engine would have crashed wooden trestles and caved many bridges along the way. In honor of Uncle Dick, the Santa Fe painted his name on the cab of the sixty-five-ton engine, #2403. The engine was assigned to the New Mexico and South Pacific section of the Santa Fe system to be used primarily between Wootton, Colorado, and Raton, New Mexico. At the time it was built, the "Uncle Dick" was the most powerful locomotive on earth. The wheels were spaced to allow the engine to readily maneuver mountain curves. Although it was more than twice as powerful as a standard locomotive, operational costs were little more than that of one.

What did the Santa Fe offer Dick Wootton for use of the Pass? What did they give him? Some say the Santa Fe offered him $50,000 for right-of-way over the Pass, but that he refused, saying just give my family and me a lifetime pass and $25 a month in groceries.[212] It's doubtful that the financially strapped Santa Fe Railroad had $50,000 to offer in 1878. The deed to the right-of-way wasn't arranged until after the tunnel was completed.

The Santa Fe did give Uncle Dick and his family a lifetime pass on the Santa Fe and twenty-five dollars a month. It was a venture on Dick's part. Maxwell hadn't fared well with his railroad interests. The year Dick died the Santa Fe was on the brink of disaster. He had no way of knowing what would or would not last for his family; but the Santa Fe did pull through. It continued to send twenty-five dollars a month to Mary and their deaf daughter, Fidelis. They enjoyed a railroad pass all their lives. In 1925 the Santa Fe raised the monthly stipend to $35. After Mrs. Wootton's death, the railroad continued to pay Fidelis until her death in 1957.

Once the Santa Fe obtained Raton Pass, it drew the attention of the financial world—to the dismay of railroad giants Jay Gould, Collis Huntington, and Leland Stanford. With the potential to be more than just a local railroad, the Santa Fe attracted enough capital to continue building.

It built a mile and a half a day in 1879 and reached Las Vegas, New Mexico, in July 1879. The mainline continued to Lamy, New Mexico; a spur line was built from there into Santa Fe (1880). The Santa Fe continued south toward Texas, west to California, and into Mexico.

Because the Santa Fe was a standard gauge railroad,[213] railroad cars could be interchanged with other rail companies for exchanged transportation routing.

If, on a sheet of graph paper, one could plot the course of railroad development in the West and that of the Santa Fe Trail's decline in usage, a case could be made for the intersecting of those lines atop Raton Pass on a December [sic] evening in 1877 [sic] at Dick Wootton's ranch. When that gentlemen's agreement was made between Santa Fe

---

[212] Twenty-five dollars a month would not have paid 1% interest on $50,000.
[213] Rails laid 4'8 ½" apart are standard gauge. Most U. S. railroads were laid using standard gauge.

Railway representative W. R. (Ray) Morley and 'Uncle Dick" Wootton, for the Santa Fe Railroad to utilize the toll road alignment over the pass, not only did one phase of history yield to another, but so too did one form of transportation technology step aside for the steam locomotive.... Rail growth and Trail decline, in a real sense, culminated on Raton Pass.[214]

First Santa Fe Railroad (A.T. & S.F) Tunnel through the Raton Mountains

---

[214] Friedman, "Railroads and the Santa Fe Trail...," *Wagon Tracks*, 18.

Changes

After the Santa Fe Railroad built a spur line into Santa Fe in 1880, business slowed down for Uncle Dick. There were still local travelers, but the bulk of transport and passenger business traveled by rail. Barlow and Sanderson's stage made its last run out of Trinidad in 1879.

Dick's road continued to be used as a highway. It was renovated, but remained the principal highway between Colorado and New Mexico more than sixty years after the first Santa Fe Railroad train crossed into New Mexico. By then few travelers remembered broken wagons, tolls, the railroad race, or the Indians, mountain men, desperados, miners, and settlers who crossed before them.

Uncle Dick's business slowed, but his family grew. By 1880 his five oldest children were married and living close enough to visit. With the birth of William and Elizabeth Wootton's little Fanny in Blossburg, New Mexico, on July 31, 1880, Uncle Dick had eleven living grandchildren.

His little son Johnie had died while Santa Fe rails were being laid on Raton Pass. Johnie's brother and namesake, John Peter, was born in December, about three weeks after the first Santa Fe engine steamed over the Pass into New Mexico.

In September 1879, Fidelis turned seven. Dick and Mary enrolled her at the School for the Deaf and Blind in Colorado Springs. It was difficult to leave their little deaf girl in boarding school far from home, but they wanted her to be as well-equipped for life as possible.

In the East, Thomas Edison worked on a light bulb idea. He never considered an experiment a failure—just a way something didn't work. He'd keep trying until he'd find a way that worked.

Settlers continued to move West. Mining offered employment, if not pockets filled with treasure. A smelter and steel mill was established in Pueblo, Colorado.

This was the time depicted in many Western novels and movies: the era of range warfare, land disputes, train robberies, vigilantes, people of note—good and bad. It was the ending era of Indian raids and warfare. New towns were springing up. Even small towns established civic organizations, churches, and one-room libraries. Some towns built an opera house. Most had at least one saloon. In some small places saloons seemed to be the chief commercial endeavor.

On September 26, 1881, the entire nation was called to silence for a National Day of Fasting and Prayer and Humiliation, as the nation mourned the assassination of President James Garfield. A member of the Half-Breed Republican faction, Garfield had been President four months when a member of the Stalwart Republican faction shot him at a Washington railway station in July.

While the President lay dying, Pat Garrett shot Billy the Kid in Ft. Sumner, New Mexico, on July 14—twelve days after Garfield was shot. Some question if it was really Billy the Kid whom Garrett shot.[215]

New Mexico's first telephone lines were being installed in Santa Fe. Trinidad, Colorado, was planning its first opera house, the Jaffra. Colorado was finalizing plans for its capitol building.

President Garfield died September 19, 1881. In the intervening months, people from all over nation donated $350,000 to a fund to benefit Garfield's family. Garfield's successor, Vice President Chester Arthur, was a Stalwart Republican. When he became President, many Americans were surprised, some angry, that Arthur set aside political division and endeavored to be President to all. His wife had died from a sudden bout of pneumonia in January 1880; so his sister Mary Arthur McElroy filled in when he needed a "First Lady."

The month President Garfield died Chief Victorio and his son-in-law Nana and their Apache warriors terrorized parts of southern New Mexico and Arizona.

---

[215] Pat Garrett's blind daughter, Elizabeth Garrett, wrote New Mexico's state song: "O Fair New Mexico".

Family

By mid-1882, Dick and Mary had two more children: Mary and Gerardus. Dick's son and daughter-in-law William and Elizabeth presented him with another granddaughter, Lillie Mae. Lillie would live to be eighty-three and a half. Gerardus lived three and a half months. His sister Mary Fannie was born almost a year after his death.

Uncle Dick taught his children to work and entrusted them with responsibility. John was a little guy when his father began to send him to the store a few miles down the road. Dick would lift John up onto a saddled horse and send him off with a sack. When John arrived at the store, he'd jump off the horse and ask the storekeeper for the items his dad wanted. The storekeeper put the purchases in the sack, tied it to the saddle horn, and helped John back up onto the horse. One time the meat sack fell off. John slid off the horse to retrieve it, but was too short to get back on. He stood by the horse until someone came along who could boost him back onto the saddle.

On Dick's sixty-eighth birthday (1884), R. L. Jr., his wife, Lucy; Eliza Ann, her husband, Judge Walker, and their three daughters came out from Trinidad to the Pass to surprise Uncle Dick and the family with a visit and birthday party. Their gift to him was a new suit of clothes.

In the heat of the summer of 1884, eleven-month-old Mary Fannie became ill. Her parents took her into Trinidad to the home of P. J. Munnecom, priest and family friend. Mary Fannie died at his home on Monday, August 12th. Dick outran cholera years ago when he high-tailed it out of Westport, but it caught up to him after all these years and took his baby.

Frank Christopher was born to Dick and Mary in August 1885, followed by their youngest child, Jesse, in March 1887. Seven weeks before Jesse's birth, his five-year-old sister, fair-headed, blue-eyed Mary (not to be confused with Mary Fannie), died three days after her mother's birthday.

Except for Joseph and Fannie, most of Dick's children lived nearby. Joseph lived in Idaho in the mid-1880's and near Emporia, Kansas, in the late 1880's. Fannie, raised by Dr. and Mrs. Burt, married in northern Colorado in 1882.

Each New Years' Day Dick's grown children came home with their families to the large home at the foot of Raton Pass. Ages of children and grandchildren overlapped and blended. There were fifteen grandchildren living in the area in 1888. Dick had fathered twenty children; eight had died. He would lose no more.

In 1885 a cataract began to dim Dick's eyesight. In early 1888 he boarded the train in Trinidad and traveled to Chicago where Dr. Olin removed the cataract from Uncle Dick's left eye. Uncle Dick remained in the city a few weeks and often visited the doctor for treatment at his residence at 3619 Indiana Avenue.

On April 21, 1888, Dick's sister Eliza Ann Hayes and her son, Will, arrived from Kentucky. She was a baby when Dick left home; he'd named his first child for her. It had been more than fifty years since he'd seen her. Dick went to town to meet Eliza and Will at the Trinidad depot. They made their home in Trinidad a few years before they moved to Dennison, Texas. (Many of Dick and her maternal and paternal relatives had settled in northern Texas.)

Young John, the oldest of Dick and Mary's sons, was the son of Dick's old age. John was born soon enough to build a solid relationship with his father, but too late to experience many of the hard times the older children had faced—a rather idyllic position. John loved life and entertained himself, perhaps too readily. Some trains were slow chugging up Raton Pass with their loads and made an easy target for a little boy with an endless supply of rocks. One minor problem: he hadn't looked far enough ahead of his pleasure to see the consequence. One day an engineer saw Uncle Dick and told him John was throwing rocks at trains.

"Okay," Uncle Dick nodded, "I'll take care of it."

Dick was never one to tolerate disrespect. The engineer knew he'd handle it. At first Dick made John stand still on a rock when a train passed by, which was often in those days. That didn't completely take care of the situation, but Dick wasn't a man of limited ideas. Hoeing required a little more focus. Dick required John to hoe in the garden when it was time for a train to pass by. Trains weren't always on time. When they did come, they were so s-l-o-w in passing. When engineers in the big black steam engines saw John hoeing rather than throwing or spinning rocks, they'd grin or laugh as they chugged past. The engineers and firemen were pleased.

In her mid-teen's Dick and Mary Pauline's second child, Ida, went by train to attend Ursuline College, a Catholic school in Tiffin, Ohio. A year or two later her younger sister, Lucy, joined her. Dick went by train to visit his girls. In the evenings, Dick entertained the nuns with firsthand accounts of the western frontier. Because light was sometimes a glare to his eye since his cataract surgery, the nuns allowed him to keep his hat on as he sat by the fire and told his stories.

Ida Wootton (right) and a friend
Photo courtesy of Ida's great-granddaughter Margaret Wilson

At times, Dick heard from his family in Kentucky. Brother Powell was practicing medicine. Their late sister Mary Catherine's son Richard D. Daniel had followed Powell's footsteps and become a physician. (Having grown up with R. L. Jr. in Kentucky, Richard came to New Mexico and practiced medicine in Fernando de Taos, and later in Mora.) Dick's brother Alexander James was in Tennessee. His brother David lived in Kentucky, where brother John had died in 1880.

One day one of Uncle Dick's boys found a letter written by Dick's mother, Fannie—a reply to a letter he'd written saying he'd soon be returning home to Kentucky. Tears welled in Dick's eyes. She'd been gone twenty-five years. Even with his Santa Fe Railroad pass, Dick never returned to Kentucky.

Better Write It Down

R. L. WOOTTON, JR. REALIZED his dad was aging; times were changing. Many of Uncle Dick's old mountain men friends were dead—only Tobin, Baker, and Boggs remained.

Foreseeing the value of an accurate account of his father's life, R. L. contacted professional history writer Howard Louis Conard and arranged for him to come to the Wootton Ranch in the summer of 1889. Conard stayed with Uncle Dick and his family. Night after night he listened to the past and recorded it for the future.

At one point Dick told Conard, "I don't feel very old, but when I look about me for my associates of the 'forties,' I find that only the mountains and I are left, and before long it will be only the mountains."[216] He spoke of the changes:

> Pleasure parties roam about over the mountains, and instead of being loaded down with firearms and ammunition, as we used to be when we ventured into the same localities, they carry lunch baskets and amateur photographing outfits....Of all the changes, the improvements, and the advance in civilization which have been made in the vast western half of the United States within the past fifty years, I have been a witness. I trust I have contributed my share toward bringing about the condition of affairs which exist today...[217]

When Dick mentioned he'd like the book dedicated to his mountain compadres of years gone by, Conard reminded him dedications were going out of fashion; but if he did want to dedicate the book, it would be better to dedicate it to someone living. Dick chose R. L., Jr. for arranging for Conard's work.

Some people read Conard's account and weigh Dick out as a braggart. On the other hand, Joseph Millard's opinion was that Wootton was naturally self-effacing. "... because he spent little time bragging to eastern writers, many of his exploits would be credited to others...he would be little-known outside his beloved wilderness because he spent his life living the adventures other men claimed...to own."[218] Howard Conard described Uncle Dick as a "genial, warm hearted old man."[219]

After the interviews, Conard returned to Chicago with the biography of Uncle Dick's western years. Dick followed for final publication arrangements. In 1890 W. E. Dibble and Company of Chicago published *"Uncle Dick" Wootton, The Pioneer Frontiersman of the Rocky Mountain Region*.

Since that time writers of western history, fiction, and drama have continued to draw from that account—directly or indirectly.

---

[216] Conard, 1890, 452.
[217] Conard, 1980, 440.
[218] Millard, "Blazer of Trails West," 91.
[219] Conard, 1890, 469.

Hoodlums in the House

The two who did the damage at Uncle Dick's place on March 3, 1890, weren't criminals. Two of Dick's young sons, eleven-year-old John and four-and-a-half-year-old Frank, got to playing with matches in an outbuilding near the house. Whether they were trying to smoke or were just playing with fire isn't clear—but it leans toward smoking. In later years, John explained the situation. There were shingles and other flammable materials that caught fire in the outbuilding, but the cat spread the fire. Somehow the cat's tail caught fire. The fire might have been contained if the cat had stayed put; but the cat took off—ran, jumped, and flew into the house through an open window. Forcing the curtains aside, the cat set them ablaze.

Mary Pauline rushed to save her sewing machine. She carried it out, and ran back in. Someone grabbed a cigar box—thinking it was one filled money with which the children played—and tossed it into the yard. It was full of clippings and mementos. The family escaped with a few clothes and pieces of furniture. Then they could only stand and watch, as the fire burned.

When the smoke cleared, part of the original three-room house was salvageable. There were only remnants of the two-story portion of the home. There was no insurance.

Santa Fe passenger train No. 4 passed the embers and reported the fire at the depot in Trinidad. When R. L. heard about the fire, he hitched up a wagon and headed out to help. At the ruins he was told that Engineer Lynch on engine #135 had stopped on his way down the mountain and taken the family to town. Uncle Dick had gone to Wootton Station about two miles away.

That night the family stayed in town with William and Eliza and their girls.

When he thought of bygone friends, family, or times, Dick sometimes felt a wave of nostalgia; but regrets weren't allowed a life of their own, weren't allowed to be a bedfellow with the life he lived in the present, never had been. With his uninsured house in shambles, Uncle Dick set about to build another. He soon moved his family into "Wootton Place," a two-story home at the end of Stonewall Avenue in Trinidad.

After they moved into town, John became an altar boy. One day the priest was late for confession—didn't show up and didn't show up. People were lining up. John wasn't at a loss. He told the other altar boy to cover for him and went into the confessional. He listened to the confessions. When the other boy saw the priest coming, he rapped on the confessional to alert John. John made a quick exit in time for the priest to continue hearing confessions.

Living in Trinidad, Uncle Dick was surrounded by family—his children and grandchildren, and relatives on Mary Pauline's side of the family—Dillettes, Lujans, McBrides, Abeytas, and Mottos.

The first summer the circus came to Pueblo, Colorado, Uncle Dick took his family up to see it. He had half a notion to follow it on up to Denver and let the kids—and himself—see it again.

Two years after Dick moved to town, his son-in-law Judge Walker died. Eliza ran a boarding house in Trinidad after her husband's death. She still had two daughters at home.

In November 1890 Dick got sick. On Thursday evening, the 12th, Trinidad's *Evening Chronicle* reported he was feeling better and would probably be out and about soon. Early the next week, both the *Chronicle* (16th) and the Santa Fe *New Mexican* (17th) gave little hope for Dick's recovery even though he'd received the best medical help available.

He recovered.

In the eastern United States the gold standard was wobbly, but industry was growing. Inventors were registering patents. George Eastman had made a twenty-five dollar box camera and was working on one that could be produced for a dollar; so everyone could afford one. Hannibal Goodwin invented celluloid film; Thomas Edison and William Dickson had just figured a way to use Goodwin's film to make a moving picture.

The Statue of Liberty had been in place since October 1886 with her invitation to the masses. Many Americans now thought she shouldn't be quite so hospitable: her invitation should be restricted a little. There'd been some effort in that direction since shortly after the Civil War. Immigration became a growing concern as the country tried to assimilate the masses with their variety of cultures, languages, religions, and political persuasions. Tenement houses were common. Slums grew. Crime increased.

In the West droughts and hard times had discouraged folks; but with news of silver strikes near Creede in 1890 and gold on Cripple Creek in 1891, hopeful people moved to Colorado.

Fear of Indian attack no longer ruled. Geronimo had surrendered back in 1886. Sitting Bull had died in South Dakota in '90. The year before, the Oklahoma Land Rush opened a portion of Indian Territory for settlement (April 1889).

As 1892 drew near, the whole United States prepared to celebrate the 400th anniversary of the discovery of America. Chicago guaranteed ten million dollars for the privilege of hosting the "World's Columbian Exposition" and won the honor. Architects and builders transformed 690 acres into a showcase of U. S. and worldwide achievements at the cost of $26,000,000. The World's Columbian Exposition was dedicated on Columbus Day, October 12, 1892, and opened in the spring of 1893. Arts, sciences, agriculture, industry, and religion were represented. New ideas awed the public. Amusements added to the pleasure. The Ferris wheel made its debut.

But, in April 1893, the U. S.' shaky financial district collapsed. The Panic of 1893 began a four-year depression. About 400 banks closed—including many in the West and South; thousands of businesses folded. Some railroads went into receivership following bankruptcy. This time the West was not as isolated.

End of the Frontier

The young nation—the United States—had come of age. On July 12, 1893, Historian Frederick Jackson Turner presented his "Frontier Thesis," to 200 historians of the American Historical Association at the World's Columbian Exposition. He declared the frontier was now ended. The first period of American history was closed. A new phase was dawning for the United States.

For more than half a century Dick and his compadres had broken ground in the Southwest, making both friends and enemies as they made pathways of possibilities for those coming after them. They established principled policies in an untamed land. There had been pioneers long before them and pioneers during their time in other places.

Uncle Dick said, "In my lifetime I've seen the change from wagon train, making fifteen miles in a day, to the railroad, covering twice that distance in an hour and hauling more freight on one train than all the freighters could deliver to Santa Fe in a whole season…I almost feel that I am no longer on the frontier and there is not a frontier to go to. In my old age I have been brought back to civilization."[220]

It was as though Richens Lacy Wootton had made a full circle. His youngest daughters, western born and raised, had the advantage of an education that included music, drama, and art.

After Ida graduated in June 1893, Lucy and she returned home to Trinidad. A note in the newspaper announced their arrival and extended a welcome invitation to visitors in their home. Twenty-five-year-old Felix Baca, whose father helped found Trinidad, visited. Before the end of the year, Ida and he were engaged.

Ida, Lucy, John, and the youngest two Wootton children, Frank and Jesse, were all home the summer the girls returned from school. Jesse, now six, would start school in the fall.

Priests encouraged fourteen-year-old John to study for the priesthood. A young priest would be returning home to France. John could go along and study there. He talked to his parents, but put off his decision because his dad wasn't feeling well—inflammation of the stomach. Uncle Dick was sick several weeks.

R. L., Jr. was home after serving his third term in the Colorado General Assembly. He'd had his real estate and insurance business in Trinidad for years and still tended his livestock. He and his Dad were close. One summer evening when R. L. came by to visit, Uncle Dick asked him to be sure the children were taken care of.

That evening, at 8:05 p.m., August 22, 1893, Uncle Dick Wootton entered the eternity of which his parents taught him.

The Beginning

---

[220] Helmers, "Uncle Dick Wootton…," *Pueblo Chieftain*, 1c.

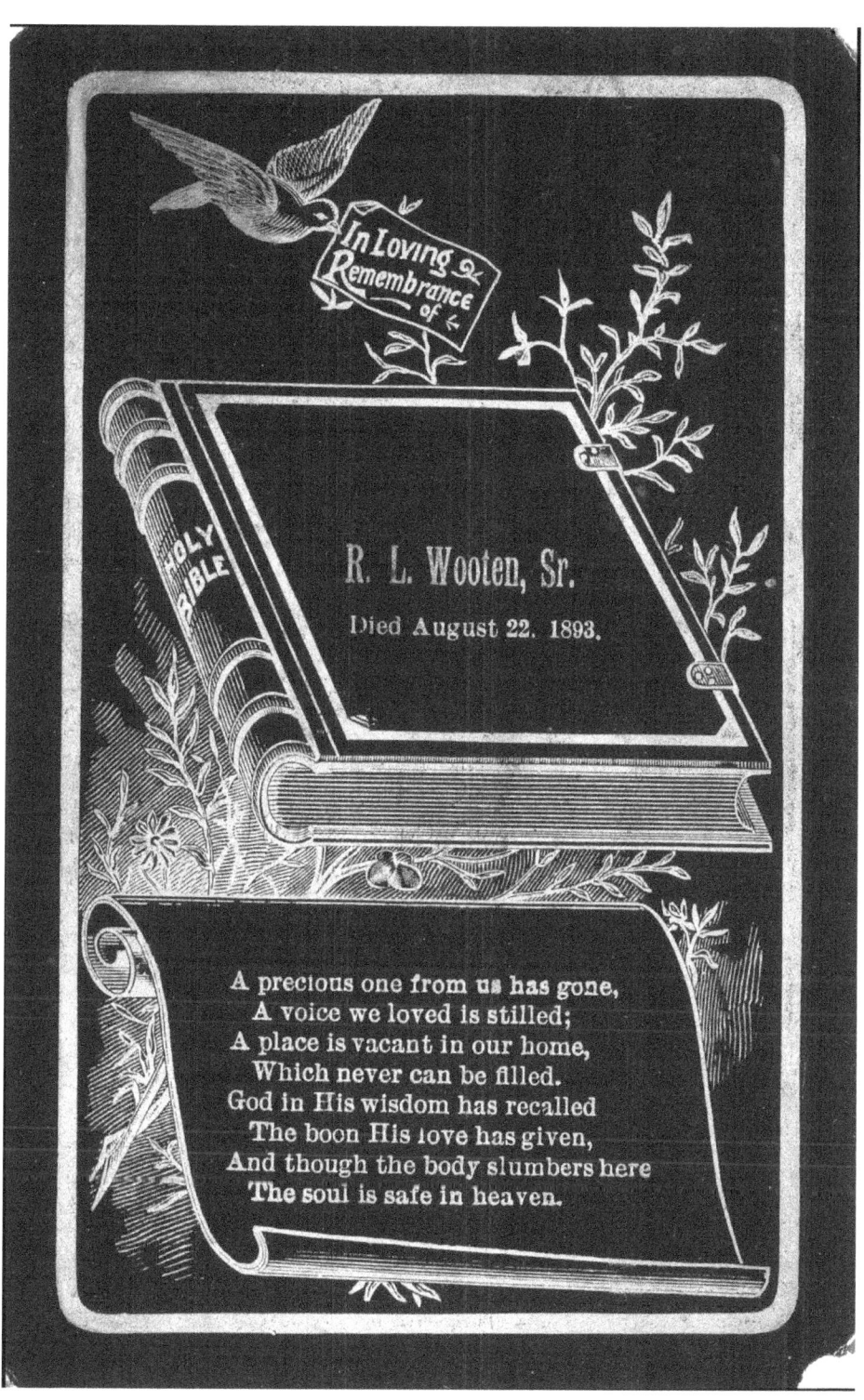

Sketches

Biographical Sketches

Compadres, Friends, and a Couple He Knew, But Didn't Care For

Albert, John David
Born: 1806, Hagerstown, Maryland
Appearance: Small man
Married: Three wives: two were Mexican or half Mexican. The first was a daughter of William Pope, who came early to the Rocky Mountain region.
Children: John said he had 26 children by his first two wives.
Died: April 24, 1899, Walsenburg, Colorado

John Albert, of Pennsylvania Dutch ancestry, came to the Rocky Mountains with a group of 60 trappers in 1834 and trapped with the American Fur Company out of Ft. Laramie.

The winter of 1836 he trapped with a party along the South Platte, as far as Cache la Poudre (northern Colorado). It snowed there on the first of December and never cleared up all winter. Snow piled up to seven feet in places near Cache la Poudre's junction with the Platte. Most of their horses froze and became the party's table fare. John and his party were stranded until spring.

In spring 1837 he went south to Bent's Fort, purchased more horses, and, in the summer, relocated in New Mexico. There he married and made his home.

John Albert was working for Simeon Turley at his Arroyo Hondo (New Mexico) mill and distillery when the Taos Massacre broke out in January 1847. Gaining momentum, the mob attacked Turley's establishment. During the siege, Albert and those at Turley's Mill barricaded themselves within the compound and fought. Most of the men in the mill died. John escaped to El Pueblo and reported the massacre to Dick Wootton and the mountain men there. It was three months—the end of April—before John recovered from his Arroyo Hondo-El Pueblo trek.

John left Taos and moved to southern Colorado and trapped. While living there, he carried mail to and from the Spanish Peaks Post Office at Cuchara Station (Colorado) every Saturday.

John Albert had many children, outlived his wives, and lived well past 90. Each time a wife died, he divided all his possessions among his children and started over.

Autobees, Charles "Charlie/Charley" (Autobees also: Orbetees, Orterbis, Autobee)
Born: 1812, St. Louis, Missouri
Parents: François and Sarah (Issman) Autobees;
François was French, Sarah a Delaware Indian
Appearance: Tall

Indian nickname: "Hoarse Voice" because his voice was scratchy

Married (Wives and children): Not necessarily in order, may have had other wives, perhaps more than one at a time.
- Picking Bones, a Cheyenne
- Serafina Avila, widow; m. Taos, New Mexico. She died at Huerfano, Colorado, 1873.

  Children of Charlie and Serafina:
  - Mariano (1837)
  - Jose Maria (1842; sometimes called Jose Tomas)
  - Francequita (1845)
  - Manuelita (1846)
  - Tomas (b.1849, Arroyo Hondo, New Mexico; m. Teodora Trujillo, 1864, 12 children)
  - Tim
- Siccamore (Syccamo, Sycamaore; d. August 1864). Various sources say she was Arapaho, Cheyenne, Blackfoot. Charlie and she had several children.
- Estefana, a Navajo. Charlie and Estefana had 3 children.
- Juanita Gomez (widow of Antansio Gomez) m. 1876

Died: June 1882, buried: St. Vrain Cemetery, SE of Avondale, Colorado

Charlie was three when his father, a lumber foreman, drowned while moving logs down the St. Lawrence River. Charlie's mother married Bartholomew Tobin. Their son Tom was born when Charlie was about eleven. Both boys lived their adult lives in the West.

Like many children of his era, Charlie was uneducated. When he was sixteen (1828) he began trapping for the American Fur Company and trapped along the headwaters of the Missouri and Columbia Rivers for about seven years. He then trapped independently and made his way to Taos, New Mexico. He trapped as far south as the Gila River (New Mexico, Arizona).

When he wasn't trapping, Charlie hauled flour and whiskey for Simeon Turley, who owned a mill and distillery at Arroyo Hondo, New Mexico. In 1837 Charlie went to St. Louis and brought his brother Tom to work for Turley.

When El Pueblo was built in 1842, Autobees was in charge of Turley's store there. He freighted goods from Independence (Missouri) to keep the store stocked. It was at El Pueblo where Charlie Autobees and Dick Wootton became well-acquainted and remained friends.

Autobees escaped Turley's Mill during the 1847 Taos Massacre. He warned Rio Hondo settlers and then took word to Bent's Fort. When he returned to Taos, Charlie sat on the jury which convicted the rebels.

After the trials Charlie farmed along Red River (New Mexico) and contracted with the Ft. Union quartermaster to supply hay to the fort. A Mexican at the fort stabbed Charlie in the back. It was a bad wound, but he recovered.

In the early 1850's Autobees moved to the Huerfano Valley (Colorado), where Wootton and he were neighbors once again. He was there in time for the Christmas Eve Massacre of 1854. The Ute stole his stock, but didn't hurt him. He was with Siccamore at the time.

The next year, 1855, Charlie was out with his family in a wagon when the Ute came upon them. He held up one finger—a sign for them to approach and talk. They didn't respond. He waved them back, but they rode toward him; so he opened fire. They shot him in the muscle of his right arm and broke his arm, but Siccamore kept his rifle loaded and stood in front of him. Charlie rested his rifle on her shoulder and shot. He said the Ute retreated after he emptied seven Ute saddles. The Autobees family returned home; Charlie's arm healed. He was still married to Serafina, but didn't bring her from Taos until 1857.

In 1856 Charlie was foreman of the adobe making crew that built Ft. Garland (Colorado).

When Dick Wootton and Charlie Autobees lived in the Huerfano Valley, Juan Chiquito often made off with some of their livestock. It wasn't a personal thing. Juan Chiquito also robbed Mexicans traveling from Ft. Laramie to New Mexico with gold in their belts. He killed some. When his son killed Felipe Archuleta on Autobees' place in 1857, Charlie's son Mariano chased the Chiquitos out of the immediate area. They settled nearby on Fountain Creek. Juan Chiquito killed an American in the summer of 1859 and another in the fall. He had a farm and a little grist mill, but his place was a refuge for Mexican murderers and the local lawless. After Wootton moved from the area, Juan Chiquito continued stealing from Autobees and threatened to kill him.

In spring 1862 Juan Chiquito sent word for Autobees and his men to meet him and his men between the St. Charles and Huerfano Rivers. Autobees showed up, but no Juan Chiquito.

In early August 1862 Juan Chiquito stole the wife (Juan's niece) of Carmel Medina (Mrs. Autobees' nephew) and the wife of Choteau Sandoval. He also stole Carmel Medina's cows and his wagon with its yoke of oxen. Even though Juan had a wife (Anastasia), he kept Sandoval's wife for himself. He gave Carmel Medina's wife, Louisa, to Jesus Romero.

Medina and Sandoval went to Charlie Autobees for help. Infuriated, Charlie and his son Mariano decided that was the last straw! They gathered about twelve men and rode to Juan Chiquito's hideout. By the time the smoke cleared, Juan Chiquito lay dead with a hole in his chest; two of his sons were escaping on horseback, and his gang were high-tailing it on foot.

Charlie and Serafina's sons rescued William Bent's son at the Sand Creek Massacre in 1864.

Charlie lived a short while with his oldest son, Mariano. He died in his 70th year. His will recognized only his children born by Serafina.

Baca, Marcelino

Born: 1808, Taos
Appearance: 6' tall
Married: Tomasa, 1838
Children:
- Jose (b. 1839, on the South Platte)
- Luis (b. 1841, Ft. Laramie)
- Elena (b. 1846, Hardscrabble, Colorado; m. Mariano Autobees son of Charlie Autobees)

Died: February 21, 1862, Battle of Valverde, New Mexico

A native New Mexican, Marcelino trapped on the Missouri for nine years. He was trapping with Jim Bridger's American Fur Co. in 1838 when the Pawnee took him captive. They prepared to sacrifice him in one of their rituals, but the chief's beautiful young daughter begged her father for Marcelino's life. The chief granted her request, and Marcelino and she married. Marcelino named her Tomasa.

Their two sons were born while Marcelino worked for Jim Bridger. The family moved south to the Pueblo/Greenhorn (Colorado) area. During the 1854 Christmas Massacre raid, the Ute stole 500 head of cattle, thirteen horses, two mules, and 117 fanegas (fanega=1.58 bushel) of corn from the Bacas. None of the family was hurt physically, but they were ruined financially. Marcelino moved to Wootton's fortress at Huerfano Village and then moved his family back home to New Mexico.

During the American Civil War, Marcelino fought as a Union man and was killed in the Battle of Valverde in southern New Mexico. He would have been 54 that year.

Baker, Jim

Born: December 19, 1818, Belleville, Illinois
Appearance: Red hair, moustache, short beard; piercing eyes; tall, thin
Married: Six Indian wives; some were "tent wives."[221]
Children: Many
Died: May 1898 (about seven months shy of his eightieth birthday), Savery, Wyoming; buried: Baker Cemetery, west of Savery, Wyoming

Wootton, who often trapped with Baker, considered him—with the exception of Kit Carson—John C. Fremont's best scout. Wootton considered Baker one of the most daring mountain men. The two came to the Rocky Mountains about the same time.

Baker returned home for a visit in 1840-41.

In his early western years Jim trapped along the Green River for Jim Bridger's fur company; but he trapped independently most of his years. For some time he lived among the Shoshone, where he married Flying Dawn, "an Indian princess," who bore him about fourteen children.

Although he continued to trap until about 1859, Baker often served as a guide or scout:
1855: Chief scout for General W. S. Harney at Ft. Laramie.
1857: Guided federal troops (on their way to the Mormon War) to Ft. Bridger.
Winter 1857-58: Led Captain Randolph Marcy from Utah across the snowy Rockies to obtain supplies at Ft. Union (New Mexico).
1865: Guided and interpreted for the Ute Indian Agency; his skills impressed his superiors.

In 1852 Jim had a store on the Green River where it met the Oregon Trail. His brother John also had a place on the Green River and raised cattle to trade with emigrants on the Oregon Trail.

Jim lived along the Blackfoot River several years before he moved to Cherry Creek

---

[221] A man sometimes had more than one Indian wife at a time. He might live in one tent with more than one wife, or he may have an individual tent for each wife—a "tent wife." Marriages were generally without what would be considered legal formalities; however, Indian tribes had varying marriage ceremonies.

(Denver-Auraria). The first year he lived at Cherry Creek, he lived in two tepees with his wife, children, and several Indians. He built a cabin and operated a ferry at Clear Creek Crossing a few miles from Denver near what would later be 53rd and Tennyson. He built a toll bridge and had a little store there until 1873.

One day in 1873 he returned from an out-of-town trip and saw a fence about a mile from his place. He asked his sons what was going on. They explained a man had set up a little ranch and built a fence to keep his cattle in.

"So that's what a fence is?"

"Yes, "that's what it is."

Well, Jim responded, he wouldn't stand for anything of the kind. He and his were getting out of there; it was getting too congested. He sold his bridge to the county commissioners, moved to Wyoming, and built a fort on the Snake River.

Barclay, Alexander

Born: May 21, 1810, England

Appearance: Cross-eyed

Wife/lived with: Teresita Sandoval Suaso Kinkead

Died: December 1855, Ft. Barclay, New Mexico; buried about a half mile south of Ft. Barclay (Of the three graves in the small stone-walled cemetery there, Alexander's in the one on the south. Rafaelita Suaso-Kinkead Kroenig's is in the middle.)

Born in England, twenty-three-year-old Alexander Barclay sailed to Canada in the spring of 1833 and settled in Ontario. In October 1836 he sold out and moved to St. Louis, a thriving community of 15,000.

There Barclay became acquainted with the Bents and accepted the position of bookkeeper for Bent-St. Vrain Company at Bent's Fort. He began work in July 1838. Dick Wootton became acquainted with Barclay while Barclay kept the books and superintended the fort's store from 1838-1842. In spring 1842, Barclay notified Bent of his resignation, effective after he took the spring load of peltry to St. Louis. That was the year the firm tried to use bull boats to transport their buffalo robes. (A bull boat was fashioned with willow framework and covered with supple hides—fairly fresh; so the willow and hides would dry to a nice snug fit. It was shaped somewhat like a large, round basket.) The boats left the fort in April, but bogged down in western Kansas. By the time all was said and done, it was December before Barclay made it back to Bent's Fort with supplies.

In the spring of 1843 he headquartered at the new El Pueblo and traded with trappers along the North Platte. He traded independently, but traveled with various men, especially Joe Doyle. At El Pueblo he met Teresita Suaso Kinkead, Doyle's mother-in-law.

Barclay and Doyle left El Pueblo. They went south to New Mexico and established Ft. Barclay near La Junta de los Rios about twenty miles north of Las Vegas. In 1855 Barclay traveled to St. Louis. Soon after his return to the fort, he died at home, age 45.

Beard, Jake

Born: January 18, 1828, Rockingham Co., Virginia, moved to St. Louis, Missouri, 1837

Married: Isabel Simpson (daughter of George and Juana Simpson), April 16, 1860

As a child, Jake moved with his family to St. Louis, where he was apprenticed to a miller.

In the winter of 1849 he left for Westport, Missouri, and, in the spring of 1850, came West on Ceran St. Vrain's wagon train. St. Vrain had four flour mills and a government contract to furnish flour for troops in New Mexico. He hired Jake and four others to come mill his grain. Jake worked the Mora, New Mexico, mill until the winter of 1852-53.

In February 1853 Jake joined Kit Carson's venture taking stock to California and seeking gold. Jake intended to stay in there; but when he took sick with chills and fever, he became so disgusted with the country he returned to the Mora area (1854). He milled flour in Mora, hauled freight, and worked at a saw mill until 1862.

Jake married George Simpson's daughter in 1860. In 1862 they moved to Joe Doyle's place in Colorado. The Beards moved to Trinidad, Colorado, in 1865. There Jake built a flour mill and a home (1868). They remained in Trinidad until they moved to California in 1900. In 1903 they moved to El Paso, Texas, and were living there in 1904.

Beaubien, Charles/Carlos (Charles Hipollyte Trotier, Sieur de Beaubien)
Born: 1800, Three Rivers, Quebec, Canada
Married: Maria Pabla Lobato (b. December 28, 1811, of an old New Mexico family; d. August 13, 1864) m. September 11, 1827, Taos, New Mexico
Children:
- Jose Narciso (October 26, 1827-January 18, 1847, Taos, New Mexico)
- Maria de la Luz Beaubien (b. June 24, 1829, Taos; m. Lucien B. Maxwell, March 1842; d. June 3, 1900, Ft. Sumner, New Mexico)
- Maria Leonora de los Dolores, (b. March 27, 1833, Taos; m. 1: Vidal Trujillo, died 2: B. J. O'Neill)
- Maria Teodora "Teodorita" (m. Frederick Mueller. There are two records of Maria Teodora: b. January 20, 1835; b. May 16, 1842, perhaps one died and another renamed.)
- Juana Catalina "Juanita" (b. July 6, 1838; m. Louis Joseph Docither Clouthier; d. November 14, 1892, Taos)
- Juan Lucas Manuel (b. June 28, 1840, Taos; d. young, before 1850)
- Maria Petra "Petrita" (b. June 28, 1844, Taos; m. ___Abreu, November 26, 1859, Taos; d. 1914)
- Juan Cristobal Pablo (b. July 1848, Taos; d. 1903)

Died: February 10, 1864, Taos, New Mexico

Charles Beaubien, a French Canadian, left Quebec to begin life on his own in St. Louis, where French was the common language. He clerked for Auguste Chouteau and volunteered for Bernard Pratte's volunteer fire department.

In December (20 or 29) 1823, when Beaubien was twenty-three, he and seventeen others applied for passports so that they could trap in New Mexico. The passports were endorsed at Council Bluffs on February 19, 1824.

In Taos, New Mexico, he opened a dry goods store to outfit trappers and supply local needs. Three years later he became a Mexican citizen and married Maria Pabla Lobato.

In an effort to strengthen its hold on its New Mexico borderland, Mexico placed land in the hands of its citizens through a land grant system. Charles Beaubien and Guadalupe Miranda applied for a grant in present-day northern New Mexico and southern Colorado. Within a week Governor Armijo approved the grant; but, before documentation was complete, Taos' Padre Antonio Martinez blocked the procedure. He argued that the land should be given to the poor, not to those rich men. He only slowed the process; the government honored the grant.

Dick Wootton was well-acquainted with Martinez, Miranda, and Beaubien. He met and accompanied Beaubien and his party when they set up one of the boundary mounds on the grant. He often smuggled goods for Beaubien.

When General Kearny set up an occupation government in New Mexico, he appointed Beaubien as a judge in the superior court. For four decades Charles Beaubien was a man of influence in northern New Mexico.

Beckwourth, James "Jim" Pierson

Born: April 6, 1798, Fredericksburg, Virginia; family moved to Missouri
Parents: Father: Revolutionary war soldier; Mother: slave on his father's plantation
Siblings: 12 siblings
Appearance: Muscular; mulatto, yellow skinned
Character: Known for exaggerating, lying, bragging, and a violent temper; courageous; efficient; skillful
Indian nicknames: "Bull's Robe," "Bloody Arm," "The Crow," "Medicine Calf"
Married or lived with:
- Crow woman
- Luisa Sandoval (later married John Brown)
- Elizabeth Lettbetter, June 1860; they had one son before she left with the child.
- Sue, an Indian, c 1864

Died: c 1866, in a Crow village

At nineteen, Jim was apprenticed to a blacksmith in St. Louis, Missouri. There he became familiar with the fur trade. He ran away from the blacksmith shop to New Orleans and joined General William Henry Ashley's trapping expedition. He trapped for Ashley and others from 1823-1826.

Early in 1829 Jim moved in with the Crow Indians, lived with them several years, became a chief, and led them on raids against the Sioux, Cheyenne, and other Crow enemies. He married at least one Crow woman and had children. He wore Indian garb and looked so much the part that trappers often thought he was a Crow. His influence kept Crow trade tied to the American Fur Company.

Jim worked for Louis Vasquez and Andrew Sublette at Ft. Vasquez on the Platte River at the mouth of Vasquez Fork (Colorado). For a time he was in charge of the fort.

He fought in the U. S. Army in the Second Seminole War in Florida. He returned West, did some scouting, some horse thieving. He went to California a couple times on horse raiding trips, and worked in trading posts until 1850. While working with John C. Fremont in

1850, Jim discovered Beckwourth Pass in the Sierra Nevadas.

Because of his braggadocio and his cutthroat trading, Jim wasn't always held in high regard among mountain men, including Wootton. Jim sometimes waited until his customers were drunk before he traded with them. One time Bill Williams saw him trading three buffalo robes and two beaver pelts for one quart of Taos lightening after the Indians were intoxicated. Wiry Williams was indignant, "No one but a low-down half-breed nigger Frenchman would stick an Indian that way."[222] At that, Jim charged Bill. When the dust settled, Jim lay unconscious on the floor.

When Denver sprouted, Beckwourth set up shop there. When the city grew more than he liked, he returned to live with the Crow. This time they poisoned their former victorious chief to keep him from leaving them. He died sometime in the mid-late 1860's.

He had dictated his adventures to T. D. Boinner and left a vivid account of Western life during his time.

Bent Family: Charles, William, George, and Robert

Silas and Martha Kerr Bent moved from Virginia. They arrived in St. Louis six days before Lewis and Clark returned from their expedition to the Pacific (1806) and settled in Carondolet. Silas held a number of high government offices. From 1813-1821 he served as Chief Justice of Missouri Territory's Supreme Court. His father had been a leader in the Boston Tea Party.

Silas and Martha had eleven children: Charles; Juliannah (b. 1801; m. Lilburn Boggs, future Missouri governor); John (b. 1803, an attorney); Lucy (b. 1805. She named her third child for her brother, Charles. Her son, in turn, named his son Charles: Charles Marion Russell, famed Western artist.); Dorcas (m. Judge William Chiles Carr of Missouri); Edward; Mary (m. Jonathan Bean, 1836); William; George; Robert; and Silas, Jr. The Bent children didn't grow up in poverty, nor did they lack education.

St. Louis was small with only three main streets running north and south; it was beautiful and cultured for that time in America. During the years Silas and Martha raised their children, St. Louis was the U. S.' western fur capital. The children were aware of the western fur trade. Four of the boys would live their adult lives in the Rocky Mountain region. The boys were fluent in English and French and became fluent in Spanish. Charles and William, perhaps George and Robert, also became fluent in Indian dialects. They were of Massachusetts Puritan stock; but because of their appearance and fluency in French, some thought they were French Canadian.

Silas Bent died on November 20, 1827. In the spring of 1832 Martha Bent gave permission for sons George (18) and Robert (16) to go to the Rockies with their brothers. They traveled west on the same wagon train as Ceran St. Vrain's younger brother Marcellin.

Charles Bent

<u>Born</u>: November 11, 1799, Charleston, Virginia (not today's West Virginia)

---

[222] Lavender, *Bent's Fort*, 228.

Parents: Silas and Martha Bent

Appearance: 5'7" tall; black hair; gray eyes; high forehead

Indian nicknames: "Gray-haired white man"; Who-pi-ve-heo (Cheyenne)

Married: Maria Ignacia Jaramillo (widow of Rumaldo Luna and sister of Mrs. Kit Carson), late 1835 or early 1836

Children:

- Alfredo (b. or bap., February 12, 1837; educated in St. Louis; m. Guadalupe Long; d. December 9, 1865, Taos; murdered by Greek George, a Mexican; left 3 children)
- George and Maria Virginia (died in infancy)
- Estafana/Estafina (b. Taos; [c 1853, Ceran St. Vrain took her to Loretto Academy in Santa Fe, where she attended school four years.]; m. Alexander Hicklin; d. September 1, 1927)
- Maria Teresina (b. November 15, 1842; m. Aloys Scheurich, May 31, 1865. Teresina also went to boarding school at Sisters of Loretto Convent, Santa Fe.)
- step-daughter: Rumalda Luna (b. c 1832; m.Tom Boggs)

Died: January 19, 1847, Taos, New Mexico, buried: Santa Fe National Cemetery, Santa Fe.

When Charles was five-and-a-half, his family moved to St. Louis. During his teens, his brother John and he attended Jefferson College in Canonsburg, Pennsylvania.

In the early 1820's Charles trapped and traded on the Missouri River for the Missouri Fur Company. He headquartered at Ft. Recovery the winter of 1823-24. In 1825 he quit working for others and partnered in the reorganized Missouri Fur Company. Three years later he traded with Indians on the Bear River and near Sweet Water (Bear) Lake. He attended the trappers' Bear Lake Rendezvous before he traveled south to trade and trap along the Platte and Arkansas Rivers.

In May 1829 Charles (age 30) and his brother William (age 20) bought goods on credit, drove to Round Grove, and joined the Santa Fe Trail spring wagon train. Charles' friend David Waldo, a member of the train, nominated Charles to lead. As wagon master, Charles led the thirty-eight-wagon train to Santa Fe. It was the first year the military escorted a spring train. The United States had no cavalry yet; so Major Bennett Riley's infantry walked alongside the train, across the Plains to the Mexican border. New Mexico was a Mexican territory until 1846.

Within five weeks of arrival in New Mexico, the brothers multiplied their investment. The next year they traveled the Trail as traders and formed a partnership with Ceran St. Vrain. That partnership became the singular most influential trading and merchandising enterprise in the 19th century Southwest.

Charles' primary position in the firm was to operate the company store in Taos, New Mexico, and make at least one round trip to the States annually. He took trade goods East and returned with merchandise for the company forts and stores. It was on such a trip in 1836 that Dick Wootton and Charles Bent met.

By 1832 Charles established Taos as home. He did enough surveying on the side to be listed as a surveyor in the 1839 New Mexico list of foreigners. Townsfolk appreciated Charles' elementary medical knowledge and often asked advice, which he gave without charge. They were glad to have access to the few medical supplies he carried in his store.

About 1835 Charles married Ignacia Jaramillo, a pretty young widow, who had a little daughter. He taught Ignacia to speak English. Ignacia's influential Taos family was related to many prominent Spanish families in the area. Spanish families in Taos were like the early French families in St. Louis: connected and intertwined. If one searched beyond the third canon among the Hispanic families in Taos—or early northern New Mexico, it would be difficult to find one unrelated, or at least one who did not share a relative in common.[223]

Although Charles maintained American citizenship, he gained political prominence in Taos. He made deep friendships with many people in various walks of life. He also gained disapproval of a few—like Padre Antonio Martinez. Occasionally New Mexico Governor Manuel Armijo gave Charles or one of his friends a reduction in tariffs on goods brought into New Mexico.

In January 1845, when Charles heard of James Polk's election as U. S. President, he wrote American Counsel Manuel Alvarez, and voiced concern about what difficulties the election could mean to New Mexico. Little did he know what it would mean to him personally. Charles was at Bent's Fort when Colonel Stephen Watts Kearny visited in late 1845. On their annual supply trip in 1846, Charles and Ceran (St. Vrain) went out of their way to see Kearny at Ft. Leavenworth. They apprised him of conditions in New Mexico.

General Stephen Kearny took New Mexico, established a code of operation, and appointed territorial officers. He chose Charles Bent first governor of New Mexico Territory.

After Kearny left, rumors of rebellion stirred in Santa Fe. With a leak of the plans and news of an American victory in Mexico, Santa Fe seemed to settle down. But rumbles of discontent stirred in Taos; Charles and a small entourage traveled to Taos. Most Taos residents were friends or relatives. His presence and influence should quell any insurrection.

That night Charles and his family heard voices. Noise grew as a clamoring mob came close to their home. The angry mob gained entrance, scalped and killed Charles—January 19, 1847. The Taos Revolt had begun.

William Wells Bent

Born: May 23, 1809, St. Louis, Missouri
Parents: Silas and Martha (Kerr) Bent
Appearance: Dark hair; strong nose; short
Character: individualistic; deeply loyal, deeply caring though not always obvious; shrewd; patient; occasional quick flares of anger
Indian Nickname: Little White Man (Cheyenne); Hook Nose (Kiowa)
Married:
- Owl Woman (Mis-stan-stur), (m. dates vary: 1835-1837; d. result of childbirth, 1847)
- Yellow Woman (Owl Woman's sister; both daughters of Cheyenne Chief Gray Thunder)
- Adelina Harvey, 1867; daughter of Alexander Harvey and a Blackfoot-Sioux

Children: William named all his children for a brother or sister. Five were Owl Woman's, one

---

[223] Ignacia Bent, Josefa Carson, and Rumalda Boggs were distant cousins of Mary Pauline Lujan Wootton.

was Yellow Woman's. There is question as to birth order of Julia and Charles: which was Owl Woman's last child, which was Yellow Woman's only child?

- Mary "Mollie" (b. January 22, 1838; m. R. M. Moore, Westport; d. 1878. Mary bore the culture of her Missouri family. She was said to be more cultured than many American ladies who settled on the frontier.)
- Robert (School: Westport 1853-1857; St. Louis until 1861; returned to Westport in summers; m. Cedar Woman)
- George
- Charles (School: Westport; after 1853 in St. Louis under guardianship of William Bernard; wounded in battle, died of malaria in an Indian camp, November 1868)
- Julia (b. July 20, 184_; m. Ed Guerrier)

Died: May 19, 1869

William built a small picket post between present-day Canon City and Pueblo, Colorado. He persuaded his brother Charles and Ceran St. Vrain on the merits of trading with Indians. The three partnered in the Bent-St. Vrain Company.

William supervised construction of the company fort near the Arkansas River. When a smallpox epidemic broke out during construction, William isolated the diseased and sent runners to Indian camps to be sure they didn't come near the fort during the outbreak. Rumor was that a Mexican making the adobe brought the disease. William contracted smallpox. Ceran St. Vrain was stricken and transported to Taos on a mule litter. As William recovered, he nursed those who couldn't be moved to help. He burned all articles touched by the disease.

Charles often referred to the fort as William's Fort. It is better known as Bent's Fort or Bent's Old Fort. William's work ethic and shrewd business skill, his hospitable nature, and his resolute purpose, were at the heart of the fort's operation.

Occasionally, William went to Taos on business; but he rarely accompanied company supply trains to Missouri. His chief interest in the business was trading with Indians in and out of Bent's Fort and supplying trappers and traders. Dick Wootton worked for him as hunter and then as a company trader when he first came West. William dealt with chiefs and was a chief in his domain. At the fort, he sometimes dressed like a chief. He adapted to customs of the region, but maintained the manners and hospitality of his upbringing.

While trapping, William rescued two Cheyenne from the Comanche. That began a lifelong friendship with the Cheyenne. He married Mis-stan-stur, a Cheyenne. After her death, he married her sister.

Except for the death of his brother Robert, the 1830's and early 1840's were good years for him. Then came Stephen Kearny and his Missouri Volunteers headed for the Mexican War. The Army appreciated the western intelligence at Bent's Fort, enjoyed rest and recreation, but preferred to be guests without remuneration.

The Army drew upon Bent's patriotic hospitality. The Army desired supplies on hand, in case they were needed; but, when they were not, the company was left holding the bag—not to mention the litter the Army left behind, at and around the fort when it moved on.

The following January (1847) Taos rebels scalped his brother Charles. Later in the year William's wife bore him another child and died. At the same time, the Indian situation appeared foreboding.

William's brother George investigated the situation. The way tribes were behaving along the Canadian it wasn't time to reopen the company's Ft. Adobe.

Then George came down sick. William did all he could, but George died in October.

The good old days had begun to change, as good old days will. With U. S. military presence in New Mexico, Ceran St. Vrain saw a market for troop supplies. William and Ceran decided to dissolve Bent-St. Vrain & Co., not with animosity, but desiring different business directions: William, the Indian trade; Ceran, troop supplies.

During the Mexican-American War, the U. S. government expected William to supply, store, clean up, bear up, and continue to help. Never did pay for everything. The government talked of buying the fort and haggled with William. It was worth the price William asked. If the government didn't think so, that was that; but William wasn't going to give the fort away. And he wasn't going to continue providing. He asked $16,000. Government representatives offered $12,000. They haggled back and forth, but never settled on a price.

There came a day in 1852 William had enough. His son George said he was despondent over the deaths of his brothers. William loaded everything he wanted to keep onto sixteen wagons and drove them out of the fort. He walked back inside and torched the few kegs of gunpowder he'd left behind. Bent's Old Fort boomed and blazed. When the last ember cooled, remnants of adobe walls sat silent on the prairie. Now there would be no more bickering over terms while the government used the fort at their convenience.[224]

He drove his wagons about thirty-five to thirty-eight miles away from the old fort. He'd build again. He hired men to hew stone for a new fort, Bent's New Stone Fort. Near the Arkansas River, it was a good location—plenty of water, plenty of wood, and a view of the countryside for miles around. Arapaho, Cheyenne and Kiowa frequented the area.

The construction crew was beginning to lay the walls in the spring of 1853 before William left to buy supplies in Missouri. While in Missouri, he obtained a contract to haul freight.

William and his traders traded in outlying Indian camps throughout the year. Now that there was no Bent-St. Vrain partnership, William took hides and trade goods East each spring. He'd purchase supplies, and return with government annuities for the Indians and supplies for his Stone Fort, which was completed the following year.[225]

In the fall of 1853 he took his three oldest children to school in Westport, Missouri and left them in the guardianship of Albert Boone—brother of Panthea Boone Boggs. (After William's sister Juliannah died, her widower married Panthea.) William thought it best for his children to adjust to Westport before going to live in the city—St. Louis—with his sister Dorcas Carr.

William seemed to have an inborn ability to work with Indians and represented them when

---

[224] With Bent's permission, Barlow and Sanderson later repaired a portion of the fort and used it as a stage station. Travelers used the walls as a message board for those coming after them. Settlers moving into the valley salvaged remnants of the old fort and used them in their homes and out buildings.

[225] Walls of the Stone Fort were 100'x135', approximately 15' high. The double-door gate allowed man or wagon to enter. Twelve rooms surrounded the central courtyard, including: two rooms for Bent family quarters; men's quarters; blacksmith shop; large storage room; a room for Bent's trader, John Sprole. William operated his new fort as a trading post five or six years.

needed, whether working with a tribe and the U. S. government, or working among tribes. In 1858 he took one tribal leader from each of the Plains Indian tribes to visit Washington, D. C.

On April 27, 1859, President Buchanan appointed him as an Indian agent. William accepted the appointment as a temporary position while he was in St. Louis in May 1859. The Senate confirmed his appointment on March 2, 1860. At the same time, William's oldest son, Robert, took out a government contract to haul annuity goods for distribution on the South Platte.

William requested the government build a fort at Pawnee Rock. As a result, Ft. Larned was under construction when he returned to St. Louis in February 1860. The government wanted to use his fort again, his New Stone Fort this time. The official asked William's price for the Stone Fort. $12,000 sounded good to him. That's the price the government offered for his other fort. No, the quartermaster wouldn't consider paying such a price.

William went to Westport for his daughter Mary's wedding to R. M. Moore on April 3, 1860.

Dickering over the fort continued. On September 9, 1860, William and Quartermaster Lt. James B. McIntyre agreed on a seven month lease at $65 per month. The government named the fort, Ft. Wise in honor of Virginia's governor and added officers' quarters and soldiers' barracks. When the Civil War began, it wasn't appropriate to have a U. S. fort named for the governor of a Confederate state; so the name was changed to Ft. Lyon in memory of General Nathaniel Lyon, who was killed in the early Civil War Battle of Wilson Creek, Missouri. Meantime William resigned as Indian agent and he and his son Robert focused their effort on his stockade at the mouth of the Purgatory. His daughter Mary and her husband moved out from Westport to join them. Sons George and Charles remained in school in Missouri.

There are two stories concerning the U. S. government lease of William's fort: 1. The government paid rent initially, stopped paying, but continued to use the fort. 2. The government hadn't paid a dime by the spring of 1864. Then the government paid past rent through the summer of 1862 and let it go at that.

During the Civil War, there was strong Southern sentiment in Missouri. Out of a population of 5000, only seventy-two Kansas City (Missouri) residents voted for Abe Lincoln. Silas, William's only surviving brother, resigned his Navy commission, but didn't join the Confederacy. Two of William's sons joined the Confederacy. George, almost eighteen, joined at Westport while there on summer vacation. Charles joined soon after. Even through all the rigmarole about the fort, William remained loyal to the Union and kept hauling its freight.

In October 1862 son George was captured at Corinth and taken to prison camp in Missouri. Son Robert was in St. Louis on business for his father when George and other Confederate prisoners were marched through town. A friend of George saw him and found Robert. Robert, in turn, went to military headquarters, where many knew his father. He secured George's release, and promised to take him West and keep him out of the War. He did. By the time they arrived home in early 1863, they found young Charles already there. Out of the Army for whatever reason, teenaged Charles seemed disgruntled, full of hatred. When Indians came by William's stockade, Charles left with them.

Robert and Mary, with her husband and child, were happy to live at the stockade. William encouraged George to stay, bought him a fine horse, made things nice for him. In spite of the fact it'd been years since he'd lived in an Indian camp, George left to live with his mother's people, the Cheyenne. William's youngest daughter, Julia, married Ed Guerrier, also half-Indian; they also had gone to live in the Cheyenne camp.

In February 1864 Secretary of War Stanton recommended the government buy William's fort; but, in March, the government decided it would be better to relocate. The government claimed William didn't have clear title to the land on which the fort was built, said the land belonged to the Indians. For the time being, however, the government was pleased to use William's fort on that land.

As the Civil War continued, Plains Indians used the situation to advantage, plundered, and killed. William was aware trouble was brewing between Indians, settlers, and the government. Tensions rose. When Chivington marched to Sand Creek in November 1864, he posted a guard on William; so William couldn't warn Chief Black Kettle and his Cheyenne. Though William's children weren't killed, his embittered son, Charles, became a "Dog Soldier" determined to drive out Americans by whatever means necessary. At one point, after a price was put on Charles' head, he went home to kill his father. Fortunately, William was in New Mexico. Not long after, in 1868, Charles was wounded while fighting the Pawnee. He caught malaria and died among his Cheyenne people.

The flood of 1866 damaged Bent's Stone Fort; so the government abandoned it to establish a new Ft. Lyon about twenty miles away. In the winter of 1866-67 William went to Washington. The quartermaster claimed the government still needed William's fort for storage and reminded William that, after all, he didn't own the land.

How does one evict the government?

William returned home. The difference in his finances: minus the cost of his trip.

Early May 1869 William started his spring train eastward, up across the New Mexico line, passed his old friend Dick Wootton's place. He passed old Bent's Fort and stopped at his place on the Purgatory. When he arrived, his daughter Mary saw how sick he was and sent for the doctor from Ft. Lyon. Pneumonia, the doctor said.

William died four days before his sixtieth birthday. His obituary in the Pueblo, Colorado, *Chieftain* estimated he left a fortune of $150,000-$200,000. But William and his brothers George, Robert, and Charles, left a legacy to the Plains and the Mountains, to the United States as a nation, which cannot be measured in dollars. It cannot be measured. They were honest men in a hard land. They paved paths, provided refuge, set standards, and gave a foothold of opportunity to countless men and women throughout the nation and some across the sea. They aided Indian nations and the United States.

George Bent

Born: April 15, 1814, St. Louis, Missouri
Indian Nickname: Little Beaver (Cheyenne)
Married: Cruz Padilla, early 1840's
Children: Robert "Elfego" (educated in St. Louis, finished school in 1854; oldtimer Jesse

Nelson said it did him no good.); and a daughter

Died: October 23, 1847, Bent's Fort on the Arkansas River; buried: outside Bent's Fort next to his brother Robert. Both brothers were reburied in St. Louis.

Like his brothers, George treated Indians with respect and gained the respect of the tribes with whom he traded. A skilled trader, he worked out of Bent's Fort and for the company store in Taos. He may have become a partner in the company; for, in 1837, Charles, William, Ceran, and he signed a claim against the government for damages from a Pawnee attack. When William was away, George often took charge of Bent's Fort, as he did in July 1844 when he fired the cannon to welcome Fremont's returning expedition.

When George became ill a few months after his brother Charles was massacred, William took him to Bent's Fort, saw to it George had every help he could provide for recovery. In spite of his watchful nursing, George died. The obituary in the *Santa Fe Republican*, November 13, 1847, said George died of "the fever." Carson's biographer called it consumption. He was thirty-three.

Attorney Frank Blair became guardian of George's son Elfego until he finished school.

Robert Bent

Born: February 23, 1816, St. Louis, Missouri
Indian Nickname: Green Bird (Cheyenne)
Appearance: Handsomest of the four western Bent brothers
Died: October 29, 1841, Bent's Fort on the Arkansas River; buried: outside Bent's Fort

After coming to the Rockies, Robert worked in and out of Bent's Fort. He'd been in the area nine years when Comanche killed him outside the fort. Men from the fort buried him near the fort walls. They covered his grave with rocks and cactus to keep the wolves away. He was twenty-five.

Boggs, Thomas "Tom" Oliver

Born: August 1824, Harmony Mission, Indian Territory
Parents: Gov. Lilburn W. and Panthea Boone Boggs; (Lilburn's first wife, Juliannah Bent, was sister of Charles and William Bent.)
Married: Rumalda Luna (daughter of Rafael and Ignacia Jaramillo Luna) m. spring 1846
Children: Charles, Minnie
Died: September 29, 1894, Clayton, New Mexico Territory

Tom was the oldest of Lilburn and Panthea Boone Boggs' ten children. Though he was not a blood relative of Charles and William Bent, Tom and his siblings called them uncle because their half-brothers, Henry and Angus, were Charles and William's nephews.

Tom was twelve when his father became governor of Missouri in 1836.

About 1845 young Tom came West. In 1846 he married Rumalda Luna, step-daughter of Charles Bent and niece of Kit Carson's wife.

Tom and Rumalda lived in various places in New Mexico, California, and Colorado. Tom worked at various occupations. He farmed, traded, ranched, and carried mail or dispatches. After the Mexican War, the family lived in California. In 1855 they returned to New Mexico, where he worked for Lucien Maxwell.

Ceran St. Vrain deeded 10,000 acres of his land grant to Tom and Rumalda Boggs. With L. A. Allen, and Charles Rict, Tom Boggs established Boggsville, Colorado (about a mile and a half southeast of Las Animas, Colorado). They raised food and stock for settlers, travelers, and for nearby Ft. Lyon. John Prowers, who'd worked with Tom at Bent's Fort and for Bent in Taos; merchant John Hough; and Kit Carson, joined them.

Boggsville was a regional center from 1863-1873. It was the county seat in 1870 when residents elected Tom Boggs sheriff. The next year he was elected to the Colorado Territorial legislature. When the railroad entered the area, Boggsville lost its prominence.

Tom was executor of Kit Carson's will in May 1868. According to the Carsons' desire, Rumalda and he assumed responsibility of raising Carsons' children.

The Boggs moved to Springer, New Mexico, in 1876 or 1877 and later to Clayton, New Mexico Territory, where they both lived until death.

Bridger, James "Jim"
Born: March 17, 1804, Richmond, Virginia; moved to St. Louis with his family, 1812
Parents: James and Chloe Bridger
Appearance: Over 6' tall, thin, rawboned; thick neck; blue-gray eyes; brown hair
Character: Friendly, generous, sensitive, serious
Nickname: "Old Gabe"—Jedediah Smith once said Bridger had the ability of the angel Gabriel when it came to leading men, hence, his nickname.
Marriages and Children:
- Cora, a Flathead Indian, 1835; 3 children; Cora died 1846.
- Ute woman, c 1846-48; she died in childbirth in 1849.
- Shoshone chief's daughter

Died: July 17, 1881, on his Missouri farm (now within Kansas City).

By the time Jim was fourteen, both his parents died. His sister went to live with a relative; Jim apprenticed to a blacksmith until he joined William Henry Ashley's trappers in 1822.

Trapping for Ashley in the Rocky Mountains, Jim was the first white man to discover the Great Salt Lake. He also discovered South Pass (Bridger Pass). In the winter of 1824-25 he saw Yellowstone's geysers (discovered by John Colter and earlier by French trappers). On his return to the States, people didn't believe his stories of water shooting up out of the earth.

By the time he was twenty-six, Bridger was a partner in the Rocky Mountain Fur Company, competitor of Astor's American Fur Company and Hudson's Bay Company.

Indians shot two arrows into his back as he was trapping in 1832. Fellow trappers removed one arrow, but were only able to remove part of the other. A piece of arrow remained lodged in the back of his neck until missionary Dr. Marcus Whitman removed it with a butcher knife in 1835.

In 1843 Jim Bridger and Louis Vasquez established Ft. Bridger on the bank of the Green River (Wyoming). They catered to Oregon Trail emigrants on their way to California or the Pacific Northwest. They offered fresh animals, a blacksmith shop, and a well-stocked store. Bridger operated the fort until the Mormons took charge in 1853. Some say they bought it;

Bridger said they drove him out.

He guided many along the Oregon Trail. He traversed the West from southern Colorado, north to the Canadian border. In the years after he left his fort, Bridger:
- guided Colonel Albert Sidney Johnston and his troops during the Mormon War (1857-58).
- guided Captain William V. Reynolds' exploration of the Yellowstone area (1859-60).
- showed South Pass to General Granville Dodge's surveyors (1865). South Pass provided a gateway across the Rockies for the Union Pacific Railway and, decades later, a route for an interstate highway.
- guided the Powder River Expedition (1865-66).
- measured the distance of the Bozeman Trail from Fort Kearny, Nebraska, to Virginia City, Montana, for the U. S. government (1866).

Jim was good natured, hospitable, and trustworthy. He was known for his tall tales—not as a liar, but as a yarn spinner/storyteller. He loved telling tales with such a serious demeanor that he often drew newcomers into his story web. Once they swallowed his tales hook, line, and sinker, he'd laugh out loud.

Jim was a bit superstitious, sometimes seemed a little rough on the edges; but he was highly respected among his peers. Though he didn't have the advantage of a formal education and was illiterate, Jim Bridger was shrewd and intelligent.

With rheumatism and failing eyesight, Jim returned East in 1868 and settled on a Missouri farm, where he died at age 77.

Brown, John

Married: Luisa Sandoval
Children: 12 sons, 3 daughters, among them:
- Matilda (1844)
- Lola (1846)
- John (1847)
- Joseph (1848)

Brown was one of the original settlers, or the originator, of Greenhorn (Colorado) settlement. He had log houses and a trading post there in the mid-1840's. Dick Wootton knew Brown in their El Pueblo years. He said Brown had hewn crude millstones of granite and set up a grist mill in a log building. It was the first grist mill in the Arkansas Valley.

Some thought John was a little odd because he claimed to be a medium.

John, Luisa, and their children left the Arkansas Valley with a group going to the San Bernardino, California, area about 1848.

Carson, Christopher "Kit" Houston

Born: December 24, 1809, two miles northwest of Richmond, Madison County, Kentucky
Parents: Lindsey and Rebecca Robinson Carson
Siblings: Each of Kit's brothers spent some time in the West.
Full siblings: Elizabeth, Nancy, Robert, Matilda, Hamilton, Hampton, Mary Ann, Sarshall, Lindsey; Half siblings from his father's first marriage: William, Sarah, Andrew, Moses,

Sophia; Siblings from his mother's second marriage: brother(s?) and sister

Appearance: Height accounts vary: 5' 4"- 5'7"; short legs, long body; light weight (accounts: 125-145 lbs.); soft blue eyes; light brown hair with a reddish cast, hair worn to his ears, sometimes to his collar; clean shaven, except for a moustache, at times; freckled face; wide forehead

Character: Good natured; modest; man of few words; spoke slowly, to the point

Married:
- Waa-nibe ("Singing Wind," "Singing Grass," "Singing Wind Grass Singing"), m. 1836; she died c 1840.
  Children: Adaline (b. c 1837); daughter (d. about age three, Taos)
- Making-out-Road, southern Cheyenne, m. c 1841-42 (The story is she divorced Kit soon after marriage. The marriage is credited by many, including Jesse Nelson a nephew by marriage, but denied by Carson's niece Teresina Bent.)
- Maria Josefa "Chipita" Jaramillo (b. March 18, 1828, Santa Cruz de la Canada, New Mexico, to Francisco and Maria Apolonia (Vigil) Jaramillo; sister of Mrs. Charles Bent; m. February 6, 1843, Taos, New Mexico; Padre Antonio Jose Martinez, officiated; George Bent and Maria de la Cruz Padilla witnessed; d. April 23, 1868, Boggsville, Colorado.) Children:
  - Charles (b. May 1, 1849/50; d. May 1851)
  - William (Julian) (b. October 1, 1852/3)
  - Teresina (b. June or July 1855; m. DeWitt Fulton Allen; d. July 6, 1916; bur. Kit Carson Cemetery, Taos)
  - Christopher Charles (b. June 12, 1858; d. May 14, 1890)
  - Charles (b. August 2, 1861; d. July 21, 1938)
  - Rebecca (b. April 13, 1864; m. Mr. Lewis; d. April 9, 1885, bur. Kit Carson Cemetery)
  - Estefana "Estafanita" (b. December 23, 1866; m. Mr. Wood; d. October 1, 1899)
  - Josephine "Josefita" (b. April 13, 1868, Boggsville, Colorado; d. October 10, 1890)

Died: May 23, 1868, Ft. Lyon, Colorado (Kit died on William Bent's last birthday.)

Before he was three years old, Kit moved with his family from Kentucky to Howard County, Missouri, where he grew up on a farm. Before he reached his teens, Kit's father was killed by a falling tree in 1818. In 1821, his mother remarried (Joseph Martin).

Kit wasn't educated. At fourteen he was apprenticed to saddle maker David Workman in Franklin, Missouri, where wagon trains outfitted for Santa Fe Trail travel. In August 1826, after working for Workman two years, Kit ran away and worked his way West on a wagon train headed to Santa Fe. His brother Robert and half-brother Andrew had been West with Sibley's Santa Fe Trail survey crew in 1825.

Concerned about his apprentice, Workman advertised in the *Missouri Intelligencer*. He described Christopher Carson as thickset, small for his age, with light hair. He offered a penny for his return. Tom Tobin and Carson, who were from the same town, often enjoyed chuckling over that article from their hometown paper.

Carson arrived in Santa Fe in November 1826 and spent the winter in Santa Fe and Taos, as teamster and cook for Mathew Kincaid, a friend of Kit's father. In the summer Kit worked as a teamster. The second winter he cooked for Ewing Young in Taos.

By 1828 Kit spoke Spanish fluently enough to accompany trader Colonel Trammell into Mexico as an interpreter. On the trip he met Robert McKnight, operator of the Santa Rita (New Mexico) copper mine. For the next few months—until August, Kit drove teams at the mine for McKnight.

He left McKnight to trap with Ewing Young's expedition through present-day Arizona, into California and back to Taos (April 1831). Kit made Taos his home base. As he trapped independently with various parties for the next few years, he gained understanding of western terrain.

About 1836 Kit married Waa-nibe, a northern Arapaho. They had two daughters: Adaline and a younger girl. Adaline was about three years old when her mother died. The younger child died in Taos when she fell into a pot of boiling soap. After Waa-nibe's death, Kit worked at Bent's Fort from September 1841-April 1842.

A good friend of Charles Bent, Kit met Mrs. Bent's sister Josefa. He wanted to marry her, but her family hesitated: Kit wasn't Catholic; and his little daughter, Adaline, was half-Indian. On January 28, 1842, Padre Antonio Martinez baptized Kit into the Catholic Church and took care of that part of the problem. But the other...Kit loved both Josefa and Adaline. He talked the matter over with Bent and decided to take Adaline to school in Missouri. She'd profit from the education and could return when she was older. In April, Kit and Adaline left the fort with the Bent-St. Vrain spring wagon train to Missouri.

In Missouri, they visited friends and relatives, while Kit arranged for Adaline to live with his sister (probably Elizabeth, possibly Mary Ann) and enrolled her in school in St. Louis.

While on a steamer going up the Missouri River, Kit met John C. Fremont, son-in-law of Missouri's long-term Congressman Thomas Hart Benton. Fremont, almost four years younger than Carson, was with the U. S. Army's Topographical Engineers and was planning a government expedition. He told Kit he hoped to get Captain Andrew Drips to guide him, but Carson told Fremont he could do the job. Fremont hired him for $100 a month.

Carson guided expeditions for Fremont, Major Beall and, when the Army of the West traveled from New Mexico to California during the Mexican War, for General Stephen Kearny. He also traveled to Washington D. C. with military dispatches.

Carson tutored Fremont concerning western life, Indians, and routes. Some found Fremont difficult to work with. Carson and Fremont did have disagreements; but Carson's skill in dealing with people dissipated the differences. When reporting his expeditions, Fremont told of Carson. In stories and books Kit became the iconic hero of the Western frontier.

Colonel Henry Inman quoted Kit, after he was shown a magazine cover depicting him in an action, "'Gentlemen, that thar may be true, but I haint got no recollection of it.'" But Inman went on to say, "there is less difference between the real Carson and his legend than is usually the case with frontier heroes. This is because Carson was really a man of many admirable qualities and few reprehensible traits and because he really did lead a strenuous and adventuresome life."[226]

---

[226] Inman, *Old Santa Fe Trail*, 174.

After Kit guided Fremont's first expedition, he returned to Taos and married Maria Josefa Jaramillo (February 6, 1843).

From July 1843-July 1844 Kit Carson and Thomas Fitzpatrick guided Fremont's second expedition from Bent's Fort,[227] through parts of the Pacific Northwest, Nevada, and California, and back to Bent's Fort. On his return Kit and Dick Owens farmed and ranched on the Little Cimarron east of Taos. Kit built a cabin, and Josefa joined him.

By the end of summer 1845 Fremont was ready for Carson and Owens to join him on another expedition. This time they trekked to California, where both Fremont and Carson became involved in Mexican War activities. Carson served in the California Battalion. He was in California at the time of the Taos Massacre. Josefa was at her sister's home in Taos the night the rebels came and scalped her brother-in-law Charles Bent.

In 1850 Kit built a small home on his place at Rayado and went back to ranching. He had quite a time trying to keep enough stock on hand for himself and the thieving Indians who came by his place. While there, Kit and Tom Goodall drove horses and mules up to Ft. Laramie and traded with emigrants on the Oregon Trail.

In March 1851 Kit went to St. Louis and picked up a load of goods for Lucien Maxwell.

In 1853 he drove sheep cross-country to the California gold field. His daughter Adaline and her husband Louey Simonds went along and stayed in California. Maxwell had also gone to California; Carson and he returned together and arrived in Taos on Christmas Day 1853.

On his arrival Kit learned he'd been appointed Indian Agent, headquartered in Taos. Over the years Carson did his best to be just, to give equitable representation of both sides, whether as liaison between the government and a tribe or between tribes. He worked among Apache, Cheyenne, Navajo, Arapaho, and Ute. In his lifetime Indians, the government, and his fellow mountain men held him in high esteem. Dick Wootton had met Kit while trapping in the 1840's, respected his abilities and principles, and enjoyed his friendship as long as they lived.

In 1860, while Kit was elk hunting in southern Colorado, his horse lost its footing going down a steep slope and dragged him. Kit developed an aneurysm in the blood vessel above his heart, which he attributed to the accident.

When Ceran St. Vrain was unable to lead the New Mexico Volunteer Infantry during the Civil War, he resigned. Kit was appointed colonel in his place. He served in the Army a little over six years, including the Battle of Valverde under General Canby, the Navajo and Apache campaigns under General Carleton, and the Battle of Adobe Walls. Although ordered to kill all braves when rounding up the Apache, Carson gave them the benefit of the doubt and granted sanctuary to those who fled to Ft. Stanton and surrendered.

He was placed in charge of Bosque Redondo until November 1864, when he was sent to Ft. Bascom. He later commanded at Ft. Garland. He could sign his name, but couldn't read or write; so various clerks performed his secretarial duties. He mustered out of the Army on November 22, 1867. Kit, Josefa, and the children moved to Boggsville, Colorado.

The U. S. government continued to call on Kit. In February 1868 he traveled by stagecoach to Washington D. C. to represent the Ute, his favorite tribe. Some Ute traveled

---

[227] Carson joined them at Ft. St. Vrain.

with him. From Washington, Kit went to Boston and New York to see if something could be done for the pain in his chest and neck. The aneurysm above his heart was causing spasms in his bronchial tubes and made him cough frequently. Breathing wasn't as easy as it used to be. Doctors in Boston and New York agreed with Colorado doctors: they could do nothing about the aneurysm on Kit's aorta. It could kill him at any time. Kit boarded a Union Pacific train in early April and traveled to Cheyenne, Wyoming. He rode the stage to Denver and a wagon to La Junta. Josefa met him in La Junta, and they rode home to Boggsville.

Kit arrived exhausted from the trip and from the frequent coughing. Two days later Josefa gave birth to Josephine, their seventh child. Ten days later she died from complications of childbirth.

As the weather warmed and the mountain snows melted, the streams began to swell. Kit found care for his children and moved across the river to the Army hospital—close enough for Dr. Henry Tilton's care; so neither of them need be concerned about having to cross the river. When the aneurysm leaked into his trachea, Kit spit up blood.

He'd been on a sick man's diet; but on May 23, 1868, he asked for and enjoyed a meal of buffalo, chile, and coffee. After eating, Kit lit his pipe and visited with the doctor and his son-in-law Aloys Scheurich. The blood vessel broke that afternoon. Kit hemorrhaged and died.

Kit and Josefa Carson were buried locally. They were reburied in Taos, New Mexico. On January 1, 1885, 1,200 people gathered at his grave in Taos for the dedication of a memorial tablet in his honor.

Edgar Hewett, preparing to write *Campfire and Trail*, interviewed Thomas Tobin:

"Did you know Kit Carson?"

"I et many a beaver tail with him," Tobin replied.

"Was Kit as fearless as they reported?"

"Wasn't afraid of hell or high water," Tom acknowledged.

"How was Kit in his private life?"

"Clean as a hound's tooth," Tobin testified.

Asked if Kit swore, Tobin answered, "Kit never swore more'n was necessary."

"Was Kit's word as good as it was said to have been?"

"Kit's word was as sure as the sun's coming up,"[228]

On June 1, 1868, the front page of the first issue of Dr. Michael Beshoar's *Colorado Weekly Chieftain* featured Kit Carson's obituary:

died at his residence on the Las Animas, on the 24th inst., of disease of the heart…From about the age of 17 years until 50, he lived the life of a hunter, trader & trapper…early became familiar with the mountains and plains from the Missouri to the Pacific…During all those years… constantly exposed to every hardship and danger. Sometimes making his home with some tribe…and assisting them in their wars against other tribes. Sometimes employed as a trapper by some mountain trader—sometimes trading on his own account…Unaided by the advantages of education or patronage,…he rose step by step until his name had become as familiar to the American people a household word….He stood…unsullied by the record of a littleness or meanness….Kindly of heart, tolerant to

---

[228] Klesinger, "Thomas Tate Tobin," 2.

all men, good in virtues of disposition…, he has passed away—dying as through his lifelong he had lived—in peace and charity with all men, and leaving behind him a name and memory to be cherished by his countrymen so long as modesty, valor, unobtrusive worth, charity and true chivalry survive among men…He leaves children of a tender age to mourn his loss.[229]

Chalifoux, Jean Baptiste
Born: Canada
Sibling: Pierre/Pedro Chalifoux

In the mid-1830's Baptiste came to the Southwest with a trapper brigade. He accompanied Wootton on the 1838-1840 expedition. Until that time he'd had a kindly outlook toward Indians. He changed his mind after he was chased and fell into a chasm.

After that trip Chalifoux never left the southern Rocky Mountains, knew the area well—especially Colorado's Spanish Peaks area. After he returned from the 1838-1840 expedition, Chalifoux and his Mexican wife opened a trading post in Embudo (early 1840's).

Dick Wootton told of a time during those years in New Mexico. Chalifoux was called to jury duty on a case in which an Indian was accused of killing a white man. The trial began; Chalifoux promptly fell asleep. He woke just in time to go with the jurors to a corner of the room to make their decision. When asked his opinion, Chalifoux didn't hesitate, "Hang him, of course; if he ain't guilty now he will be." His legs had healed, but his opinion was permanently altered.

At one time he lived on the Cuchara River between LaVeta and Walsenburg and raised corn and beans. About 1854, Chalifoux lived in a dugout downstream from Dick Wootton's place at Huerfano Village.

In 1859 he lived for a time near Grey's Creek, where he and companions built houses; but, through the years, he especially enjoyed wandering about.

Claymore, Auguste "Gus" (sometimes called Clermont)
Died: 1879, Nine Mile Bottom on the Purgatory River, Colorado

Claymore was dubbed "Last of the Trappers." When the beaver market plummeted, Claymore didn't turn to other pursuits like other trappers. He just kept on trapping.

In 1838 or 1839 Snake Indians attacked Claymore and bashed his head in. They didn't scalp him, but crushed his skull enough that part of his brain showed. His trapping companions found him and waited for him to die; but he recovered, lived more than 40 years.

In 1860 Claymore and "old Chalefou" (Baptiste Chalifoux) had a cabin in the Trinidad, Colorado, area.

In his latter years Claymore lived with Ben Ryder and Jesse Nelson on the Purgatoire River. One day he went camping and didn't come back; so Ryder sent his boys out to look for him. They found his burro and cart six miles from Nelson's house. They saw logs on the fire; nearby sat Claymore, dead.

---

[229] Mitchell, "…Death of Kit Carson," 2.

"Gus" Claymore and his cart

Doyle, Joseph "Joe" Bainbridge
Born: July 10, 1817, Mt. Pleasant, Virginia
Parents: Alexander and Jane Evans Doyle
Married: Maria de la Cruz "Cruzita" Suaso (c 1830-March 1, 1865; daughter of Manuel Antonio and Teresita Sandoval Suaso), October 14, 1844, Taos. Padre Martinez officiated.
Children: The first four were born in Mora Co., New Mexico.
- James "Jim" Quinn (b. December 1849; d. 1885, Trinidad, Colorado)
- Frances Teresa "Fannie" (b. December 5, 1852; m. Paul Berry, Jake Beard's nephew)
- Florence Ann "Flora" (b. 1855)
- Alexander Greene (b. May 1858; d. in the mid-1860's, Doyle's Ranch)
- Jose Lino (b. La Junta [Watrous], New Mexico, October 5, 1860)
- Jacob R. (m. Maria Estefan Gutierrez)
- possibly also Elizabeth

Died: March 10, 1864, Denver; buried: Doyle's Ranch (Colorado)

Born in Virginia, Joseph Doyle moved with his family to Illinois and then to St. Louis.

Like Dick Wootton, Doyle came West with Bent-St. Vrain Company. He began work for Bent in July 1839, the month he turned twenty-two. The next four years he learned by doing—traded with Indians, accompanied supply trains going East, and worked at the fort.

Wootton and Doyle met when Dick returned to Bent's Fort after his two-year trapping expedition. They became better acquainted at El Pueblo (Colorado), where they were neighbors farming, ranching, and trading. They remained lifelong friends.

In 1846 Doyle left El Pueblo with Alexander Barclay and built Ft. Barclay near the junction of the Mountain and Cimarron Branches of the Santa Fe Trail—in New Mexico. Mrs. Doyle's mother, Teresita, was with Barclay; so it was somewhat of a family endeavor.

Joe Doyle and Dick Wootton returned to Colorado in the early 1850's, settled in the Huerfano Valley, and were neighbors once again. When one was gone, the other looked out for his family. Doyle moved his family back to New Mexico after the 1854 El Pueblo Christmas Massacre.

From Ft. Barclay, he corresponded with Wootton and proposed a cross-country freighting partnership. Early in 1856, they began hauling government freight from Missouri to Ft. Union (New Mexico) and from there to outlying military posts. Their last run together was to Salt Lake City in the autumn of 1858.

Joe sold Ft. Barclay to his brother-in-law William Kroenig and returned to Colorado. He cultivated a 600 acre ranch, dug an irrigation system, and built a flour mill and a large clapboard house, which he called "Casa Blanca." He found a ready market for his cattle, sheep, and farm products in Pueblo, Denver, Canon City, at Ft. Union, and Ft. Garland.

In 1859 Doyle brought O. J. Goldrick from St. Louis to teach his children. But Goldrick went to Denver and opened the first school in the present state of Colorado.

In the early 1860's Dick Wootton and Doyle once again lived in the same vicinity. It was on Doyle's Ranch where Dick, widowed, married Fannie Brown in 1863.

Joe Doyle was a judge and commissioner in Huerfano County. He was elected to represent the county in the Colorado Territorial Legislature. In March 1864, while serving in the legislature, he suffered a heart attack. He died two or three days later.

Although he was known for his generosity and kindness, even to his competitors, Joe Doyle left an estate of over $100,000. There were many hands in the Doyle pot. Wootton continued as an overseer on Doyle's Ranch until after his wife Fannie died following childbirth in November 1864. Shortly after Fannie's death, Dick left to build a toll road across Raton Pass, leaving those with interests in the Doyle legacy to sort out their roles.

Mrs. Doyle died March 1, 1865—less than a year after Joe. Her oldest child was fourteen. There were rumors that Mrs. Doyle was poisoned because some were afraid Wootton would come back and marry her, and they would lose their share of the Doyle wealth. Mrs. Doyle's mother, Teresita Suaso, remained on the Doyle ranch until her death in 1894.

Fisher, Robert "Bob"
Born: 1807, Virginia
Parents: William and Nancy Fisher
Appearance: strong, tall, about 180 lbs.
Character: Dealt honorably; serious; obstinate when pushed, combative when angered
Married: Romualda Lopez (daughter of Ramon and Maria de la Luz Lopez), May 8, 1842
Children:
- Antonio Jorge "George" (b. April 1843, d. July 21, 1893, Colfax County, New Mexico)
- Antonia Josefa or Juana (b. May 17, 1844)
- Jose Melquiades "Joe" (b. August 31, 1845)

- Alejandro (b. July 18, 1847, Taos; d. October 23, 1905, Union County, New Mexico)
- Maria Preciliana (b. September 2, 1848)
- Norberto (b. May 24, 1850)
- Maria Trinidad

Died: California, 1852

At age seventeen Robert Fisher arrived in Taos on a wagon train with about 80 men. At first, he trapped. He worked many years for Bent-St. Vrain in and out of Bent's Fort. He was a strong and loyal Bent supporter.

In the early days of trapping and trading in New Mexico, many men became Mexican citizens for convenience sake—usually for business or marriage. In order to become a citizen one must be baptized in the Roman Catholic Church. For whatever reason, Robert was baptized in Taos seven years after his arrival.

In the late 1830's George Simpson and Bob joined Bill Williams on a trapping expedition into present-day Wyoming, Utah, and Nevada. On that trip Fisher and Simpson decided to learn the Indian trade and go in business for themselves.

They partnered (1842) with Francisco Conn, Mathew Kinkead and Joseph Mantz and established El Pueblo in the area of present-day Pueblo, Colorado. There was plenty of good water and grazing grass nearby. At El Pueblo Robert Fisher and David Spaulding worked for Simeon Turley. In 1843 Fisher sold out at El Pueblo and moved to nearby Hardscrabble.

In May 1842 Robert had married Romualda Lopez, one of Jose Ramon and Maria de la Luz Lopez' seven daughters. Three of Romualda's sisters married French trappers. She was Dolores Wootton's aunt and great-aunt of Mary Pauline Wootton.

In 1845 John Hatcher and he helped construct Bent-St. Vrain's Adobe Walls along the Red (Canadian) River in the Texas panhandle.

Robert was with a Bent trading party in Colorado when the Taos Rebellion broke out. When he heard about Charles Bent's assassination, he was concerned Romualda and their three small children may have been attacked. They survived. When it came time to try the offenders in Taos, Robert was chosen foreman of one of the petit juries.

William Bent sent Robert Fisher and Kit Carson to reopen Adobe Walls in the fall of 1849. Once again Comanche opposition squelched the effort. The men started back to Bent's Fort, but Apache ran off all but two of their mules; so the men walked back to the fort. Robert's work for Bent ended August 10, 1849, as Bent prepared to abandon Old Bent's Fort.

Fisher was one of the parties of trappers and soldiers who attempted to rescue Mrs. White, her child, and nurse in 1849.

In April 1850 he sold his Taos home and moved to Rayado near Kit Carson's place. Later in the year the gold fields of California lured him to try his hand at prospecting. Robert left for California with George Simpson before his last daughter was born. Romualda and the children remained in New Mexico. When Simpson returned, he brought Romualda word that Robert died in California.

Fitzpatrick, Thomas "Tom"
Born: 1799, Ireland

Appearance: Medium height, slim; dark brown hair (turned white during an adventure in 1832)
Character: Decisive; good common sense
Indian Nicknames: "White Hair," "Broken Hand" (The story is told that while he was being pursued, he attempted to remove his rifle cover, but shot and mutilated his left hand.)
Married: daughter of John Poisal and a Snake or Arapaho woman
Children: Two
Died: 1854, age 55 of pneumonia

After receiving a good education, Thomas Fitzpatrick came to the United States as a teenager. In the spring of 1823 he joined William Ashley and his trappers.

In 1830 Fitzpatrick, Jim Bridger, Henry Fraeb, Jean Baptiste Gervais, and Milton Sublette bought out Smith, Jackson, and Sublette's fur company. They renamed it the Rocky Mountain Fur Company. Fitzpatrick and Jedediah Smith were traveling for the company on the Santa Fe Trail when Comanche killed Smith. When the trapping trade waned, Fitzpatrick often served as a guide. He accompanied Fremont on his second expedition in 1843.

When Tom arrived at Bent's Fort on October 14, 1846, he learned he was in charge of the new Upper Platte Indian Agency, on the Arkansas, Kansas, and Platte Rivers. Headquartered at Bent's Fort, he served the Arapaho, Kiowa, Cheyenne, Sioux, and Shoshone.

During the Mexican-American War, he started to guide General Kearny to the Pacific, but was sent back to carry dispatches to Washington. After the war he returned to the Upper Platte Agency. In an attempt to establish hunting boundaries for the various tribes and to mediate safe travel for emigrants, he requested government funds for a conference at Ft. Laramie. The U. S. granted his request. U. S. government agents met with 10,000 Indians representing nine tribes at a conference at Ft. Laramie in the autumn of 1851.

Guerrier, William "Bill" (also spelled Garey, Guerier)
Married: Cheyenne woman, daughter of Gray Thunder
Child: Edmund "Ed" (m. Julia Bent, daughter of William Bent)

Bill Guerrier, a seasoned trader, is perhaps best known for the way he died. He was up at Ft. Laramie trading with the Sioux on his own account. As was the custom with traders, he had many goods on display. Several Indians were standing around when an old Indian came to buy gun powder. A spark from Bill's pipe fell into a keg of gun powder, ignited it, and blew Bill and the Indians standing around into Kingdom come. Some of the knives he'd brought to trade shot into a nearby tree where they stuck. But, as one old-timer summed it up: as for Bill, the Indians "couldn't find nothing of him."

Hatcher, John L.
From: Ohio
Appearance: Small-sized
Nickname: "Freckled Hand" (Cheyenne)
Character: Good natured, cheerful; lively; talkative; fearless

John Hatcher worked for Bent—hunting, trapping, trading. He farmed in the Trinidad,

Colorado, area long before the town existed. Indians let him stay long enough to raise his crop in 1846, then drove him out in time to harvest his crops. (Some say 1847.)

John was good natured, but laziness in an employee sometimes got the best of him. When he'd had all he could take, he'd lash out his bullwhip and let the man have it.

One time he traveled with a group across the Plains and met an old Kiowa squaw at the Canadian River. She was so happy to see Hatcher; she hugged him and wept. Many years before, when young Hatcher traded among her people, she'd adopted him as her own son.

John Hatcher and Robert Fisher were good friends. They helped build Adobe Walls in 1845. In 1847 Hatcher did what he could to help in the trial and hangings after the Taos Revolt.

He hunted and guided for military and exploratory expeditions in 1845, 1850, and 1851. In early 1853 Hatcher traveled with Maxwell's group to the California gold field. When he returned, Hatcher freighted on the Santa Fe Trail several years. In 1858 he held off Comanche Chief Old Wolf and 300 warriors when they attacked him near Wagon Mound, New Mexico. He grappled with the chief and held a knife to his throat

the warriors rode out of sight.

In the early 1860's it was reported Hatcher made it rich in the state of Durango, Mexico.

Hicklin, Alexander "Zan"
Born: c 1809; Lafayette County, Missouri
Character: brave, generous, happy; "sharp, keen mind"
Married: Estafana Bent (daughter of Charles and Ignacia Bent), October 20, 1856
Children: Alexander, Jr., Thomas
Died: February 13, 1874, at his ranch on the Greenhorn River, Colorado

Zan Hicklin was about thirty-seven when he arrived in New Mexico with a commercial wagon train. When Colonel Doniphan arrived to fight the Mexican War, Zan joined his Army. After the war he lived in California and New Mexico.

Zan married Charles Bent's daughter, Estafana, in 1856. About two years later they settled on the Greenhorn River about twenty-five miles from Pueblo, Colorado. There he established a ranch and built a Mexican style hacienda, where he and Estafana lived the rest of his life. Because they were a happy couple and always welcomed those who chose to drop-in, their home was a favorite stop for many.

A staunch Democrat, Zan Hicklin was a Southern sympathizer during Civil War and a friend of William Green Russell (of the Green Russell Party), who attempted to leave Denver to aid the Confederate cause.

Dick Wootton enjoyed Zan's wit and thought he was one of the best practical jokers around. He wasn't a literate man, but lived well without a classroom education and communicated easily with people of all stations. Folks were glad to know him.

Kinkead, Matthew (also spelled Kincaid)
Born: 1795, Madison County, Kentucky
Father: David Kinkead

Married or lived with: Teresita Sandoval Suaso (b. c1811, New Mexico; m. Manuel Suaso c1825, then with Kinkead, then with Barclay; d. c1894, age 83, Doyle Ranch, Colorado)
Children: Andres, Rafaela (Rafaelita)
Died: near Sacramento, California

When he was a lad, Matthew's family moved often before settling in Boones Lick, Missouri. As a teen he served in the War of 1812.

Kinkead came to New Mexico in 1824, and in 1825, began a distillery business in Taos with William Workman, a friend from Boones Lick. To boost business opportunity, Kinkead became a Mexican citizen in 1829. As a citizen, he was eligible for a Mexican land grant and was one of many who received the Mora Valley Land Grant (New Mexico) in 1835.

In the early 1840's, Kinkead and his friend Edmond "Francisco" Conn left the Mora Valley to join George Simpson, Robert Fisher, and Joseph Mantz in building El Pueblo. At El Pueblo he lived with Teresita Suaso and had two children, Andres and Rafaela. In 1847 he left for California. He took his son, Andres, and left Teresita and Rafaela behind.

Kinkead was a shrewd businessman and had a reputation for knowing when to buy and when to sell. Rumors made their way back to New Mexico that Kinkead became wealthy in California.

Kroenig, William

Born: c 1825, Germany
Married:
- Rafaelita Kinkead (daughter of Mathew Kinkead and Teresita Suaso; d. childbirth, c1858. Children: a son (d. young); Fannie (b. c 1858; m. Frank Meredith Jones [A. T. & S. F. survey team], December 1879)
- Louisa Watrous (daughter of Samuel B. Watrous)

Died: Near Ft. Barclay, New Mexico, c1896

In the Maxwell Land Grant Case Kroenig testified he came to New Mexico in 1849. He was educated in Germany, where he studied for the Jesuit priesthood; but he left for America before taking orders. Soon after his arrival William Kroenig traveled to Colorado and New Mexico, where he first worked as a merchant for Maxwell and Quinn. When the rescue party was organized to search for survivors of the White Massacre, he joined in.

Working in the mercantile business, Kroenig recognized the advantage of trading with Indians and went in business for himself. In August or September 1853, Kroenig, Autobees, Levin Mitchell and Wootton began to settle in the Huerfano Valley. At the Greenhorn Kroenig raised corn and beans to trade with Indians. He traded some goods near Ft. Laramie. He preferred to trade for livestock, which Indians obtained from emigrants, rather than for hides and pelts

By 1856 he'd accumulated a sizeable herd. He went south into New Mexico and purchased land at La Junta de los Rios (near Ft. Barclay) from Barclay and Doyle. In 1858 he purchased all interests in Ft. Barclay.

After the death of his first wife, William married Louisa Watrous, whose father had a large ranch east of his place. Kroenig built nine lakes on his property and stocked them with fish, while maintaining his occupation as a merchandiser.

In the 1860 Mora, New Mexico, census, he was listed as a merchant at Golondrias. At the same time he partnered with Ben B. Field in a commission store in Denver. In the early 1860's they also partnered in the Field Ranch, which Field operated on the Huerfano River (Colorado).

In the fall of 1866 William Kroenig and the sutler from Ft. Union, Captain John William Moore, opened the Mystic Copper Mine near the summit of Mt. Baldy, New Mexico. They figured they'd profit more by supplying miners than by mining. Moore opened a store; and Kroenig built a sawmill in a little mining town, which soon boomed. Moore named it Elizabethtown for his four-year-old daughter Elizabeth Catherine Moore. Elizabethtown (E-town) became the county seat of the new Colfax County, New Mexico.

Kroenig had a spacious home built on his La Junta de los Rios ranch, which he named Phoenix Ranch. He also partnered with Las Vegas, New Mexico, businessman Charles Ilfeld.

LeDuc, Maurice

Father: Maurice LeDuc
Appearance: Thin; short—about 5'8"; broad shouldered, stooped when aged; clean-shaven; blue eye—one eyed; blond.
Married:
- Sioux lady
- Elena, a Mexican

Children: At least two children by the Sioux and at least two by Elena
Died: 1880

When Maurice LeDuc was with his Sioux wife, he lived in San Geronimo, New Mexico. However, when he married pretty Elena in a Catholic ceremony performed by a priest, his Sioux wife didn't take kindly to the idea. She packed up all she could carry, took their children and Maurice's pony back to her Sioux nation.

Dick Wootton became well-acquainted with Maurice at El Pueblo. Maurice was one of the Barclay-Doyle party that moved south from El Pueblo on April 23, 1848, to build Ft. Barclay in New Mexico Territory. Maurice remained at Barclay until October 15, 1853, when he and Elena and their two children returned to El Pueblo with Doyle, Simpson, Sandoval, and others. He lived in the El Pueblo area at the time of the 1854 Christmas Eve Massacre.

In 1859 he hunted with a large party, including Claymore, Goodall, Levanway (Joseph Barnoy), and others. They came upon an area littered with the bleaching bones of the animals the Ute stole from Marcelino Baca during the Christmas Massacre in 1854.

In 1861-63 LeDuc lived on Hardscrabble Creek, trapped when trapping was good, worked at what he could when it wasn't, and bided his time until it was.

Before he sold his land grant, Lucien Maxwell invited Maurice to come stay at his place in Cimarron, New Mexico. Maurice took him up on the invitation, even moved to Ft. Sumner, New Mexico, with Maxwell when he did sell.

In his latter years Maurice had a mobile home—a cart and a sorrel horse—with which he moved from place to place.

With his little cart and horse, he was in-and-out of Charlie Autobees' place on the Huerfano in the late 1870's. Then he lived in Trinidad with an old trapper friend named Bill. One to rove, Maurice left Trinidad after about a year and went to Maxwell's place at Ft. Sumner though Maxwell was dead. Maurice didn't stay long. He packed up his mule and headed north to his son's place in Cimarron. There was a heavy snowstorm, and Maurice was never heard from again.

LeFevre, Manuel (also spelled Lefebvre)
Born: June 19, 1805, St. Louis, Missouri
Parents: Augustin and Felicité (Vaillancourt) Lefebvre (Felicité d. June 1811)
Married: Maria Teodora Lopez (daughter of Ramon and Maria de la Luz Martin Lopez), December 1, 1827, Taos, New Mexico
Children:
- Maria Dolores (m. Dick Wootton)
- Jose Vicente
- Francisco Antonio
- Maria Francisca Guillerma (m. Charles D. Williams; he came to New Mexico, August 19, 1846, as a soldier in Kearny's army)
- Maria Pacifica
- Maria de la Luz (m. Charles Fracker)
- Maria Leonora (m. Dr. David Harmon)
- Maria Teodora
- Manuel Carlos
- Jose Manuel

Died: Near Ocate, Mora, New Mexico

As captain of a brigade of trappers, LeFevre led them from Carondolet (in St. Louis) to Taos, New Mexico—the Southwestern fur trading center. Among those in his brigade were Alarid Blanco and Antoine Dillette, who became his brothers-in-law in New Mexico. Each married a daughter of Ramon and Maria de la Luz Lopez, who were also the parents of Robert Fisher's wife. Manuel married Maria Teodora; Alarid married Maria Guadalupe (1832); Antoine married Maria Victoria (1836). Marrying into local families, many trappers and traders became related in the far-reaching Hispanic family connections of the area. Some French Canadian trappers who came to the Southwest were already related by birth.

In January 1827, a month after his marriage, LeFevre went trapping with twenty-two men, including Ceran St. Vrain. He trapped for years with Taos as his home base.

He was Dick Wootton's first father-in-law.

Leroux, Antoine (also written LeRoux)
Born: 1801, St. Louis, Missouri
(He was a childhood friend and neighbor of Antoine Robidoux.)
Parents: Louis William LeRoux D'Esneval and Elena Josi Sale dit Lajoie; Elena's mother was from New Mexico.

Siblings: Sylvestre Veral Leroux (Came to the Rocky Mountains c1840); Elena; Marie. Antoine was the youngest.

Married: Juana Catalina Vigil (daughter of Juan de Jesus Vijil Montes and Juana Catarina Valdez de Vijil), November 4, 1833

Children:
- Maria Pablita (b. September 21, 1834, Taos, New Mexico; m. Pedro Valdez)
- Luis Gonzaga (b. c 1836; d. 1898, Ocate, New Mexico)
- Juan de Jesus/Jean (b. September 3, 1838)
- Maria Elena (b. October 14, 1840, Taos; m. Alfredo Elfego Branch)
- Maria Deluvina (b. May 7, 1842; d. in infancy)
- Jose David (b. May 24, 1844; d. in infancy)
- Maria Mariquita Teresa (b. June 3, 1847, Arroyo Hondo, New Mexico; m. Leopoldo Chene, January 28, 1864, Taos)
- Caroline/Catarina (age 1, 1850 NM Census, d. young)
- Maria Ysabel (b. March 7, 1851, Arroyo Hondo)

Died: June 30, 1861, at his ranch near Taos (between Rio Pueblo and Rio Lucero); died of spear wounds complicated by asthma.

Antoine Leroux trapped with William Ashley and Major Andrew Henry on the upper Missouri before coming to New Mexico in 1824. He trapped along the Rio Grande, the Arkansas River, and the Gila River (in 1826).

Leroux served on the jury at the Taos Massacre trials in 1847.

Leroux, Carson, Tobin, Wootton, and other mountain men accompanied Major Grier in his search for survivors of the White Massacre in northeastern New Mexico. Some blamed Leroux for the halt which allowed time for Mrs. White's murder. Though Leroux wasn't Dick Wootton's favorite person, Wootton stood by Leroux and averred the delay was neither Leroux's choice, nor fault.

Leroux became a skilled guide. He guided:
- Colonel Philip St. George Cooke and his battalion from Santa Fe to California during the Mexican War (late 1846).
- (With Dick Wootton) Colonel Newby into Navajoland (1848).
- U. S. Commissioner John Russell Bartlett from San Diego, California to New Mexico, when Bartlett surveyed the boundary between the U. S. and Mexico (April 1852).
- Captain J. W. Gunnison's expedition over Cochetopa Pass (Colorado).
- A. W. Whipple in his railroad survey.
- The 1858 Marcy-Loring party that took supplies from Ft. Union to Johnston's Utah unit.

L'Esperance, Pierre (Pedro Esperanza)

Born: c1791, Canada; came from near Sorrel, Quebec

Appearance: Blue eyes; light complexion; about 6' tall; not a fat man, but strong and sturdy like those in his family of origin

Died: 1879, age 88

Pierre trapped with a party of about fifteen who trapped along the Missouri River and into the Rocky Mountains in the early 1820's. When they reached present-day southeastern Wyoming, they turned south. They trapped as they went, until they reached the Spanish borderlands. Spain had few soldiers for the size of its territory, but they found L'Esperance, LeDoux, Bijou, Gremer, Duchesne and their brigade. They disarmed them and escorted them to Taos. Many, if not all, of the brigade remained in the New Mexico/southern Colorado area. Some married into local families.

At one time L'Esperance lived with French trapper Antoine Dillette and his family in Mora, New Mexico. Antoine's daughter—Dick Wootton's mother-in-law—remembered L'Esperance brewed beer while he was living with them.

L'Esperance settled in Tecolote (near Las Vegas, New Mexico). He had a ranch and built the first sawmill in the area. He used a vertical motion reciprocating saw.

Having no children of his own, L'Esperance wrote his namesake nephew in 1857 and invited him to come live with him. His eighteen-year-old nephew accepted the offer, joined him, and added a circular saw to the mill machinery. (Nephew Pedro was born June 29, 1839, in Sorrel, Quebec Canada to Joseph and Mary L'Esperance.)

Maxwell, Lucien Bonaparte

Born: September 14, 1818, Kaskaskia, Illinois

Parents: Hugh H. and Marie Odile (Menard) Maxwell (Hugh was Irish; he was a well-to-do merchant, died in 1834. Marie was French. Her father, Colonel Pierre Menard, figured in the early fur trade and was a partner in the Missouri Fur Company. A prominent Illinois politician, he served as Lt. Governor.

Appearance: 5'10 ½" tall; blue eyes; fair complexion; wavy brown hair

Character: Kind, but a strong character—seldom showed anger, but when he did, his anger was violent; enjoyed gambling

Married: Ana Maria de la Luz Beaubien (daughter of Charles and Maria Pabla Lovato Beaubien) m. either May 27, 1842, or June 3, 1844, Taos

Children:
- Peter Menard (b. April 27, 1848, Taos; d. June 21, 1898, Ft. Sumner, New Mexico)
- Virginia (b. December 12, 1850; d. September 7, 1915, El Paso, Texas)
- Sofia
- Emilia (b. 1852, Rayado, New Mexico; d. 1884 Ft. Sumner)
- Maria Leonar (b. 1856, Rayado)
- Verenisa (b. August 3, 1860; d. in infancy)
- Paulita (b. 1864, Mora; d. 1929, Ft. Sumner)
- Odile Berenisa (b. July 25, 1869; d. 1935, Cimarron, New Mexico)
- Julian.

Died: July 25, 1875, Ft. Sumner, New Mexico, buried there

Lucien Maxwell came West after his father's death. His mother was a Menard; Ceran St. Vrain's brother Savinien had married a Menard; so Lucien had a contact when he arrived in the Southwest in the winter of 1841-42. Upon arrival he worked at Ft. St. Vrain (Colorado).

When John C. Fremont came through in 1842 on his first expedition, Maxwell hired on as chief hunter. In 1845 Maxwell again accompanied Fremont, this time to California. Between the two expeditions Lucien married Charles Beaubien's daughter Luz, built a cabin on the Ponil River near Cimarron, New Mexico, and farmed.

In 1841 Luz's father and Guadalupe Miranda had petitioned the Mexican government for a land grant in northeastern New Mexico. Governor Manuel Armijo granted them the Beaubien-Miranda Land Grant, the largest land grant in North America. Miranda left the area about the time the U. S. gained control of New Mexico. Beaubien planned for his son, Narciso, to manage the grant; but he was killed during the 1847 Taos Revolt. Beaubien had no other sons at the time; so chose his son-in-law Lucien Maxwell to fill the post.

In June 1848 Maxwell led a party of twelve men across Manco de Burro Pass. Ute ambushed them, shot Maxwell in the back of the head, wounded all but one of the others, killed a few, and kidnapped two children accompanying the party. The survivors walked toward Taos and were rescued about thirty miles east of Taos. Maxwell spent the rest of the year recuperating and working for his father-in-law.

In 1849 Lucien Maxwell and Kit Carson established homes at Rayado, New Mexico, about eleven miles south of Cimarron on the Santa Fe Trail. Maxwell's home was large and lavish: carpets, velvet drapes, mirrors, gold framed pictures, a grand piano, and beautiful furniture. He had space enough and china, silver, and crystal enough to serve 100.

When Major Beall, commander in Santa Fe, ordered dragoons be stationed at Taos, 1st Lt. Judd, in charge of artillery, balked. Rayado, where Maxwell lived, was at the juncture of the Santa Fe and Taos Trails. He helped persuade the Army it was a strategic location for a military post. Soldiers liked the place and were glad for the change. They hoped to build a frontier post which would bring in some money; so they could invest in the countryside.

Rayado Post was established in 1850. Major Grier commanded the 43 soldiers of Companies G & I of the 1st Dragoons stationed there. Their primary assignment was to protect against Indian attack. At times the soldiers hunted bands of wolves that preyed on settlers' or travelers' animals.

The post was stocked with 45 horses. Maxwell supplied the post with horses, cattle, sheep, hay, grain, and much of the lodging. He received $2,400-$3,400 per year for quarters and stables and $20-$30 a ton for hay. After fifteen months, the Army ordered the post to be closed, but agreed to leave fourteen soldiers and a non-commissioned officer at Rayado if Maxwell would provide quarters and provisions without charge. Some Rayado soldiers helped build Ft. Union.

Soon after Kit Carson left for California in 1853 Maxwell also drove sheep to sell in the gold fields. They returned to New Mexico together and arrived home Christmas Day 1853.

While Maxwell farmed and ranched, there was always the threat of Indian thievery. He sold out at Rayado in 1858. With his profits, he purchased shares of the Beaubien-Miranda Land Grant and moved to Cimarron City, New Mexico. "Uncle Jack" Holland built Maxwell another large home—more spacious than the one he'd built him in Rayado. The Cimarron home was comprised of two individual buildings connected by a large adobe hallway. Floors were hardwood. The rooms were as lavish as Maxwell's Rayado home. There was room for family, servants, and guests, spacious rooms for dancing and entertaining. Maxwell had his game room for billiards and gambling, kept gold dust and coins on hand in the bottom drawer of his downstairs bedroom—never locked the drawer and never had a problem with theft.

In Cimarron, Maxwell became postmaster and Indian Agent. Although the Ute had attacked him in 1848, he made friends of his enemies. When the Kiowa and Comanche beat them near Cimarron and stole their horses, Maxwell gave them horses from his own herd and gained their perpetual friendship. They called him "Maxwell, friend of the Ute."

After Maxwell's father-in-law died in February 1864, Lucien and Luz bought the remaining land grant shares which they hadn't inherited, including those belonging to Charles Bent's children (settled in court May 3, 1866). The Beaubien-Miranda Land Grant became the Maxwell Land Grant. It included about 1,714,765 acres—a bit larger than the state of Delaware, plus half the state of Rhode Island. From his vast land grant Maxwell gave Dick Wootton 2,500 acres to build a toll road across Raton Pass in exchange for perpetual free passage. Raton Pass was the gateway to Maxwell's Land Grant.

At the height of his prosperity, Maxwell employed 500 people, cultivated thousands of acres, and raised thousands of cattle, sheep and horses. Maxwell built a grist mill near his Cimarron home, ground his wheat and sold much to the U. S. government for military use.

Lucien and Luz sponsored the building of Immaculate Conception Church in Cimarron, a gift to the community in memory of their children Julian and Verenisa. Bishop Jean Lamy dedicated the church.

Elizabethtown, on Maxwell's grant, became county seat of the new Colfax County. He was appointed county probate judge.

He worked with many families—set them up with a herd and a small ranch to operate on shares. He didn't call for his shares with any particular regularity, only when the military needed more than he had handy. Then he'd call his shareholders in, hear their account, and ask them to bring in his share. He generally did business on a verbal basis.

In 1870 Maxwell sold his Land Grant to a group of Colorado investors for $650,000-$750,000. Accounts vary. Three months later the investors sold the grant to an English company for $1,350,000. In October (1870) Maxwell purchased the military post at Ft. Sumner and moved there. Later in the year he applied for and was granted a charter to establish the 1st National Bank in Santa Fe. He sold his interest in the bank the next year and invested $250,000 in a company building the Texas Pacific Railway. That investment failed.

Five-and-a-half years after selling his grant, Maxwell died in Fort Sumner. He was 56.

The editor of the *Las Vegas Gazette* (New Mexico) eulogized him: "Against Lucien B. Maxwell, no man can say aught, and he died after an active and eventful life, probably without an enemy in the world. Of few words, unassuming and unpretentious, his deeds were the best exponent of the man. He was hospitable and generous and upright, and dispensed large wealth acquired by industry and genius with an open hand to the stranger and the needy."

Metcalf, Archibald
Born: 1815, New York state

Married: Maria de la Luz Trujillo (b. c1830, daughter of Jose Francisco Trujillo and Maria Natividad Sandoval; sister of Vicente Trujillo.), c 1843 or 1845
Died: 1848, Ft. Laramie

Archibald arrived in St. Louis in 1840 and traveled West on a trading expedition with John Baptiste Richard. In 1841 he settled on the Greenhorn (Colorado) and worked with Marcelino Baca, John Brown, and Bill New. He moved to the South Platte (Colorado) for a spell, but returned to Greenhorn.

Luz was young when they married. In her later years, she said she married him because her mother told her to. Her parents did require Metcalf to be baptized Catholic before they allowed him to marry Luz. Archibald and Luz lived on the Greenhorn until 1846 and were involved in various ventures, including trading with Indians near Manitou Springs (Colorado).[230] In 1846 Apache attacked him on his way to Taos. He returned home and moved his family to Santa Fe.

He was one of St. Vrain's volunteers in the 1847 Taos Revolt and was sheriff in Taos for a short time during the time of the massacre trials.

He died of cholera at Ft. Laramie the next year. He was about thirty-three. After his death, Luz married George Whittlesey. In 1855 she married Abram Ledoux's son Felipe.

New, William
Born: 1802, Illinois
Married: Mary
Children: Three children
Died: 1851

William New was working at Bent's Fort when Dick Wootton arrived in 1836. After that he managed Ft. St. Vrain until Ceran St. Vrain's brother Marcellin was placed in charge of the fort in the autumn of 1837.

New trapped independently for a few years, lived at El Pueblo in 1842, and in 1850 built a place near Carson's at Rayado, New Mexico. Jicarilla Apache killed him there, at his home.

Owens, Richard "Dick" Lemmon
Character: used good judgment
Married: Indian woman (while living at Greenhorn)
Children: At least two

Dick Owens was in the West as a free trapper at least as early as 1834. Most of his early western years were spent north of Ft. St. Vrain. He went to Ft. Walla Walla (Washington) with Wyeth and returned with Captain Joseph Thing. He was in and out of Ft. Hall from December 1834-late February 1836.

Owens and seventeen men accompanied Captain Thing (1835) in an effort to establish friendly relations with the Nez Percé and Flathead Indians on the Salmon River. After two

---

[230] West of present-day Colorado Springs, Colorado, Manitou Soda Springs had long been enjoyed by Indians, New Mexicans, and mountain men, to soak hides for preservation. The springs were also used for medicinal purposes.

bands of Blackfoot Indians attacked their camp and stole their goods, Thing's expedition returned to Ft. Hall. Later in the year Owens was trapping with Joseph Gale's party when Blackfoot attacked again. The trappers were on the open prairie near Pierre's Hole. The Blackfoot, hiding nearby in brush, shot and wounded Owens and several others. They lodged an arrow in his foot. With a rifle, they shot him three times in the other leg: in the calf, the shinbone, and the thigh. Owens was still hobbling around on crutches, recuperating from the attack, when he met Kit Carson. After that they often trapped together as free trappers and became close, lifelong friends. Owens was at Lucien Fontenelle's trapping camp on the Powder River in February 1838. In the spring he trapped with Carson along the Laramie River, then spent the winter at Ft. Davy Crockett.

In 1841 Owens established a place on Greenhorn Creek (south of Pueblo, Colorado). While living there in the early 1840's, Dick Owens and a trapper named John Burroughs (Burris) met up with a grizzly bear. Each man fired. Both men missed. Each man eyed a lone cedar and ran for it. Owens, ahead of Burroughs, reached the only safety available. The bear snatched Burroughs from his low perch, mauled him, and went for Owens. Burroughs crawled to his gun and shot the bear just as it grasped Owens left hand in his mouth. As the bear fell to the ground, it bit off some of Owens' fingers. Both men survived; but each had scars to bear witness to their story.

In 1845 Owens and Carson farmed on the Little Cimarron River east of Taos. They also spent time together with pathfinder John C. Fremont. Owens was with Fremont's 3rd Expedition and was one of eight captains in Fremont's California Battalion in November 1846.

Ryder, Ben
Born: c 1800-1806
Married: Josie (Josefa) "Chipeta" Tafoya (a widow; she and her first husband, Manuel, had two children. She was a large stout woman and a good midwife.)
Children:
- Robert (b. El Pueblo, Colorado)
- Ben (b. El Pueblo)
- Willie (b. Napeste)
- Catarina (b. La Junta de los Rios, New Mexico; m. Jesus Chacon)
- James (b. Trinidad, Colorado)
- Polly (m. Encarnacion Martines)
- Lorenza (m. Ignacio Gurule)
- Anna (m. Juan Garcia)

Died: May 1886, Walsenburg, Colorado

In his early adult years Ben trapped and worked at Bent's Fort as a carpenter. In the early 1850's he worked for Dick Wootton at Huerfano (Colorado). His wife, Chipeta, worked for Dolores Wootton.

After the El Pueblo Massacre, the Ryders moved to Ft. Barclay, New Mexico, and lived there during the years Dick Wootton headquartered at Ft. Barclay. When he left, they remained. Later, they became some of the first settlers in the Trinidad, Colorado, area. For many years they lived on their ranch south of El Moro along the Animas River.

Ben lived near Jesse Nelson and worked for him about six years at Nine Mile Bottom.

About 1880-81 he moved to Walsenburg. He was a little over 80 when he died there in 1886.

Sabille, John (Jean Sybille)

Born: c 1784 (In 1860 or '61 John said he was 77.)

Appearance: Thin; small, lightweight man—wiry built; whiskered face plus a long beard; agile

Married or lived with: Indian wives

Died: After 1862

John Sabille said he grew up in a wealthy family—one of St. Louis' founding families. He came to the Rocky Mountains about 1810 or a little before. He was one of the French trappers who helped build Ft. Vasquez.

He learned to trade among the Indians, especially the Arapaho, Brule Sioux, Cheyenne, and Mountain Ute. Wherever he went, he was at home because he had a wife in each Indian tribe with which he traded. He was still camping and trading in his mid-seventies.

Although Sabille was about five years older than Dick Wootton's father, he called Dick Wootton his friend.

St. Vrain Family: Ceran, Marcellin, Rel

In the 1790's Jacques de Lassus St. Vrain, a native of French Flanders and former officer in the French navy, left France and followed his parents to America. His father had been a wealthy man of influence in Louis XVI's council. In 1790 Jacques' parents and two youngest siblings sailed to America to escape the French Revolution (1789-1799). During those years thousands of aristocrats were beheaded on the guillotine.

Jacques arrived in New Orleans and obtained a land grant near the Mississippi River in present-day southeastern Missouri, which was owned by France. In 1795 he went upstream to Nouvelle Bourbon, where his family had settled, and from there to Spanish Lake about fourteen miles above St. Louis. In Spanish Lake he built his home and brewery. Jacques married Marie Felicité Dubreuil. They had ten children.

Until the U. S. purchased Louisiana Territory, Jacques supported his family with income from his brewery and his involvement in politics. Afterward, the brewery and land speculation were his sole means of support. In 1813 the brewery caught fire. Then his land speculations failed.

When Jacques died in 1818, Felicité and some of the children went to live with his brother Charles Auguste and his family on their farm. The older children were sent to various people.

Of Jacques' six sons—Savinien, Dumatil, Ceran, Felix, Charles, and Marcellin—at least four—Felix, Charles, Ceran and Marcellin—pioneered in the westward movement.

The older brothers, Felix and Charles, traded with Indians along the Mississippi. About 1830 Felix was appointed to succeed Thomas Forsythe as Indian agent for the Sacs and

Foxes. Charles worked among them with Felix and interpreted for Governor Reynolds during negotiations with the Black Hawk. When the Black Hawk declared war, they killed Felix, cut off his hands and feet and ate portions of his heart in order to gain his courageous spirit. Charles moved to the Rocky Mountains; it was reported that Indians killed him.

Ceran and Marcellin pioneered in the Southwest. Of the four brothers, Ceran was the most prominent in Southwestern history. He played a prominent role in Dick Wootton's life.

Ceran De Hault De Lassus de St. Vrain

Born: May 5, 1802, Spanish Lake, Missouri
Parents: Jacques Marcellin Ceran and Marie Felicité (Dubreuil) de Hault de Lassus de St. Vrain
Siblings: Sisters and five brothers; Ceran was the fourth child.
Appearance: Round face; expressive wide-set dark, expressive eyes—often sparkled good-naturedly, occasionally flashed with anger; black hair and beard.
Character: a man of his word; shrewd, honest businessman.
Indian Nickname: Black Beard
Marriages and Children:
- Maria Dolores Luna
  Child: Vicente (b. May 10, 1827)
- Maria Ignacia Trujillo
  Child: Joseph Felix (b. November 1, 1844)
- Luisa Branch of Mora, New Mexico
  Child: Felicitas/Felicité

Named his gun: Silver Heels (Men often named their guns.)
Died: 6 p.m., October 28, 1870, Mora, New Mexico

When Ceran was born, the U. S. had not yet purchased the Louisiana Territory from France; so he was born in and grew up in a French community. He spoke fluent French

His father died when Ceran was a teen. Being one of the older children, Ceran was sent to live with family friend Bernard Pratte, Sr. in St. Louis. As Ceran clerked at Bernard Pratte and Co., he became acquainted with trappers and traders, their needs and adventures.

In 1823 Ceran joined a group of Hudson's Bay trappers on an expedition into New Mexico. When he returned to St. Louis in 1824, he partnered with François Guerin. They bought trade goods on credit from Pratte and took them to Santa Fe over the Santa Fe Trail.

They didn't start until fall (1824); by the time they arrived, business was slow. They took their goods on to Taos; but after thirty-seven days, they still had stock. Guerin sold out to St. Vrain for $100, three mules, and Ceran's promise to pay what was owed Pratte. Ceran figured he'd pack up and go south into Mexico if he couldn't sell the rest of the goods to trappers when they came back to town. To help pay down the debt owed Pratte, he sent a mule and some pelts by Guerin.

Ceran didn't find Taos as difficult as some did. He grew up Catholic; so he was familiar with the Catholic influence in the settlement. He spoke French and English; so he could speak with men like Beaubien, Dillette, Blanco, LeFevre and other Frenchmen who lived there or used Taos as a base camp. During the slow business months, he learned to speak Spanish. By midsummer (1825) he sold enough goods to satisfy his debt to Pratte and earn a nice profit for himself.

He trapped and traded; but trading and supplying goods became his primary occupation. On August 29, 1826, he applied for a passport to trade in Sonora. On September 30, 1828, he again applied for and received a passport to trade in Chihuahua and Sonora, Mexico.

The Mexicans, as many who write unfamiliar names, wrote names to suit their language. Pronouncing "v" as "b," some of their documents record St. Vrain's name: Seberiano Sambran.

In late 1830 Ceran St. Vrain and Charles and William Bent formed a business partnership: Bent-St. Vrain & Company. They and their company influenced many young men who followed the Santa Fe Trail, including, but far from limited to: Maxwell, Simpson, Wootton, Carson, Boggs, Fisher, and Barclay. Bent-St. Vrain & Co. operated trading forts and company stores. When they began the partnership, New Mexico tariffs were high and the market for goods was low. Even at that, business was better in New Mexico than in Missouri. By the end of the decade, the company was sending $20,000-$40,000 worth of furs to St. Louis annually.

In February 1831 St. Vrain applied for and became a Mexican citizen to facilitate business. His primary focus was the Santa Fe store; but he also traveled to each of the company's forts: Ft. St. Vrain, Adobe Walls, and Bent's Fort. At Bent's Fort he welcomed travelers, visited mountain men, or went out and traded with Indians. He sometimes traveled with the annual supply trains to and from the States, sometimes traded goods in Mexico.

From 1834-1838 Ceran was American consul in Santa Fe. He relinquished the position.

When Fremont wrote of his second expedition (summer 1843), he spoke of Ceran being married to a daughter of Beaubien. However, the marriages of Charles Beaubien's daughters are accounted for unless there was another child, not documented. By early 1844 Ignacia Trujillo was his wife; their son Felix was born in November 1844.[231]

In January 1844 Taos alcalde Cornelio Vigil and Ceran St. Vrain received the Vigil-St. Vrain Land Grant north and east of Taos and south of the Arkansas River. Charles Bent couldn't apply for a grant—he wasn't a Mexican citizen; but he was involved some way. In March, Vigil and St. Vrain assigned Bent a sixth interest in the grant.

In 1846 Washington D. C. was abuzz with Manifest Destiny and possible war with Mexico. Charles Bent and Ceran left Taos and arrived at Ft. Leavenworth, Kansas, on June 28 to apprise Colonel Stephen Kearny of the general and particular situations and attitudes in New Mexico. From there they sailed to St. Louis. Charles returned to New Mexico; Ceran remained in St. Louis until August 24. He headed home to Santa Fe with a wagon train loaded with trade goods. By the time he arrived, Kearny had taken New Mexico "without a shot." Born French, Ceran had become an American when the U. S. purchased Louisiana Territory. He'd taken Mexican citizenship for business purpose. Now he was an American

---

[231] Felix was educated in St. Louis. He lived first at Carondolet; then he and William Bent's boys—George and Charlie—went to Mr. Clarkson's and boarded together. From there he went to Webster College.

citizen again.

New Mexicans seemed to take the United States' presence calmly, but the situation blew to thunder in January 1847 with the assassination of Charles Bent and many others.

When news of the massacre reached Ceran in Santa Fe, he organized volunteers to accompany Colonel Sterling Price to Taos. Among his volunteers were mountain men, traders, New Mexicans, and Mexicans. When he arrived in Taos, Dick Wootton and other mountain men from El Pueblo joined him. Ceran interpreted during the Taos Massacre trials.

After Charles Bent's death, Ceran St. Vrain and William Bent reorganized their company. In the summer of 1847 St. Vrain traveled to St. Louis and offered to sell Bent's Fort to the government. Major Swords and Captain Enos, who often visited the fort, advised the government to reject the offer. They didn't think grazing was sufficient, and wood had to be hauled five to eight miles. The U. S. didn't buy the fort, but continued to use it. Ceran established a second store in Santa Fe, but soon sold it, lock, stock, and barrel, to Joab Houghton and a partner.

Ceran noticed the Indian trade was changing. Yet New Mexico seemed an open venture. New settlers were arriving; there was an Army to feed and supply. It seemed time to get out of the company business. Bent-St. Vrain and Co. dissolved.

Ceran contracted to supply 1,000,000 pounds of flour to the U. S. Army for each of the next three years. In order to fill the contract, he built gristmills in grain producing New Mexico valleys at Mora, Peralta, and Taos. He moved to Mora.

In the fall of 1849 he was a representative to the territorial convention in Santa Fe. Rails were rapidly connecting in the eastern U. S., and he hoped a railroad would build into New Mexico. About 1854 St. Vrain asked Kit to sign an endorsement letter. He thought Kit Carson's connections would help attract a railroad. In the early 1850's Secretary of War Jefferson Davis and others also had visions of a Southern railway connecting the Atlantic and Pacific, but the Civil War interrupted. New Mexico would have no railroad in Ceran's lifetime.

In the late 1850's St. Vrain moved to New York City. He intended to retire there; but he'd worn out shoes in New Mexico. He returned. In January 1858 he bought a portion of the Sangre de Cristo Land Grant from Steve Lee's widow. In addition to his store, mill, and distillery, he built a gristmill at Beaubien's Culebra settlement and established a store at Canon City (Colorado).

When the Civil War came to New Mexico, St. Vrain was commissioned Colonel of the First New Mexico Cavalry. He began to select officers and recruit soldiers, but realized the task was heavier than he could handle at the time. He resigned. Kit Carson was named to fill his position. Ceran stayed in Mora and continued to mill flour and sell supplies to the Army. He published the *Santa Fe Gazette*, a Mora newspaper.

One day, while sitting in front of his Mora store, smoking a cigar, Ceran had a stroke. He lived several weeks in his paralyzed state. At 6 p.m. on October 28, 1870, Ceran St. Vrain died, age 68. His wife, Luisa, survived him.

More than 2,000 attended his military funeral in Mora. The Ft. Union regimental band played. Pallbearers were Ft. Union's commanding general and his staff. Ceran, like Charles

Bent and Kit Carson, had quit the Catholic Church years before because of run-ins with Padre Martinez. Kit and he had read themselves out of the Catholic Church because of the Padre; so he wasn't buried in the Catholic cemetery. The Masonic fraternity buried him in the family cemetery in Mora.

Marcellin St. Vrain

Born: October 14, 1815, Spanish Lake, near St. Louis, Missouri
Parents: Jacques and Marie Felicité (Dubreuil) St. Vrain
Appearance: 5'6'or 7" tall; about 115 pounds; black eyes; curly black hair
Character: ability to make friends easily
Married: May have had the first two at the same time:
- Tall Pawnee Woman
- Rel c 1839
- Elizabeth Jane Murphy, June 26, 1849, Florissant, St. Louis County, Missouri

Children: Four with Rel (See Rel St. Vrain Bransford.); ten with Elizabeth:
- Isadora (b. November 21, 1851)
- Teresa Emma (b. July 4, 1854; d. April 1873)
- Eugene William (b. March 7, 1856; d. September 18, 1929)
- Marie Felicité (b. May 10, 1858; d. March 1, 1926)
- Sarah Helen (b. April 18, 1860; d. July 1862)
- Celess (b. April 15, 1863; d. September 8, 1941)
- Leona Ann (b. August 31, 1865; d. March 1889)
- Paul Augustus (b. March 16, 1868)
- twins: James and Elizabeth (b. January 6, 1871)

Died: March 3, 1871, on his farm six miles south of New London, Ralls County, Missouri

Marcellin St. Vrain, thirteen years his brother Ceran's junior, joined Ceran in the Southwest in 1832. Although he wasn't a Bent-St. Vrain partner, he was a chief trader and was in charge of Ft. St. Vrain for a few years. He sometimes led a company supply train.

About 1848 Marcellin and an Indian wrestled at Bent's Fort. Marcellin didn't just best him; he accidently killed him. At the time, circumstances didn't matter. His brother Ceran and the Bent brothers knew Marcellin's life wasn't work a plug nickel if he ventured outside the fort. They advised him to return to Missouri. Persuaded, Marcellin entrusted his wife, Rel, and their children to the care of his brother Ceran and left for Missouri.

In Missouri he established a farm, became a miller, and—in June 1849—remarried. Two years later he returned to New Mexico for his two sons and took them home to Missouri.

Rel St. Vrain Bransford

Born: 1825, a twin
Married:
- Marcellin St. Vrain, c 1839; Children:
  - Child (b. c1840, lived 18 days)
  - Felix (b. June 17, 1842, Ft. St. Vrain, Colorado; d. 1864, of smallpox at Vicksburg

during Civil War, was a Confederate soldier)
- Charles (b. October 17, 1844, Ft. St. Vrain; drafted into Union service, Civil War; m. Mary Jane Cope, October 19, 1871, Missouri; d. February 19, 1936)
- Mary (b. March 9, 1846, Ft. St. Vrain [St. Vrain Bible had her year 1848.Brother Charles thought Mary changed it. He said she was two years younger than he.]; m. General E.B. Sopris, Trinidad, Colorado)

• William Allen Bransford, August 6, 1859, Mora, New Mexico; Children:
Alexander, Virginia, Anna, Amelia, William, Charles, Jefferson

Died: April 12, 1886

Some say Rel was Sioux; others say she was Blackfoot. Dick Wootton always told his children she was a Blackfoot. She was a twin. In perfectly acceptable Indian style, Marcellin St. Vrain was going to marry both girls. But, the story is told that Rel's twin was jealous and hung herself before the wedding.

All was going well for Marcellin, Rel, and the children until he accidently killed an Indian. Advised to leave, he returned to Missouri. He left Rel and the kids in Mora in Ceran's care.

Rel often walked to the top of a hill to look for him; but when he returned (c 1851), it was to take their sons to Missouri, where he'd remarried. Rel became a Catholic and married William "Bill" Bransford, who worked for her brother-in-law Ceran.

Bransford came to the Rocky Mountain region in 1844 and often worked for Bent-St. Vrain—sometimes at Bent's Fort, sometimes at Ft. St. Vrain (1844-1849), and later at the company store in Taos. He was a head trader, a dependable man.

Late in the summer of 1846 Bransford was at Leavenworth where he met General Stephen Kearny. Kearny needed a seasoned man to accompany him and his soldiers across the Plains. He couldn't hire him out-and-out; so he purchased a herd of cattle for Bransford to drive. Thus, Bransford traveled with him across the Plains and into New Mexico and gave what help was needed. Bransford returned to Bent's Fort and was on hand to help Bent-St. Vrain in the Vermijo (New Mexico) area during and after the 1847 Taos Rebellion.

Bransford clerked for Ceran St. Vrain in Taos, lived in Taos and in Mora, where he married Rel. Bill, Rel, and the kids moved to Trinidad about 1865, after Wootton settled at the base of Raton Pass. In January 1881 Bill was appointed Las Animas County coroner (1881-82). In 1883 he gave testimony for the Maxwell Land Grant case. He was 71.

Rel and Bill died in Trinidad—he at the home of Felipe Baca the day after Christmas 1883.

Silva, Jesus
Born: c 1819/20, Taos

On September 19, 1877, Jesus testified before Colfax County (New Mexico) Notary Public Harry Whigham concerning the Maxwell Land Grant issue. At the time, he said he was 58 years old. He testified again in 1885 and gave record of his work: As a boy, he worked for his uncle. As a man he worked three-and-a-half years for William Bent, traveling from fort to fort trading with Indians. He spoke Cheyenne and knew sign language.

He worked for Archibald Metcalf two years and eight months.

He hunted and supplied meat for Lucien Maxwell at Rayado. He had also worked for Beaubien, Maxwell's father-in-law and acted both as hunter and guide for troops. During the time he worked for Beaubien, Jesus accompanied him, Cornelio Vigil, and others to set up mounds to mark border extremities of the Beaubien-Miranda Land Grant.

Dick Wootton became acquainted with Jesus in Taos about 1840. They often met in New Mexico and on the Arkansas. They were together when they testified in the land grant case.

Simpson, George Semmes
Born: May 7, 1818, St. Louis, Missouri
Parents: Dr. Robert and Brecia Smith Simpson
Appearance: Small build; wore a beard
Married: Juana "Juanita" Suaso (b. December 26, c1829, daughter of Manuel Antonio and Teresita Suaso Sandoval. Mrs. Simpson, Mrs. Joe Doyle, and Mrs. William Kroenig were sisters. Juana died c 1916 in California.)
Children:
- Isabel (b. June 2, 1844; m. Jacob Beard)
- Joseph Robert (b. March 19, 1846; m. 1: Maria J. Pacheco, 2: Maria Josepha Garcia)
- Pedro Advinuela (b. August 1, 1848, Ft. Barclay, New Mexico; m. Flora Jennings)
- Joseph Merced (b. September 24, 1850; m. Serafina Long)
- Alexander Barclay (b. October 20, 1853, Mora, New Mexico)
- Jennie Maria (b. October 28, 1858; m. Ernest Camp)
- Ann Maria (b. July 18, 1860, Mora)
- Lucy (b. April 4, 1863, Doyle's Ranch; m. Samuel Anderson Pawley)
- Virginia (b. April 4, 1863, Doyle's Ranch; m. Norris T. Cavalier)
- Raphaela Semmes (b. March 25, 1870; m. Burgess Lee Gordon)

Died: September 7, 1885, Trinidad, Colorado; buried: on Simpson's Rest, near Trinidad

The fourth of seven children, George was the first to survive infancy. His parents doted on him. They provided George with a top notch education. His father, a doctor and druggist, had banking and mercantile interests.

After a failed romance, young George attempted suicide using laudanum. To give him a fresh perspective, his parents outfitted him for a trip West in 1838.

George trapped independently, often with Bill Williams. He trapped in present-day Idaho, Utah, Nevada, and back around to Bent's Fort. At the fort he learned the Indian trade.

In 1842 he helped establish El Pueblo with financial help from his father. While living at El Pueblo, George married Juana Suaso, a hard working young lady. They moved thirty miles upstream to Hardscrabble (Colorado) in 1844, then back to El Pueblo before moving to Ft. Barclay (New Mexico). Juana's mother, Teresita, and sister Cruz Doyle and family lived there. After George misappropriated funds from Alexander Barclay and Joe Doyle in the autumn of 1848, he left to visit in St. Louis. Juana and their three children remained in New Mexico. George's mother and Barclay persuaded him to return.

On his return George contracted cholera on a Mississippi steamer during the cholera epidemic of 1849. When anyone died on the steamer, the crew took them off the boat and buried them on the bank of the Mississippi. George instructed the crew that, if he died, they were to ship his body to his father, Dr. Robert Simpson in St. Louis.

When George appeared to be dead, the crew put his body in a coffin and packed it with ice to preserve it and keep it from stinking before they reached St. Louis. Before they arrived, someone saw the ice moving. With help, the person removed the ice and uncovered George. He'd passed the climax and was well on his way to recovery.

George returned to New Mexico, spent some time in California during the gold rush, returned to Ft. Barclay, and then moved to Huerfano Village (Colorado).

He traded out of Bent's Ft. a few months when Dick Wootton was there in the late fall of 1855. He clerked in Mora (New Mexico) in 1860 before he moved to Doyle's Ranch (Colorado). He and his family moved to the new town of Trinidad (Colorado) in the mid-1860's and remained there the rest of his life.

During the times George was gone in the early years of marriage, Juana lived in Mora, New Mexico. She supported the children with help from Doyle and Barclay and George's parents, as well as by teaching children to read and write. Every year George's parents sent a load of provisions. They wanted the children come live with them, but Juana didn't want to part with her children. Even in old age, she worked hard and looked out for others.

George was elected Las Animas County Clerk in 1867. In his Trinidad years, he wrote poetry and articles. Some were published in the Trinidad and Pueblo newspapers. He continued to receive an annuity from his parents for many years.

For a while George had a problem with alcohol, but quit before his death at age 67. He requested that he be buried on the nearby mountain where he and a few settlers had been attacked during a time of Indian trouble. They'd drawn the Indians away from Trinidad. By hiding in caves in the mountain, they survived; but the Indians kept them up there two weeks.

A monument was placed on top of his grave on the mountain known as Simpson's Rest.

Tharp Family: William, Edward, Louis

William "Bill" Tharp

<u>Born</u>: 1817, St. Louis
<u>Married</u>: Antonia Luna (called a half-wit; had lived with Jim Beckwourth)
<u>Children</u>: Two children
<u>Died</u>: May 1847, Walnut Creek

William Tharp came to the Rocky Mountain region in 1841. He got his western start working for Bent-St. Vrain. For three years he traveled East with the Bent supply trains.

In 1844 he made El Pueblo home base and worked as an independent trader. He partnered with various men, including Joe Doyle.

On May 5, 1847, William left Pueblo, headed for St. Louis. Among the goods, he was taking was a load of furs, robes, and buckskins for Dick Wootton. At Walnut Creek (near Great Bend, Kansas), Comanche attacked and killed Tharp, scalped and mutilated him, and stole his cargo.

Edward Tharp

Born: 1824

Died: c 1845; El Pueblo

Edward came West five years after his older brother William. James Waters killed him at El Pueblo when the two got in a dispute over Waters' wife.

Louis Tharp

Louis, an older Tharp brother, came to El Pueblo after his brother William was murdered. He came to handle William's store and settle his affairs. He left El Pueblo for St. Louis on February 25, 1848, and was robbed by Indians.

Tobin, Thomas "Tom" Tate

Born: May 1, 1823; Tobin came from Boones Lick, Missouri.

Parents: Bartholomew (Irish) and Sarah (a Delaware Indian) Tobin

Siblings: Among his siblings was his half-brother: Charles Autobees

Appearance: 5'7" tall

Character: A man of his word, as well as of few words.

Married:
- Pasquala Maria Bernal in the 1840's—after 1846; she died 1886.
  Children:
  - Pasqualita (m. Kit Carson's son William)
  - Narciso
  - Thomas, Jr.
- Rosita Quintana (no children)

Died: May 16, 1904; buried: Ft. Garland, Colorado

In 1837, when he was fourteen, Tom came West with his half-brother Charlie Autobees. His first job was with Simeon Turley at his mill and distillery in Arroyo Hondo, New Mexico. During the Taos and Arroyo Hondo massacres in January 1847, Tom escaped and reported the situation to Colonel Sterling Price in Santa Fe. He returned to fight the rebels.

A couple years later he searched with the party looking for Mrs. White, her daughter and nurse after Indians massacred their party in eastern New Mexico. His friends among the mountain men said he "could track a grasshopper through sagebrush."

Tom Tobin did some trapping, and scouting. He guided many, including Colonel Henry Inman, Major William Grier, and Colonel Sterling Price. General Stephen Kearny and Charles Bent said Tobin, Carson, and Wootton could be relied on in combat: they followed instructions and assessed and reported situations accurately.

Tom rid Colorado of the ruthless Espinosa Gang, who held up stages, killed passengers, invaded ranches, and killed settlers. The government put a $2,500 price tag on their heads. Tom, a sure shot with pistol and rifle, had an idea where to look and went after them. When he finished with them, the Espinosa Gang were done killing. He either went prepared or found a gunny sack among the gangs' gear. It would have been quite a chore for one man to

bring back all the bodies; so he just brought back their heads in a gunny sack. Reports vary:
- Tom received nothing.
- The federal government rewarded him $500 up front; the Colorado Territorial government paid him $1000 later.
- A grandson said he received $400 cash, a buckskin coat, and a Henry rifle.
- Another grandson vouched for the coat and the rifle. He had them and a paper with his grandfather's x, signifying Tobin had been granted $1000 reward. Whether Tom received the money or just the promise became the subject of fireside chats.

Tom lived at Ft. Garland, Colorado, many years and died there twenty-two years after the death of his brother Charlie Autobees. Tom was 81.

Towne, Charles "Charley/Charlie" (also spelled Town)
Born: St. Louis, Missouri
Married: Maria Antonia Montano, March 6, 1845
Died: June 1848, Manco de Burro Pass

Charley Towne was with Jim Beckwourth in 1841. Like Wootton, Towne was one of the men often in and out of El Pueblo in its early days.

In 1843 he joined Fremont, Carson, and Alex Godey on Fremont's second expedition. He joined them at El Pueblo and returned there July 1, 1844.

In 1847 he rode with the troops to help break up the Taos Revolt and was a juror in the trials that followed. The following year—June 1848—he was with Lucien Maxwell's party at Manco de Burro Pass when Apache ambushed them. They killed Charley.

Turley, Simeon
Born: 1806, Kentucky; grew up in Boones Lick, Missouri, where he knew William Workman, Carson, and Kinkead
Among his siblings: Jesse B. Turley
Died: January 22, 1847, Arroyo Hondo, New Mexico

Turley had a trading post at El Pueblo and hired men like Charlie Autobees and Robert Fisher to run the business and haul goods from the States. His primary venture was his productive grain mill and distillery at his Arroyo Hondo ranch. There he raised sheep and created a small industry using spinning wheels and looms to provide yarn and cloth for the local market. He employed local Mexicans and Indians, as well as young men from the States.

Turley settled in the Taos area in 1830 and felt he was among friends. However, when he received word of the 1847 Taos Massacre, he did close his gates. The mob, hundreds of men strong, closed in on his place. For two days Turley and his employees held out inside the stockade. The rebels killed him.

Waters, James Wesley
Born: June 1813, upper New York state
Married: Candelaria

Died: September 20, 1889, at his home in San Bernardino, California

James Waters came West in 1835. He hunted, trapped, and went overland to California. He returned with abalone shells to trade with the Indians.

In the 1840's Waters made his home at El Pueblo, where Dick Wootton and he were well-acquainted. Early in 1848 Waters and his friend Edward Tharp got into an argument over Water's wife and fought to the death—Tharp's. Waters fled. He hid, and his friends brought him food until he went to Greenhorn. There he worked for John Brown. When Brown went to California the next year, Waters went with him, Calvin Briggs, John Burroughs (Burris), and their party. Brown and Waters remained lifelong associates. In California, Waters became one of the early settlers of the San Bernardino area and helped build the opera house there in 1881.

Watrous, Samuel B.
Born: 1808, Montpelier, Vermont
Parents: Erastus and Nancy (Bowman) Watrous
Married:
- Tomacita/Tomasita
- Rose Chapin (d. in childbirth)
- Josephine Chapin (b. c1842; Rose Chapin's sister)

Children:
- Joseph B. (partnered with his father in cross-country freighting)
- Emeteria (m. George Gregg)
- Louisa (m. William Kroenig)
- Belina (b. c1853; m. Carl Wildenstein; d. c1924),
- Samuel, Jr. (b. 1855)
- Maria Antonia (m. James Johnson) May be same as or different than Mary Antonette
- Rose/Rosa

Died: 1886, New Mexico; suicide

About 1849 Samuel Watrous purchased an interest in the John Scolly Grant and built his home and store in the Mora Valley (New Mexico), in an area known as La Junta de los Rios.

Watrous was in the Huerfano Valley (Colorado) for a time with Doyle and Wootton and moved back to New Mexico about the same time they did. Headquartered at La Junta de los Rios, he farmed, ranched, and freighted. From 1856-1864, he freighted cross-country. The area where he located his home and store became Watrous, New Mexico.

When U. S. officials rounded up men and required them to take the oath of allegiance to the Union, they pulled in Watrous and Wootton.

When the Santa Fe Railroad built into New Mexico, Watrous donated land for a right-of-way through his property.

Williams, William "Bill" Sherley
Born: June 3, 1787, Horse Creek, Rutherford County, North Carolina
Parents: Joseph and Sarah Musick Williams, both predominantly Welsh (Sarah was of Lewis

stock, same stock as Meriwether Lewis of the Lewis and Clark Expedition.

Appearance: Red hair; blue-gray eyes; about 6'1" tall; thin/sinewy; tanned, weather-beaten skin, leathered by years in the Southwestern outdoors; bony face, pockmarked from smallpox

Character: Honest; great friend, but an implacable enemy; helpful to men starting careers in the mountains; fond of children; good speaker, at times eccentric speech or manners; good sense of humor. Dick Wootton considered him "warm-hearted, brave, and generous."[232]

Nicknames: Parson Bill, Old Bill Williams

Married or lived with:
- An Osage lady (died before Bill moved to the Southwest); Children: Mary and Sarah (b. September 15, 1814; m. Mr. Mathews)
- Antonia Baca (widow with 3 children) of Taos, New Mexico; Child: Jose (b. c 1834)

Died: March 1849

When Bill was six, the Spanish opened an area of their upper Louisiana Territory to settlers. Bill's dad sold his 650 acres in North Carolina and took advantage of the opportunity. With a group of family members, he moved his family toward Missouri where the family eventually settled. In August 1796 the Spanish government granted him about 680 acres in St. Louis County.

Fourth of nine children, Bill was nine by the time the family settled on their land grant. The children had little opportunity for formal education; but Bill's mother was knowledgeable and taught her children. Besides a basic education, she taught them Latin and the fundamentals of her Baptist faith. She saw to it Bill was far from illiterate.

Bill and his brothers were allowed freedom to hunt, trap, and range far. When he was sixteen Bill ranged 200 miles from home while hunting and visited an Osage village. He enjoyed his visit and went back home to say goodbye to his family. He moved in with the Osage Big Hill band, learned their language, and became part of their community.

From 1805 until about 1825 Bill lived with the Osage, hunted, and trapped westward, trading among Indians. Some say Bill did missionary work and was a circuit preacher in Missouri; others say he just helped teach missionaries the Osage language and interpreted for them. He wrote a 2,000 word Osage-English dictionary, which enabled missionaries to write *Osage First Lines of Writing*, a book of grammar and familiar phrases of the Osage language.

While among the Osage, Bill married and had two daughters. In later years he lived among the Ute. Uncle Dick Wootton remembered, "He had been so much among the Indians that he used to look and talk like an Indian, and had imbibed a great many of their superstitions and peculiar notions."[233] Bill was a little older than Dick's father.

During the War of 1812, Bill worked as scout for the Mounted Rangers along the Mississippi River. From time-to-time thereafter he guided or interpreted for the military in the Osage region. From May 1817 to the end of June 1818, Bill was official interpreter for Indian Agent George C. Sibley at the government's small military and trading post at Ft.

---

[232] Conard, 1980, 185.
[233] Conard, *Uncle Dick Wootton*, 1890, 201.

Osage.

Bill's father died in 1820 and left him 40 Missouri acres, which Bill sold. In 1823 he opened a trading post with Paul Baillio on the Neosho River; the business failed by the end of the year.

Bill trapped independently along the Columbia River during the winter of 1824-25, but was back home in the Osage village by the end of May. He assigned power of attorney to his brother James and made preparations to leave. Before the end of summer 1825, he left.

Appointed to survey a trade road from Ft. Osage to Santa Fe, George Sibley chose Bill to interpret and hunt for the expedition. Bill was the signing interpreter for the Council Grove Treaty and the treaty with the Kansa at Sora Kansa Creek, August 16, 1825.

When the expedition arrived in Taos, Bill remained to trap and trade. Taos became his home base, as he trapped far north, south, and west. He often left town with a blanket, rifle, knife, and six five-pound traps hung across his back. A few weeks later he'd return loaded with pelts. He'd sell the pelts, live off the profit, and head out again. He conferred on himself the degree of M. T., Master of Trapping. Sometimes he marked his pelts, "Bill Williams, Master Trapper."

On trapping or trading expeditions, Bill occasionally preached on Sundays to the other men. Saturday night he'd tell them he was going to preach to them next day, wanted them to clean up, and come hear him. They would.

He would give a regular first class sermon at the appointed time and apparently with utmost sincerity and earnestness. He would then say off the hyms [sic] one verse at a time and the men would most heartily sing them. When he said 'We will now kneel in prayer', every one reverently got down on his knees. The whole meeting was conducted solomly [sic] and there was no levity about it, either on the part of Wms. [sic] or any of his hearers, who respected the man.[234]

Being much among the Indians, Williams' high pitched voice had picked up mannerisms and expressions of some of the tribes he'd lived among. Like most mountain men, Bill spoke several Indian languages, as well as English, Spanish, and French. He had a knowledge of Latin and Greek. Like many mountain men, he had a good understanding of politics, history, and literature.

For a short time Bill tried his hand at storekeeping in Taos, but soon became exasperated at the local manner of haggling over prices. One day he emptied the store, put most of his goods out along the street, and threw bolts of calico out his door. "Take the ___ stuff since I can't sell it to you." People grabbed the goods, and Old Bill headed back to the mountains.

He always carried a small magnifying glass, which he used to advantage among Indians. When he thought an Indian was lying to him, Bill took out the glass, looked at the person through the glass, acting as though the glass enabled him to see the truth in the other person. He created great respect for his glass and its ability. Men didn't dare lie to Old Bill's glass.

He lived with the Ute about three years. Then, in the summer of 1841, he returned to Missouri to visit his mother, brothers, and sisters. He stayed through the winter. In early spring he outfitted in St. Louis and headed West, this time on a trading expedition.

---

[234] Cragin, *Early Far West Notebook,* Santa Fe, No. 26.

Bill was up at El Pueblo visiting other mountain men when U. S. Pathfinder John Fremont visited after his return from Oregon in 1845. Considered an old-timer among the mountain men, Bill had traveled extensively throughout the Rocky Mountain region and knew all the mountain passes. Fremont engaged his services, and those of Kit Carson, to guide him on a 3rd expedition. When it came time to cross the great Salt Desert, Fremont had ideas of his own. On October 27, after a hearty disagreement between Fremont and his guides, Bill decided Fremont could cross the desert as he pleased and left.

Micajah McGehee, a member of an expedition led by Williams, described him:

Though a most indefatigable walker, he never could walk on a straight line, but went staggering along, first on one side and then the other. He was an expert horseman …He rode leaning forward upon the pommel, with his rifle before him, his stirrups ridiculously short, and his breeches rubbed up to his knees, leaving his legs bare even in freezing cold weather. He wore a loose monkey-jacket or a buckskin hunting-shirt, and for his head-covering a blanket-cap, the two top corners drawn up into two wolfish, satyr-like ears,[235]

Bill never seemed to hold his rifle steady, but never missed the mark with his first shot. He wandered around the Rockies, trapping, hunting, guiding, living in and out of settlements.

During the summer of 1847, he guided and guarded troop wagons on the Santa Fe Trail, as they crossed the Plains with supplies for the Mexican-American War. In the spring of 1848 he and other mountain men were called to accompany Major Reynolds in a campaign against the Apache and Ute, who had been raiding northern New Mexico settlements. Indians had chased two companies of soldiers out of the Raton hills (New Mexico). After three battles, thirty-six Indians and two soldiers were dead. Bill's elbow was shot and shattered. Many were wounded, but the military won.

Bill was at El Pueblo in November 1848 when Fremont came through on his fourth expedition. Kit Carson, Fremont's usual guide, was in Taos. No one at Bent's Fort or El Pueblo wanted to guide Fremont in such weather. He asked Bill; no one knew the mountains like Bill Williams. Williams was hesitant, but finally agreed to go.

In the mountains Fremont wanted to try a different direction. Williams told Fremont they couldn't possibly go the direction he wanted. Fremont refused Williams' advice, put him to the rear, and made Alex Godey head guide. The expedition forged on—not necessarily ahead—in the snow packed winter Rockies at the price of lives, livestock, and equipment.

Fremont laid the blame for the disaster on Bill. The Kern brothers, who traveled with the expedition laid responsibility solely at Fremont's feet. Experienced guide and mountain man Antoine Leroux wrote E. M. Kern that there was no way any sensible mountain man would go the way Fremont chose—no trapper or Indian ever knew any path to exist that way.

The Kern brothers hoped to recover their instruments, medical gear, and papers they'd had to cache in the mountains. The end of February 1849, Bill, Dr. Kern, and a few Mexicans retraced their path up the Rio Grande into the San Juan Mountains to recover the goods. Unknown to Bill and Dr. Kern, Major B. L. Beall and his 1st Dragoons from Taos had just whipped the Ute.

---

[235] Hafen and Hafen, *Fremont's Fourth Expedition*, 144.

After Bill and Dr. Kern recovered the gear, they turned back toward Taos. They passed a Ute camp in the early evening and traveled about a half mile further before making camp. The men were sitting by the campfire when about a dozen Ute arrived. The two men thought nothing of it. Bill had lived among the Ute; he spoke their language. Without warning one Ute lifted his rifle and shot Bill in the forehead. Another shot cracked and a bullet sped into Dr. Kern's heart.

There were conjectures: The Ute attacked because Bill helped the soldiers in the Raton hills last spring. Or: Not realizing who they were shooting, they shot two white men in retaliation for Lt. Whittlesey trouncing them. As a whole, the Ute, mourned Old Bill's death.

Williams, Arizona, Williams Mountains, Williams River, Bill Williams Mountain, and the Bill Williams Fork of the Colorado were named for him.

Military Acquaintances

During the Taos Rebellion, the Mexican War, and while freighting for the U. S. Government, Dick Wootton became acquainted with many soldiers and officers, among them:

Canby, General Edward Richard Sprigg
<u>Born</u>: November 9, 1817, Piatt's Landing, Kentucky
<u>Parents</u>: Israel and Elizabeth Piatt Canby
<u>Died</u>: April 11, 1873, Siskiyou, California

Canby served in the Seminole War (Florida), the Mexican War, the Mormon War (Utah), and the American Civil War. During the Civil War he was a Union officer at Valverde, New Mexico, then in New York. Between those two assignments he was appointed commander of the Department of New Mexico. He was promoted and assigned to Union command; he captured Mobile, Alabama. After the war he worked in the Reconstruction effort.

After the Battle of Glorieta, Mrs. Canby, who was in Santa Fe, visited hospitalized wounded soldiers of both sides and did what she could to help care for them.

Canby had survived many years of military service when he died in California at the hands of Modoc Indians. In the midst of peace negotiations under a flag of truce, Modoc Chief Captain Jack, stood up and shot Canby in the face—below his left eye. When Canby tried to stand to escape, another Modoc finished him off. This incensed the American public. President Grant, who'd been encouraged to try a peaceful approach with the Modoc, ordered a strong counterattack. By June 1, 1873, the Modoc surrendered; Captain Jack was captured.

Doniphan, Colonel Alexander William
<u>Born</u>: July 9, 1808, Kentucky
<u>Appearance</u>: 6'4" tall; red-headed
<u>Married</u>: Elizabeth Thorton, December 21, 1837
<u>Died</u>: August 8, 1887

Alexander Doniphan was a Missouri attorney, a state legislator (1836 and 1840), and a militia soldier before he led Missouri volunteers to New Mexico in the Mexican-American War. He commanded victorious troops at the Battle of Brazito (southern New Mexico). After the war he returned to his Missouri law practice and, in 1854, served in the state legislature.

Although Doniphan was a slaveholder when the Civil War erupted, he favored neutrality for his state. Desiring a plan to gradually eliminate slavery, he met with a group in Washington D. C. in 1861 to try to avert war.

Johnston, General Albert Sydney
Born: 1803; Washington, Kentucky
Married: Henrietta Preston; Eliza Griffin
Died: April 6, 1862; in action at the Battle of Shiloh, Tennessee; buried in New Orleans, reinterred in Austin, Texas (Texas State Cemetery)

Johnston graduated from West Point when Dick Wootton was ten. By the time Dick met him, Johnston had fought in the Black Hawk War and the Texas War for Independence. He'd been Secretary of War for the Republic of Texas and had also fought in the Mexican War.

For a short time Johnston stayed out of the Army and became a planter. By the mid-1850's he was back in the Army, stationed in New Mexico, where Wootton knew him. In 1858 Wootton and Doyle freighted supplies into Utah, where Johnston led troops in the Mormon War.

Johnston remained in the U. S. Army until the outbreak of the Civil War, when he joined the Confederacy. He was considered one of the South's greatest generals. At the Battle of Shiloh a gunshot severed an artery behind his right knee. He bled to death.

Price, Sterling
Born: September 20, 1809, Prince Edward County, Virginia
Nickname: Ole Pappy Price
Married: Martha Head, May 1833
Died: September 1867, Missouri; died of cholera

Price was admitted to the bar before he moved to Missouri (c1830) where he fought against the Mormons at the governor's request. He served three terms in the Missouri General Assembly and one term as U. S. Congressman. He resigned his position to serve in the Mexican-American War as Brigadier General. When General Stephen W. Kearny went to California, Price was in charge of New Mexico. He led troops to quell the 1847 Taos Rebellion. Dick Wootton and other mountain men fought alongside him there.

In 1852 Sterling Price became governor of Missouri.

Price chaired the Missouri secession convention in February 1861. Missouri took a neutral path, but broke with the Union later in 1861 when Union commander Nathaniel Lyon seized the state militia camp. Price accepted command of the Missouri guard and became a Confederate Major General. Rather than surrender when the war ended, he took his troops to live in exile in Mexico. He died soon after he returned to Missouri.

Sibley, Colonel Henry Hopkins

Born: May 25, 1816, Natchitoches, Louisiana
Parents: Samuel Hopkins (son of Dr. John Sibley of the Long Expedition) and Margaret McDonald Sibley
Died: August 23, 1886, Fredericksburg, Virginia

A graduate of West Point, Sibley fought in the Seminole and Mexican Wars before being stationed in New Mexico, where he commanded at Ft. Union. Dick Wootton knew him in New Mexico. When the Civil War broke out, Major Sibley left his command and joined the Confederacy. He persuaded Southern leaders to push to gain the entire southern U. S. from the Atlantic to the Pacific—to obtain a western seacoast and the western mineral fields. In San Antonio he organized Texas volunteers for the Confederacy.

He was victor at the Battle of Valverde, but lost the Battle of Glorieta. He commanded other brigades during the Civil War. After the war, he sailed to Egypt where he became a general in the Khedive's army.

Railroad Acquaintances

During the years the A.T. & S. F. (Santa Fe Railroad) trains steamed past Dick Wootton's place, he became well-acquainted with scores of railroad men—locomotive engineers and firemen, conductors, brakemen, officials, line and signal maintainers; station agents; engineers who planned the line and the tunnel. Among those whose life stories remain public:

Morley, William Raymond "Ray"

Born: 1846, Massachusetts; orphaned and raised in Iowa by an uncle
Married: Ada McPherson, 1873
Character: Would do jobs at personal expense, put the welfare of his job above his own; resourceful
Died: January 3, 1883, near La Cruz, Chihuahua, Mexico, Mexican Central Railroad line; buried Las Vegas, New Mexico Territory

During the Civil War, Morley marched with General Sherman's Union troops. After the war he studied two years at Iowa State University and became a civil engineer.

In 1871 Morley went to work for the Maxwell Land Grant Company, headquartered in Cimarron, New Mexico. He became executive vice-president in 1872. That year he encouraged former classmate Attorney Frank Springer to locate in the Cimarron area. In 1874 the two purchased Cimarron's newspaper and hired Will Dawson as editor. Their press wasn't dominated by the Santa Fe Ring, which had ties to the Maxwell Land Grant Co. The men soon found themselves at odds with both factions of the Colfax County War.

Morley worked for the Santa Fe Railroad from about 1875-1880 or 1881. George B. Lake, Lewis Kingman, and Morley were responsible for much surveying and laying out of the Santa Fe lines in parts of Colorado, New Mexico, and beyond.

Dick Wootton and Morley became well-acquainted when Morley surveyed the route over Raton Pass; he enjoyed their friendship. The Santa Fe's chief engineer, A. A. Robinson, pegged Morley as "a warm friend and a good hater."

One thing those who corresponded with Morley remembered was his poor penmanship. In fact, Robinson recommended Morley buy a typewriter when they were first manufactured so that those he corresponded with could save time deciphering and not be so prone to profanity.

When Thomas Nickerson became president of the Mexican Central Railroad, he sent for Morley to be his chief engineer. Morley was extremely diligent and cautious with firearms. One day, however, while building the Mexican Central system, Morley and A. A. Robinson (general superintendent of the line) were driving with a party of surveyors when Morley was accidentally shot and killed.

Robinson, Albert Alonzo

Born: October 21, 1844, South Reading, Vermont
Died: 1918

After Albert's father died, the family moved to Wisconsin, where Albert farmed to support the family. Determined to obtain a college education, he attended a local academy and saved money until he could afford to enter the University of Michigan in 1865. During his college years, he surveyed near the Great Lakes for the government. Between loans and part time jobs, he was able to graduate in 1869. He worked for the St. Joseph and Denver City Railroad that year.

After he earned his Master's degree in 1871, he hired on as engineer for the Atchison, Topeka & Santa Fe Railroad and became chief engineer. He later became vice-president and general manager of the engineering department. In his twenty-two years with the Santa Fe, Robinson built 5,074.1 miles of mainline.

He left the Santa Fe when the company fell into the hands of financers whose ideas and methods veered from the Santa Fe's established ways. From 1893 until his retirement in 1906, Robinson was president of the Mexican Central Railway.

Strong, William Barstow

Born: May 16, 1837, Brownington, Vermont; grew up in Beloit, Wisconsin
Character: Generous; courteous, hand-shaking, goodwill sort of guy; trustworthy and deeply loyal—he expected the same of others.
Died: August 3, 1913, Los Angeles

William Strong graduated from Bell's Business College in Chicago, and immediately began railroading in Milton, Wisconsin (March 1855), as telegraph operator and station agent. He worked as station agent in Whitewater and Monroe, Wisconsin, before he became a general agent in the Chicago, Milwaukee & St. Paul Railway's Southwestern Division.

The year the Civil War ended, the McGregor Western Railway appointed him assistant superintendent. Strong remained with McGregor until 1867. He again changed lines and became general western agent for Chicago & Northwestern line, headquartered in Iowa.

Three years later he accepted the Chicago, Burlington, and Quincy railroad's offer of assistant general superintendent in Council Bluffs. When the line merged with the Burlington & Missouri in 1872, Strong became superintendent of the consolidated line. From 1874-1875 he was general superintendent of the Michigan Central in Chicago. He returned to Burlington and worked two years.

With all his experience with various railroad lines, William Strong became general manager of the Atchison, Topeka & Santa Fe (Santa Fe) railroad, November 1, 1877. A few weeks later, on December 17, he was elected company vice-president. On July 12, 1881, Strong became president and director, with an office in Boston.

During his years with the Santa Fe, Strong pushed with determination to expand the Santa Fe. He accomplished his ambitious plans with the help of his skilled and dedicated engineer, Albert A. Robinson. Under their leadership the Santa Fe laid rails into New Mexico, across Arizona, and into California.

During Strong's years the Santa Fe Hospital Association originated and the Fred Harvey system and the Santa Fe began working together. Strong founded Santa Fe reading rooms for employees. He hoped it would make their lives more enjoyable and reflect in their jobs. He took pride in the cleanliness of the Santa Fe line. Cleanliness remained a top priority for the line as long as it was the Santa Fe. He retired from the company in September 1889. He moved first to Wisconsin, then to California. Barstow, California, is named for him.

WILLIAM BARSTOW STRONG

LEWIS KINGMAN

W. R. MORLEY

Settlement Citizens

Beshoar, Dr. Michael
Born: February 1833, Lewistown, Mifflin County, Pennsylvania
Parents: Daniel and Susan Rothrock Beshoar
Married: Anna E. Maupin, 1872
Children: (listed in his obituary)
- Mrs. W. D. Guiley (of Chicago)
- Mrs. E. W. Fox (of Maryland)
- Dr. Ben Beshoar

- Dr. John Beshoar
- Bertram Beshoar (of Trinidad, Colorado)

Died: 11:15 p.m., September 5, 1904; at home 611 E. Main, Trinidad, Colorado

Interested in medicine since childhood, Michael Beshoar earned his medical degree from the University of Michigan in 1853. He began medical practice in Pocahontas, Arkansas—about twenty miles south of the Missouri line. While there, he served two terms in the Arkansas legislature.

When the Civil War fired up, young Dr. Beshoar signed on as surgeon for the Seventh Arkansas infantry. In 1862 he was medical director under General Hardy until after the Battle of Shiloh, when he was transferred to the Department of the Mississippi. In late 1863 Union soldiers captured him and marched him to St. Louis. He was allowed to study post-graduate courses at St. Louis Medical College and act as physician at Benton Barracks and surgeon at Jefferson Barracks. He was released and placed in charge of the Fort Kearny hospital (Nebraska).

In 1866 Dr. Beshoar resigned the Ft. Kearny post and attempted to settle in Denver, but Denver and the *Rocky Mountain News* weren't welcoming "galvanized Yankees." Dr. Beshoar picked up his medical bag, moved to Pueblo Colorado, and established the first drug store between Denver and Santa Fe. While maintaining his Pueblo interests, he moved to the new settlement of Trinidad, Colorado. He opened a medical practice and drug store there (1867). In 1868, while living in Trinidad, he began publishing the *Chieftain* in Pueblo, Colorado.

Dr. Beshoar was a prominent southeastern Colorado citizen the remainder of his life. Active in politics as a Democrat, Dr. Beshoar served as Las Animas County coroner, assessor, and clerk. For seven years he was county judge, served four terms as the county superintendent of schools, and served one term in the Colorado House of Representatives.

In Trinidad he donated land for a hospital and participated in and led community organizations. He founded the Early Settlers' Association and presided over it until his death. He knew many of the old trappers and traders and was one of the area's old timers himself.

In addition to civic involvements, Dr. Beshoar kept informed of medical innovations. It was said that, although he was the oldest practicing Colorado physician at the time of his death, he was as aware of new medical procedures as recent graduates. He practiced medicine in Trinidad and Las Animas County. He belonged to local, state, and national medical associations and held office in some. At one time Dr. Beshoar was a member of Colorado's State Board of Health.

He died of sudden heart failure. Trinidad schools closed for his funeral. High school students marched behind his hearse. Father Pinto officiated at Dr. Beshoar's funeral at the Catholic Church with the Elks lodge participating.

The Woottons knew him well and respected him enough that his photo had a place in a family album.

Byers, William Newton

Born: February 22, 1831, Madison County, Ohio

Parents: Moses W. and Mary A. Brandenburg Byers
Married: Elizabeth Minerva Sumner, 1854
Children: Frank S.; Mary Eva (m. William F. Robinson)
Died: March 1903, Denver, Colorado; died following a stroke.

William Byers had more exposure to western life than to journalism when he arrived in Denver-Auraria on April 17, 1859. He'd helped with the Oregon-Washington boundary survey and went to the California Gold Rush. After that he became a member of the bar and served in the Nebraska legislature.

Byers was involved in real estate in Omaha (Nebraska) when he heard news of Rocky Mountain gold (Colorado). Having been in California, he knew gold rush towns need a newspaper. He purchased a used printing press in Bellevue, Nebraska, sold advertising copy in Omaha, engaged helpers, and packed what he needed into two wagons. On March 8, 1859, he and his employees started out for gold country. Mrs. Byers remained in Nebraska until her husband established his business.

The men traveled to Ft. Kearny and cross country to Cherry Creek (Colorado). Byers didn't know where he'd set up his press, but knew he was headed to the Rocky Mountains. He'd already named his newspaper *Rocky Mountain News*. Before he arrived, Byers wrote two pages of generic news—including the Nebraska advertising—for his first edition.

When bearded Byers arrived in Auraria, he looked for a place to set up shop. Dick Wootton offered to rent him part of the upstairs of his new building. Byers took it. He and his men hauled the press and supplies upstairs. Then Byers scoured the twin towns for local news to add to his pre-written copy. Snow fell, but Byers gathered news and went to press. The first issue of the *Rocky Mountain News* rolled off the press on April 23, 1859. Twenty minutes later Colorado's second newspaper, the *Cherry Creek Pioneer*, hit the streets; but the *Pioneer* was short-lived.

Byers may not have been a veteran journalist; but he became one. He reported crime and disorderliness, from minor infractions to murders and duels. It was not a time of political correctness of expression. Byers wielded his pen to draw people to Cherry Creek and to promote the growth he preferred for the region—whether showering laurels or scathing disapproval.

By spring 1864 the *Rocky Mountain News* was being printed on a 3,000 pound steam-powered printing press in a new facility along Cherry Creek. Flooding devastated much in Colorado that spring. It didn't make an exception when it came to Byers' new building and press, washed them downstream. John Chivington rowed his boat across town and rescued Byers and his family off the roof of their house.

During Civil War years William Byers used his ink for the Union though he sharply criticized the governor for outfitting Union volunteers before receiving approval from Washington. After the war, he made it clear galvanized Yankees were not welcome in Denver.

William N. Byers' words helped shape the character of his town as it grew into a city. He died in March 1903. His newspaper lived on until February 27, 2009.

Bent-St. Vrain & Company

Bent-St. Vrain Company was an alliance between Charles and William Bent and Ceran St. Vrain. Later their younger brothers, George and Robert Bent and Marcellin St. Vrain, worked for the company. The company owned Bent's Fort, Ft. St. Vrain, Adobe Walls, a farm in Missouri, and stores in Taos and Santa Fe. As they developed trade among trappers, traders, Mexicans and Indians for hundreds of miles around their establishments, St. Vrain and the Bent brothers did their best to maintain a position of neutrality.

Bent-St. Vrain rivaled the American Fur Company in the Rocky Mountain Fur trade. The legacy of Bent-St. Vrain to the Southwest and to the nation reached far beyond clanking coffers. With dignity, Bent-St. Vrain imparted opportunity and values, as they played their part in the lives of individuals and the forging of the nation.

Influential in the New Mexico political arena and well-acquainted with the Southwest, Ceran and Charles helped pave the way for the U. S. to enter the Southwest.

After Charles was massacred in 1847, Ceran and William reorganized the company and changed the name to St. Vrain & Bent. They dissolved the partnership in 1849 or 1850.

Bent's Fort

Built near the Arkansas River on the U. S. Mexican border, Bent's Fort was close enough to the mountains to outfit and trade with trappers and traders. Yet, it was on the Plains with easy access for the Indian trade, grazing for livestock, and hunting for sustenance. Some tribes considered the area home. Others, including Arapaho, Cheyenne, Kiowa, Comanche, Crow, Prairie Apache, Ute, and Shoshone, passed through.

William Bent told Jared Sanderson, who ran a stage line out of the fort, that construction of the fort was started in 1828 and completed in 1832.

Ft. St. Vrain

Ft. St. Vrain was located about fifteen miles east of the Rocky Mountain foothills on the east bank of the South Platte, about a mile from St. Vrain Creek (northern Colorado). Although reports of construction vary, one person of the era reported it in operation in May 1837. First named Ft. Lookout, it was changed to Ft. George for George Bent, then Ft. St. Vrain when Marcellin St. Vrain was in charge. The fort measured 130' (north-south walls) x 60' (east-west walls). In the far West only Ft. Laramie and Bent's Fort were larger. Circular bastions guarded the southwest and northwest corners of the fort.

In 1842 Bent-St. Vrain established a weekly express service between Ft. St. Vrain, Bent's Fort, and the company store in Taos; mountain men rode as couriers.

Bent-St. Vrain abandoned the fort in 1845.

Adobe Walls

After reaching a peace agreement with the Comanche and Kiowa, Bent-St. Vrain built Adobe Walls as a stronghold from which to trade with Plains Indians in the Texas Panhandle. The adobe fortress was built about a half mile from the Canadian River, near a small creek, surrounded by cottonwood trees in Hutchinson County, Texas. Piñon and cedar trees grew on the nearby bluffs. The walls were about three feet thick and eighty feet square with a tower on each corner. The height is reported to have been nine or eighteen or twenty feet high. The walls had portholes. The gate was in the center of the south wall. Like Bent's Fort, buildings lined the inner walls.

Adobe Walls was never as successful as Bent's Fort or Ft. St. Vrain.

Bent's Farm and Ranches

In 1842 Bent-St. Vrain purchased a farm about six miles southwest of Westport, Missouri, for an eastern transshipment port. Farm fields provided fodder for trail animals and wild western horses, which the company drove East for taming and resale. Farm buildings provided storage for wagons and trade goods and room to repair over-the-road wagons. The partners chose Angus Boggs, the Bent's twenty-two-year-old nephew—son of their late sister Juliannah—to manage the farm. The number of farm employees required impacted growth of the Westport community.

The company also had ranches on the Vermijo and Ponil in New Mexico.

Restored Bent's Fort, near La Junta, Colorado

The Westward Movement: Exploration

Early Exploration and Trade in the American Southwest

Spaniards colonized the American Southwest more than 200 years before Americans began to traffic in the area. New Mexico was Spain's buffer zone, her border child. As early as 1650 Spain regulated New Mexico trade. Frenchmen came trapping and trading in the 1700's, anyway. They'd learned of New Mexico from Indians on the Missouri River as early as 1714 and arrived in Santa Fe by 1719.

The Mallet brothers headed toward Santa Fe in 1739, but lost their pack animals in a river crossing. Even though they had nothing to trade when they arrived, the locals welcomed them; and the Spanish government resented them.

The Spanish government sent supply trains from Mexico into New Mexico every three years. New Mexico's pleas for provisions, clergy, and troop protection seemed to fall on deaf ears; so New Mexicans found ways to live, to enjoy life with what they had and did not have.

Spain's New World government was centralized in Mexico City, from whence New Mexico governors were appointed. Once a governor was in office, authorities were too far away to control his day-to-day actions. When the central government decided to replace a governor, it didn't matter if he'd served well or been a despot, the man was replaced. Although it was against the law, some government jobs, even that of soldier, were sold to the highest bidder. Financially, governors had little to work with, few soldiers, and few supplies.

The Spanish government made ordinances pertaining to trade. Bribes could sometimes influence the interpretation—or complete neglect—of ordinances.

More French traders came—in 1744, 1748, 1750, 1752—from Quebec, St. Louis, New Orleans, the Great Lakes region, from a variety of places by a variety of routes. Spanish officials often confiscated goods and jailed traders. Yet, when they returned home, trappers and traders emphasized the commercial opportunities in poorly supplied New Mexico. French trappers continued to arrive as the century ended and on into the early 1800's. Jacques Clamorgan organized the Spanish Commercial Exploration Company in St. Louis in 1794. In August 1807 he went across Kansas to Santa Fe and sold his goods.

Frenchmen adapted to New Mexico communities with ease. Those who came to the Southwest were from Canada (C), St. Louis (SL), France (F), or other locales. Among them: Joe Manuel Allen (C), born cj 1797; Luis Ambrule (SL),m. in Taos, 1824; Michel/Miguel Arcenó (C), m. in Taos, 1825; Joseph Barnoy, nicknamed Levanway; Charles Beaubien (C); Luis Bergand or Bergaud, m. in Taos, 1830; Yara; Joseph Bijou; Joseph Bissonette; Antonio Blanchard, also called Brashal/Brachal, m. in Taos, 1826; William Blanc/Guillermo Blanco (C), son of Augustin and Margaret Robinson Blanc; Enrique Boné, m. Francisca Varela; Victor Bordeaux/Bordaux/Bardaux (F); John/Juan O. Bristol, m. in Taos, 1826; Francisco Broune (SL), son of George and Mary Dewitt Broune; Anastasio Carier (C), m. in Taos, 1824; Jean/Juan Chantet; Jean Baptiste Chalifoux (Charlifoux/Charlefoux/Challifou/

Charlefou) and his brother Pierre/Pedro Chalifoux (C); Pierre/Pedro Charette/ Charrette, m. Margarita L.; had a son, Pedro, b. 1828; Josef Charvet; John/Juan Chaubelón, m. in Taos, 1827; Francisco Chunt/Lut (F); Michel/Miguel Desmaraes (C), m. in Taos, 1848; Alarid/ Enrique Blanc/Blanco, son of Francisco Blanc and Amable Colorada, married Ramon Lopez' daughter Guadalupe, February 16, 1832, Taos; Antoine Dillette (C), (Diett, Grillette, Gillette; his Canadian relatives who moved to U. S. Atlantic states used the name St. Mars—b. Three Rivers Canada, m. Maria Victoria Lopez; Duchesne, often drunk when he was old; Amado Duque (F) m. at San Miguel, New Mexico, 1848; Luis Fornier (F); Lame Vidal; Joseph/Jose Grenier (C) (Grignier, Grignet, Grine; pronounced Greenya), son of Jean Baptiste Grenier, m. in Taos, first: Maria Juana Rodarte, second: Manuela Sanchez ; Jean Baptiste Grenier (Grignet, Grignier); Naptiste (Bautista) Guerra/Guarra (possibly same as Charra); Jean/Juan Jeantet (from Bordeaux, France); Luis Lachoné (SL) m. in Taos, 1841; François/Francisco Laforet; Anastasio Larié (C), sometimes spelled Cariel; Antoine Ledoux, m. Polonia Lucero; Pierre L'Esperance; brothers Paul and Pierre Mallet, first known Frenchmen in New Mexico; Abram and Joaquin Ledoux; Isidore/Isidoro Robiçous; brothers François/Francisco, Joseph III, Isidore, Antoine (b. 1794), Louis, and Michel Robidoux (SL); Jean Sybille/John Sabille; Bautista Brison Sanserman (C), son of Alexo Brison, m. in Taos, August 1824; François Turcotte, scalped at Turley's Mill; Jean Vaillant (F), arrived in New Mexico 1824.

In 1804 William Morrison, American merchant from Kaskaskia—the capital of Illinois at the time—sent Jean Baptiste LaLande with pack animals loaded with goods to sell or trade in Santa Fe. LaLande sold the goods, married and settled in New Mexico. Back in the States, Morrison wondered what happened to his trader and his merchandise. In 1805 Mr. Purcell came to trade in New Mexico and likewise settled in and made himself at home.

After its 1803 Louisiana Purchase, the United States sent explorers into its new land, which bordered New Mexico and included a tiny piece of New Mexico's northeast corner.

United States Enters the Southwest
Pike Expedition

In 1806-07 Zebulon Montgomery Pike led a U. S. Government authorized expedition to the newly acquired southwestern territory. He traveled part of the future Santa Fe Trail route. At the great bend of the Arkansas River, he turned northwest (toward Pike's Peak, Colorado), then south toward the Sangre de Cristo Mountains. He mapped his route and journaled his findings.

Pike and his men crossed the Sangre de Cristo Mountains into Spanish territory and built a stockade. Spanish soldiers found them and took them captive to Santa Fe. After a few months the Spaniards released the explorers, but had confiscated Pike's journal and papers. On his return to the U. S., Pike published what he remembered about the southwest, its resources, and what he thought was a practical way to travel there. His note of needs in New Mexico settlements and the exorbitant prices paid for merchandise stirred American interest.

More Traders

About the time of Pike's exploration, Jacques Clamorgan left St. Louis for Spanish territory. After he traded goods in Santa Fe, he rode south and traded in Chihuahua, Mexico.

In the early 1800's only those authorized by the U. S. government were allowed to trade with Indians on American soil. About the time of the War of 1812, Manuel Lisa, who'd been trapping along the Missouri River, obtained permission to trade in the southwest on the American side. He sent merchandise with Charles Saguinet, but Indians overtook Saguinet and stole the goods.

Several tried their hand at trading in New Mexico, but found it impossible to establish trade while New Mexico was under Spanish rule. Spanish authorities kept an eye out for intruders. Many, like Robert McKnight, James Baird, and Samuel Chambers, thought Hidalgo's 1810 declaration of independence removed foreign trade restrictions in New Mexico. Apparently they didn't receive the word that Hidalgo was arrested and executed in July 1811.[236] When they arrived in New Mexico, they were captured and jailed, some for years—until Mexico became independent of Spain.

Long Expedition

After the U. S. began to recover from the War of 1812, the government authorized another exploratory expedition of its' western acquisition. Major Stephen Harriman Long, his brother David Long, and botanist Dr. Edwin James led the expedition. They return home with notes on inhabitants, animals, plants, and geological formations. Long returned with a less promising report than Pike. It was Long's opinion that the country wasn't fit for cultivation.

Long estimated the chief value of western land was to keep U. S. population from overextending itself and to act as a buffer from enemies. He called the U. S.' acquisition the "Great American Desert." American text books repeated his assessment.

Dodge Expedition

The U. S. authorized a third southwestern expedition in 1835. Colonel Henry Dodge led 120 dragoons on a path similar to Long's and held councils with Indians in the U. S.'s southwestern territory.

Kearny Expedition

Judging by the number of trappers and traders they saw, southwestern Indians thought "white men" were a sparse tribe, an easy prey. The U. S. Government hoped that seeing U. S. military strength would deter Indian attacks on travelers and settlers. For that purpose, in 1845, Colonel Stephen Watts Kearny led 280 U. S. dragoons from Ft. Leavenworth (Kansas) to Ft. Laramie (Wyoming), and south to El Pueblo (Colorado) before returning by way of the Santa Fe Trail.

Fremont Expeditions

John Charles Fremont, "the Great American Pathfinder" led a series of exploratory expeditions. All except his last expedition were for the U. S. government. His father-in-law,

---

[236] Hidalgo's name: Miguel Gregorio Antonio Ignacio Hidalgo Costilla y Gallaga Mandarte Villaseñor.

Thomas Hart Benton—Missouri's veteran U. S. Congressman, was a strong advocate of westward expansion. To enhance each expedition, Fremont recruited knowledgeable men to accompany him.

First Expedition: June 10-September 3, 1842

Fremont explored the eastern slopes of the Rocky Mountains, north to the Platte River, and into Wyoming. Kit Carson guided; Lucien Maxwell hunted.

When mountain man Jim Bridger met the group, he warned them to be alert for Indians, particularly Sioux and northern Cheyenne. The previous August they'd killed several trappers, including his partner Henry Fraeb. Carson knew Bridger's character, listened, and made a will. Fremont had no respect for the admonition and disdained Carson's action, but Carson had a way with Fremont. He knew how to work with him; so they weathered flurries of differing opinion.

Second Expedition: July 1843-July 1844

Fremont engaged Kit Carson and Thomas Fitzpatrick as guides. William Gilpin, later Colorado Territory's first governor, was also with the expedition.

This military and geographic expedition covered some of the same route traveled by Pike and Long, but explored beyond. From the northwest corner of Colorado, Fremont followed the Little Snake River into North Park, south to the headwaters of the Colorado, Arkansas and South Platte Rivers. From there they trekked north through part of present-day Wyoming, west to the Great Salt Lake, along the Oregon Trail to Ft. Vancouver, and south through California. They returned to Bent's Fort on July 2, 1844. Having seen the West in this year of good rainfall, Fremont's report encouraged Americans to move westward.

Third Expedition

In spring 1845 Fremont started on a third U. S. backed expedition. Where he was headed wasn't clear to all. Some said he was going to survey a railroad route; others said he was going to the area near Bent's Fort, still others said he was headed to California, a possession of Mexico.

In present-day Colorado Fremont divided his men into two groups. He sent one party to explore the Canadian River route from New Mexico to the States. He kept the second party with himself. Those 60 men and he followed the Arkansas River, crossed the Continental Divide, continued to the headwaters of the White River, and on to the Great Salt Lake. Kit Carson and Bill Williams had been guiding the expedition, but Williams and Fremont disagreed concerning the route. The difference became so great that Williams refused to guide Fremont any further.

The expedition continued on without him and, in December 1845, arrived in California, where Fremont encouraged Americans living there to revolt against Mexico. In spring 1846 Mexican officials ordered him to leave. He went north to Oregon. In May 1846 the U. S. declared war with Mexico. At Klamath Lake, Oregon, Fremont received dispatches and returned to California to rekindle revolutionary sparks.

When settlers in the Sacramento Valley (California) captured the village of Sonoma, Fremont joined them. On July 4, 1846, he raised a flag with a grizzly bear emblem proclaiming California a republic. Three days later an American squadron occupied Monterrey and proclaimed U. S. victory. They included San Francisco and Sonoma in their victory.

Commodore Robert Stockton mustered Fremont and the men of his expedition as Navy Mounted Riflemen to help in the conquest and occupation of southern California. By the middle of August they had pretty well wrapped up the Mexican-American War in California.

Fourth Expedition: 1848-1849

The 1848 expedition was an attempt to find a central route for a railway. It was conducted in the dead of winter to obtain a realistic idea of conditions. It was not government funded. Men in Fremont's Fourth Expedition:
* = traveled with Fremont in his California campaign or in the Mexican War in California
^ = each ^ represents a previous expedition on which this man accompanied Fremont
/ = fatality of this expedition
\ = killed retrieving baggage

^/Antoine Moreau ("Morel"); *Billy Bacon; */Benjamin Beadle; ^Thomas E. Breckenridge; */Carver; ^Josiah Ferguson; Frederick Creutzfeldt, botanist; Ike Cooper; Julius Ducatel; Captain Andrew Cathcart; John C. Fremont; */George Hubbard; ^^Charles Pruess, topographer;*Joseph Stepperfeldt, gunsmith; ^/Henry King; Thomas S. Martin; Theodore McNaab; /Elijah T. Andrews; ^/Vincent Tabeau ("Sorrel"); ^^*Charles Taplin; ^*Lorenzo D. Vincenthaller "Haller"; Micajah McGehee; ^\Bill Williams, guide; ^/Henry J. Wise; /Henry Rohrer; ^^^/Raphael Proue; John Scott, seasoned mountain man; Gregorio, Joaquin, and Manuel—California Indians; ^^*Alex Godey and his fourteen-year-old nephew Theodore McNabb; Jackson Saunders, Fremont's orderly and personal chef (one of the Benton's free black servants); \Dr. Benjamin Kern and brothers ^*Edward and Richard, expedition artists

Gunnison Exploration

In 1853 Congress directed exploration of a feasible railroad route through Colorado along the 38th parallel. In June Captain John W. Gunnison led the exploration party into Colorado, along the Mountain Branch of the Santa Fe Trail. They then traveled south into the San Luis Valley, followed the Gunnison to the Grand River, and west into Utah. There, in October, Piute Indians killed Captain Gunnison and some of his men. Lt. Edward Beckwith led the remaining men to complete the survey.

Trails

El Camino Real (The Royal Highway)

El Camino Real was the 1,500 mile route Juan de Onate took from Mexico City to Santa Fe. In February 1598 he led settlers from Zacatecas, Mexico—a rich silver mine area, across the Chihuahua desert to the Rio Grande. In April they camped near future Ft. Seldon. (It remained a favorite campsite for 300 years.) They then traveled 80 miles across Jornada del Muerto, and followed the Rio Grande to Socorro, to Isleta Pueblo, and to the junction of the Rio Chama with the Rio Grande.

Onate's route, El Camino Real, was the supply route between Chihuahua mines and military headquarters, as well as between Mexico City and Santa Fe; but it was never an improved road. The original route originated near Mexico City in Teotihuacan, a city contemporary with Rome. Its citizens used the route to New Mexico, where they obtained turquoise. Their route extended south to Peru, where they traded the turquoise. The Spanish followed those preexisting routes.

Every three years a supply train picked up supplies at the port of Vera Cruz, Mexico, freighted them to Mexico City and on to New Mexico. The Spanish crown required supply trips be made every three years to supply New Mexico priests and missions. The suppliers also carried mail and sold goods to New Mexicans. A round trip took about eighteen months: twelve months for the trip and six months to distribute goods. Supply trains arrived in late October or early November.

The town of Chihuahua, Mexico, grew up around a Spanish mission in northern Mexico. By the early 1700's supply caravans traveled from Chihuahua to Santa Fe. At first, the trip from Chihuahua required sixteen weeks of travel. It was shortened to about six weeks.

When the Santa Fe Trail opened, New Mexicans preferred the quality, availability, and prices of American goods. New Mexico no longer depended on Mexico or El Camino Real. Many Santa Fe Trail goods traveled El Camino Real to be sold in Chihuahua. The approximate 550 mile portion between Santa Fe and Chihuahua was sometimes referred to as the Chihuahua Trail.

Old Spanish Trail

William Wolfskill was the first recorded American to travel the complete Spanish Trail. Explorers, trappers, and the Spanish had previously traveled portions of the trail. An extension of the Santa Fe Trail, the Spanish Trail wound northwest from Santa Fe and Taos into present-day southern Colorado and Utah, southwest across southern Nevada, on to Los Angeles, California. There were plenty of watering holes along the route, and it was far enough north to avoid Apache raids.

It was a trail used primarily by traders. Horse thieves, who traveled to California and returned to New Mexico and Colorado to sell horses, found the Old Spanish Trail convenient.

Goodnight Trail (Goodnight-Loving Trail)

Charles Goodnight stood 6' tall and weighed over 200 pounds. His short beard resembled President Grant's. He walked with a limp after his feet had frozen while he freighted on the Plains. He tried his hand as a Texas Ranger. In 1856 he became a cattleman.

Ten years later he and Oliver Loving, a trail driver in his fifties, formed a cattle business partnership, which developed into a large operation. The men established the Goodnight-Loving Trail, a cattle-driving trail which originated in Young County, Texas. In 1866 it followed the Butterfield Overland Mail Route, then trailed the east side of the Pecos River into New Mexico, to Ft. Sumner, and northwest to Las Vegas. From Las Vegas it followed the Santa Fe Trail to Trinidad, Colorado. It then went north through Pueblo to Denver.

In June 1866 Goodnight, Loving, and sixteen cowboys drove 2,000 head of cattle from Texas to Ft. Sumner, New Mexico, and made a good profit selling most of the cattle to the government for eight cents a pound on the hoof. They drove the remaining cattle to Denver. When they reached Raton Pass, Goodnight was incensed that Uncle Dick charged for the cattle to cross the toll road. When all was said and done, Goodnight paid. But, in 1867, he rerouted his cattle; so he wouldn't have to pay. Goodnight altered his New Mexico route: north from the Canadian River, toward Capulin and Folsom, across Trinchera Pass, into Colorado. Goodnight himself only made one more drive over that trail.

Goodnight owned a ranch, about 40 miles northeast of Trinidad, Colorado. He used it as a relay station for his cattle drives. From Trinchera Pass, the cattle were driven to the ranch. The trail proceeded from the ranch to Pueblo and Greeley, Colorado. It followed Crow Creek to Cheyenne, Wyoming, where his cowboys delivered cattle at the Union Station.

Cattlemen used Goodnight's trail until 1879 or 1880.

Santa Fe Trail

Mexican Independence

When Mexico gained independence from Spain in September 1821, it took along all of Spain's southwestern territory in North America. Spain lost its grip on the American Southwest, and Mexico took hold. New Mexico remained a borderland territory, not a state of Mexico.

When Mexican independence was proclaimed in New Mexico, there were at least three trading parties near the border: William Becknell's party of Missourians; Hugh Glenn and Jacob Fowler with a group of trappers and traders (along the Arkansas River); John McKnight and Thomas James with eleven men (They intended to attempt trade in New Mexico and find out about John's brother Robert, a trader imprisoned by the Spanish).

Jubilant in their new measure of freedom, Mexican soldiers welcomed William Becknell, the first trader they found near their border. Mexico relaxed trade restrictions, which Spain had clutched. but was unprepared for the influx of traffic that came.[237]

On January 6, 1822, Santa Fe formally celebrated freedom from Spain. Artillery salutes wakened the dawn. A little girl in angel dress and carrying a sword in her right hand led a citizens' double-file parade. Two children, also dressed as angels with rich fineries, walked behind her. The two carried a baby dressed like the Virgin to symbolize "Independence and the Purity of our Cause." Church bells rang.

New Mexico Governor Facundo Melgares invited American visitors to offer any ideas they had to enhance the festivity. Thomas James, of the McKnight party, joined in. With the help of others, he spliced enough pine trees to construct a 70' liberty pole.

Artillery fired salutes.

Tesuque Indians danced in the Plaza. The general public made merry—for better or worse, as each saw fit.

Father of the Santa Fe Trail

In 1821 William Becknell and his party of four left Arrow Rock, Missouri, with pack mules laden with goods to trade with Indians. They hoped to trade for horses and mules, do a little trapping, and catch some wild animals to add to their profit. Indebted, Becknell hoped to get his pocketbook above water. He needed this trip to be a success.

His plans changed when Mexican soldiers met them. Becknell had traveled more than 100 miles south of Raton Pass and was already in New Mexico. These soldiers, however, weren't like those who'd met Americans in the past. Delighted with their independence from Spain,

---

[237] Once Santa Fe Trail trade began to grow, Mexico couldn't seem to regulate the number of traders. New Mexico Governor Manuel Armijo, during his three terms of office between 1827 and 1846, taxed trade in one way or another to generate revenue for New Mexico.

they welcomed Becknell to New Mexico.

The first New Mexico settlement the traders entered was San Miguel del Vado,[238] less than 60 miles from Santa Fe. (San Miguel became a customs port of entry on the Santa Fe Trail.) Becknell arrived in Santa Fe on November 16; some of his men remain in San Miguel. New Mexicans quickly relieved Becknell's mules of their loads. In spite of eighteen inches of snow on the ground, Becknell's party left San Miguel for the States on December 13, 1821. Two traders, who arrived in San Miguel by a different route, returned with them.

By January 29, 1822, Becknell arrived in Franklin, Missouri. Four of his party claimed to have returned with $3000 worth of goods, a 2000% profit. Profit reports vary from 600% to 2000%. Whatever the case, they had enough to pay bills and to arouse interest in Santa Fe trade. Other men soon trekked the same path to profit.

Even though traders made a large profit, New Mexicans saved. Traders' merchandise cost them less than merchandise from Mexico. Spain had long held New Mexico in its clutches and prohibited trade which did not originate in Spanish controlled Mexico.

In 1822 Becknell returned to Santa Fe with three wagons loaded with goods. He thought Raton Pass was impassable for wagons and avoided it. Becknell opted to cross the Arkansas River near present-day Dodge City, Kansas, and cut across the dry, flat hunting ground of the Kiowa and Comanche. That route became the Cimarron Cut-Off or the Dry Branch of the Santa Fe Trail. Becknell is known as the Father of the Santa Fe Trail because he was the first to cross the route with wagons.

When Becknell traveled the Cimarron Cut-Off, he and his party ran out of water. They became so thirsty they killed their dogs and drank the blood. The warm blood didn't assuage thirst. They killed a buffalo that had been to water and drank the fluid from its stomach.

Route

According to Dick Wootton 300 miles of the Santa Fe Trail were pretty rugged, but the first 500 miles were the most difficult because of mud holes and the need to cross and re-cross streams. Travelers made necessary road repairs as they went. If there were mud holes, travelers gathered prairie grass and filled them. Those who traveled over the mountains sometimes had to get out their axes to clear brush or timber from their path or to use as fill when needed.

The eastern terminus of the Santa Fe Trail began in Franklin, Missouri; it moved to Independence, and later to Westport, Missouri. There were two primary branches of the Trail: Cimarron Cut-Off and Mountain Branch. Other roads branched off to southern New Mexico, Mexico, Ft. Leavenworth, Oregon, northern Colorado, Utah, and California. There were also variations of the main branch: The Granada/ Ft. Union Road and Aubrey's Cut-Off.

Ft. Union Cut-Off was a military road, which turned off of the Mountain Branch at Grenada, east of Big Timbers/Bent's New Stone Fort, Colorado. It cut a direct path southwest to Ft. Union. Aubrey's Cutoff, pioneered by Francis Xavier Aubrey, went further into Kansas than the Dry Route, but left the Mountain Branch at Aubrey's Crossing (Kansas). It rejoined

---

[238] San Miguel had a distinctive weather pattern which often surprised traders. A storm that thundered, rained, and sometimes hailed on San Miguel may hit and pass over, only to turn around and hit again.

the Cimarron Cut-Off near Upper (Flag) Creek, Oklahoma. It avoided the most treacherous parts of the Dry Route and the Mountain Branch (Raton Pass). Aubrey's route had wood in two places, more than was available on the Cimarron route. Aubrey's route fell into disuse and was covered with grass by the time Joe Watrous traveled it in 1861. Watrous reopened the road; it continued to be used in springtime as long as the Cimarron Cut-Off was alive. Both fell into disuse after Dick Wootton built his toll road across Raton Pass.

Cimarron Cut-Off/Dry Branch

The Dry Route crossed the Arkansas River at various points, primarily the Lower, Middle, and Upper Crossings. The condition of the river influenced which spot was chosen to cross. Joe Watrous, who freighted across the Dry Route in the 1850's and early '60's, only saw the Arkansas River dry twice at the crossing, once in 1853 and again in 1863. He dug trenches in the river sand—deep enough for water to ooze up and fill the trenches with water for his stock. He said the water came up pretty clear.

Henry Smith's party also crossed the Cut-Off in 1863. He said they found little water or good grazing grass en route. Ordinarily most of the Dry Branch had grass. Freighters and traders expected extra Indian trouble the summer of 1863 because of the severe drought on the Plains, but government annuities to the Indians relieved the situation.

The Dry Route cut across the tip of the panhandle in Indian Territory (Oklahoma) and traveled southwest across northern New Mexico until it rejoined the Mountain Route near La Junta (Watrous), a few miles from Ft. Union and about a half mile from Ft. Barclay. The Trail was in use about thirty years before either fort was built.

The Dry Route advantage was that it cut 55-65 miles (accounts vary up to 100 miles) off the trip and eliminated the need to cross Raton Pass. The disadvantages were Indian raids and the lack of water and wood. For a time raiders from Texas and Arkansas robbed travelers on the Cimarron Cut-Off. It was a dangerous route throughout Civil War years. As for lack of wood, dry buffalo chips and cow chips were the chief fuel used on the Cimarron Cut-Off.

After the Cut-Off left the Arkansas River, there was a stretch of about 60 miles where there was no water source. Traders called it the 'hornada,' their rendition of the Spanish phrase jornada del muerto, journey of death. Some carried water in small kegs hung under their wagons. Those who traveled the Cut-Off were wise to carry enough water for man and animal. Bleached bones scattered along the Jornada testified of some who didn't.

In dry seasons water could be scarce or distasteful in other areas along the Dry Route. It was common for travelers to report mirages of beautiful lakes. At times water was so scarce a train set up camp a distance from water; so animals wouldn't smell the water before they were unhitched. If they were close enough to smell water, thirsty animals headed for the water and drug their wagons right after them, often bogging them in the mud.

In early Santa Fe Trail years the dry Cimarron Cut-Off was sometimes difficult to follow; but 1834 was such a wet year that wagons rutted tracks and made the Trail easy to discern. By 1836 the Dry Route was the primary route for Santa Fe traders and remained so until the season of 1864. Use diminished after Dick Wootton built his road over Raton Pass in 1865. By 1868 the Dry Route was dead. Grass grew back over the ruts of 1834.

Mountain Branch (Raton Route)

William Becknell's first trip into New Mexico was across the Mountain Route's Raton Pass. The Mountain Branch had good access to water and wood. Grass was good. Indian raids were less. It was farther than the Dry Route; but, until 1865, the main drawback was the Raton mountain crossing. In 1865 Uncle Dick Wootton built a twenty-seven mile toll road up and over Raton Pass. When the railroad entered New Mexico, it followed Wootton's route—steam engines needed water and the coal resources found in the Raton Mountains.

Entire Route

Though other places in the vicinity contributed to the Santa Fe Trail, Franklin, Missouri, is considered the original eastern terminus. It was about 150 miles from St. Louis.

Traders relied heavily on St. Louis merchandise. St. Louis enriched and was enriched by Santa Fe Trail trade, but it was never a point on the Trail. The eastern terminus moved west to Independence. From there travelers could travel to the Southwest on the Santa Fe Trail or the Northwest on the Oregon Trail. The Oregon Trail followed the Santa Fe Trail about 53 miles before coursing northwest.

By 1845 Westport Landing (Kansas City) on the Missouri border became the eastern port.

The Santa Fe Trail began as one trail, forked in two directions, and rejoined. These major landmarks and points along the Santa Fe Trail were not all part of the Trail at its inception. Others were no longer a part of the Trail in its latter years; but each was a point at one time:

Franklin
Boones Lick
Arrow Rock
Harvey Spring
Grand Pass
Tabo Creek Crossing
Lexington
Ft. Osage
Little Blue River Crossing
Independence
Westport/Kansas City
Elm Grove Camp (Thus far the Santa Fe and Oregon trails are together.)
Lone Elm/Round Grove Campground
Black Jack
Palmyra Well
110 Mile Creek
Bridge (Switzler's) Creek
Big John Spring
Council Grove, on the Neosho River about 110 miles from Kansas City, the easiest portion of the trip. Many used Council Grove's hardwood for wagon repairs.
Elm Creek

Diamond Spring
Six Mile Creek Crossing
Lost Spring, campsite with water
Cottonwood Creek Crossing, campsite with water
Little Arkansas Crossing, campsite with water
Owl Creek
Little Cow Creek (Chavez Creek, Jarvis Creek)
Cow Creek Crossing, campsite with water
Plum Buttes
Great Bend of the Arkansas: an area with dangerous quicksand; about 120 miles from Council Grove. Between the two points were many cottonwood-lined streams to cross. Rolling grassy plains provided good grazing.
Walnut Creek (Fort Zarah was built in this area.)
Pawnee Rock, about fourteen miles southwest of Great Bend. The red colored sandstone rock was originally about 100' high, but with use and time was reduced to about half of that. Many engraved their names on Pawnee Rock. It was named Pawnee because there a band of Pawnee surprised a band of Cheyenne and scalped them. Dick Wootton said, "There have been more people killed along that portion [Pawnee Rock vicinity] of the old trail than have lost their lives at the hands of the Indians in any other spot in the West."[239]
Ash Creek Crossing, campsite with water
Pawnee River, campsite with water
Coon Creek Crossing, campsite with water
Lower Crossing
Ft. Dodge: plenty of hay in the nearby river bottom. The fort began with a few huts and tents.
Caches: about 90 miles from Pawnee Rock. A group of trappers buried goods here until they could retrieve them. Forts Atkinson and Mann were built nearby.
Point of Rocks
Middle Crossing
Point of Rocks
Upper Crossing

To travel the Cimarron Dry Cut-Off, wagons crossed the Arkansas River at various points from Lower to Upper Crossing. From there the route headed southwest across the tip of Indian Territory (Oklahoma) and into northeastern New Mexico. The Mountain Branch continued west along the north bank of the Arkansas River before turning south.

Cimarron/Dry-Cut-Off
Jornada, 50-60 miles of sand desert
Sand Creek
Lower (Cimarron) Springs
Middle (Cimarron) Springs (Kansas)
Willow Bar (Oklahoma)

---

[239] Conard, *Uncle Dick Wootton*, 1980, 37.

Wolf Mountain
Upper (Flag) Spring
Inscription Rock
Cold Springs
Cedar Creek (Camp Nichols nearby)
McNees Creek (New Mexico)
Turkey Creek
Rabbit Ears Creek Camp (near Mt. Dora)r
Round Mound
Whetstone Creek
Point of Rocks)
Red (Canadian) River
Ocate Creek
Santa Clara Springs and Wagon Mound
Wolf Creek

Mountain Branch
Choteau's Island
Indian Mound
Aubrey's Crossing (Kansas)
Bent's New Stone Fort (Colorado)
Bent's Fort. Here the road forks: one follows the Arkansas to Pueblo to Denver; the other follows the main Mountain Route, crosses and follows the Arkansas and then
(follow) Timpas Creek
Iron Springs
Hole-in-the Rock
Trinidad, cross the Purgatoire River
Wootton
Raton Pass
Willow Springs (New Mexico)
Clifton House
Rayado (with a never failing stream)
Cimarron
Rock Crossing of the Canadian

At La Junta (Watrous), New Mexico, on the Mora River the Mountain and Cimarron Branches of the Santa Fe Trail rejoined about a half mile from Ft. Barclay (few miles from Ft. Union, on the Mountain Branch) and continued on to Santa Fe:
Las Vegas, about twenty miles from La Junta
Tecolote
Bernal Springs
San Miguel del Bado (Vado)

San Jose del Bado
Pecos
Pigeon's Ranch
Glorieta
Apache Canyon
Rock Corral
Santa Fe

Except for a few bridges, some mound markings made by Sibley's crew in 1825, Dick Wootton's Raton Pass toll road, and a few spots in Apache Canyon (New Mexico) which were shored up by Army Engineers, the Santa Fe Trail was an unimproved road.

Travel Time

Weather permitting, a loaded wagon train could travel about fifteen miles per day, possibly a little more if pulled by mules, a little less if pulled by oxen. Weather, wagon repair, and the temperament and effort of wagon master, employees, and teams played into the time equation.

Though trains traveled at various times, the annual Santa Fe Trail caravan formed in May, weather and conditions permitting. If things went well, a train leaving Bent's Fort could reach Westport in about six weeks. It took about two weeks longer from Santa Fe.

Santa Fe

Spanish colonists established Santa Fe in 1610. Under Governor Pedro de Peralta the site was surveyed and plans made for the Plaza and the Governors Palace. During years of Spanish rule, people knew their station. The highest class were those born in Spain or were of pure Spanish ancestry. The next class were those of mixed ancestry: Spanish and Indian, or if coming from Mexico, possibly Spanish and African. Lowest in the pecking order were those who had no Spanish blood. True Spaniards were top choice for government positions.

Nestled in the Sangre de Cristo Mountains, Santa Fe had been Spain's royal city, capital of Spain's New Mexico for over 200 years. Now it was capital of Mexico's New Mexico, which included all of present-day Arizona and parts of Colorado, Nevada and California.

The Palace of the Governors faced the Plaza in the center of town. The Palace and Plaza were the center of Santa Fe commerce, military, and politics. Spanish was the primary language.

Undersupplied under Spain and Mexico, Santa Fe was the original object of Santa Fe Trail trade. Santa Fe Trail caravans rolled to a stop along the Plaza, where farmers, ranchers, and homemakers sold their wares—wood, cheese, vegetables, fruits, meats, hay. Dirt paths wound away from the Plaza to homes, where each family raised its garden and animals. Many had at least one fruit tree. Santa Fe's air was clean, clear—except for the fragrance of piñon wood burning in kivas or hornos.

Neither man, nor beast seemed in a hurry. That nettled some newcomers. But, in this land of mañana/tomorrow, why hurry? New Mexicans were accustomed to waiting three years for supplies and mail. Sure, the government was overbearing at times. There were Indian raids.

Crops weren't always what they hoped. Time and again they'd been thrown into the lap of hardship, or ingenuity, of making do. New Mexico wasn't only the land of mañana; it was also the land of ahora—the land of now. Now they stopped to greet one another on the Plaza, in the yard, on the road. When the Catholic church bell rang, they stopped now to pray. They stopped for funerals now. Now they danced at weddings. They knew how to celebrate; anything out of the ordinary was reason enough to celebrate: A holy day? Sure. Trappers returning? Why not? A wagon train's arrival? Guests must be welcomed. They brought fiddles and guitars and celebrated with a fandango. If they had jewelry, they wore it. They wore cheery clothing; they liked bright colors, and not just for clothing. If there was any way the women could add ornamentation to their dresses, it was done. There was no class or culture division when it came to celebration; those from all stations in life celebrated as one. New Mexicans could cheer; they could mourn; they could clap; they could sing.

New Mexico: Trail's End

When traders arrived in New Mexico, it had two main regions: Rio Arriba and Rio Abajo. There were three departments within the two regions: Santa Fe and Santa Cruz in Rio Arriba; Albuquerque in Rio Abajo. There were sixteen towns large enough to have a community government.

Small matters were judged locally. If a matter required civil or criminal court judgment, the parties had to travel to Mexico. Unless their superiors interrupted, New Mexico authorities took care of justice themselves. A single adobe room could well-serve as a community jail—one room for any, for all. Cellmates could spend their time congenially or not. That wasn't a concern to the community. If a captive had business during the day, he could tend to it and return when done. If there was a fandango, prisoners were often allowed to go as long as they returned after the dance.

Writing *The Commerce of the Prairies*, Josiah Gregg noted that, except for a typhoid epidemic in 1837-39 and an 1840 small pox epidemic, which killed about ten percent of New Mexico's population, New Mexicans experienced little of the febrile diseases found in the Mississippi Valley. As a whole, New Mexicans lived long. Many lived into their nineties, some past a hundred. Gregg said some became so wizened they resembled mummies. Their vivid memories of long ago events testified to their longevity. The old ones were a source of life to the young, who honored their elders' experience-procured wisdom and their memories, which provided roots in the continuity of life. New Mexicans honored age.

The weather? Of the world's seven temperate zones, New Mexico has five. New Mexico was more arid than any of the states in the Union at the time. The sun shone in brilliance— dancing, beaming through the day. Like a kaleidoscope, sunrises and sunsets changed colors of the sky. In anticipation of the day or in a last goodbye, the sun cast light plays across the landscape. The rain, when it came, came quickly, often preceded by dazzling displays of lightening and booming claps of thunder. Rain came in torrents or in a rich steady flow; it didn't mist. It didn't drizzle for twenty-four hours. The sky puckered up and rained and cleared. Summer rains washed the sky, freshened the air. They came. They went. The sun shone again, and the sky seemed a deeper, richer blue. New Mexico was not muggy, humid. In winter there was snow, sometimes as early as mid-October. Snow came to many areas in New Mexico. Except in high mountain altitudes, it didn't last long. The sunshine couldn't stand to stay away and melted lingering, sparkling snow crystals. Snow was over by the end of winter—unless it decided to play a late April Fool joke on New Mexicans and surprise them with a skiff of snow some unusual day in April or even one in early May. It had to be rare enough to take them by surprise, and it was.

Most buildings were built of thick adobe/mud blocks. Some were plastered. Adobe made a home interior cooler in the summer and warmer in winter. It worked well for the climate and was readily available to even the poorest in the community. Most homes had a kiva—a rounded, elevated fireplace in the corner of a room. Many had an horno for baking outdoors.

An adobe home

Arrival of a Wagon Train

Nearing Santa Fe triggered a mixture of feelings for traders. The journey would be complete. There'd be a warm welcome, relaxation, enjoyment of a settlement, profit. But there were also inspections and possible changes in custom charges or demands. Some traders spoke Spanish or made-do. Others hired interpreters. Some bypassed personal involvement and hired a local dealer to take their goods through customs.

Traders and their crew usually took time to clean-up, slick-down before pulling into town. As they neared town, the smell of piñon smoke wafted through the air from Santa Fe hearths.

Locals were always pleased to see a caravan rolling into an otherwise ordinary day. In true Hispanic style, news of the sight of an incoming caravan quickly rustled through the settlement. By the time a caravan rolled to a stop along the Plaza, locals were on hand with a warm greeting.

Trade Goods

Some popular items traders brought into New Mexico were kitchen utensils, pots, coffee grinders, knives, scissors, paper, cloth and sewing notions—buttons, needles, thread, thimbles; hand tools—shovels, axes, hoes; razors and razor straps. The Mexican government banned some items at times, items like gunpowder, tobacco, candle wicking, and lead or iron. Sometimes certain items were allowed, but at a higher tariff.

In return, New Mexicans offered mules, pelts, wool, blankets, and silver. Silver could be put in green rawhide pouches, which dried around the silver to make nice tight bundles for transport.

Value of the Trail

The War of 1812 and reconstruction had taken a financial toll on the young United States. The Napoleonic Wars, which drained Europe, also affected the U. S. Then the year with no summer (1816) hurt U. S. agriculture. The struggling young United States succumbed to the Financial Panic of 1819. The Bank of St. Louis, founded two years earlier, went belly up. The Bank of Missouri floundered two years later, 1821. In an effort to buoy its economy, the Missouri legislature allowed paper money to be issued on the state's credit; but most merchants refused the printed promise. Specie (money in coin form) was scarce in Missouri and throughout the nation.

Enter the Santa Fe Trail trade with its silver, mules, and goods. New Mexico welcomed merchandise; Missouri welcomed silver. Soon Congressman Thomas Hart Benton's Missouri was up and running. Mexican silver dollars became Missouri's circulating specie. The federal government decided Missouri was a good choice for its personal banking.

In 1824 in the *Niles Register*, Missouri Governor Alexander McNair promoted Santa Fe trade, not only for hunting, trapping, and trade profits, but also to promote good relations with Indians and Mexicans. He saw it as an opportunity to spread democracy.

The fur trade nurtured St. Louis. The Santa Fe trade helped transform it into a refined city. Though the wagon making business flourished in numerous places in the nation, there were thirty-two wagon makers in St. Louis. St. Louis supplied many trade goods. By the 1840's the city boasted a public school and some paved streets.

New Mexico mules and burros were taken to Missouri. Missourians bred them and sold them for use on farms and western trails. The mule became a Missouri icon. Large mules sold for $145 each in 1863.

Tradesmen, manufacturers, merchants and farmers profited as they supplied goods, animals, wagons, and stagecoaches. Mail service expanded. Many enterprises begun as a result of the Santa Fe trade far outlasted the Trail.

In the 1840's commission merchants offered their services to Santa Fe Trail traders. For a fee they would obtain merchandise locally or as far away as New York and Philadelphia. They dealt with manufacturers and saw that merchandise was readily available. Some also supervised loading of wagons. Some arranged loans. There were at least four commission firms in Westport.

Thousands of gold seekers traveled the Trail on their way to western gold fields.

Military protection was often needed. Considering the wide expanse, the government constructed forts sparingly, but strategically. By 1860 annual freighting across the Trail had become a multimillion dollar business. The Civil War interfered a bit with trade, but it began to pick up midway through the war. After the war, Trail business mushroomed. A toll bridge at Council Grove reported 4,584 carriages and wagons crossed between May and November of 1865—5,000 in 1866.

Prairie settlements sprang up and flourished along the Santa Fe Trail, spreading population into the United States' Louisiana Purchase land. Western farm and ranch products, minerals, animals, hides, and buffalo pelts enriched the young nation.

The Santa Fe Trail was the first transcontinental route. In 1833 it branched to California; in 1841 the Oregon Trail began with the Trail and branched northwest to the Pacific Northwest. (Some date the Oregon Trail 1841, some 1842.) In 1847 the Mormons branched a trail to Utah. Each trail added an avenue of commerce or settlement and strengthened the young United States. The Trail played into the hands of Manifest Destiny and expansion of the U. S. The West offered opportunity for minds and methods, room for people to put feet to new ideas.

As the young nation matured, railroads forged their way westward. The Atchison, Topeka, and Santa Fe Railway built its mainline alongside the Trail. In later years asphalt ribboned highways along the route.

For almost 60 years the Santa Fe Trail directly enriched economy throughout the United States, as well as in England and in parts of Europe.

Traders

Americans, New Mexicans, Mexicans, and French were the main traders on the Santa Fe Trail. Some made trading a lifelong career; others traded only a few seasons—or one. Some did business in the Southwest long enough to garner capital for a better life, went back home and never returned. Others—whether they came alone or with their family—made the Southwest their permanent home.

Not every trader was successful every time; not every trader was successful. At times goods, animals, and lives were lost to weather or attack en route. Sometimes the Mexican government confiscated goods. The Mexican government tried various ways to regulate trade; but each time Mexico set up an obstacle, traders found a way around it—sometimes resorting to smuggling goods or paying someone to smuggle for them.

Soon after the Santa Fe Trail opened, New Mexico traders joined Americans traveling the Trail, between Missouri and Santa Fe and between Santa Fe and Chihuahua. They traded Chihuahua silver for American goods, but also included their own merchandise—wool, hides, mules, woven dry goods, and other items. Some New Mexico dons required young men under their influence to work as bullwhackers on their trips. Some were paid as little as eight dollars for the entire trip to the States and back.

Provisions for the Journey

Professional wagon masters generally employed one or more hunters for the journey;

otherwise, individuals hunted and shared with others as needed. Buffalo was the primary target for their table; but when they needed meat, game was game—antelope, rabbit, deer.

Water was of primary importance; it was scarce in some areas. A guide who knew water sources was invaluable. In choosing a campsite, travelers wanted not only a safe camping spot, but also a good, safe water source, if at all possible. A clear, running stream was a plus. They tried to avoid muddy banks, swamps, and murky ponds where germs or mosquitoes could multiply. If water wasn't clear enough to drink plain or clear after it was sieved through a handkerchief, travelers boiled it. Any scum was skimmed from the surface. It was always wise to stock up on water from a fresh source.

In the 1860's R. M. Rolfe listed needs for a crew of twenty-eight men for 60 days:[240]

30 sacks flour, 98 lbs. each
2,500 lbs. bacon 20 sacks
1 sack 50c coffee, 125 lbs.
2 sacks $1 sugar, 250 lbs.
1 sack 75c beans, 2 bushels
1 sack dried apples, 103 lbs.
10 lbs. soda
6 boxes matches
1 sack 50c salt, 100 lbs.
20 lbs. soap
Sheet and Lariat rope 32 ½ lbs.
1 keg $1.50 vinegar, 5 gal.
3 10-gal. water kegs
1 lb. candles
4 boxes ground pepper
24 qt. cans wagon grease
1 lb. ground mustard
2 lbs. ox nails
1 oz. shoeing hammer
1 oz. shoeing rasp
1 oz. shoeing pincers
Total Cost: $768.62

Traders packed with care:
- Flour, 100 pound weight, was packed in double canvas bags.
- Sugar was tightly sealed in waterproof bags of gutta-percha or India rubber.
- Bacon, 100 pound slabs, was packed either in a strong sack, or—for hot weather—in a box, covered with bran. Well-cured pork could be packed and kept the same way.
- Butter had to be boiled. Any scum must be skimmed off the top until the butter was as clear as oil. Then it was poured into a tin container and soldered shut. In that manner it

---

[240] Walker, *Wagonmasters*, 119, 120.

could be preserved a long time with only slight change in taste.
- Dried meats and vegetables could be kept in pieces or ground into a powder. They were eaten in the dried state or reconstituted when needed. Either way, dried products had a long shelf life. Dried meat ground to powder was called pemmican. Some liked to mix pemmican with flour and boil it.
- Travelers provided their own medicines—common items in a traveling medicine chest: opium, quinine, and a cathartic.

Thomas Hart Benton

Thomas Hart Benton was elected U. S. Senator from Missouri in 1821, the year William Becknell made his first trip to Santa Fe. Benton was well aware his state was the gateway to Santa Fe trade. At a time of tottering national economy, he wisely championed the westward movement from his Washington post.

Alphonso Westmore wrote Missouri Congressman John Scott of the need to mark the Santa Fe Trail. Besides markers, the Trail needed right-of-way through Indian country and into Mexican territory. Benton would present the ideas to Congress, but wanted to be informed before he sought Congressional help. He contacted Augustus Storrs, who'd traveled the Santa Fe Trail. Storrs answers to Benton's twenty-two questions were published for Congress in early 1825. Benton persuaded representatives of the farming South and manufacturing North that all would benefit, and they did. Southern grown cotton and Northern manufactured cloth would find a market at the end of the Santa Fe Trail.

Benton remained an eloquent, tenacious expansionist during the thirty years he represented Missouri. Among his interests were the Santa Fe Trail, the Homestead Act, a central railroad route to the Pacific, and obtaining Texas and California for the United States. He was influential in implementing western exploratory expeditions led by his son-in-law, John C. Fremont.

Survey

On March 3, 1825, President Monroe signed a bill, which commissioned a Santa Fe Trail survey team. The bill allotted money for wages, markers, treaty negotiations, and payments to Indian tribes in exchange for perpetual right-of-way from the Missouri border to the U. S.-Mexican border.

On Thursday, July 17, 1825, the forty-man survey crew left Ft. Osage to measure the distance to Santa Fe via the Cimarron Branch of the Santa Fe Trail. Seven drove wagons; thirty-three rode horseback. Flies pestered them all month.

Benjamin H. Reeves, George C. Sibley and Thomas Mather were commissioners in charge of the expedition. They would be paid eight dollars a day upon completion of the survey. Other crew members who held positions were: Archibald Gamble, secretary; Joseph Cromwell Brown, surveyor from Virginia; Bill Williams, interpreter and guide. Stephen Cooper, familiar with the Santa Fe Trail, piloted the expedition.

On Friday, August 5, the crew camped along the Neosho River. The campsite had excellent pasture and a grove of ash, oak, cottonwood, hickory, and walnut. On the evening of August 8, Bill Williams and Archibald Gamble brought about 50 chiefs, headmen, and warriors of the Great Osage and the Little Osage into camp. Among the chiefs were "Handsome Bird" (Shin-gawassa), "White Hair" (Pa-hu-sha), and two called "Foolish Chief" (Ca-he-ga-shinga and Ca-he-ge-wa-tonega). That evening survey commissioners explained their purpose and desire to mark a road through Osage land and to have free use of that road forever. They offered $800 for the privilege. After discussing the proposal among themselves, the chiefs accepted the offer. On Wednesday the 10th, Bill Williams read and explained the treaty. Each side signed; each side received a copy. The principal Osage chief received the copy for his tribe.

After the Council Grove Treaty, Bill Williams rode to find the Kansa Indians. The remaining survey crew moved west and camped on the banks of Dry Turkey Creek (eastern Kansas). On Monday, August 15th, Shone-gee-ne-gare, great chief of the Kansa, and about 50 Kansa met with survey commissioners. The commissioners offered the Kansa the same deal they'd offered the Osage. The Kansa agreed to the terms. Next day the Kansa and the commissioners signed a treaty to allow survey and passage through Kansa land.

George Sibley's survey crew arrived in Taos, New Mexico, on Sunday, October 30, 1825. Because of the terrain and inclement weather, they went to Taos before Santa Fe.

They'd already surveyed the Trail, but Sibley rode down to Santa Fe to get permission from the governor. The Mexican government in Santa Fe wouldn't give permission to survey until June and wouldn't allow the Trail to be marked in any way.

The crew made some mound markers along the Trail, but they were of little use. In May 1827 George Sibley and a party of twelve traveled the Santa Fe Trail to correct some of the 1825 survey and shorten the route. They worked two months.

Freighters and Wagon Masters

Freighters were of various nationalities. Most Santa Fe Trail freighters were of English or Scotch ancestry; most were Protestants, more Baptists than other denominations. Some wagon masters held worship services; some would not travel on Sundays.

A wagon master (major domo) was responsible for freight, crew, route, and train. He supervised the loading of goods to make certain: weight was centered in the wagon, fragile items were secure, and items susceptible to water damage were protected. It was his responsibility to hire muleskinners or bullwhackers, hunter(s), an assistant wagon master, and three or four extra men should any of the others become ill or desert.

He often rode ahead of the train because he was responsible for daily campsites, water supply. He watched for Indians and kept an eye open for good grazing for the animals at meal and camp stops. He had to be able to shoe oxen and mules, repair wagons and wagon wheels. He prepared supplies for sick or injured men or animals. Although a good wagon master delegated tasks, he had to be able to perform them if another could not.

The owner of a wagon train was responsible for the goods, wagons, and animals in his train, whether he owned them or had them on credit. If they were stolen or suffered mishap, he suffered the loss. When he freighted goods for someone, he gave the owner of the goods a bill of lading, in which he assumed responsibility for goods entrusted to him. There were two exceptions: He was not responsible for acts of Providence, such as flood or tornado, nor for what might be termed acts of war, such as Indian attack. However, he was expected to do all within his power to protect the merchandise even in exceptional situations.

Because a loaded wagon train often carried merchandise worth thousands of dollars, mutiny was as much a possibility on the Plains as on the sea. Many a major domo was killed for his train.

In 1859 a bullwhacker could earn $40 per month plus rations. A Midwest farmhand earned $8 a month. Many who worked for their passage on a wagon train became well-known Southwestern citizens.

As more traders entered the market, the market extended south to Chihuahua, Mexico. After the Mexican War, need for freighters increased as the U. S. Army required supplies in its newly acquired territory. More merchants began to rely on freighters to transport goods, rather than making trips themselves. When the Santa Fe Trail gave way to the railroad, wagon freighting became localized. Wagons hauled freight from railroad stations to areas not serviced by rail.

Trail Animals

Mules, horses, and oxen were used on the Santa Fe Trail. Some early traders used horses, but horses couldn't hold up under the load-pulling strain day after day like mules and oxen could. Mules and oxen had advantages and disadvantages.

The foremost problem with mules was their price and the fact Indians were more apt to steal mules and horses. Indians had little use for oxen; they couldn't ride them; for eating, they preferred the taste of buffalo. In the 1840's a pair of mules cost about ten times the price of a pair of oxen. In the 1860's the price was down to three-six times the cost of oxen. Even the tack for mules was more expensive. But, mules could pull a wagon fifteen-twenty miles a day. Oxen were a bit slower at twelve-fifteen miles per day.

Saddles and packs seldom created a sore in a mule's tough hide. Cattle diseases didn't seem to bother them like they did oxen. Traders figured a mule had a trail-working life of at least eighteen years. Mules were more temperamental than horses or oxen; they did seem to know their own mind. They were also more sensitive to trouble. Mules handled weather better than oxen. Oxen didn't pull as well in hot weather and didn't always survive cold weather extremes.

When Major Bennett Riley was ordered to accompany the annual trade caravan in 1829, the Army couldn't afford mules; so Riley introduced oxen to Santa Fe Trail travel. The only problem Riley noted using oxen was that their feet became tender at times. That hindered their ability to pull. Oxen used on the Trail were usually at least four years old, but they weren't the size of those used on New England farms. Generally, they were ordinary range oxen from Texas or present-day Oklahoma. As a whole, oxen were gentler than mules. They did stampede more easily than mules, but katy-bar-the-door once they got started.

Wagons

When a wagon train rolled across the Plains, the cotton or linen canvas tops reminded people of a fleet of ships sailing on the sea; so a covered wagon was often called a prairie schooner.

Wagons were produced by builders in many states. Joseph Murphy in Missouri built his of hardwood and marked them with a painted "J. Murphy." Schuttler wagons were manufactured in Illinois, Studebakers in Indiana. Pittsburg was home to Conestoga wagons. Because other manufacturers built similar wagons, Conestoga became a generic term for a covered wagon. A genuine Conestoga could be spotted by its blue wagon bed, its red wheels and running gear.

Wagon volumes varied. A Studebaker bed, for instance, was 190 cubic feet, while a Murphy wagon held 345 cubic feet. Conestoga wagons were built to handle two to three tons of freight weight. It was the most popular wagon style in early days of the Santa Fe Trail. But, with changing Mexican regulations, traders preferred larger flat bottomed wagons, known as "Santa Fe." Freighters found the larger wagons more cost effective. In the 1840's a Murphy wagon cost about $140. The "Santa Fe" sold for about $160 in the 1860's.

Traders often sold the wagons rather than haul them home. They preferred to return to the States with silver and mules rather than with bulky cargo, which attracted Indians. If the price of iron was up, they could burn their wagons, sell the iron, and still come out ahead.

Over the years improvements were added to wagons. To extend wheel life, blacksmiths forged iron rims to fit the wooden wheels. Iron axles began replacing wooden axles about 1845. Wagon tongues changed. They were engineered to have a "drop tongue," which enabled more freedom of movement to facilitate travel across rivers, up banks, over hills.

To cut expenses, freighters began to tow empty wagons in tandem. One team could pull at least two empty wagons. As a result, in the 1860's some wagon makers redesigned their wagons to eliminate the overhang at the front and rear of the wagon. The change included a tongue adaptation to facilitate tandem towing.

When Santa Fe Trail travel began, wagons weren't equipped with brakes. Drivers were left to their ingenuity. Some men attached logs and chains to the rear wheel to slow momentum. Others used a "rough lock"—a chain wrapped around the rear spokes and fastened to the wagon body. Sometimes a drag brake/shoe brake was used. It was a metal skid—sometimes studded—placed under the rear wheel and chained to the body. Mormons came up the "Mormon brake." They chained a log under the wagon bed to keep both the front and rear wheels off the ground. By the early 1860's wagon brakes were invented. They allowed drivers to brake by operating levers.

Freighters and traders were prepared to handle wagon repairs. When wagon wheels dried and shrunk, the iron rim wobbled off. Men soaked the wheel to swell the wood, then refit it in the iron rim. If they weren't near water, they wedged a wood shim between the wheel and the iron. The best method was to reheat the iron, fit the hot iron on the wooden wheel, and dip it in cold water to shrink the rim to fit the wheel. That sort of repair wasn't available out on the Trail. Men carried hardwood to fashion a replacement axle, spoke, bow, or tongue, if needed. They kept a bucket of grease—usually meat fat—hanging from the rear axle to lubricate the hubs.

Dangers and Diseases along the Trail

1. Wind ranged from welcome to sandstorm to tornado and was accentuated by heat or cold. Trail caravans crossed portions of "tornado alley" as they crossed the Plains. Men observed the face of the sky and learned to chain wagons together at night if the sky indicated the possibility of a tornado. Wagons had tossed, and men had learned.

2. Hail ripped open wagons' canvas covers and frightened animals, causing them to stampede, sometimes resulting in injury of death of man or animal.

3. Lightning strikes occasionally started a prairie fire, which trail men fought. Thunder could cause a stampede. Heavy rain collected in wagon ruts and made prairie earth boggy. One summer William Bent's train waited a month for the prairie to dry enough; so the train could travel forward. He traveled a little way down the road and bogged down for another month.

4. Snow, early or late, could surprise travelers, cover tracks or pile up in mountain canyons. On the Cimarron Branch men were known to burn their wagons' wood to keep from freezing.

5. Water: Extra water affected crossings of streams or rivers; in some places there was lack of water for man or beast.

6. Insects—flies, buffalo gnats, grasshoppers and multiplying mosquitoes—pestered man and beast. Horned toads, lizards, and prairie dogs lived along the Trail.

7. Diseases: malaria spread by mosquitoes; cholera and typhoid, contracted from contaminated food or water.

8. Accidents, including broken bones, serious cuts, falls, gunshot, sometimes maimed, killed, or led to death. There were many graves along the Trail, often spoiled by coyotes.

9. Raids: When wagons began to roll across the Trail, Indian raids began and cost lives and revenue. During the Mexican War and Civil War, Indian raids increased. Raiders also came from Missouri, Texas, and Arkansas.

Stagecoach Travel

A one way trip between Santa Fe and Independence cost $250, including accommodations and board. Each passenger was allowed 40 pounds of baggage. Each extra pound cost 50 cents. As for accommodations, passengers slept in the stage as it traveled. They ate fresh meat along the Trail. Should wild game be unavailable, the stage carried a ready supply of hardtack and pork. In later years saloons, stage stops, and hotels sprang up along the route; so food options expanded to items available in different locales. Even then, the meat was generally wild game.

Nine passengers could squeeze inside a coach; two more could ride on top. If weather and Indians allowed and the coach had no breakdowns, it could travel from Independence to Santa Fe in two weeks, traveling round the clock. Drivers preferred to drive through the worst of Indian country at night. Indians preferred to attack early in the day and seldom attacked at night.

Passengers who wanted to stretch their legs were allowed to walk along the stage as long as they could keep up. If the stretch between stops had been particularly wearing on the team and they needed a little relief, passengers were required to walk a spell and give the animals a break.

Window flaps inside the coach were often lowered to protect from dust, sun, or storms; in winter they were kept down for warmth. At such times, passengers had no view of the landscape. If a storm was bad enough, the stage stopped—especially on Raton Pass. When lightning flashed and thunder boomed on Raton Pass in the summer, passengers found what shelter they could outside the coach. No one wanted to take the chance of being near a spooked team on the Pass. During winter storms, many coaches turned over on Raton Pass. Though the route improved once Uncle Dick built his road in 1865, the Pass could still be hazardous in adverse weather.

Barlow & Sanderson began their stage route across Raton Pass a couple years before Dick Wootton built his road. Their business began in 1860 with a line from the Missouri Pacific Railway terminus at Otterville, Kansas, to Kansas City. It was a partnership company, not a stock company. The Civil War interfered with operations; but the company continued to expand and was servicing Trinidad, Colorado, in 1862. Barlow sold out to Sanderson. Colonel Jared L. Sanderson, superintendent and general manager of the stage line, lived with his wife at old Bent's Fort for about twenty years beginning in 1861. William Bent gave them permission to use what was left of his fort. The Sandersons kept the dwelling rooms and main wall in good repair. The old fort was the stage's principal home station and was used as a repair shop on their line. The location was good—about 600 miles from Kansas City and about 400 miles from Santa Fe.

Their stage drivers drove from home station to home station and changed teams at every swing station. Every fourth station was a home station. The placement of stations depended on where they found water. Swing stations were about ten to twelve miles apart. Some stage stations were twenty miles apart. Where the terrain was easier, four teams pulled a coach. On difficult or mountain terrain, six teams were used.

Some of the home stations along the Santa Fe Trail were: Kansas City; Olathe; 144 Mile Creek; Council Grove; the Little Arkansas; Cow Creek—where Bat Masterson's brother Bill operated an eating house and built a stone corral; Ft. Zarah; Ft. Larned; Ft. Dodge; Cimarron Crossing; Aubrey; Bluff Station; Big Sandy; old Ft. Lyon; new Ft. Lyon; Bent's Old Fort; Timpas; Iron Springs—operated for a time by Wootton's son-in-law Thomas Young; Hole in the Rock; Hole in the Prairie; Gray's Ranch—until Trinidad became a station, then in Judge Walker's place; Clifton House. Dick Wootton's place on Raton Pass was not a home station, but a swing station. In New Mexico there were also stations at Cimarron and Sapello.

Barlow & Sanderson's last run out of Trinidad was in 1879, the year the Santa Fe Railroad arrived in Lamy, New Mexico, eighteen miles from Santa Fe. The company continued. It had branched out in many directions, including Colorado mining communities—places the rail hadn't reached. It had trouble with robberies and attempted robberies in its latter years.

Mail

In the summer of 1850 mail stages from Ft. Union to the Arkansas River were guarded by eight men, each equipped with a rifle, a Colt revolver, and a hunting knife. In 1857 the number of escorts was increased to one officer and twenty to thirty soldiers. It was later reduced to one officer and fifteen to twenty soldiers.

When General John Garland became department commander (New Mexico), he sent soldiers in wagons. He thought that provided better defense and required less animals across the Dry Route. No mail was lost while soldiers escorted mail under Garland's command (1853-1858). In May 1858 escorts were discontinued. They started again in the fall of 1859.

END OF THE TRAIL—THE OLD FONDA

Railroad Influence

Little by little railroads established new railheads as rails spiked their way across the Plains. When the railhead reached Las Vegas, New Mexico, July 4, 1879, the old Trail was all but done. For the next seven months, Otero, Seller & Company continued to haul freight from Las Vegas to Santa Fe. On February 9, 1880, the first steam engine chuffed into Santa Fe and ended the need for the Santa Fe Trail. Portions of the Trail continued to be used as local highways for many years.

SANTA FE DEPOT AT ALBUQUERQUE IN 1880

Western Indians

Indians, like early European peoples, were by no means one nation, one people. They spoke diverse languages and dialects, worshipped their own gods, dressed in their own manner, worked their own way, played their own games, honored their distinct values, ruled by their own code. Each played and fought. Some lived on the move; others remained primarily in one place. A few Indians farmed. Each tribe operated as a nation unto itself. Even their arrows and footprints were distinct.

There were also similarities. In the nomadic tribes, men made arrows, hunted, stole, and warred as they deemed appropriate. Women cooked, tended the children, prepared game, scraped and prepared buffalo hides, sewed clothing, made tepees, kept house, and, together with the children, gathered firewood or buffalo chips. They cheered the men in battle and helped gather the spoils. Boys were trained to follow their fathers, girls to follow their mothers.

As a part of intertribal wars, Plains Indians captured women and children belonging to other tribes, kept them as slaves, traded them to another tribe, or made them a part of their own people. After the Spanish arrived in the Southwest, Indians found a new market for captives, as well as new captives to take. The Spanish purchased captives, not only as servants, but with an eye to converting them to Catholicism and to the Spanish language and way of life. They usually freed slaves at the time of marriage. Raised away from their tribe, often with a new Spanish name, captives married in the Spanish community. The Spanish called the offspring of mixed marriages Genizaros; later they called them Mexicans. By the time of the Santa Fe Trail, the Mexican Republic ordered all people in New Mexico to be called Mexicans. They were no longer to be called Spanish; for they now belonged to Mexico. But New Mexicans kept their distinctions, regardless of what they were called.

Impact of Horses

Horses transformed the lives of American Indians. Before they had horses, women and dogs bore the burdens. Indians traveled on foot, hunted on foot. Men chased buffalo off an incline; warriors waiting below killed the wounded animals. Many men died or were wounded in the process. In winter they chased buffalo onto ice. When the large animals lost their footing, hunters could kill an entire herd. That method also injured many men, cost some their lives. Travel was slow; so, whether hunting or gathering, Indians had to live close to their activity. Few ventured far onto the Plains. The size of tepees was limited to the size women and dogs could carry in addition to other items they transported when moving to the next food source. Only headmen had large teepees.

Then Spaniards arrived. Hernán Cortés disembarked in Mexico with ten stallions and six mares and changed the history of America. Spanish policy strictly prohibited providing Indians with horses or guns. Spaniards, however, did need workers to care for their horses. Indian workers learned to ride and care for horses. And, what was to be done when a horse would stray off now and then? Some true strays became ancestors of western mavericks. Others made their way into Indian camps. Not knowing what they were at first, Indians called them big dogs.

In 1680 Pueblo Indians revolted in New Mexico. Spanish settlers fled toward Mexico, abandoning their silver ore, horses, and mules. Indians snatched up the horses and mules and made the most of the opportunity. Within fifty years Indians as far away as the Comanche and Shoshone were building up herds of horses. Comanche on horseback began to find their way to the goods of the Spanish and the Apache.

A little more than a century after the Pueblo Revolt—in the autumn of 1787—Blackfoot Indians descended with war whoops on a Spanish pack train. Surprised and terrified, the Spaniards hit the trail, left their silver ore cargo and all else behind. Delighted with the thirty horses and dozen mules, the Indians cared for little else. Indians began to measure their wealth in horses. If a warring tribe was expected at night, horses used for buffalo hunting were taken into the tepee; and the women slept outside. It was considered a manly feat to steal horses, especially another's prized horse. Comanche were perhaps the most skilled horse thieves. By the mid-nineteenth century, Comanche lore had it that the great spirit made horses for them; and the Comanche were the ones who had given the horse to the white men. They learned the land far south into Mexico and as far east as the Gulf of Mexico. They knew land formations, water sources, settlements.

Indians seemed born to ride. They learned in childhood. Boys learned to shoot with precision while riding. While riding, warriors could keep four or five arrows in the air at one time. Horses opened the Great Plains for hunting, raiding, and warring. Travel was no longer limited. Able to hunt at great distances, warriors took more game; tribes had more to eat. With more hides, they could make tepees two and three times larger than before. They had plenty of horses and mules to carry tepees and the poles required when it was time to move camp. With horses, Indians could move a camp up to thirty miles in one day.

Women followed along on hunts. They were on hand to identify their husband's kill by identifying his arrow. They dressed the meat on site. A good hunter needed a few wives to dress all his kill. After the hunt, they enjoyed a victory meal and ate the gut meat before carting hides and meat back to camp. Some tribes left the heart behind, thinking it helped replenish the herd.

With increased hunting, Indians had hides to trade. In the 1840's they traded 100,000 hides a year to traders. In return they enjoyed knives, pots, guns and steel hatchets, needles, blankets and cloth, tobacco and liquor, and other items. It was no longer a problem to travel a hundred miles to trade or raid. Some Indians became rich, powerful; but their raids impoverished other Indians.

Primary Tribes along the Santa Fe Trail

In 1840 it was estimated that approximately 300,000 Indians lived in the western U. S. There were at least thirty distinct tribes, each with its own language. There were hundreds of dialects.

Indians most commonly encountered along the Santa Fe Trail were the Osage and Kansa

(Kaw), Pawnee, Comanche, Kiowa, Cheyenne, Arapaho, Plains Apache, Ute, Jicarilla Apache, and occasionally the Sioux. Pueblo Indians lived near the Trail's end.

Plains Indians moved about as they hunted on lands near the Santa Fe Trail. They considered stealing a brave and honorable profession. Slow-moving, encumbered wagon trains were easy prey. Sometimes Indians approached a wagon train and asked for or demanded gifts; other times they attacked, killed, stole, burned.

Apache

Long before trappers and traders came into the Southwest, the roving Apache migrated from Canada, across the Plains, into New Mexico (including Arizona), and Mexico. When they obtained horses, they became excellent horsemen.

Mescalero Apache lived primarily in southern New Mexico within easy reach of travelers going south into Mexico or across southern New Mexico headed for California.

Jicarilla Apache roved in northeastern New Mexico, especially along the Cimarron, Ponil and Vermejo Rivers where wagon trains frequently passed and where game was plentiful—rabbit, turkey, eagle, beaver, antelope, deer, elk, and buffalo.

The Apache made a treaty with the U. S. in 1851. It seemed to have little effect.

Arapaho

Though they were fierce and roamed when hunting and warring, the Arapaho were a generous, relatively friendly people. They were Dick Wootton's favorite tribe. There was more than one band, one in present-day Colorado, the other in present-day Wyoming and Montana. Among the Plains Indians Arapaho were second in height only to the Cheyenne.

Following their Chief Little Raven's advice, Arapaho stayed out of united Indian wars in the 1870's—for the most part.

Cheyenne

Before becoming Plains Indians, the Cheyenne farmed in Minnesota and Western Wisconsin. Rather than submit to nearby tribes, they moved toward the Black Hills of Dakota. Later they moved south. Some stopped in present-day Wyoming; others moved near the Arkansas River (Colorado). In the Arkansas River area they encountered a new enemy, the Kiowa. In their new home, the Cheyenne often allied with the Arapaho.

The Cheyenne were a tall, trim people—the tallest of all Plains Indians. They were proud and firm willed, with a taste for war. As the Comanche learned horsemanship from childhood, the Cheyenne learned endurance. In 1821 Jacob Fowler noted he saw Cheyenne children running across snow a foot deep to play on the frozen Arkansas River, "all as naked as the coame in the World...all tho the frost was very seveer..."[241]

Cheyenne women were known for their exceptionally clean housekeeping.

The Cheyenne enjoyed their friends; William Bent was one. He married into their tribe. When the Cheyenne heard William's brother Charles had been massacred, they held a

---

[241] Lavender, 123.

powwow and decided to ride for revenge. Had it not been for William's insistence, the Cheyenne would have equalized things in Taos according to their calculations of equality.

In the mid-1840's the southern Cheyenne's hunting netted little; Bent tried to help. He knew he couldn't sustain them; so he spoke to them about farming. Chief Yellow Wolf understood the merits, but the young bucks wouldn't give up hunting and raiding. Yellow Wolf knew the women and old people would be unable to protect farms from other tribes when the young men roamed. He suggested the government build them a fort like Bent's where they could flee, if necessary. But William couldn't even get the government to pay for the military use of his own fort.

Comanche

Each Comanche war chief owned hundreds of horses. No Comanche chief or warrior would ride a mare because they considered males superior.

As the finest horsemen among all Indians, Comanche counted wealth in horses. Each year the Honey-Eater band of Comanche raided down the Rio Grande and into Mexico. They usually went in September, while grass was good enough for grazing, and weather was neither too hot, nor too cold for travel. They knew every settlement along their route, knew the land, the watering holes, the distance. They knew where to find good horses, women, children, and livestock. One man led; warriors were assigned tasks. Enough women traveled along to set up and pack the tepees, gather fuel, prepare meals, and care for the horses.

Trained to ride from childhood, a Comanche could drop to the side of his speeding horse at a moment's notice, leaving only one foot visible from the other side. He was able to ride any distance in that manner and shoot an arrow or use a fourteen-foot lance as skillfully and accurately as if he were mounted upright. Often an entire Comanche band approached an enemy or victim riding in this manner. They appeared to be merely a herd of horses. When ready to straddle the horse again, the warrior used his overhanging foot to pull himself upright. It was extremely difficult to return Comanche fire when a warrior shot from under his horse's neck or belly. Mountain men learned to watch for "wild horses" that could only be seen on one side.

Comanche enjoyed painting themselves in bright colors: white, yellow, red, blue, or any other color a man preferred, unless it was for war; then the paint was black. They rode armed: wood lances; flint battle-axes; bows and arrows; decorated buffalo hide shields; and, if they could get them, rifles, machetes, knives. Comanche, Kiowa, and Apache were considered the fiercest of the fierce. Comanche were a favorite of none of the old traders and mountain men.

Comanche's primary habitat was along the upper Arkansas River, central and western Kansas, and Texas. When most of the Comanche moved to a reservation, the Kwahadi band held out. They had never signed a treaty with the United States. Their great leader Quanah Parker was the half-breed son of Cynthia Parker, who was abducted by Comanche when she was a child. Quanah and his warriors raided Colonel Ronald Mackenzie's camp and defeated him. But, in September 1874, Colonel Mackenzie went into Palo Duro Canyon (Texas) on the Red River and attacked a camp of Comanche, Kiowa, and Cheyenne. Soldiers caught them off guard, burned their camp and drove off or killed the livestock, including their pride: their horses. With no provisions, no shelter, and no horses, Quanah and his Kwahadi band surrendered in 1875.

Comanche were said to be the shortest of the southwestern Indians.

Kiowa

Driven out by rival tribes in the upper Missouri River region, Kiowa migrated to the Black Hills. There they learned from the Crow and schooled themselves in the ways of Plains Indians. When they moved to the southern Plains in the late 1700s, the Kiowa fought and made peace with the Comanche. After that, they were often confederate in battle. Both were known for their wealth of horses and horsemanship. Ferocious and cruel, together or apart, both were the scourge of any traveler or settler along the northern Pecos River. In Santa Fe Trail days the Kiowa's general habitat was the upper Arkansas River, upper Canadian River, and the headwaters of the Red River; but they ranged as suited them. With tepees and horses, they lived on the move.

Eventually the Kiowa settled on an Oklahoma reservation. In 1871, 70-year-old Chief Sitting Bear, leader of the Kaitsenko—Society of the Ten Bravest, and several others, including chiefs, left the reservation and raided Texas settlements. They attacked a wagon train, killed the wagon master and his six teamsters. They stole forty-one of his mules and rode to Ft. Sill to collect their government allotments. When one chief bragged about the massacre, soldiers arrested Sitting Bear and two others. When soldiers came to take Sitting Bear to trial, he stabbed one guard and stole his rifle. As he fumbled to get a cartridge in the chamber, another soldier shot him.

Kiowa attacks didn't stop until the end of the Red River War of 1874-75.

Osage and Kaw (Kansa)

These tribes hunted on the Plains, lived in permanent homes in eastern Kansas, and grew gardens near their villages. In 1825 the Osage and Kansa signed a treaty with the U. S., granting right-of-way travel on the Santa Fe Trail.

Pawnee

The Pawnee lived on the Missouri River near the mouth of the Platte River but wandered and hunted all over present-day Kansas. They farmed near their homes in northeastern Kansas and eastern Nebraska. Corn, beans, and squash were staple crops for many Indians who farmed.

Pueblo

Established in permanent settlements, Pueblo Indians built pueblo style homes in New Mexico. They farmed, made pottery, blankets, and turquoise jewelry. Their gardens were often the target of Indian raids.

They established an annual trade fair in Taos to trade goods with other tribes, Spaniards, and trappers before the existence of the Santa Fe Trail.

Ute

Nomadic Indians, the Ute were most often at home in the mountain regions of present-day New Mexico, Colorado, and Utah. They often banded with Comanche when raiding. Arapaho were their traditional enemy.

Chipeta

Kit Carson considered Ute the best marksmen among the Indians. Old Bill Williams lived among them for a time. They were Lucien Maxwell's favorite tribe. They enjoyed going to see Dick Wootton on Raton Pass.

There were Indian agencies for the Ute at Abiquiu and Cimarron, New Mexico. Ute and the U. S. made two treaties in 1868. One provided a reservation in southwest Colorado. The other offered gifts—money and livestock— and cash annuities to move onto the reservation.

Chief Ouray and his wife Chipeta were great leaders among the Ute in the mid-1800s. In 1874 the U. S. government offered Chief Ouray $1,000 a year for ten years for a salary and $25,000 a year to the tribe to maintain their Colorado agency.

After the Meeker Massacre, the Washington Treaty of 1880 removed the Ute to a reservation in eastern Utah. Then their former neighbors had rest from Ute raids. Chief Ouray died before the move, but Chipeta moved with the remainder of the tribe.

Indians and Newcomers

Although America appeared to be a vast empty land when Conquistadors, colonists, and settlers arrived, the sparse native population had a lifestyle that enjoyed use of the entire land, when desired. Indian tribes moved from place-to-place, into areas of other tribes. Wars began and continued.

In the Southwest, Spaniards and Indians met and, after many difficult experiences, had learned to co-exist by the time Americans arrived. The first method Spaniards tried was assimilation. They attempted to convert and educate Indians; so they could all be one culture. It worked somewhat with Pueblo Indians though they maintained their own society.

Next the Spaniards tried retaliation: you steal from me; I steal from you. When Indians kidnapped and enslaved women and children; the Spaniards did likewise. Before long, it was such a common practice that each blamed the other for starting it. They never did get all the wrinkles ironed out before Mexico gained independence from Spain and carried along Spain's New World colonies and Indian troubles. Mexicans never did settle Indian relations and were having trouble with the Navajo when the United States inherited the situation.

The Louisiana Purchase included the land of the Plains Indians. With the Mexican-American War and the Gadsden Purchase, the U. S. also gained lands of southwestern Indians. In early American colonial days, Indians were considered separate nations. Many churchmen and humanitarians favored assimilation; others spoke of segregation. Soldiers who saw Indians in action thought they'd refuse assimilation and spoke of extermination. Many Indians moved or were moved west of the Mississippi.

Roaming Indians seemed to have an unwritten code: If another tribe had something they wanted, they went after it. If others were killed in the process, well, they were dead. Braves hunted, traded, stole, killed whatever was necessary with varying degrees of stealth and skill.

When mountain men came into the Southwest, they were like another tribe entering the area, a tribe unto themselves. Though many worked independently, they could be counted on to act as a unit. They were a mixture of nationalities with similar goals. They hunted and trapped, like the Indians, for meat and pelts. They understood the trade system and relied heavily on Indians trading pelts. When freighting, mountain men knew where to "let" bags of sugar or flour drop off a wagon for nearby Indians. They also understood the unwritten Indian law: kill before you're killed. It was Uncle Dick's opinion that if white men hadn't interfered, Indian tribes would have eventually killed one another off. One killing seemed to call for another in the age old standard of retribution.

Barton H. Barbour, wrote in "Kit Carson and the 'Americanization' of New Mexico,"
violence was part and parcel of Indian life on the plains and in the mountains. Bitter intertribal animosity and bloodshed were common, fueled by traditional hatreds, horse thefts, kidnappings and murders, territorial squabbling, and competition for economic resources such as game or access to fur traders. American trappers had to be prepared for

violence if they were to survive in that environment..."[242]

Settlers didn't cotton to "sharing" their crops, their wives, or their children. Indians attacked wagon trains on the Plains, raided settlers, stole from them, killed them, treated them similarly to the way tribes treated one another. Settlers didn't seem to get it. They didn't seem to understand the law: kill before you're killed.

Hostility and raiding were their manner of life. Extra opportunity presented itself during the Mexican-American War with more military supply wagons on the Trail. Inexperienced drivers replaced seasoned drivers, who enlisted in the Army. Raids increased. During the summer of 1847 Comanche, Kiowa, and Pawnee killed 47 Americans, destroyed 330 American wagons, and stole 6,500 animals. Kiowa and Comanche found hunting whites easier and more profitable than killing buffalo. Navajo and Apache raided in New Mexico; Ute raided in New Mexico and southern Colorado. Neither the Arapaho, nor the southern Cheyenne were too friendly that year. It perpetrated a chain reaction: Some Americans began to shoot Indians on sight. Indian women wailed for warriors to revenge. Warriors attacked. Americans retaliated.

In the early 1850's Commissioner Emory spoke of killing the Indians. Lives of many who lived elsewhere were unaffected directly by the whole situation. Reformers forgot colonial history, but did pay attention. From their distant view, they encouraged passivity. They suggested that Indians hardly knew right from wrong like they did; so they shouldn't be held responsible for their actions. An experienced Indian fighter spoke of the Apache:

> It is all very well to argue that the Indian knows no better, that he merely possesses the teachings of his race, that his cruelties are the results of untaught savage disposition, etc.; but...is it true policy that intelligent, Christian people should be sacrificed, year after year, and their massacres, excused on the ground that the murderers were only Indians?...Must we forever continue to accept the...theories of parlor readers on Indian character?...The American savage is no idiot. He knows right from wrong, and is quite as cognizant of the fact...as the most instructed of our race. If the reader should feel a particle of doubt on this point, all he has to do is to commit a wrong upon an Apache, and he will very soon become convinced that the savage is quite as much aware of the fact as he can be...The capacity to discriminate between right and wrong is not the exclusive property of christianized people.[243]

Like the Spanish and Mexicans before them, the American Army found they needed more men to withstand attacks in the large southwestern space. In 1852 Comanche attacked every small party that traveled between San Antonio and El Paso—to within three miles of Ft. Bliss (Texas). They set prairie fires to burn grazing to hinder wagon trains and the Army. From 1846-1850 New Mexicans reported the Apache cost them: 31,581 horned cattle, 7,050 horses, 453,293 sheep, and 12,887 mules. Apache seemed to have cattle rustling down to a science, making off with entire herds in one fell swoop and slipping away from the scene with skill and speed. They sometimes traveled more than a thousand miles from the scene. The Army

---

[242] Barbour, *New Mexican Lives*, 183, 184.
[243] Horgan, *Great River*, 846.

tried talks, made treaties. It seemed like no sooner than they got back to the fort and caught their breath, raids or thefts started back up again.

In 1854 Sioux captured Ft. Laramie and killed all the men on hand. General W. S. Harney went after them and whipped them at Ash Hollow. After that, trouble escalated between the Sioux and the Americans until Sitting Bull's warriors were stopped years later.

By the mid-1850's William Bent and Indian Agent Thomas Fitzpatrick realized tribes had become accustomed to a lifestyle they couldn't sustain. Though traders still bought buffalo pelts, the beaver market was gone. The market, which enriched Indians and traders, had changed. Bent and Fitzpatrick were concerned that the Indians they dealt with were becoming beggars, dependent on American charity.

Wendell Phillips, a Massachusetts abolitionist, demanded the government forget about a transcontintental railroad and set up a department to watch out for the Indians. In 1859 U. S. Army Captain Randolph Marcy's friend, who'd lived among Southwestern Indians twenty-five years, gave his opinion:

They are the most onsartainest varmints in all creation, and I reckon tha'r not mor'n half human; for you never seed a human, arter you'd fed and treated him to the best fixins in your lodge, jist turn round and steal all your horses, or ary other thing he could lay his hands on. No, not adzackly. He would feel kinder grateful, and ask you to spread a blanket in his lodge ef you ever passed that-a-way. But the Inju he don't care shucks for you, and is ready to do you a heap of mischief as soon as he quits your feed. No, Captain,' he continued,' it's not the right way to give um presents to buy peace; but ef I war governor of these yeer United States, I'll tell you what I'd do. I'd invite um all to a big feast, and make b'lieve I wanted to have a big talk; and as soon as I got um all together, I'd pitch in and sculp about half of um, and then t'other half would be might glad to make a peace that would stick. That's the way I'd make a treaty with the dog'ond, red-bellied varmints; and as sure as you're born, Captain, that's the only way.'"[244]

Captain Marcy didn't think that showed good faith. He thought it'd be better to meet them on the battlefield and take care of the matter. His friend disagreed:

Tain't no use to talk about honor with them, Captain; they hain't got no such thing in um; and they won't show fair fight, any way you can fix it. Don't they kill and sculp a white man when-are they get the better on him? The mean varmints, they'll never behave themselves until you give um a clean out and out licking. They can't understand white folks' ways, and they won't learn um; and ef you treat um decently, they think you ar afeard. You may epend on't, Cap. The only way to treat Injuns is to thrash them well at first, then the balance will sorter take to you and behave themselves.[245]

Artist Vincent Colyer felt certain peace would be obtained by honest dealing with Indians. Chief Ouray was an example of an Indian chief who honored honest dealing.

Captain Charles Christy, stationed at Ft. Zarah in 1867, wasn't persuaded:

Expressing sympathy for the Indian is to my mind worse than the habit women have of sending flowers to a wife-murderer. There has been a noticeable tendency among some storywriters, and among those of the Fennimore Cooper kind in particular, to throw a

---

[244] Marcy, *Prairie Traveler*, 211, 212.
[245] Marcy, 212.

hero's halo around the Indian…I have been among the Indians nearly all my life, and have seen them under all conditions, but I cannot say that I can recall any one of the whole lot who, by any stretch of the imagination, could be called a hero….All the old scouts and Indian fighters will say the same…I am satisfied that Cooper's Indian tale… have indirectly caused the deaths of hundreds of whites and reds. The stories invested the Indian with many excellent qualities which he did not possess, and created a sentiment for him … unmerited and which protected him when deserving punishment. Elated at escaping so frequently the penalty of his misdeeds the noble red man felt encouraged to repeat and increase his outrages, until finally it became necessary to kill off a lot of them.[246]

Christy met Indians after the Huning Massacre; he said:

when the winter set in and they decided to quit the warpath and become 'good' Indians again until spring, they came into the fort to get their winter's supplies from the government and began boasting about what they had done, and saying it would only take the next summer for them to clean out every fort in the country. They never wearied of bragging of their deviltries and telling how brave they were. Many a time when they were boasting, I have made them angry by saying jeeringly:

'What—do you call yourselves brave? Bah!...You say you are braves and then you go out and kill a lot of women and children. That is not the work of braves—it is the work of cowards!...it is very brave for big bucks like you, well-armed with guns and sharp knives, to go in and kill those women…You kill them and take their scalps and then you go back to your lodges and have a scalp-dance….And when you are in your lodges, safe from all danger, and with your bellies full of buffalo-meat, it is then you tell your children how brave you have been to take those scalps and you pat yourselves on the breast and sing. Bah—you are not men, you are only old squaws! Why don't you fight us white dogs face to face when you meet us?...You are afraid to meet us face to face like men!' Whew! But they would…be fighting mad! They would stride forward, shaking their fists high in the air and say: 'Never mind. We will meet you some day and then we will kill you all!'[247]

During the Civil War, Indians took advantage of the scarcity of soldiers. There were appeals; but Washington D. C. was distant from western life—in miles, culture, and manner of communication. The struggling young nation tried. At the end of the war, Washington did focus more earnestly on taming the West. When the situation became his duty, William Tecumseh Sherman, Civil War general who burned his way through the South, developed his military view: "The more we can kill this year, the less will have to be killed the next war,…they all have to be killed or be maintained as a species of paupers."[248]

The U. S. government divided responsibility for Indian affairs: Military stationed in Indian country received orders from the War Department, The Department of the Interior controlled Indian agencies. So, while Indians were on the warpath, they could, at times, still stop by the Indian agency and receive provisions.

Indians didn't want to adopt a different lifestyle. The forefathers of some had raised crops, but their tribes had moved to the Plains. They were now accustomed to a roving life. They

---

[246] Simmons, *On the Santa Fe Trail*, 111.
[247] Simmons, *On the Santa Fe Trail*, 116, 117.
[248] Capps, *The Indians*, 192.

resented encroachment on hunting land, land they'd moved onto before the white man came. When they'd had enough, Indians went on the warpath, striking terror and instilling fear. They stole horses, cattle, women, and children; attacked wagon trains and stagecoaches; burned homes; mutilated, murdered, used familiar methods, but upped the scale.

The Mexican border was no border to them. Indians stole 10,000 horses annually in New Mexico, Texas, and Mexico. They were known to tie Mexican wagon masters upside down on wagon wheels. They'd keep a man's head a foot off the ground, build a fire under his head, and cook his brains until they burst out of his head.[249] When they kidnapped women and children, they generally kept them alive unless they whined or made too much of a to-do. Women generally became concubines and/or slaves. Children were often beaten and abused, traded off, made slaves, or raised to be part of the tribe.

In the mid-1860's trouble brewed, and trouble boiled, not just in Colorado and New Mexico, but from Texas to Minnesota. Though they still fought among themselves, Indian tribes banded with enemy tribes to resist the white man.

---

[249] Horgan, 847.

Indian Wars

There were few soldiers stationed in the West compared to the number of Indian braves, especially during the American Civil War. One soldier sent to Mesilla, New Mexico, in 1862 noticed, "What the Confederates failed to appropriate, the Apaches destroyed. The inhabitants were literally starving and utterly demoralized."[250]

When Confederate General Sibley returned to Richmond after his New Mexico campaign, he reported Navajos had driven off hundreds of thousands of the New Mexicans' sheep. He encouraged systematic action against both the Navajo and the Apache.

Not all Indians were aggressive without provocation. The Pueblo Indians lived along the Rio Grande, raised livestock and crops, traded, and were also the objects of Indian raids.

Buffalo Soldiers

During the Civil War, thousands of "colored Negroes," as they were called in that era, joined the Union Army. Few deserted. There were no black officers. Few could read or write. After the war; many reenlisted. More joined. Men of all races and many nationalities found the military a place to earn the necessities of life, plus a small income—a start in life.

After the Civil War, black soldiers formed the 9th and 10th cavalry and the 24th and 25th infantry units. Plains Indians dubbed them "buffalo soldiers." A favorite Indian amusement was to put on a soldier's cap, coat, and blue pants, and mimic black soldiers' walk and talk.

Buffalo Soldiers served from Texas to Montana and the Dakotas—primarily in New Mexico, Arizona, Texas, and Indian Territory. They protected travelers and men laying railroad tracks. They fought Indians, helped build towns, and constructed telegraph lines. The 9th cavalry was stationed in New Mexico—at Fort Union in the north and forts Seldon, Stanton, and Bayard in the south.

In spite of rheumatism, Major Albert P. Morrow shared hardships as one of them at Ft. Bayard. They doggedly chased Chief Victorio and his braves in the Apache Wars. Eighteen buffalo soldiers received Medals of Honor for service in the Indian Wars of 1879-1881.

The 10th Cavalry were garrisoned in Texas at forts Bliss (El Paso), Davis, Stockton, and Quitman. Tall Colonel Benjamin H. Grierson—a full-bearded, kindhearted, mild man—commanded Ft. Davis. Although he'd led in the Civil War (Grierson's Raid), some of his officers thought him too easy going with both his troops and the enemy.

Navajo; Bosque Redondo; Apache

NAVAJO are Athapaskan Indians who migrated from Canada to the Southwest. They were well established raiders long before the U. S. entered the area. In 1845 Mexico's New Mexico Governor Manuel Armijo lamented that Navajos were consuming the Territory little by little.

---

[250] Horgan, 831.

On August 19, 1846, Stephen Kearny proclaimed New Mexico a U. S. territory and promised to protect New Mexicans.

In March 1848 Colonel Newby, accompanied by Antoine Leroux and Dick Wootton, left Santa Fe with six companies of soldiers to encourage better Navajo behavior toward other New Mexicans. In a powwow the Navajo promised to return all Mexican captives and bring 3,000 sheep to replace the ones they'd stolen. Twenty-seven days later they brought in five children and less than a hundred rams and signed a peace treaty.

In February 1849 Lt. Col. John M. Washington wrote the War Department that Indians must control themselves or be controlled, must cultivate and earn an honest living or be destroyed.

On August 31, 1849, soldiers and two U. S. representatives rode to Navajo country to explain the U. S. plan to open the land to settlers. During the course of events, a Mexican guide claimed the Navajo stole his horse. Argument and skirmish erupted. Soldiers shot and killed seven Navajo, including leader Narbona. The incident set off further skirmishes between Navajo and the U. S.

On September 9, 1849, Mariano Martinez, chief of one Navajo group, signed his "X" on a peace treaty in the presence of Lt. Col. Washington and Indian Agent James S. Calhoun. It was an agreement to submit to U. S. jurisdiction, to allow the U. S. to set boundaries, to return all captives and stolen property, and to be at peace.

Trouble continued:

1851, Arizona: Ft. Defiance, the first fort in Navajo country was built. Navajo were accustomed to Spanish and Mexican rule, both ill-equipped to deal with the distant Navajo. American rule was more active. Navajo now had to negotiate with U. S. officers for use of land and water. The Army at Ft. Defiance was like a thorn in their flesh—especially to chiefs and rich herdsmen like Manuelito. More skirmishes.

1858: Manuelito found 60 head of livestock shot and thought soldiers killed them. He informed the major at Ft. Defiance that the grass and water belonged to him and the Navajo. After that 160 Zuni Indians helped soldiers burn Manuelito's village and fields. In turn, Manuelito resolved to drive soldiers away from the fort.

1860: Headman Manuelito and medicine man Barboncito led 1,000 Navajo to attack Ft. Defiance. Soldiers repelled the attack, but abandoned the fort in 1861. The attack prompted the U. S. Army to change tactics: it adopted a policy of total war against the Navajo.

1861: With U. S. military attention focused on the Civil War, Navajo and other Indians found opportunity to increase raiding. When raids multiplied, General Canby resorted to basic military tactic: colonize or destroy. He thought if he moved the Navajo away from familiar territory, he could retrain them. Before his plan materialized, he was transferred to Civil War duty and replaced by General James H. Carleton. The Navajo situation was his order of business. New Mexico Governor Connelly backed Carleton's effort to move raiding Indians to a reservation.

Winter 1862-1863: Colonel J. Francisco Chavez ordered Navajo to come to terms by July 20, 1863. If they didn't, he vowed they'd then be treated as hostile people.

July 20, 1863: July 20 came and went without Navajo compliance.

July 1863: When the Civil War began, Kit Carson had resigned his position as Indian agent and joined the New Mexico regiment. Although the Civil War was short lived in New Mexico, Carson remained a soldier. Carleton considered Carson his most qualified soldier and placed him in charge of the Navajo campaign. He ordered Carson to go forward with a "Scorch the Earth Policy." With Ute guides, Carson led soldiers into Navajoland (present-day Four Corners area). Ute scouts found and killed some Navajo, captured some; but the Navajo were hardy.

Summer 1863-Spring 1864: The Army's "Scorch the Earth Policy" was unrelenting pressure and presence until surrender—a battle of attrition. They stopped wells, burned crops, killed livestock, and destroyed homes while Navajo headmen Barboncito, Manuelito, and Ganado Mucho hid in hills, valleys, and among rocks. Navajo fled for refuge in Canyon de Chelly.

January 1864: Ordered to shoot anyone who attempted escape, soldiers blocked the entrance to Canyon de Chelly. Kit Carson ordered troops to march into the canyon. They destroyed thousands of peach trees, pride of the Navajos. Carson didn't enter the canyon himself. Soldiers killed twenty-three Navajo and brought out 234, surrendered or captured. About two-thirds of the Navajo surrendered by the time soldiers completed the campaign.

March 1864: At Ft. Defiance, hundreds of Navajo awaited relocation to Bosque Redondo on the Pecos River in east central New Mexico. Having held out during the military campaign, many weakened Navajo died at Ft. Defiance before the tribe left to Bosque Redondo. More than 100 of those who left the fort died from rigors of the journey, called "The Long Walk." They walked through a blizzard on March 21.

New Mexicans, who'd long endured the brunt, destruction, and heartache of Navajo attacks came out to meet them as they passed by. They hurled insults, rocks, whatever was at hand. Other Indians who'd suffered at their hands also met them. Soldiers killed three Navajo who didn't keep up; those soldiers were court-martialed. Each received a dishonorable discharged.

1864-1868: About 8,000 Navajo lived at Bosque Redondo. At times they were allowed to hunt, allowed to leave the confines of Bosque Redondo. In addition, the provost marshal at Ft. Sumner allowed many Navajo to return to Navajoland for a temporary time during these years. People as far as Las Vegas (New Mexico) wanted the Navajo moved because, when allowed to leave the confines, they raided settlers all around the area. New Mexicans complained the Bosque was just giving the Navajo a center of operations.

Placed in charge of Bosque Redondo, Kit Carson divided the Navajo into ten villages. Each village had its headman, overseer, and subchief to provide the people representation.

The government effort got off on a bad foot at Bosque Redondo. Officers in charge didn't know Navajo wouldn't live in a dwelling where someone died. In addition, the tribe was larger than anticipated; so the government started with inadequate rations. Then crops failed. When other years proved to be poor farming years, the Navajo weren't persuaded farming was a better way of life. They preferred raiding to farming, anyway. Life was hard. Many died. When Carleton inspected Bosque Redondo, he saw firsthand that the Navajo hadn't raised enough food to meet their needs. He had cattle driven to the reservation and ordered full government rations.

General William T. Sherman and S. F. Tappan of the 1866 Peace Commission visited Bosque Redondo. They concluded Navajo should be returned to Navajoland.

Treaty of 1868: At one point General Sherman considered relocating the Navajo to a reservation in Kansas or Oklahoma. Navajo headmen, like Barboncito, Manuelito, Armijo, and Ganado Mucho, insisted they return to their land with its four sacred mountains in northeast Arizona and northwest New Mexico. The treaty did something no other Indian treaty did: it allowed the Indian to return home. In 1878, 1880 and 1884 the U. S. government added land to the Navajo reservation for their increasing numbers. Theirs became the largest reservation in the U. S.

The U. S. gave the Navajo 13,000 sheep. The government agreed to establish an Indian agency for them and to provide each Navajo with sheep, goats, corn, flour, seed, and tools for the next ten years. Schools would be provided for children ages six-sixteen. Some provisions continued to be renewed. In exchange, the Navajo agreed to never again war against the United States.

As the group walked home, they formed a ten mile procession. The fort was closed and sold.

1880's: Navajo owned 30,000 horses and more than 1,000,000 sheep.

By the end of the century, the tribe doubled in number from its Bosque Redondo days.

BOSQUE REDONDO was located along the Pecos River, which offered fish, duck, and beaver. Carleton had found what he thought was good land on which to segregate the Navajo. It was much more fertile than the Navajo's high desert country. The land Carleton chose was a forty square mile plat called Bosque Redondo, about five miles from Ft. Sumner and 180 miles southeast of Santa Fe. The idea of segregation didn't originate with Carleton. Beale, Canby, Neighbors, and Steck had recommended the same thing.

Cottonwood trees lined the riverbank; the soil was dark and rich. Carleton thought the soil was better than soil along the Missouri River Valley. Comanche, Kiowa, Mescalero Apache, and other Indians frequented the area. It was a place where antelope, deer, and wild turkey roamed—what better choice could Carleton make? There was enough land for all the Athapaskan Indian family—the Navajo and Apache. Carleton had already had Carson move about 400 Mescalero Apaches to the Bosque in 1863. But not all families get along; the Apache and Navajo did not, had not. Way outnumbered, the Apache left.

The government objective had been to teach the Navajo and Apache to be self-sufficient; so they'd quit raiding settlers. New Mexicans had called for the protection General Kearny promised when they became U. S. citizens.

Carleton was determined to make the experiment work. It was costing the government a million dollars a year. Still, Carleton was certain if he could administer law and order in the territory, New Mexico towns, farms, and ranches could flourish. He did bring about change that others from Spain, Mexico, and the United States had failed to work in New Mexico.

APACHE were Athapaskan Indians who migrated from Canada between 1300 and 1400 into lands inhabited by Pueblo Indians. Apache and Navajo were bitter enemies.

In the summers of 1861 and 1862, Apache raided New Mexico residents. As Apache plundering and killing continued into the winter of 1862-1863, General John R. West was ordered to resist Gila Apache west of Mesilla, New Mexico. Colonel Kit Carson was ordered to rein in the Mescalero Apache and move them to Ft. Stanton. In March he took 400 Mescalero Apache to Bosque Redondo in east central New Mexico.

With the Apache under control, miners in southern New Mexico resumed mining in 1863. Southern New Mexico settlers farmed again.

After the Navajo arrived at Bosque Redondo, however, the Mescalero Apache left in 1864. They returned to their familiar haunts and took up their old raiding profession.

Within six weeks—in 1866—Apache killed twenty men in New Mexico's Guadalupe Mountains and on Texas' El Paso-San Antonio route.

In 1869 the Army regathered some Mescalero who'd left Bosque Redondo and confined them at Ft. Stanton. Four years later they were given a reservation on the eastern slope of the Sacramento Mountains, New Mexico.

In 1874 Apache Chief Cochise requested his Chiricahua Apache be given the land in their home area. The government granted his request, and Cochise honored his word. His people honored him and kept peace until his death in 1874. Other Apache continued to receive government rations while they continued to raid in Arizona, New Mexico, Texas, and across the border into Mexico. After Cochise's death, his Chiricahua increased activity. When they raided, Apache left behind enough animals to reproduce and enough people to tend them; so there would be more available next time around.

Pursued by 9th and 10th Cavalry Buffalo Soldiers (1879-1880), Mimbres Apache Chief Victorio and his warriors rode south into Mexico four times. Victorio was in his late 70's, possibly 80. When Victorio and his band rode across the border into Mexico in late October 1879, Major Albert P. Morrow and 100 of the 9th Cavalry crossed the border after them. They found the Apache, but didn't find enough water to sustain the troop; they returned to New Mexico.

Apache raided in Mexico, robbed, killed, and reinforced their band. By adding warriors who left the Mescalero Apache reservation and others, they more than doubled the size of their band. In January 1880, after the Mexican army got riled up over two bloody massacres, the Apache figured folks in the San Andres Mountains might be missing them and rode back across the American border.

American Colonel Edward Hatch was determined to catch Victorio. In early April 1880, he came close to getting a bead on him; but water in that arid land played a hand. Apache controlled one water hole; soldiers drank from another. When gypsum in the water made the soldiers sick, Victorio closed in on them. They fought all night until Colonel Grierson and his 10th Cavalry arrived to reinforce them.

Apache raided, plundered, killed in the Black and Mogollon Ranges in May 1880. After Chief Victorio was shot in the leg, the band rode back across the border into Mexico. That summer Colonel Grierson and his troops guarded water holes along the border. In late July 1880 Victorio crossed the Rio Grande back into New Mexico.

Knowing Victorio and 150 warriors were in the area, Grierson, his teenage son, two officers, and twenty-one Buffalo Soldier cavalrymen were at Tinaja de las Palmas in Quitman Canyon to fortify the water hole on the morning of July 30. They held off the Apache until relief columns arrived from east and west. Nevertheless, on August 2, 1880, Victorio rode north and escaped the soldiers. In pursuit, Grierson and 10th Cavalrymen covered sixty-five miles in twenty-one hours.

On August 6, 1880, Grierson and his men guarded Rattlesnake Springs. They exchanged fire with the Apache, but didn't give up the spring. The same day infantry escorting a provision train from Ft. Davis rebuffed Apache who attacked the train. Grierson and his cavalry arrived to relieve the soldiers. Victorio and his band headed south into Mexico.

Mexican Colonel Joaquin Terrazas and his 350 soldiers found Victorio and his band at Tres Castillos, Mexico, on October 15, 1880. The Mexicans killed Victorio, sixty-two of his warriors, and eighteen women and children.

After Victorio's death, Nana led the band until they were captured and taken to San Carlos Reservation in Arizona. In May 1885 some Apache and a few leaders, including Nana, Mangas, and Geronimo, escaped and killed at least eighty-five people. They raided and plundered for more than a year before being removed far from their southwestern land.

Mail and the Pony Express

In 1860 U. S. mail from the East could be sent to the Southwest by overland stage or the Pony Express. Otherwise, it must be shipped to Panama, carried across the Isthmus, shipped up the Pacific coast to San Francisco, and transported overland to its destination.

Stage lines provided passenger service, but their primary profit was in mail service. John Butterfield's stage line was the first to span the distance from Missouri to the Pacific.

Butterfield's Southern Overland Express

Congress discussed the need for cross-country mail service in 1857. They awarded a contract to John Butterfield, a New Yorker with experience in stage management. Butterfield supervised the choice of route, the construction of 200 stage stations along the 2,795 mile route, and the purchase of horses, mules, and coaches. He hired employees. In eighteen months the "Butterfield Stage" was ready to roll.

The Pacific Railroad reached Tipton, Missouri, in August 1858. (Through mergers, the Pacific Railroad became part of the Union Pacific Railroad.) The first Butterfield Stage left Tipton on September 16, 1858, and arrived in San Francisco, California, on October 10th.

Mule or horse drawn—depending on the terrain, the stage traveled from Tipton, Missouri, into Tennessee for a stop in Memphis, on through Arkansas, Oklahoma, and Texas. From El Paso, Texas, the Butterfield Trail followed the Rio Grande into southern New Mexico. The first coach arrived in New Mexico on September 28, 1858. From Mesilla, New Mexico, the route headed west across southern New Mexico into southern California, and north to the San Francisco terminus. The stage carried mail for twenty cents per ounce.

A stage left each terminus on Monday and Thursday mornings. A one-way ticket for the entire three-and-a-half week trip cost $200; otherwise, a passenger paid fifteen cents a mile. The two daily meals were an extra charge. Ordinarily, the trip took about twenty-five days. With all the bouncing and jarring of a stagecoach ride, some passengers who traveled the entire distance ended up with boils by the time they reached the end of the line.

A driver and a conductor accompanied each coach. If a driver was unable to continue his section of the run, it was the prescribed duty of the keeper of the stage station to take over for him. The Butterfield Stage Company made it standard practice not to carry gold or silver; so they wouldn't be such a temptation to highwaymen.

After southern states began to secede from the Union early in 1861, Congress opted out of doing business on Butterfield's southern route.

Pony Express

The Pony Express was a cross-country courier system, which belonged to Alexander Majors, William Hepburn Russell, and William B. Waddell, who previously partnered in contract freighting. At the peak of their freight operation in the 1850's, they employed 5,000 men, owned about 3,500 wagons, and hauled 16,000,000 pounds of freight in one year.

Alexander Majors became a byword for energy and integrity among freighters. He was a Christian man, a man of temperance. He gave each man a small Bible and set aside each Sunday to worship the Lord Jesus Christ. He required every employee to sign a commitment to sobriety and a promise not to use profanity, not to be cruel to the animals, and not to gamble. If a man broke his commitment, he was subject to dismissal. Majors believed industrious gentlemen made the best employees. He insisted men obey orders promptly. Although he was strict, he wasn't harsh. Majors treated men with kindness and respect; he was well-liked wherever he traveled.

Charles Fremont had seen the Bent-St. Vrain courier system in operation when he visited El Pueblo and reported it on his return to the States. Some think Russell, Majors, and Waddell may have put the cross-country courier idea into action as a result. Riding day and night, express riders were able to cross the country from Missouri to the Pacific faster than a stagecoach.

Russell, Majors, and Waddell set up manned express stations every ten to fifteen miles on their route from St. Joseph, Missouri, to San Francisco, California. The route was: St. Joseph Missouri; Ft. Kearny, Nebraska; Ft. Laramie and Ft. Bridger, Wyoming; Salt Lake City, Utah; Camp Floyd, Carson City, and Washoe City, Nevada; across the Sierra Nevadas to Placerville, Sacramento, and San Francisco, California. It was a more central route than Butterfield's line.

Horses were changed at every station. Riders changed about every seventy-five miles. Man and mail could not weigh over 175 pounds total. When riders arrived at a station, their next mount was saddled, ready to go. The Pony Express began cross-country mail service April 3, 1860. Expressmen of the first trip rode the entire distance in eight days and four hours—twenty hours ahead of their projected timetable.

Riders were sometimes shot. For their daring, speed, and steadfastness, a rider earned $100-$150 a month, many times the wage of a farm laborer. In the beginning, mail carried the full distance cost $5.00 per half ounce. The charge was reduced to $1.00 to encourage business. Monthly operation costs to maintain the Pony Express were about $30,000.

On October 24, 1861, Eastern and Western telegraph lines[251] connected at Salt Lake City. After that, Pony Express mail service dwindled. Congress appropriated a million dollar subsidy to help defray cost of mail service over the central route; but Russell, Majors, and Waddell sold out before they received the first $100,000 payment. Ben Holladay purchased their assets and expanded stage service to California and other western destinations. In 1866, when he realized he would soon be competing with the railroad, Holladay sold out to Wells Fargo.

---

[251] Indians called the telegraph "talking wires."

Railroads

When Dick Wootton left home in 1834, there wasn't one mile of railroad track on the American continent.

There had been attempts to build railroads since the 1700's. In England Richard Trevithick built a steam locomotive and, in 1804, hauled ten tons of coal at five miles per hour. A few years later George Stephenson built a steam engine for England's first public steam railway—the Stockton & Darlington Railway, which opened in 1825. Stephenson became a leading influence in the development of Britain's railway.

The first American railroad was a quarry road—the Quincy. It was powered by gravity downhill and by horse power uphill. The first American railroad for public use was the Baltimore & Ohio's little thirteen mile rail run. It used British engines. They proved unsatisfactory for the grades and curves needed for American terrain; so Americans began building engines. Peter Cooper designed a little engine he named "Tom Thumb." Men doubted trains could pull uphill and around curves, but "Tom Thumb" was the little engine that did. In 1830 it pulled four-and-a-half tons at varying grades and around curves. "Tom Thumb" gave three dozen passengers a thirteen mile ride from Baltimore to Sellicott's Mills and back in just over two hours.

The year Dick Wootton left Independence, Henry Campbell patented the "American type" engine that had two pair of large driving wheels, which added power. Many railroads adopted the English rail gauge: 56 ½" between rails. It became the "standard" gauge used in the United States. Some railroads, especially in mountainous areas, used a narrow gauge: 3' apart. Train cars built for a certain gauge could travel on any tracks built of the same gauge; so railroad cars need not be unloaded and reloaded in order for goods to reach the destination.

Railroad companies began to spring up and build local roads. In the 1850's local roads began connecting and incorporating. Because rails were such a boon to transportation, they became a key element during the Civil War. Each side tried to disable rails of the other. The Gray Ghost—John Singleton Mosby—and his Virginia Rangers destroyed Union rails to aid Robert E. Lee.

Railroad expansion braked for the Civil War; but plans continued to be made. From 1862-1866, the Pacific Railway Acts helped provide funds for the first transcontinental railway. The Union Pacific and Central Pacific Railways built that road along the 32nd parallel. Bonds granted by the U. S. government were not outright gifts, but debts due, payable.

At the beginning of 1865 the U. S. had 35,085 miles of track. Except for a few miles in the Pacific Coast area, there were none west of the Missouri River. After the Civil War, on July 10, 1865, track was laid westward from Omaha, Nebraska. As railheads moved westward, farms and settlements began to dot the prairies. Remote areas became more accessible. Trains provided safer, quicker travel than wagon trains and stagecoaches.

Congress granted some railroads right-of-way—ownership of specified public land along the path of the rails. A railroad could build on or sell the land to help defray construction costs. States and territories were interested in railroads to help increase population and taxation. Some railroads advertised in Europe for emigrants to settle along their lines. Some offered special land purchase deals. European speculators were also involved in some railroad lines.

Railroads extended markets and united industry: Farmers and ranchers could ship products hundreds of miles. Fruits, vegetables, and dairy products could arrive miles away in time to be served fresh. Raw materials were easily shipped to factories. Industry, in turn, found customers along distant rails. Early trains were short, often consisting of only eight cars, but, a boxcar could hold about as much as four wagons. (A standard box car measured 40' x 6' x 7' in 1880.).

Americans became more dependent on one another economically and more unified in communication and information. News and learning spread among passengers and workers—at depots and freight stations and into the community; the nation became more intertwined.

A. T. & S. F. Railway, "The Santa Fe"

Cyrus K. Holliday dreamed of a railroad that would replace the Mountain Branch of the Santa Fe Trail. As a member of the Kansas Territorial Senate, Holliday wrote and helped pass a charter that would enable him to build a railroad in Kansas. On February 11, 1859, he obtained a charter to build his Atchison and Topeka line. In 1863 the charter was modified to give him authority to build toward Santa Fe. To reflect the change, he renamed his company the Atchison, Topeka and Santa Fe Railway. It was more often referred to as the A. T. & S. F. or the Santa Fe.

The Civil War broke out before Holliday obtained sufficient funds to build. As president of the company from September 1860 until January 1864, Holliday held onto his hopes and worked enthusiastically to attract financing. After he served as president, he became secretary of the company. He was then director for thirty-seven years. Whatever his position, Holliday worked with enthusiasm and industry to accomplish his objective.

For nine years Holliday attempted to find capital in the U. S. and in foreign countries. At times it appeared like a go; then the financer would back out. In 1867 George K. Beach of New York agreed to build a section of the road, but backed out and assigned his contract to T. J. Peters of Cincinnati. Peters hired engineer Albert A. Robinson to set the first stake and mark the route.

Kansas' Senator Edmund G. Ross broke ground for the A. T. & S. F. in 1869. When the first thirteen miles were complete to Wakarusa, Peters borrowed a locomotive and a coach to try it out. The engineer sped down the rails and arrived in Wakarusa in just a little more than thirty minutes.

From Wakarusa tracks were laid to Burlingame, Kansas, then on to Topeka, a total of forty-nine miles. Rails tracked on toward the state line and toward Granada, Colorado. On March 3, 1863, the Kansas Territorial legislature set aside 2,931,247 acres of Kansas land for the railroad that reached the state line by March 1873. The road was to start at Atchison, Kansas, and go in the direction of Santa Fe, New Mexico. Within seven months of the deadline, the Santa Fe had completed sixty-one miles, but had 400 miles left to build. With great effort, but no reduction in quality, crews laid rails to the state line by December 28, 1872. Fifty pound steel rails were the standard.

As the Santa Fe built westward, it advertised at home and abroad to draw settlers along its rails. Then the Financial Panic of '73 hit. Five thousand businesses went bankrupt. The A. T. & S. F. had no money for construction and little for maintenance. The Northern Pacific Railway began to crumble and made investors leery of financing railroads. By compromising with its bondholders, the Santa Fe hung on. In 1874 grasshoppers chewed up fields in many parts of the U. S., cutting deep into farmers' pockets. Before Kansas farmers recovered, drought stunted crops. The Santa Fe took many settlers back East free of charge, yet managed to keep building southwestward. It continued advertising. Without sufficient population a railroad couldn't profit. The company established a land department and provided half-price tickets for incoming settlers. It helped provide ocean transport for laborers and settlers. Home seekers grasped the hope of opportunity. The Santa Fe's semi-monthly excursions brought 10-50 passenger cars filled with settlers to form the population nucleus along their rails in Kansas. More than 10,000 Russian Mennonites moved onto the Plains.

From its inception the Santa Fe system wasn't just attempting to build a railroad. It had the vision of Manifest Destiny. Its mission was to supplement the achievements of the mountain men and military men who made inroads into the American Southwest. The Santa Fe's mission was to help colonize and develop the Southwest by providing transportation, facilities, and employment.

After drawing emigrants to fill the Plains, the Santa Fe employed artists and photographers, whose work encouraged tourists to ride Santa Fe coaches and enjoy the Southwest. They promoted Hot Springs in New Mexico, the Grand Canyon in Arizona, and other Southwestern sites. Their calendars highlighted the Southwest. To make travel more enjoyable, the Santa Fe worked with Fred Harvey, who provided dining and hotel services.

A. A. Robinson and his crew of engineers laid out the line from Granada to Pueblo, Colorado, in 1875. Contractors Long and Shepardson oversaw the work as laborers laid the rails. Once a month, paymaster James Moore paid wages from the pay car; Edward Wilder was treasurer.

After a full day's work, laborers slept with their Winchesters under the stars; for it was evident Indians were near. Knowing Indians' "fancy for long hair," the men kept theirs shorn close. No sense tempting Indians with a long scalp. Employees enlisted fellow worker John Atkinson to be camp barber. He cut hair in the evenings after work.

Las Animas, Colorado, was the only populated place between Dodge City, Kansas, and Pueblo, Colorado. There was an eating house at Lakin. Other than that, there were only section houses at siding stations and a warehouse at La Junta, Colorado.[252] Beyond Dodge City there weren't many sidings that would hold more than thirty cars to wait for an oncoming train to pass.

The Santa Fe faced competition from the Denver and Rio Grande, also called the D. & R. G., or the Rio Grande. That line planned to build from Denver to Mexico City. Both roads

---

[252] The railroad reached La Junta, Colorado, in 1875.

planned to enter New Mexico though Raton Pass and the Royal Gorge. At each place there was room for only one line. The Santa Fe had considered following the Cimarron Route of the Santa Fe Trail, but the Mountain Branch offered more water and vast coal fields, both essentials for steam locomotives. In addition, there was more potential for development of railroad traffic along the Mountain Branch. Some farms were already established in the Arkansas Valley. There were also ranches, farms, and mines in northern New Mexico.

William B. Strong was A. T. & S. F. manager in charge of getting the railroad into New Mexico. He heard that the territorial legislature required any railroad entering the territory to have cash up front to cover ten percent of the proposed line. That was far beyond the Santa Fe's ability; but it didn't stop Strong. He jumped on a Barlow & Sanderson stage, crossed Raton Pass, passed Wagon Mound and Las Vegas, and arrived in Santa Fe. With prominent northern New Mexico businessman Miguel Otero, Colorado Governor Pitkin, and Colonel Nut, Strong went to the capitol to see what could be done. The problem appeared more formidable than he'd realized. Representatives from the Southern Pacific had just lobbied for the passage of the California Act. Not only did it require the 10% down, it also required that the board of directors of any railroad doing business in New Mexico must be from California. That should halt both the A. T. & S. F. and the D. & R. G. The men lobbied for the act to be amended or repealed. Because the act wasn't yet in effect, the former incorporation act would be in effect for a short time. The men found a territorial bill that would allow the railroad to enter New Mexico under the name of an existing corporation. They quickly incorporated as the New Mexico and Southern Pacific Railway Company. The A. T. & S. F. would be able to build and operate in New Mexico under that charter. While working in Santa Fe, Strong's representatives were also able to add a line to the legislation that exempted his railroad from territorial taxes for six years.

The board of directors back in Boston had only provided Strong $20,000; but Strong was a visionary. He instructed Chief Engineer, A. A. Robinson, up in Pueblo, to build toward New Mexico. Robinson said there was no way he could build across the state for $20,000. That wouldn't even cover costs for two miles of track over Raton Pass once he got there, but Strong wasn't deterred. He figured if he got his foot in the door, there'd be a way.

The Santa Fe crew laid an x-shaped frog track at La Junta early in 1878 and set their course toward New Mexico. The Rio Grande (D. & R. G.) had connected Colorado Springs and Pueblo in June 1872. The Panic of '73 slowed its progress; but the Rio Grande persevered and, by April 1876, laid rails to El Moro, within five miles of Trinidad, Colorado. The company planned to sell land and build its own town at El Moro. That made Trinidad folks madder than hops. They'd established farms, businesses, bank, church. The next couple years the D. & R. G. concentrated its effort and investment building across La Veta Pass toward Alamosa, Colorado.

In 1877 both the Santa Fe and Rio Grande surveyed a line into New Mexico. Santa Fe's President Nickerson was cautious, conservative; but William Strong persuaded him this was no time to conserve. Strong seized moments; this was a time for all or nothing. He knew Raton Pass was the gateway to Santa Fe and points beyond. Strong had already begun to think of rails to the Pacific and lines spidering across the western map. He envisioned development of ranches, farms, new communities, mines—gold, silver, turquoise, copper, and coal. A railroad would be able to transport passengers, freight, and the U. S. mail—an attractive hand of cards. On February 26, 1878, President Nickerson authorized an initial amount to grade surveys in the spring. Strong immediately instructed engineer A. A. Robinson to get to Raton Pass and hold it! The Santa Fe had been preparing for such an opportune hour. The Santa Fe and Rio Grande had broken into one another's telegraph codes and knew what the other was up to.

Santa Fe's A. A. Robinson and Ray Morley boarded a Rio Grande train at Pueblo. They hid their faces when they realized the Rio Grande's Chief Engineer J. A. McMurtie and J. R. DeRemer were on board. All four men got off at El Moro. The Rio Grande men went to a hotel. The Santa Fe men hired a buggy and rushed to Raton Pass, as Strong instructed.

Dick Wootton was getting ready for bed when Robinson and Morley arrived. They explained the situation. A messenger from Trinidad came to Dick's to warn the Santa Fe men that McMurtie and DeRemer would be there with a work crew by dawn. Some young men from Trinidad were still at Wootton's after a dance. Others arrived from Trinidad.

Prepared with shovels and lanterns, Robinson, Morley, the Trinidad crew, and Wootton began grading a Santa Fe line to establish the Santa Fe's right of prior construction. They were working when DeRemer, McMurtie, and their grading crew arrived before dawn. They weren't about to turn around. Wootton watched to see the argument didn't get out of hand and kept working with the Santa Fe men. The Rio Grande didn't have a leg to stand on. The Santa Fe clearly had support of the owner and the right of prior construction. They left without bloodshed.

The Santa Fe finished laying track from La Junta to Wootton, Colorado on November 1, 1878. Ordinarily, engineers wound around a steep mountain to ascend the grade gradually. On Raton Pass there was no space to wind around. It would take months to bore a tunnel; so they built a switchback to enable trains to cross the Pass. It was finished on December 1, 1878. On December 7th the first Santa Fe engine chugged over Raton Pass and into New Mexico. The ascent was so difficult that engines had a hard time pulling as much as thirty-three tons up the mountain. In the mid-to-late 1870's freight cars could carry a maximum of fifteen tons; so engines weren't pulling much more than themselves over the Pass.[253]

The Santa Fe ordered a custom built engine from the Baldwin Locomotive Works to work Raton Pass. At the time it was most powerful locomotive on earth. Because the engine was too heavy to cross many railroad trestles, Baldwin shipped the fifty-seven-ton engine in parts. As a token of appreciation, the Santa Fe named the engine, #2403, "Uncle Dick."

While the Santa Fe bored a 200' tunnel through the mountain in 1879, trains from the north brought supplies over the switchback to those working on the south end.

The Rio Grande and the Santa Fe met again in a struggle for right-of-way through the Royal Gorge, which led to Colorado mines. Stories of the struggle varied with the telling, then and now. Morley, Holbrook, and Kingman had done some rudimentary surveys in 1877. In 1879 the Santa Fe worked in the area under the charter "Canon and San Juan Railroad."

---

[253] The railroad facilitated transportation of New Mexico's copper, coal, potash, lumber, wool, and cattle. By 1900 as many as 60 trains traversed Raton Pass daily.

In the early morning hours Ray Morley rode from La Junta to Canon City, Colorado. He arrived at the Royal Gorge with more than one hundred men and began work. When D. & R. G. men arrived, they didn't turn back. There was no proprietor to throw in with either line as there had been on Raton Pass. The D. & R. G. men just went further down the canyon and started work. Each railroad constructed a fort and continued work. They called in troops and shed blood—two died—before the case went to court. Rather than continue lengthy expenditures of manpower, time, and money, the Santa Fe left the Gorge to the Rio Grande and concentrated effort on building to the Pacific. At first, the Santa Fe chose Guaymas, Mexico, for its Pacific port.

Ray Morley had done preliminary surveying around Tucson, Arizona. He recommended building to that point, then across the 32nd parallel to the Pacific, rather than across central Arizona. There were more mineral resources near Tucson. Morley thought there was more opportunity for population growth there than along a Grand Canyon route.

While fighting the D. & R. G., the A. T. & S. F. had continued to build toward Santa Fe. It arrived a mile from Las Vegas, New Mexico, at twelve noon on July 4, 1879.

Las Vegas was made a division headquarters with a round house to service engines.[254] On August 1, 1879, the Santa Fe purchased Montezuma Hot Springs north of Las Vegas on the banks of the Gallinas River. There they built and elaborately furnished a 300 room hotel. The building was planned and built to provide each room with several hours of sunlight daily.[255] Nine ponds in the nearby Gallinas Canyon annually provided 50,000 tons of ice for the ice market.[256]

From Las Vegas, the A. T. & S. F. continued toward Santa Fe. The work crew blasted the steep grade at Glorieta, New Mexico, in the summer of 1880. Some of the men had difficulty working at the high altitude and were taken to the hospital in Santa Fe. When A. T. & S. F. tracks reached Lamy, New Mexico—eighteen miles from Santa Fe, the rails turned south toward Albuquerque. Ray Morley didn't think Santa Fe's terrain was expedient for a mainline. Back in 1867 Palmer of the D. & R. G. had suggested it would be best to put a branch line into Santa Fe. The town hired a surveyor to see if there was a way around the decision, but he agreed with Morley and Palmer. After that, the community raised funds; so a branch line was constructed from Lamy to Santa Fe. People in Santa Fe were accustomed to mail orders from places like Chicago taking months to arrive. They appreciated the speed of rail service.

Enroute to Albuquerque, the Santa Fe serviced existing turquoise and coal mines. The railroad intended to build directly into Albuquerque; but, at $1,000 an acre, the needed land was too expensive. They purchased nearby land and built the line two miles from town. The

---

[254] The roundhouse included 19 service stalls in 1899 and 34 in 1917. By 1908, 30 freight and passenger trains (15 each direction) passed through Las Vegas daily. Freight trains averaged 1,700 cars of freight; passenger trains carried an average of 1,100 passengers.

[255] There were 200 guest rooms. The enterprise required 325 employees. Fred Harvey was in charge of the 500 seat dining room, where a 25 member band played during meals. The Santa Fe provided a two-story 42'x200' hot springs bath house and a mud house for guests. An average of 1,000 bathed in the springs daily. Every hour 30 carriages met guests arriving on the train from Las Vegas. The inn caught fire in the early 1880's, but was rebuilt.

[256] Ice, cut and stored in icehouses, was sold to the Santa Fe Railroad and other western lines. Before mechanical refrigeration, the ice was used in railroad dining cars and in hauling freight.

train arrived on April 15, 1880. Albuquerque business moved toward the rails.

Moving on from Albuquerque, the Santa Fe crew had trouble laying track near Isleta, New Mexico. The rails they laid during the day, Indians destroyed during the night. The crew made no progress until missionary Fr. Dourchee talked to the Indians. On a smaller scale, the railroad had had some similar trouble near Las Vegas, New Mexico.

In June 1881, Santa Fe tracks reached El Paso, Texas. In 1882 they connected line to Guaymas, Mexico. In August 1883 it crossed the Colorado River at Needles, California, and began laying rails across the hot California desert. Tracks arrived in Los Angeles late in 1885 and in San Diego in 1886.

In 1886 the company gained an outlet at Galveston, Texas, and extended its line into Denver. With William Barstow Strong at the helm, the company added thousands of miles of branch lines. In 1887 the Santa Fe expanded eastward from the Missouri River to Chicago and began service there in April 1888.

When the Santa Fe set its eyes on Raton Pass at the end of 1877, it had a 786 mile system, including spur lines and 65 miles of leased line. Twelve years later the Santa Fe was a transcontinental system, including the Great Lakes (Chicago), the Gulf of Mexico (Galveston), the Pacific (Guaymus, Mexico, and San Diego and Los Angeles, California), and the central Rockies (Denver). It had branches to communities, mines, and industries off the mainline. Chicago to Los Angeles was its mainline.

Bad crops in Kansas, the cost of expansion coupled with competition from other railroad lines,[257] changes in legislation, and the Panic of 1893 resulted in temporary financial trouble for the Santa Fe. William Strong, by then president of the line, raised $11,000,000 to meet the principal and heavy interest due; but when the board of directors broke out into a bitter quarrel, Strong and his supporters left the matter to the directors.

A. T. & S. F. stock plummeted. Stockholders lost about $60,000,000, and the railroad went into receivership. The Santa Fe reorganized under the direction of new president, Edward Payson Ripley, who took charge on January 1, 1896. Ripley turned the situation around and built up the railroad empire that men like Holliday, Morley, Robinson, and Strong began. In 1896 the A. T. & S. F. had 6,445 miles of track, 11,000 in 1920. In 1960 the Santa Fe operated 12,992 miles of rails, never scrimping on service or safety in the workplace—for workers and passengers and for the freight they hauled.

The Santa Fe fulfilled its goal to replace the Old Santa Fe Trail and helped develop the Southwest. It encouraged camaraderie among its employees, helped populate the Southwest, and provided awareness of Southwestern art, culture, and people.

In the 1880's and 1890's most Southwestern Indians lived on reservations. With the wild West tamer and more accessible, tourists traveled West. They sat on plush seats—the Santa Fe saw to comfort, even provided more leg room than most lines—and looked out the window at lands they'd heard of. Passenger cars were equipped with wood or coal stoves for heat and oil lamps or candles for light.

After World War II, more Americans purchased autos and provided their own

---

[257] Between 1885 and 1887 the Rock Island Railroad laid 1,300 miles of rail, and the Missouri Pacific built 1,071miles of rail in area serviced by the Santa Fe.

transportation. Air travel increased. The number of passenger trains on the Santa Fe mainline reduced to four trains each way daily. Odd numbered trains traveled West to Los Angeles; even numbered ones traveled East to Chicago. Though railroaders generally referred to them by number, the general public knew them better by name: "The Grand Canyon Line" (#23, #24) was the common man's train with a more affordable fare. The Super Chief (#19, #20) and El Capitan (#17, #18) were sleeper-coach trains. In summer The Chief was all coach; the El Cap was all sleeper. Numbers 7 and 8 were primarily mail trains with space for passengers in the rear car—used primarily by employees dead-heading home or to their next run.

Revenue from mail service helped subsidize passenger service. Until the early 1970's mail within the U. S. traveled primarily by rail. Air mail was available, but at an increased rate. After the U. S. began to shift mail from rail to air, Amtrak took over U. S. passenger service. In 1995 the Burlington Northern absorbed the A. T. & S. F. Railway.

Fred Harvey

Frederick Henry Harvey migrated to the United States from England when he was fifteen and found work in a New York café. In the 1850's he and a partner established a café in St. Louis; the business failed during the Civil War. After the War, He moved to Kansas and worked as a freight agent for the Burlington Railway.

Because his job required travel, Harvey ate at various places along the railroad line. When he began to have problems with indigestion, he realized the need for a food service system. Burlington officials were too busy to consider his food service proposition; so he took his ideas to the Santa Fe. Santa Fe officials thought Harvey's idea worthwhile and gave him the go-ahead.

In 1876 Fred Harvey opened his first eating house in Topeka, Kansas, while he was still working for Burlington. By 1882 his restaurant business was successful enough for him to quit his railroad job and begin following the Santa Fe line. He dotted it at intervals with Harvey restaurants and hotels. His establishments were clean, the food excellent, and the service great. "Harvey Girls" and Harvey waiters served customers. Harvey hired almost 5,000 Eastern and Midwestern girls to work in his restaurants and Harvey houses. When they hired on, girls signed a contract that they wouldn't marry for at least one year. They lived and worked under the strict supervision of matrons. Many of the girls did marry afterward and raised families in the West.

Western cuisine didn't always suit the taste of travelers, but they did enjoy Fred Harvey's hospitality and table. The Harvey system operated all Santa Fe Railroad dining cars. In addition, Harvey had lunch counters, lounges, hotels, restaurants, and newsstands along the Santa Fe line. Before trains included a dining car, menu orders were taken on the train and wired to the Harvey restaurant at the next depot stop. When the train arrived, meals were ready.

"Fred Harvey" became known throughout the world for fine service. Although the Santa Fe and Harvey companies were separate businesses, they were linked by work and reputation.

Raton Pass

At an altitude of 7863', Raton Pass is the low point in the mountain range between Colorado and New Mexico. Some call it the threshold to New Mexico. The natural pathway was traversed on foot, then with pack animals, followed by wagons, trains, and motor vehicles.

In 1870, after Spaniards heard that Frenchmen from the Mississippi area were coming to trade with Indians, Pedro Villasur led a party of Spaniards across Raton Pass to intercept any Frenchmen wandering toward New Mexico. Doubtless others crossed before Villasur, but he is the first on record. Indians, Spaniards, trappers, mountain men, traders, all knew of Raton Pass.

William Becknell crossed Raton Pass in 1821 when he entered New Mexico with his loaded pack mules. When he returned with wagons the next year, he chose to circumvent the Pass. Until Dick Wootton built a road over Raton Pass, most wagons from the States traveled the Cimarron Route of the Santa Fe Trail in order to bypass the mountain.

In 1846 Stephen Kearny led Missouri Volunteers over Raton Pass because there was more water available for a company than on the Cimarron Route. Colonel John T. Hughes reported, however, that in some areas wagons had to be tied with ropes and hoisted up a mountain ridge, eased over, and let down on the other side.

Lt. James W. Abert had to stop on the mountain because the wheel of a trader's wagon had rolled off the edge and caused the wagon to overturn. Its goods had rolled out and down the side of the mountain. Another driver moved his wagon out of the way and put a piece of wood under the wheels to hold them in place. The wagon, however, was filled with over 5,000 pounds of freight and rolled backwards down the hill. It crushed a few trees in its path until it hit a strong pine, which held the wagon in place.

Abert noticed grizzly bears on the Pass. Infantryman George Gibson noticed Raton Pass' cool mountain air, pure water, and good fishing. He caught a mess of trout to add to provisions.

By the time the Army of the West crossed Raton Pass with their wagons and animals, the men were so exhausted that Kearny allowed them to take a Sabbath rest—the first they'd had enroute. While they were there, as is often the case in the summer, a brief rain showered the mountain and left a brilliant rainbow above the peaks.

When Colonel Sterling Price led the 2nd Missouri Mounted Volunteers to New Mexico, he chose the Cimarron Cutoff. His company had a hard go of it for lack of water.

Matt Field, who crossed Raton Pass before Wootton built his toll road, described the Pass: The whole scene was a most admirable mingling of lovely with the wild and terrible. Splintered and rifted trees and tottering rocks above, hung beetling over the ravine while, like a very laughing child sporting unconsciously near some object of fear, the bright little stream danced gaily over the pebbles. Huge stones were lying around, from whose forms we could trace the gaps above from whence they had fallen. Dark and tangled thickets were near, where the berries hung sought for food by the grizzly bear.[258]

By 1854 the Mountain Branch of the Santa Fe Trail across Raton Pass was seldom used in comparison to the Cimarron Cutoff. It could be and was still crossed, but trees had to be removed from the path and repairs had to be made where mountain rainstorms had washed across and cut into the terrain. In 1854 Lieutenant Craig's party spent several days repairing the path enough to cross and be on their way.

When Dick Wootton traversed Raton Pass with wagons on his way to Denver in 1858, it took him almost a month to travel the 50 miles on either side of, up, and over the Pass.

The route crossed and re-crossed the steep banks of Raton Creek eighteen times. Snow often filled arroyos in winter. Men who knew the Pass carried #50 shovels to clear their way. Stages and wagons that crossed the Pass knew what it was to be stuck in the snow for days.

A portion of Dick Wootton's road across the Raton Mountains

---

[258] Sabin, *Kit Carson Days*, 226, 227.

Dick Wootton's Family

Except for Fidelis, Dick's adult children spoke fluent English and Spanish. Fidelis and some of her siblings also used sign language. Their home on Raton Pass is referred to as the house at the Pass, Wootton Ranch, and Raton Pass.

First Wife: Dolores LeFevre Wootton
Born: June 29, 1828, Taos, New Mexico
Parents: Manuel and Maria Teodora Lopez LeFevre
Married: March 6, 1848, Taos, New Mexico Territory
Children:
- Eliza Ann,
- Richens Lacy, Jr.,
- Frances Dolores,
- Lorett, possibly Loretta (b. c March 1853, Taos; d. between late 1860-1864),
- George (b. early 1854, Taos; moved with family to Raton Pass, 1865, d. before 1870, Raton Pass),
- Jose Manuel (b. April 29, 1855, Huerfano Village [Colorado]; d. at his grandparents' home, Taos, buried July 14, 1855, Our Lady of Guadalupe Parish Cemetery, Taos)

Died: May 6, 1855

Dick and Dolores married two months before her twentieth birthday. They lived first in Taos, then in Huerfano Village (Colorado), where Dolores died after the birth of Jose Manuel. She is buried at the base of the hill where Rumaldo Cordova was buried after El Pueblo Massacre.

Three of Dick and Dolores' children lived to adulthood:

Eliza Ann
Born: February 1, 1849, Fernandez de Taos, New Mexico; baptized February 24, 1849.
Married: William Ryland Walker (b. December 16, 1828, Richmond, Virginia; d. 6:55 p.m., March 30, 1892, Trinidad, Colorado) m. Monday, January 30, 1865.
Children:
- Frances Virginia "Jennie" (b .July 15, 1867; m. Dolan B. Smith, Albert M. Horn),
- Mary Eliza "Lizzie" (b. June 1869; m. __ Johnson),
- Olive Agnes "Ollie" (b. January 1874; m. __ VanKirk).

Died: January 28, 1914, Trinidad, Colorado; died after a second stroke

As Dick's oldest child, Eliza often took upon herself to help extra with her siblings or in the home when one of her mothers died. A caring spirit was part of her nature all of her life.

Like her father, Eliza had an acute awareness of people and events and recalled them vividly in later years. As a child, she met traders, trappers, and scouts when they visited her father. Some, like Carson, became famous, others became forgotten. Sometimes the men stayed in their home for days or weeks. That's the way folks did in the old West.

Eliza attended Mr. Mayberry's small school at Ft. Barclay during her father's freighting years. In Auraria, she attended Mr. Goldrick's Union School, the first school in Colorado. In her teens, she attended boarding school in Canon City, Colorado. But the day before her sixteenth birthday she married William Ryland Walker, twenty years her senior.

William came to the Southwest as a soldier with the 2nd U. S. Cavalry during the Mexican War. After the war, he served at Fort Union in the 2nd regiment of dragoons until 1853. After his discharge, he remained in New Mexico.

Jacob and Isabel Beard witnessed William and Eliza's marriage at the home of Alexander W. Robb in Huerfano County, Colorado Territory. Richard Skeratt officiated.

At first, William and Eliza lived with Dick and the family at Raton Pass. While Dick built the toll road, Eliza cared for her siblings in their make-do quarters. The Walkers moved into Trinidad, where they operated a hotel and stage station. In October 1868 Rev. Elial Jay Rice, a Methodist minister from Kansas, rented a room in their U. S. Hotel and preached his first sermon in Trinidad. That was the first of regular Protestant services in town.

In 1876-1877 William was president of the Trinidad school district. Eliza was operating a boarding house. She continued to take in boarders after William's death.

Richens Lacy "R. L." Jr.

Born: March 21 or 26, 1850, San Fernandez de Taos, New Mexico. (His sister Eliza said March 26. "Sketches and Portraitures" of Colorado's 9th General Assembly [1893] and R. L.'s obituary and tombstone date his birth March 21, 1851. But, he was baptized July 28, 1850 [Taos Baptismal records], and the 1850 NM Territorial Census lists him as 1/12.)

Appearance: Tall; broad shouldered like his father, but not broad-faced, finer featured than his father; dark hair, "inclined to curl"; blue-gray eyes.

Character: Daring, courageous, but described as a "Christian gentleman"; his manners and values combined those of his French/Spanish and Southern grandparents; seasoned frontiersman.

Married:
- Florence Walker (m. 1872, Trinidad; d. 1877, buried Catholic Cemetery, Trinidad)
  Children: Jerome D., Edward, Fannie. All died young.
- Lucy May Huntley (b.1861 to Dr. and Mrs. E. D. Huntley; m. 1879, Trinidad; d. 1932, Albuquerque, New Mexico) No children

Died: January 26, 1925, Albuquerque, New Mexico; buried: Fairview Cemetery, Albuquerque

1854: Moved with family from Taos to Huerfano Village.
1857-58: Attended Mr. Mayberry's school at Ft. Barclay.
Spring 1859: Went with his Uncle Joseph Wootton to Kentucky to be educated.
1866: Graduated from Lafayette College, Christian County, Kentucky; returned to Colorado. His speech bewrayed his Southern exposure; it was always, "Good mornin', suh."
1866-67: Led a twenty-one-wagon train from Trinidad to the new Ft. Lyon.

1867-69: Wagon boss on an ox-train for Beard & Walker, who freighted across the Plains.

1869: Clerked for Thatcher Brothers in Trinidad. Later in the year opened a general store.

1870: Moved across the state line into Colfax County, New Mexico. Ranched at the head of the Trinchera and had a mercantile business.

1872: Sold mercantile business and returned to Trinidad. Continued to ranch and opened a real estate business in partnership with E. Brigham in Trinidad.

1872: Married Florence "Flora" Walker. Birth and death of three children, 1873-77.

In 1870's: Las Animas County Assessor, Colorado.

1876-78: Undersheriff, Las Animas County, Colorado. Florence died 1877.

1878-80: Las Animas County Sheriff. Captured a band of horse thieves; arrested Clay Allison.

1879: Married Lucy May Huntley.

1879-1887: E. Brigham and R. L. added insurance to their real estate business. R. L. continued the business until 1900.

1881: Secretary and Vice-Grand of Odd Fellows in Trinidad.

1882: Chosen Treasurer of W.G. Rifenburg Hose Co. No 3.

1886: Built a lake and resort park near Trinidad, planted trees there, and, after that, yearly cut ice for market. Continued as a stockman.

1889-94: A lifelong Democrat, he represented Las Animas and Bent Counties in Colorado's 7th, 8th, 9th General Assemblies. (Elected 1889, 1891, and 1993.) Was a Democratic-Populist nominee for Speaker of Colorado's 9th General Assembly, but was defeated by one vote. As a representative, he was tenaciously accountable concerning expenditure of public money.

1900: Remained in the Trinidad area until all but his two youngest siblings were of age (Frank was fifteen and Jesse, thirteen). Moved to El Paso, Texas. Worked in real estate in El Paso and mined in Mexico.

May 16, 1903, El Paso: Mayor C. R. Morehead announced the appointment of R. L. Wootton as El Paso Chief of Police. The council's unanimous decision was made in an executive session the previous afternoon. R. L. served as Chief of Police, 1903-1905.

Spring 1905-1925: Moved to Albuquerque, New Mexico. There he was involved in insurance, real estate, and law enforcement. He was Bernalillo County undersheriff for four years under Rafael Garcia, and under Felipe Zamora 1923-25. R. L. and Lucy were members of the Methodist Episcopal Church.

January 20, 1925: Off duty, R. L. went to mail a job telegram. Boarding a streetcar, he lost his footing, slipped, and fell off. The streetcar ran over him and fractured his skull. He died six days later at St. Joseph's Hospital, Albuquerque. Lucy survived him.

Frances Dolores

<u>Born</u>: April 14, 1852, Fernando de Taos, New Mexico; baptized May 30, 1852, Taos.

<u>Married</u>: Thomas H. "Brigham" Young, about 16 years her senior (b. c1835/1836, Missouri), August 17, 1865; Rev. J. D. Patterson officiated.

<u>Children</u>:
- Albert (1866),

- Minerva (1868),
- Henry (c 1870/71),
- George (c 1872/73),
- William R. (c 1874/75),
- R. L. "Dick" (c 1876/77),
- John (c 1878/79),
- L. (Lottie or Lily c 1882/83),
- Another died young.

Died: January 2, 1904, Trinidad, Colorado (another article says February 2, 1904)

Dolores was three when her mother died. Her dad kept the children with him at first and then took them to their maternal grandparents in Taos until he remarried.

When Dolores was six and a half, Uncle Dick decided to move the family back to Kentucky. They ended up settling in Auraria, where she attended Mr. Goldrick's Union School. She was almost eight when her new mother died. The family moved to the Pueblo area. Her dad remarried when she was eleven and a half, but a year later that mother died.

Dolores attended Mrs. Leslie's school on the Huerfano River until her marriage to Thomas "Brigham" Young at Gray's Ranch in Huerfano County, Colorado Territory.

They first lived at Iron Springs stage station (near Thatcher, between Bent's Old Fort and Trinidad), where Thomas was stationmaster. Indians had attacked shortly before he became stationmaster. At times he was a stage stationmaster. At times he ranched, raising cattle and horses in Las Animas County, Colorado.

Dolores lived at 424 University Street in Trinidad, Colorado, when she died at age 51. Rev. Buhrman officiated at her funeral in the Methodist Church South. Burial was in Trinidad's Masonic Cemetery, with graveside services by the Fraternal Union, of which she was a member. Her brother, R. L. Jr., wired from El Paso that he was unable to attend.

Second Wife: Mary Ann Manning Wootton

Mary Ann was a widow traveling with a Missouri emigrant train that stopped to winter at Bent's Fort in the winter of 1855-56. Dick met Mary Ann at the fort, where they married. Two of their three children survived to adulthood. Frank (b. March 25, 1860, Auraria, Colorado) died at the Wootton house on Raton Pass about 1873.

Mary Ann died in Auraria (Denver, Colorado) the day her third son, Frank, was born.

Joseph E.

Born: December 1856, Ft. Barclay, New Mexico; named for his father's youngest brother

Married:
- Alice Phillips, February 2, 1878, Holy Trinity Church, Trinidad, Colorado. (Witnesses: Federico Lujan and Maria A. Gillet) They had no children. Divorced.
- Nellie
  Children of Joseph and Nellie:
    - Eva E. (b. August 1885, Idaho),

- Cora C. (b. August 1889, Kansas),
- Freddie E. (b. January 1895, Kansas),
- Lena May (b. January 1898 Kansas; m. Settimo Trapani),
- James C.

Died: 1947, Kansas; buried: Mt. Muncie Cemetery, Lansing, Leavenworth, Kansas

When Trinidad tongues didn't approve of Joseph's divorce of Alice and marriage to Nellie, he and Nellie left the area. At one time Joseph was a farmer. They went to Idaho. but later settled near Emporia, Kansas. They lived in Chicago for a time. In 1940 Nellie and Joseph lived with their daughter May, her husband, and children in Leavenworth, Kansas.

William Michael/Michael William, "Bill," (as a child sometimes called Willie)

Born: 1858, Ft. Barclay, New Mexico
Married: Mary Elizabeth McDougall (b. September 1862; parents: Lloyd and Nancy Lamorie McDougal), October 10, 1879, Trinidad, Colorado Territory
Children:
- Fanny F. (b. July 31, 1880; m. Walter Saxon),
- Lillie Mae (b. May 25, 1882; m. __ Jones),
- William R. (b. June 29, 1884; m. Lois O. Abston),
- James (b. April 1888; m. Bessie Cunningham),
- Arthur Jay (b. January 6, 1891; m. Susan Clementine Baer),
- Alfred Adolph (b. December 24, 1894; m. Stella Baer),
- Oliver (b. August 9, 1898; m. Violet Donmiller).

Died: May 14, 1899, Hastings, Colorado

Bill was a baby when his family moved to Cherry Creek (Colorado) His mother died when he was not yet two. He was six when he and his family moved to Raton Pass. Bill lived in southern Colorado and northern New Mexico the remainder of his life.

On October 10, 1879, he married Mary Elizabeth McDougal of Kansas. Their witnesses were Jesus Maria Lujan (brother of Mary Pauline Wootton) and Maria del Reyes Salazar (married Jesus Maria Lujan).

At the time of his death, Bill was a weigh boss at the Hastings mine, Victor Cole and Coke Co.'s principal camp. The day he died, Bill had been drinking and, according to one report, "creating a disturbance." It was common for men at that time and place to wear a revolver. Camp constable Joe Johnson ordered Bill to hand over his revolver. As Bill reached to hand it over, Johnson shot him in the brain. Bill died almost instantly. Johnson said Bill was drawing on him, claimed self-defense, and was acquitted. But Johnson killed again, killed Postmaster Johnny Fox. The community was ready to lynch him, but they tried and convicted him. Johnson was executed at Canon City, Colorado.

At the time of Bill's death, his seven children ranged in age from nine months to almost nineteen years. His son William went to work in the mine to help support the family. Fannie and Lillie Mae were already married.

Third Wife: Fannie B. Brown Wootton

Married: October 5, 1863, Doyle's Ranch, Colorado Territory
Died: October 17, 1864, as a result of childbirth, one year and twelve days after marriage; buried: Doyle Cemetery, Doyle's Ranch.

Frances "Fannie" Virginia
Born: October 17, 1864; named for her mother and paternal grandmother
Married:
- Owen DeKalb Williams, February 6, 1882; divorced
  Children: Walter Charles Williams (b. October 5, 1885) and perhaps another son
- A. G. Fitzgerald, March 10, 1891, Aspen, Colorado; divorced
- Phillip Franklin Irving, 1895
  Child one child in the 1900 census, none recorded in 1910

Died: February 17, 1937, Aspen, Colorado

When Fannie was born, her oldest brother was in Kentucky. Her sister Eliza was at boarding school. Her other siblings were home. Her Grandpa Wootton died the year before her birth, her Uncle Samuel in August and her Grandma Wootton in September, the year of her birth. Her father's farm crops had failed. It's reported that, at some point, the government confiscated his property because he was a Southern sympathizer.

For whatever reason, her father allowed Dr. Walter Burt and his wife to care for her. Whether Dick originally intended it to be short-term or not, Fannie lived with the Burts, as their only child. The Burts moved from the Pueblo area and, by 1880, lived in Granite, Colorado. Fannie used her Wootton name when she married Mrs. Burt's brother Owen D. Williams. She divorced Williams, married and divorced A. G. Fitzgerald, then married Canadian born Phillip Irving. Irving was a sheriff in the early years of their marriage. They lived in Aspen in 1910.

Fourth Wife: Mary Pauline Lujan Wootton

Born: January 25, 1855, Mora, New Mexico, to Jose Guadalupe and Maria de la Luz Dillette Lujan
Appearance: Dark hair, blue eyes
Character: An independent spirit; devoted to family and religion; enjoyed social groups
Married: December 18, 1871, Wootton Ranch, Wootton, Colorado
Children:
- Mary Fidelis
- Ida Dillon
- Lucy Anne
- John Peter (Johnie) (b. December 31, 1875; d. September 4, 1878)
- John Peter
- Mary (b. Monday, February 28, 1881; d. Friday, January 1887)
- Gerardus (b. Saturday, May 20, 1882; d. Saturday, September 9, 1882; funeral the next

afternoon at the Catholic Church, Trinidad.)
- Mary Fannie (b. Tuesday, September 4, 1883; d. Monday, Aug 11, 1884. Mary Fannie and at least one other sibling died of cholera.)
- Frank Christopher
- Jesse Joseph

Died: March 2, 1935, following a stroke, Albuquerque, New Mexico; buried next to Uncle Dick (Catholic Cemetery, Trinidad, Colorado)

Mary Pauline Lujan married Dick Wootton a week before Christmas in 1871; she would be seventeen in January. Her mother was a first cousin of Dick's first wife, Dolores; Mary Pauline had known the family all her life.

The family story is that her father left for California when she was very young and returned on July 4th years later. Like many area mothers, her mother, Luz, kept the home fires burning during her husband's absence.

Dick and Mary Pauline had ten children; four died in infancy or childhood.

Mary Pauline survived Dick by more than forty years. She was active in Trinidad society and the Catholic church; she was a staunch Catholic. After Dick's death, she enjoyed traveling by train to see family in New Mexico, her son Jesse in California, and her sister Louise in Oklahoma.

After she left Trinidad, she lived for a short time with her daughter Ida in Albuquerque. After a stroke and illness of about three months, Mary Pauline died at Ida's home. Five of her ten children survived her: "Dellie" and Ida of Albuquerque; sons John of Las Vegas, New Mexico, Frank of Coalmont, Colorado, and Jesse of Santa Barbara, California. Her funeral was at the Catholic Church in Trinidad. Pallbearers: F. E. Dunlavy; cousin by marriage Teodoro Abeyta; nephew Will G. Lujan; Frank E. Tafoya; Henry Abbott; John J. Marty.

Mary Fidelis "Dellie"

Born: Friday, September 20, 1872, Wootton, Colorado
Character: Helpful, caring; but had an independent streak
Died: March 7, 1957, Las Vegas, New Mexico, had dropsy a short time before her death; buried: Mt. Calvary Cemetery, Las Vegas, New Mexico

Her family called her both Dellie and Fidelis. At the age of three she contracted scarlet fever, which deafened her for life and left some paralysis on her right side. Fidelis attended Colorado School for the Deaf and Blind in Colorado Springs, 1880-1892.

After finishing school, Dellie traveled and visited family. At times she lived with her mother, at other times with her sister Ida.

As the siblings aged, Frank said to John, "What are we going to do about Dellie?"

"Oh, she'll outlive us all," he replied.

She did. She lived with her niece Marguerite Wootton Archuleta and family when she died in Las Vegas, New Mexico. She'd outlived all Uncle Dick's children.

Ida Dillon

Born: Monday February 9, 1874

Married: Felix Baca (b. Trinidad, Colorado, June 7, 1868, to Felipe and Dolores Baca), February 4, 1894, Trinidad, Colorado

Children:
- Lucy Ligouri (b. November 18, 1894; m. George B. Scott; d. October 6, 1962, Albuquerque, New Mexico)
- Felipe Arturo (b. March 21, 1896; d. July 10, 1896)
- Stella Marie (b. September 4, 1901; d. May 14, 1903)
- William Bertram (Bert) (b. October 4, 1904; d. November 1964, Ft. Lyon, Colorado)

Nickname: Her grandchildren called her "Mammy."

Died: January 8, 1950; buried: Sunset Memorial Park, Albuquerque, New Mexico

As a teen, Ida went to Ursuline College in Tiffin, Ohio. For the Easter program in 1893, she played a piano trio with Lillie Kaup and Ella Watts and took part in the reenactment of the story of Christ's crucifixion and resurrection. Ida graduated on June 19, 1893, and returned home to Trinidad as an artist, teacher, and pianist.

On February 4, 1894, Ida married Felix Baca, son of one of Trinidad's founders. Her maternal Uncle Jesus Maria Lujan, a well-known chef, made the wedding cake as his gift to the couple.

Before their first anniversary, Felix had surgery in Chicago (October 1894) and remained there seven weeks to recuperate before he returned to Trinidad.

Felix had graduated from Notre Dame in 1889 and earned his law degree at NWU in Evanston, Illinois. He was a practicing attorney in Trinidad.

About 1902 or '03 Felix opened a law office in Albuquerque, New Mexico. When their daughter Stella died, the family lived at 1032 E. 1st Street.

Their son Bertram won first prize among 96 contestants in the territorial baby fair show in September 1906. His prize was a decorated brass bed.

In 1920 New Mexico Governor O. A. Larrazolo appointed Felix as Judge of New Mexico's 7th Judicial District. Felix was a lifelong Republican.

After her sister Lucy's death in 1920, Ida helped raise Lucy's boys, Bobbie and Sandy.

In March 1925 Felix traveled to Pueblo, Colorado, for surgery. The surgery seemed a success; but, on April 1st, Felix died. Ida, Lucy, Bertram, two grandchildren and three siblings survived him. Both children were married.

After Felix's death, Ida was Bernalillo County (New Mexico) Clerk from 1927-30. In 1931 she was Deputy County Clerk. She was an unsuccessful candidate for Secretary of State. She helped organize scholarships for deserving girls to the University of New Mexico.

Ida died in Albuquerque, New Mexico, following a stroke in 1950.

Lucy Anne

Born: Wednesday, July 11, 1877, Wootton, Colorado

Married: Alexander "Alec" Patterson Meiklejohn, 8 p.m. October 21, 1907

Children:
- Robert "Bobby" Hutton (b. August 7, 1908)
- Alexander "Sandy" Patterson, Jr. (b. August 21, 1913)

Died: Died of peritonitis; 1 a.m., May 13, 1920, at home, Mora, New Mexico

Lucy attended school in Trinidad before joining her sister Ida at Ursuline College in Tiffin, Ohio. After her father died, Lucy stayed home with her mother and worked at a dry goods store until marriage to her longtime beau, Alec Meiklejohn.

With Father Brunner officiating, Lucy and Alec were married in the drawing room of her mother's home on Colorado Avenue in Trinidad, Colorado. Lucy wore a white Paris muslin gown and carried white roses. A wedding supper followed the ceremony, and gifts were opened. The next day Alec and Lucy boarded the train for Las Vegas, New Mexico, where he worked for the Santa Fe Railroad.

They moved to Mora, New Mexico, where Lucy died at age 42. Her brother John and family were living in nearby Cleveland, New Mexico.

John Peter

Born: December 29, 1878, Wootton home, Wootton, Colorado; named for his late brother Johnie

Physical Appearance: Blue eyes, brown hair;

Married:
- Mary Violet Rankin of Denver, divorced by 1910
- Elizabeth "Bessie" Fuss (b. December 5, 1892, Cleveland, New Mexico; daughter of Joseph J. and Margaret Ann "Maggie" Murphy Allen Fuss; d. June 30, 1936, Albuquerque, New Mexico, died of peritonitis following surgery for benign uterine tumors; buried: Mt. Calvary Cemetery, Las Vegas, New Mexico), m. July 17, 1913, Cleveland, New Mexico

Children:
- Dorothy Marguerite (b. June 7, 1914; m. Fidel Archuleta)
- John Peter (b. August 3, 1916; m. Eileen Wilson)
- Mary Pauline (b. November 13, 1918—prematurely during the 1918 flu epidemic. She was so small she was snuggled into a shoebox by the stove to keep warm enough to survive. She lived longest of John's children; m. Clarence Chandler),
- Robert Milton (b. December 6, 1920; the first of John's children to die)
- William Leslie (b. February 6, 1923; m. Stella Fram)
- Frances Loraine (b. December 11, 1925; m. Fred Niehans)
- Evelyn Louise (b. October 9, 1929; died last of her siblings; m. Joseph Harris)
- Richens Lacy (b. October 23, 1932; m. Evelyn Bailey)
- Joseph Gerald (b. February 15, 1936, Uncle Dick's youngest grandchild; m. Glenda Scott)

Died: August 7, 1953, A. T. & S. F Hospital (Memorial Hospital), Albuquerque (John's home at the time: 315 Railroad, Las Vegas, New Mexico); buried: Mt. Calvary Cemetery, Las Vegas, New Mexico.

John was born the month the first Santa Fe Railroad engine steamed across Raton Pass. He was a people person. He loved to have his dad with him, even if his dad was just sitting in a chair. Uncle Dick was strict with his children, but John told his children it didn't hurt when his dad spanked him because of his (Uncle Dick's) missing fingers.

John, with the help of his younger brother Frank, was instrumental in burning down the Wootton house at the Pass. The two brothers were playing with fire in an outbuilding.

John graduated from Tillotson Academy in Trinidad. He enjoyed drama, music, community, family, sports, correspondence, journaling, photography—both photographing and developing, woodworking, fishing and camping, horticulture, pies, and politics. His sister Ida was Republican; John was Democrat.

During his lifetime, John worked in mercantile businesses, ranched, served as undersheriff, and worked for the Santa Fe Railroad, once in his early years as a fireman and for the last twenty-seven years of his life as a Special Officer/Agent.

He was handy and meticulous, and expected the same of his children. Like his father, he expected his children to be responsible. They learned, but they also learned his love of life. Even though his wife died when the nine children were young—ages four months to twenty-two years, he expected them to grow up with and retain strong family ties.

John had diabetes and high blood pressure several years. In 1953, while in Raton, New Mexico, he had an aneurism or stroke. His sixteen-year-old son, Joe, drove him to Las Vegas. His daughter Pauline and son-in-law Clarence drove him on to the A. T. & S. F. Hospital in Albuquerque. He lived a short time; but doctors were unable to save him. He was 74.

Mary

Born: Monday, February 28, 1881, Wootton, Colorado

Died: Friday, January 28, 1887, 4 a.m.; funeral Catholic Church, Trinidad, 2 p.m. January 29.

When Mary was born she already had eleven living nieces and nephews.

Fair-skinned, round-faced, blue-eyed Mary wore her light brown hair short and curly. She was just a little more than two years younger than her brother John, who seemed to have no problem thinking of things to do.

Mary, with the family, welcomed baby brother Gerardus and sister Fannie. They died at ages four months and eleven months, respectively. Deaths during childbirth and in infancy were common. It was good Mary and John had one another to play with. Baby Frank was born when she was 4 ½. Another baby—the last—was on the way when she became ill. Mary died one month to the day short of her sixth birthday. John was eight.

Frank Christopher

Born: Monday, Aug 10, 1885, Wootton, Colorado

Married: Willa May Tynes, July 10, 1904, Trinidad, Colorado

Children:
- Richens Lacy (b. May 9, 1905; m. Charlotte Fredricka Deckard)
- Frank Christopher, Jr. (b. May 11, 1906; m. Olive Johnson)
- Helen Jenette (b. August 14, 1908; m. John Hamilton)
- Dorothy May (b. August 21, 1914, m. Charles O'Wells)

Died: January 12, 1957, Denver (lived at 350 S. Lipan, Denver, Colorado, at the time of his death); buried: Crown Hill Cemetery, Denver

The family moved to Trinidad before Frank started school. He was seven when Dick died.

Frank married Willa May Tynes at his mother's Trinidad home. May wore white silk and carried a bouquet of roses into the parlor decorated with fern and carnations. Dinner was served to guests following the ceremony.

They made their first home with his mother at 346 Colorado Avenue, Trinidad. He worked for White House Mercantile Company. He later became a miner, mining mechanic, and electrician.

Frank, May, and their family lived at Tabasco, Colorado, when the 1,200 miners' strike broke out at Hastings and Tabasco in October 1913. During the four hour bombardment, strikers from Berwind Canyon shot and killed Hastings guard Angus Alexander. Stray bullets fired and struck Frank and May's home five or six times while May was fixing breakfast. The shots wounded two of their children. Frank and May were called to testify in February 1914.

The family moved to the Denver area about 1932 and remained there. In 1954 Frank and May celebrated their 50th wedding anniversary at the Methodist Church in Trinidad.

Jesse Joseph

Born: Saturday, March 19, 1887, Trinidad, Colorado
Married:
- Ethel Lucille Owen, June 18, 1904, Raton, New Mexico; divorced. (She married Walter Hunter, September 5, 1919.)
  Children: (Leroy and Chrystella took their stepfather's surname.)
  - Jesse Owen (b. May 1, 1905; m. Lorraine H. Kittler; Margaret Todd)
  - Leroy Lawrence (b. January 4, 1908; Minnie Fetterhoff Thurston)
  - Chrystella Pauline (b. December 31, 1910; m. Joe Bacon)
- Jennie Catharine Cavaleto, August 27, 1921, Ventura, California
  Child: Marjorie (b. April 8, 1922; m. Alfred N. Smith; Bartley Sanders Durant)

Died: July 19, 1945, Colorado Springs, Colorado; died of tuberculosis; buried: Santa Barbara, California

Jesse, the youngest of Uncle Dick's twenty children, was six when his father died. He was seventeen when he went across the state line and married Ethel Owen in New Mexico.

The young couple settled in Trinidad, where Jesse worked for the Trinidad *Chronicle News*. Sometimes they lived with his mother; their children were born in her home. When Ethel had a period of poor health after they moved from the area, she sent their daughter, Chrystella, to live with Mrs. Wootton.

Jesse was a linotype operator for the *Albuquerque Morning Journal* and the *Albuquerque Citizen*, as he had been for the *Chronicle News*.

After Ethel and Jesse divorced, he served in the Army during World War I from 1917-1919. After the war he had a printing business in Santa Barbara, California, where he met and married Jennie Cavaleto. They lived there in the 1920's and '30's.

Jesse developed tuberculosis as a result of his World War I service. As the disease progressed, he moved to the Union Printers' Home in Colorado Springs, Colorado, where he died, age 58.

Simple List of Uncle Dick's Ancestors

F. = Father
M. = Mother

Number 1 is the child of number 2; 2 is the child of 3; 3 is the child of 4, etc.

1. Richens Lacy "Uncle Dick" Wootton
 2.F. David Christopher Wootton (b. 1789 VA)
  3.F. John Wootton (b. VA)
   4.F. Samuel Wootton (b. 1725 Glasgow Scotland)
   4.M. Sarah Powell (b. c 1730)
  3.M. Mary Christopher (b. c 1766)
   4.F. David Christopher (b. 1730 VA)
    5.F. Nicolas Christopher (b. c 1680)
    5.M. Anna/Annie Bowman
   4.M. Elizabeth Grigg (b. 1726 VA)
    5.F. James Grigg (b. 1693 VA)
     6.F. William Grigg (b. c 1666 VA)
      7.F. William Grigg (b. 1693 England)
      7.M. Elizabeth or Frances Burwell
     6.M. Susannah Lockett (b. 1671 VA)
      7.F. Thomas Lockett (b. 1645 VA)
      7.M. Margaret Osborne (b. 1649 VA)
       8.F. Thomas Osborne (b. 1615 England)
       8.M. Martha Jones
    5.M. Frances
 2.F. Frances "Fannie" Virginia Brame (b. 1795 VA)
  3.F. Richens Brame (b. 1769)
   4.F. John Brame (b. 1746 VA)
    5.F. Richens/Richins Brame (b. 1722 VA)
     6.F. Richens/Richins Brame/Brim (b. 1689 VA)
      7.F. John Brame/Brim (b. 1644 England)
       8.F. Nichi (Nicholas) Brim/Breame (b. 1602 England)
        9.F. David/Davy Bryn/Brend/Brim (b. 1571 England)
         10.F. John Brend (d. 1580 England)
          11.F. John Bren (b. c 1516 England)
          11.M. Johan Aldous (b. c.1520 England)
           12.F. Robert Aldous
         10.M. Mary Monfylde

      9.M. Ames King
     8.M. Anne Bogin (b. 1606 England)
    7.M. Mary Dabney (b. 1656 Ireland)
   6.M. Hannah Cheedle (b. 1694 VA)
  5.M. Susannah Chiles (b. 1724 VA)
   6.F. Walter Chiles (b. 1699 VA)
    7.F. Captain Henry Chiles (b. 1671 VA)
     8.F. Walter Chiles II (b. 1631 England)
      9. F. Walter Chiles (b. 1608 England)
      9. M Elizabeth (d. 1672 VA)
     8. M. Susannah Brooke/Brooks (b. c 1634-England)
   6.M. Mary Falkner
 4.M. Mary Norment (VA)
  5.F. William Norment (b. 1737 VA; his father: J. or T. b.Scotland)
  5.M. Mary Richardson Chandler (b. 1739 VA)
3.M. Catherine (?Lacy) (b. 1773 VA)

Raton Pass House in Later Years

Colonel James A. Owenby had been one of the A. T. &S. F. Raton Pass survey crew. He wasn't a military man, but a mining promoter. He became an organizer and promoter of the Wootton Land and Fuel Company with coal mining interests near Wootton, Colorado. Owenby operated the company from 1906-1915. In 1906 the company acquired the Wootton ranch and other nearby Las Animas County, Colorado, properties.

With help from Eliza Wootton Walker, Owenby built a replica of Uncle Dick's Raton Pass home around the original walls. It became Owenby's personal home, but there were private suites for the three primary investors:

1) John Pierpont Morgan, an American financier in New York (helped organize the American Steel Corporation; helped finance A.T. & T., International Harvester, and General Electric)
2) Ogden M. Mills, of New York, was Morgan's friend and financial advisor.
3) Ben P. Cheney, of Boston, was the son of an early founder of the Santa Fe Railroad.

Company mines began operation in 1909 and closed in 1913 when many southern Colorado mines temporarily shut down for a miners' strike. In 1923 title was transferred to the Rocky Mountain Coal & Iron Co. Colorado Fuel & Iron acquired the title in 1932 and changed the name to Colorado Fuel & Iron Steel Corporation.

After Colonel Owenby moved, Albert Berg and his family became caretakers, followed by Albert's son Don Berg and his wife, Katherine, and family.

Over the decades heavy traffic on the nearby interstate took its toll on the foundation and old adobe walls. The replica house was demolished.

ALBUM

Uncle Dick at Home, Raton Pass

Mary Pauline Lujan Wootton
(about the time of her marriage to Richens Lacy "Uncle Dick" Wootton)

Richens Lacy Wootton
In his trapper garb

Mary Pauline Lujan Wootton

Wootton's Original Raton Pass Home, built 1865

Above: Dick Wootton's first home on Raton Pass
Below: His last Raton Pass home

Dick Wootton's Home, Raton Pass

Wootton Ranch, Raton Pass
From a stereo view card

Richens Lacy "Uncle Dick" Wootton
From a small tintype picture

Mary Pauline Lujan Wootton
Widow of Uncle Dick Wootton

"Uncle Dick" Wootton with granddaughter Minerva "Minnie" Young
On the porch of Dick's Raton Pass Home

("Cuthand" can be seen on his left hand.)

Eliza Ann Wootton Walker
Uncle Dick's firstborn

Photo courtesy of Eliza's great-great-granddaughter Glenna McLaughlin Lawrence

Hon. Richens Lacy Wootton, Jr.

Above: Richens Lacy "Uncle Dick" Wootton
Below: Mary Pauline Wootton and her mother, Maria de la Luz Dillette Lujan

Top left: Minerva Young with her brother and mother, Frances Dolores Wootton Young
Top right: Frances' funeral card, January 7, 1904

Bottom: R. L. Wootton, Jr., Chief of Police (El Paso); Mary Pauline and Fidelis Wootton

Richens Lacy Wootten
Chief of Police, El Paso, Texas

Lucy, John, and Mary Wootton, children of Uncle Dick and Mary Pauline Wootton

Left to right: Back: John P. Wootton, (seated) Fidelis "Dellie" Wootton, Frank Wootton. Standing in front: Jesse Wootton

Ida Dillon Wootton   John Peter Wootton, Sr.
Ida's photo courtesy of her great-granddaughter Margaret Wilson

Frank and Jesse Wootton

(Four of Uncle Dick and Mary Pauline Wootton's children in birth order)

Mrs. Felix (Ida Wootton) Baca

Alexander "Alec" Meiklejohn and his bride Lucy Wootton Meiklejohn

In front of her mother's home, Trinidad, Colorado

Daughters of Uncle Dick and Mary Pauline Wootton

Left: Ida Wootton Baca
Right: Lucy Wootton Meiklejohn with her son Robert "Bobby"

Elizabeth "Bessie" Fuss Wootton, wife of John Peter Wootton, Sr.

Left to right: Mary Pauline Wootton, granddaughter Lucy Baca, son-in-law Alec Meiklejohn, daughter Fidelis Wootton, daughter-in-law Bessie Fuss Wootton

May Tynes Wootton, wife of Frank C. Wootton

Above: Ida (Wootton) and Felix Baca and daughters baby Stella and Lucy

Below: Felix Baca and son Bertram "Bert"

Above: May Tynes Wootton with sons Frank, Jr., and Richens at their mining camp home

Below: Under-sheriff John Wootton, Sr., (left), Mora, New Mexico

Left:
John Peter Wootton, Sr.
and granddaughter Janelle Wootton

Below:
John Peter Wootton, Sr., c late 1940's

Uncle Dick Wootton's mother, Frances "Fannie" Virginia Brame Wootton

David and Fannie Wootton's Faith

David and Fannie Brame Wootton were members of the Presbyterian Church at the time of their deaths in 1863 and 1864. Fannie's tombstone, recorded in a letter from descendant Bill Dorris III:

> Frances daug. Of C. & R. Brame, born in Mecklenburg Co. VA June 14, 1795 married D. C. Wooton [sic] 2/2/1815 moved to Christian Co. KY with her husband and children in 1830-She was early impressed with the importance of laying up treasures in Heaven. Sought and obtained religion and joined the Presbyterian Church in which she lived a constant membership until her death Sept. 15, 1864

The basic premise of their Scottish Presbyterian faith :

> There is one God, " in three different but equal persons: Father, Son, and Holy Spirit. …the Bible is the Word of God…there is no better guide on earth as to what we should believe and how we should live…everyone is born a sinner, and as such is subject to God's wrath and the punishment of death, which means eternal separation from God in Hell. …Jesus Christ, the only Son of God, alone paid the penalty for sin and as such is the only Redeemer of men. Having risen from the grave Jesus Christ now resides in Heaven from where he rules the nations until the day of His glorious return, a day which will usher in His judgement [sic]…Repentance of sin and turning to faith to accept Jesus Christ as Saviour is the only way of salvation from the wrath of God and His ultimate eternal punishment."[259]

Bible verses pertaining to repentance and salvation: Romans 3:10;3:23; 6:23; 5:8; John 3:16; 3:36; Ephesians 2:8-10; Romans 10:9, 10, 13; I Corinthians 2:9.

---

[259] "Our Beliefs," Reformed Presbyterian Church of Scotland. 2017.

David Christopher Wootton, Jr. (Uncle Dick Wootton's brother) with Nannie Wootton Ledford (daughter—on left), Nellie Ledford Dorris (granddaughter), W. R. Dorris (great-grandson)

Photo courtesy of David Christopher's great-great-grandson William "Bill" Dorris

Alexander James Wootton, brother of Richens Lacy Uncle Dick Wootton

Photo courtesy of his great-grandson Robert Wootton

Top (on left): Mary Pauline Wootton's brother Jesus Maria Lujan
Bottom: (left) Deputy Sheriff Teodoro Abeyta, husband of Amelia McBride (Mrs. Wootton's cousin); (right) Wootton family friend Dr. Michael Beshoar, Trinidad, Colorado

Mrs. Frank (Louise) Sivyer and her children
(Louise—sister of Mary Pauline Lujan Wootton)

Mrs. George C. (Piedad) McBride and daughters.
Left to right: Amelia, Eliza, Piedad, and Jennie

(Piedad—Mary Pauline Wootton's maternal aunt)

Mr. and Mrs. (Eliza McBride) Rocco Motto

Rocco was a civic-minded Trinidad, Colorado, storekeeper.

Above: Engine 2403, the "Uncle Dick," photographed in Albuquerque, New Mexico, 1916

Below: Mrs. Wootton's last home in Trinidad, Colorado

Right front: Linotype operator Jesse J. Wootton

Fidelis Wootton second to left of man with letters on shirt
First Reunion Deaf Department Colo School for the D. & B. 1874-1904

Wootton Family
Mora County, NM
c 1909

Left to right:

Back: Lucy Baca, Mary Pauline and Fidelis Wootton
Middle: Bert Baca, Luz Diflette Lujan, Bobby and Lucy (Wootton) Meiklejohn
Front: Jesse Jr. and John P. Wootton, Sr., Ida (Wootton) Baca

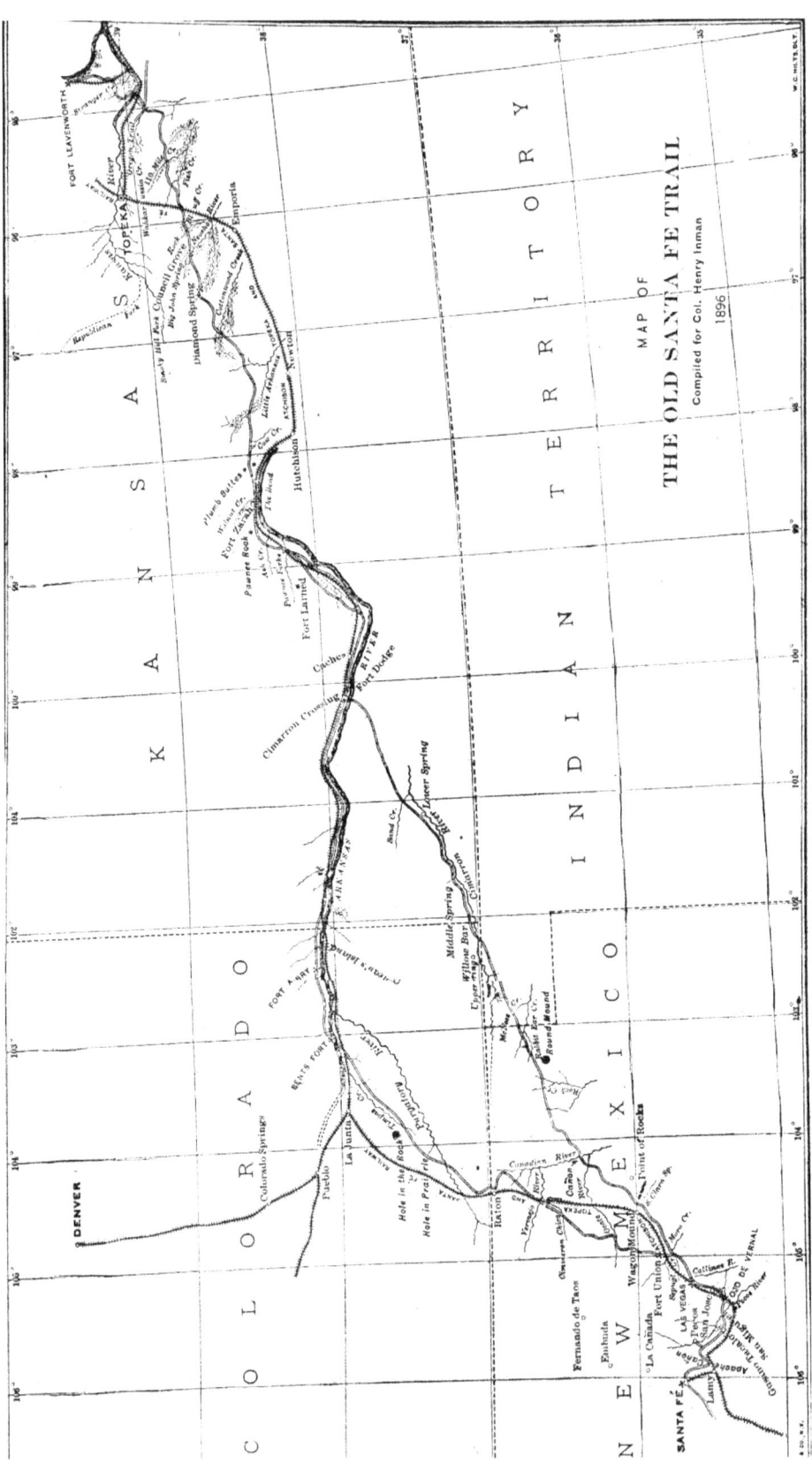

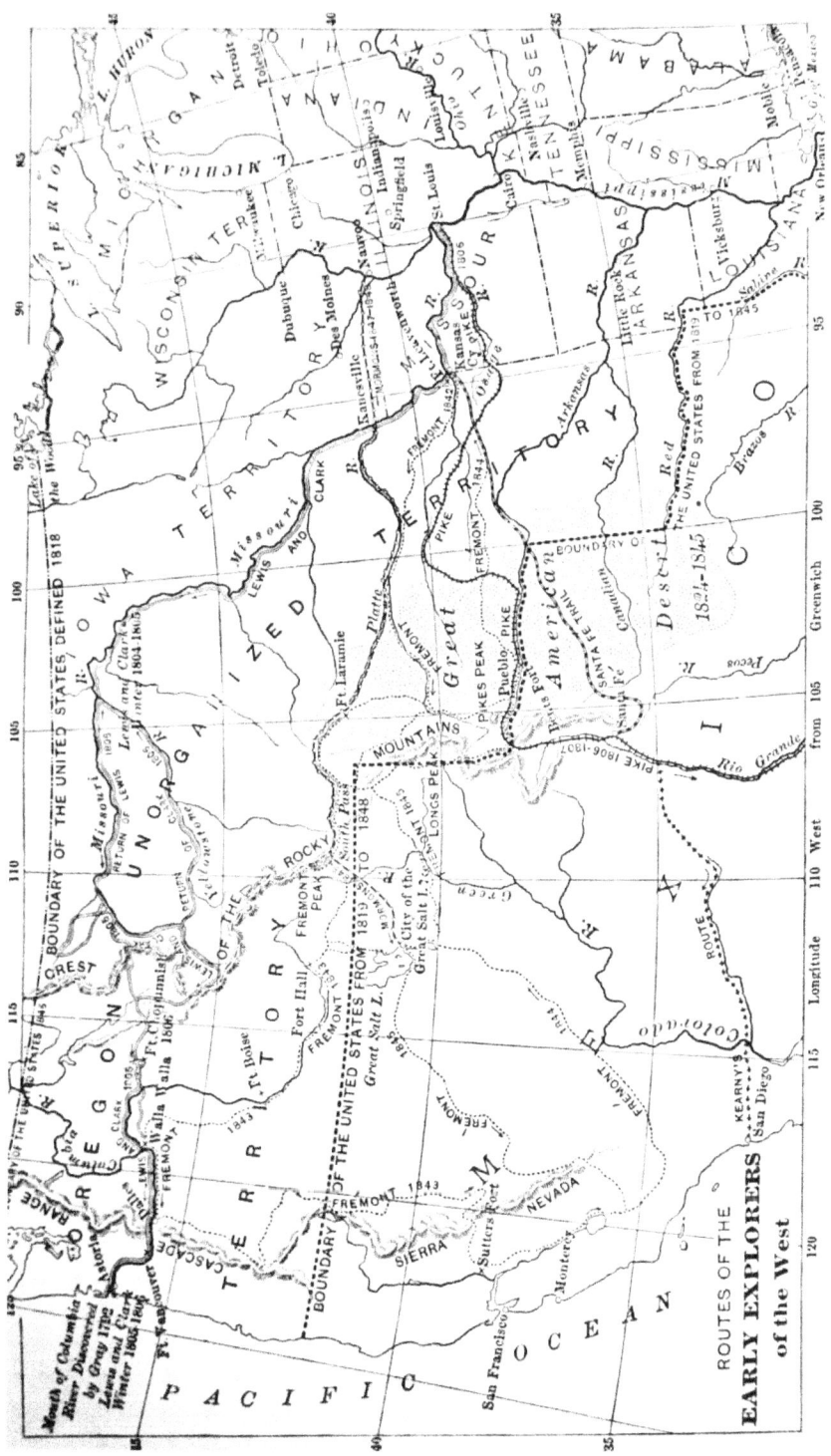

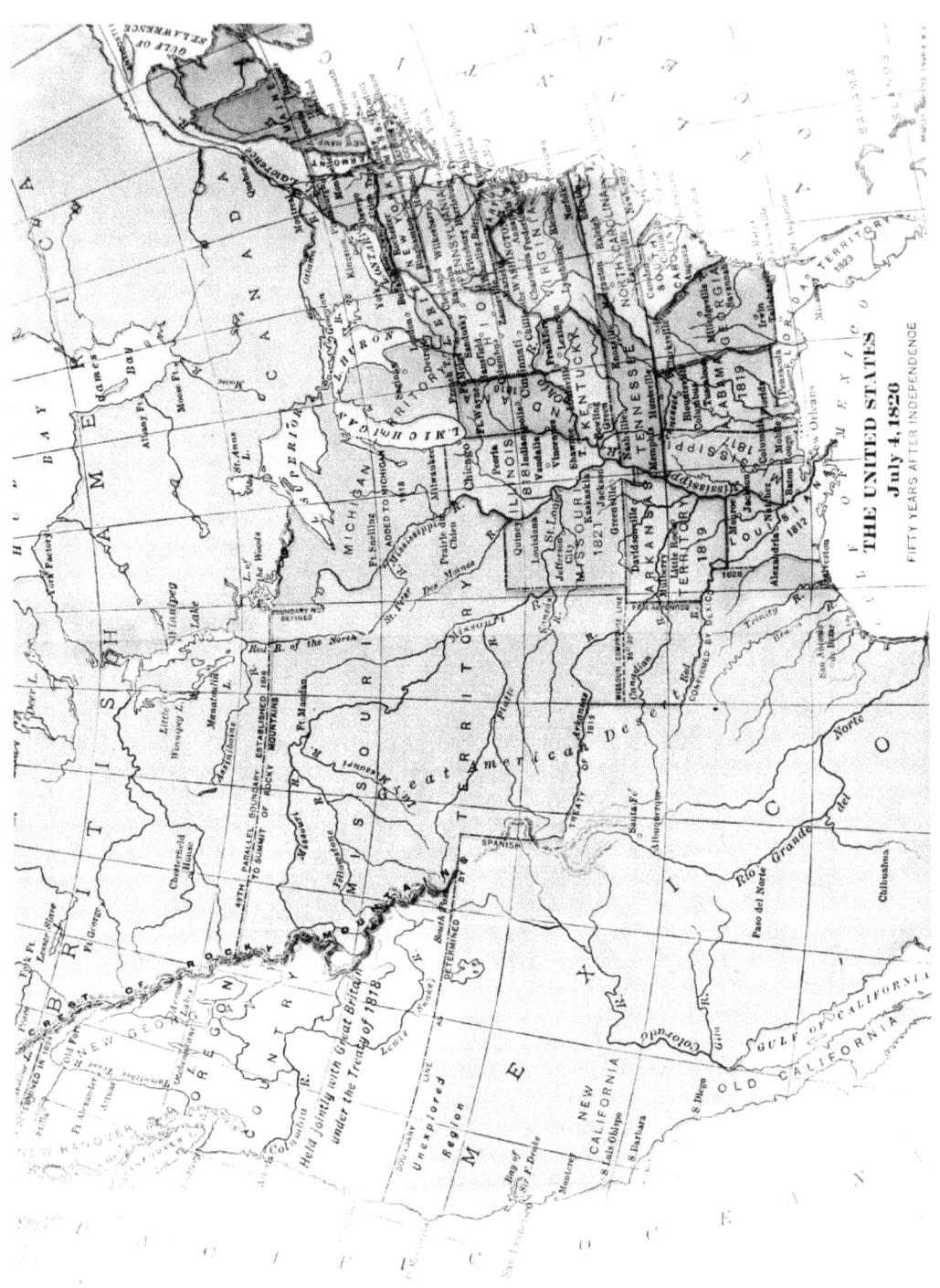

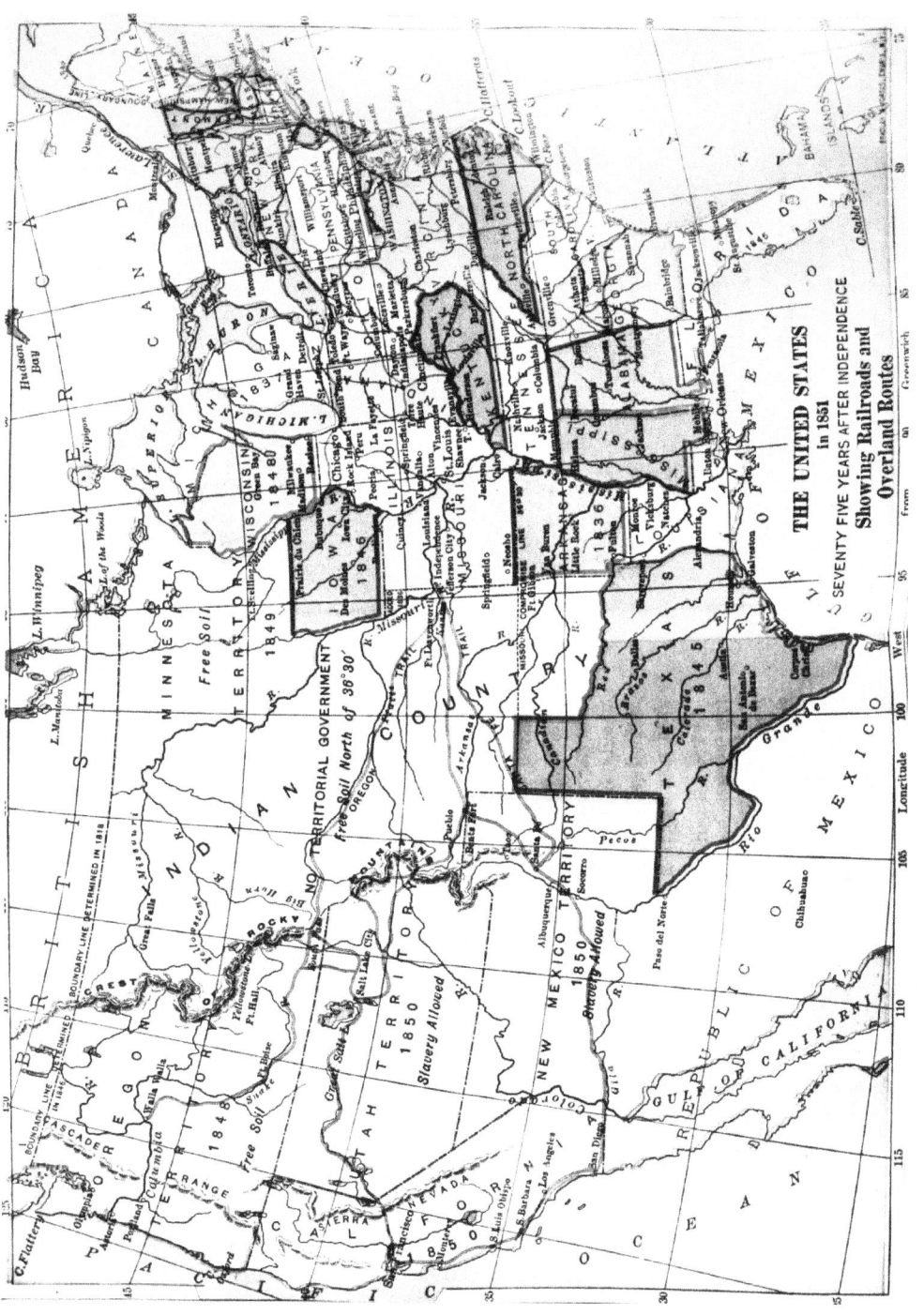

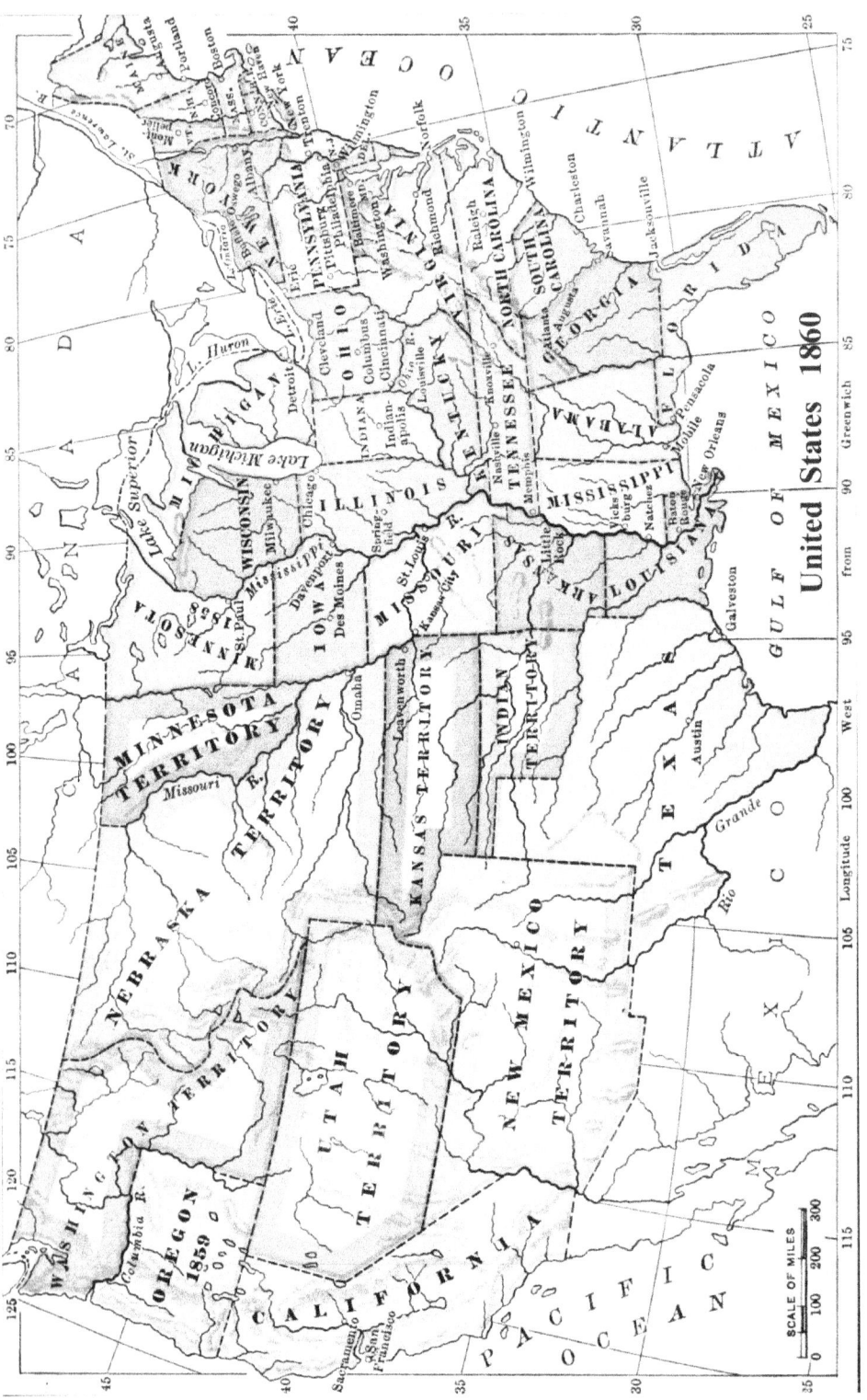

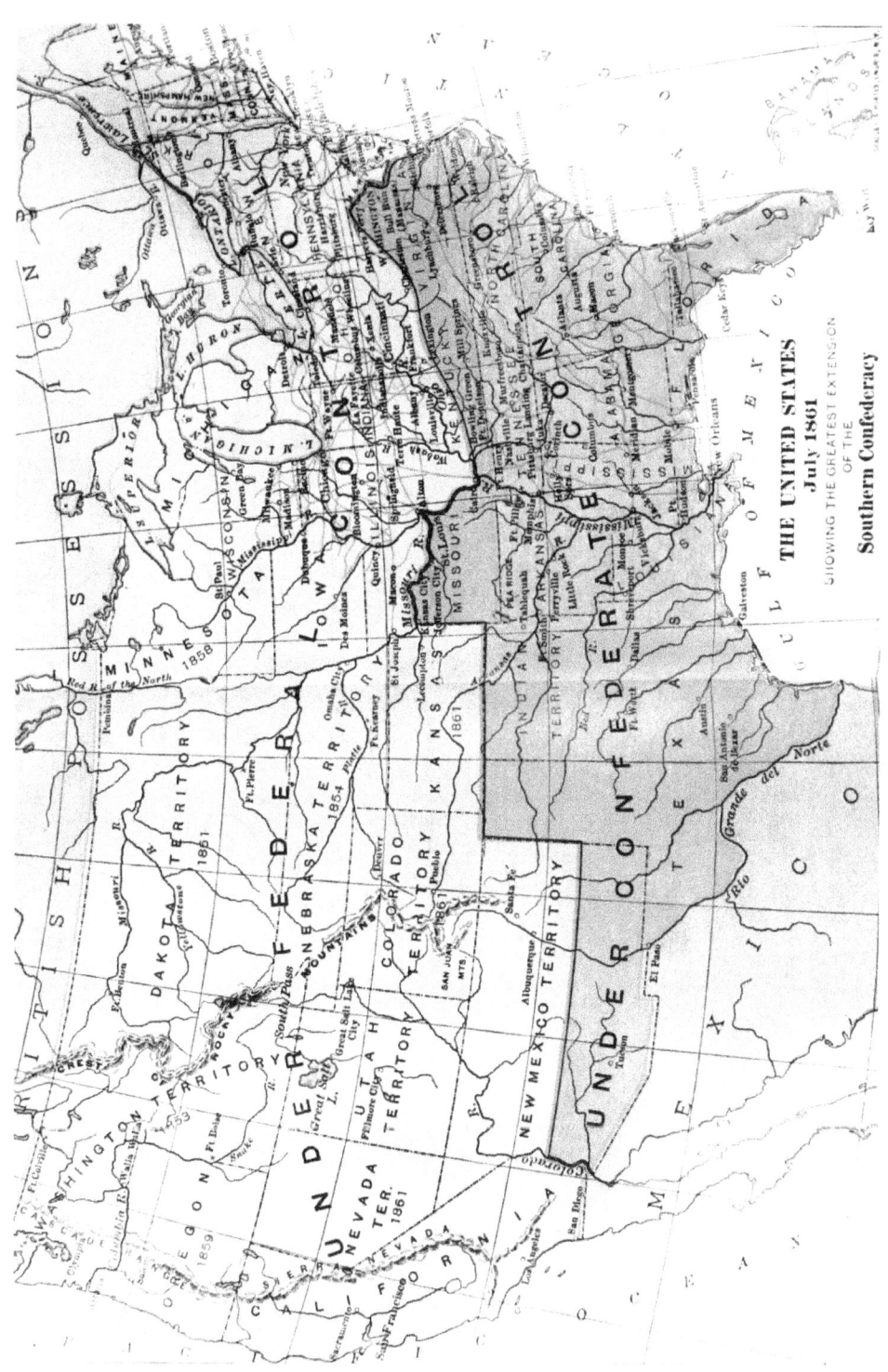

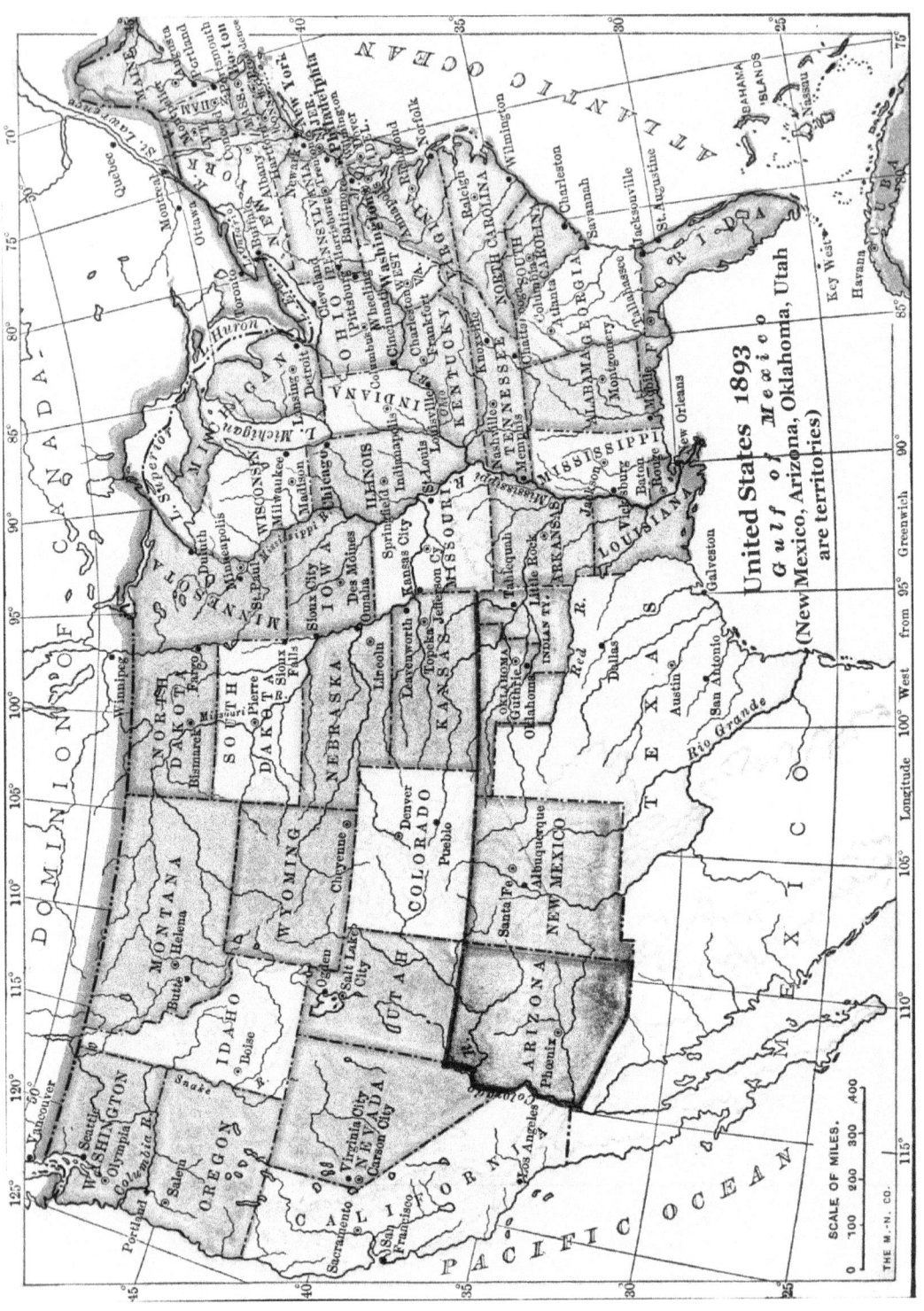

Timeline

When no specific month or date is given, the event occurred in that year or season, but not necessarily in the order recorded. Present-day States may be included in parenthesis.

1816 (leap year), "The Year without a Summer"
- May 6, Boydton Parish, Virginia: Richens Lacy Wootton is born.
- May 6: William Colgate and others organize the American Bible Society.
- May 6: Kenner Levee collapses and floods parts of New Orleans.
- James Madison is U. S. President. Last December he presented his four national goals:
    - Tariff protection for U. S. industry (Tariff passed in 1816 doubles 1812 tariff rates.)
    - Better travel system (The nation has only a few dirt roads for buggy travel.)
    - National currency (The first federal bank failed in 1811; the government now banks with private banks in various states. Under Madison, Congress will realize the value of unified national currency and authorize a Second National Bank.)
    - Stronger military
- 1816 is the midpoint in the Dalton Minimum, which affects weather from 1795 into the 1820's. (The great volcanic activity from 1812-1817 didn't affect weather patterns as much as the eruption of Mt. Tabora on the Isle of Sumbawa, Dutch East Indies. From April 5-15, 1815, Mt. Tabora spewed ash and sulfuric gases into the atmosphere, blocking areas of sunlight.)
    - The Dalton Minimum is an extended period of the sun's low magnetic activity. It resembles the Maunder Minimum (c 1645-1715), which brought about 70 years of colder weather to the northern hemisphere.
    - As a result, in the summer of 1816, drought and frosts wreak havoc on crops in eastern Canada, northeastern United States, Europe, and areas of China and Japan. On August 22, frost hits seaboard states from New England to North Carolina. Rain, floods, and frost blight crops in northern Europe, which is trying to regain strength after the Napoleonic Wars. Food riots break out in France and Great Britain.
- June 18, 1st anniversary of Napoleon Bonaparte's defeat at the Battle of Waterloo; Napoleon lives in exile on the island of Saint Helena.
- Washington, D. C.: Congress passes an act to exclude foreign fur traders.
- Autumn, Sterling, Massachusetts: Mary Sawyer's lamb follows her to school. As a result, Sarah Hale wrote "Mary Had a Little Lamb."
- This is the Federalist Party's last year in U. S. politics. Rufus King of New York is the party's last Presidential candidate. Originally nationalist, Federalists lean toward states' rights. The emerging Republican-Democrat Party represents national unity.

- December 4: Fifty-eight-year-old James Monroe wins the U. S. Presidential election. He was President Madison's Secretary of State.
  - Monroe's aim: a national bond. Believing in the importance of a central national government, he will focus on reconstruction of the capitol and the White House (burned by the British during the War of 1812).
  - During Monroe's tenure, 1817-1825, the U. S. opens more western lands. Industrial opportunities increase.
- December 11: Indiana is admitted to the United States.
- France: René Laënnec invents the stethoscope.
- December: American Colonization Society organizes the return of freed slaves to Africa.

1817

- Mecklenburg County, Virginia: Richens Wootton's brother John Christopher is born.
- New Mexico: Spanish soldiers arrest the Chouteau-DeMun trapping brigade (set out in 1815), take them to Santa Fe, and keep them in custody 44 days. (Some members of the Chouteau-DeMun party: Joseph Bijou, Joseph Philibert, and Etienne Provost, whose mother was a Menard. Prominent in St. Louis, the Chouteau family is connected to the DeMun, Cabanné, Pratte, Berthold, and Gratiot families of St. Louis. All will figure in the Westward movement.)
- March, Washington, D. C.: Alabama is divided: the eastern part retains the Alabama name; the western portion is named Mississippi.
- April 15, Hartford, Connecticut: Gallaudet, first American school for the deaf, opens.
- April 28: England and the U. S. form the Rush-Bagot Agreement. Except for law enforcement, both nations agree to disarm on the Great Lakes. There is no legal boundary between the U. S. and Canada.
- Summer: President Monroe travels throughout the northeastern United States, as far west as Detroit. This is the first such trip for an American President.
- July 4, Rome, New York: Construction of the Erie Canal begins.
- July 12: Henry David Thoreau is born.
- July 18, England: British author Jane Austen dies.
- December 10, Washington, D. C.: Mississippi is admitted to the Union.
- December: President Monroe sends Major General Andrew Jackson, of War of 1812 fame, to quell fighting between Georgia settlers and Seminole Indians.
- Cadmium, lithium, and selenium are discovered.
- United States population is 8,900,000.

1818

- January 1, Washington, D. C.: Reconstruction complete, the White House reopens.
- April 4: Congress decides not to add stripes to the American flag for each state admitted to the Union, as originally planned. The American flag will have one stripe for each of the thirteen original states and one star for every other state.
- Sunday, May 10: Paul Revere dies.
- On the Ohio River (West Virginia): The federally funded Great National Pike reaches

Wheeling. This first national road is also known as the Cumberland or National Road. Begun in Cumberland, Maryland, in 1811, it will extend to Vandalia, Illinois.

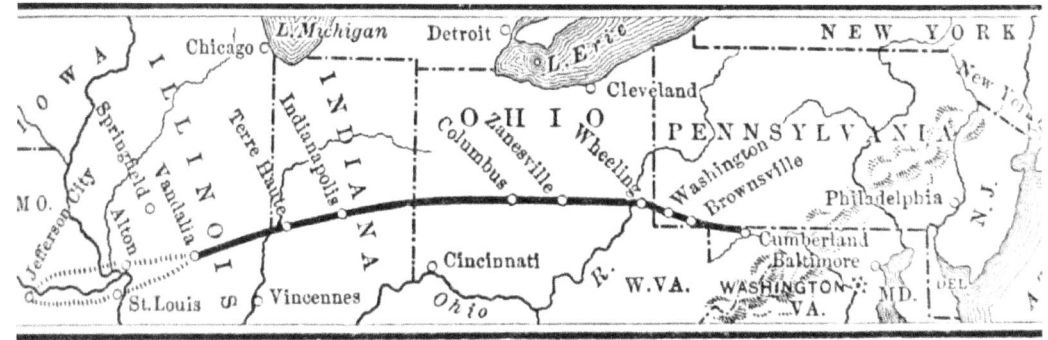

THE CUMBERLAND OR NATIONAL ROAD

- A network of postal roads is forming.
- Convention of 1818: The U. S. and Britain set the boundary between the U. S. and Canada at the 49th parallel from Minnesota to the Stony (Rocky) Mountains.
- Sunday, November 8, Mecklenburg County, Virginia: Richens Wootton's sister, Mary Catherine, is born. Richens is four-and-a-half.
- December 3, Washington, D. C.: Illinois becomes a state, its capital: Kaskaskia. The addition of Illinois balances the number of free and slave states.

1819

- January 17, South America: Simon Bolivar declares the Republic of Great Colombia free from Spain and leads a force of Venezuelan troops to overthrow Spanish rule.
- February 22: By treaty Spain cedes Florida to the U. S. in exchange for cancellation of $5,000,000 worth of debts owed American citizens.
- Washington, D. C., *McCullouch v. Maryland*: John Marshall, Chief Justice of the Supreme Court, rules in favor of the constitutionality of the formation of the Bank of the United States. The case sets two precedents:
  - Union over state: In issues where state and federal disagree, federal wins.
  - Flexibility of the U. S. Constitution: Congress has implied powers, as well as those spelled out in the U. S. Constitution.
- As a result of spending and speculation following the War of 1812, the United States comes face-to-face with the Financial Panic of 1819.
- May 22, Savannah, Georgia: The *Savannah*, which uses both steam and sails, leaves for Liverpool, England. It will arrive June 20. It is the first steamship to cross the Atlantic.
  - As steamboats are refined, the United States will utilize its river systems more. Steamboats going south on the Mississippi River generally average twenty-five miles per hour; going north to St. Louis, the speed is cut to an average of about sixteen miles per hour.
  - This year a passenger expects to pay $100 to travel from Pittsburgh to New

- Orleans. With all the innovations in steam travel, a traveler in the 1830's will be able to travel the same distance for $15 to $30.
- May 24, Kensington Palace, England: Princess Victoria is born.
- May 30, Pittsburg, Pennsylvania: Leaving by steamboat, Major Stephen H. Long and his expedition begin a western exploration expedition.
- May 31: Walt Whitman (American poet) is born. (1819-1892).
- Franklin, Missouri: The *Missouri Intelligencer* begins publication.
- Andrew Jackson's men complete the first Southern highway, a military road from Florence, Alabama, to the Gulf Coast near New Orleans.
- American inventor Oliver Evans dies. His specialty was mill machinery and steam engines. He designed a self-propelled land vehicle and suggested steam-powered stagecoaches would someday enable man to travel up to fifteen or twenty miles per hour.
- New Hampshire adopts religious tolerance laws.
- December 14: Alabama is admitted to the Union.

1820
- Thirteen U. S. cities boast a population of at least 8,000.
- Monday, February 28: Richens Wootton's brother Thomas is born.
- March 15: The Missouri Compromise sets boundaries on the expansion of slavery in the U. S. west of the Mississippi River. Among other matters, the Compromise allows Maine admittance to the Union as a Free State and Missouri as a slave state.
- Spring and summer: Following the Platte River, Major Stephen H. Long and party explore (Colorado) the Rockies (Rocky Mountains), thence to the Arkansas and Canadian Rivers.
- U. S. Land Act of 1820 sets standards for the sale of unsettled federal land. Minimum purchase: Eighty acres. Price per acre: $1.25 cash, no credit.
- Missouri: American frontiersman Daniel Boone dies in his 80's.
- The Mexican government grants Missouri banker Moses Austin's request to allow him to establish a colony of Americans in Texas.
- Unopposed, President Monroe is re-elected. His is the "Era of Good Feelings."
- November 17: Looking for a new seal-fishing area, twenty-one-year-old American Captain Nathaniel Palmer of Connecticut discovers Antarctica.

1821
- May 5, Island of Saint Helena: Napoleon Bonaparte I of France dies of cancer.
- Texas: Following the death of his father, Moses, Stephen F. Austin carries out his father's plan to establish an American colony in Texas. He organizes and leads 300 families to settle on the banks of the Brazos River. Over the next fifteen years the Mexican government will give more land grants and allow more settlers in Texas.
- Sequoya, a Cherokee fascinated by the white man's ability to communicate in writing, completes a writing system for his people. (He worked on it twelve years.) His main desire: to preserve Cherokee history and culture in writing. The Cherokee learn to read and write and publish books and newspapers for interest and education.

- The North West Fur Company and Hudson's Bay Company merge under the Hudson's Bay name.
  - The North West Fur Company began in Canada (1783) and absorbed John Jacob Astor's (American immigrant from Germany) Pacific Fur Company. Company Trappers and traders made inroad treks across the Canadian West to the Pacific Ocean.
  - Hudson's Bay Company, chartered in England in 1670, will establish Fort Vancouver on the Columbia River and monopolize the Canadian fur trade from 1838-1859.
- August: Major William Bradford grants Hugh Glenn license to trade with Indians along the Arkansas River and its tributaries. (The U. S. War Department operates "factories"—a type of trading post—for trade with some tribes. Individual traders must compete with these government posts. The War Department grants few trade licenses to private individuals.)
- August 10, Washington, D. C.: Missouri becomes the twenty-fourth state.
- August 24: Treaty of Cordoba between Spain and Mexico establishes Mexican independence.
- American Colonization Society buys land from tribesmen on Africa's northwest coast, names it Monrovia (renamed Liberia) in honor of President Monroe. The first group of 130 freed slaves moves to the free land created for them in their native Africa.
- September 1, Arrow Rock, Missouri: William Becknell and a few men leave to trade goods with Indians.
- September 25: As planned in Cincinnati last spring, Jacob Fowler (1764-1849) arrived at Hugh Glenn's trading post on the Verdigris River (Oklahoma) to finalize preparations. They leave today on an expedition to the headwaters of the Arkansas River.
- September 27, Mexico City: Mexico proclaims independence from Spain and takes Spain's new world territory in present-day states of Colorado, New Mexico, Utah, Arizona, Nevada, Kansas, Wyoming, California, Texas, and Oklahoma. When word of independence reaches Santa Fe, officials welcome American traders. The Mexican government releases American Robert McKnight and other foreign trappers and traders imprisoned in New Mexico under Spanish rule.
- October 4, Mexico: Mexico adopts a constitution for its new federated states, excluding New Mexico. New Mexico remains a territory without rights to draw up a constitution.
- October 21 (Colorado): William Becknell and traders follow the Purgatoire River.
- November 13, New Mexico: Mexican soldiers meet Becknell's party. Missourians can't speak Spanish; soldiers can't speak English, but the Missourians interpret the soldiers' actions as friendly and hospitable. They camp together tonight. Tomorrow they will travel together to San Miguel, a major New Mexico settlement.
- November 14, Purgatory/Purgatoire River (southeast Colorado): Lewis Dawson of

the Glenn-Fowler party wounds a grizzly. The bear turns on Dawson and mauls him severely. Dawson dies next day.
- Monday, November 19: The Glenn-Fowler party meets a Kiowa chief accompanied by 30-50 warriors. The warriors camp with them, ride with them next day, send two runners to their band. By nightfall hundreds of Kiowa arrive and set up about 200 lodges, which house twelve to twenty each. There is no trouble.
  - Wednesday, November 21: Comanche arrive and set up 350 lodges. Cheyenne and Arapaho men, women, and children begin arriving. Fowler figures this must be some sort of rendezvous. There are now 10,000-18,000 Indians in the encampment.
  - Friday, November 23: Assuming Glenn-Fowler came with goods from the President of the United States, Comanche and Cheyenne intend to kill the traders and steal the goods. Kiowa, having made friends of these white men, won't allow it. Arapaho side with the Kiowa; that settles the issue and averts war and murder.
  - The Glenn-Fowler party divides; some go upstream to trap in the mountains. Others hear of opportunity in Santa Fe and head south. Glenn and Fowler will return to the U. S. next summer and make no further trips to Santa Fe.
- Trapper Jacques LaRamee disappears. Jim Bridger joins a search party. All they find is a broken beaver trap and LaRamee's partially constructed cabin. Two years later an Arapaho tells Bridger the Arapaho killed LaRamee and put his body in the river under the ice near a beaver dam.
- November 16, Santa Fe: William Becknell arrives. His trading is a huge success. More traders, who were near the New Mexico border, arrive and enjoy large profit.
- Santa Fe, New Mexico: Governor Facundo Melgares invites William Becknell to visit, receives him with Spanish courtesy, asks much about the United States, and encourages immigration and trade. The population of Santa Fe is about 5,000.

1822
- January 6, Santa Fe, New Mexico: Governor Facundo Melgares leads New Mexicans in official celebration of independence from Spain. In preparation, many buildings have been whitewashed. At the church, vessels and hangings are laid out for this day.
  - At dawn a cannon booms the dawn of independence from Spain.
  - In the morning all ages celebrate with a parade.
  - Celebration climaxes in the evening with a ball at the Palace of the Governors, decorated for the occasion.
- January 29, Missouri: William Becknell returns from New Mexico. In the *Missouri Intelligencer* Becknell encourages Santa Fe trade. He reports plenty of money and mules in New Mexico, but advises traders to take first-rate goods, not to try to clear out old or damaged stock.
- February, March, St. Louis: Newspaper advertisements announce General William Ashley desires to employ 100 men to accompany him for one, two, or three years on his expedition to the source of the Missouri River.
- April 27, Point Pleasant, Ohio: Hiram Ulysses Grant (Civil War General; U. S.

President) is born. Disliking his initials, he'll change his name to Ulysses Simpson Grant.
- Washington, D. C.: Responding to frontier settlers and the American Fur Company lobby, Congress changes Indian trade requirements. Government factories will no longer compete with traders. Permits become easier to obtain; the Superintendent of Indian Trade generously issues licenses.
- Colonel Benjamin Cooper leads a group of traders to Santa Fe.
- July 16, Virginia: Richens' brother David Christopher Wootton, Jr. is born.
- Santa Fe, New Mexico: William Becknell returns with three wagons of trade goods. William Wolfskill accompanies him. Because wagon traffic begins this year, 1822 is considered the official beginning of the Santa Fe Trail.
- Fall: Robert McKnight, James Baird, and Samuel Chambers—imprisoned by Spain more than nine years for trading in New Mexico—gather goods and return to Santa Fe. Caught in a Kansas blizzard, the men eat most of their animals. In the spring they bury their goods, go to Taos, return with more animals, and retrieve their goods. When they finally reach Santa Fe with their goods, they enjoy a hefty profit.
  - Baird and McKnight figure they have as much opportunity in New Mexico as in their own country. Disgusted with the U. S. for not doing more on their behalf during their years of imprisonment, the men have returned not only to trade, but also to become Mexican citizens. They have already resided in Mexico the number of years prescribed for citizenship.
- Santa Fe Trail: About seventy traders travel to Santa Fe this year.
- St. Louis, Missouri, flourishes with the Southwestern trapping and trading boom.
- October 4, Delaware, Ohio: Rutherford Birchard Hayes is born (Civil War Ohio Volunteer; Ohio representative; Ohio governor; 19th U. S. President).

1823
- 1822 and 1823, New Mexico: Governor Jose Antonio Viscarra leads campaigns against the Navajo, who are harassing New Mexicans.
- May 4: Blackfoot Indians kill four of Andrew Henry's trappers and drive the rest of the group back to their Yellowstone encampment.
- May 30, Pryor's Fork: Blackfoot Indians attack trappers. They hack Michael Immell and Robert Jones to pieces, kill five of their trappers, and make off with the trappers' twenty bales of furs and every one of their horses and traps.
- New Mexico: Bartolome Baca becomes governor and will be in office until 1825.
- December 2: In his annual Congressional address President James Monroe presents his foreign policy: the Monroe Doctrine.
- New York City: Gaslight is introduced into the city. It was introduced in Boston last year, but will not reach Philadelphia until 1835.

1824
- May 11, Washington D. C.: The Bureau of Indian Affairs opens as a division of the War Department. It replaces the Office of Superintendent of Indian Trade (1806-1822).

- May: Sylvestre Pratte, son of Bernard Pratte, leads 100 men to New Mexico and the southern Rocky Mountains. Sylvester Pattie and his twenty-year-old son, James Ohio Pattie, are among them. After the death of his wife, Sylvester Pattie and son left Kentucky for the Rockies.
- May 16: Alexander Le Grande leads a wagon train westward across the Missouri River. This is considered the first full-scale wagon train on the Santa Fe Trail.
- At the request of Congress, President Monroe invites Lafayette, Marquis de Marie Jean Paul Joseph Roche Yves Gilbert du Motier Lafayette, to visit the United States. He spends more than a year in the U. S. and visits all twenty-four states.
    - A wealthy young man at the time of the Revolutionary War, Lafayette outfitted his own ship, sailed to join the American cause, and served as a loyal officer in the American army. He has been absent from the United States 40 years.
    - Congress gives Lafayette $200,000 and 24,000 acres in Florida.
- Concerned about the influx of foreign trappers, the Mexican government bans trapping beaver in New Mexico.
- United States: Woodbridge and Willard's new textbook refers to the Plains as a desert.
- Along the Pecos River, New Mexico: Comanche raid settlements and take captives: three Spanish women, an American, and the daughter of a former New Mexico governor. With only 120 soldiers for the entire New Mexico territory, Governor Bartolome Baca asks and receives help from American trappers and traders. They rescue two of the five captives; ten Americans die in the rescue. This places traders in good favor in Santa Fe—for now.
- Santa Cruz, New Mexico: William Becknell and ten trappers stock up and leave to trap on the Green River (Colorado). Before he leaves, Becknell writes Governor Baca that he has "nothing to Dew" with those who are trapping in the Taos area.
- November, Missouri: Augustus Storrs tells Missouri's Senator Thomas H. Benton that he returned with a Santa Fe Trail caravan bringing $10,044 worth of furs. Another eighty-one-man caravan traveled the Santa Fe Trail in 1824 with twenty-five wagons loaded with $30,000 worth of trade goods and returned with furs worth $10,000, plus $80,000 in gold and silver.
- November, Franklin, Missouri: Ceran St. Vrain and François Guerin buy goods on credit from Bernard Pratte and make their first trading trip via the Santa Fe Trail.
- Washington, D. C.: Congress raises tariff rates.
- There are 1,347 Americans in Texas with 443 slaves.
- December (Salt Lake, Utah): Jim Bridger finds a large salt lake.
- December 25: Richens' brother William W. Wootton is born.

1825
- March 3, Washington, D. C.: President Monroe authorizes a survey expedition to mark the Santa Fe Trail.
- Washington, D. C.: John Quincy Adams becomes U. S. President.
- Friday, June 17: Lafayette joins the celebration as the cornerstone is laid for the

monument at Bunker Hill.
- Lower Rio Grande, Texas: This is a wet year. Rain raises the river and slows interaction between Mexico and its northern colony of Texas. Meanwhile, Comanche are stealing horses from Texas settlers.
- Santa Fe, New Mexico: Governor Bartolome Baca grants Sylvester Pattie permission to trap along the Gila River in southern New Mexico and to operate the Santa Rita copper mine in the same area. The mine has been producing copper since at least 1790. Pattie was one of the Americans who helped rescue captives taken by the Comanche last year.
- October 26: The Erie Canal opens. The 363 mile canal links the Great Lakes with the Atlantic Ocean. With the importation of raw materials and exportation of finished goods, New York City becomes the busiest U. S. port and the nation's financial center.
- United States: The introduction of mechanically produced glass makes glass readily available at more affordable prices.
- November, Taos, New Mexico: Antoine Robidoux returns from Missouri with four of his brothers. Joseph III, François, Isidore, Antoine, Louis (leaves New Mexico for California in late 1843), and Michel Robidoux are all sons of the late Joseph Robidoux II (d. 1809).
- United States population is 11,252,237.

1826
- Santa Fe, New Mexico: Antonio Narbona, former Colonel of Chihuahua, Mexico, is governor of New Mexico (1825-27).
- April 8: Henry Clay and John Randolph duel. Clay challenged Virginia Representative Randolph to a duel because Randolph called President Adams and Secretary of State Clay a "coalition between the black-leg and the Puritan." Both men survive.
- Missouri: Christopher "Kit" Carson leaves for New Mexico via the Santa Fe Trail.
- July 4, 50th Anniversary of the Declaration of Independence: Former Presidents Thomas Jefferson, age eighty-three, and John Adams, age ninety, die.
- Willow Valley (Utah): William Ashley holds a trappers' rendezvous. He had one last year; this one is more organized. The rendezvous becomes an annual affair, which attracts hundreds of mountain men and trappers and thousands of Indians. A rendezvous lasts about a week and gives everyone time for business (buying and selling pelts, tools, ponies, trapping supplies, knives, etc.) and recreation (wrestling, drinking, gambling, horse racing, storytelling—factual and fabricated, shooting competition, and other competitive events).
- July 23: Alexander James Wootton is born. His brother Richens is ten.
- August 1, Santa Fe, New Mexico: After trapping through parts of present-day Arizona and Colorado since March, James Ohio Pattie and his trapper brigade arrive with a load of fine beaver pelts. Because the men trapped without a license, Governor Narbona confiscates the furs.

- August, Santa Fe, New Mexico: A large number of trappers are in town buying horses, repairing gear, and enjoying the benefits of town. Among them are Bill Williams, Tom Smith, Milton Sublette, Ceran St. Vrain, Sylvestre Pratte, Alexander Branch, Michel Robidoux, and many Frenchmen.
- August 29, New Mexico: Bill Williams and Ceran St. Vrain and thirty-five others apply for passports to trade in Sonora, Mexico.
- On the Arkansas River (Colorado): Charles and William Bent build a small picket post trading post between present-day Pueblo and the foothills. (Some date this later.)
- About midnight, desert (near Phoenix, Arizona): Papagos Indians kill all but three of Michel Robidoux's trapping party. The next night survivors, James Pattie, another trapper, and wounded Michel Robidoux, see lights in the distance. They look like campfires. The men walk to the camp and find Ewing Young and his band of twenty-nine trappers, including Milton Sublette and Tom Smith. Hearing the report and being true to the trappers' code (let no Indian depredation go unpunished), the trappers lay an ambush for the Papagos next day. They kill 110 Papagos, loot and burn the Indian camp. They return to bury the dismembered bodies of Robidoux's slain trappers.

1827
- January, Taos (New Mexico): Ceran St. Vrain and twenty-two trappers leave on a trapping expedition.
- Washington, D. C.: Reconstruction of the U. S. Capitol is complete (British burned the capitol in August 1814).
- Tennessee: Future Texas leader Sam Houston becomes governor of Tennessee.
- New Mexico: Governor Manuel Armijo of Albuquerque cracks down on trapping in New Mexico. Armijo is 6' tall, well built (heavier later). His lips are full. His eyes and demeanor reveal a touch of arrogance. He often wears a sky blue uniform, decorated with gold and silver.
- July 3: Jedediah Strong Smith and his men, who have been exploring southwestern trapping grounds, return for the annual trapper rendezvous.
- Carey and Lee's new *Atlas* includes what they consider America's large desert: The Plains.
- Summer: Mojave Indians attack Jedediah Strong Smith and his men as they cross the Colorado River enroute to California. They kill ten of Smith's men. (Accounts vary from ten to more than twelve.)
- October 1, North Park on the Platte River: Having been bitten by a rabid dog, Sylvestre S. Pratte, leader of a trapping expedition, dies. The group chooses twenty-five-year-old Ceran St. Vrain, former employee of Sylvestre's dad, Bernard, to take charge. Bill Williams is also with the expedition.
- California: Richard Campbell and a party of trappers arrive from New Mexico.
- Fort Leavenworth is established to protect Santa Fe Trail travelers.

1828
- March, New York: An earthquake rattles for several minutes.

- April 21: Noah Webster publishes his expanded two-volume dictionary, *American Dictionary of the American Language*. (He has worked on the two-volume dictionary about twenty years.) He first published his one-volume dictionary in 1806.
- May 19, Washington, D. C.: President John Q. Adams signs the Tariff of Abominations. This effort to protect New England industry angers those not involved in manufacturing. The nations' farmers have neither protections, nor subsidies.
- Washington, D. C.: Sequoya (Cherokee) arrives to represent Western Indian tribes.
- July 13: Indians steal furs and massacre all but four men in Jedediah Smith's trapping expedition traveling to Ft. Vancouver. Survivors escape to Ft. Vancouver. Dr. John McLoughlin of the Hudson's Bay Company recovers the stolen furs.
- Saturday, July 19: Richens Wootton's brother Samuel F. Wootton is born.
- Sylvester Pattie, his son James Ohio Pattie, and twenty-two trappers, who left Taos (New Mexico) the end of 1827, trap along the Gila River. The group splits. Jesse Ferguson, Richard Laughlin, William Pope, Nathaniel Pryor, Edmund Russell, and Isaac Slover stay with the Patties and follow the Colorado River overland toward San Diego, California. Mexicans capture them on the Baja Peninsula and imprison them in San Diego. Sylvester dies in prison. During a smallpox epidemic the California governor learns that James has vaccine, which belonged to Sylvester. He frees James to vaccinate people in California. James will later return home to Kentucky.
- North side of the Arkansas River, near the U. S.-Mexican border: Charles and William Bent and Ceran St. Vrain begin construction on a fort. (William said construction began in 1828.)
- Late August, Cimarron/Dry Branch of the Santa Fe Trail: Traveling to the States, Mr. McNess and Daniel Munroe ride ahead of the wagon train. While the men sleep, a small band of Comanche kill McNees and leave Munroe for dead. When the train arrives, the traders, including Colonel Marmaduke and Milton Sublette, bury McNees and load Munroe into a wagon. Munroe soon dies. After burying him, the traders sight about six Indians and open fire. They kill all but one—a custom some tribes follow of leaving one to carry the news. After hearing the survivor's report, Comanche chase the wagon train, catch up, and steal most of the train's 1,000 head of horses and mules.
- Two weeks later, on the Santa Fe Trail: Comanche attack a wagon train heading East. They kill and scalp train captain John Means, who had been riding rear guard. They then dog the travelers until nightfall. Under cover of darkness, they stampede the train's 150 animals. Surviving members of the train walk toward Missouri. Unable to carry their silver, they cache it on Chouteau's Island. After walking more than 400 miles in thirty-two days, five survivors arrive in Missouri.
- As a result of raids this summer, Santa Fe Trail traders request military protection, just as the government protects ships at sea.
- Ewing Young leads a party of trappers, including Kit Carson, from Taos to California.
- Ortiz Mountains (thirty to thirty-five miles southwest of Santa Fe, New Mexico):

Gold is discovered. Miners rush to the mountains. Only New Mexico citizens are allowed to work the mines.
- December 28: Rachel Jackson, age sixty-one, dies of a heart attack following her husband's election to the U. S. presidency. Andrew Jackson attributes her death to politicians' verbal attacks during the campaign.

1829
- March 4: Andrew Jackson succeeds John Q. Adams as U. S. President.
  - President Jackson assigns Major Bennett Riley to command four infantry companies to escort wagon trains on the Santa Fe Trail as far as the border of Mexico. This is the first military escort on the Santa Fe Trail. The U. S. has no cavalry. (When Congress adjourned without acting on the matter, Samuel C. Lamme, David Waldo, and a small group of traders appealed directly to President Jackson, who was well-acquainted with Indian action. Jackson contacted the War Department and arranged the escort.)
- Because matters between Mexico and Spain are somewhat restless, Mexico orders Spanish nationals to leave New Mexico or pay bribes for immunity. Ten men and six women leave. They travel East on the Santa Fe Trail with the wagon train belonging to Charles and William Bent and brothers David and William Waldo.
- June 3, Ft. Leavenworth (Kansas): Captain Bennett Riley and approximately 200 infantrymen leave to escort Santa Fe Trail traders. The infantry's limited budget doesn't allow the purchase of mules; oxen pull the infantry's supply wagons.
- June 11, Round Grove: Because of Indian trouble last year, only thirty-eight wagons are waiting when the U. S. infantry arrives to escort the Santa Fe Trail spring caravan.
- Mexican President Guerrero abolishes Negro slavery in Mexico.
  - Texan Stephen Austin protests: When Americans were allowed to settle in Texas, it was understood slavery would be allowed. The Mexican government allows slavery to continue in Texas.
- Sailor Samuel Colt (born 1814) makes a wooden model revolver, which he later perfects and patents. Colt's is the first successful repeating revolver. He will build a factory and produce revolvers in his hometown, Hartford, Connecticut.
- Richens Wootton's brother Powell C. is born. Richens is thirteen.

1830
- January, Washington, D. C.: The Webster-Hayne Debate begins in Congress and continues almost two weeks—the issue: nullification and states' rights.
- April 6: Mexico bans further American immigration into Texas.
- Jim Bridger, Thomas Fitzpatrick, Henry Fraeb, Jean Baptiste Gervais, and Milton Sublette, "Thunderbolt of the Rockies," buy out David Jackson, Jedediah Strong Smith, and William Sublette's fur business and rename it Rocky Mountain Fur Company. William and Milton are two of the five Sublette brothers.
- May 28: President Jackson signs the Indian Removal Act, which Secretary of War John C. Calhoun proposed in 1828. The act calls for resettlement of all Indians living

east of the Mississippi River to lands west of the Mississippi. During Jackson's two terms, the U. S. and Indian tribes sign 94 treaties—some successful, some not. Most Indians will move into present-day Arkansas, Oklahoma, Kansas, or Nebraska.
- Spring, Santa Fe Trail: Soldiers do not escort wagon trains this year. Having heard of last year's profits, more traders head to Santa Fe. Josiah Gregg estimates about $120,000 worth of merchandise travels across the Trail to Santa Fe this year. About one-sixth of the goods are taken further south into Mexico.
- July, Mecklenburg County, Virginia: David and Frances Wootton sell their land to James Jones and move to Christian County, Kentucky.
- Peter Cooper completes Tom Thumb, the first commercial steam locomotive to operate in the United States. (Cooper has already become rich manufacturing isinglass, glue, and gelatin. He will pioneer in development of American iron and will promote telegraph companies and the underwater Atlantic cable.)
- August 4, Santa Fe, New Mexico: Bent-St. Vrain wagons arrive with the Santa Fe Trail trade caravan. A few days before, in late July, a Mexican customs inspector and a band of soldiers surprised traders at the headwaters of Red River and charged over 50% duty on goods brought into New Mexico. Ceran St. Vrain estimates the duty is closer to 60% of the cost of his goods. By October traders return to Missouri, but with less profit than anticipated because of the tariff and this year's sluggish market.
- October 5, Fairfield, Vermont: Chester Alan Arthur is born (U. S. President, 1881-1885).
- December, Santa Fe, New Mexico: Charles Bent arrives with a second load of goods brought over the Santa Fe Trail this year.

1831
- January 1: American journalist William Lloyd Garrison begins publishing *The Liberator*, an antislavery newspaper.
- May: Charles Bent is in Missouri loading wagons with trade goods.
- May 27, Council Grove: Approximately 200 people travel in the spring caravan to Santa Fe. There are almost one hundred wagons loaded with trade goods, about a dozen smaller vehicles, and two wagons supporting cannons—one four-pound, one six-pound.
  - Among those traveling West are Josiah Gregg, first known health seeker, and some Spanish ladies returning home to New Mexico. (Mexico banished Spaniards in 1829). Gregg notes that two French ladies previously traveled cross-country on the Santa Fe Trail to Santa Fe. (They became residents of Chihuahua, Mexico.)
- May 27, Santa Fe Trail: Comanche lance and kill thirty-two-year-old Jedediah Strong Smith, trapper and pathfinder. Smith and his train, including two of his brothers and William Sublette, David E. Jackson, Thomas Fitzpatrick, E. S. Minter, and others were traveling to Santa Fe. They were not with the annual spring caravan.
  - A learned man, Jedediah Smith journaled his travels. He never traveled without his rifle and his Bible.

- Once a grizzly bear attacked Smith and tore his scalp loose; but his compadres sewed his scalp back on with a needle and thread.
- July 4: Former U. S. President James Monroe, age seventy-three, dies.
- Washington, D. C.: Congress asks for an account of the fur trade and concludes that, because of the elements, privation, and Indian attack, trapping is a dangerous enterprise that often costs the health or life of the trapper-trader.
- August, South Hampton County, Virginia: Slave Nat Turner leads a slave rebellion.
- Cyrus Hall McCormick (1809-1884) invents a reaping machine. He'll improve it before he patents it in 1834. Even then, it will be awhile before his machine is in common use.
- September 10: Charles Bent leads a ten-wagon train across the Santa Fe Trail. This is his second trip this year. Most of this train's employees are New Mexicans.
  - With them is Albert Pike, a young teacher from Massachusetts. He is the first known Western tourist. When Pike leaves Independence (Missouri), he considers himself an educated man; but he soon realizes a formal education without practical common sense is of little value in the West. (Pike will be an Arkansas attorney; a soldier in the Mexican War; a Confederate general. In that capacity he will make alliances with a group of Plains Indians and lead a Cherokee brigade in Civil War battles.)
- November 19, Orange, Ohio: James Abram Garfield (20th U. S. President) is born.

1832
- May: Ceran St. Vrain sends traders to Chihuahua and Sonora, Mexico.
- New Orleans: Cholera strikes.
- William Lloyd Garrison organizes the American Anti-Slavery Society. He will continue anti-slavery efforts until emancipation is proclaimed.
- July, Washington, D. C.: Congress approves further tariffs.
- South Carolina protests the tariffs of 1828 and 1832 and passes a Nullification Act.
- July, Battle of Pierre's Hole (Wyoming): After the annual trader rendezvous, Milton Sublette and a party of trappers encounter about 200 Blackfoot. A Flathead with Sublette kills a Blackfoot chief under the flag of truce. Fighting ensues; Pickney Sublette is killed.
- August, Massachusetts: The first U. S. school for the blind opens.
- New Mexico: Bishop Zubria arrives on a visit from Durango, Chihuahua, Mexico. He is appalled at New Mexico poverty, but he finds no effective way to raise revenue.
- Bent's Fort (Colorado): Charles Bent brings word to Ceran St. Vrain that Black Hawk Indians killed his brother Felix St. Vrain.
- October 6, Christian County, Kentucky: Richens' sister Eliza Ann Wootton is born.
- November 26: New York City's first streetcar (horse-drawn) begins operation.
- November 29, Germantown, Pennsylvania: Author Louisa May Alcott is born.

1833, "The Winter the Stars Fell"
- January, Santa Fe Trail (Texas Panhandle): Indians attack Santa Fe Trail traders returning to Missouri with profits. They kill all but ten traders and all the animals.

Traders abandon their goods and walk. Five follow the Dry Route toward Missouri; five follow the Canadian River. Those who follow the Dry Route arrive in Missouri by March 3rd, the date their story is published in the *Missouri Intelligencer*. Of the other five, two disappear; three reach a Creek Indian camp.

- Washington, D. C.: Congressman Henry Clay of Kentucky appeases the North and South with the Compromise Tariff of 1833.
- Bradford's *Atlas* portrays the Plains as a desert.
- Southwestern shore of Lake Michigan: For two years a village has been growing up around Ft. Dearborn. Now 500-600 people live there and are optimistic their village may continue growing. They call it Chicago.

CHICAGO IN 1833

- Ortiz Mountains, New Mexico: Veins of gold—the source of the gold found in the Ortiz Mountains in 1828—are found on the land grant that belongs to Jose Francisco Ortiz. The Sierra de Oro mine opens. Up to 3,000 miners work the placer deposits in the Ortiz and San Pedro mountains. This is sometimes considered the first gold strike west of the Mississippi; however, gold was mined in the hills south of Santa Fe in 1749-54. In the 17th century lead and silver were mined in the area.
- June 19, Council Grove: Because of rain, the Santa Fe Trail spring caravan leaves late. Ft. Leavenworth soldiers meet the caravan and escort the train as far as the Arkansas River. This spring, wagons rut a trail in the damp sod, which future trains will follow.
    - William Donoho, his wife Mary, and their nine-month-old daughter travel with the train. They will remain in Santa Fe a few years.
- Cutthroat Gap Massacre, Wichita Mountains (Oklahoma): Osage cut the heads off some of their Kiowa enemies, put them in cooking kettles and set the kettles in a row.
- August 20, North Bend, Ohio: Benjamin Harrison is born. He will serve in the Army and the Senate before becoming the 23rd President of the United States, 1889-1893.
- November 12: A meteor shower illuminates the night sky from the Atlantic to the Pacific. Indians call this the "winter the stars fell." On this night Ouray, great Ute chief, is born in New Mexico. (Some say he was born the 13th.)

1834

- Mississippi: Richens Wootton arrives to work on his uncle's plantation.
- May, Missouri: About eighty wagons comprise the spring caravan heading for Santa Fe. Included in the freight is a printing press for Don Ramon Abreu of New Mexico.
- Spring (Wyoming): Bill Sublette and Robert Campbell begin building Ft. Laramie on the Laramie River near the junction with the North Platte. The fort will be ready for business by the end of summer. Buffalo are abundant along the Platte all year.
- Oregon: Missionary Jason Lee arrives. He will return to the States in four years; his lectures will draw immigrants to Oregon.
- Summer, Santa Fe, New Mexico: Antonio Barreiro publishes New Mexico's first newspaper, *El Crespusculo de la Libertad (The Dawn of the Liberty)*, on Don Ramon Abreu's new press.
- Santa Fe, New Mexico: Ceran St. Vrain is appointed U. S. consul (1834-1838).
- October 14: Henry Blair patents a corn planter. He can't write his name; he signs "X."
- In prison for debt incurred developing his idea, Charles Goodyear continues figuring how to make India rubber useful. In 1839 he will discover how to vulcanize rubber. He will continue to perfect his process until he makes rubber a useful commodity.

1835

- Mexico: Antonio Lopez de Santa Ana appoints Army Colonel Albino Perez governor of New Mexico. Perez is the first outsider appointed governor of New Mexico since Mexico gained control of New Mexico. Middle-aged Perez is tall, well educated, and courteous. He is a polished politician and enjoys society—except for common New Mexicans.
- Christian County, Kentucky: Richens' brother, Joseph Edward Wootton, is born.
- April 6, west bank of the Gallinas River, New Mexico: Thirty-five people from San Miguel del Vado establish Las Vegas on the Santa Fe Trail.
  - An 1821 land petition for settlement of the area was granted in 1823. Because of Indian trouble, the settlement only lasted until 1827. The Mexican government granted another petition in 1833.
    - Las Vegas citizens trade eggs, milk, cheese, and fresh mutton with freighters who stop at their settlement. Soon stores will spring up; the town will have more to offer. Las Vegas merchants Francisco Lopez, Charles Blanchard, and Miguel Romero and sons, and others become Santa Fe Trail traders and transport their own goods.
- May, Missouri: The annual Santa Fe Trail caravan leaves with about 75 wagons. They will return in October.
- Summer: The Presbyterian Church appoints Samuel Parker and Dr. Marcus Whitman, a medical doctor with eight years' experience, as missionaries to the Pacific Northwest. Whitman and Parker travel Northwest with Lucien Fontenelle's fur caravan.
- Texas: About 18,000 Americans with about 2,000 slaves live in Texas. Cotton is an

important Texas product.
- John Marshall, Chief Justice of the Supreme Court, dies. He was appointed to the bench February 4, 1801. He was often opposed. At times there was talk of his impeachment, but he remained in office until death. His strong decisions set precedents supporting national government and made the Supreme Court a power to be reckoned with.
- October 2, Battle of Gonzales: Texas' war for independence from Mexico begins.
- October 20, New Mexico: The Mora Land Grant gives land along the Mora River to seventy-five families.
- November 3, Texas: American settlers in Texas organize a provisional government.
- November, New Mexico: Having purchased Don Ramon Abreu's printing press, Padre Antonio Martinez begins publishing school materials and other pamphlets.
- December 11: Colonel Benjamin Milam leads Texans and captures San Antonio.
- The United States now boasts more than 1,000 miles of railroad lines.
- Because of the War of 1812, the national debt was $127,000,000 when Richens Wootton was born. It is now paid in full.

1836
- February 25: Samuel Colt patents a revolver. It allows one to shoot without having to reload after each shot.
- March 2: Texas declares independence from Mexico.
- March 6, Texas: General Antonio Lopez de Santa Ana and his Mexican troops defeat Texans at the Alamo and recapture San Antonio. Mexicans kill all men in the Alamo, including frontiersmen Jim Bowie and Davy Crockett.
- March 27, Palm Sunday, Goliad, Texas: After the Battle of Coleto, Texas General Fannin and his troops surrender. Mexican General Santa Ana orders soldiers to shoot more than 340 surrendered Texans. Soldiers burn the bodies and leave them to the elements. Less than thirty of the surrendered escape death. The massacre arouses sympathy in the U. S., England, and France and outrages Texans. It fuels the fire to fight for independence.
- April 21, Battle of San Jacinto: Sam Houston and his Texans defeat Mexican troops under General Santa Ana and gain Texas' independence. Almost half of Santa Ana's army dies in the battle. Texans capture him and his remaining soldiers.
- May, northern Texas: Comanche kidnap nine-year-old Cynthia Ann Parker from her home after killing her father. Search for Cynthia will be futile until 1860.
- Independence, Missouri: Richens Wootton joins a Bent-St. Vrain wagon train. Along the way, his name is changed to Dick.
- June 3, Goliad, Texas: As they pass through Goliad, General Thomas J. Rusk and his men see charred remains of Goliad Massacre victims. They stop and bury the bodies.
- June 15: Arkansas is admitted to the Union.
- Northeastern U. S.: The first U. S. trade union convention convenes. Workers want less work hours. They ask for ten-hour work days, education for all, monopolies controlled, and debtors' prisons abolished.

- June 28, Virginia: Former President James Madison, who worked diligently during the drafting of the Constitution and the Bill of Rights, dies at age eighty-five. His wife, Dolley, will live thirteen more years.
- July 11: President Jackson's Specie Circular requires gold or silver to purchase public lands. Bank notes are no longer acceptable. This requirement will take effect after the election and will curb western land speculation.
- July, New Mexico: In an effort to stop raids, Governor Albino Perez leads a campaign against the Navajo.
- New Mexico, Mexican Decree of 1836: Governor Perez levies heavier taxes on New Mexicans and restricts their rights.
- East side of the Platte River (Colorado): About 1836 Fort Lupton is built. It serves in the fur trade business about ten years before being abandoned. Walls of the 100' x 100' fort are four feet thick at the base. (Some date it 1837.)
- Bent's Fort (Colorado): Richens "Dick" Wootton arrives.
- Bent's Fort: Three to four weeks after arrival Dick Wootton trades with the Sioux.
- September 1 (Walla Walla, Washington): Missionary Dr. and Mrs. (Narcissa) Whitman arrive. The Whitmans and Mr. and Mrs. H. H. (Eliza) Spalding establish mission stations in Oregon Territory.
- September 5, Republic of Texas: Sam Houston is elected President.

1837
- January 26: Michigan is admitted to the Union.
- March 18, Caldwell, New Jersey: Grover Cleveland (U. S. President, 1885-1889, 1893-1897) is born.
- Dick Wootton makes his first trip into Taos, New Mexico.
- April 22, Southwestern New Mexico: Johnson kills Apache chief Juan Campo. As a result, Santa Rita copper mine closes. Mine owners Courcier and McKnight enlist the help of James Kirker, a man well-acquainted with Apache ways. (Accounts vary: Kirker was: 1) a former Apache captive; 2) a trader among them. Sources also vary concerning: 1) his name: James, John; 2) time of mine closure.)
  - Kirker gathers twenty-three men of various nationalities, but primarily Delaware and Shawnee Indians. They attack Chief Mangas Coloradas' Apache village, kill fifty-five, capture nine, take 400 head of stock, and destroy the village.
  - Kirker's fame as an Indian fighter spreads. In 1839 the Governor of Chihuahua, Mexico, will call on Kirker to help fight Apache raiders in Chihuahua. There, farms, missions, ranches, and mines suffer; some shut down because of the raids. The governor offers $100 bounty for each Apache scalp, but doesn't pay Kirker for the 182 scalps he brings in. The Governor's breach will come back to haunt his state when Kirker helps the Americans in the Mexican-American War.
- President Andrew Jackson establishes diplomatic relations with the Republic of Texas.
- Martin Van Buren becomes U. S. President and inherits a national financial crisis, the Panic of 1837. Banks close throughout the U. S. on May 10. Depression begins. Van

- Buren refuses governmental intervention. Gradually the economy recovers.
  - The financial panic, combined with good reports of those who have been to Oregon, encourages many to migrate to the Pacific Northwest.
- May 1837 (near Platteville, Colorado): New Ft. St. Vrain is open.
- May 27, Homer (Troy Grove), Illinois: James Butler "Wild Bill" Hickok is born.
- June: Dick Wootton organizes a trapper brigade. They leave on a nine-month expedition.
- On the South Platte River (northern Colorado): Ft. Vasquez is in operation. Built as a trading fort, it serves Arapaho, Cheyenne, Sioux, Ute, trappers, traders, and travelers. It has one watchtower, about thirty-six feet high, on the northwest corner. (Construction dates vary.)
- June 28, England: Queen Victoria is crowned and begins her sixty-three year reign over the British Empire. This begins the Victorian Era.
- John Deere invents a steel plow strong enough to turn American prairie sod.
- Pawnee attack a Bent-St. Vrain wagon train led by Marcellin St. Vrain. Ceran St. Vrain, Charles, William, and George Bent file a claim for damages with the U. S. government.
- Summer: In spite of the great depression, the Bank of Missouri opens its doors. During the Panic of 1837 a shortage of specie permeates the United States. Santa Fe Trail trade keeps the Missouri bank alive and healthy. As one of the soundest banks in the nation, the Bank of Missouri becomes a bank of deposit for the U. S. government.
- Forty-eight Cheyenne braves ride south on a scalping and horse rustling party. Kiowa Chief Sitting Bear (in his thirties) and his warriors don't appreciate the visit. They kill all forty-eight of the Cheyenne Bow String Society, not leaving one messenger. Warriors scalp and strip the Cheyenne and lay them in a row on the prairie. No one sees—until a group of Arapaho visit the Kiowa and recognize some scalps on display. They report to the Cheyenne, who plan retaliation.
- August 3, New Mexico: Tired of heavy Mexican taxes and poor military protection, New Mexicans rebel against Mexican rule. The Rebellion of 1837 (Chimayo Revolt) originates in Santa Cruz de la Cañada and spreads to Taos and Santa Fe.
- August 9, New Mexico: Rebels behead Governor Albino Perez. On the 10th they choose Jose Gonzales, buffalo hunter and northern leader of the rebellion, as governor.
- September to the end of January 1838: Manuel Armijo, a former New Mexico governor, raises an army in southern New Mexico and returns to Santa Fe as the "savior of Mexican rule." He appoints himself governor. The Battle of Pojoaque follows; Jose Gonzales is killed.
- Christian County, Kentucky: Dick's last sibling, Frances E. Wootton, is born.
- Dick Wootton and his trapping companions winter in Wyoming.
- The population of the United States is 15,900,000.
- A smallpox epidemic sweeps through the Comanche and Kiowa tribes.

- Winter 1837-38, near the fork of the Whiterock and Uinta Rivers: Antoine Robidoux builds Ft. Uinta (Ft. Robidoux) to supply trappers. His supplies come from New Mexico.

1838

- January 28, New Mexico: The last of the Rebellion of 1837 is squelched.
- Spring, New Mexico: Bill Williams and Dick Wootton trap together.
- Spring: Fewer traders head to Santa Fe this spring. Some blame the Chimayo Revolt. Others don't want to pay Mexico's high tariff.
- Green River (Wyoming): Jim Bridger and Louis Vasquez establish Ft. Bridger.
- Southwest: George Simpson arrives.
- March 7, Sweden: "Swedish Nightingale" Jenny Lind (October 6, 1820-November 2, 1887) debuts at the Stockholm Opera.
- May 10, Maryland: John Wilkes Booth is born.
- Thursday, June 14, Christian County, Kentucky: Dick's brother William Wootton dies.
- Summer, Westport, Missouri: Dick Wootton sells peltry.
- Bent's Fort (Colorado): Preparing to meet the Kiowa, Cheyenne trade buffalo robes for muzzle-loading flintlocks: five robes per gun.
- Wolf Creek, Indian Territory (about 140 miles NW of Oklahoma City): Cheyenne find the Kiowa. Not interested in taking prisoners, Cheyenne kill thirty Kiowa, who are hunting buffalo. Next they find and kill a dozen women digging roots. Battle begins between Cheyenne and Kiowa warriors; several die. Cheyenne cannot storm the Kiowa camp because Kiowa women make defensive breastworks in the sand, cut down trees, and form barricades. At sundown the Cheyenne return north.
- New Mexico: Having withstood years of Comanche and Kiowa raids, the last seventeen survivors at Pecos Pueblo leave home to join the tribe at Jemez Pueblo.
- September: Dick Wootton and nineteen men leave on a trapping expedition.
- October 27, Missouri: Governor Lilburn Boggs issues the Extermination Order, ordering Mormons to leave the state. (c 1832 Mormons moved into Jackson County. Residents said Mormons set up a printing press and talked about building a temple and taking over.)
- Winter 1838-39, "Trail of Tears": Despite outraged protests of many Americans to Congress, most Cherokee are removed to Indian Territory. Traveling with John Ross, the last group begins the journey in December. They carry Cherokee records. Hundreds of Cherokee have escaped and are hiding in Tennessee.

1839

- March, Indian Territory (Oklahoma): Cherokee traveling with John Ross arrive. It is estimated that more than 3,000 Cherokee died in stockades and on the Trail of Tears.
- April, Indian Territory: Cherokee begin rebuilding their nation. They build homes and prepare to plant crops.
- Spring: Manuel Alvarez joins the annual Santa Fe Trail wagon train. He has eight to ten wagons filled with merchandise purchased primarily in New York City and

- Philadelphia.
- Santa Fe, New Mexico: Manuel Alvarez becomes U. S. consul. Charles Bent offers assistance, but finds Alvarez capable and working toward good U. S.-New Mexico relations. A native of Spain, Alvarez has been in America since 1818-19. He speaks English fluently and is the successful proprietor of a Santa Fe store.
- Tuecto, New Mexico: A gold mine opens. Soon the little town has twenty-two stores with business at a brisker pace than in Santa Fe.
- Santa Rita del Cobre in the land of the Chiricahua Apache, southern New Mexico: Copper mines, closed because of Apache raids, reopen.
- June 13: On the way to Oregon, the Peoria Party from Illinois meets Charles Bent's wagon train. Bent and about thirty-five men are headed East with about 200 head of Bent's sheep and ten wagons loaded with pelts.
- Early morning, July 3 or 4, Bent's Fort (Colorado): Bent's horse guard drives 40-50 horses and mules to pasture outside the fort. Yelling and shrieking, Comanche spring from hiding and rush at the animals in an attempt to stampede and rustle them. Quickly assessing the situation, the guard rounds up the cattle and speeds them toward the fort. Almost there, he is struck in the heart by three arrows. Bent's men bury him outside the fort. Comanche return to Texas with thirty-seven of Bent's animals.
- July 6, Bent's Fort (Colorado): The Peoria Party arrives. After being well received and entertained, the party resumes their journey to Oregon on July 11th.
- Santa Fe Trail, New Mexico: Governor Manuel Armijo charges a flat $500 duty on each wagonload of goods entering New Mexico, regardless of wagon size or value of goods.
- August, on the South Platte River (northern Colorado): Bent-St. Vrain, Vasquez-Sublette, and Lupton have trading forts within ten miles of each other.
- September 6 (Oklahoma): Cherokee, one of the "Five Civilized Tribes," unify, adopt a constitution, and choose Tahlequah as their capital.
- December 10: Through American consul Manuel Alvarez, Charles Bent requests Governor Armijo do something about the Taos murder of American Semon [sic] Nash. Four Americans have been murdered in the last few years with no retribution.

1840
- New Mexico: Governor Armijo reports to the Mexican President in Mexico City that he has long considered American built forts near the New Mexico border a danger to New Mexico government—especially the fort of Charles Bent.
- February 10, England: Queen Victoria marries Prince Albert.
- Early afternoon, May 7, Mississippi: Great Natchez Tornado injures 209, kills 317.
- San Antonio, Texas: A delegate of Texans and Comanche meet to discuss terms of relationship. Texans asked the Comanche to bring 200 kidnapped Texans, including the child Cynthia Ann Parker. Comanche bring one boy and one young girl. When Texans see the mutilated girl, they take the Comanche peace delegation captive to guarantee return of all hostages. Fighting breaks out; twenty Comanche are killed. In

retaliation, Comanche torture many of their Texan hostages to death.
- Comanche help the Kiowa make peace with nearby tribes; so they will not need to wage war with others at the same time they work Texas over.
- Indians hold a preliminary powwow seventy miles east of Bent's Fort. For two weeks, they ride and inform scattered bands that a Big Council will be held along the river six miles below Bent's Fort. Some bands remain at the camp several days, enjoy sports, games, and gambling. Many visit Bent's Fort; Bent won't sell them whiskey while they're at such a gathering.
  - At the council tribes exchange gifts. Comanche and Kiowa give hundreds of horses; everyone able to ride receives at least one horse. In return, Cheyenne present rifles and other gifts to the Comanche and Kiowa.

- June 12, Independence, Missouri: The *Daily Missouri Republican* announces Bent-St. Vrain wagons have arrived with thirty packs of beaver pelts, one pack of deerskins, about 15,000 buffalo robes, and twelve sacks of buffalo tongues. The merchandise will be taken by steamboat to St. Louis.
- Midsummer, Tahlequah, Indian Territory (Oklahoma): Cherokee meet and adopt the constitution they drafted last year.
- Gunnison River, near the mouth of the Uncompahgre (Colorado): Antoine Robidoux establishes Ft. Uncompahgre, a trading post. The Ute will drive him out in a few years.
- Santa Fe Trail: A trader on the Santa Fe Trail loses 400 mules in a surprise snowstorm.
- Fall: Dick Wootton saves the life of an Arapaho.
- Sioux sell 24,000,000 acres to the U. S. Government for $1,665,000 up front, plus an amount to be paid in annuities. The government builds brick houses for Sioux who are willing to exchange a nomadic life for a farming lifestyle. After that, many Sioux buy merchandise on credit. When annuities arrive, merchants collect from the government payment. After their debts are paid, many Sioux have little left.
- December: Scotchman David Livingstone (March 19, 1813-1873) sails for Africa. He will become a renowned missionary and explorer.

1841
- January 8, Taos, New Mexico: Charles Beaubien and Guadalupe Miranda petition the Governor of New Mexico for a land grant in northern New Mexico. Padre Antonio Martinez attempts to block it.
- Spring: Dick Wootton joins a trading expedition into Mexico.
- March 4, Washington, D. C.: William Henry Harrison, age sixty-eight, begins his term as U. S. President. He catches cold at his inauguration and dies of pneumonia on April 4th. Vice-President John Tyler succeeds him.
- Dick Wootton drives sheep to Kansas City.
- U. S.: Erastus Bigelow perfects a power loom invented in 1839 for manufacturing carpets.
- U. S.: Cyrus Hall McCormick, who patented his reaper in 1834 and continued to

improve the machine, sells two reapers—his first sales.
- June 6, Texas: President Lamar sends the Texan-Santa Fe Expedition into New Mexico.
- June 10, Independence, Missouri: Charles Bent arrives with eighteen wagonloads of merchandise. He left Bent's Fort in April.
- July 2, Santa Fe, New Mexico: After a little less than two months on the Trail, the annual Santa Fe Trail trade caravan arrives.
- Indian Territory (Oklahoma): The Cherokee Nation begins a public school system. Within three years they will have eighteen schools. The year after that they will begin publishing the territory's first newspaper, *Cherokee Advocate*.
- October 26, Santa Fe: Having been detained in New Mexico waiting a passport, Don Manuel Alvarez leaves for Missouri with a small group of men and sixty-seven animals.
- November 24, Cottonwood Creek near Council Grove, Santa Fe Trail: A severe snowstorm overtakes Don Manuel Alvarez and his men. The storm leaves a three-foot blanket of snow. Two men and forty mules freeze to death. Previously, and repeatedly in the future, travelers suffer loss from severe storms in the same area.
- December 13, Independence, Missouri: Manuel Alvarez and those of his party able to travel arrive. Alvarez sends aid to those left behind.

1842

- Texas: Replacing Mirabeau Lamar, Sam Houston is again President.
- (Colorado): El Pueblo is built.
- June 10-September 3: Kit Carson guides John C. Fremont of the U. S. Topographical Corps on his first exploration of the West.
- China: The Treaty of Nanking officially ends the Opium War. As a result, Hong Kong belongs to Great Britain; five Chinese ports open to British trade.
- Massachusetts limits factory workers twelve years of age and under to ten-hour workdays.
- Valley of the Arkansas River (Colorado): Dick Wootton establishes a farm.
- August 9, Ashburton Treaty between the U. S. and Great Britain: Daniel Webster and Lord Ashburton negotiate a treaty settling the boundary between Canada and Maine. The treaty provides mutual extradition of criminals and restraint of slave trade.
- August 16, Texas: President Sam Houston commissions Charles Alexander Warfield, colonel in the Texas army. Warfield is the son of a successful New Orleans businessman. Assigned to lead an expedition into New Mexico and on to Chihuahua, Mexico, Warfield enlists the help of John McDaniel in St. Louis.
- September 10: America's "First Lady," Letitia Tyler, age fifty-one, dies.
- December, New Mexico: On his way to the States, Dr. Marcus Whitman visits Charles Bent. In the States, Whitman encourages people to settle in the Pacific Northwest.

1843

- January 10, Clay County, Missouri: Alexander Franklin "Frank" James is born.

- January 29, Niles, Ohio: Future U. S. President (1897-1901) William McKinley is born.
- February 16, Texas: President Sam Houston authorizes Colonel Jacob Snively to recruit volunteers to loot Mexican caravans on the Santa Fe Trail.
- February 13-22, New Mexico: Charles Beaubien and a party mark the boundaries of the Beaubien-Miranda Land Grant. Dick Wootton accompanies them.
- April 10, Little Cow Creek (Kansas): Texas recruit John McDaniel leads in the robbery and murder of Don Antonio Jose Chavez.
- Late April (Colorado): Dick Wootton traps along the Arkansas.
- About 350 traders travel the Santa Fe Trail with about $450,000 worth of merchandise. They take about half of the goods further south into Mexico.
- Mexico: Cherokee statesman Sequoya dies searching for lost Cherokee.
  - Sequoia trees are named in his honor.
- Great Migration of 1843: Dr. Marcus Whitman leads emigrants to the Pacific Northwest.
- Travelers encounter flooding on the Plains.
- July 1843-July 1844: Kit Carson and Thomas Fitzpatrick guide John Fremont on his second western expedition.
- August 6, Ft. Bird (Texas): Jacob Snively's band, organized to intercept Mexican traders on the Santa Fe Trail, disbands.
- August 7, Mexico: Because of raids on Mexicans, Mexican President Santa Ana closes Mexican customs houses connected with Santa Fe Trail trade.
- (Northern Colorado): Dick Wootton trades with the Cheyenne.
- Flechado Pass, New Mexico: Ute kill twelve Mexicans. Among the dead are Matias Mestas and Pedro Trujillo, husband of Chipeta Miera. Many have been killed at this location over the years.
- August 26, St. Louis, Missouri: Charles Bent and Ceran St. Vrain sign a contract to supply Philip St. George Cooke and his U. S. dragoons.
- Winter 1843, New Mexico: Dick Wootton trades with the Ute.
- December 30, New Mexico: Steve Lee and Narciso Beaubien are granted the Sangre de Cristo Land Grant north of Taos.

1844
- January, New Mexico: The Mexican government grants Ceran St. Vrain and Cornelio Vigil a portion of land east of the Sangre de Cristo Grant.
- March 31, Mexico: Mexican President Santa Ana repeals his act (August 1843) that closed Mexican customs houses.
- 8:45 a.m., Friday, May 24, Washington, D. C.: Samuel F. B. Morse sends the first message on his telegraph system: "What hath God wrought!" (*Bible*, Numbers 23:23)
  - Known for painting and sculpting, Morse brought an early camera from Paris, learned to photograph, and taught photography. Among his students: Mathew Brady, famed Civil War photographer.
- June 26: Widowed U. S. President Tyler marries Julia Gardiner.

- New Mexico: New Mexico's printing press returns to Santa Fe, where Donaciano Vigil edits the official publication *La Verdad* (*The Truth*).
- July 2, Bent's Fort (Colorado): John Fremont's second exploration expedition returns.
- Treaty of Wanghia: This first treaty between the U. S. and China allows trade.
- Washington, D. C.: The U. S. government passes the Townsite Act of 1844.
- Josiah Gregg, who trafficked in Santa Fe Trail trade from 1831-1840, publishes *Commerce of the Prairies*, his account of the trade.
- Fall, winter: Dick Wootton trades with Indians and smuggles goods into New Mexico.

1845
- March 1, Washington, D. C.: President Tyler signs Congress' joint resolution to allow Texas to become a state of the Union. It will be admitted on December 29th.
- March 3: Florida is admitted to the Union.
- March 4, Washington, D. C.: James Knox Polk takes office as U. S. President (1845-1849). His focus: national expansion.
- Hutchinson County, Texas: Bent-St. Vrain builds Adobe Walls. (Date accounts vary.)
- Spring, New Mexico: (Southern New Mexico:) Apache threaten travel on El Camino Real into Mexico. (Western New Mexico:) Navajo raid, steal goods, kidnap. Governor Armijo doesn't have sufficient troops to control the situation. Next year raids increase.
- Dick Wootton drives buffaloes to Kansas City.
- May 18, Ft. Leavenworth (Kansas): Colonel Stephen W. Kearny and 280 U. S. dragoons leave on an expedition to the Rocky Mountain region.
- John Fremont treks toward California on a third expedition.
- June 8, Tennessee: Former U. S. President Andrew Jackson, age seventy-eight, dies at home. He battled tuberculosis and dropsy for years.
- Summer, south of El Pueblo (Colorado): Dick Wootton builds a cabin.
- August, Santa Fe Trail: Colonel Kearny and his dragoons return to Ft. Leavenworth.
- Ireland: The Potato Famine begins. Irish immigration to the U. S. increases. Before the famine ends in 1847, it will kill about 750,000 Irish.
- October, Rio Grande del Norte: Dick Wootton and Alex Barclay trade with the Ute.
- October 10, Annapolis, Maryland: The U. S. Naval Academy opens. West Point Military Academy was established in 1802.
- U. S. postage for a letter is five cents prepaid for up to 300 miles. Beyond that, it costs ten cents. From 1792-1845 postage was based on distance and cost up to twenty-five cents.
- Washington, D. C.: President Polk sends John Slidell to Mexico.

1846
- February 1-March 1, Goshen's Hole (Wyoming): Dick Wootton and other traders hole up during a blizzard.
- February 26, Scott County, Iowa: William Frederick "Buffalo Bill" Cody is born

- (1846-1917).
- Spring: More than 400 wagons, estimated to be loaded with more than $1,750,000 worth of goods, travel west on the Santa Fe Trail.
- May 13, Washington, D. C.: Congress declares war against Mexico.
- May, Missouri: Governor John C. Edwards calls for volunteers for the Army of the West.
- June 15: The Oregon Treaty between the U. S. and Great Britain establishes the boundary between U. S. and British territory at the 49th parallel in the Pacific Northwest. Vancouver Island goes to the British.
- June 30, Ft. Leavenworth (Kansas): The Army of the West leaves, marching westward.
- Richard M. Hoe produces a steam cylinder press, which enables a larger quantity of newspapers to be printed in less time. Hoe will continue improving his press' efficiency.
- Sierra Grande, Colfax County (New Mexico): Dick Wootton trades with the Ute.
- Pawnee Rock area (Kansas): Chiefs Little Wolf and Sitting Wolf lead Comanche warriors to attack U. S. troops traveling to Mexico. Frightened by Indian war whoops, military horses bolt. Comanche kill all riders separated from the unit.
- Bent's Fort (Colorado): The Army of the West arrives.
- Santa Fe, New Mexico: Don Manuel Alvarez, U. S. counsel in Santa Fe, encourages Governor Manuel Armijo not to oppose Americans when they arrive.
- July 30: Opinion divides regionally when the Walker Tariff lowers the tariff on most items and admits some items duty free. President Polk gladly signs the tariff; it ends some protection and allows farmers to sell to Britain. For the most part, New England and Mid-Atlantic states resist; Southern and Western states approve.
- Summer (Colorado): Twenty-eight Mormon families cross the Plains and settle near El Pueblo.
- July 31, Bent's Fort (Colorado): Most of the Army of the West leave.
- August (Colorado): On his way to California and Oregon, Francis Parkman stops at Bent's Fort and El Pueblo. He's gathering information for his book *The California and Oregon Trail* (*The Oregon Trail*).
- August 15, Las Vegas, New Mexico: Kearny's army enters the Plaza.
- August: Missouri congressman Sterling Price resigns and raises a Second Missouri Mounted Volunteer Infantry to fight in the Mexican-American War.
- August 18, Santa Fe, New Mexico: The Army of the West arrives.
- August 19, Santa Fe: Kearny proclaims his governing code.
- August 22, Santa Fe: Kearny defines the boundaries of New Mexico.
- Thursday, September 10: Elias Howe patents the sewing machine. He demonstrated his machine in Boston last year, but hasn't sold any. His machine can sew 250 lockstitches per minute, outdoing the work of five skilled seamstresses.

The first Howe sewing machine

- September 20-24, northern Mexico: The Battle of Monterey is fought.
- Late September, Santa Fe, New Mexico: Kearny makes governmental appointments.
- September 25, Santa Fe: Kearny and most troops leave for California.
- October, near the Arkansas River Crossing, Santa Fe Trail: Pawnee attack a small, ill-equipped wagon train. They allow traders to leave on foot, but take the animals and what supplies they want. With no desire to be weighed down, they dump the flour and save the cloth bags. The prairie breeze scatters flour across the prairie like an early snowstorm.
- Mid-October, near Mora, New Mexico: Apache camp, kill horses and cattle, and allow their stock to take over private fields. They whip those who try to drive out their stock. A boy is reported seriously wounded; Governor Bent charges Colonel Doniphan to act.
- Late October: George and Jacob Donner lead an Illinois emigrant party on a new trail to California. Snowstorms stop them in the Sierra Nevada Mountains. Dead bodies of fellow travelers sustain survivors until rescuers arrive in February 1847.
- Italian chemist Ascanio Sobrero discovers nitroglycerin, which explodes twenty-five times faster than gunpowder and is more than twice as powerful.
- October 26, New Mexico: Colonel Doniphan places Colonel Sterling Price in command of Santa Fe. Intending to stop Navajo raids, Doniphan sends Major Gilpin with 180 men to northwest Navajo country. He and his troop head for southern Navajo country.
- October 26, New Mexico: Unimpressed by U. S. regulations, Navajo raid Albuquerque and some villages south of Albuquerque. They kill several people and scatter and steal what they can of 5,000 sheep.
- November 22, Ojo del Oso/Bear Spring (New Mexico): Navajo chiefs sign a peace treaty with Colonels Doniphan and Gilpin. This is the first U. S. treaty with the Navajo.
- December 23, Santa Fe (New Mexico): Rumors are astir of a plot to kill Americans.

- December 25, New Mexico: American soldiers win the Battle of Brazito near El Paso.
- December 28: Iowa is admitted to the Union.

1847
- The U. S. Army contracts to carry mail to New Mexico. Mail travels from Fort Leavenworth to Santa Fe on the Santa Fe Trail, 1847-1849.
- January 14, Santa Fe, New Mexico: Governor Charles Bent and party leave for Taos.
- January 19, Taos, New Mexico: The Taos Revolt begins.
- January 24 or 25, El Pueblo (Colorado): John Albert arrives with news of the Taos Revolt/Massacre. Trappers, including Dick Wootton, prepare to leave for Taos.
- February 3, Taos, New Mexico: U. S. troops arrive.
- February 3, Taos: Dick Wootton joins the Battle of Taos.
- February 28: Dick Wootton couriers a military dispatch from Mexico to Santa Fe.
- March 29, Mexico: U. S. General Winfield Scott captures Vera Cruz.
- April, Taos, New Mexico: Taos Massacre assassins are tried.
- May: A company of Third Missouri Mounted Volunteers under Colonel John Ralls rides southwest to join the Mexican-American War.
- The American Medical Association is founded.
- Santa Fe Trail, along the Arkansas River (Kansas): Fort Mann is established in a handy location for those in need of wagon repairs. The commander reports 12,000 people and 3,000 wagons pass the fort this year.
- Summer, Santa Fe Trail: Apache, Comanche, Kiowa and Pawnee raid travelers. Known losses to Indian attack: forty-seven killed, 330 wagons destroyed, 6,500 animals stolen. Comanche and Kiowa encourage Cheyenne to join the raids: killing whites is a very profitable venture and is easier than killing buffalo.
- Summer: Ute war in Colorado. Navajo and Apache raid in New Mexico.
- September 5, Clay County, Missouri: Jesse Woodson James is born to Robert Sallee and Zerelda (Cole) James.
- September 14, 15: General Winfield Scott's U. S. troops enter and occupy Mexico City.
- October 23, Bent's Fort (Colorado): George Bent dies.
- November 29, about 2 p. m., Waiilatpu Mission, Oregon Territory: Cayuse Indians massacre thirteen, including Marcus and Narcissa Whitman.
- December, Santa Fe, New Mexico: The first sawmill in the area is built.
- December 22, New Mexico: Twenty-three-year-old Francis X. Aubrey leaves Santa Fe in an effort to make record time traveling the complete Santa Fe Trail—from Santa Fe to Independence, Missouri. He arrives in Independence on January 5th.
  - Aubrey is an energetic man, full of life. His deep foghorn voice belies his 5'2" stature. He has black hair, a moustache, and full goatee. Though he has piercing, alert eyes, he is a man of thoughtful kindness.

1848
- California: John A. Sutter, pioneer trader in the Sacramento Valley, hires James W.

Marshall to help build a sawmill. While doing carpentry work, Marshall discovers gold nuggets. When news of his discovery spreads, the California Gold Rush begins.
- February 2: The Mexican War ends with the Treaty of Guadalupe Hidalgo.
- February 23, Washington, D. C.: While serving in Congress, former President John Quincy Adams, age eighty-one, dies when stricken with paralysis. His wife, Louisa Johnson Adams, will survive him four years.
- Monday, March 6, Taos, New Mexico: Dick Wootton marries Dolores LeFevre and is appointed temporary sheriff.
- March 19, Monmouth, Illinois: Wyatt Earp (buffalo hunter, Indian fighter, and Kansas and Arizona lawman) is born. (March 19, 1848-January 13, 1929)
- March, New Mexico: Dick Wootton and Antoine Leroux guide Colonel Newby into Navajo country.
- May 19, Santa Fe, New Mexico: Francis X. Aubrey leaves for Independence. He arrives on May 28th and breaks his Santa Fe Trail travel record by almost six days.
- Comanche attack a Bent-St. Vrain wagon train. Bent's men repel the attack and kill Chief Red Arm. They scalp one dead warrior—a gift for the Cheyenne. It is a favorable thing to receive a scalp to dance over.
- July 4: President Polk announces ratification of the Treaty of Guadalupe Hidalgo. This officially ends the Mexican-American War. Remaining troops will leave Mexico in less than a month.
- September 12, Santa Fe: Francis X. Aubrey wagers $1,000 he can travel from Santa Fe to Independence in six days. With fresh mounts prepared along the way, he arrives bedraggled in Independence five days and sixteen hours later—September 17th.
- Santa Fe Trail: A U. S. government train loses 800 oxen—frozen to death.
- November 22, St. Joseph, Missouri: There's no question: there is gold in California. Joseph Wittman escorted John Sutter's wife and daughter to California and has returned with quarts of California gold to be assayed. The chemist's verdict: pure gold.
- November, Bent's Fort (Colorado): About 3,500 Indians camp around the fort in about 600 lodges and wait for U. S. government annuities.
- November: John C. Fremont begins a fourth exploration expedition.

1849
- January 23, Kentucky: Dick Wootton's sister Mary Catherine Daniel, dies.
- February 1, Taos, New Mexico: Dick Wootton's first child is born.
- Early March, Taos, New Mexico: Ute kill Bill Williams and Dr. Benjamin Kern.
- Washington, D. C.: During his term, President Polk helps put the national monetary system back under federal control.
- Washington, D. C.: Zachary Taylor, second cousin of former U. S. President James Madison, becomes President.
- Spring: The first rush of California gold seekers cross the Plains.
- June 15, Tennessee: Three months after leaving Presidential office, fifty-three-year-old James K. Polk dies. Some attribute his death to the stress of his years in office.

- Cholera takes a heavy toll on Southern Cheyenne. Northern Cheyenne are little affected.
- July 12: America's beloved former first lady Dolley Payne Madison, age eighty-one, dies. She rescued the Declaration of Independence, many of her husband's papers, and many items of national importance when the British burned the White House in August 1814.
- (Colorado): On the way to the California gold fields, Georgia miners find gold at the headwaters of Cache la Poudre, on Cherry Creek and Ralston Creek. Green Russell and party, also from Georgia, find gold on the Sweetwater and the North Platte.
- James S. Calhoun, first U. S. Indian agent in New Mexico, commends Pueblo Indians to Washington. He cites the industry of these settled people and asks protection for them and their property.
- August 21, Bent's Fort (Colorado): William Bent torches Bent's Fort.
- October 29, Taos, New Mexico: Messengers report the White Massacre.
- November 28, Santa Fe: The Santa Fe *New Mexican* publishes its first edition.
- Washington, D. C.: The Bureau of Indian Affairs moves from the War Department to the new Department of the Interior.

1850
- Taos, New Mexico: Dick Wootton and Charles D. Williams partner in a store.
- The U. S. Post Office Department takes over mail service to Santa Fe. Eight-passenger stagecoaches will carry both passengers and mail. The arrangement will last fifteen years. Near Wagon Mound, New Mexico: Kiowa attack the first mail-passenger stage, kill the driver and eight guards, and burn the stage. There were no passengers.
- March 21 or 26, Taos, New Mexico: Richens L. Wootton, Jr. is born.
- Ft. Atkinson is built near old Ft. Mann.
- Near Cimarron, New Mexico: Rayado Post is established to protect travelers.
- June 5, Alabama: Pat Garrett (New Mexico lawman) is born.
- July 9, Washington, D. C.: President Zachary Taylor, age sixty-five, dies in the White House. Millard Fillmore takes office the next day.
- Near Wagon Mound, New Mexico: Apache attack a stagecoach. The ten men from the coach use their fallen horses as a barricade and hold off the Apache until Ute arrive the next day and join the Apache. Later, members of a wagon train pass by and see the ten dead bodies and remains of the stagecoach.
- September: California is admitted to the Union as a state. New Mexico and Arizona become territories.
- The 1850 U. S. census reports the population of New Mexico: 61,547.
  - Population of Santa Fe, 4,500; Fernando de Taos, 800; Abiquiu, 1,800
  - There are eight teachers and 466 pupils in New Mexico. All education is private.
- Santa Fe: Ft. Marcy's Baptist chaplain, Hiram W. Read, establishes a school in town.
- September 20, Washington, D. C.: The Compromise of 1850 (a series of bills) is passed in a stopgap attempt to compromise between slavery and anti-slavery factions.

- John C. Calhoun, longtime Southern representative, dies.

1851
- Independence, Missouri: The estimated population is 2,500.
- Southwestern New Mexico Territory: For years Apache have raided. This year miners at Piños Altos have had enough. They whip Apache leader Mangas Coloradas. That stirs up unprecedented warfare that will continue thirty-five years. Apache leaders Nana, Geronimo, and Victorio will take up the torch after Mangas Coloradas' death in 1863.
- Dick Wootton goes to St. Louis for merchandise.
- Santa Fe, New Mexico Territory: Jean B. Lamy of France arrives to be the Roman Catholic Bishop. He attempts to reform the local priesthood and educational system begun by Padre Martinez of Taos in the 1830's.
- France: Louis Napoleon Bonaparte (nephew of Napoleon Bonaparte), elected to serve a four-year term as French President in 1848, assumes a ten-year right to the office. Next year he will establish the Second French Empire and declare himself Emperor.
- New Mexico Territory: Forts Fillmore, Defiance, and Conrad are built. (Ft. Conrad, at the foot of Valverde Mesa in southern New Mexico, protects travelers on the Jornado del Muerto section of El Camino Real. Ft. Fillmore, built under Lt. Col. Edwin V. Sumner's direction, protects travelers between El Paso, Texas, and Las Cruces, New Mexico.)
- August 2, near the junction of the Cimarron and Mountain branches of the Santa Fe Trail: Colonel E. B. Alexander and his men begin building Ft. Union.
- Autumn, Ft. Laramie: At the request of Indian Agent Thomas Fitzpatrick, Congress authorizes funds for a conference at Ft. Laramie. Ten thousand Indians representing nine tribes meet with U. S. government agents.
  - Sioux, Crow, Shoshone, and Cheyenne are among the tribes represented. Comanche and Kiowa have sent word they'll not come because they own too many fine horses to risk them among so many fine horse thieves.
  - U. S. government representatives offer the tribes represented an annuity payment of $50,000 per year for fifty years in exchange for permission to establish military posts and safe roads. The Senate ratifies the agreement for ten-fifteen years.
- Friday, December 12, Christian County, Kentucky: Dick's brother Thomas dies.

1852
- April 14, Taos, New Mexico Territory: Frances Dolores Wootton is born.
- Harriet Beecher Stowe's anti-slavery book *Uncle Tom's Cabin* is published. It began to appear last year in installment form.
- Late May, Santa Fe: Sick with scurvy and jaundice, New Mexico Governor James S. Calhoun leaves for Missouri.
- June, Ute Creek, San Luis Valley (Colorado): The U. S. builds Ft. Massachusetts at the western base of Mt. Blanca. Ute are not intimidated; attacks continue.
  - Ft. Massachusetts is the first regularly staffed military post in what will later be

the state of Colorado. It will remain in service until 1858.
- Ft. Leavenworth: A 500-wagon train, including wagons hauling U. S. government supplies, and a train led by Francis Aubrey leave enroute to Ft. Union and Santa Fe.
  - Ft. Leavenworth is a small, primarily tent settlement with much wagon activity.
  - On this train freight is hauled from Leavenworth to Santa Fe at $10.00 per hundred. Teamsters earn twenty-five dollars per month, plus meals. Passengers, except children, pay $250 for the trip. Children travel half fare.
  - While the train camps near Pawnee Rock, Indians stampede and rustle the train's 200 Army horses. Riders go back to Ft. Leavenworth and return with replacement horses.
  - Babies are born while the wagon train is enroute. One member of the train dies and is buried in the wagon ruts. To keep her body from desecration, members of the train drive over the ruts to obliterate evidence of a grave.
- Thursday, June 24, Taos (New Mexico): Dick Wootton leaves, driving sheep to California.
- Summer, fifteen miles south of Taos on the Santa Fe-Taos road: Cantonment Burgwin is built to protect travelers from Jicarilla Apache and Ute. It is named for Captain John Burgwin, killed in the Battle of Taos. It will be renamed Ft. Burgwin (mid-1850's) and will serve until 1860. The fort is surrounded by mountains.
- June 30, Santa Fe Trail, near Independence, Missouri: New Mexico Governor James S. Calhoun dies. President Fillmore appoints William Carr Lane (St. Louis' first elected mayor) in his place. Lane leaves St. Louis in July, travels forty days, and arrives in Santa Fe on September 9. Having endured the rigors of the Trail, Lane urges Washington to:
  - provide monthly stage and mail service between Santa Fe and Missouri.
  - establish manned stations every forty to forty-five miles along the Trail—places where travelers can find shelter and supplies.
  - dig wells where water is scarce along the Cimarron Cut-Off.
- Laguna Pueblo, New Mexico Territory: Baptist Samuel Gorman establishes a school for Indian children.
- Fall, stage station, two miles from Ft. Union (New Mexico): Indians attack, burn the stage station and stables, scalp a stock tender, and steal the station's horses. Ft. Union soldiers arrive and drive Indians away. Soldiers return to the fort next day.
- October 9, Sacramento Valley, California: Wootton and crew arrive with 8,900 sheep.
- Henry Clay, the Great Compromiser, and Daniel Webster, the great Northern orator, die.
- Santa Fe, New Mexico Territory: Catholic Bishop Jean B. Lamy organizes a boys' school. He will open a Catholic school for girls next year.

1853
- About March, Taos, New Mexico Territory: Lorett Wootton is born.
- March 30: Former First Lady Abigail Fillmore, age fifty-five, dies after taking cold

and becoming ill at the inauguration of President Franklin Pierce.
- Taos, New Mexico Territory: Dick Wootton arrives home from California.
- (Colorado): Construction begins on William Bent's new Stone Fort.
- Near the junction of the Santa Fe and Oregon Trails (Kansas): Fort Riley is built.
- Summer, Council Grove (Kansas): This is now a settlement with about twenty houses—some framed, some log. There is also a Methodist mission house made of local limestone. Indian villages dot the landscape up and down the nearby stream.
- Santa Fe: David Meriwether, imprisoned by the Spanish in 1820 for attempting to trade in New Mexico, returns as appointed governor. Born in Virginia and transplanted to Kentucky, Meriwether served as U. S. Representative from Kentucky before his New Mexico appointment. He is now fifty-three and will serve until 1857.
- Congress has authorized John Williams Gunnison to explore a feasible railroad route along the 38th parallel. He begins his journey with an expedition party.
- On the bank across from Dona Ana, southwest New Mexico Territory: Ft. Thorn is built to guard the San Diego road. It will serve from 1853-59.
- July 8, Japan: Commodore Matthew Calbraith Perry and his U. S. Navy ships arrive in Tokyo Bay, a port closed to outside trade more than 100 years. Perry boldly refuses to deal with emissaries, but respectfully presents his documents to the two princes, who represent the emperor. To give the emperor time, Perry leaves Japan and sails to China, but will return in February.
- August or September (Colorado): Dick Wootton, Charlie Autobees, Levin Mitchell and William Kroenig begin to establish Huerfano village.
- October, along the Sevier River (Utah): Piute Indians kill Captain John W. Gunnison and several of his men. Lt. Edward G. Beckwith and the survivors complete the government survey.
- October 31: The U. S. military 9th Department is renamed the Department of New Mexico.
- November 26: William Bartholomew (changed to Barclay) Masterson is born. "Bat" will figure as a gunfighter, buffalo hunter, scout, and lawman in Kansas, Colorado, and New York. (Years given for birth vary: 1850-1859. He died October 25, 1921.)
- December 30: Gadsden Treaty/Purchase negotiated by James Gadsen, settles the border dispute between the U. S. and Mexico. Franklin Pierce is U. S. President; Antonio Lopez de Santa Ana is president of Mexico. The U. S. pays Mexico $10,000,000 for the disputed boundary land. This land offers the U. S. the possibility of a southern railroad route. As a result of the treaty, westward immigration from the Southern states increases.

1854

- January 15, Santa Fe: A Baptist church opens. This is the first organized religious group in New Mexico other than Catholic or Native American.
- February, Japan: Commodore Perry returns. After a few weeks the Japanese sign a treaty that allows the U. S. the right to trade in the ports of Shimoda and Hakodate.
- Spring (Colorado): One Cheyenne visits a Kiowa camp. On his return, he brings

- smallpox to his clan near Bent's Stone Fort.
- Cholera spreads again.
- About March, Taos (New Mexico): George Wootton is born.
- May 22: Introduced in January, the Kansas-Nebraska Act passes. The Act separates and organizes the territories of Kansas and Nebraska and allows each to choose whether to be a free or slave territory. If either chooses slavery, the Fugitive Slave Law will apply. Some interpret this as an undoing of the Compromise of 1850. Sectional dissension grows between North and South.
- Between Socorro and Las Cruces (southern New Mexico): The U. S. government replaces Ft. Conrad with Ft. Craig. The twenty-two-building fort will house two companies and serve from 1854-1884.
- The U. S. Government creates the office of Surveyor General. The office will be in charge of settling land grant questions in New Mexico.
    - Problems arose after Kearny proclaimed property protection. Some landowners didn't realize the need to have land claims validated: hadn't Mr. Kearny said they were guaranteed? Others didn't know how to protect their rights and couldn't afford legal fees to have someone else do it. Many lost land.
    - The Surveyor General acknowledges land grants given Pueblo Indians. Some pueblos don't have documentation to support their claims. The U. S. government considers the fact they've remained in the same place so long to be documentation enough. It will honor land claims of seventeen Indian pueblos.
- Santa Fe, New Mexico Territory: Bishop Lamy unfrocks Padre Antonio Jose Martinez.
- Summer, outside of Ft. Laramie (Wyoming): Waiting for annuities, a Sioux kills a cow. Seeking recompense, the owner reports the loss. Under the Ft. Laramie Treaty, Americans are to punish their own; Indians are to punish their own. Lt. John L. Grattan attempts to arrest the warrior; the Sioux will not turn him over. They shoot twenty-four arrows into Grattan's body and kill his thirty soldiers. Neither the Army, nor the Sioux are willing to let the situation go at that. The Ft. Laramie Treaty goes down the drain.
- August, Santa Fe: During an argument, attorney and newspaperman Richard Hanson Weightman stabs Francis Xavier Aubrey to death. Born in Quebec, Canada, in 1824, Aubrey traveled the Santa Fe Trail twenty-seven times in nine years. He pioneered the Santa Fe Trail's Aubrey Cut-Off.
- Fall: President Pierce appoints A. H. Reeder governor of Kansas Territory. When Reeder calls for an election of territorial legislators, proponents of slavery cross the Missouri border into Kansas—tents and all. There are only 831 legal voters in Kansas. More than 6,000 cast votes, resulting in a pro-slavery legislature.
- Christmas Massacre, El Pueblo (Colorado): Led by Chief Tierra Blanca/Blanco, Ute gain entrance to El Pueblo and massacre the inhabitants.

1855
- January, El Pueblo (Colorado): Ute return. Arapaho pursue and defeat them.

- Sunday, April 29, Huerfano Village (Colorado): Jose Manuel Wootton is born.
- May 6, Huerfano Village (Colorado): Dolores Wootton dies.
- July 14, Taos, New Mexico Territory: Jose Manuel Wootton dies.
- Congress allots $100,000 to improve two roads from Fort Riley on the Platte River—to Bent's Fort, and to Bridger's Pass (Wyoming).
- March 19, near Lincoln, New Mexico Territory: To protect settlers and travelers from the Apache, General John Garland selects a sight for Ft. Stanton. (Kit Carson will headquarter there during his expedition against the Mescalero Apache. Stanton will operate as a fort until 1896, when it will become a hospital for tubercular patients. For a short time during World War II, it will be a POW camp.)
- Santa Fe Trail trade is valued at $5,000,000 in 1855.

1856

- Winter 1855-56, Bent's Fort (Colorado): Dick Wootton marries Mary Ann Manning.
- March 1, Ft. Union (New Mexico): Wootton leaves, leading a thirty-six-wagon train to Kansas City.
- April 29, Indianola, Texas: Thirty-four Egyptian camels arrive for the U. S. Camel Corps.
- "Patent Pool" Agreement: Others improved Elias Howe's patented sewing machine and were earning profit. By the end of 1854 Howe won a series of legal battles concerning patent rights. This year a Patent Pool Agreement sets a precedent for future patents. Sewing machine manufacturers will pay $5 per machine to Elias Howe for his invention patent and to Isaac Singer for his improvements on Howe's invention.
- April, North Platte: U. S. troops and Cheyenne begin a prolonged conflict. Source of the problem: The Cheyenne, in possession of four Army horses, return three. Little Wolf refuses to give up the fourth. He claims it wasn't one of the Army horses, but doesn't say where the fourth horse is. The Army commander orders the arrest of three Cheyenne. One escapes; one is shot attempting escape; Wolf Fire is imprisoned. As they flee toward the Black Hills, Wolf Fire's family come upon an unsuspecting trapper—Ganier—and kill him. Other Cheyenne flee toward the Arkansas River to join the Southern Cheyenne. The Army finds the deserted lodges of the Northern Cheyenne and confiscates the property.
- New Mexico Territory: Dick Wootton moves his family to Ft. Barclay.
- San Miguel County (New Mexico): Chief Esaquipa and a band of Comanche camp on the banks of the Gallinas River and steal corn from area ranchers. They require rancher Alex Hatch to contribute an ox and other supplies. Soon after the Comanche leave, a band of Kiowa stop at the ranch for food on their way to war with the Navajo.
  - Thievery, or "what belongs to one belongs to all," is a common practice among Indians. At times, when an outlying settler begins to prosper, a band of Indians ride in on a night raid, massacre the family, and steal stock or provisions or kidnap women and/or children.

- End of August: On their way to war with the Pawnee, Cheyenne see a mail stage approaching. Urged to ask the driver for tobacco, two of the young men take out after the stage. The driver assumes the worst, shoots at the Indians, and speeds off—but not before the Indians whip up their bows and shoot arrows into the driver's arm.
    - When they hear the driver's shot, other Indians hurry to see what's happening. Indian leaders quirt the two young men for shooting the driver. Next day troops from Fort Kearny charge the Indian camp. The Cheyenne flee; ten are killed.
    - Within a couple weeks, Cheyenne attack four groups of travelers, take captives, and kill. Among the dead: Utah's Congressional delegate Almon Babbitt, two women, two children, six men. Cheyenne take two women and one child captive.
- Fall (Bent's Fort): William Bent dispenses annuities to the Southern Cheyenne.
- September 25: In his annual report, Indian Agent Thomas S. Twiss relates summer problems. He also reports the Northern Cheyenne have come to him; all is well now.
- September 25: In his annual report Superintendent of Indian Affairs Alfred Cumming writes that the Comanche have been spending winter months raiding and stealing in Texas as far as the Rio Grande. They then return north, hunt buffalo, and wait for government annuities. Cumming reports the Kiowa and Comanche are insolent, consider white men far beneath them, and despise government officers.
- December 28, Staunton, Virginia: Woodrow Wilson (U. S. President 1913-1921) is born.
- December 1856, Ft. Barclay, New Mexico Territory: Joseph Wootton is born.
- Winter 1856-57 is a hard winter. One government-contracted freight train takes eleven months to travel between Ft. Leavenworth and Utah. Flour is the train's chief commodity.

1857

- March 4: After defeating candidate John C. Fremont of the new Republican Party, James Buchanan takes office as U. S. President. Buchanan is the only bachelor President to date.
- Spring (Solomon River, northern Kansas): Having hashed over grievances in winter camp, many bands of Northern and Southern Cheyenne unite. Cheyenne medicine men persuade warriors their power will render white men's guns powerless against the warriors. Cheyenne ask Sioux to join them against the white. The Sioux not only refuse, Sioux Chief Long Chin relates the incident to mountain man Tim Goodale when their paths cross at Ash Hollow.
- Kansas City: Eight hundred and sixty-five thousand pounds of wool arrive from New Mexico. By 1859 New Mexico wool gains such a reputation that buyers from Boston and New York will be on hand to buy the wool as soon as it arrives on Santa Fe Trail wagon trains.
- Spring: Antoine Lebrie, Leandro Beral, Louis Clouthier, and Leon Constantin drive William Bent's thirty-two-wagon train across the Plains and distribute presents from the U. S. government to the Plains Indians in exchange for peace. Each wagon, pulled by five yoke of oxen, carries 5,000 pounds of goods. Cheyenne, Kiowa, Comanche,

Arapaho, and some Apache receive the goods near the Arkansas River (near Ft. Dodge, Kansas). After distribution, Bent takes the wagons to Missouri to restock. He travels on to Washington, D. C. to make his report as Indian agent. He returns to Missouri, picks up merchandise, and goes back to his Stone Fort.
- Colonel E. V. Sumner commissions Lt. John Pope to survey the shortest practical route between Ft. Leavenworth (Kansas) and Ft. Union (New Mexico). Pope's route, the Ft. Leavenworth Trail/Road, is a compromise between the Mountain Branch and the Cimarron Branch of the Santa Fe Trail.
- Spring: Cheyenne raid emigrants along the Platte River.
- New York City's first passenger elevator begins service.
- May 20, Ft. Leavenworth (Kansas): Colonel E. V. Sumner leaves with eight companies of cavalry. His orders are to find the Cheyenne and "bring them to terms." If that doesn't work, soldiers are to "chastise them properly." Sumner dispatches Major John Sedgwick and four companies to check the Arkansas River area. (Fall Leaf, a Delaware Indian who worked with Fremont in 1853, guides.) Sumner and the remaining companies scout the Platte River, then turn south at Ft. Laramie (Wyoming).
  - Major Sedgwick (born September 13, 1813, Cornwall Hollow, Connecticut) graduated from West Point, served in the Seminole and Mexican Wars, and in the 1st Cavalry. During the Civil War, he will command the Army of the Potomac's V and VI Corps. He will command at Seven Days' Battles, Antietam, Chancellorsville, Fair Oaks, and Gettysburg. A leader who actually leads, Sedgwick will be shot and killed at the forefront of battle at Spotsylvania, May 9, 1864. He never marries.
  - Born in Boston, January 30, 1797, Edwin Vose Sumner is affectionately called "Bull o' the Woods." Some say his voice when commanding troops inspired the nickname. Others connect the name to his military tenacity, his toughing it out to victory. Others claim the nickname was born when a musket ball hit him upside the head and didn't seem to leave much of a dent. Sumner served in the Mexican War and will serve as Major General of volunteers in the Civil War.
- June, Cheyenne River area: A Blackfoot war party kills a party of Sioux.
- July 4 (Colorado): Unable to locate Cheyenne bands, Colonel Sumner and Major Sedgwick meet on the South Platte and search on together.
- About 10 a.m., July 29, Solomon's Fork, Kansas Territory: Colonel Sumner's scouts see a small band of Cheyenne and report to Sumner. Suddenly, Sumner and Sedgwick face hundreds of warriors, drawn for battle. Sumner estimates there are 300 warriors; some soldiers figure there are 900. Many warriors have rifles and revolvers; all are armed and have mounts. Sumner speaks to his soldiers of his confidence in them and their united effort and orders troops forward. Soldiers charge with bayonets and kill about thirty Cheyenne. Warriors flee, but not before they kill two soldiers and wound eight soldiers and Lt. James Elwell Brown "J. E. B." Stuart (of Civil War fame).

- Colonel Sumner cares for his wounded and rests the troops and animals before continuing pursuit. He's unaware the Cheyenne are camped nearby.
- July 31, about fifteen miles from the battlefield (above): Sumner's troop finds the Indian camp. Cheyenne have taken about half their lodges; 171 remain. Soldiers destroy those. Sumner moves along the Arkansas River to protect the road near Ft. Atkinson (Kansas).
- Ft. Atkinson (Kansas): On his arrival, Colonel Sumner learns that the annual gifts for the Cheyenne are on their way to Bent's (Stone) Fort for distribution. Knowing the gifts include guns and ammunition, he leaves to intercept provisions.
- Utah Territory: Appointment of Alfred Cumming as governor triggers the Mormon War, also called the Utah War.
- August 2, about 11 a.m.: About 150 Cheyenne attack nineteen men driving cattle to Salt Lake for the Utah Expedition. They kill William Sandburn and wound another. They drive off all 824 cattle and drive off or kill eighteen of the twenty horses and mules. That night survivors reach Ft. Kearny (Nebraska) and report the incident. Survivors think they wounded four or five Cheyenne and killed two.
- August 3: Soldiers from Ft. Kearny find Mr. Sandburn's body stripped, scalped, and molested. After they bury him, soldiers search for the cattle, but find only forty-three. They return to the fort the next day.
- August, Eastern United States: The Panic of 1857 begins after the closure of the Ohio Life Insurance and Trust Company. The Panic follows inflated prosperity in the early 1850's and will impede westward expansion of railroads.
- August 9: Colonel Sumner reports not one woman or child has been harmed during his expedition.
- September: Secretary of War John B. Floyd sends Sumner word that the Cheyenne Campaign is ended. Colonel Sumner replies, expressing disappointment that a job so well begun cannot be finished. He addresses the issue of arms, ammunition, and provisions sent to the very tribe from whom the government wanted protection.
- September 7-11, Mountain Meadows Massacre, Utah Territory: Mormons and Indians attack an emigrant train traveling toward California.
- September 12: Lieutenant E. G. Marshall of Ft. Kearny reports to Adjutant General S. Cooper that approximately 150 Cheyenne killed three U. S. government contracted teamsters near Ash Hollow and took a supply of U. S. arms and ammunition.
- September 15, Ft. Kearny (Nebraska): Lieutenant E. G. Marshall writes Adjutant General Cooper, confirms his report of September 12th, and adds that fifty head of cattle were also run off. Yesterday, the Cheyenne came within a mile of the fort; today, Cheyenne line the road west of the fort. The boldness of the Cheyenne has persuaded Marshall they're aware that Ft. Kearny is only a one-company post—a defensive, not an offensive position. He warns his superior trouble is only beginning.
- September 15, Cincinnati, Ohio: William H. Taft (U. S. President 1909-1913) is born.
- Winter 1857-1858: Captain Randolph B. Marcy and his troop march from Ft. Bridger

(Wyoming) to Ft. Union (New Mexico) to obtain supplies to rescue Albert S. Johnston's Mormon War troops.
- Because of the Mormon War, this is the most profitable year for those freighting to Utah.

1858
- February 9: Dr. L. J. Russell and his brother William Greeneberry Russell organize a party of gold seekers—the Green Russell Party.
- March, Canadian River country, New Mexico Territory: Comanche kill Mr. Bushman, Sam Watrous' ranch foreman.
- April, near the Platte Bridge, Kansas Territory (Colorado): Blackfoot Indians steal horses from the Arapaho. In his annual report, Indian Agent Thomas S. Twiss reports some Indians strictly observe their agreement not to attack their neighbors; but he's had quite a time with the Crow and Blackfoot, who keep attacking Sioux, Cheyenne, and Arapaho in his agency. Twiss suggests military reservations are the only worthwhile avenue the government has to change the disposition of some tribes. He thinks that would save millions of dollars the country spends as a result of some tribes' behavior.
- May 11: Minnesota becomes a state.
- May, Lawrence (Kansas): The Lawrence Party leave in search of Cherry Creek gold.
- (Loveland, Colorado): Mariano Modeno builds a cabin and fortification for his family. In 1862 his stone Ft. Namaqua will become a fortified station for the Overland Stage.
- Summer, North Platte River below Ft. Laramie: William Bent distributes government goods to five tribes. His men drive the wagons into a circle and chain the wheels together; so goods can be unpacked and divided into piles, one for each tribe. Piles are not equal, but appropriate to each tribe. Bent calls the chiefs and points to their pile of goods. The chiefs, in turn, call their young men to bear the goods.
- August 5: A transatlantic cable connects telegraph service between Europe and the United States. It operates successfully only a few weeks. Cyrus West Field, who conceived the idea, and his associates Peter Cooper, Marshall Robert, Moses Taylor, and Chandler White do not give up until they have a successful lasting cable (1866).
- New Mexico Territory (southern Colorado): Ft. Garland is built in an open valley six miles south of Ft. Massachusetts. It replaces that poorly located fort and guards local residents and those traveling Sangre de Cristo Pass.
- August 17 (Colorado): Indian Agent Robert C. Miller reports from Bent's Fort:
  - Cheyenne tell him their battle with Col. Sumner last year taught them a lesson. Older members of the tribe want the Great Father in Washington to give them land, farming tools, and people to teach them to use them.
  - Comanche and Kiowa have different ideas. Miller tells the Kiowa if they don't stop attacks, the Great Father will stop their presents and come punish them. Chief To-Hosea says the White Father is a coward: his men are weak; he's no match for the chief's warriors. Kiowa are willing to send delegates to

Washington. (In sixty days Indian delegates meet Agent Miller for the trip to Washington.)
- Cheyenne want land at the headwaters of the South Platte. Kiowa and Comanche prefer the Red River area. Miller confers with Indian Agent Kit Carson in Taos before he goes to Washington. Kit knows the entire area and will be able to advise him.
- August 21-October 15: In a series of public debates Stephen A. Douglas and Abraham Lincoln vie for the position of U. S. Senator from Illinois. Douglas is re-elected, but Lincoln gains national fame.
- John L. Mason patents a glass jar with a rubber seal and glass top. The Mason jar enables people to preserve food in a manner more like the fresh product.
- Early September, Salt Lake City (Utah): Wootton and Doyle arrive with supplies.
- September 15: Butterfield Southern Overland Mail Co. mail coaches leave St. Louis and San Francisco—the company's first cross-country runs.
- September 24, east side of Cherry Creek, Kansas Territory (Colorado): Traders John Smith and William McGaa help the Lawrence Party form St. Charles Town Association.
- September 28: The first Butterfield stage enters southern New Mexico.
- Ft. Barclay, New Mexico Territory: William Wootton is born.
- October 20-30, Cherry Creek (Colorado): Gold-seekers discuss formation of a town company on the west side of Cherry Creek.
- Seeing Donati's Comet with its two curved tails, Indians along the Santa Fe Trail say this will be a hard winter.
- October 27, New York City: Theodore Roosevelt (U. S. President 1901-1909) is born.
- October 29, Cherry Creek, Kansas Territory: A severe snowstorm hits.
- November 1, west side of Cherry Creek (Colorado): Gold-seekers name their town site Auraria Town Company.
- New Mexico Territory: Dick Wootton and family leave Ft. Barclay.
- December (Colorado): With immigrants moving to the Cherry Creek area, Cheyenne and Arapaho are concerned about hunting grounds near the Arkansas and Platte Rivers. They appoint William Bent to represent them. He listens and writes Superintendent of Indian Affairs Robinson in St. Louis to explain the situation. He'll see Robinson in the spring, but hopes Robinson will be kind and do something for the Indians this winter.
- Friday, December 24, Auraria (Colorado): Wootton family arrives.

1859
- January 1 (Colorado): Auraria boasts fifty cabins; Denver has about twenty.
- January 1: The *Journal of Commerce* reports goods received in the States from New Mexico and the mountains in 1858: Wool: 1,051,000 lbs.; goatskins: 55,000; dressed deerskins: 60,000; dry hides: 61,857; specie in boxes: 1,527,789; an estimated $50,000 worth of furs and skins, also, furs and buffalo robes.

- January 7, Idaho Springs (Colorado): George Andrew Jackson journals that he discovered gold here today. Born about 1824, George hales from Glasgow, Missouri. Jackson, James Sanders, and Tom L. Golden are the Chicago Party. Jackson had worked the California gold fields, made a fortune, and lost it. Jackson and Tom Golden found Golden City and remain in the area until the Civil War. Jackson will join the Confederacy. After the war he will return to mine in Ouray, Colorado, and remain until his death.
- January 15, Boulder Canyon (Colorado): Gold is discovered. Before the end of February, prospectors also strike gold in Deadwood and Gold Hill.
- Auraria (Colorado): Wootton builds the first two-story building in the area.
- February 2 (Colorado): Indian Agent Thomas Twiss writes the Office of Indian Affairs. Because of emigration into the South Platte area, he recommends a treaty of provision be made with the Indians and offers to submit a plan.
- February 14: Oregon is admitted to the Union.
- March 8, Nebraska: W. N. Byers and associates leave the little town of Omaha with plans to establish a newspaper in the Rocky Mountain region.
- Sierra Mountains, Nevada: First discovered in 1856, the Comstock Lode, rich in gold and silver, is rediscovered. Virginia City booms.
- South of Auraria (Colorado): D. C. Oakes and Street open a steam-powered lumber mill.
- April 17, Auraria (Colorado): W. N. Byers arrives and rents part of Dick Wootton's building for the first home of his *Rocky Mountain News*.
- April 18, Leavenworth, Kansas: The first Leavenworth & Pikes Peak Express Company coach leaves for Denver. Two coaches travel together on this first run and arrive May 17.
- April 21, Auraria (Colorado): R. L. Wootton becomes an agent for the Arapaho Express.
- May 6, Clear Creek, west of Denver (Colorado): John H. Gregory discovers the Gregory Lode. He works his claim and prospects as late as August 27. He then sells out and returns home with his earnings to ease his wife's workload and provide his children with a good education. In less than three months, 20,000-30,000 men begin to prospect in the vicinity of Gregory Gulch. It becomes known as the "The Richest Square Mile on Earth."
- Near the mouth of the Pawnee River (Kansas): Ft. Larned is established.
- Summer (Colorado): Indian Agent William Bent brings government goods from the States to distribute to the Indians.
- San Luis Valley (Colorado): Settlers from New Mexico begin milling flour.
- Sunday afternoon, August 28, Titusville, Pennsylvania: Uncle Billy Smith has been helping Edwin L. Drake drill for oil. They stopped work yesterday afternoon and plan to start again Monday; but this afternoon, Uncle Billy finds dark liquid near the surface. Excitedly, he dips into the well and draws out oil. This first U. S. oil well is sixty-nine feet deep.

- When refined into kerosene, the oil will transform the lighting of homes. Americans will soon light their homes with kerosene, rather than with candles or whale blubber oil. Oil will lubricate machinery in the coming War.
- This year 2,000 barrels of oil will be produced in the U. S., 500,000 in 1860, and more than 2,000,000 in 1861.
- September 5, Kansas Territory (Colorado): Citizens of Arapahoe County vote down the proposed state constitution (vote: 2,007 to 164).
- Mid-September: A stagecoach carries $40,000 worth of gold from the Colorado gold district to the States.
- September (Colorado): Auraria-Denver appeals to Congress for military protection from Indian ravages to travelers.
- September 18, Treaty Council on the Upper Platte (Upper Platte Indian Agency was at Ft. Laramie, Wyoming): Thirteen chiefs (Arapaho: Black Bear, Cut Nose, Friday, Little Owl, Medicine Man; Cheyenne: Big Wolf, White Cow, White Crow; Sioux: Bold Bear, Man Afraid of His Horses, Sitting Bear, Stabber, Standing Elk) and sixty-five principal men from the Arapaho, Cheyenne, and Sioux tribes meet with Indian Agent Thomas S. Twiss. Much is offered: lump cash sum, goods, and annual money—as long as the President sees fit—for doctors, teachers, fences, building and agricultural supplies. In exchange Indians agree to remain on their land, cede other lands, and pay for any wrongs they commit. The treaty must be ratified by Congress and signed by the President. It is not.
- October 3, Auraria (Colorado): Owen J. Goldrick opens a public school.
- October 3, Auraria, Kansas Territory (Colorado): Arapahoe County election of officers is held. Officers elected: John H. Kehler, sheriff; C. R. Bissel, probate judge; L. W. Bliss, treasurer; D. C. Collier, attorney; E. F. Clewell, registrar of deeds; J. Farrell, C. A. Lawrence, R. L. Wootton, supervisors; B. D. Williams, territorial delegate to Congress.
- October 5 (Colorado): Cheyenne and Arapaho appeal to U. S. Indian Agent William Bent. He commends them to the Superintendent of Indian Affairs for their determined effort to get along with white men and with other tribes. He notes that swift negotiations are important: Indians are irritated by the number of immigrants to their hunting grounds in the gold region. Kiowa and Comanche are another matter. Having met strong opposition in Texas, the Comanche now live between the Arkansas and Canadian Rivers. Bent saw 2,500 of them at Walnut Creek on September 16. They seemed to want peace; but Bent drew a different conclusion from their actions. He notes Comanche are willing in the presence of troops; but once troops are out of sight, they're ever ready to attack emigrants. Emigrants now travel the Santa Fe Trail in large numbers in all seasons. Bent recommends the military maintain a force among the Comanche at all times.
- Sunday evening, October 16, Harper's Ferry, Virginia: To secure arms, Connecticut native John Brown leads abolitionists in a raid of the federal arsenal. They work through the night and free some slaves. By morning they kill five men and control

town and federal facilities.
  - Brown has been active in anti-slavery issues in Kansas. In 1856 he killed five pro-slavery men near Pottawatomie Creek, Kansas.
- October 17, Monday night, Harper's Ferry, Virginia: The Virginia Militia arrives. On Tuesday, Colonel Robert E. Lee and J. E. B. Stuart lead ninety U. S. Marines, recapture the arsenal, and arrest John Brown. Two of Brown's sons die in the fight.
- October (Colorado): Snow starts piling up in the mountains; most prospectors leave Gregory Gulch for the winter. At least 2,000 men remain at work.
- October, Denver-Auraria (Colorado): Residents continue efforts to become a territory.
- October 24: In twenty-seven precincts 1,852 vote for provisional government, 280 against. Elected territorial officers: R. W. Steele, first Governor of the Territory of Jefferson (Colorado); Lucien Bliss, Secretary; R. L. Wootton, Treasurer; Sam McLean, Attorney General; Oscar B. Totten; Clerk of the Supreme Court; A. J. Allison, Chief Justice; John M. Odell and E. Fitzgerald, Associate Justices; Hickory Rogers, Marshal; H. H. McAfee, Superintendent of Public Schools.
- November, Auraria, Kansas Territory (Colorado): A. E. Pierce of the Auraria Post Office News Depot opens a small circulating library.
- November 21: Future outlaw Tom Horn is born (Hung in Cheyenne, Wyoming, November 1903).
- November 22: *Missouri Democrat* reports there are 500 houses in Denver-Auraria.
- December 2, Charleston, South Carolina: Tried and condemned for murder and treason, John Brown hangs.
- November 23: "Billy the Kid" is born. (Birthdate on his tombstone: November 23.) Some say his name is William Henry Roberts. As a youth, he will be called William Bonney or William Antrim. (One version: William Bonney was born to Catherine McCarthy in New York City. Another, his name: William Henry Roberts, born December 31, near Buffalo Gap, Taylor Co., Texas, to James Henry and Mary Adeline Dunn Roberts. Another: Katherine Ann Bonney Antrim was Billy's maternal aunt, who raised him after his father left and his mother died.)
- December 4, Cold Spring, Cimarron Cutoff (New Mexico): Twenty Kiowa attack an escorted mail wagon and exchange fire for hours. Kiowa and Comanche raids increase.
- In 1859 mining districts spring up throughout the Colorado mountains in Arapahoe City, Auraria, Baden City, Boulder, Central City, Cheyenne Pass City, Colorado City, Denver, Douglas City, Fountain, Golden, Golden Gate City, Highland City, Montana City, Mount Vernon City, Red Rock, Russellville, and Sacramento City.
- Winter 1859-60, Bent's Stone Fort (Colorado): With increase in immigration, William Bent doesn't think he'll be able to continue his Indian trade much longer.

1860
- Near Boulder (Colorado): Mines produce coal for the local market at one dollar a bushel.

- West Texas: Indians raid.
- Sunday, March 25, Auraria (Colorado): Frank Wootton is born; his mother dies.
- April 3: The first Pony Express riders leave Sacramento, California, and St. Joseph, Missouri. Harry Roff rides east from Sacramento; H. Wallace rides from St. Joe. Wallace arrives in Sacramento in eight days and four hours.
- April 5 (Colorado): Auraria and Denver become one: Denver City.
- April 6, California Gulch (Colorado): The Leadville gold boom begins.
- Spring: Antoine Lebrie, Leon Constantin, Leandro Beral, and Louis Clouthier take robes to Kansas City for William Bent. On their return they move to Hardscrabble (Colorado).
- May 9: Because of continuing Comanche and Kiowa depredations and hostilities in Texas and along the Santa Fe Trail, Colonel E. V. Sumner orders Major Sedgwick to lead a campaign against them. These Indians have threatened Santa Fe Trail travel since its inception. In 1853 they made a ten-year treaty with the U. S. through Indian Agent Thomas Fitzpatrick. They receive an $18,000 annuity, but they are the primary source of Indian trouble this year. (The treaty was renewable for an extra five years.)
    - Sumner corresponds with Sedgwick. From his experienced vantage point, he instructs Sedgwick: At this stage, it will be impossible to discern between actions of individuals. Sedgwick must treat them, not as individuals, but as a whole. Sumner attempts to insure that battles be fought among men without danger to women and children. Nonetheless, Sumner makes his directive clear: pursue, attack. There is to be no parlay until they have been punished.
- Pease/Peace River, Texas: U. S. forces (cavalry, Texas Rangers, Tonkawa scouts, and civilian volunteers) surprise a Comanche camp. About to be shot, one brave holds up a baby. This is not a brave, but a blue-eyed woman. Her husband, Chief Peta Nocona, and their two teenage sons, Quanah and Pecos, escaped. Soldiers think this may be Cynthia Parker, abducted by Comanche in 1836. They take the woman and her baby daughter to Cynthia's uncle Isaac Parker. He attempts to talk to her, but she speaks little English. About to give up, he says maybe this is a mistake and adds, "Poor Cynthia Ann." The sun-darkened woman with short, greasy hair replies, "Me Cynthia." Texans welcome her, give her land and a pension. She never smiles and often rides off to look for her sons. About four years after her rescue, Cynthia's daughter, Topasannah, dies of a fever. Cynthia dies soon afterward. Her oldest son, Quanah, will be a famous Comanche chief. Although his name means fragrant, he will never allow any warrior to mock his name, nor give him any name other than Quanah, the name given him by his mother.
- July 1 (Colorado): Men plan the village of Pueblo.
- (Colorado): Dick Wootton divides his time between Pueblo and Denver.
- Southwest New Mexico: Ft. Maclane opens and serves from 1860-65.
- Summer, San Juan Mountains (Colorado), Utah Territory: Prospectors discover gold.
- July 19 (Colorado): Apache, Arapaho, and Cheyenne camp around Bent's Fort to receive annuities, including blankets, cloth, calico, hoop iron, axes, rifles, and other

provisions. At this time, Major Sedgwick considers Arapaho and Cheyenne friendly.
- (Northeast of Canon City, Colorado): Gabriel Bowen finds an oil spring. Nothing is done about the find.
- Near Gallup, New Mexico Territory: Ft. Fauntleroy is established as a tent camp. It is manned by the 2nd Regiment of New Mexico Volunteers. (When Thomas Fauntleroy joins the confederacy, the fort will be renamed. Abandoned during the Civil War, it will reopen nearby as Ft. Wingate in 1868.)
- Congress recognizes William Bent's share in the St. Vrain Vigil Land Grant.
- October 22, Ft. Wise (Colorado): Major Sedgwick reports problems with scurvy among soldiers building Fort Wise. They've had no vegetables since May 15.
- April 24-October, Council Grove, Kansas: Merchant Seth Hayes counts 3,519 men, 2,667 wagons, and 478 horses pass through town.
- November 6, U. S. Presidential election: Abraham Lincoln defeats John Bell of the Constitutional Union Party and Democrat Stephen A. Douglas. Lincoln's Vice-President is Hannibal Hamlin of Maine.
  - Born near Hodgenville, Kentucky, Lincoln spent his childhood in Kentucky and Indiana. His formal education provided foundational reading, arithmetic and writing. Beyond that he was primarily self-taught. He read of and was impressed by George Washington's life and the battles for freedom. In 1830 his family moved to Illinois.
  - Abraham Lincoln is a man of deep faith, reads his Bible often, knows it well, and will keep a copy on his Presidential desk for frequent admonition and direction. Though Lincoln has a firm will, some say he has a childlike reliance upon God.
  - Thin-boned, long-limbed Lincoln is 6'4" tall, has black hair, expressive gray eyes.
  - He served in the military and performed various jobs before becoming a lawyer, a state representative, and a U. S. Congressman. His hard work and honesty have earned him respect and the nickname "Honest Abe."
  - Since 1837 Lincoln has left no question concerning his view against slavery.
- November 30, near Fort Lupton (Colorado): Patrick Waters shoots Thomas R. Freeman. The People's Court tries and convicts him for murder. He will be hung December 21st.
- December 20: South Carolina secedes from the United States.
- December 26: Union troops move to Fort Sumter, South Carolina.
- December, New Mexico Territory, Mountain Branch, Santa Fe Trail: Comanche and Kiowa war parties trouble travelers south of Raton Pass. Thomas Fauntleroy, head of the Department of New Mexico, charges Ft. Union commander Lt. Col. George B. Crittenden to take care of the matter. Indians flee. Crittenden's soldiers pursue.

1861
- By 1861 there are fifteen U. S. cities of 8,000 or more: Brooklyn, Chicago, Cincinnati, Detroit, Galveston, Indianapolis, Kansas City, Minneapolis, Milwaukee, New Orleans, Portland, St. Paul, St. Louis, Salt Lake City, San Francisco, and

- Seattle. Those east of the Mississippi River are connected by telegraph and railway.
- January 2, ten miles north of Cold Spring on the Cimarron River, New Mexico Territory: Ft. Union soldiers surprise a Kiowa-Comanche village. Indians wound three soldiers and flee. Soldiers kill ten Indians, capture 40 horses, and burn the Indians' village.
- January 29: Kansas becomes a state.
- January: Mississippi, Florida, Alabama, Louisiana and Georgia secede from the Union.
- February 4, Montgomery, Alabama: Seceded states organize the Confederate States of America.
- February 9: Jefferson Davis of Mississippi is chosen provisional President of the Confederacy and will be inaugurated February 18th. In November he will be elected Confederate President. Politically, Davis follows in the footsteps of John C. Calhoun. A strong Constitutionalist, he believes in strict interpretation of the constitution. He strongly defends States Rights.
  - Born in Christian County, Kentucky, in 1808, Davis grew up in Mississippi. He graduated from Transylvania University (Kentucky) and the U. S. Military Academy. Davis married Lt. Col. Zachary Taylor's daughter in 1835. (Taylor became U. S. President in 1849.)
  - After early years in the military, Davis served in the U. S. House of Representatives, the Mexican War, the U. S. Senate, and as Secretary of War (under President Franklin Pierce). As Secretary of War, Davis improved military tactics and weapons. He also organized exploration of possible railroad routes from the Mississippi River to the Pacific Ocean. He approved the Army's experimental use of camels.
  - When Mississippi seceded from the Union, Davis resigned from the U. S. Senate.
- February 18: The Arapaho, Cheyenne, and United States make the Fort Wise Treaty.
  - Cheyenne and Arapaho agree to good behavior, to give road right-of-way, and to relinquish all lands they claim as their own, except a tract reserved for their use.
  - The United States agrees to
    - divide the land according to Cheyenne and Arapaho request and to provide $450,000 for land improvements (houses, fences, etc.).
    - furnish and deliver items necessary for farming.
    - pay $5,000 per year for five years. The money is to be used to set up a sawmill, grain mill, etc., and to build homes for a skilled miller, engineer, farmers, interpreter, or mechanics should the Indians need such help.
    - pay each of the two tribes $15,000 per year for fifteen years. If Indians fail to work at improving their condition, the treaty allows the President of the United States to withdrawn this payment.
    - continue to pay previous annuities until promises are fulfilled.
  - Members of the tribe who do not join with the main Arapaho and Cheyenne tribes within one year will not receive benefits.

- Authorized treaty representatives:
  - United States: Commissioners Albert G. Boone and F. B. Culver
  - Arapaho: Ho-ha-ca-che (Little Raven), Ac-ker-ba-the (Storm), Che-ne-na-e-te (Shave Head), and Ma-na-sa-te (Big Mouth).
  - Cheyenne: Mo-ta-va-to (Black Kettle), Vo-ki-vokamast (White Antelope), Avo-na-co (Lean Bear), O-ne-a-ha-ket (Little Wolf), Na-ko-hais-tah (Tall Bear), A-am-a-na-co (Left Hand).
- U. S. interpreters:
  - John Simpson Smith, trapper and mountain man, husband of an Indian, and an organizer of the Denver Town Company.
  - Robert Bent, son of William Bent and Mis-stan-stur, daughter of Cheyenne Chief Gray Thunder.
- Cheyenne and Arapaho, who live in northern Colorado and Kansas on the plains above the Arkansas River, cede their lands to the U. S. government. A portion of land along the Arkansas River is made into a reservation for them.
- February 28: Colorado Territory is created.
- March 4, Washington, D. C.: Abraham Lincoln is inaugurated U. S. President.
- March: Confederates make provision for a Constitution and currency.
- March 22: President Lincoln appoints William Gilpin Governor of Colorado Territory.
- April 12 a.m., Ft. Sumter, South Carolina: The American Civil War begins.
- April 15: The U. S. declares war on the Confederacy. President Lincoln calls for troops.
- April 17: Virginia hoped for compromise between North and South. Now that war is declared, Virginia secedes from the Union and joins the Confederacy.
  - During this bloody battle of brothers, Virginia will be hit hard. It is a natural pathway between North and South. The Confederate capital will move to Richmond. Richmond's proximity to Washington, D. C. makes Virginia's position strategic.
- April 19: President Lincoln orders a naval blockade of Confederate states.
- April 20: Although he was offered field command of Union troops, Colonel Robert E. Lee of Virginia resigns his U. S. Army position. Lee's desire and support has been for a preserved nation, but his loyalties lie with his native state.
- April, New Mexico Territory: William W. Loring resigns command of the Department of New Mexico to join the Confederacy. E. R. S. Canby replaces him and will hold the position June 1861-June 1862.
- May 6, Dick Wootton's 45th birthday: The Confederacy declares war on the Union.
- May-July: Paiute Indians' disruption of Pony Express service costs the company $75,000.
- May 20: North Carolina wants to remain with the Union, but will not supply troops to fight Confederates as Lincoln requests. The state secedes from the Union.
- New Mexico Territory: Republican Henry Connelly replaces Democrat Abraham

Rencher, who has been territorial governor since 1857.
- June, New Mexico Territory: In charge of Ft. Union, Edward Canby orders Major William Chapman to organize parties of New Mexicans to help patrol the Santa Fe Trail.
- July 1, New Mexico Territory: John Baylor of the Texas militia occupies Mesilla.
- July 21: The South defeats the North at the first Battle of Bull Run.
- August, New Mexico Territory: John Baylor claims all of New Mexico south of the 34th parallel as Arizona Territory for the Confederacy.
- Santa Fe Trail trade is down this year because of the Confederate invasion in New Mexico and guerilla activity in Missouri and Kansas.
- September 26: President Lincoln proclaims this a day of national fasting and prayer.
- October 24: The Overland Telegraph Company and the Pacific Telegraph Company join wires in Salt Lake City. Indians call the telegraph "talking wires."
- 1861, Europe: Italians unite under Victor Emmanuel II and form the Kingdom of Italy.
- New Mexico Territory: The U. S. Indian Agency in Taos moves to Cimarron.

1862
- January 18, Virginia: Former President John Tyler, age seventy-one, dies before he is able to assume his elected position as Confederate Congressman. Last year Tyler headed a Peace Convention that went to Washington D. C. in an unsuccessful attempt to avert Civil War.
- February 7, New Mexico Territory: Confederate Major Henry Sibley and his Texas Volunteers march north along the Rio Grande.
- February 19, 20, 1862 Ft. Craig (New Mexico): Union Colonel Edward Canby attacks Sibley's Rebel troop.
- Early morning, February 21, Battle of Valverde, New Mexico Territory: Union Colonel Ben Roberts leads a charge on Sibley's Confederate troops. Confederates win.
- February 22: Marching 400 miles in thirteen days, John Slough and John Milton Chivington (1821-1894) lead the First Colorado Regiment of Union volunteers south from Camp Weld, over Raton Pass, into New Mexico.
- March 4, Santa Fe (New Mexico): Governor Henry Connelly and other pro-Union government officials leave.
- March 7, Aubrey, Kansas: William Clarke Quantrill and his raiders attack and kill three men. Guerillas keep things stirred up on the eastern end of the Santa Fe Trail.
- March 9, Atlantic seacoast: The *Monitor* and the *Merrimack* battle.
- March 10, New Mexico Territory: An advance unit of Confederate soldiers occupies Santa Fe. Major Sibley officially captures the capitol on March 23.
- March 26-28 (Wednesday-Friday), Apache Canyon, New Mexico Territory: The Battle of Glorieta rages indecisively until Union Volunteers destroy the Confederate supply train.
- April 6, 7, Tennessee: North and South clash at the Battle of Shiloh.

- April 11, New Mexico Territory: Union forces reoccupy Santa Fe.
- April 15, about forty miles northwest of Tucson (Arizona): Union and Confederate forces meet at the Battle of Picacho Peak.
- April 15: Battle of Peralta, south of Albuquerque (New Mexico): Canby's Ft. Craig force and Sibley's retreating Confederates fight the last Civil War battle in New Mexico.
- April 21, Washington, D. C.: President Lincoln signs a bill to prohibit private coinage.
  - Clark, Gruber and Co. of Denver continues to mint coins until the end of the year. After negotiations, the government pays $25,000 for the Denver mint in April 1863. The government had appropriated $75,000 to build a mint, but chose to buy the Clark and Gruber mint already in operation.
- May 16, Denver (Colorado): Dr. John Evans arrives to replace Governor Gilpin. His first words to his constituents: "Let us pray."
  - Evans, from Illinois, helped found Northwestern University. As a physician, he discovered cholera is an infectious disease.
- May: No longer concerned about formation of new slave states, the U. S. Congress passes the Homestead Act. Any head of family over twenty-one years of age may gain title to 160 acres of public land. The head of a family can obtain title to the land by living on the land five years and making improvements or by paying $1.25 per acre. Other enactments, like the Desert Land Act of 1877 will further encourage settlement of public lands.
- Plains Indians attack stage stations in Kansas.
- Summer, Denver (Colorado): Emigration picks up, but most emigrants pass through to Idaho's Salmon River Mines.
- July 22, Denver (Colorado): *Rocky Mountain News* announces the organization of a board of trustees in charge of building Denver Seminary. The two-story facility will be built at 14th and Arapahoe.
- July 24, Kinderhook, New York: Former U. S. President Martin Van Buren dies on his estate. He was the first president born in the independent United States.
- Denver (Colorado): Southern sympathizers are encouraged to leave.
- Colorado Territory (near Canon City): A. M. Cassedy and James A. McCandless drill a 50'oil well. This is the first oil drilling in the U. S. since the Pennsylvania find.
- August 17, Minnesota: Four Sioux braves—Breaking Up, Brown Wind, Killing Ghost, and Runs Against Something When Crawling—stop at Robinson Jones' farm to help themselves to eggs. One doesn't want to steal; the other three say he's a coward. He says he'll kill a white man to prove he isn't afraid.
  - Farmer Jones sees them coming and flees with his family to his son-in-law's house. The braves follow and kill Farmer Jones, his wife, his daughter, his son-in-law and one other. The braves hurry back to the reservation on stolen horses.
  - The Sioux realize the gravity of the situation. Several Sioux villages gather for council. Throughout the night, chiefs deliberate: turn the guilty parties over or go

on the offensive? Going on the offensive wins out. The Minnesota Massacre ensues.
- August 18, before daybreak, Minnesota: Sioux war parties leave their reservation to attack white settlers. Some women and children are alone on farms while men are away fighting the Civil War. The Sioux spare a few settlers and take a few captive. For the most part, anyone white is killed on the spot. They kill approximately 450 settlers.
  - Of those taken captive, some are killed. Some are tortured—like the young girl whose legs are slashed open in front of her mother.
  - Sioux attack the Eastlick family, kill Mr. Eastlick and two of his sons, and wound Mrs. Eastlick. She instructs her eleven-year-old son, Merton, to flee with his baby brother. Merton carries the baby until he finds refuge 50 miles away. Mrs. Eastlick lives and rejoins them.
  - Not all Sioux are attacking. A few friendly warriors warn a group of missionaries and teachers to flee with their families. More than two dozen escape.
  - Some attribute partial cause of the massacre to the fact that Indian Agent Thomas Galbraith did not distribute government annuities on time when Sioux were on the brink of starvation. Others say Agent Galbraith honored those who followed the agency's prescribed directives for annuities above those who did not.
  - Much of the general American population thought the government should pursue peace with the Sioux. This uprising stirs sentiment against western Indians and breeds or feeds the thought that maybe the only thing they understand is force.
  - Sioux raids in the Dakotas, Minnesota, and Iowa embolden other tribes.
- Minnesota: The governor sends forces to quell the Sioux revolt. Troops defeat Sioux resistance at Wood Lake. Sioux return 269 captives.
- Pecos River, east-central New Mexico Territory: Ft. Sumner is built.
- August 29: North and South meet at Manasseh for the second Battle of Bull Run.
- September 2: The U. S. ordered that Confederate guerillas be treated as outlaws because of their activity in Kansas and Missouri. That roused Southern sympathizers to join the guerillas. Quantrill and his guerillas soon control Kansas City, Missouri. Today, Quantrill's men raid Olathe, Kansas, on the Santa Fe Trail. They kill six men and steal every wagon in town and many from nearby farms to transport confiscated goods back to Missouri. Ft. Leavenworth soldiers pursue them and kill two raiders.
- September, Denver (Colorado): Because Indians have killed many on the Salmon River Mines route, residents organize a cavalry for home protection.
- September 17: The North defeats the South at the Battle of Antietam.
- September 18: James Henry Carleton (1814-1873) is appointed commander of the Department of New Mexico (until June 27, 1865).
- September 22: President Lincoln announces he will free slaves on January 1st if seceded states do not return to the Union by that time.
- Early October: Quantrill's Raiders kill fifteen soldiers guarding a Santa Fe Trail wagon train, then raid Shawnee, Kansas, stealing, killing, and burning. They will

- winter in Kansas, but their raids will disrupt lives and trade on the Santa Fe Trail again next year.
- October, New Mexico Territory: Colonel James Carleton orders Kit Carson to gather the Mescalero Apache and bring them to the Bosque Redondo Reservation.
- November 4: Richard Gatling patents his Gatling gun. It can shoot 1,200 shots per minute.
- Near Trinidad, Colorado Territory: Coal is found.
- Colorado Territory: The Butte Valley settlement is a "secesh" stronghold.
- The U. S. Department of Agriculture is established.
- Cooke's Canyon, Southern New Mexico Territory (300 yards from Cooke's Spring—the only water hole in 40 miles): Under General James H. Carleton the California Column builds Ft. Cummings on the most treacherous four-mile stretch of the Butterfield Stage Route. Danger is so great from the Mimbres and Chiricahua Apache that no one is allowed to be alone outside the fort. The fort is manned primarily by buffalo soldiers. Soldiers patrol the area to protect or escort travelers, supply trains, and stagecoaches. Ft. Cummings operates 1862-1870, 1882-1885.
- December 1, Auraria side of Denver (Colorado): Denver's first free public school opens.
- December 26, Mankato, Minnesota: Thirty-eight Sioux warriors hang for their part in the Minnesota Massacre. Two hundred sixty-five were on the execution list; President Lincoln studied each individual's report and reduced the number to thirty-eight. He used care relaying the unfamiliar sounding Sioux names to the telegraph operator; so no one would be executed by mistake.
  - The three chiefs responsible for the Massacre are still at large. Chief Shakopee and Chief Medicine Bottom fled to Canada. (They will be found, tied to a dogsled, brought back to the States, and executed on November 11, 1865.) Chief Little Crow is hiding in North Dakota. (When he returns to Minnesota next summer, a farmer will recognize him, shoot, and kill him.)

1863
- January 1: President Lincoln issues the Emancipation Proclamation declaring freedom for slaves in all states.
- February, Washington, D. C.: In an attempt to quell trouble between Indians and whites, President Lincoln sends for a delegation of Ute, Cheyenne, and Arapaho leaders.
- February 24: Arizona is created out of the western portion of New Mexico Territory.
- March 3: Idaho Territory is formed from Dakota, Nebraska, Washington, and Utah.
- March 3: President Lincoln signs a draft act: males aged 20-45 must either sign for military service or pay $300 to have someone serve in their place.
- March, Bosque Redondo Reservation (New Mexico): Mescalero Apache arrive.
- March 27, 11:30 a.m., White House, Washington, D. C.: President Lincoln meets with fifteen Indian chiefs.
- April 19, windy morning, Denver (Colorado): A drunken man at the Cherokee Hotel

kicks over a stove about 3 a.m. Wind picks up the flames. Over the next three hours, fire practically guts the center of town. Much of the business district is destroyed.
  - Townspeople rebuild with limited supplies. Children sift through ruins for used nails. They find them, pound them straight, and sell them.
- Washington D. C.: April 30th is proclaimed a day of national fasting, humiliation and prayer.
- April, Council Grove, Kansas: More wagon trains pass through to Santa Fe this spring than in the past two years.
- May 2, Battle of Chancellorsville: General Stonewall Jackson is wounded; his left arm must be amputated. Pneumonia follows; he dies May 10.
- May 4: Battle of Chancellorsville ends, a victory for the Confederacy.
- June 19: Virginia divides into two states: A group of northwestern counties, loyal to the Union, become West Virginia. Concerning slavery in Virginia:
  - Many of various nationalities came to the colonies as indentured servants. Africans came to Jamestown, Virginia, as indentured servants in 1619. Slave trade began decades later when Africans were brought into the colony and sold as slaves. In 1778 Virginia abolished participation in the African slave trade, but not in slavery. About half of Virginia's population was slaves at the beginning of the Civil War.
- Near Elephant Butte, New Mexico Territory: Ft. McRae opens (serves 1863-1879).
- North of Tucumcari (eastern New Mexico): Ft. Bascom is built (serves 1863-70). Wages for Ft. Bascom soldiers in 1866 will be eleven dollars per month, plus rations.
- Near Silver City, New Mexico Territory: Ft. Bayard is established near Santa Rita del Cobre (copper mines) to protect miners, settlers, and travelers from Apache raids. One cavalry and two infantry companies are stationed here. After the Civil War, Ft. Bayard's cavalry will war against Apache leaders Victorio and Geronimo. Bayard will continue as a military fort until the end of the century, when it will be converted to a leading medical center treating tubercular patients.
- July 1-3: Union victory at Gettysburg is a turning point in the Civil War.
- July 4: Vicksburg, a major Confederate port on the Mississippi, falls to Union forces after a 47 day siege.
- July 13-16, New York: Protestors riot following the first lottery draw (July 11) for the federal draft act (March 3). One thousand are killed.
- Summer: Drought on the central Plains.
- Summer, Colorado Territory: Cheyenne and Kiowa add to their supply of horses and arms in a series of raids on settlers. Governor John Evans wires Washington for aid.
- Montana: A gold rush draws prospectors.
- The U. S. government reduces postage for letters to a uniform three cents per ounce. Free mail delivery begins in some eastern cities.
- August 21, Lawrence, Kansas: William Clarke Quantrill and his raiders, including Frank and Jesse James, murder about 150 people.
- Friday, September 18, Christian County, Kentucky: Dick Wootton's father, David C.

- Wootton—age 74, dies.
- Fall, 1863, near La Porte (northern Colorado): The 1st Colorado Cavalry establishes Camp Collins to protect travelers from Sioux, Cheyenne, and other Indians. It is named in honor of Colonel William O. Collins, an officer at Ft. Laramie.
  - The Overland Stage Trail from Denver to California travels north through La Porte (Colorado) and Virginia Dale to Fort Laramie (Wyoming).
- September, New Territory: A band of 800 Navajo steal in Mora and San Miguel Counties. Hilario Gonzales and Francisco Lopes of Las Vegas lead about seventy volunteers in pursuit. They kill six Indians and recover 10,000 stolen sheep about twenty miles west of Ft. Sumner. Kiowa and Apache often raid in San Miguel County.
- Monday, October 5, Doyle Ranch (Colorado): Dick Wootton marries Fannie Brown.
- 1863-64, New Mexico Territory: The U. S. and Navajo war.
- November 19, Gettysburg, Pennsylvania: President Lincoln delivers the Gettysburg Address. He returns home sick. (Edward Everett also spoke at the Gettysburg dedication.)
- November 26: The Union celebrates Thanksgiving, a new national holiday.
  - Following Union victory at Gettysburg, President Lincoln set aside the fourth Thursday of November as a national holiday to celebrate with thanks. This is not the first American Thanksgiving. Thanksgiving was celebrated at Berkeley Hundred Plantation, Virginia, in 1619 and in 1621 by the Pilgrims in Massachusetts.
- Mexico City, Mexico: Napoleon III's French troops enter. Embroiled in Civil War, the United States does not interfere.
  - June 1864: Maximillian of Austria becomes Emperor of Mexico.
  - After the Civil War, U. S. Secretary of War William Seward will send troops to the Mexican border and order the French to leave. They remain. In 1867 Benito Pablo Juarez, native-born Mexican Indian from Oaxaca, will regain power for the Mexican people.
- December 1, Texas: Thomas Edward "Black Jack" Ketchum is born. He'll begin his career as a rancher/cowboy, but will become an outlaw in northeastern New Mexico and southern Colorado. He will hang for it in Clayton, New Mexico Territory, April 26, 1901.
- December 2, Andover, Massachusetts: Former first lady Jane Pierce, age 57, dies. All her children preceded her in death.

1864
- February 10, Taos, New Mexico Territory: Charles Beaubien dies.
- February 25: Anna Symmes Harrison, eighty-nine-year-old widow of former President William Henry Harrison, dies.
- New Mexico Territory: Navajo are moved to Bosque Redondo Reservation.
- Union forces secure the Missouri-Kansas border from Rebel raids. That encourages Santa Fe Trail travel.

- May 11, Yellow Tavern, Virginia: Confederate General Jeb Stuart, age thirty-one, is mortally wounded in the abdomen while battling Sheridan's force. He will die tomorrow night.
- May 19, 20, and a few days previous, Colorado Territory: Abnormal rainfall and hail cause floods at Camp Collins, in Denver, and in the Fountain Valley.
- May 26: Montana Territory is formed from Idaho Territory.
- Northeastern Colorado Territory: Ft. Sedgwick is established.
- Walnut Creek on the mouth of the Arkansas River (Kansas): Fort Zarah is established to escort and protect travelers. It is seldom manned by more than fifteen-twenty soldiers.
- July, Ft. Larned (Kansas): Kiowa raid and steal 172 animals belonging to the U. S. Army.
- Summer: Indians raid from the Rio Grande to Montana.
- August 4, Washington, D. C.: President Lincoln proclaims this a day of national fasting, prayer, and humiliation before God.
- August 19, near Cimarron Springs (Kansas): Indians kill ten men, burn wagons, steal cattle.
- August 21, near Ft. Atkinson (Kansas): Indians attack five caravans, kill a wagon master, and rustle several hundred animals.
- August, Denver, Colorado Territory: Because of Indian trouble, John Chivington institutes martial law. In Colorado Territory all eastward travel stops for more than a month.
- August: William Bent writes the Cheyenne and asks them to consider a council of peace. Dog Soldiers don't like his idea, but the old chiefs send word on August 29, that the council has decided, under certain conditions, to consider peace.
- August 29: General George McClellan and George Pendleton are nominated to run against Abraham Lincoln and Andrew Johnson for U. S. President and Vice-President.
- French scientist Louis Pasteur introduces a heating process, pasteurization, to the wine industry. Pasteurization proves beneficial to preservation of food and milk.
- September 2, Georgia: Union General William T. Sherman leads troops into Atlanta.
- Thursday, September 15, Christian County, Kentucky: Dick Wootton's mother dies.
- September 25, Pawnee River (Kansas): Ft. Larned troops find a camp of about 4,000 Arapaho, Cheyenne, and Kiowa. A fight ensues; two soldiers and nine Indians die.
- September 28, Camp Weld, Colorado Territory: Cheyenne and Arapaho chiefs meet with Governor John Evans and his delegation.
- October, Colorado Territory: Indian attacks do not stop.
- Mid-October, Denver area (Colorado): Snow begins early and continues; the season's last snowfall is May 1, 1865.
- October 17, Colorado Territory: Frances Virginia Wootton is born. Her mother dies.
- October 23, Missouri: Major General Sterling Price's Confederate forces had marched from Jefferson City and gained victory at Independence. Today Union

Major General Samuel R. Curtis' forces defeat them at the Battle of Westport.
- October 31: Nevada becomes the 36th U. S. state.
- November 8: The United States re-elects Abraham Lincoln president.
- November 15: Union General W. T. Sherman and his troops begin their "March to the Sea." On December 21st they capture Savannah, Georgia; Sherman presents it to President Lincoln as a Christmas gift.
- November 24: The Union celebrates Thanksgiving.
- November 26, first Battle of Adobe Walls, Texas Panhandle: Kit Carson leads the 1st N. M. Cavalry against Kiowa and Comanche. Soldiers retreat.
- November 29, Sand Creek Massacre, Colorado Territory: John Chivington and his forces surprise the Cheyenne and offer no quarter.

1865
- January and February, northern Colorado Territory: Approximately 1,500 Southern Cheyenne join Northern Cheyenne. They loot stores in Julesburg and attack the stage station, burn stage stations northeast of Denver, kill forty-five soldiers at Camp Larkin (Ft. Sedgwick), and raid every settler within eighty miles west of the camp. They kill people, steal cattle and wagons. Before they destroy 100 miles of telegraph lines, the governor wires Washington for troops.
- February 8, Denver, Colorado: Martial law continues in effect until the Julesburg road reopens.
- February 10, Colorado Territory: The legislature approves an act incorporating R. L. Wootton's "Trinidad and Ratoon [sic] Mountain Wagon Road Company."
- Raton Pass: Dick Wootton begins work on the Raton Pass Toll Road.
- March 4, Washington, D. C.: In his inaugural address President Lincoln speaks of his desire to help the nation heal after the Civil War; so there can be lasting peace. He wants care for the widows, orphans, and wounded.
- March: U. S. Congress begins investigation of the Sand Creek Massacre.
- On the Plains: The winter thaw is late.
- April 9, Courthouse, Appomattox, Virginia: Confederate General Robert E. Lee surrenders. Thousands of Confederates from all stations in life escape to refuge in Mexico and other Latin American countries.
- April 14, Washington, D. C.: John Wilkes Booth assassinates President Lincoln (shot on the 14th, died on the 15th). Andrew Johnson will succeed Lincoln as President.
- May 10, Irwinville, Georgia: Confederate President Jefferson Davis is captured and imprisoned. When news reaches Denver, bands play in the street all afternoon.
- May 13, Battle of Palmito Hill (area of Brownsville, Texas): Not knowing the Civil War ended, Confederate and Union forces fight their last battle. Though the War was lost, Confederate troops win the battle.
- May 29: President Johnson appoints provisional governors for Southern states. He offers amnesty for all who take an oath of allegiance to the Union—except Confederate leaders.
- Wootton, Colorado: Dick Wootton's toll road is open for business.

- End of the Civil War frees troops for service in western states.
  - Troops build Camp Tyler (Ft. Morgan, Colorado) and other forts.
- Across from Mt. Robledo (north of Las Cruces, New Mexico): Built on high ground, adobe Ft. Seldon is named for Colonel Henry Raymond Selden (active in Civil War service in New Mexico; commander of Ft. Union at his death in 1865). The area has long been a campground. The Spanish used it. In 1853 the U. S. Army had Camp Robledo there.
  - One company of infantry and one of cavalry (total of 125-185 men) man the fort. They protect Mesilla Valley settlers, travelers on Jornada del Muerto, and miners traveling to Silver City and Piños Altos. To supplement their diet, soldiers hunt deer and fowl. Nearby land is good for farming and grazing.
  - Not intimidated by the fort, Indians often camp nearby. Once a band divided forces: one group drew soldiers away from the fort; the other stole the Army's cattle herd.
  - When the railroad comes, General William T. Sherman and other military men will attempt to make Ft. Selden the regional military center. El Paso's Ft. Bliss will be chosen, instead. As a child, Douglas MacArthur (World War II General) will live at Ft. Selden. The fort will close in 1892.
- Santa Fe Trail, between Ft. Larned and Ft. Union: Indian attacks are frequent. The Army limits travel between the forts to the first fifteen days of each month.
- Kit Carson oversees construction of Ft. Aubrey. Colonel A. H. Pfeiffer will command the fort. Indians killed Pfeiffer's wife when he was stationed at Ft. McRae.
- June 1, Washington, D. C.: President Johnson proclaims this a day of national fasting, prayer, and humiliation before God.
- Kansas: Fort Dodge is established.
- July 27: The Military Division of the Pacific is created to replace the Department of New Mexico and several other military departments.
- Colorado Territory: Grasshoppers destroy crops.
- New Mexico: For three years insects, drought, and floods have spoiled many crops.
- Britain: Sir Joseph Lister grasps the connection of infection and germs. He begins use of antiseptics in surgical procedures. Until this time it was common for infection and death to follow the simplest surgical procedures. Lister first tried to sterilize the surrounding air. He soon realized instruments, dressings, and surgeons' hands must also be sterile. Percentage of postoperative deaths falls from up to 50% to 2-3%.
- September 8, New England: Asa Mercer of Seattle distributes a circular, inviting widows and orphan daughters of Union soldiers to sail to Washington Territory. Adult fare is $125-$150; children travel half price. He promises employment to women of good character. He doesn't mention the predominantly male population of the Pacific Northwest is looking for brides.
- October 18, Little Arkansas River: U. S. government commissioners make a treaty with the Kiowa and Comanche. William Bent is one of the commissioners.
- November 2, Corsica, Ohio: Warren G. Harding (U. S. President, 1921-1923) is born.

- December 18, Washington, D. C.: Amendment Thirteen is added to the U. S. Constitution. It forbids slavery and involuntary servitude in the U. S. or any place under U. S. jurisdiction, except as punishment for a convicted crime. It is the first amendment added since 1804.

1866
- 1866-67, Santa Fe Trail: Soldiers escort all wagon trains from Ft. Larned (on the border of Comanche country) westward.
- Christian County, Kentucky: R. L. Wootton, Jr. graduates from Lafayette College.
- Near an old stone corral, south of the Little Arkansas Crossing (Kansas): The U. S. government establishes Camp Grierson. It functions a short time in 1866, just long enough to protect wagon trains crossing the Arkansas.
- June: Charles Goodnight and Oliver Loving drive longhorns over Raton Pass.
- Wells Fargo & Co. purchases Holladay Overland Mail Co. (5,000 miles of stage line) and becomes the preeminent stage line transporting passengers and gold from western mining camps.
- William Henry Jackson travels West as a wagon driver. He'll leave, but return as photographer for General William Palmer.
    - Before becoming a commercial photographer in Denver (1879-1898), Jackson photographs (1873-1876) the Rocky Mountain region for F. V. Hayden, who will publish an atlas in 1881. Jackson is the first to photograph Yellowstone. He will illustrate several books. (d. 1942, age 99)
- Taos County, New Mexico Territory: Ft. Lowell serves from 1866-69.
- August, Ft. Garland, Colorado Territory: Kit Carson takes command of the post.
- October, Cimarron, New Mexico Territory: Copper is found.
- October, Tecolote, New Mexico Territory: Lt. DeHague and Lt. Richard Russell establish a trading post. E. M. Moore already sells goods in the little adobe village, and George Moore and David Winternitz operate a $75,000 freight business there. Russell and DeHague purchase goods from C. H. Kitchen in nearby Las Vegas and from C. H. Moore at Ft. Union. They trade locally, in Las Vegas, at Ft. Union, and as far as Ft. Defiance.
    - With the help of Hispanic laborers, Richard hauls wagon loads of salt from a salt-sink near Tecolote. There is a purer salt-sink in Texas, but the government forbids Americans to travel there because of Indian hostilities.
    - Mrs. Russell has plush red furniture and a fine stove with an oven, hauled by wagon from Leavenworth. Local women bake food in hornos outdoors.
- December 21, Fetterman Massacre, Bozeman Trail (Wyoming): Captain William J. Fetterman and eighty soldiers under his command attempt to rescue soldiers being attacked while gathering firewood. Fetterman and his soldiers are killed, scalped, and stripped. Earlier in the year Fetterman, angry because of Indian raids in spite of a treaty, said if he had eighty men, he'd ride through the whole Sioux nation.
- Robert Leroy Parker (Beaver, Utah) and Harry Longabaugh (Plainfield, New Jersey) are born this year. The boys will grow up to be horse thieves, cattle rustlers, train and

bank robbers. As part of the "Wild Bunch" of 1896-1901, they will be known as "Butch Cassidy" and the "Sundance Kid," respectively. (The "Wild Bunch" will include Harry Tracy; Elzy Lay; Ben Kilpatrick, the "Tall Texan;" and others.)

1867

- February 25, Washington, D. C.: U. S. Congress orders the survey of a canal through Panama to link the Atlantic and Pacific oceans.
- February, Pepin, Wisconsin: Laura Elizabeth Ingalls (Laura Ingalls Wilder) is born. Among other works, Laura will write The Little House Books, based on her family and her pioneer childhood.
- March 1, Washington, D. C.: Congress overrides President Johnson's veto and adds Nebraska to the Union; the vote for Colorado statehood doesn't make it past the veto.
- March 2: Regardless of President Johnson's veto, Congress passes the first of a series of Reconstruction Acts following the Civil War.
  - The first act divides southern states into five districts under martial law: 1) North and South Carolina 2) Virginia 3) Alabama, Florida, Georgia 4) Mississippi, Arkansas 5) Louisiana, Texas. Restoration of civil government will be allowed when states are readmitted to the Union. The policy opens the door for "carpetbagger'" influence in Southern politics.
  - North and South Carolina, Arkansas, Florida, Louisiana, and Alabama are allowed readmittance. Tennessee was readmitted in 1866. Mississippi, Virginia, Georgia, and Texas will not be readmitted until 1870.
- March 23, Washington, D. C.: Congress overrides President Johnson's veto and passes a second Reconstruction Act. (Others will follow in July and March 1868.) The act requires qualified voters to register and vote on readmission to the Union.
- March 30: U. S. Secretary of State, William H. Seward, agrees to purchase Alaska from Russia for $7,200,000. Some Americans can't imagine what the U. S. wants with the big cold land—and at such a price! Some call it Seward's Folly, others Seward's Icebox. Congress approves the purchase on April 9 and concludes the transaction in October.
- April, Ft. Larned (Kansas): Major General Winfield Scott Hancock and his troop hold council with the Cheyenne. His purpose: remind the Cheyenne of the treaty made with the U. S. in 1865, in which they agreed to remain south of the Arkansas River. After the council, Cheyenne travel north and burn a stage station on the Smoky Hill Route. In return, Hancock burns tepees and Indian belongings left behind. Infuriated, Cheyenne step up raids.
- June, Ft. Wallace (Kansas): Chief Roman Nose leads an attack against the fort and kills several soldiers. He also attacks a nearby stage station while he is in the area.
- June-November, Camp Grierson, Kansas: Because of raids, the camp reopens for the freighting season. A unit of the 10th Cavalry mans the camp; cholera kills many soldiers.
- Southeastern Colorado: The U. S. government builds its own Ft. Lyon.
- U. S. Congress amends the Townsite Act of 1844. To keep speculators from buying

- large tracts of land and not developing them, the Townsite Act of 1867 requires at least one hundred people per townsite offer (320 acres of land at $1.25 per acre).
- July 15, England: Hoping to make a safe explosive, Alfred Bernhard Nobel has long been experimenting with nitroglycerin. In 1864 he patented a detonating cap to use when exploding nitroglycerin. Today, at a rock quarry, he demonstrates his new invention: dynamite. This transforming invention will make Nobel a rich man.
    - He will establish a multimillion dollar trust fund and use his riches to reward those who invent or write for the peaceful good of mankind. He intends dynamite to be used for good purposes and will be disappointed when it is used otherwise.
- New Mexico Territory: Comanche attack Oliver Loving and a Mr. Wilson, who were scouting for the Goodnight-Loving outfit. Wounded, Loving waits five days for help. He is taken to Ft. Sumner, but his shattered wrist doesn't heal. A doctor amputates Loving's arm above the elbow; gangrene sets in. Loving dies about three weeks later. (b. 1812; d. September 21, 1867). He is buried at Ft. Sumner. Honoring Loving's request, his son Joe and partner, Goodnight, will bury him in Weatherford, Texas, on March 4, 1868.
- September, Kansas, about 3 p. m.: Franz Hunning and his wagon train approach Plum Buttes (between Cow Creek and the Great Bend of the Arkansas). War whoops fill the air as 200 Cheyenne and a few Arapaho and Kiowa sweep down upon the train. The train circles for defense to no avail. Warriors murder and scalp Hunning's mother-in-law and brother-in-law, disembowel them and cut off their breasts. They quarter the old lady and pile her parts on top of her clothes. Hunning flees to Ft. Zarah for help.
    - Sparsely manned Ft. Zarah has few mounts. A scout and companion ride ahead of the infantry to assess the situation. They find bloody goods strewn across the landscape, wagon covers riddled with bullet holes, and wheel spokes cut in pieces. Much is burnt. Hunning's mother-in-law and brother-in-law are so mutilated the soldier thinks they are both female.
- Abilene, Kansas: Texas cattlemen had been driving cattle to eastern markets through Missouri, angering farmers. When the railhead reaches Abilene, Joseph M. McCoy builds cattle yards and loading chutes. Taking advantage of the shorter distance, Texas cattlemen drive 35,000 cattle on the Chisholm Trail north to the Kansas railhead.
    - Jesse Chisholm, trader with the Wichita Indians, had a store near the mouth of the Arkansas River. He drove into Indian Territory often enough to leave wagon tracks. Cowboys driving cattle from Waco and Ft. Worth, Texas, followed Chisholm's wagon tracks when they reached them and called their whole trail after his name.
- Near Socorro, New Mexico Territory: Silver is discovered.
- October, Kansas: Five Plains Indian tribes meet with a U. S. Peace Commission and accept the Medicine Lodge Treaty. Kiowa Chief Satanta (White Bear) signs the treaty, but continues raiding settlements.

- November 7, Cimarron, New Mexico Territory: Lucien Maxwell gives Dick Wootton a quit claim deed to Raton Pass property.
- November 25, Washington, D. C.: The House of Representatives impeaches President Andrew Johnson. Accusations include: removal and replacement of Secretary of War Stanton; unlawful disbursement of War Department money; causing General Emory (in charge of the Washington Department) to disobey orders. Impeachment proceedings continue into late spring 1868. Johnson is acquitted.
- December 9, Colorado Territory: Denver becomes the permanent capital of Colorado.
- Tuesday, December 14, Exchange Hotel, Santa Fe: Colonel William L. Rynerson shoots and kills New Mexico Territory's Chief Justice John P. Slough. On December 17 Rynerson pleads self-defense, is acquitted, and will lead a lengthy political career.
    - Censured by Legislative Council on the 16th, Slough had called Dona Ana County's Legislator William Rynerson "a thief in the army, a thief out of the army, a coward, and an S. O. B."[260]

1868
- January: Colorado's mining industry begins a new era when a smelter opens at Blackhawk, west of Denver, near Central City. The smelter is capable of separating embedded gold from some types of rock.
    - Chemistry professor and metallurgist Nathaniel Peter Hill studied area minerals and geological formations and sent ore samples to Wales for analysis. Last spring he organized a smelting company; later in the year he began construction of the Blackhawk smelter.
- March 2: Ouray is appointed Chief of the Ute nation.
- U. S. representatives and northern Plains Indians accept the Ft. Laramie Treaty.
- May 12 – November 13, New Mexico Territory: Army engineer Captain N. S. Davis directs hundreds of men digging a ditch for the Moreno Water and Mining Company. Water will flow through the ditch to the Moreno Valley gold fields. Distance: approximately forty miles. Cost: $300,000.
- May, Kansas: The railhead reaches Sheridan.
- May 23, Ft. Lyon (Colorado): Kit Carson dies.
- June 1, near Lancaster, Pennsylvania: Former President James Buchanan dies.
- June 1, Ft. Sumner, New Mexico Territory: The U. S. and the Navajo sign the Treaty of Bosque Redondo. Barboncito, Armijo and other chiefs and headmen represent the Navajo; Peace Commissioners W. T. Sherman and Samuel F. Tappan represent the U. S.
- June, Colorado: Dick Wootton lays out a road from Pond Creek, Kansas, to Bent's Fort.
- July 11: Surveyors begin survey of the New Mexico-Colorado border.
- July 28: The Fourteenth Amendment to the U. S. Constitution is ratified. Its five sections pertain to civil rights of every born or naturalized U. S. citizen;

---

[260] UNM University Libraries, https://nmstatehood.unm.edu/node/72227.

representation; limitations for those who have been involved in insurrection or crime; acknowledgement of the public debt; power to enforce the amendment.
- August 27, Smoky Hills (Colorado): Indians kill twelve families near Harker.
- August 30, Ft. Lyon (Colorado): Captain Penrose reports Indian hostilities from Ft. Dodge to Ft. Lyon, from Ft. Lyon to Denver, and in the Smoky Hill area.
- September, northwest of Ft. Wallace (Colorado): Battle of Beecher Island is fought. Chief Roman Nose dies.
- October 9, east of Ft. Lyon (Colorado): Indians capture two-year-old Willie Blinn and his mother, Clara.
- October 21, California: An earthquake shakes San Francisco.
- November 27, upper Washita River (Oklahoma): George Custer and his U. S. 7th Cavalry kill at least forty Indians, including Cheyenne Chief Black Kettle (escaped Sand Creek).
- Christmas, December 25: President Johnson proclaims amnesty for all Confederates.

1869
- January 25, New Mexico Territory: The New Mexico legislature creates Colfax County, named in honor of U. S. Vice-President, Schuyler Colfax. Elizabethtown is the county seat.
- May 10, Promontory Point, northern Utah: A golden spike joins the rails of the Union Pacific and Central Pacific, completing the first transcontinental rail line.
- May 19, Colorado Territory: William Bent dies of pneumonia.
- Santa Fe: William Anderson Pile replaces New Mexico Governor Robert Byington Mitchell and remains in office until 1871.
- Indian Territory (Oklahoma): Fort Sill is established.
- July 8: Telegraph lines for military use are completed from Ft. Leavenworth to Santa Fe.
- Sunday afternoon, July 11, Summit Springs, Colorado Territory: William "Buffalo Bill" Cody acts as scout for Major (General) Eugene A. Carr. Carr and his soldiers defeat the intrepid Dog Soldiers ten miles from Sterling, Colorado.
- Santa Fe (New Mexico): Jean Baptiste Lamy directs construction of St. Francis Cathedral (Cathedral Basilica of St Francis of Assisi). It is built around La Parroquia, which replaced a church on the site destroyed during the 1680 Pueblo Revolt. Jean Bouquet, Lamy's friend from France, helps cut stone quarried from Lamy, New Mexico. A stonecutter and stonemason, Bouquet came to New Mexico c 1855.
- Black Friday, September 24: In an attempt to corner the gold market, Jay Gould and James Fisk, Jr., place the U. S. in a state of financial emergency.
- By early fall, Kansas: Rails have reached Fort Wallace.
- October 8, Concord, New Hampshire: Former President Franklin Pierce, age 64, dies.
- December 10, Wyoming Territory: Territorial Legislature votes to allow women to vote and hold office. The *Cheyenne Leader* expects this to attract settlers, especially women, to the predominately male state. Women throughout the U. S. won't have equal voting rights until the Nineteenth Amendment is ratified in August 1920.

- Colorado Territory: Edward C. McCook is Governor (1869-1873). He succeeds Alexander C. Hunt (1867-69). McCook will govern again from 1874-1875.

1870

- January 26: Congress allows Virginia to send Congressional representation to Congress.
  - Virginia, birthplace of many presidents and early Americans, experienced such war destruction and indebtedness it will be forty to fifty years before recovery seems a reality.
- January 28: Lucien Maxwell sells his Maxwell Land Grant.
- February 23: Mississippi is allowed representation in Congress for the first time since it seceded from the Union. Hiram R. Revels, a Mississippi black man will begin his term in Congress on February 25.
- New Mexico Territory: Elizabethtown, Colfax County seat, becomes the first incorporated town in New Mexico Territory. The county seat will move to Cimarron in 1872, to Springer in 1882, and finally to Raton in 1897.
  - Elizabethtown is a thriving community with a newspaper, *The Lantern*—begun last year; two hotels; five stores; two churches; and a drugstore. There is enough business for seven bars and three dance halls. The town is gaining a rough reputation.
- March 30: Amendment Fifteen is added to the U. S. Constitution. It pertains to voting rights "regardless of race, color, or previous condition of servitude."
- Spring, State archives, Palace of the Governors, Santa Fe: Much of the Spanish Archives of New Mexico disappear.
- Nathan Cook Meeker, *New York Tribune* agricultural editor, advertises for emigrants to form an irrigated agricultural colony in Colorado. Meeker chooses 200 of those who respond to help form Greeley Colony (named for his editor in chief, Horace Greeley). Colonists will transform thousands of acres of arid land into land producing potatoes, corn, wheat, oats, and alfalfa.
- June: The Denver Pacific Railroad links Denver, Colorado, to Cheyenne, Wyoming.
- June 22: Congress creates the Department of Justice.
- June, Colorado Territory: Las Animas County reports a case against Dick Wootton for selling liquor without paying taxes. Prosecution is suspended when payment is made.
- July 15: Congress allows Georgia Congressional representation.
- August 15, Denver: The Kansas Pacific Railroad has linked Denver with Kansas City. Today a train arrives.
- October 12: General Robert Edward Lee, age sixty-three, dies. Although Lee took the oath of allegiance and applied for reinstatement of his U. S. citizenship, he dies without it. It will be 105 years before his citizenship is reinstated. On August 5, 1975, President Gerald Ford will sign a bill granting U. S. citizenship to Robert E. Lee. On October 17, 1978, President Jimmy Carter will sign a bill reinstating Jefferson Davis' citizenship.

- October 28, 6 p. m., Mora, New Mexico Territory: Ceran St. Vrain dies, age sixty-eight.

1871
- January, New Mexico Territory: James Buckley, "Coal Oil Jimmy," dies. In his lifetime Jimmy enjoyed robbing stages and murdering in the Las Vegas and Elizabethtown areas.
- Reverend Morton asks for and obtains a special clause added to his life insurance policy to permit him to move to Denver, Colorado Territory, and remain insured.
  - Some life insurance companies grant certain travel coverage, but few, if any, cover death if: 1) caused by hostile Indians, 2) a result of violating the law, 3) the insured is involved in a duel.
  - Companies prefer not to insure miners or railroad workers. Most companies make it policy not to insure west of the 100th meridian. This allows a person to hang onto his insurance premiums about as far as Dodge (Dodge City, Kansas). In the mid-to-late 1870's life insurance companies will begin changing policy.
- Europe: French overthrow Napoleon III and establish the Third Republic.
- Phineas Taylor Barnum opens his "Great Travelling [sic] Museum, Menagerie, Caravan, and Hippodrome."
- March 3: The Indian Appropriation Act nullifies all Indian treaties and declares Indians wards of the government.
- Colorado Territory: General William J. Palmer founds Colorado Springs.
- March 3, near New London, Missouri: Marcellin St. Vrain, age fifty-five, dies.
- June 13, Canon City (Colorado): Colorado Territorial Prison admits its first inmate.
- Kiowa Chief Sitting Bear, age seventy, breaks out of the Kiowa reservation. Other chiefs and he attack Texas settlements. After they attack a ten-wagon train (hauling grain), kill its seven men, and steal forty-one mules, they ride to Fort Sill to pick up government allotments. Things would've gone better for them if one chief hadn't bragged about the attack. Soldiers arrest Sitting Bear and two others and send them to Texas for trial. (Sitting Bear will attempt escape, attempt to kill, and be killed.)
- Golden, Colorado Territory: Colorado School of Mines is established.
- October 8, Illinois: The Great Chicago fire breaks out and burns for twenty-four hours.
- Italy: Rome is made the nation's capital.
- 1869-1871, Kansas: Western cattlemen drive 1,500,000 cattle into Abilene for sale and shipment.
- Monday, December 18, Wootton Ranch (Colorado): Dick Wootton marries Mary Pauline Lujan.

1872
- July 4, Plymouth, Vermont: Calvin Coolidge (30th U. S. President, 1923-1929) is born.
- Washington, D. C.: Congress creates the first national park: Yellowstone Park.
- Summer: Enterprising dry goods salesman Aaron Montgomery Ward comes up with

an idea to cut out middleman profit and sell directly to customers. He purchases $1,600 worth of goods and begins a mail order business in a room less than 200 feet square. His catalog is a simple list of 167 items. Catalogs are just the thing for far-flung towns, farms, and ranches. Within three years Montgomery Ward & Co. will offer 2,000 items in a seventy-two page pocket-sized catalog.
- New Mexico Territory: Henri Lambert, former cook for President Lincoln and General Grant, moves from Elizabethtown to Cimarron. There he builds the St. James Hotel at a cost of $17,000. The St. James will be home to at least twenty-six murders before Cimarron City sees quieter days.
- Friday, September 20, Wootton Ranch (Colorado): Mary Fidelis Wootton is born.
- Fall: The Santa Fe Railroad has laid track from Wichita to Newton, Kansas.

1873
- January 17 (Oregon): Fifty Modoc Indians defeat Lt. Col. Frank Wheaton's army of 309. The Modoc War, between the Modoc and the U. S., begins. It will be fought in southern Oregon and northern California until June 1874.
- Easter Sunday: Ute Chief Rafael is on the warpath because government agents keep trying to make his tribe move.
- 1873-1878: Grasshopper raids besiege Colorado and Kansas. The mining industry helps Colorado survive economically.
- Texas: A Congressional commission begins investigation of Indian atrocities. Reports of Indians attacking their homes call settlers away from registering complaints.
- New Mexico Territory ships 29,000 pounds of lead to eastern states.
- September 17, 18, 19: Stocks plummet (17th). Jay Cooke and Company, the era's financial rock, closes its doors in New York, Washington, D. C., and Philadelphia (18th). September 19th is the U. S.' second Black Friday. The New York Stock Exchange closes for ten days. The financial boom, begun after the Civil War, comes to a halt. Financial depression begins and lasts almost six years. Five thousand businesses bankrupt.
    - Cooke's company floated bonds to help Union operations during the Civil War and was involved in railroad securities. Cooke found himself needing more money than he could raise in the U. S. He tried, but couldn't obtain funds in Europe. Because of the Franco Prussian War, Europe has troubles of its own.
- Buffalo hunters kill buffalo for hides alone.
- The United States opens its doors to 473,000 immigrants.
- Colorado Territory: Samuel E. Elbert is governor (1873-74).

1874
- February 9, Wootton, Colorado Territory: Ida Dillon Wootton is born.
- March 8, Buffalo, New York: Former President Millard Fillmore, age seventy-four, dies. He was president two years and eight months.
- May 21, about 9:30 a.m., Colorado Territory: Fire breaks out in Central City (Gregory Gulch) and destroys most of the town by midafternoon.

- About 9:30 two or three Chinamen, who operate a laundry in Dostal Alley behind Main Street, rush out to draw attention to their shanty. They were burning incense to an idol. The incense sticks sent bits of curled paper blazing up the chimney, but not all went up the chimney. Some ignited dry woodwork in the shanty.
- Last year a small fire heightened awareness of fire danger in the community of closely built frame buildings; so they'd devised a fire plan. Now the community rouses into action. A fire bell calls the fireguard. Men form a water brigade and grab the new red fire buckets, but the gulch is dry. They find well water. Fire fighters demolish frame buildings in the fire's path to keep the fire from jumping. But fire dances and leaps across the fifty foot main street. It careens, crackling down both sides of city streets. People, hands laden with assorted goods, rescue what they can. Firefighters from other areas hear of the fire by telegraph and arrive by noon. Before suppertime the fire is under control. About 150 downtown buildings are destroyed. After a two-three hour battle to save it, the large, two-year-old Teller House stands. People gather there, grateful to God the battle's over and that they and their friends are alive.
- June 27, Adobe Walls, Texas: Comanche leader Isa-tai and Comanche Chief Quanah Parker lead about 300 warriors to attack twenty-eight hunters. Outnumbered, but well-armed, hunters withstand the attack. This second Battle of Adobe Walls is a last straw between Comanche and the U. S. government. Comanche spread out over the Texas Plains and renew attacks. Citizens appeal to the U. S. government for protection. U. S. determination to settle things once for all leads to the Red River War.
- Summer 1874-June 1875, eastern New Mexico and Texas Panhandle, Red River War: Major William R. Price of Ft. Union, Col. Nelson A. Miles of Ft. Dodge, Lt. Col. John W. Davidson of Ft. Sill, Col. Ronald S. Mackenzie of Ft. Concho, and Lt. Col. George P. Buell of Ft. Griffin circle the Red River region to prevent Indian escape. U. S. Cavalry subdues Plains tribes and requires them to agree to move to Indian reservations.
  - Late September, Palo Duro Canyon, Texas: In an attempt to break Comanche resistance, Col. Ronald Mackenzie attacks a Comanche camp at the headwaters of Red River. Few Indians are killed. Mackenzie and his troops set fire to Comanche lodges and destroy their food supply. Unable to handle the more than 1,400 Comanche horses, soldiers drive the horses into a nearby canyon and shoot them—the pride of the Comanche.
  - There are many skirmishes in the Red River War. Soldiers and Indians are persistent. Quanah Parker and his Quahadi Comanche band are the last to surrender. They surrender at Ft. Sill in June 1875. The Red River War marks the final defeat of the Kiowa and Comanche.
- New Mexico Territory ships 7,122 pounds of copper ore, 200,400 pounds of copper and twenty-five bars of bullion eastward.

- August 10, West Branch, Iowa: Herbert C. Hoover (U. S. President 1929-1933) is born.
- November 24: Joseph Glidden is granted the patent for barbed wire.
- November 30, Oxfordshire, England: Winston Churchill is born.

1875
- New Mexico Territory: A military telegraph line is completed from Santa Fe to Mesilla.
- Spring, Black Hills (South Dakota): The U. S. Government sends Mr. Jenny, a geologist, to survey on the Sioux reservation. Sioux do not consider surveyors, cavalry, and infantry who accompany Jenny, a simple survey team. They prepare to defend their land.
- May 17, Kentucky: Churchill Downs hosts the first Kentucky Derby.
- Leadville, Colorado Territory: While digging a water ditch for a gold mine, two men discover lead carbonate. For years Leadville will supply the majority of U. S. lead and silver.
- June, southwestern Indian Territory (Oklahoma): After surrender, Chief Quanah Parker's Comanche band moves to a reservation near Fort Sill. Quanah encourages his people to get an education, learn to farm, and lease their land for grazing. Under Parker's leadership his entire band sets a standard for other tribes as they become citizens of the United States.
- June, Santa Fe (New Mexico): Governor Marshall Giddings dies in the Palace of the Governors. He has been governor since 1871.
- July, New Mexico Territory: Samuel Beach Axtell is appointed governor. His years (1875-1878) in office will be marked by corruption and disorder.
  - In his early fifties, Axtell has graying hair and dark eyes.
- July 25, Ft. Sumner, New Mexico Territory: Lucien B. Maxwell dies.
- August 3, Colorado Territory: The Purgatoire River floods—the worst since 1864.
- September 14, New Mexico Territory: Rev. T. J. Tolby is found dead. His murder ignites the Colfax County War.
- Last week of December, Chimayo, New Mexico: Patricio Baca, considered northern New Mexico's most accomplished horse thief, is killed.
- December 31, Wootton, Colorado Territory: John Peter Wootton is born.

1876
- January, New Mexico Territory: Governor Samuel Axtell moves Colfax County district court from Cimarron to Taos.
- Colorado Territory: Peter Magnes has raised sugar beets near Denver for years. He and a committee of men encourage construction of sugar beet factories. Magnes predicts more money can be made in Colorado from the manufacture of sugar than from all the gold mined in the state. (April 19, 1959, *Rocky Mountain News*: Colorado gold produced 1858/59-1959: $905,956,200. Colorado beet sugar produced 1901-59: $1,551,480,000.)
- June, Philadelphia, Fairmount Park, Centennial Exposition (May 10-November 10):

Alexander Graham Bell shows his new invention: the telephone. In 1878 New Haven, Connecticut, will have the first telephone exchange and serve twenty-one customers.
- June 17, near Rosebud Creek, Montana: Sioux and U. S. military (under General Crooke) fight the Battle of the Rosebud. The Army retreats from the well-armed Sioux.
- June 25, Battle of the Little Bighorn (Montana): Sitting Bull and his Sioux warriors wipe out American troops under "Long Hair," General George Armstrong Custer. About 136 Sioux are killed, 160 wounded. Sioux women carry off their dead and wounded, take what they want from dead soldiers, and slash some soldier bodies. News of the battle stirs Americans; troops are sent immediately. Sitting Bull and many flee to Canada; he remains there five years. Some surrender; some are caught.
  - Sioux considered Custer and his 7th Cavalry protectors of Black Hills gold seekers and railroad surveyors on the Yellowstone.
  - June 6, Dakota Territory: *Bismarck Tribune* reports the massacre and includes names of soldiers killed. Including a *Bismarck Tribune* reporter, soldiers, and Indian scouts, 261 men are listed—including Custer, two of his brothers, and his brother-in-law. Bodies of Lt. Harrington, Lt. Sturgis, and Col. Porter are not found.
- South of present-day Florence, Colorado: Isaac Canfield discovers oil. This is the beginning of oil production in the Florence Field.
- New Mexico Territory: The Indian Agency in Cimarron closes.
- Trinidad, Las Animas County, Colorado Territory: Mrs. Wootton's uncle is Las Animas County Sheriff (his second term). R. L. Wootton, Jr. is undersheriff.
- The U. S. sends the Apache to White Mountain reservation in Arizona. Geronimo and a band of southern Chiricahua Apache continue to raid and terrorize southern Arizona, New Mexico, and parts of Mexico for another decade. (His Indian name is Goyathlay, "one who yawns"; Mexicans call him Geronimo.)
- August 1: Colorado is admitted to the Union. John L. Routt becomes the first state governor (1875-1879). The seven territorial governors were Republican.
- August 2, Deadwood, Dakota Territory: Jack McCall shoots James Butler "Wild Bill" Hickok in the back. Hickok has been a lawman, has helped slaves escape, and has driven freight across the Santa Fe Trail.
- September 7, Northfield, Minnesota: In an attempt to rob the bank, the Younger and James Gang enter a death trap. This marks the end of their exploits as a gang.
- October, New Mexico Territory: Juan Gonzalez should have stuck to horse thieving in Lincoln County. He is killed in Albuquerque, as he attempts to rob a store.

1877
- U. S. President Rutherford B. Hayes takes office. He immediately orders Federal troops to leave the South. During his term big business grows, technology advances, immigration soars.
- April: The last of the post-Civil War occupation troops leave the South. Carpetbag

rule (dominated 1865-1870) ends in all Southern states.
- Monday, June 11: Lucy Wootton is born.
- Idaho and Montana: The Nez Percé Indian War is fought. Chief Joseph is captured.
- Telegraph service reaches El Paso, Texas, and San Diego, California.
- Thomas Edison invents the phonograph. His first recording: "Mary Had a Little Lamb."
- Boulder, Colorado: University of Colorado begins with forty-four students and two professors.
- September 7, Ft. Robinson, Nebraska: Chief Crazy Horse, of the Minneconjou band of Oglala Sioux, is killed.
- September 24: Dick Wootton gives testimony of Maxwell Land Grant boundaries.

1878
- Trinidad, Las Animas County, Colorado: R. L. Wootton, Jr. is sheriff. Miguel Antonio Otero is treasurer.
- A yellow fever epidemic kills 14,000 in the U. S. (states hardest hit: Alabama, Louisiana, Mississippi and Tennessee).
- January 1, Florence, Kansas: The first Harvey House opens.
- January 14: The U. S. Supreme Court rules it is unconstitutional for state laws to demand any railroad to supply equal accommodations regardless of race or color.
- February 18, Lincoln County, New Mexico Territory: Attorney John H. Tunstall, an Englishman with investments in Lincoln County, is shot and killed on his way to Lincoln. His murder ignites the Lincoln County War, in which Billy the Kid gains notoriety.
- February 26, Raton Pass (Colorado): Dick Wootton grants the Atchison, Topeka, and Santa Fe Railway right-of-access over Raton Pass.
- April-July: Ute Indians move to a reservation.
- June, Snake River area (southern Idaho and Oregon): Bannock Indians kill settlers and appropriate or destroy settlers' property. This begins the Bannock-Paiute Uprising.
- Leadville, Colorado: New discoveries of gold draw thousands. By fall 1879, 15,000 miners mine the area.
- July 14-19, Lincoln County, New Mexico Territory: Lincoln County War bursts into action. (By the time it's over Billy the Kid will be on the lam, and Attorney Alexander A. McSween will be dead.) After he came to Lincoln County this spring, McSween exposed Lawrence G. Murphy and James J. Dolan's business practices and connection with the Santa Fe Ring. Headquartered in Santa Fe, the Ring is highly influential at all levels of government in various parts of the territory
- September 4, Wootton, Colorado: Two-year-old John Wootton dies at home.
- September 27: Appointed to replace Samuel Axtell as New Mexico Governor, Lew Wallace leaves Trinidad, Colorado, on his way to Santa Fe. Wallace travels by train to Trinidad, by buckboard across Raton Pass and the Vermejo (New Mexico) to Cimarron. He stays a day and night as guest of attorneys Frank W. Springer and

- William D. Lee, a friend from Indiana. (President Harrison will appoint Lee as judge of the Second Judicial District of New Mexico.)
- Sunday, September 29, about 9 p. m., Santa Fe: Lew Wallace arrives. He spends the night at the United States Hotel on the Plaza.
- September 30, Santa Fe (New Mexico): Lew Wallace's first task is to present Samuel Axtell with Presidential papers suspending him from office. Axtell expects him. Wallace explains his business. They agree the official papers will be presented tomorrow.
  - Cimarron (New Mexico): When residents learn of Axtell's dismissal, they rejoice in the streets with dancing, fireworks, and shots—shotguns and pistols: 50 guns fire into the air.
- September 30: 3:15 p.m. Santa Fe: Lew Wallace qualifies as governor. Washington has briefed Wallace and hopes that, with his experience, he will be able to end the Lincoln County War. Wallace's record: attorney; Mexican War soldier; Major General in the Civil War; chairman of the inquiry of Anderson Prison. He also served on a court-martial concerning Lincoln's assassination.
- October 1, Santa Fe, New Mexico Territory: Lew Wallace takes office (1878-1881). First on his agenda: private interviews with leaders of rival factions involved in New Mexico turmoil. He reports to Secretary of the Interior Carl Schurz and requests President Hayes' approval of the use martial law and the appointment of a military commission.
- September/October, Colorado: Meeker Massacre.
- October 7: President Hayes authorizes use of federal troops to bring order in Lincoln County, New Mexico Territory. The feud has turned into outright range war.
- October 11, Texas State Penitentiary: Imprisoned for his raids, Kiowa Chief Satanta, "White Bear," jumps from a window to his death.
- November 1: The Santa Fe Railroad finishes laying track from Pueblo, Colorado, to the New Mexico-Colorado line.
- December 7, Raton Pass: The first train crosses into New Mexico.
- Sunday, December 29, Wootton, Colorado: John Peter Wootton is born.

1879
- New York City: F. W. Woolworth opens his first five-and-ten-cent store. He founds the F. W. Woolworth Company chain of stores.
- Cerillos, New Mexico Territory: Coal is mined.
- February 13: The Santa Fe Railroad's first passenger train chugs across Raton Pass and into New Mexico. (At the height of operations the depot at Raton, New Mexico, will welcome 60 trains daily.)
- February 24, Colorado: Denver's first telephone company begins business with 161 customers. New York City boasts 252 phones. By 1884 telephone poles become a problem in New York City. (City fathers decide telephone wires must go underground.)
- February 28: The "Black Exodus of '79" begins. Thousands of blacks migrate

westward. In the 1870's and 1880's, former slave Benjamin Singleton leads thousands of blacks from the South to form all-black communities on the Kansas prairies.
- March 13, New Mexico Territory: Billy the Kid writes Governor Lew Wallace and offers to testify in exchange for immunity.
- March 14, Ulm, Germany: Albert Einstein is born to Hermann and Paulina Koch Einstein.
- March 17, Lincoln (New Mexico): Governor Lew Wallace meets with Billy the Kid.
- Colorado: Frederick W. Pitkin, another of the long line of Colorado Republican governors, takes office (1879-1883).
- April: Apache Chief Victorio and some of his warriors escape the reservation and terrorize parts of New Mexico and Arizona, killing as they go.
- April, New Mexico Territory: Keeping his word to Governor Wallace, Billy the Kid arrives in Lincoln to testify before the Lincoln County Grand Jury concerning legal violations in Lincoln County.
- May 7, California: Policy between the U. S. and China allows free immigration. Chinese immigration into California has reached such proportions that California enacts a new constitution that bans employment of Chinese.
- June 14, Palace of the Governors, Santa Fe: A reception and military ball welcome and honor visiting Civil War hero Lieutenant General Phil H. Sheridan.
- July 1, New Mexico Territory: Train tracks reach Las Vegas, largest town in the territory.
- July 4, 12 noon, Las Vegas, New Mexico Territory: Decorated with flags, ribbons, and evergreens, two Santa Fe Railroad locomotives arrive in Las Vegas. Dan Daley is at the throttle; Charlie Brooks is conductor. A local brass band plays as the train arrives in the block. Townspeople will celebrate the event tonight with two balls.
  - The track is one mile from the business center. Residents and merchants ford the Gallinas River to meet trains until a bridge is built. Soon the town will have streetcars—pulled by horses, or mules—to transport passengers between the depot and the business center. For one dollar a person can buy twenty-five streetcar tickets. At the height of operation, streetcars meet trains and leave the depot every ten minutes between 7 a. m. and 9 p. m. An electric trolley system will replace animal-drawn streetcars (1901-1927).
  - With the opening of rail service more people move into New Mexico. Las Vegas' growing businesses and surrounding ranches attract many. Among the newcomers are ranchers, farmers, and other fine upstanding citizens, as well as those who enjoy less legal restraint, including many troublemakers from Dodge City, Kansas. Rascals and outlaws—some homegrown, some from other places—find the large territory an easy hiding place and haunt for their shenanigans. Some members of the Dodge City Gang find prominent positions in Las Vegas: H. G. Neill, alias, Hoodoo Brown, justice of the peace; Joe Carson, city marshal/deputy sheriff; Dave Mather, alias, "Mysterious Dave," and J. J. Webb,

policemen. Other outlaws in Las Vegas: "Caribou Brown, Dirty-face Mike, Scar-face Charlie, Pawnee Bill, Kickapoo George, Jack-knife Jack, Flyspeck Sam, Hatchet-face Kit, Durango Kid, Cockeyed Frank, Rattlesnake Sam, Split-nose Mike, Web-fingered Billy, Wink the Barber, Double-out Sam, Jimmie the Duck, Flapjack Bill, Buckskin Joe, Cold-deck George, Pegleg Dick, Red River Tom, Hog Jones, Long Lon, Soapy Smith, Stuttering Tom, and Tommy the Poet."[261]

- About a year after the arrival of the railroad, Las Vegas vies for title of wildest of the Wild West. In one month the newspaper reports 29 killings, whether murdered, shot in self-defense, or in correction by the Las Vegas Vigilance Committee.
- Las Vegas, New Mexico Territory: Dr. John "Doc" Holliday opens a dentist office, but once again finds gambling more attractive than dentistry. "Doc" opens a saloon on Center Street in the new section of Las Vegas, near the Santa Fe railway depot.
- July 26-29, Five miles from Las Vegas, New Mexico Territory: Jesse James enjoys a secret vacation at hot springs owned by childhood friend Scott Moore and wife, Minnie. Jesse likes the area, considers changing his name and bringing his family to live here.
  - Years later, Bob Ford, who shot Jesse in the back, will move to Las Vegas and open a saloon on the north side of Bridge Street about halfway between the Plaza and the Gallinas River. Residents consider him a coward and don't encourage his presence in their community. He moves on.
- Las Vegas, New Mexico Territory: I. H. Hulbert installs the first telephone in the Territory. The telephone line connects his drug store on the Plaza to his branch store on the new Railroad Avenue, which fronts the railroad tracks. In 1880 County Commissioners in Las Vegas refuse to have phones installed in government offices. They reason that the new invention will be of little use because it can't speak Spanish.
- White Oaks, New Mexico Territory: Gold is discovered. From 1879 to 1906 almost $3,000,000 worth of gold and silver will be mined in the area.
- Wootton, Colorado: Sixteen-year-old Albert E. McCready, arrives from Brockville, Ontario, Canada, and finds his first job as a toll tender for Uncle Dick Wootton. He works at the Pass for a year.
- Late August, Las Vegas, New Mexico Territory: "Doc" Holliday shoots an outlaw on Center Street and leaves town.
- October 14, Ojo Caliente, Arizona Territory: Apache Chief Victorio and his band steal a herd of horses from 9th Cavalry Company E. They murder five buffalo soldiers and stake their bodies to the ground.
- Near the end of October, New Mexico Territory: Governor Lew Wallace visits Ojo Caliente, where Apache raid repeatedly. Residents are glad to see the governor and show him the results of the most recent raid: Sixteen bodies of men, women and children—some appallingly mutilated—lie before the church altar.

---

[261] Joseph Miller, *New Mexico*, 235.

- December 4, Cañoncito, New Mexico Territory: Bartender Frank Page settles the issue of twenty-five cents owed for a drink by killing "Rattlesnake Bill" Johnson. People who live in the area breathe a sigh of relief that the Rattlesnake is dead.

1880
- January: Thomas Edison patents a light bulb, which he developed in December. The world dubs him the Wizard of Menlo Park.
- Friday, February 6, Ouray, Colorado: Camped between Ouray and civilization, hostile Indians block the passage of supply wagons. The military promises prompt aid.
- Midnight, February 7, Las Vegas, New Mexico Territory: Discontent with the slow wheels of justice, a group of orderly, but determined, citizens march from Railroad Avenue to the jail. They gather more volunteers as they walk. When the blocks-long line of men arrives, the jailor hands them his keys. Citizens walk John Dorsey, Thomas "Tom" Jefferson Henry, and James Lowe (alias James West) to the center of the Plaza and hang them from the windmill. (The three men and a number of others came to Las Vegas for a good time on January 22. Drunk, they became involved in a bloody shootout and escaped, but surrendered when promised protection and a fair trial.)
- February 9, New Mexico Territory: First railroad train enters Santa Fe.
- February 10: In an effort to reach Santa Fe, Denver and Rio Grande Western Railroad enters New Mexico Territory from a north-central approach.
- April 22, Albuquerque, New Mexico Territory: Santa Fe Railroad arrives.
- May, New Mexico Territory: Indians kill settlers, burn homes, drive off stock. As a result, some towns organize militias.
- July 7-15: Ulysses and Julia Grant visit New Mexico and Colorado. The Grants have been on a world tour since he finished his U. S. presidential term.
- New Mexico Territory: The Maxwell Land Grant Company sells 320 acres for the townsite of Raton.
- August 24, near the Pine River, southwestern Colorado Territory: Great Ute Chief Ouray dies of Bright's disease. He is buried at Ignacio, Colorado. Soon his people, including his wife, Chipeta, move to a Utah reservation. (Two dates given for his death: August 24, 27.)
    - Because he was born on the night of a meteor shower, his parents named him Ouray, "the Arrow." Ouray's father was Uncompahgre Ute, his mother Apache. Raised among the Spanish, Ouray spoke Spanish, Ute, Apache, and English. Ouray had one child, a son—Parso ("Apple" because of his round face), who was kidnapped by the Sioux and never returned.
    - Though raised as a Tabequache Ute, Chipeta was Kiowa-Apache. Her Ute name was White Singing Bird.
- *Ben Hur*, written by New Mexico Governor Lew Wallace, is published.
- 1880-1882, Trinidad, Las Animas County, Colorado: Mrs. Wootton's Uncle Jose Luis Dillett is twice elected county assessor.

- October, Tres Castillas Mountains, Mexico: Chief Victorio dies. He and his warriors terrorized parts of New Mexico, Arizona and northern Mexico. Nana succeeds him and fights eight more battles before being reconfined to a reservation. Victorio ("Apache Wolf") was born in 1825. Death date accounts vary: October 14 or 15, 1880 or 1881.
- October 28, Santa Fe (New Mexico): President Rutherford B. Hayes visits. This is the first time an acting president has visited New Mexico.
- December 5, New Mexico Territory: Santa Fe enjoys its first gaslights.
- December 20 or 23, Stinking Springs, De Baca County, New Mexico Territory: Pat Garrett captures Billy the Kid, Billy's sidekick Tom Pickett, and others. Billy's pal Charles Bowdre dies under fire. Billy is jailed in Las Vegas and then transferred to Santa Fe. Tom Pickett will live until May 14, 1934, and die in Arizona.

1881

- January 1, New Mexico Territory: Billy the Kid writes Governor Wallace, "I would like to see you for a few moments if you can spare the time."[262]
- January 10, New Mexico Territory: Alfred Graves kills double agent Porter "Port" Stockton. Porter had frequented northeastern New Mexico, where Dick Wootton was well-acquainted with him and his ways. Sometimes a marshal, sometimes a thieving member of the Stockton gang, Porter had moved to northwestern New Mexico. Infuriated because of Porter's murder, his brother Ike vows vengeance. With a band of outlaw buddies, Ike begins a short reign of terror known as the San Juan County War. They gun down several men on Ike's list before a sheriff and deputy apprehend him.
- Thinking a man should not be President more than one term, President Hayes declines a second term nomination. James A. Garfield becomes President of the United States.
- February 23, Denver, Colorado: Colorado Electric Co., Colorado's first electric generating firm, begins producing electricity. Electric lights illuminate city streets. Soon a few homes and businesses begin using lights.
- February 28, Wootton, Colorado: Mary Wootton is born.
- March 17, Santa Fe, New Mexico Territory: Governor Lew Wallace resigns. Lionel Allen Sheldon will replace him and hold office until 1885.
- March 27, Lincoln, New Mexico Territory: Billy the Kid writes the last of his six letters to Governor Wallace. He reminds the governor of their deal in 1879: testimony for immunity. Billy is scheduled for criminal trial.
- Dillon Canyon, about three miles west of Raton (New Mexico): Santa Fe Railroad geologist James T. Gardiner discovers coal. In 1882 the Old Gardiner Mine (Blossburg No. 4) will begin producing; the town of Gardiner will flourish until the late 1930's.
- April 16, New Mexico Territory: Hung in Raton today is James J. Devine—along

---

[262] Horn, "Soldier-Statesman," 214.

with his string of aliases: James Johnson, Curran, and Jones.
- April 30, New Mexico: Before he leaves office, Governor Wallace signs a death warrant for Billy the Kid. He's two days too late: Billy escaped the Lincoln County Jail the 28th.
- May 6, Wootton's 65th birthday, New Mexico Territory: A. W. Archibald, Deputy Surveyor, completes his survey of the Maxwell Land Grant in the ongoing U. S. investigation of the Grant. The survey began August 24, 1879.
- May 30: Lew Wallace returns home to Crawfordsville, Indiana, in a Pullman car on the Santa Fe Railroad—a more comfortable ride than his trip to Santa Fe less than three years ago. He will return West from time to time on mining business.
- June 4, New Mexico Territory: Territorial Governor Lionel Sheldon arrives.
- North of Colorado Springs, Colorado: Colorado's greatest train robbery occurs when robbers get away with $105,000 cash and $40,000 in jewelry. The crime is never solved.
- July 2, Railway station, Washington, D. C.: Charles J. Guiteau shoots President James Garfield, who was about to leave for his 25th Williams College reunion.
- July 14, night, Ft. Sumner, New Mexico Territory: Sheriff Pat Garrett shoots and kills "Billy the Kid" in the Maxwell home. The body is buried the next day. Billy's tombstone sets his death date: July 15. Some claim Billy didn't die that night. They claim another was shot and buried in his place and that Billy escaped and quietly lived out his years to a ripe old age.
  - On guard outside, deputies Poe and McKinney hear a gunshot, rush to the house, and find Garrett at the door. He tells them it was Billy; he thinks he shot him. Poe looks at the lifeless body and tells Garrett he shot the wrong man. Garrett was sure it was Billy, says he knew his voice.
- July 17, Missouri: Jim Bridger dies on his farm.
- Raton, New Mexico Territory: New Mexico's first public high school is founded.
- Blossburg, about five miles northeast of Raton, New Mexico Territory: The Santa Fe Railroad and the Raton Coal and Coking Co. open a coal mine. At its height, the town of Blossburg has a population of 1,000. It will have a school, a band, stores, a newspaper—*Blossburg Pioneer*, two churches—Catholic and Methodist, and bars.
  - Miners supplement income by homesteading on Johnson Mesa, about sixteen miles east of Raton. When out of work, men farm. When the men are needed at the mine, carrier pigeons bring a message from Blossburg to a specified building on Johnson Mesa.
- September 19: President Garfield, age forty-nine, dies. Vice-President Chester A. Arthur becomes U. S. President. Because of Garfield's death, September 26 is proclaimed a national day of fasting, prayer, and humiliation.
- September 27: Ike Stockton, leader of the Stockton Gang, dies after leg amputation. The Durango, Colorado, sheriff and deputy shot the 5'4" Stockton in the leg while trying to apprehend him. Stockton's Gang scatters. Some were later hanged in Socorro, New Mexico—well-known for its lynching street, Death Alley.

- October 3-8, Albuquerque: New Mexico holds its first territorial fair.
- October 26, Wednesday afternoon, OK Corral, Tombstone, Arizona Territory: Virgil Earp with his brothers Wyatt and Morgan, and Doc Holliday, attempt to arrest the Clanton Gang. A bullet hits Morgan's shoulder; one wounds Virgil's leg; another grazes Doc's hip. On the Clanton side, Frank and Tom McLaury and Billy Clanton die. Billy Claiborne and Ike Clanton quickly retreat. Not all gang members are present.
- November, New Mexico Territory: Santa Fe gets its first telephone.
- November, Shakespeare, New Mexico Territory: Horse thieves "Russian Bill" Telfrin and Sandy King are hanged.
- December 1: Despite mixed public opinion whether the Earps should have shot the Clanton Gang, the judge rules that they acted in the line of duty.
- December 3, Las Vegas, New Mexico Territory: They won't need as many meals at the jail tomorrow. David Rudabaugh, John Joseph Webb, Frank Kearney, William Goodman, Jack Kelly, S. Schroeder, and Tom "Tex" Quinlan break out of the jail and scatter. Rudabaugh heads for Mexico.
  - Captured at Stinking Springs with Billy the Kid, Rudabaugh had been sentenced and was in jail waiting hanging. Although he'd been a Las Vegas peace officer, he was also a gunman and thief—robbed stages and trains and stole horses. He escaped hanging this time; but in February 1886 citizens of Hidalgo de Parral, Mexico, will shoot and behead him.
- Denver, Colorado: H. A. W. Tabor opens the Tabor Opera House.
- The population of the United States is fifty-one and a half million.
- Trinidad, Colorado: In the early 1880's Bat Masterson serves as marshal for one year.

1882
- January 30, Hyde Park, New York: Franklin Delano Roosevelt is born (U. S. President, 1933-1945).
- February 12, Trinidad, Colorado: Visiting son R. L., Jr. and daughter Eliza Walker, Uncle Dick Wootton reports that spots of bare ground—where snow is melting near his Raton Pass home—are alive with young grasshoppers. The area had no grasshoppers last year.
- March 24, Las Vegas (New Mexico): Tired of gangs, hoodlums, and outlaws, citizens hang a sign: "Notice to thieves, thugs, fakirs and bunko-steerers among whom are J. J. Harlin, alias 'Off Wheeler,' Saw Dust Charlie, Wm. Hedges, Billy the Kid, Billy Mullin, Little Jack the Cutter, Pock-marked Kid and about twenty others: if found within the limits of this city after ten o'clock p.m. this night you will be invited to attend a grand necktie party, the expense of which will be borne by 100 substantial citizens."[263]
- Pueblo, Colorado: Colorado Fuel & Iron Corporation establishes a smelter and steel mill.

---

[263] Joseph Miller, 235.

- April 3, St. Joseph, Missouri: Bob Ford shoots and kills Jesse James.
  - The James Gang ranged in Missouri, Iowa, Illinois, Kentucky, Alabama, Arkansas, Texas, Kansas, and Colorado. Their heyday was 1866-1876, but their activities weren't limited to those years.
- Saturday, May 20, Wootton, Colorado: Gerardus Wootton is born.
- Near Avondale, Colorado: Charles Autobees dies.
- Dodge City, Kansas: "The Cowboy Capital" bustles. During cattle-selling season, herds of cattle arrive almost daily from Texas and other free-range grazing areas. Cowhands celebrate the end of the weeks-long drive, spend hard earned pay to enjoy proffered entertainments: a cowboy band, dancing, drinking, and gambling.
- July 12 or 13, Turkey Creek Canyon, Arizona Territory desert: Thirty-two-year-old John Peters Ringo—Johnny Ringo, a gunman involved with the Clanton Gang, is found dead.
- July 16, Springfield, Illinois: President Lincoln's widow, Mary Todd Lincoln, age sixty-three, dies of a stroke. She's been living with her sister.
- Saturday, September 9, 1 p. m., Wootton, Colorado: Gerardus Wootton dies.
- A. J. (Jim) Stinson drives 20,000 cattle in eight herds from west-central Texas into New Mexico's Estancia Valley. The Stinson Trail across New Mexico is named for him.
- New Mexico Territory: Miguel A. Otero's Las Vegas Telephone Company, which boasts 173 telephones, branches out. One branch, in the 100 block of Albuquerque's Railroad Avenue (Central), has fifty subscribers. Over the next four years, Albuquerque phones decrease to thirty-two. At the end of 1886 the Albuquerque phone company closes; the town will have no phone service until later in 1887.
- Shoe factory worker Jan Ernst Matzelinger invents a shoe-lasting machine that revolutionizes shoe manufacturing. (Parts of shoes have been sewn by machine since 1851.)

1883

- California: The Santa Fe Railway completes tracks into Needles.
- January 16: The Pendleton Civil Service Act creates the Civil Service Commission and provides merit examinations for civil service jobs.
- Congress overrides the recommendation of the president's commission to lower tariffs; it raises tariffs.
- New Mexico Territory: Apache kidnap Judge H. C. McComas' little son Charles. United States troops trail the Apache into Mexico.
- 1883-1885: James B. Grant is Colorado's first Democrat governor.
- Colorado: Dick Wootton testifies in the Maxwell Land Grant Case in Federal Court.
- Cimarron City, New Mexico Territory: William Frederick "Buffalo Bill" Cody organizes his "Wild West Circus," also known as the Wild West Show. His show tours the U. S. and Europe with entertaining performances, which depict a version of the American West. Sometimes "Buffalo Bill" returns to Cimarron for Christmas, where he enjoys giving Christmas parties for children at the St. James Hotel.

- July 4, Anaheim, California: The first U. S.-born ostrich hatches. Ostrich feathers are used in fashion. The feather industry in New York alone has increased from $500,000 to $5,000,000 in the past five-and-a-half years. Ostrich farms spring up in the U. S. Ostrich feathers will continue to be a lucrative business until after World War I.
- July 29, Dovia, Italy: Benito Mussolini is born.
- September 4, Trinidad, Colorado: Mary Fannie Wootton is born.
- U. S. postage for a letter is reduced to two cents per ounce.
- November 1: R. L. Wootton, Jr. testifies in the Maxwell Land Grant hearings.
- November 18: Railroads in the U. S. and Canada begin the use of standard time zones to facilitate scheduling. The Standard Time Act will be enacted in the U. S. in 1918.

1884
- January 22, Socorro, New Mexico Territory: Joe Fowler hangs from a cottonwood tree. Rumor had it Fowler killed more than twenty men. Fowler was known in Texas, Kansas, and New Mexico, sometimes as a rancher, sometimes as a bartender, always as a gambler. He made a mistake taking up ranching near Socorro. Folks there didn't take it kindly when, in the fall of 1883, he stabbed and killed Joseph Cale. It took Cale three days to die. Folks didn't care if Fowler was drunk or not; the jury convicted him. His attorney appealed his case, but townsfolk didn't see the sense in waiting around and giving Fowler room and board. A mob gathered, decided Fowler's number was next.
- May 8, Lamar, Missouri: Harry S. Truman (33rd U. S. President, 1945-1953) is born.
- July 4, Springer, New Mexico Territory: Robber "Red" McLaughlin celebrates Independence Day by breaking out jail.
- July 4 and 5, Kansas: To celebrate Independence Day, Dodge City hosts the first known bull fight in the United States.
- July 4, Paris, France: The Statue of Liberty is presented to the American people. F. A. Bartholdi designed the statue and worked with many to build it. Funds were raised in the U. S. and France.
- Las Vegas, New Mexico Territory: The Santa Fe Railway establishes a company hospital on Hot Springs Boulevard, two miles north of town.
- Chicago, Illinois: The first skyscraper, the ten-story Home Insurance Building, is built. Since the 1871 Chicago Fire, architects have learned to build steel framework to support high structures.
- Cattle king John Chisum dies.
  - Chisum, originally from Tennessee, filed bankruptcy soon after the Civil War. He moved to New Mexico and began raising cattle on a ranch that spread from near Ft. Sumner, south 200 miles. He left no question whether other settlers were welcome in his area; they were not. He saw to it they understood.
  - From 1870-1881 Chisum claimed he owned the largest number of cattle in the world. In 1878, at the height of his success, he had more than 100,000 head of cattle. After that, cattle rustlers and Indian raiders took their toll on his herd and competition of other ranchers began to take a slice of his market.

- August 10, off the Atlantic Coast: A 5.5 earthquake affects coastal areas from Virginia to Maine and is felt as far inland as Cleveland, Ohio.
- August 11, Trinidad, Colorado: Mary Fannie Wootton dies.
- Santa Fe: New Mexico constructs a state penitentiary.
- December 1, near Frisco, New Mexico Territory: Angry because of the arrest of Charles McCarty, who'd been terrorizing New Mexicans, eighty Texas cowboys attempt to kill Deputy Sheriff Elfego Baca. He holds them off.

1885
- March 4: Grover Cleveland, a bachelor, begins his first term as U. S. President.
- March, Raton, New Mexico Territory: Bat Masterson's brother James is run out of town.
- March 13, Springer, New Mexico Territory: Horse thief Ernest Anthony dies in jail.
- March 13, Springer, New Mexico Territory: John Curry, Tom "Red River" Whealington, and Dick Rogers are killed trying to help a friend escape from jail.
- Colorado again chooses a Republican governor: Benjamin H. Eaton (1885-1887).
- May, Arizona Territory: Nana, Geronimo, and other Apache break out of San Carlos Reservation. Before they're recaptured, they raid, loot, and kill (eighty-five U. S. citizens, including ten soldiers, twelve White Mountain Apache and an unknown number of Mexicans).
- July 23: Former U. S. President Ulysses S. Grant dies, age sixty-three. The last year of his life Grant wrote his memoirs. He completed the work four days before his death.
- August 10, Wootton, Colorado: Frank Christopher Wootton is born.
- September 7, Trinidad, Colorado: George Simpson dies.

1886
- April 20, New Mexico Territory: Blossburg floods.
- May, Walsenburg, Colorado: Dick Wootton's friend Ben Ryder dies.
- June 2: U. S. President Grover Cleveland marries Frances Folsom of Buffalo, New York. This is the first wedding of a President in the White House.
- September 3, Las Vegas, New Mexico Territory: The Tamme Opera House opens with a grand ball, concert and banquet. Fort Union's 10th infantry band plays the promenade.
  - Charles "Charlie" Tamme arrived in Las Vegas in 1879. George M. Ward and he opened a saloon-billiard hall, did well, and sold. Tamme and Henry P. Browne dreamed of and built the two-story (75'x130') stone Tamme (Duncan) Opera House to seat 1,000. It will be used for a variety of events; so the opera seats are removable. The building houses doctors' and attorneys' offices, the Western Union office, a flower shop, and a saloon. (In 1888 the saloon orders a large mirror, which requires an entire railroad boxcar for shipping.)
- September 3, Skeleton Canyon (southwest New Mexico/southeast Arizona): Geronimo surrenders. He and about 500 Chiricahua Apache are sent by rail to Ft. Pickens, Florida. One group of Apache returns to Arizona next year. Geronimo and

- his men will be transferred to Mt. Vernon Barracks, Alabama. Geronimo will be moved to Ft. Sill, where he will remain until his death in 1909.
- October 28, Liberty Island, New York: The Statue of Liberty is dedicated. It arrived in crates from France in May 1885.
- November 18: Former U. S. President Chester Arthur, age fifty-six, dies less than a year after leaving office. In the early years of his presidency Arthur was diagnosed with Bright's disease, but kept the matter quiet while in office.

1887
- January 28, Trinidad, Colorado: Dick Wootton's daughter Mary dies.
- March 8: New Mexico Attorney Frank Springer begins a four-day presentation before the U. S. Supreme Court in behalf of the Maxwell Land Grant Company.
- March 19: Dick Wootton's last child is born.
- April 18, Washington, D. C.: The U. S. Supreme Court rules in favor of the Maxwell Land Grant Company.
- The A. B. Dick Company produces a mimeograph machine invented by Thomas Edison.
- Congress passes the Interstate Commerce Act, which creates the Interstate Commerce Commission. This allows the federal government to investigate complaints about rates and practices of interstate railroads.
- An act of Congress allows individual Indians to own property within a reservation.
- July 17: Dorothea Lynde Dix dies. Born in 1802, she was in charge of Union women nurses during the Civil War. After the war, she traveled until her eightieth year, working to better prison conditions and care for the mentally ill.
- August 25, near Rangley, Colorado: Indians and American forces fight their last battle in Colorado. Troops sent by the governor meet Uintah Reservation Ute who have harassed settlers in the Meeker area. Two soldiers and eight Indians die.
- October 31, near Denver: Ft. Logan begins as a twenty-six tent camp. It will be a receiving station during World War I, then a military training camp. It will continue in service until after World War II.
- November 8, Glenwood Springs, Colorado: In his thirties, John "Doc" Holliday dies. Diagnosed with tuberculosis at a young age, the Georgia-born dentist moved to the dry western climate.
- Santa Fe: New Mexico opens a state school for the deaf.
- 1887-1889. Colorado: Democrat Alva Adams is governor.

1888
- January, Cimarron, New Mexico Territory: Fire destroys the part of the Maxwell House that the Maxwell's used to entertain.
- Overextended, Maxwell Land Grant Company reorganizes again.
- Chicago, Illinois: Dick Wootton has cataract surgery.
- March 11-14: A great blizzard blows in the northern U. S. from Wyoming and Montana through New England. Hundreds die.
- April 21, Trinidad, Colorado: Merchants complain of dust. They want a sprinkling

cart to settle dust on the streets.
- Oskaloosa, Kansas: Voters elect Mayor Mary Lowman and an all-woman town council—a first in the United States.

1889
- January 12, Santa Fe: J. Francisco Chavez and Albert Fountain, leaders of the Territorial Senate and House of Representatives, are given thirty-six hours to be out-of-town if they want to leave alive.
- March 9: Dick Wootton receives verification of Maxwell's quit claim deed.
- April 20, Braunau, Austria: Adolf Hitler is born.
- Noon, April 22, Oklahoma Land Rush: Having purchased over 3,000,000 acres of Indian Territory from Creek and Seminole Indians, the U. S. Government opens almost two-thirds of the land for settlement. Thousands rush in. In September 1893 another strip of land will be opened in the Cherokee, Tonkawa, and Pawnee areas.
- Santa Fe: L. Bradford Prince follows Edmund G. Ross (1885-1889) as governor of New Mexico Territory.
- April 26, San Miguel County, New Mexico Territory: Las Gorras Blancas/"The White Caps" protest use of the Las Vegas Land Grant. Chief concerns: land titles and property rights. (San Miguel is the largest New Mexico county, both in population and land area.)
  - They wear white hoods and work at night: shoot cattle, burn barns, destroy crops, equipment, haystacks, and other property. As their first protest, they demolish four miles of new fence, built by two English ranchers near San Geronimo.
  - Their acts are against anyone doing anything they consider inappropriate use of the land grant. In June and July they destroy the crops, equipment, sawmill and fences of Jose Ignacio Lujan, who fenced his place near San Ignacio. They allow no fencing.
  - They wreck railroad property, burn bridges, and threaten people not to sell timber for railroad ties. People are not to work for anyone unless Las Gorras Blancas approve the work and wage.
  - Under Juan Jose Herrera, Las Gorras Blancas will affiliate with national labor group Knights of Labor. They call themselves Los Caballeros de Labor and attempt to attract the working class. By the end of 1890 they are a political party in San Miguel County: El Partido del Pueblo Unido. Pinkerton detectives oversee the next election.
  - In July 1890, they are reported to the Secretary of the Interior for: destruction of life (wounding, killing) and property (hundreds of miles of fence, farm implements, crops, homes). By 1892, armed posses bring them under control.
- Pueblo, Colorado: Union Depot, a grand railroad depot, is built.
- Summer, Willow Gap (Creede), southern Colorado: Nicholas C. Creede finds a rich vein of silver and exclaims, "Holy Moses!" That becomes the mine's name. More prospectors arrive in spring. By summer a tent town springs up. Mines open in Bachelor, Spar City, and Sunnydale. Within a year mines produce $6,000,000 worth

- of silver.
- Summer, Wootton, Colorado: Writer Howard Louis Conard arrives.
- North Dakota and South Dakota (both November 2), Montana (November 8), and Washington (November 11) become states while Benjamin Harrison is President. He is the grandson of former President William Henry Harrison.
- Oklahoma Territory's first oil producing well is drilled.
- October, Trinidad, Colorado: J. F. Cook and Oliver Aultman open their Photograph Gallery on the corner of Main and Animas Streets.
- 1889-1894, Colorado: R. L. Wootton, Jr. represents Las Animas County in the state legislature's 7th, 8th, and 9th General Assemblies.
- November 30: Wisconsin requires the use of English for school-aged children 7-14.
- Colorado's sixth state governor is Republican Job A. Cooper (1889-1891).

1890
- January 25, New York City: "Nellie Bly" (Journalist Elizabeth Cochran) returns from her trip around the world. She left November 14, 1889, and traveled by ship, train, hand cart, and burro to complete the trip in 72 days, 6 hours, 11 minutes, and 14 seconds.
- January 25: United Mine Workers of America is founded.
- Saturday, March 1, Wootton, Colorado: The Wootton house burns.
- About 30 miles northwest of Raton, New Mexico Territory: Maxwell Land Grant Company creates the town of Catskill. This welcoming community-minded town thrives about a dozen years. Daily, in Catskill's heyday:
  - Workers in five sawmills fill and ship thirty to fifty flatcar-loads of lumber.
  - Workers burn 3,000 cords of wood into charcoal in beehive-shaped brick ovens; the charcoal is shipped by rail to smelters.
- July 2: In an effort to protect the public against monopolies, President Benjamin Harrison signs the Sherman Antitrust Act.
- July 3 and 10: Idaho and Wyoming become the 33rd and 34th U. S. states. Some states allow women to vote on some local issues, such as whether a railroad should be allowed through their parish. Wyoming has allowed women to vote on all issues since 1869.
- Henry Ford, a machinist in his twenties, works on a gas-powered engine. It will be three years before he completes a successful gas engine and three more before he makes a gas-powered automobile.
- October 1: Congress passes the McKinley Tariff Act, which raises tariffs to an all-time high.
- Trinidad, Colorado: Teodoro Abeyta (husband of Mrs. Wootton's cousin Amelia McBride) is Deputy Sheriff.
- October 14, Denison, Texas: Dwight David Eisenhower (World War II five-star general; U. S. President 1953-1961) is born.
- Chicago, Illinois: W. E. Dibble & Co. publishes *Uncle Dick Wootton*.
- November 22, Lille, France: Charles de Gaulle is born.

- December 6-8, Santa Fe: Dick Wootton promotes his memoirs at the Exchange Hotel. (This was originally La Fonda.)
  - In the first years of American Occupation (1846-1848), it was the United States Hotel; it became the Exchange Hotel in 1878. In 1919 the original building will be demolished and a new La Fonda will be built on the same location.
  - The hotel has welcomed travelers since the early 1800's. In the early years it was a rendezvous place for trappers, traders, and pioneers. There, merchants, soldiers and politicians met, dined and discussed. There, murderers killed several.
- December 10, South Dakota: Sioux Chief Sitting Bull dies.
- 1890 U. S. Census lists population of:
  - Arizona   59,620
  - Colorado   412,198 (more than double 1880's 199,327)
  - Idaho   84,385
  - Montana   132,159
  - Nevada   45,761
  - New Mexico   153,593
  - North Dakota   182,719
  - South Dakota   328,808
  - Utah   207,905
  - Wyoming   60,705

  The combined population of Pennsylvania and Illinois is more than the population of these ten plus Oregon, Washington, California, Nebraska, Kansas, Texas, Oklahoma.
  - U. S. population more than tripled in the past fifty years. 1890 population is 62,622,250.
- December, South Dakota: The U. S. 7th Cavalry and the Sioux fight the Battle of Wounded Knee.

1891
- February, El Paso, Texas: Uncle Dick Wootton takes subscriptions for his book.
- February, Albuquerque (New Mexico): Dick Wootton returns to sell his book.
- February 27, New Mexico Territory: Ft. Union closes.
- Colorado: Former Territorial Governor John L. Routt returns to office.
- March 3: Congress establishes the Court of Private Land Claims to deal with southwestern land grant claims. Over the next thirteen and a half years, titles to almost 2,000,000 acres of land will be validated.
- March 9-12, southern coast, England: Storm sinks fourteen ships.
- Whitcomb L. Judson patents a gadget to be used in place of buttons. He calls it a zipper.
- West of Colorado Springs, Colorado: Cowboy Robert Womack from Kentucky discovers gold. Under the influence of alcohol, he sells his rights for $500. His mine will produce about $5,000,000 worth of gold.
  - Owners of the land stake off an eighty-acre townsite for the boomtown they call

- Cripple Creek. Real estate sales, transportation, milling, and business will prosper. Many men become millionaires as a result of Womack's find.
- June 20, Ames, Colorado: This week the switch is turned on at the nation's first alternating current electrical power plant. AC power proves successful.
  - Direct current electricity had long been used in the U. S. Scientist George Westinghouse and miner L. L. Nunn persuaded directors of Westinghouse Electric Co. to advance them $15,000,000 to build an AC power plant. (Westinghouse has worked with AC in the laboratory.) Nunn staked $100,000 in gold that Westinghouse's idea would work. Engineers and equipment traveled by train, wagon, and burro to complete construction at the Ames site.
- August 14, Nashville, Tennessee: Sarah Polk, eighty-seven, dies. She survived her husband, President James K. Polk, by forty-two years. They had no children.
- October 28, Trinidad, Colorado: Richens L. Wootton, John Conkle, and A. Mansbach of the Old Timers' Committee collect money for the survey of a railroad line. They write letters to solicit contributions from people along the proposed line. They'll keep the subscription list open until several leading financial men return to town.
- Berlin, Germany: Dr. Robert Koch, who began to link certain bacteria with certain diseases, opens the Institute for Infectious Diseases.
- December 29: Thomas Edison patents the radio.

1892
- January 1, New York: Ellis Island begins accepting immigrants to the U. S. Fifteen-year-old Annie Moore, traveling from Ireland with her two brothers, is the first immigrant to set foot on Ellis Island.
- January: James Naismith publishes rules for playing basketball. The 1st official basketball game is played at the Young Men's' Christian Association, Springfield, Massachusetts.
- May 12, Santa Fe New Mexico Territory: Fire destroys the New Mexico capitol and many documents.
- July, Homestead, Pennsylvania: Carnegie Steel Mill calls in 300 Pinkerton detectives to break up a strike. In a bloody battle, striking workers defeat the Pinkerton men. The Pennsylvania militia is called to protect the mills.
- American financier Jay Gould dies. He leaves a fortune of about $72,000,000. Because of his business dealings connected with Black Friday in 1869, some consider him "the most hated man in America."
- People are concerned about the U. S. Treasury's dwindling gold reserve.
- October 5, Coffeyville, Kansas: The Dalton Gang overextends itself in an effort to rob two banks in the same town at the same time. The town is expecting them. Bob and Grat Dalton, Bill Powers, and Dick Broadwell are killed. Emmett Dalton is wounded on this his twenty-first birthday. Four townspeople are killed.
- October 23, Chicago, Illinois: The World's Columbian Exposition opens in celebration of the 400th Anniversary of Columbus' discovery of America.
- Autumn, Brussels, Belgium: At the suggestion of the United States, nations meet for

an international monetary conference. U. S. representatives encourage the use of silver among nations. There is no decisive action.
- Rudolf Diesel patents his design for a diesel engine.

1893, "A Year of Storms"
- January, Hawaii: A coup d'état deposes Queen Liliuokalani and ends royalty rule in Hawaii.
- January 17, Fremont, Ohio: Former U. S. President Rutherford B. Hayes dies—age 70.
- February 12: Omar Bradley, who will etch his name in military history, is born.
- February 14: Hawaii requests an annexation treaty with the United States. The treaty provides for the U. S. to assume up to $3,250,000 of Hawaiian debt, to support the deposed royalty, and to regulate Chinese immigration. It will be ratified in July 1898.
- March 4: Grover Cleveland becomes U. S. President in time to inherit the financial Panic of 1893. In Colorado, Davis H. Waite, of the Populist Party, becomes governor.
- May, Las Vegas, New Mexico Territory: Vicente Silva murders his brother-in-law Gabriel Sandoval and his own wife, Telesfora on May 19. Silva's own gang robs and kills him. Some say the gang was partial to Telesfora. Others say they didn't have a problem with the murders, but thought Silva should have paid them more than $10 each to bury the bodies. Others say they were tired of bloodshed; so, after they buried Telesfora, they killed Silva (b. 1845, Albuquerque).
  - For years Silva's gang (known as "Vincente Silva and the Forty Thieves" and "La Sociedad de Bandidos de Nuevo Mexico") has terrorized the Las Vegas area. They operated under cover of Silva's Imperial saloon (a block from the old Las Vegas Plaza) and specialized in murder, rape, robbery, and cattle rustling.
  - Some local supporters have felt the gang helped even the score concerning land deals made by Americans on Spanish/Mexican grant lands —especially the Las Vegas Land Grant.
  - Silva's Thieves: Eugenio Alarid (policeman); Genovevo Avila; Sostenes Lucero; Jose Chavez y Chavez (former associate of Billy the Kid); Nestor Herrera; Guadalupe "El Lechuza" Caballero; Leandro and Nestor Gallegos; Manuel "El Mellado" Gonzolez y Blea (in charge of Silva's home north of Las Vegas; talked when arrested); Zenon Maes; Martin "El Moro" Gonzolez y Blea; Cecilio Lucero (hung on a telephone pole); experienced cattle rustlers: Tomas Lucero (lived until the 1940's) and his twin, Juan de Dios Lucero (The two worked for Silva from San Miguel County north into southern Colorado.); Patricio Maes (suspected of being a traitor; hung from Bridge Street bridge in Las Vegas, October 23, 1892); German Maestas (gang member who was hung legally: After he killed his common law wife and her lover with the help of Juan Vialpando, German was taken into custody near Lamy, New Mexico, and hung in Las Vegas, May 25, 1894.); Manuel Maldonado (Silva's handyman); Florentino Medran; Hilario Mares; Jose F. "Piedra Lumbre" Montoya (stonemason by day); Gabriel Petal; Libado Polanco (secretary); Acasio and Procopio Rael; Antonio Rael (murdered

by gang members); Juan Romero; Ricardo "El Romo" Romero; Remigio "El Gavilan" Sandoval; Dionicio "Candelas" Sisneros (Silva's cook); Julian Trujillo; Francisco "El Indio" Ulibarri (full blood Comanche); J. M. Vialpando; Antonio Jose "El Mico" ("El Patas de Rana") Valdez; Marcos Varela (Silva's nephew and bartender); Jesus Vialpando (hung November 19, 1895, Santa Fe).

- May 5: Because of the Financial Panic, speculators in New York City rush to exchange stocks for gold.
- Colorado: Coupled with the Sherman Silver Purchase Act and failing mines and businesses, the Panic of '93 impoverishes Horace Tabor (1830-1899), who enjoyed success and renown in the Denver area. Throughout Colorado, silver miners hang President Cleveland in effigy.
- July 12: Historian Frederick J. Turner declares America's frontier period is finished.
- July, Colorado Springs, Colorado: Katharine L. Bates writes "America the Beautiful."
- August 22: Four hurricanes blow simultaneously: near Nova Scotia; west of the Cape Verde Islands; between Bermuda and the Bahamas; northeast of the Lesser Antilles. This is the first record of four hurricanes at once. Before their fury is spent, a hurricane hits New York City and another (the "Sea Islands Hurricane") hits Georgia and South Carolina. One thousand or more die.
- Tuesday, August 22, 8:05 p. m., Trinidad, Colorado: Richens Lacy Wootton dies.
- Friday, August 25, Trinidad Colorado: Dick Wootton's funeral is held at the Catholic Church. He is buried in the Catholic Cemetery.

1901
- R. L. Wootton, Jr. receives word of the death of his father's brother Powell Wootton of Lafayette, Kentucky. (Dick's brothers David and Alexander James died last year.) Dr. Powell Wootton practiced medicine in Lafayette for 50 years (Family clipping):
his practice extended all over that portion of the country…Many a poor family has been assisted by his deeds of charity, and in his practice as a physician he never refused a call. Much of his practice was gratuitous, and the suffering poor, black, as well as white, knew that in him they always had a friend who would respond to their calls, if necessary, without…price.
He owned a farm and was also a successful agriculturist…Dr. Wootton had been a member of the Baptist church from the time the Lafayette church was established, and was a leader in church work as in all things else.

1906
- April 27, Dennison, Texas: Dick Wootton's last surviving sibling, Eliza Hayes, dies. She will be buried in Dennison's Fairmont Cemetery.

1928
- Friday, July 6, 10:30 a.m., south highway, Wootton, Colorado: Judge A. W. McHendrie delivers the dedication address for the Daughters of the American Revolution marker commemorating Dick Wootton's toll gate site. The marker's bronze plate is set in volcanic rock.

1935

- March 2, Albuquerque, New Mexico: Mary Pauline Wootton, 80-year-old widow of Uncle Dick Wootton, dies at the home of their daughter Ida Baca. Twenty grandchildren and eight great-grandchildren survive her.

1936

- February 15, Las Vegas, New Mexico: Uncle Dick Wootton's youngest grandchild, Joseph Gerald Wootton, is born. (Uncle Dick had 56 grandchildren.)

1937

- June 12, *Canon City Record*:
  The steeply curving roadway over the Raton mountains, once an engineering triumph, but now outmoded, is slated to be abandoned and replaced by a new highway which will eliminate the steep climb and winding route…When this is completed the famous old Raton pass road will fade into oblivion. It was first opened up in 1865 when Uncle Dick Wooton [sic],…established a toll road across the mountains. Up to the present the original route of the old toll road has been maintained, for the most part.[264]

- June 22, Trinidad, Colorado: *Trinidad Chronicle News* announces the dedication this weekend of Fort Wootton in Memorial Square. It will be dedicated to war veterans.
  it carries the name of Richens L. (Uncle Dick) Wootton who tended the tollgate near the Colorado-New Mexico line from the mid '60's to middle '80's, and whose career is linked intimately with the pioneer history of southern Colorado. For 'Uncle Dick' Wootton truly belonged to the Trinidad community. He lived here and died here and his family lived after him in this community. It was different with Kit Carson. He was a national figure… Kit Carson belonged to the nation…Wootton however was truly a community pioneer. A modernized old Wootton house still stands near where the famous tollgate swung open to admit the wagon trains and freighting caravans enroute overland to and from Santa Fe and other places in Colorado and New Mexico.[265]

1940

- January 20, Santa Fe, New Mexico: New Mexico State Highway Commission awards a $344,532.72 contract to Cook and Ransom of Ottawa, Kansas, to build the New Mexico side of U. S. Highway 85 over Raton Pass. Work must be begun within ten days from the date of the work order. The company is allowed 250 weather-working days to complete the job. Colorado finished its portion from Morley to the state line about a year ago.

1942

- July 23, Raton, New Mexico: The new Raton Pass road needs final coat and minor repairs. Advertisements are out for bids. New Mexico State Engineer Burton G. Dwyre doubts anything will be done now that the country is at war (World War II).

---

[264] "Historic Highway …To Be Abandoned," *Canon City Record*, June 17, 1937.
[265] "Fort Wootton," *Trinidad Chronicle News*, June 22, 1937.

Port of Entry on Raton Pass

- The state highway department is in charge of the old Raton Pass road.

1957
- March 7, Las Vegas, New Mexico: Dick Wootton's last surviving child, Mary Fidelis Wootton, dies at the home of her niece Marguerite Wootton Archuleta.

1961
- October 22, Raton, New Mexico: Raton Pass is registered as a National Historic Landmark. The landmark plaque is presented to the city.

1965
- Saturday, September 11, Summit of Raton Pass: New Mexico and Colorado businessmen and politicians, including New Mexico Governor Jack Campbell and Charles Shumate (representing Colorado John Love), dedicate a four-lane, divided highway over Raton Pass on Interstate 25. The eight miles of highway cost almost $6,000,000.

2008
- Three of Dick Wootton's grandchildren die. Oldest of the three, Leroy Lawrence Hunter, dies in Texas, March 2, age 100.

2010
- February 26, Las Vegas, New Mexico: Dick Wootton's last surviving grandchild, Evelyn Wootton Harris, dies, following a stroke.

Bibliography

Bibliography

If online source does not include copyright date, access date is included for reference.

"1840-1849," "1850-59." The Henry Ford~http://www.TheHenryFord.org. (access 1 February 2014).
Along the Route. Chicago: Rand McNally, 1960: pp. 3-6.
"Albert Sidney Johnston." (12 January 1999). www.findagrave.com/cgi-bin/fg.cgi?page=gr&Grid =4334.
Alberts, Don E. "Sibley Campaign." *Handbook of Texas Online*. Texas State Historical Association. (15 June 2010). http:// tshaonline.org/handbook/online/articles/SS/ qds3.html
Alberts, Don E., ed., *Rebels on the Rio Grande: The Civil War Journal of A. B. Peticolas*. Albuquerque: University of New Mexico Press, 1984.
"An Old Pioneer Gone." *Daily News*, August 23, 1893.
Anderson, H. Allen. "Adobe Walls, TX." *Handbook of Texas Online*. Texas State Historical Association. (9 June 2010). http:// www.tshaonline.org/handbook/online/ articles/hra10.
Andrist, Ralph K., ed. *History of the Making of the Nation*. New York: American Heritage Publishing Co., Inc., 1968.
------. *History of the Confident Years*. New York: American Heritage Publishing Co., Inc., 1969.
Arellano, Anselmo F. "The Never-Ending Land Grant Struggle." *La Herencia del Norte*. Santa Fe: Gran Via, Inc., Summer 1996: pp. 15-17.
Arellano, Anselmo F., and Julian Jose Vigil. *Las Vegas Grandes on the Gallinas 1835-1985*. Las Vegas, NM: Editorial Telerana, 1985.
Armitage, Merle. *Operations Santa Fe*. New York: Duell, Sloan & Pearce, 1948.
Ascherman, Arla. "El Valle de los Rancheros," Pueblo, CO: County Historical Society. (June 1994). http://www. pueblo history. org.
Baca, Elmo. "Pecos Valley Villages Stand Proud." *New Mexico Magazine*. Vol. 68, No. 10. Oct. 1990: pp. 87-95.
Baker, Fred. "Colorado, New Mexico Hail New Road Over Raton Pass." *The Denver Post,* September 12, 1965.
Barbour, Barton H. "Kit Carson and the 'Americanization' of New Mexico." *New Mexican Lives: Profiles and Historical Stories*. ed. Richard W. Etulain. Albuquerque: University of New Mexico Press, 2002.
Baxter, John O. *Las Carnederas*. Albuquerque: University of New Mexico Press, 1987.
Beaty, Opal Waymire. "Christmas on the Old Trails." *New Mexico Magazine*. Vol. 43, Nos. 11- 12. Albuquerque: Department of Development, November-December 1965: pp. 8-11.
Becknell, William. "The Journals of Captain Thomas Becknell from Boone's Lick to Santa Fe and Santa Cruz to Green River." *Missouri Historical Review*. Vol. 4, No. 2. Jan. 1910: pp. 65-84.
"Bent's Old Fort: Official Map and Guide." National Park Service, U.S. Department of the Interior, 1994.
Berg, Al. "Old Wootton Ranch Linked With Pioneer History of Area." *Chronicle News*, September 29, 1952: p. 2.
Berry, Jim. *The Maxwell Land Grant*. Norman, OK: University of Oklahoma Press, 1961.
Beshoar, Dr. Michael, ed. "Uncle John Albert." *Cattleman's Advertiser: Trinidad Daily Advertiser*, Feb. 2, 1885.
Beshoar, Michael, M.D. *All about Trinidad and Las Animas County, Colorado: Their History, Industries, Resources, Etc.* Denver: Times Stearn Printing House and Blank Book Manufacturing, 1882.
Blair, John S., ed. *The Washington Law Reporter*. Vol. XV No. 25. Washington, D. C., June 22, 1887: p 389.
Bledsoe, S. T. "Texas: Its History, Resources and Opportunities." *The Santa Fe Magazine*. Vol. XXV, No. 4. Chicago: Railway Exchange, March 1931: pp. 14, 15.
Borneman, Walter R. *Rival Rails*. New York: Random House, 2010.
Bowman, Charles W. *The History of Bent County: History of the Arkansas Valley*. Chicago: O. L. Baskin & Co., 1881.
Bradley, Glenn D. "Builders of the Santa Fe: Lewis Kingman—A Man Who Made Good." *The Santa Fe Magazine.* Vol. VIII, No. 5. Chicago: Railway Exchange, April 1914: pp. 21-23.
-----. "Builders of the Santa Fe: William B. Strong—A Railroad Napoleon." *The Santa Fe Magazine*. Vol. VIII, No. 10. Chicago: Railway Exchange, September 1914: pp. 17-21.
------. "Builders of the Santa Fe: William R. Morley—A Man Without Fear." *The Santa Fe Magazine*. Vol. IX, No. 5. Chicago: Railway Exchange, April 1915: pp. 17- 20.
------. "Famous Landmarks Along The Trail." *Santa Fe Employes' Magazine*. Vol. VI, No. 10. Chicago: Railway Exchange, September 1912: pp. 25-29.
------. "Famous Frontier Fights: The Defense of Beecher's Island." *The Santa Fe Magazine*. Vol. XXIII, No. 8. Chicago: Railway Exchange, July 1929: pp. 13-21.
------. "'Uncle Dick' Wootton." *Santa Fe Employes' Magazine*. Vol. V, No. 2. Chicago: Railway Exchange, January 1911: pp. 25-36.
------. "When Camels Were Freighters in the Southwest." *The Santa Fe Magazine*. Vol. XXIII, No. 11. Chicago: Railway Exchange, October 1929: pp. 13-18.

Bradley, Glenn Danford. *Winning the Southwest: A Story of Conquest*. Chicago: A. C. McClurg & Co., 1912.
Breckenridge, Thomas E. "The Story of a Famous Expedition." *Cosmopolitan Magazine*, August 1896: p. 400.
Broadhead, Edward. *Fort Pueblo*. Pueblo, CO: Pueblo County Historical Society, 1995.
------. "Robert Fisher 1807-1852." Pueblo, CO: Pueblo County Historical Society. http://www.pueblohistory.org/history/robert fisher.htm. (access 4 April 2004).
Brown, William E. *The Santa Fe Trail*. St. Louis: Patrice Press, 1988.
Bullis, Don. *New Mexico: A Biographical Dictionary 1540-1980*. Volume 1. Los Ranchos de Albuquerque: Rio Grande Books, 2007.
Calkins, Carroll C., ed. *The Story of America*. Pleasantville, NY: Readers' Digest Association, Inc., 1975.
Canon, Benton. "The History of Georgia Colony," Site: Pueblo County, CO. (2002-2012). http://www.kmitch.com/Huerfano/ geogcol.htm.
Capps, Benjamin. *The Indians*. New York: Time-Life Books, 1973.
Carruth, Gorton. *The Encyclopedia of American Facts and Dates*. New York: Harper and Row, 1987.
Carter, Harvey Lewis. *Dear Old Kit, Memoirs of Kit Carson*. Norman, OK: University of Oklahoma Press, 1968.
Carter, Harvey L. "The Divergent Paths of Fremont's 'Three Marshals.'" *New Mexico Historical Review*. XLVIII, No. 1. Albuquerque: University of New Mexico, January 1973: pp. 5-26.
------. "How Kit Carson Resolved a Moral Dilemma." *New Mexico*. Vol. 50, Nos. 9-10. Albuquerque: New Mexico Dept. of Development, September/October 1972: pp. 9-13.
Chapman, Arthur. *The Story of Colorado*. San Francisco: Rand McNally & Company, 1924.
Chavez, Fray Angelico. "The Mora Country." *New Mexico*. Vol. 50, Nos. 1-2. Albuquerque: New Mexico Dept. of Development, January/February 1972: pp. 32-37.
------. "Ruts of the Santa Fe Trail." *New Mexico*. Vol. 50, Nos. 7-8. Albuquerque: New Mexico Dept. of Development, July/August 1972: pp.18-29, 43-45.
Clark, Anna Nolan. "He Blazed the Trail." *New Mexico Magazine*. Vol. 19, No. 2. Albuquerque: Valley Printing Co., February 1941: pp. 21-23, 38-40.
Cleaveland, Agnes Morley. *No Life for a Lady*. Boston: Houghton, Mifflin, Co., 1941.
Cleaveland, Norman. "Clay Allison's Cimarron." *New Mexico*. Vol. 52, Nos. 3-4. Albuquerque: New Mexico Department of Development, March/April 1974: pp. 11-14, 38-48.
Cleaveland, Norman, with George Fitzpatrick. *The Morleys*. Albuquerque: Calvin Horn Publisher, Inc., 1971.
Clum, Mr. John P. "Santa Fe in the 70s." *New Mexico Historical Review*. Vol. II. Santa Fe: Historical Society at the Museum Press, 1927: p. 382.
Coggan, Catherine. "Once dynamic Dawson still a living memory." *New Mexico Magazine*. Vol. 79, No. 9. Santa Fe: New Mexico Magazine, September 2001: p. 80.
Colonial Virginia: A Picture Book to Remember Her By. New York: Crescent Books, 1979.
Colorado Families: A Territorial Heritage. Denver: Colorado Genealogical Society, 1981.
"Colorado Governors Since 1861," http://www.colorado.gov. (20 April 2001).
"Colorado State Archives Colorado History Chronology," www.coloradospringsdirectory.com, (access 13 September 2007).
"Colorful Chapter in State's History Was Railroads' Battle for Raton Pass." *Albuquerque Journal*, July 2, 1954.
Conard, Howard Louis. *Uncle Dick Wootton*. Chicago: W. E. Dibble and Co., 1890.
------. *Uncle Dick Wootton*, ed. Milton Milo Quaife. Lincoln, NE: University of Nebraska Press, 1980.
Connelly, Thomas. "The American Camel Experiment A Reappraisal." *Handbook of Texas Online*. Texas State Historical Association. http://www.tsha.utexas.edu/ handbook/online/articles/CC/quc1.html. (access 4 October 2006).
Conner, Buck. "Jim Baker Party," http://www.klesinger.com. (access 2002).
"Construction of the A. T. & S. F. R. R. Over the Raton Mountains." *The Santa Fe Magazine*. Vol. XXXII. Chicago, February 1939: pp. 7-9.
Cordry, Dee. "True Heart: The Story of Edmund Guerrier." www.ionet.net/~okhombre/edmund.html. (access 24 January 2007).
Craig, Katherine L. *Craig's Brief History of Colorado for Teachers and Students*. Denver: Welch-Haffner Printing Co., 1923.
Cragin, Frances W. *Early Far West Notebook*. Colorado Springs, CO: Property of Colorado Pioneer Museum.
------. *Early Far West Notebook*. Santa Fe: Property of New Mexico State Archives.
Cramer, Joseph L. "Manco Burro Pass: New Mexico or Colorado?" *New Mexico Historical Review*. Vol. XLIII, No. 2. Albuquerque: University of New Mexico, April 1968: p. 155.
Curtis, Olga. "The Exit to Wootton." *The Denver Post Empire Magazine*, December 12, 1970.
C.W.A. Workers. "La Plata Huerfano and Mesa Counties C.W.A. 1933-1934." Interviews for State Historical Society of Colorado.
Daily News, Evening, August 25, 1893.
Daniel, Clifton, ed. director. *Chronicle of America*. Mount Kisco, NY: Chronicle Publications, 1989.

Dary, David. *The Santa Fe Trail: Its History, Legends and Lore*. New York: Penguin Putnam, Inc., 2000.

Davis, Herndon. "Once Upon a Time…," "Raton Pass." *The Denver Post*, April 8, 1951.

"Daylight Saving Time." *IDEA*. (2008). http://webexhibits.org/daylightsaving/d.html.

"Detour to the Cherokee Trail." Ft. Collins, CO: Ft. Collins Museum, n.d.: p. 3.

Devitt, Steve. "Navajo Myth: Finding the true story of the Long Walk proves difficult." *Daily Times*, May 29, 2002: p. 5.

DeWitt, Dave. *Discover New Mexico*. Belen, NM: Sunbelt Press, May 1979.

Dickey, Roland F. "Lew Wallace: One of 'Them Literary Fellers.'" *New Mexico Magazine*. Vol. 63, No. 1. Albuquerque: Albuquerque, Dept. of Development, January 1985: pp. 15-17.

Doniphan, Colonel A. W. "Official Report of the Battle of Sacramento." *Documentary History of the Mexican War*. ed. by Steven R. Butler. Richardson. Texas: Descendants of Mexican War Veterans, 1995: pp. 105-107. http://www.dmwv.org/mexwar/documents/sacra.htm. (access 15 November 2013).

Duffus, R. L. *The Santa Fe Trail*. New York: David McKay Co., Inc., 1930.

Dunlop, Richard. *Great Trails of the West*. New York: Abingdon Press, 1971.

Ellis, Richard N., ed. *New Mexico Historic Documents*. Albuquerque: University of New Mexico Press, 1975.

Emmett, Chris. *Fort Union and the Winning of the Southwest*. Norman, OK: University of Oklahoma Press, 1965.

"Employes [sic] Long in the Service." *The Santa Fe Magazine*. Vol. VIII, No. 10. Chicago, Sept. 1914: p. 43.

Fairbanks, Jonathan, and Clyde Edwin Tuck. *Past and Present of Greene County Missouri: Early and Recent History and Genealogical Records of Many of the Representative Citizens*. Indianapolis: A. W. Bowen and Co., 1915.

"Famous Woodsmen of Other Days, No. 56: 'Uncle Dick' Wootton, Part III." *Hunting and Fishing*. Vol. VII, No. 7. Boston: National Sportsman, Inc., July, 1930: pp. 15, 28, 47, 48.

Favour, Alpheus H. *Old Bill Williams: Mountain Man*. Chapel Hill, NC: University of North Carolina Press, 1936.

Featherstone, William. "Report from Bents Old Fort." *La Junta Tribune Democrat*, November 30, 1968: p.4, c. 3.

"First Work To Start On Raton Pass Highway." *Chronicle News*, February 8, 1940.

Fitzpatrick, George, ed. "Frontier Forts of New Mexico." *New Mexico Magazine*. Vol. 38, No. 2. Albuquerque: Department of Development, February 1960: pp. 28, 40.

------. "They Took the Train." *New Mexico Magazine*. Vol. 42, Nos. 6-7. Albuquerque: Department of Development, June-July 1964: pp. 2-4.

Flora, Stephenie, compiler. "Whitman Massacre." (2004). http://www.oregonpioneers.com/whitman [1, 2, 4]

Flynn, A. J., and L. R. Hafen. "Early Education in Colorado." *The Colorado Magazine*. Vol. XII, No. 1. Denver: State Historical Society of Colorado, Jan. 1935: pp. 15, 16, 18, 19.

"Fort Union." National Park Service, U.S. Department of the Interior, 2002.

"Fort Wootton." *Chronicle News*, Trinidad, Colorado, June 22, 1937.

Foster, George, H., and Peter C. Weiglin. *The Harvey House Cookbook: Memories of Dining along the Santa Fe Railroad*. Atlanta: Longstreet Press, Inc., 1992.

Friedman, Frederick S. "Railroads and the Santa Fe Trail: A Transition in Technology." *Wagon Tracks*. Vol. 13, No. 2. Woodson, KS: Santa Fe Trail Association, February 1999: pp. 18-22.

F. R. W. "Still More About Wootton." *The Denver Post Empire Magazine*, March 23, 1952: p. 23.

Gardner, Mark. "Race for Raton Pass." *New Mexico Magazine*. Vol. 83, No. 5. Santa Fe: New Mexico Tourism Department, May 2005: pp. 32-37.

Garrard, Lewis H. *Wah-to-yah*. Norman, OK: University of Oklahoma Press, 1962.

Gaston, Joseph. "The Whitman Massacre, Centennial History of Oregon," Excerpt from: *The Centennial History of Oregon 1811-1911*. Vol. I. Chicago: S. J. Clarke Company, 1912. http://gesswhoto.com/centennial-whitman-massacre. (access 19 July 2008).

Glasser, Harry O. "The Magic Story of Gasoline." *The Santa Fe Magazine*. Vol. XXV, No. 4. Chicago: Railway Exchange, March 1931: pp. 39, 40.

Goldrick, O. J. "The First School in Denver." *The Colorado Magazine*. VI. Denver: State Historical Society of Colorado, 1929: pp. 72-74.

Goodale, F. D., ed. *The Evening Chronicle*. Vol. 2. October 28, 1891, p. 4, col. 2. November 12, 1891, p. 4, col. 3. November 16, 1891, p. 4, col. 3. Trinidad, CO: Chronicle Publishing Co.

Grant, Blanche C., A.B. *When Old Trails Were New*. New York: Press of the Pioneers, Inc., 1934.

Gray, Vikki. (2004). www.ghostseekers.com/SanLuisValley/sanluisvalleyP-S.htm.

"Great New Mexico Pedigree Database," Albuquerque: Hispanic Genealogical Research Center of New Mexico. www.hgrc-nm.org/. (access 2009).

Greever, William S. "Railway Development in the Southwest." *New Mexico Historical Review*. Vol. XXXII, No. 2. Albuquerque: Historical Society of New Mexico and University of New Mexico Press, April 1957: pp. 160-163.

Gregg, Andrew K. *New Mexico in the Nineteenth Century*. Albuquerque: University of New Mexico Press, 1968.

Gregg, Josiah. *The Commerce of the Prairies*. Lincoln, NE: University of Nebraska Press, 1967.

Guild, Thelma S., and Harvey L. Carter. *Kit Carson A Pattern for Heroes*. Lincoln, NE: University of Nebraska Press, 1948.

Gutierrez, Priscilla Shannon. "Charles 'Carlos' Hipolite Beaubien: More Than A Name On A Land Grant." No. 74. Santa Fe: Historical Society of New Mexico, January 2008, pp. 1-3.

First National Bank in Trinidad 125th Anniversary. Trinidad, CO.

Flint, Shirley Cushing, and Richard Flint. "Watrous." New Mexico Office of the State Historian. www.newmexicohistory.org/ places/watrous. (access 2012).

"Fort Bridger." http://userpages.aug.com/bdobson/bridger.html. (access January 2009).

Hafen, Leroy R. Hafen. *Fur Trappers and Traders of the Far Southwest*. Logan, UT: Utah State University Press, 1997.

Hafen, LeRoy R., ed. et al. *The Mountain Men and the Fur Trade of the Far West: Biographical Sketches of the Participants*. Glendale, CA: Arthur H. Clark & Co. 1965.

Hafen, LeRoy R., and Harvey Carter. *Mountain Men and the Fur Traders of the Far West*. Lincoln, NE: University of Nebraska Press, 1982.

Hafen, LeRoy R., and Ann W. Hafen, ed. *Central Route to the Pacific*. Vol. VII. Glendale, CA: Arthur H. Clark Company, 1957.

------. *Fremont's Fourth Expedition: a Documentary Account of The Disaster of 1848-1849*. Vol. XI. Glendale, CA: Arthur H. Clark Company, 1960.

------. *Relations with the Plains Indians, 1857-1861*. Vol. IX. Glendale, CA: Arthur H. Clark Company, 1959.

------. *Reports from Colorado: The Wildman Letters, 1859-1865*. Vol. XIII. Glendale, CA: Arthur H. Clark Company, 1961.

------. *To the Rockies and Oregon, 1839-1842*. Vol. III. Glendale, CA: Arthur H. Clark Company, 1955.

------. *Old Spanish Trail*. Vol. I. Glendale, CA: Arthur H. Clark Company, 1954.

Haley, J. Evetts. *Charles Goodnight: Cowman and Plainsman*. Norman, OK: University of Oklahoma Press, 1949.

Hall, Ernest W. "The Red Captain of the Santa Fe." *The Santa Fe Magazine*. Vol. XV, No. 3. Chicago: Railway Exchange, February 1921: p. 27.

Hall, Frank. *History of the State of Colorado*. Vol. II. Chicago: Blakely Printing Company, 1890.

Hart, Herbert M. *Old Forts of the Southwest*. Seattle: Superior Publishing Company, 1964.

Hayes, Marita. "D. C. Oakes: Early Colorado Booster." *The Colorado Magazine*. Vol. XXXI, No. 3. Denver: State Historical Society of Colorado, July 1954: p. 223.

Helmers, Dow. "Uncle Dick Wootton built toll road on Raton Pass." *Pueblo Chieftain*, May 26, 1974: p. 1c.

Helton, Jim H. "From an Old-Timer." *The Santa Fe Magazine*. Vol. XXVIII, No. 12. Chicago: Railway Exchange, November 1934: p. 42.

Hertzog, Peter. *A Directory of New Mexico Desperados*. Santa Fe: Press of the Territorian, 1965.

Hewett, Edgar L. *Campfire and Trails*. Albuquerque: University of New Mexico Press, 1945.

Hicks, John D., and George E. Mowry. *A Short History of American Democracy*. Boston: Houghton Mifflin Company, 1956.

Hill, W. E. "America Owes Its Development to the Railroads." *The Santa Fe Magazine*. Vol. XXVIII, No. 12. Chicago, November 1934: pp. 13-16.

"Historic Highway Over Raton Pass To Be Abandoned." *Canon City Record*, June 17, 1937.

"History of Butch Cassidy LeRoy Parker." http://www.utah.com/oldwest/butch_ cassidy. htm. (access: 3 February 2014).

"History of Colorado in the Civil War." http://2ndcoloradocavalry.com/cavhistory. html. (access 4 February 2009).

History of New Mexico. Vol. I. Los Angeles: Pacific States Publishing Co., 1907.

Holbrook, Stewart H. *The Story of American Railroads*. New York: Random House, 1945.

Horgan, Paul. *Great River: The Rio Grande in North American History*. New York: Holt, Rinehart and Winston, 1954.

Horn, Calvin. "Soldier-Statesman." *New Mexico Magazine*. Vol. 41, No. 10. Albuquerque: Department of Development, October 1963: pp. 16, 17, 34, 35.

http://www.logancountychamber.com/tourismsummitsprings.html. (access 6 November 2006).

Huning, Franz. *Trader on the Santa Fe Trail, The Memoirs of Franz Huning*. Albuquerque: Calvin Horn Publisher, Inc., 1973.

Hunt, Aurora, "Letters to Lincoln." *New Mexico Magazine*. Vol. 39, No. 2. Albuquerque: Dept. of Development, February 1961: pp. 3-5, 36, 38.

Hurd, Charles W. "Origin and Development of the Santa Fe Trail." *The Santa Fe Magazine*, Vol. XV, No. 10. Chicago: Railway Exchange, September 1921: pp. 17-27.

Hurst, James. "Geronimo's Surrender – Skeleton Canyon 1886." (9 January 2003) www.southernnewmexico.com. Clovis, NM: Stone Monkey Marketing, 2015.

Hyslop, Stephen G. *Bound for Santa Fe*. Norman, OK: University of Oklahoma Press, 2002.

Inman, Col. Henry. *The Old Santa Fe Trail*. Topeka: Crane & Co., 1914.

Jameson, J. Franklin, Ph. D. *Dictionary of United States History 1492-1899*. Boston: Puritan Publishing Co., 1899.

Jameson, W. C. *Billy the Kid Beyond the Grave*. Dallas: Taylor Trade Publishing, 2005.

Jarrell, John. "Sibley and the Confederate Dream." *New Mexico Magazine.* Vol. 54, No. 8. Albuquerque: Dept. of Development, August 1976, pp. 18-22.

Jeffries, Olen C., "The Pecos, River of Romance." *New Mexico Magazine*. Vol. 45, Nos. 6-7. Albuquerque: Dept. of Development, June-July 1967: pp. 26-28, 34.

"Jenny Lind 1820-1867." *Women in History: A Biographical Encyclopedia*. Gale Research. (2002). http://www.encyclopedia.com/topic/Jenny_Lind.

Jezer, Marty. *The Making of America: Opening of the Western Frontier*. San Mateo, CA: Bluewood Books, 2001.

"John Spotswood Garland." www.findagrave.-com/cgibin/fg.cgi?page=gr&GRid=10643676. (access 20 March 2005).

Keleher, William A. *Maxwell Land Grant: A New Mexico Item.* Albuquerque: University of New Mexico Press, 1942.

------. *The Fabulous Frontier: Twelve New Mexico Items*. Santa Fe: Rydal Press, 1942.

------. *Violence in Lincoln County 1869-1881*. Albuquerque: University of New Mexico Press, 1982.

Kendall, John. *History of New Orleans*. Chicago: Lewis Publishing Co., 1922.

"Ketchum, Thomas Edward 'Black Jack'." http://www.findagrave.com/cgi-bin/fg.cgi?page=gr&GRid=2435. (access 1 Jan 2001).

Ketchum, Richard M., ed. *The American Heritage of the Pioneer Spirit*. New York: American Heritage Publishing Company, Inc., 1959.

Kopp, April. "Uncle Dick Wootton: Frontiersman blazes trail to Raton." *New Mexico Magazine*. Vol. 67, No. 3. Albuquerque: Dept. of Development, March 1989: pp. 52, 54-58.

Lamar, Howard R., ed. *The Reader's Encyclopedia of the American West*. New York: Thomas Y. Crowell Company, 1977.

Lamm, Gene. "A Brief History of the Village of Cimarron to 1900." Cimarron, NM: Cimarron Chamber of Commerce, Cimarron Historical Society, 1998.

Las Vegas *Daily Optic*. Special Centennial Edition, July 27, 1979: Sec. 1-5.

Lavender, David. *Bent's Fort*. Lincoln, NE: University of Nebraska Press, 1972.

------, *The Southwest*. New York: Harper and Row, Publishers, 1980.

Laycock, George. *The Mountain Men*. Guilford, CT: Lyons Press, 1996.

LeCompte, Janet. *Pueblo, Hardscrabble, Greenhorn: Society on the High Plains, 1832-1856*. Norman, OK: University of Oklahoma Press, 1978.

Lee, W. Storrs, ed. *Colorado: A Literary Chronicle*. New York: Funk & Wagnalls, 1970.

Logsdon, Paul. "Traces of the Santa Fe Trail." *New Mexico Magazine*. Vol. 60, No. 2. Albuquerque: Dept. of Development, February 1982: pp. 46-48.

Lossing, Benson J., LL.D. *Matthew Brady's Illustrated History of the Civil War*. New York: Fairfax Press, n.d. (Originally published as *A History of the Civil War*, 1912.)

Lyon, Fern. "The Colfax County War: a Timetable." *New Mexico*. Vol. 52, Nos. 3-4. Santa Fe: New Mexico Department of Development, March/April 1974: p. 10.

Macy, Guy E. "Organization and Early Development of Pueblo County." *The Colorado Magazine*. Vol. XVI, No. 2. Denver: State Historical Society of Colorado, March 1939.

Malone, Daisy Roberts. "Uncle Dick Wooten." *Pueblo Star Journal*, May 31, 1953.

Marcy, Randolph B. *The Prairie Traveler*. Bedford, MA: Applewood Books, n.d. (originally published 1859).

Marshall, James. *Santa Fe: the Railroad that Built an Empire*. New York: Random House, 1945.

Martin, Clay. "Butterfield Trail." *New Mexico Magazine*. Vol. 80, No. 11. Santa Fe: New Mexico Magazine, November 2002: pp. 52-56.

Martin, Gene and Mary. *Trail Dust*. Boulder, CO: Johnson Publishing Company, 1972.

Massengil, Pat, compiler. "Littleton School District No. 6." (modified 18 June 2003). http://www.littletongov.org/history.

McCall, Col. George Archibald. *New Mexico in 1850: A Military View*. Norman, OK: University of Oklahoma Press, 1968.

McGrath, Maria Davies. *The Real Pioneers*. Vol. II., Vol. III. Denver: Denver Museum, 1934.

McKinnan, Bess. "The Raton Pass Toll Road." *New Mexico Historical Review*. Vol. II. Santa Fe: Historical Society of New Mexico at the Museum Press, 1927: pp. 83-89.

McMaster, John Bach. *School History of the United States*. New York: American Book Company, 1897.

McMechen, Edgar C. "The Model of Auraria-Denver, Colorado." *The Colorado Magazine*. Vol. XII, No. 4, Denver: State Historical Society of Colorado, July 1935.

Media Solutions. Salt Lake City: University of Utah. (2004). http://www.media.utah.edu/ home/home.html.

Melzer, Richard. *Images of America Fred Harvey Houses of the Southwest*. Charleston, SC: Arcadia Publishing, 2008.
"Memorias," *New Mexico Magazine*. http://www,webmail.newmexico.travel/memorias.php. (access 1 March 2009).
Millard, Joseph. "Blazer of Trails West," pp 89-104, McQuitty—Wootton Collection.
Miller, Joseph. *New Mexico: A Guide to the Colorful State*. New York: Hastings House, 1962.
Miller, William Lee. *President Lincoln: The Duty of a Statesman*. New York: Alfred A. Knopf, 2008.
Mitchell, Karen, contributor. "*Colorado Weekly Chieftain*, June 1, 1868: Death of Kit Carson." Site: Pueblo County, CO. (2002-2012). http://www.kmitch.com/Pueblo/ news1868.html.
Mitchell, Karen. "Taos County, New Mexico, 1847 Revolt." Site: Pueblo County, CO. (2002-2012). http://www.kmitch.com/ Taos/revolt1847.html.
Mix, Larry and Carolyn. St. Johns, KS: Santa Fe Trail Research Site. (1995-2015). http://www.santafetrailresearch.com.
Monnett, John H., and Michael McCarthy. *Colorado Profiles*. Evergreen, CO: Cordillera Press, Inc., 1987.
Montgomery, D. H. *The Leading Facts of American History*. Boston: Ginn and Company, 1910.
Montoya, Maria E. *Translating Property: The Maxwell Land Grant and the Conflict of land in the American West 1840-1900*. Berkeley, CA: University of California Press, 2002.
Moody, Ralph. *Stagecoach West*. New York: Thomas Y. Crowell Company, 1967.
Motto, Scytha. *Old Houses of New Mexico and the People Who Built Them*. Albuquerque: Calvin Horne Publisher, Inc., 1972.
Mumey, Nola. *History of the Early Settlements of Denver*. Glendale, CA: Arthur Clark Co., 1942.
Munkres, Robert L. "Tales of Old Fort Laramie," *The National Tombstone Epitaph*, November 1981, http://www.muskingum.edu/~rmunkres/military/Laramie/Tales. (access 24 January 2007).
Murphy, Lawrence R. *Lucien Bonaparte Maxwell: Napoleon of the Southwest*. Norman, OK: University of Oklahoma Press, 1983.
Murphy, Maurice. "Santa Fe Capitalization Is Ideal: With High Margin of Safety." *The Santa Fe Magazine*. XXIII. November 1929, pp. 34-36.
"Museum of Colorado Prisons." Canon City, CO: Museum of Colorado Prisons, n.d., p. 2.
Myrick, David. *New Mexico's Railroads*. Albuquerque: University of New Mexico Press, 1990.
"New Mexico." http://www.coloradomosb297.org/newmexico.html. (access 4 February 2009).
"Night Warning Gives Santa Fe Lead...." *The New Mexico Sentinel*, December 29, 1937.
"NOAA Revisits Historic Hurricanes." U.S. Dept. of Commerce. http://www.noaanews.noaa. gov/stories. (access 30 July 2003).
Noble, David Grant. *Pueblos, Villages, Forts & Trails*. Albuquerque: University of New Mexico Press, 1994.
"Obituary: 'Uncle' Dick Wootton's Widow Dies." *The Santa Fe Magazine*. Vol. XXIX, No. 5. Chicago: Railway Exchange, April 1935, p. 24.
Otero, Miguel Antonio. *My Life on the Frontier 1864-1882*. Albuquerque: University of New Mexico Press, 1987.
"Our Beliefs," Reformed Presbyterian Church of Scotland, 2017.
Padilla, Jerry. "Quien a Hierro Vive a Hierro Muerre." *La Herencia Del Norte*. Santa Fe: La Herencia Del Norte Gran Via, Inc., Summer 1996: pp. 22, 23.
Parkhill, Forbes. *The Blazed Trail of Antoine Leroux*. Los Angeles: Westernlore Press, 1965.
Pearson, Jim Berry. *The Maxwell Land Grant*. Norman, OK: University of Oklahoma Press, 1961.
Perrigo, Lynn I. *The American Southwest Its People and Cultures*. Albuquerque: University of New Mexico Press, 1971.
Pettibone, W. H. "Reminiscent of early Days On the Santa Fe." *The Santa Fe Magazine*. Vol. VIII, No. 10. Chicago, September 1914: p. 45.
Pierce, James H. "With the Green Russell Party " *The Trail*. Volume XIII, No. Twelve. Denver: Societies of Daughters of Colorado and The Territorial Daughters, May 1921: pp. 5-9.
Poling-Kempes, Lesley. *The Harvey Girls: Women Who Opened the West*. New York: Paragon House, 1989.
Quintana, Patricio G. "The Three Forts." *New Mexico Magazine*. Vol. 40, No.10. Albuquerque: Dept. of Development, October 1962: pp. 29-31.
Raton: 2004 Visitor's Guide. Raton, NM, 2004.
"Raton Leads In Movement To Preserve Old Pass Highway" *Chronicle News*, July 23, 1942.
Raton New Mexico 2001 Visitor's Guide. Raton, NM: Raton Chamber and Economic Development Council, Inc., 2001.
"Raton Pass Hairpin Road To Be Rerouted." *The Denver Post*, January 25, 1940.
"Raton Pass, New Mexico." Google Earth, March 29, 2014.
Regents of the University of California. "Dawson Family Papers." Dawson Family Papers Collection Number: MSS 0240. La Jolla, CA: Online Archive of California, University of California San Diego. (2009). http://www.oac.cdlib.org/ findaid/ark:/ 13030/tf3k4006bd/.

"Reshaw's Bridge." (8 November 2014). http://www.wyohistory.org/taxonomy /term/272/feed. (access 21 November 2015).

Richardson, T. C. "Goodnight-Loving Trail." *Handbook of Texas Online*. Texas State Historical Association. (15 June 2010). http://www.tsha.utexas.org/handbook/ online/articles/ayg02.

Rittenhouse, Jack D. *Maverick Tales of the Southwest*. Albuquerque: University of New Mexico Press, 1987.

Rocky Mountain News. 1859: May 7, p. 4, col. 3.; May 14, p. 3, col.1.; June 11, p. 3, col. 3.; August 6, p. 1, col. 1.

Rocky Mountain News. Centennial Edition. Sunday, April 19, 1959.

Ross, George E. *Know Your Presidents and Their Wives*. Chicago: Rand McNally & Company, 1960.

Russell, Marian, as dictated to Mrs. Hal Russell. *Land of Enchantment: Memoirs of Marian Russell Along the Santa Fe Trail*. Albuquerque: University of New Mexico Press, 1981.

Ryus, William Henry. *The Second William Penn: A True Account of Incidents that Happened Along the Old Santa Fe Trail in the Sixties*. Ft. Davis, TX: Frontier Book Co., 1968.

Sabin, Edwin L. *Kit Carson Days 1809-1868*. Lincoln, NE: University of Nebraska Press, 1995.

"Santa Fe Trail, National Scenic Byway." America's Byways, Scenic and Historic Byway Program: New Mexico State Highway & Transportation Dept. Raton, NM: The Raton/Colfax County Hispano Chamber of Commerce. n.d.

"Santa Fe Trail, Official Map and Guide." National Park Service, U.S. Department of the Interior, 1995.

Savvy, Cee. "The Trail to Santa Fe." *Enchantment Voice of New Mexico's 17 Rural Electric Cooperatives*. Statewide ed. Vol. 30, No. 2. Santa Fe, New Mexico, June 1979.

Segale, Sister Blandina. *At the End of the Santa Fe Trail*. Columbus, OH: Columbian Press, 1932.

Serna, Louis F. "The Outlaws of Cimarron." *La Herencia del Norte:* Santa Fe: Gran Via, Inc. Summer 1996, p. 27.

Settle, Raymond W. and Mary Lund. *Saddles and Spurs: The Pony Express Saga*. Harrisburg, PA: Stackpole Co., 1955.

Shaw, Miss Luella. "Proceedings of Company 'A'." *True History of Some of the Pioneers of Colorado*. Denver: Press of Harper Co., 1909. (9 August 2011). Colorado Genealogy, 2015. http://www.coloradogenealogy.com/ pioneer/ proceedings_ company_a.htm. (access 2015)

Sherman, James E. and Barbara H. *Ghost Towns and Mining Camps of New Mexico*. Norman, OK: University of Oklahoma Press, 1975.

Sifakis, Stewart. "Who Was in the Civil War." CivilWarTalk Network. (1997-2014). http://www.civilwarhome. com.

Simmons, Marc. *New Mexico: An Interpretive History*. Albuquerque: University of New Mexico Press, 1988.

------. *When Six-Guns Ruled, Outlaw Tales of the Southwest.* Santa Fe: Ancient City Press, 1990.

Simmons, Marc, ed. *On The Santa Fe Trail*. Lawrence, KS: University of Kansas Press, 1986.

Simpson, Lt. James H., Frank McNitt, ed. *Navaho Expedition.* Norman, OK: University of Oklahoma Press, 1964.

Smiley, Jerome C. *History of Denver*. Denver: Denver Times, Times-Sun Publishing Co., 1901.

Smith, Honora DeBusk. "Early Life in Trinidad and the Purgatory Valley." (master's thesis, University of Colorado, 1930). 70-73, 100, 167-169.

Smith, R. Gess. "The Whitman Massacre as recalled by Mary Marsh Cason." *A Place Called Oregon: History & Genealogy*. http://gesswhoto.com/whitman.html. (access 19 July 2008).

Snow, William J. "Utah Indians and Spanish Slave Trade." *Utah Historical Quarterly*. Vol. II, No. 3. Salt Lake City: Utah Historical Society. 1929.

"Southern Ute Tribe," *Travelhost*. Vol. 47, No. 1, 2013: p. 13.

Sprague, Marshall. *Colorado: A Bicentennial History*. New York: W. W. Norton and Company, Inc., 1976.

Stone, Wilbur Fiske. "Michael Beshoar, M.D." contributed by Joy Fisher. (21 December 2008). Extracted from Wilbur Fiske Stone *History of Colorado Illustrated*. Volume III. Chicago: The S. J. Clarke Publishing Company, 1918. http://files.usgwarchives.org/co/lasanimas/bios/ beshoar86nbs.txt.

Swords, C. L., and W. C. Edwards, Compilers and Publishers. "Richens L. Wootton, Jr." *Sketches and Portraitures of the State Officers and Members of the Ninth General Assembly of Colorado*. Denver: Carson, Hurst and Harper, Printers and Engravers, 1893.

Taylor, Morris F. *Trinidad, Colorado Territory*. Pueblo, CO: O'Brien Printing and Stationery Co., 1966.

------. *First Mail West*. Albuquerque: University of New Mexico Press, 1971.

------. *O. P. McMains and the Maxwell Land Grant Conflict*. Tucson: University of Arizona Press, 1979.

"The Families of Charles and William Bent." La Junta, CO: Bent's Old Fort National Historic Site, n.d.

"The Great New Mexico Pedigree Database." Albuquerque: Hispanic Genealogical Research Center of New Mexico. (2005-2014). http://www.hgrc-nm.org.

"The Maxwell (Beaubien-Maxwell) Land Grant and the Colfax County War." Copyright: Sangres.com.http:// sangres.com/ historymaxwelllandgrant.htm. (access 17 July 2008).

"The Mountain Men." History Channel, 22 August 2007.

Thompson, Jerry. "Sibley, Henry Hopkins." *Handbook of Texas Online*. Texas State Historical Association. (15 June 2010). http://www.tshaonline.org/handbook/ online/articlefsi01.

Thompson, Slason. *A Short History of American Railways*. Chicago: Tucker-Kenworthy Co., 1925.

Tracy, Deborah. "Defiance named...," *Daily Times*, November 3, 1991, p. F2.

Trego, Frank H. *Boulevarded Old Trails in the Great Southwest*. New York: Greenberg, 1929.

Trinidad Daily News, October 13, 1890, p. 1, Col. 3.

Twitchell, Ralph Emerson. *Old Santa Fe*. Chicago: Rio Grande Press Inc., 1963.

"Uncle Dick." *New Mexico Magazine*. Vol. 67, No. 3. Albuquerque: Department of Development, March 1989, p. 52-58.

"Uncle Dick Treated on Christmas Day, 1858." *Rocky Mountain News.* 80th Anniversary Edition, April 23, 1939.

UNM University Libraries. (2011). https://nmstatehood.unm.edu/node/72227. (also:) https://nmstatehood.unm.edu/node/72230.

Utley, Robert M. *Ft. Union and the Santa Fe Trail*. Studies Series No. 89. El Paso: Western Press, University of Texas at El Paso, 1989.

------, "The Buffalo Soldiers and Victorio." *New Mexico Magazine*. Vol. 62 No. 3, Albuquerque: Dept. of Development, March 1984, pp. 47-50, 53, 54.

"Veteran Santa Fe Railroad Engineer Once Was Wootton Tollgate Tender." *Chronicle News*, September 29, 1952.

Vickers, W. B. *History of the City of Denver: Arapahoe County, and Colorado*. Chicago: O. L. Baskin & Co., 1880.

Warburton, Jay. http://www.ghosttowns.com/states/co/summitspringsbattlefield.html. (access 6 November 2006).

Ward, Josiah M. "Dick Wootton Knew When He Had Enough." Magazine Section. *The Denver Post*, January 4, 1920.

Walker, Henry Pickering. *The Wagonmasters*. Norman, OK: University of Oklahoma Press, 1986.

"A Walking Tour of Old Town, Cimarron, New Mexico in the 1800s." Cimarron Historical Society, n.d.

Walter, Bob. "Fort Wallace." Wichita, KS: Skyways. http://skyways.lib.ks.us/history/ wallace (access 30 May 1997).

Waters, L. L. *Steel Trails to Santa Fe*. Lawrence, KS: University of Kansas Press, 1950.

Webb, Dave. *Santa Fe Trail Adventures.* Dodge City, KS: Kansas Heritage Center, 2000.

Weber, David J. *The Taos Trappers.* Norman, OK: University of Oklahoma Press, 1971.

Weiser, Kathy. "Colorado Legends Central City: Boom & Bust." *Legends of America*. (2003-present). http://www.legendsof america.com/CO-CentralCity.html.

West, Corporal Joe. "Buffalo Soldiers in Settlement of the Southwest." Lecture at San Juan College, Farmington, NM. February 20, 2004, 7:30 p.m.

Wharton, J. E. History. *The City of Denver.* with D. O. Wilhelm. *Business Directory of the City of Denver*. Denver: Byers and Dailey Printers, News Office, 1866.

Wheeler, Keith. *The Townsmen.* Alexandria, VA: Time-Life Books, Inc. 1978.

"Widow of 'Uncle Dick' Wootton Died at Albuquerque, N.M., Saturday, Funeral in Trinidad Tomorrow A. M." *Chronicle News*, March 4, 1935.

Willard, James F. "A Raton Pass Mountain Road Toll Book." *The Colorado Magazine*. Vol. VII, No. 2. Denver: State Historical Society of Colorado. March 1930, pp. 77-83.

"William Sherley Williams." (2003). http://www.allthingswilliam.com.

Williams, Jerry L., ed. *New Mexico in Maps*. Albuquerque: University of New Mexico Press, 1986.

Wommack, Linda R. "Chief Ouray: The Indian for Peace." *The Ute Pass Vacation Guide.* Florissant, CO: Diamond Graphic Source, 2005: pp. 61, 62.

Wood, Betty. "Trip of the Month Arroyo Hondo." *New Mexico Magazine*. Vol. 39, No. 2. Albuquerque: Dept. of Development, February 1961: p. 35.

Woodward, Arthur. "Trapper Jim Waters." City of San Bernardino, CA. (2000-2015). https://www.ci.san-bernardino.ca.us/about/history/jimwaters.asp. (article first published: Los Angeles Corral of Westerners, 1955).

Workers of the Writers' Program of the Work Projects Administration in the State of New Mexico. *A Guide to the Colorful State.* New York: Hastings House Pub., 1962.

The World Book Encyclopedia. 21 vols. Chicago: Field Enterprises, 1975.

Zamonski, Stanley, and Teddy Keller. *The Fifty-Niners: A Diary of Denver.* Denver: Sage Books, 1961.

Zimmerman, Emily. "Jim Bridger." http://xroads.virginia.edu/-hyper/HNS/mtmen/ jimbrid.html. (access 29 August 2006).

TABLE OF CASES

The United States, Appellant, v. The Maxwell Land Grant Company, et al., United States Circuit Court, The District of Colorado, Printed Book of Testimony, Supreme Court of the United States, No. 974, October term, 1886.

PRIVATE INDIVIDUALS AND COLLECTIONS

Berg, Catherine, Trinidad, Colorado, interview, a.m. 200_.; Brame Papers—author's private collection combined with the gift collection of the late Lois Brame; Harris, Evelyn Wootton, granddaughter of Richens L. Wootton, interviews; Humphries, Sharon, "Glorieta Pass," New Mexico History Presentation, Farmington, New Mexico, December 3, 1992; McLaughlin, Opal Smith, great-granddaughter of Eliza Wootton Walker, interviews, 1991, 1992; Wilson, Norma Scott, great-granddaughter of Richens L. Wootton, telephone interview; Wootton, John P., Jr., grandson of Richens and Mary Pauline Wootton; Author's clipping and photo collection.

PHOTO CREDITS
William Dorris III, Glenna Lawrence, Margaret Wilson, Robert Wootton
Photos, illustrations, and maps from works in public domain are noted in the Table of Contents and included in the Bibliography. Those are part of the author's collection. Undocumented photos are author's photography or are part of the author's collection.

COVER PHOTO CREDITS:
Insert of Uncle Dick, Conard, *Uncle Dick Wootton,* 1890.
Front and Back Landscapes, Shadow, Janelle Wootton McQuitty

Index

The purpose of this index is to catalogue what is available in the book. It is extensive, including names of most people and places, regardless of whether or not they are well-known; but it is not all-inclusive. It does not list every time words of larger volume (ex: Dick Wootton, branches of the Santa Fe Trail, Santa Fe, Denver, etc.) are mentioned. It is my hope, that enough references are included to direct readers and that, by including less well-known names, also, readers may be helped in their area of research or interest.

A

A. Y. Mine, 131
A.B. Dick Company, 469
Abbott, Henry, 335
Abert, Lt. James, 327
Abeyta, Amelia McBride, 374
Abeyta, Teodoro, 335, 374, 471
Abiquiu, 62, 64, 74, 97, 305, 420
Abreu, Ramon, 406, 407
Ac-ker-ba-the (Storm), 437
Adams, Alva, 469
Adams, John, 399
Adams, John Q., viii, 398, 399, 401, 402, 419
Adams, Louisa Johnson, 419
Adamson, Cecilia, 95
Adamson, William, 101
Adobe, 1, 7- 9, 31, 46, 51, 59, 168, 217, 225, 247, 273, 284, 289
Adobe Walls, 79, 155, 186, 226, 239, 241, 253, 272, 273, 415, 445, 455
Adriance, Jacob, 129
Alamo, 407
Albert, John, 53, 54, 215, 418
Albuquerque, 56, 61, 73, 99, 107, 142, 324, 330, 331, 336, 417, 439, 462, 465, 472
Albuquerque Citizen, 339
Albuquerque Morning Journal, 339
Albuquerque Post, 139
Alcott, Louisa May, 404
Alderdice, Susanna and family, 179
Aldous, Robert and Johan, 340
Alexander, E.B./Colonel, 101, 421
Alexander, Major, 169
Allen, DeWitt Fulton, 232
Allen, Joe Manuel, 274
Allen,, L.A., 230

Allison, A.J., 433
Allison, Bill, 105
Allison, Clay, 192, 331
Allison's Fort, 106
Altman & Cook Photo Gallery, 471
Alvarez, Manuel, 29, 224, 410, 411, 413, 416
Ambrule, Luis, 274
Amendment to U.S. Constitution, 447, 450-452
American Anti-Slavery Society, 404
American Bible Society, 391
American Colonization Society, 392, 395
American Fur Company, 11, 215, 216, 218, 221, 230, 272, 397
American Medical Association, 418
Anthony, Ernest, 468
Anthony, Major, 153
Anthony, Scott, 156
Antietam, 427
Antrim, William, aka Billy the Kid, 433
Apache, 22, 36, 37, 62, 68, 73, 81, 86, 87, 94, 98, 101, 127, 148, 149, 165, 166, 204, 234, 239, 249, 260, 272, 279, 301-303, 307, 311, 314-316, 408, 411, 415, 417, 418, 420, 422, 427, 434, 441-443, 457, 460-462, 466, 468
Apache Canyon, 140, 141, 287, 438
Appomattox, 164, 445
Aragon, Juan "Shoco", 96, 98
Arapaho, 15, 19, 23, 31, 39, 69, 73, 92, 97, 98, 101, 106, 112, 114, 116, 127, 148, 149, 152-154, 157, 166, 171, 216, 226, 234, 240, 251, 272, 302, 305, 307, 396, 409, 412, 424, 427, 429, 430, 432, 434, 436, 437, 441, 444, 449
Arapaho Express, 431
Arcenó, Michel, 274
Archibald, A.W., 464
Archuleta, Diego, 44, 45, 56, 58, 60

Archuleta, Felipe, 217
Archuleta, Fidel, 337
Archuleta, Marguerite Wootton, 335
Arizona Territory of the Confederacy, 135. 438
Arkansas River, 5, 6, 13, 18, 19, 24, 29-32, 37, 54, 69, 76, 88-90, 106, 152, 154, 158, 164, 166, 177, 225, 226, 229, 245, 253, 272, 275, 277, 281-283, 285, 298, 302-304, 395, 400, 401, 405, 427, 428, 437, 444, 446, 448, 449
Arkansas Valley, 31, 39, 92, 102, 231, 322
Armijo, Manuel/Governor, 23, 26-29, 32, 43-45, 66, 221, 224, 247, 311, 400, 409, 411, 415, 416
Army of the West, 42, 44, 233, 327, 416
Arrow Rock, 281, 284, 395
Arroyo Hondo, 53, 215, 216, 245, 259, 260
Arthur, Chester A., 204, 403, 464, 469
Articles of Confederation, iii
Ash Creek, 105, 285
Ash Hollow, 308, 426, 428
Ashburton Treaty, 413
Ashburton, Lord, 413
Ashley, William, 15, 221, 230, 240, 245, 396, 399
Astor, John Jacob, 395
Atchison, Kansas, 111, 153, 320
Atwood, J.W., 96
Aubrey Crossing; Cut-Off, 282, 286, 424
Aubrey/Aubry, Francis X., 104, 282, 418, 419, 422, 424
Auraria, 113, 115-118, 120, 123-127, 129, 131, 132, 138, 219, 270, 430-434, 441
Auraria Town Company, 115
Austen, Jane, 392
Austin, Moses, 394
Austin, Stephen, 394, 402
Austin, William, 54
Autobees, Charles/Charlie, 33, 53, 55, 59, 74, 87, 89, 96, 98, 100, 113, 216, 242, 243, 259, 423, 466
Autobees, Charlie: Wives of: Picking Bones, Serafina Avila, Siccamore, Estefana, Juanita Gomez, 216
Autobees, Francequita, 216
Autobees, François and Sarah (Issman), 215
Autobees, Jose Maria, 216

Autobees, Manuelita, 216
Autobees, Mariano, 216, 217
Autobees, Serafina, 217
Autobees, Tim, 216
Autobees, Tomas/Tom, 98, 216
Axtell, Samuel B., 193, 456, 458, 459

B

Babbitt, Almon, 426
Baca, Bartolome, 397-399
Baca, Bertram, 336, 367, 381
Baca, Elena, 217
Baca, Elfego, 468
Baca, Felipe, 166, 256
Baca, Felipe and Dolores, 336
Baca, Felipe Arturo, 336
Baca, Felix, 210, 336, 361, 367, 367
Baca, Ida Wootton, 335, 338, 361, 363, 367, 381
Baca, Jose, 34
Baca, Jose (Marcelino's son), 217
Baca, Lucy Ligouri, 336, 365, 367, 381
Baca, Luis, 34
Baca, Luis (Marcelino's son), 217
Baca, Marcelino, 34, 94-96, 217, 243, 249
Baca, Patricio, 456
Baca, Stella Marie, 336, 367
Baca, Tomasa, 34, 94, 217
Bacon, Joe, 339
Bacon's Rebellion, iii
Baer, Stella, 333
Baer, Susan Clementine, 333
Baillio, Paul, 262
Baird, James, 276, 397
Baird, Spruce, 66
Bakeman, Ike, 152
Baker, Jim, 132, 207, 218
Baldwin Locomotive Works, 201, 323
Baldy Mountain, 165
Bank of Missouri, 18, 290, 409
Bank of St. Louis, 290
Bannock Indians, 458
Bannock-Paiute Uprising, 458
Baptiste, John, 5, 249
Barceló, Gertrudis/La Tulles, 48
Barclay, Alexander, 34, 39, 40, 89, 101, 102, 219, 237, 257, 415

Barela, Jose "Viejito", 94-96
Barker, A.H., 115
Barlow & Sanderson, 160, 167, 180, 181, 203, 298, 322
Barnoy, Joseph/Levanway, 243, 274
Barnum, P.T., vi, 453
Barreiro, Antonio, 406
Bartholdi, F.A., 467
Bartlett, John Russell, 245
Barton, Kid, 181
Bates, Katharine, 475
Battle of Adobe Walls, 234, 455
Battle of Antietam, 142, 440
Battle of Beecher Island, 171-173, 451
Battle of Brazito, 265, 418
Battle of Bull Run, 142, 438, 440
Battle of Coleto, 407
Battle of Glorieta, 142, 146, 148, 166, 265, 267, 438
Battle of Gonzales, 407
Battle of Monterey, 417
Battle of Mora, 56
Battle of Palmito Hill, 445
Battle of Peralta, 142
Battle of Picacho Peak, 439
Battle of Pierre's Hole, 404
Battle of Pojoaque, 409
Battle of Sacramento, 61
Battle of San Jacinto, 407
Battle of Shiloh, 142, 266, 269, 438
Battle of Taos, 418, 422
Battle of the Little Bighorn, 186, 457
Battle of the Rosebud, 457
Battle of Valverde, 139, 217, 234, 267, 438
Battle of Wilson Creek, 227
Battle of Wounded Knee, 472
Baylor, John, 135, 438
Beach, George K., 320
Beall, B.L./Major, 73, 233, 247, 264
Bear Creek, 151
Bear Lake Rendezvous, 223
Bear River, 223
Beard & Walker, 331
Beard, Isabel, 330
Beard, Isabel Simpson, 220
Beard, Jake, 166, 167, 220, 237, 257, 330
Beaubien & Muller, 132

Beaubien, Charles, 29, 32, 35, 47, 53, 59, 70, 132, 193, 220, 257, 274, 412, 443
Beaubien, Juan Cristobal Pablo, 220
Beaubien, Juanita, 220
Beaubien, Leonora, 220
Beaubien, Luz (see Luz Maxwell), 220
Beaubien, Maria Pabla/Mrs. Charles, 52, 220
Beaubien, Narciso, 50, 52, 59, 220, 247
Beaubien, Petrita, 220
Beaubien, Teodora, 220
Beaubien-Miranda Land Grant, 52, 191, 247, 248, 257, 414
Beck, John, 113, 114
Becknell, William, 281, 282, 284, 293, 327, 395-398
Beckwith, Edward/Lt., 278, 423
Beckwith, Jim, 34
Beckwourth, Elizabeth Lettbetter, 221
Beckwourth, Jim, 53, 125, 127, 156, 221, 222, 258, 260
Beckwourth, Sue, 221
Beecher Island, 173, 179
Beecher, Fredrick, 173
Bell, Alexander Graham, 190, 457
Bell, John, 435
Benedict, Kirby, 181
Bennet & Wyatt, 119
Bennet, Hiram, 119
Bent, Alfredo, 51, 223
Bent, Cedar Woman, 225
Bent, Charles, 1-3, 6, 13, 18, 29, 34, 35, 39, 43, 47, 48, 50-55, 58-60, 176, 222-225, 228, 229, 253, 254, 272, 302, 400-404, 409, 411, 413, 418
Bent, Charles (William's son), 154, 156-158, 225, 227, 228
Bent, Cruz/Mrs. George, 43, 166, 228, 232
Bent, Estafana/Estafina, 223
Bent, George, 43, 53, 222, 226, 228, 232, 272, 409, 418
Bent, George (William's son), 152, 154, 156-158, 225, 227
Bent, Ignacia/Mrs. Charles, 43, 50, 51, 59, 232
Bent, Julia, 225
Bent, Martha, 222
Bent, Mary, 176
Bent, Mary "Mollie", 225, 227

Bent, Mis-stan-stur/Owl Woman, 224
Bent, Robert, 24, 222, 225, 228, 229, 272
Bent, Robert (William's son), 225, 227, 437
Bent, Robert (George's son), 166, 228, 229
Bent, Silas and Martha Kerr, 222, 223, 224
Bent, Silas and Martha, children of, 222
Bent, Teresina, 51, 223
Bent, William, vi, 1, 8, 11, 43, 44, 55, 89, 107, 152, 154, 156-158, 164, 176, 222, 223, 225, 226, 229, 239, 254, 272, 297, 298, 302, 308, 400-402, 409, 426, 429, 430-435, 444, 446, 451
Bent, Yellow Woman, 224, 225
Bent's Fort, 1, 6-8, 10, 13-15, 19, 22, 23, 29, 31, 34, 38, 53, 55, 71, 112, 114, 175, 215, 216, 219, 224, 228, 229, 237, 239, 240, 249, 250, 253-256, 272, 277, 286, 408, 410-412, 420, 429, 434
Benton Barracks, 269
Benton, Thomas H., 34, 47, 67, 277, 290, 293, 398
Bent's Big Timbers (see also Stone Fort), 115
Bent's Fort, 11, 13, 18, 22, 24, 29, 34, 35, 43-45, 55, 56, 59, 96, 100, 161, 176, 177, 225, 226, 233, 240, 272, 287, 298, 332, 416, 419, 425
Bent-St. Vrain & Co., 1, 10, 11, 13-15, 32, 34, 36, 38, 55, 56, 58, 103, 219, 225, 226, 233, 237, 239, 253-255, 258, 272, 273, 318, 403, 407, 409, 411, 412, 419
Beral, Leandro, 426, 434
Berg, Albert, 162, 342
Berg, Don, 342
Berg, Katherine, 342
Bergand or Bergaud, Luis, 274
Berkeley Hundred Plantation, Virginia, 443
Bernal Springs, 141, 286
Bernard Pratte and Co., 252
Bernard, William, 225
Berry, Paul, 237
Beshoar, Anna E. Maupin, 269
Beshoar, Daniel and Susan Rothrock, 269
Beshoar, Michael, 167, 235, 269, 270, 374
Beshoar, Michael, children of:, 269, 270
Biencroff, Thomas, 121
Big (Gageby) Creek, 177
Big Bend, 105, 158

Big Gip, 179
Big John Spring, 284
Big Sandy Station, 177
Big Timber, 149
Bigelow, Erastus, 412
Bijou Creek, 171
Bijou, Joseph, 246, 274, 392
Bill of Rights, 408
Billy the Kid, 203, 433, 458, 460, 463-465, 474
Bismarck Tribune, 457
Bissel, C.R., 432
Bissonette, Joseph, 34, 274
Black Exodus of '79, 459
Black Friday, 181, 183, 451, 454, 473
Black Hawk (Delaware Indian), 69
Black Hawk Indians, 404
Black Hawk War, 266
Black Hills, 302, 304, 425, 456, 457
Black Jack (point on Santa Fe Trail), 284
Black Kettle, 153, 154, 157, 437
Black Sun, 179
Blackfoot, 20, 216, 249, 301, 397, 404, 427, 429
Blackfoot River, 218
Blackhawk smelter, 450
Blair, Frank, 47, 58, 229
Blair, Henry, 406
Blake & Williams', 120, 125
Blake, Charles, 115, 125, 126
Blanc/Blanco, William, 274
Blanchard (Brashall/Brachal), Antonio, 274
Blanchard, Charles, 406
Blanco, Alarid, 62, 244, 252, 275
Blanco, Maria Guadalupe Lopez, 244
Blind school (first U.S. school for), 404
Blinn, Clara and Willie, 176, 451
Bliss, Lucien, 131, 432, 433
Blossburg, 203, 463, 464, 468
Blossburg Pioneer, 464
Boggs, Angus, 273
Boggs, Juliannah Bent, 222, 226, 229, 273
Boggs, Lilburn, 222, 229, 410
Boggs, Panthea Boone, 226, 229
Boggs, Rumalda/Mrs. Tom, 43, 50, 51, 59, 175, 223, 229, 230

Boggs, Thomas/Tom, 43, 47, 71, 132, 175, 207, 223, 229
Boggsville, 175, 230, 232, 234, 235
Bogin, Anne, 340
Bolivar, Simon, 393
Bonaparte, Louis Napoleon, 421
Bonaparte, Napoleon, 391, 394
Boné, Enrique, 274
Bonney, William aka Billy the Kid, 433
Boone, Albert, 132, 152, 236. 437
Boone, A.G., 152
Boone, Daniel, vi, 132, 394
Boones Lick, Missouri, 242, 259, 260, 284
Booth, John Wilkes, 164, 410, 445
Bordeaux, Charles, 34
Bordeaux/Bordaux/Bardaux, Victor, 274
Bosque Redondo, 148, 149, 165, 234, 313, 314, 315, 441, 443
Bosse, 153
Boston Journal, 126
Boston Tea Party, 222
Boulder (Colorado), 431, 433
Bouquet, Jean, 451
Bowdre, Charles, 463
Bowen, Gabriel, 435
Bowie, Jim, 407
Bowman, Anna/Annie, 340
Bozeman Trail, 172, 231, 447
Bradford, Allen/Judge, 145-147, 470
Bradford, Tom, 186
Bradford, William, 395
Bradley, Omar, 474
Brady, Mathew, 414
Brame, Catherine, ix
Brame, Frances "Fannie" Virginia, 340
Brame, James Dabney, ix
Brame, John, 340
Brame, John T., ix
Brame, Joseph and Jane, ix
Brame, Richens, iii, ix, 340
Brame, Richens/Richins, 340
Brame/Brim, John, iii, 340
Brame/Brim, Richens/Richins, 340
Branch, Alexander, 400
Branch, Alfredo Elfego, 245
Bransford, William, 55, 59, 166, 167, 193, 256
Bransford, Children of William/Bill and Rel: Alexander, Virginia, Anna, Amelia, William, Charles, Jefferson, 256
Bransford, Rel St. Vrain, 166, 255, 256
Brave
    Breaking Up, 439
    Brown Wind, 439
    Killing Ghost, 439
    Runs Against Something When Crawling, 439
Brazos River, 394
Bread Riots, 14
Bren, John, 340
Brend, John, 340
Brewer, David, 194
Bridge (Switzler's) Creek, 284
Bridger, James and Chloe, 230
Bridger, Jim, 24, 218, 230, 231, 240, 277, 396, 398, 402, 410, 464
Bridger Pass, 425
Briggs, Calvin, 15, 33, 261
Brigham, E., 331
Brim/Breame, Nichi (Nicholas), 340
Bristol, John O., 274
Broadwell, Dick, 473
Brooke/Brooks, Susannah, 341
Broune, Francisco, 274
Brown, Captain, 55
Brown, Hoodoo (H.G. Neill), 460
Brown, John, 33, 35, 100, 112, 231, 249, 261
Brown, John (Civil War John Brown), 432, 433
Brown, Joseph, 231
Brown, Joseph Cromwell, 293
Brown, Lola, 231
Brown, Luisa, 33
Brown, Matilda, 231
Browne, Henry P., 468
Brownell, William, 193
Brunner, Father, 337
Bryn/Brend/Brim, David, 340
Buchanan, James, 47, 133, 227, 426, 450
Buckley, James/Coal Oil Jimmy, 453
Buddee & Jacobs, 127
Buell, George, 455
Buffalo Soldiers, 173, 174, 189, 311, 315
Buhrman, Rev., 332
Bull Bear, 153

Bunker Hill, 399
Bureau of Indian Affairs, 397, 420
Burgwin, John, 56, 57, 58, 422
Burlington & Missouri Railroad, 268
Burlington Railway, 326
Burns, W.T., 195
Burris/Burroughs, John, 15, 34, 36, 250, 261
Burt, Dr. and Mrs. Walter, 160, 183, 205, 334
Burwell, Elizabeth or Frances, 340
Bushman, Mr., 429
Butte Valley settlement, 441
Butterfield, John, 317
Butterfield's Southern Overland Express, 280, 317, 318, 430, 441, 447
Byers, Elizabeth/Mrs. William N. 131, 270
Byers, Frank S., 270
Byers, Mary Eva, 270
Byers, Moses and Mary Brandenburg, 271
Byers, William N., 123, 124, 127, 132, 142, 150, 155, 167, 270, 431

C

Cabeza de Vaca, Luis Maria, 23
Cache la Poudre, 175, 215, 420
Cale, Joseph, 467
Calhoun, James S., 312, 420, 421, 422
Calhoun, John, 66, 67, 110, 402, 421, 436
California Charlie, 96
California Gold Rush (gold fields), 34, 83, 270, 419
California Gulch, 131, 135, 434
Camino Real, 28, 279, 415, 421
Camp Floyd, 318
Camp Grierson, 447, 448
Camp Robledo, 446
Camp Weld, 153, 438, 444
Camp, Ernest, 257
Campbell, Henry, 319
Campbell, Jack, 477
Campbell, Richard, 400
Campbell, Robert, 406
Canadian River, 37, 77, 79, 241, 277, 280, 304, 405, 429
Canby, Edward, 139-141, 234, 265, 312, 314, 437-439
Canby, Israel and Elizabeth Piatt, 265
Canby, Mrs. Edward, 265

Canfield, Isaac, 457
Canon & San Juan Railroad (a name used by the A.T. & S.F.), 323
Canon City, 147, 238, 254, 324, 330, 333, 435, 439, 453
Cañoncito, 44-46, 462
Cantrell, John, 114, 115, 121
Canyon de Chelly, 97, 313
Cardenas, Manuel, 192, 193
Carier, Anastasio, 274
Carleton, James H., 102, 148, 155, 234, 312-314, 440, 441
Carnegie Steel Mill, 473
Carondolet, 222, 244
Carpenter, Louis H., 173
Carpetbag rule, 458
Carr, Dorcas Bent, 226
Carr, Eugene, 179, 451
Carr, William Chiles, 222
Carson, Adaline, 232, 233
Carson, Charles, 232
Carson, Christopher Charles, 232
Carson, Christopher/Kit, vi, 15, 29, 41, 43, 71-73, 76, 78, 86, 126, 143, 148, 154, 158, 170, 171, 175, 218, 220, 223, 230, 235, 239, 247, 250, 254, 259, 260, 277, 305, 306, 313, 315, 399, 401, 430, 441, 445-447, 450, 476
Carson, Christopher/Kit,siblings of, 231
Carson, Estefana "Estafanita", 232
Carson, Joe, 460
Carson, Josefa Jaramillo/Mrs. Kit, 43, 50, 51, 59, 232, 234
Carson, Josephine "Josefita", 232
Carson, Lindsey and Rebecca Robinson, 231
Carson, Rebecca, 232
Carson, Teresina, 232
Carson, Waa-nibe, 232
Carson, William (Julian), 232
Carter, Jimmy, 452
Cassedy, A.M., 439
Castoreum, 16
Catskill, 471
Cavalry, 176, 223, 316, 434
Cavanaugh, Dr., 112
Cayuse Indians, 418
Cedar Creek, 286
Central City, 129, 131, 454

Central Pacific Railroad, 178, 319, 451
Central Route to the Pacific, 71, 87, 318
Chalifoux, Jean Baptiste, 19, 20, 22, 59, 89, 236, 274
Chalifoux, Pierre/Pedro, 236, 275
Chambers, Samuel, 276, 397
Chancellorsville, 149, 427, 442
Chandler, Clarence, 337
Chandler, Mary Richardson, 341
Chantet, Jean/Juan, 274
Chapman, John, 74
Chapman, William, 438
Charette/ Charrette, Pierre, 275
Charvet, Josef, 275
Chase, Salmon P., vi
Chattanooga, 149
Chaubelón, John/Juan, 275
Chaves, Pablo, 58
Chavez, Antonio Jose, 29, 30, 414
Chavez, J. Francisco/Colonel, 312, 470
Chavez, Lt. Colonel Manuel, 140, 141
Cheedle, Hannah, 341
Chene, Leopoldo, 245
Che-ne-na-e-te (Shave Head), 437
Cheney, Ben P., 342
Cherokee, 20, 96, 114, 401, 404, 410-412
Cherokee Advocate, 413
Cherokee Trail, 144, 145
Cherry Creek, 113-116, 118, 119, 121, 123-127, 129, 130, 132, 133, 135, 150, 218, 270, 271, 420, 429, 430
Cherry Creek Pioneer, 123
Cherry, Lt., 188
Cheyenne, 12, 24, 31, 35, 55, 80, 89, 98, 101, 108, 116, 127, 148, 149, 152-154, 156-158, 166, 171, 172, 176, 179, 189, 216, 221, 223, 225, 226, 228, 232, 234, 240, 251, 256, 272, 277, 285, 302, 303, 307, 396, 409, 410, 412, 418-420, 421, 423, 426, 427-430, 432, 434, 436, 437, 441- 445, 448, 449, 451, 452
Cheyenne Bow String Society, 409
Cheyenne Leader, 451
Cheyenne River, 427
Cheyenne, Wyoming, 235, 280, 433, 452
Chicago, 182, 268, 205, 325, 405, 432, 473
Chicago & Northwestern Railroad, 268
Chicago, Burlington, & Quincy Railroad, 268

Chicago *Democrat*, 41
Chicago Fire, 467
Chicago, Milwaukee & St. Paul Railway, 268
Chicago Party, 431
Chickamauga, 149
Chicorica, 18, 35, 193
Chief Big Wolf, 152
Chief Black Kettle, 152, 153, 156, 228, 451
Chief Captain Jack, 265
Chief Cochise, 315
Chief Conniach, 169, 170, 187, 189
Chief Crazy Horse, 458
Chief Esaquipa, 425
Chief Gray Thunder, 224, 240
Chief Guero, 97
Chief Handsome Bird, 294
Chief Johnson, 188
Chief Joseph, 458
Chief Juan Campo, 13, 408
Chief Lean Bear, 148
Chief Left Hand, 145, 153, 157, 437
Chief Little Crow, 441
Chief Little Raven, 302, 437
Chief Little Turtle, 151
Chief Little Wolf, 416, 425, 437
Chief Long Chin, 426
Chief Mangas Coloradas, 316, 408, 421
Chief Mariano Martinez, 312
Chief Medicine Bottom, 441
Chief Old Wolf, 241
Chief One-Eye, 157
Chief Ouray, 148, 183, 184, 189, 305, 308, 405, 450, 462
Chief Peta Nocona, 434
Chief Quanah Parker, 186, 303, 434, 455, 456
Chief Rafael, 454
Chief Red Arm, 419
Chief Roman Nose, 151, 171-173, 448, 451
Chief Satanta (White Bear), 449, 459
Chief Shakopee, 441
Chief Shone-gee-ne-gare, 294
Chief Sitting Bear, 304, 409, 453
Chief Sitting Buffalo, 21
Chief Sitting Bull, 209, 308, 457, 472
Chief Sitting Wolf, 416
Chief Spotted Wolf, 148
Chief Tierra Blanca, 94, 97, 424

Chief To-Hosea, 429
Chief Two-Face, 152
Chief Uncotash, 83, 84
Chief Victorio, 204, 311, 315, 316, 421, 442, 460, 461, 463
Chief White Antelope, 157, 437
Chief White Hair (Pa-hu-sha), 294
Chief Yellow Wolf, 157, 303
Chihuahua, 28, 46, 61, 253, 267, 276, 279, 291, 295, 403, 404, 408, 413
Chihuahua Trail, 279
Chiles, Captain Henry, 341
Chiles, Susannah, 341
Chiles, Walter, 341
Chiles, Walter II, 24, 341
Chisholm Trail, 449
Chisum, John, 467
Chivington, John M., 140, 141, 150-158, 228, 271, 438, 444, 445
Cholera, 80, 82, 88, 205, 249, 257, 266, 297, 335, 404, 424, 439, 448
Chouteau, Auguste, 220
Chouteau's Island, 286, 401
Chouteau-DeMun, 392
Christian County, Kentucky, viii, ix, 330, 403, 404, 409, 410, 421, 436, 442, 444, 447
Christopher, David and Mary, 340
Christopher, Nicolas, 340
Christy, Charles/Captain, 308
Chronicle News/Evening Chronicle (Trinidad), 209, 339, 476
Chunt/Lut, Francisco, 275
Churchill, Winston, 456
Cimarron (on Santa Fe Trail), 286
Cimarron City, 113, 161, 165, 170, 185, 191-193, 199, 200, 243, 246, 267, 298, 305, 420, 447, 450, 454, 466, 469
Cimarron Crossing, 5, 298
Cimarron Cut-Off/Dry Branch, 5, 6, 30, 76, 165, 282, 283, 293, 297, 401, 427
Cimarron Mountains, 75
Cimarron River, 250, 436
Cincinnati Commercial, 126
Cisneros, Felipe, 94
Civil Service Act, 466
Civil Service Commission, 466

Civil War, 102, 108, 111, 134, 140, 142, 146, 148, 164, 167, 176, 198, 209, 218, 227, 228, 234, 241, 254, 265-269, 271, 283, 291, 297, 298, 309, 311, 312, 319, 320, 326, 404, 427, 431, 435, 437-440, 442, 443, 445, 446, 448, 454, 469
Claiborne, Billy, 465
Claim jump war (brief), 131
Clamorgan, Jacques, 274, 276
Clanton Gang, 465, 466
Clanton, Billy, 465
Clanton, Ike, 465
Clark, Gruber & Co., 131, 439
Clark, P.H., 114
Clay, Henry, ix, 66, 67, 110, 399, 405, 422
Claymore, Auguste, 19, 20, 22, 228, 236, 243
Clear Creek Crossing, 219
Cleveland, Grover, 408, 468, 474, 475
Cleveland, New Mexico, 337
Clewell, E.F., 432
Clifton House, 286, 298
Clinton, De Witt, viii
Clouthier, Louis, 426, 434
Coal Creek, 92
Cochetopa Pass, 71, 245
Cochran, Elizabeth/"Nellie Bly", 471
Cody, William/"Buffalo Bill", 415, 451, 466
Cold Springs, 286, 433, 436
Coleman, James and Nancy, viii
Colfax County War, 190, 191, 267, 456
Colfax, Schuyler, 451
Colgate, William, 391
Collier, D.C., 129, 432
Collins, William, 443
Colorado 100-dayers, 153
Colorado City, 138, 153, 171
Colorado Electric Co, 463
Colorado Fuel & Iron Co., 342, 465
Colorado General Assembly, 210, 331, 471
Colorado Pike's Peakers/Volunteers, 140-142, 438
Colorado River, 21, 325, 400, 401
Colorado School for the Deaf and Blind, 203, 335, 380
Colorado School of Mines, 453
Colorado Springs, 114, 143, 147, 203, 322, 335, 339, 453, 464, 472, 475

Colorado Territorial Legislature, 238
Colorado Territorial Prison, 453
Colorado, names of some mining districts, 433
Colt, Samuel, vi, 402, 407
Columbia River, 20, 35, 216, 263, 395
Columbia River Valley, 35
Colyer, Vincent, 308
Comanche, 4, 5, 13, 24, 48, 68, 78, 79, 90,
    107, 129, 149, 152, 154, 155, 157, 160, 166,
    175, 185, 186, 225, 229, 239, 240, 248, 258,
    272, 273, 282, 301-307, 314, 396, 398, 399,
    401, 403, 407, 409- 411, 418, 419, 421,
    425, 426, 429, 430, 432-436, 445-447, 449,
    455, 456, 475
Compromise of 1850, 68, 106, 420, 424
Comstock Lode, 431
Conard, Howard Louis, 75, 207, 471
Conejos (Colorado), 145
Confederate, 135, 139-142, 227, 241, 255,
    266, 311, 436-439, 442, 444, 445
Confederate States of America, 134, 140, 436
Conkle, John, 473
Conn, Francisco, 31, 239, 242
Connelly, Henry, 38, 139, 140, 312, 437, 438
Connor, Joe, 152
Conquistadors, 306
Constantin, Leon, 426, 434
Constitutional Union Party, 435
Continental Divide, 83, 277
Cook, D.D., 119
Cooke, Jay, 454
Cooke, Philip St. George, 29, 30, 44, 245, 414
Cooke's Spring, 441
Coolidge, Calvin, 453
Coon Creek, 4, 285
Cooper, Benjamin, 397
Cooper, Job A., 471
Cooper, Peter, 429
Cooper, Peter (and "Tom Thumb"), 319, 403
Cooper, S./Adjutant General, 428
Cordova, Rumaldo, 94, 95, 98
Cortés, Hernan, 300
Cortes, Manuel, 58
Cortez, Jose, 69
Cottonwood Creek Crossing, 285
Council Grove, 3, 106, 284, 285, 291, 298,
    403, 405, 413, 423, 435, 442

Council Grove Treaty, 263, 294
Court of Private Land Claims, 472
Cow Creek, 158, 285, 298, 449
Cow, Mrs. Patrick O'Leary's, 182
Cow Springs, 64
Cowboy Capital, 466
Cox, James, 195
Craig, Lt., 328
Creede, 209, 470
Creede, Nicholas, 470
Creek Indians, 405, 470
Cripple Creek, 209, 473
Crittenden, George, 435
Crockett, Davy, 407
Crow Creek, 280
Crow Indians, 221, 304, 421
Cubero Post, 139, 142
Cuchara River, 236
Cucharas, 189
Culver, F.B., 437
Cumberland/National Road, 393
Cumming, Alfred, 110, 426, 428
Cummings, Alexander, 166
Curry, John, 468
Curtis, Samuel, 154, 445
Custer, George, 186, 451, 457
Cuthand, 24, 39, 107, 353
Cutthroat Gap Massacre, 405

D

Dabney, Mary, 341
Daily Missouri Republican, 412
Dalton, Bob, Emmet, and Grat, 473
Dalton Gang, 473
Dalton Minimum, 391
Dame, William H., 110
Daniel, Mary Catherine Wootton, 206, 419
Daniel, Richard, 206
Daughters of the American Revolution, 475
Davidson, John W., 455
Davis, Jefferson, vi, 134, 139, 140, 176, 254,
    436, 445, 452
Davis, N.S., 450
Dawson, John, 197
Dawson, Lewis, 395
Dawson, Will, 267
de Gaulle, Charles, 471

Deadwood, Dakota Territory, 457
Death Alley, 464
Declaration of Independence, 399, 420
Deere, John, 18, 409
DeHague, Lt., 447
Del Norte, 73, 74
Delaware, 37, 69, 215, 248, 259, 408
DeLisle, Frank, 56
Democrat Party, 435, 437
Democratic Review, 41
Denver, 11, 113, 116-118, 120, 123-127, 129-135, 138, 142, 144, 145, 149-154, 156, 157, 159, 165, 167, 175, 181, 208, 219, 222, 235, 237, 241, 243, 269, 270, 280, 286, 325, 328, 339, 430, 431-434, 439-441, 443-447, 450, 452, 453, 456, 459, 463, 465
Denver City Constitutional Convention, 120
Denver Hall, 120, 125
Denver, James/Governor, 115
Denver Ladies Union Aid, 131
Denver Pacific Railroad, 452
Denver Seminary, 439
Denver Town Company, 115, 437
DeRemer, J.R., 199, 200, 323
Deseret, 110
Desert Land Act, 439
Desmaraes, Michel, 275
Devil's Gate, 161, 162
Devine, James J., 463
Diamond Springs, 149, 285
Dickson, William, 209
Diesel, Rudolf, 474
Digger, 22, 85
Dillette, Antoine, 62, 244, 246, 252, 275
Dillette/Dillett, Jose Luis/Louis, 181, 183, 462
Dillette, Victoria Lopez, 244
Dillette/Gillet, Maria A., 332
Disturnell, James, 68
Dix, Dorothea, 469
Dodge City, 30, 167, 282, 321, 453, 466, 467
Dodge City Gang, 460
Dodge Expedition, 276
Dodge, Francis Safford, 189
Dodge, Granville, 231
Dodge, Henry, 276
Dodson, Doc, 150, 151

Dog Soldiers, 12, 152, 157, 158, 178, 179, 228, 444, 451
Dolan, James, 458
Dolores, Coxo, 96
Donati's Comet, 430
Doniphan, Alexander, 47, 61, 62, 241, 265, 417
Doniphan, Elizabeth Thorton, 265
Donner, George and Jacob, 417
Donner Pass, 85
Donoho, William, Mary, and daughter, 405
Doolittle, James, 158
Dorris, Nellie Ledford and son William, 372
Dorsey, John, 462
Douglas, Stephen, 67, 430, 435
Doyle, Alexander and Jane Evans, 237
Doyle, Alexander Greene, 237
Doyle, Cruz/Mrs. Joe, 33, 99, 160, 237, 257
Doyle, Fannie, 237
Doyle, Flora, 237
Doyle, Jacob, 237
Doyle, James "Jim" Quinn, 237
Doyle, Jose Lino, 237
Doyle, Joseph/Joe, 33, 40, 88-90, 92, 93, 95-97, 99, 101, 102, 108, 110-112, 127, 132, 147, 160, 219, 220, 237, 238, 242, 257, 258, 266, 430
Doyle, Richard, 133
Drake, Edwin, 431
Drips, Andrew, 233
Duchesne, 246, 275
Dunlavy, F.E., 335
Dunn, William, 132
Duque, Amado, 275
Duran, Augustin, 48
Durango, Colorado, 464
Durant, Bartley Sanders, 339
Dwyre, Burton, 476

E

Earp, Morgan, 465
Earp, Virgil, 465
Earp, Wyatt, 419, 465
Earthquake, 400, 451, 468
Eastlick family, 440
Eastman, George, 209
Eaton, Benjamin, 468

Edison, Thomas, 203, 209, 458, 462, 469, 473
Edwards, John C., 416
Einstein, Hermann and Paulina, 460
Einstien, Albert, i, 460
Eisenhower, Dwight D., 471
El Crespusculo de la Libertad, 406
El Moro, 198, 199, 250, 322, 323, 474
El Partido del Pueblo Unido, 470
El Paso, 28, 30, 142, 220, 246, 307, 317, 325, 331, 421, 446, 472
El Paso-San Antonio route, 315
El Pueblo, 31, 33-36, 39, 40, 53-55, 62, 71, 72, 90, 93-95, 98, 100, 113, 215, 216, 219, 231, 237, 239, 242, 243, 249, 250, 257, 258-261, 264, 276, 318, 413, 416, 418
El Pueblo Massacre, 218, 238, 243, 250, 424
Elbert, Samuel, 454
Electoral College, 190
Elephant Corral, 125
Elizabethtown, 165, 191, 243, 248, 451-454
Elk Grove (California), 85
Elkins & Marmon, 193
Ellis Island, 473
Elm Creek, 284
Emancipation Proclamation, 441
Emory, Commissioner, 307
Emory, General, 450
Encinas, Juan de Dios, 98
Engle, William, 200
Enos, Captain, 254
Era of Good Feelings, 394
Erie Canal, viii, 392, 399
Espinosa Gang, 259
Estancia Valley, 466
Estes (Istuss/Istess), Bob/Asa, 34, 44, 59
Eubanks family, 152
Evans, John, 142, 148, 153-155, 439, 442, 444
Evans, Oliver, 394
Evans, Thomas, 134
Everett, Edward, 67, 443
Exchange Hotel, 450, 472
Extermination Order, 410

F

F. W. Woolworth Company, 459
Fagan's Camp, 144, 145
Fair Oaks, 427
Falkner, Mary, 341
Fall Leaf, 114, 427
Fannin, General, 407
Farrell, J., 432
Father of the Santa Fe Trail, 282
Fauntleroy, Thomas, 435
Federalist Party, 391
Ferguson, Jesse, 401
Ferris wheel, 209
Fetterman Massacre, 447
Fetterman, William, 447
Field, Ben B., 243
Field, Cyrus W., 429
Field, Matt, 327
Fillmore, Abigail, 422
Fillmore, Millard/President, 110, 420, 422, 454
Financial Panic 1819, 290, 393
Finch, Duane D., 196
Fisher, Alejandro, 238
Fisher, Antonia J., 238
Fisher, George, 238
Fisher, George W., 129
Fisher, Joe, 238
Fisher, Maria Preciliana, 239
Fisher, Maria Trinidad, 239
Fisher, Norberto, 239
Fisher, Robert, 31, 33, 35, 59, 62, 70, 76, 78, 83, 112, 239, 241, 242, 244, 260
Fisher, Romualda, 33, 83, 238, 239
Fisher, William and Nancy, 238
Fisher's Peak, 198
Fisk, James, Jr., 181, 451
Fitzgerald, A.G., 334
Fitzgerald, E., 433
Fitzgerald, John, 59
Fitzpatrick, Thomas/Tom, 43, 44, 101, 112, 240, 277, 308, 402, 403, 421, 434
Flathead Indians, 249, 404
Florence Field (oil), 457
Floyd, John B., 428
Flying Dawn, 218
Fontenelle, Lucien, 250, 406
Foolish Chief, 294
Ford, Bob, 461, 466
Ford, Gerald, 452
Fornier, Luis, 275

Forsythe, George, 172, 173
Forsythe's Scouts, 173, 179
Fort Wise Treaty, 436
Foster, Lafayette, 158
Fountain Creek, 31, 94, 95, 150, 217
Fountain Qui Bouille, 144
Fountain River, 92, 150
Fountain Valley, 181, 444
Fountain, Albert, 470
Fowler, Jacob, 281, 302, 395
Fowler, Joe, 467
Fox, Johnny, 333
Fracker, Charles, 244
Fraeb, Henry, 24, 240, 277, 402
Franklin, Missouri, ix, 232, 282, 284, 394, 398
Freeman, Thomas, 435
Freighter/freighters, 99, 108, 110, 154, 177, 180, 283, 294, 296
Fremont, Jessie, 72
Fremont, John C./Pathfinder, 34, 41, 49, 71, 72, 106, 218, 221, 233, 246, 250, 263, 276-278, 293, 426
Fremont's California Battalion, 250
Fremont's First Expedition, 277, 413
Fremont's Fourth Expedition, 264, 278, 419
Fremont's Second Expedition, 234, 240, 260, 277, 414, 415
Fremont's Third Expedition, 250, 264, 277, 415
Ft. Atkinson, 420, 428, 444
Ft. Aubrey, 446
Ft. Barclay, 40, 78, 83, 88, 99, 101-103, 108, 109, 113, 181, 219, 237, 238, 242, 243, 250, 257, 258, 283, 286, 330, 425, 426, 430
Ft. Bascom, 234, 442
Ft. Bayard, 311, 442
Ft. Bliss, 307, 311, 446
Ft. Bridger, 110, 111, 218, 230, 318, 410, 428
Ft. Burgwin/Cantonment Burgwin, 96, 422
Ft. Chambers, 152
Ft. Collins/Camp Collins, 150, 443, 444
Ft. Concho, 455
Ft. Conrad, 421, 424
Ft. Craig, 139, 140, 424, 438, 439
Ft. Cummings, 441
Ft. Davis, 311, 316
Ft. Davy Crockett, 250

Ft. Dearborn, 405
Ft. Defiance, 312, 313, 421, 447
Ft. Dodge, 175, 285, 298, 427, 446
Ft. Fauntleroy, 435
Ft. Fillmore, 135, 421
Ft. Garland, 170, 189, 217, 234, 238, 259, 429, 447
Ft. George, 272
Ft. Griffin, 455
Ft. Hall, 249
Ft. Hayes, 172
Ft. Kearny, 123, 152, 158, 231, 269, 270, 318, 426, 428
Ft. Laramie, 11, 13, 14, 80, 111, 215, 217, 218, 234, 240, 242, 249, 272, 276, 308, 318, 406, 421, 427, 429, 432, 443
Ft. Laramie Treaty, 176, 424, 450
Ft. Larned, 149, 151, 227, 298, 431, 444, 446-448
Ft. Leavenworth, 39, 42, 172, 178, 224, 253, 276, 282, 400, 402, 415, 418, 422, 426, 427, 440
Ft. Leavenworth Trail/Road, 427
Ft. Logan, 469
Ft. Lookout, 272
Ft. Lowell, 447
Ft. Lupton, 14, 408, 435
Ft. Lyon, 149, 152-154, 157, 158, 164, 175, 176, 177, 227, 228, 230, 232, 298, 330, 448, 450, 451
Ft. Maclane, 434
Ft. Mann, 418, 420
Ft. Marcy, 46, 420
Ft. Massachusetts, 89, 421, 429
Ft. McRae, 442, 446
Ft. Morgan/Camp Tyler, 446
Ft. Namaqua, 429
Ft. Osage, 262, 263, 284, 293
Ft. Pickens, 468
Ft. Quitman, 311
Ft. Recovery, 223
Ft. Riley, 423, 425
Ft. Robidoux (Ft.Uinta), 410
Ft. Robinson, 458
Ft. Sedgwick/Camp Larkin, 179, 444, 445
Ft. Seldon, 279, 311, 446
Ft. Sill, 186, 304, 451, 453, 455, 456, 469

Ft. St. Vrain, 14, 34, 38, 246, 249, 253, 255, 256, 272, 409
Ft. Stanton, 234, 311, 315, 425
Ft. Steele, 188
Ft. Stockton, 311
Ft. Sumner, 148, 165, 191, 203, 220, 244, 246, 248, 280, 313, 314, 440, 443, 449, 456, 464
Ft. Thorn, 423
Ft. Uncompahgre, 412
Ft. Union, 96, 99, 102, 107, 109, 113, 136, 139-143, 162, 165, 177, 193, 216, 218, 238, 243, 245, 247, 254, 267, 283, 286, 298, 311, 421, 422, 425, 427, 429, 435, 436, 438, 446, 447, 472
Ft. Union Road, 282
Ft. Vancouver, 277, 395
Ft. Vasquez, 14, 221, 251, 409, 411
Ft. Walla Walla, 249
Ft. Wallace, 149, 172, 173, 176, 448, 451
Ft. Wingate, 435
Ft. Wise, 227
Ft. Zarah, 285, 298, 308, 444, 449
Fulton, Robert, vi
Funk, Dr. Z. E., 196
Fuss, Joseph J. and "Maggie" Murphy, 337

G

Gadsen Purchase, 68, 306, 423
Gadsen, James, 423
Galbraith, Thomas, 440
Galisteo, 140, 141
Gallaudet, 392
Gallinas River, 324, 406, 425, 460, 461
Galvanized Yankees, 167, 269, 271
Galveston, Texas, 325
Gamble, Archibald, 293
Ganado Mucho (Navajo headman), 313, 314
Garcia, Jose Manuel, 60
Garcia, Rafael, 331
Gardiner, James T., 463
Gardiner, Julia, 414
Garfield, James, 203, 204, 404, 463, 464
Garland, John, 298, 425
Garrard, Lewis, 62
Garrett, Elizabeth, 204
Garrett, Pat, 203, 420, 463, 464
Garrison, William Lloyd, 403, 404

Gatling gun, 441
Gatling, Richard, 441
Geronimo, 209, 316, 421, 442, 457, 468, 470
Gervais, Jean Baptiste, 240, 402
Gettysburg, 149, 427, 442, 443
Gettysburg Address, 443
Gettysburg of the West, 142
Gibson, George, 327
Gibson, Thomas, 123
Giddings, Marshall, 456
Gila River, 21, 66, 73, 216, 245, 399, 401
Gilmore, Charlie "Chuck-a-luck", 117
Gilpin, William, 47, 134, 135, 140, 142-144, 277, 417, 437, 439
Glenn, Hugh, 281, 395
Glenn-Fowler, 396
Glidden, Joseph, 183, 456
Glorieta (on Santa Fe Trail), 287
Glorieta Mesa, 141
Glorieta Pass, 141, 142
Gobacks, 124
Godey, Alex, 71, 106, 260, 264, 278
Golden, Tom L., 431
Golden, Colorado, 161, 453
Goldrick, Owen J., 127-129, 132, 432
Goliad Massacre, 407
Gonzales, Francisco, 97
Gonzales, Hilario, 28, 443
Gonzales, Jose, 409
Gonzales, Jose Maria Elias, 28
Gonzalez, Juan, 457
Goodale, Tim, 426
Goodall, Tom, 234, 243
Goodman, William, 465
Goodnight, Charles, 133, 164, 280, 447
Goodnight-Loving Trail, 280
Goodwin, Hannibal, 209
Goodyear, Charles, 406
Gorman, Samuel, 422
Goshen's Hole, 40, 415
Gould, Jay, 181, 201, 451, 473
Grand Canyon, 37, 321, 326
Grand Pass, 284
Grand River, 18, 37, 84, 278
Grant, James B., 466
Grant, Ulysses, 137, 193, 265, 280, 396, 468
Grant, Ulysses and Julia, 462

501

Grass, Tom, 96
Grattan, John L./Lt., 424
Graves, Alfred, 463
Gray's Ranch, 298, 332
Great American Desert, vi, 1, 276
Great Bend, 114, 258, 285, 449
Great Chicago fire, 453
Great Natchez tornado, 411
Greek George, 223
Greeley Colony, 452
Greeley, Colorado, 188, 280
Greeley, Horace, vi, 126, 138, 452
Green, Charlotte, 8
Green, Dick, 8, 56, 57
Green River, 18, 19, 38, 84, 218, 230, 398, 410
Green Russell Party, 113-115
Green, Tom, 139
Greenhorn, 35, 54, 94, 100, 113, 143, 181, 218, 231, 241, 242, 249, 261
Greenhorn Creek, 250
Gregg, George, 261
Gregg, Josiah, 288, 403, 415
Gregory Diggings, 127
Gregory Gulch (Central City), 431, 433, 454
Gregory Mine, 125
Gregory, John H., 125, 431
Grenier, Jean Baptiste, 275
Grenier, Joseph, 275
Grey's Creek, 236
Griego, Pancho, 192
Grier, William, 76-78, 82, 245, 247, 259
Grierson, Benjamin/Colonel, 311, 315
Grigg, Elizabeth, 340
Grigg, James, 340
Grigg, William, 340
Guadalupe Mountains, 315
Guadalupita, New Mexico, 166
Guerin, François, 252, 398
Guerra/Guarra (possibly same as Charra, Napiste/Bautista, 275
Guerrero, Mexican President, 402
Guerrier, Bill, 33, 112, 240
Guerrier, Ed, 152, 154, 157, 225, 228, 240
Guerrier, Julia Bent, 154, 157, 228, 240
Guinard, Louis, 34
Guiteau, Charles J., 464

Gunnison Exploration, 278
Gunnison, John, 87, 245, 278, 423
Gunnison River, 84, 412

H

Haddon, Frank, 196
Haight, Isaac C., 110
Haish, Jacob, 183
Hale, Sarah, 391
Half-Breed Republican, 203
Hamilton, John, 338
Hamlin, Hannibal, 435
Hancock, Winfield Scott, 137, 448
Harding, Warren, 446
Hardscrabble, 239
Hardscrabble Creek, 243
Harmon, Dr. David, 244
Harney, W.S., 218, 308
Harper's Ferry, 432
Harris, Evelyn Wootton, 477
Harris, Joseph, 337
Harrison, Anna, 443
Harrison, Benjamin, 405, 471
Harrison, Charles, 133
Harrison, William/President, 24, 412, 459, 471
Harvey, Adelina, 224
Harvey, Fred, 269, 321, 326
Harvey Girls, 326
Harvey House, 458
Harvey Spring, 284
Harwood, Willliam, 55
Hastings Mine, 333
Hatch, Edward/Colonel, 315
Hatcher, John, 43, 59, 71, 86, 166, 239, 240
Hatfield, William, 54
Hawken, Samuel, 132
Hawkins, John, 34
Hayden, F.V., 447
Hayes, Eliza Ann Wootton, 205, 475
Hayes, Rutherford, 190, 397, 457, 459, 463, 474
Hayes, Seth, 106, 435
Hayes, Will, 205
Hayne, Robert, viii
Head, Mark, 55
Heavy Furred Wolf, 179

Henderson, John, 197
Hendley, Israel, 56
Henry, Andrew, 245, 397
Henry, Tom, 462
Heredia, General, 61
Herring, Valentine/Rube, 33
Hicklin, Alexander, Jr, 241
Hicklin, Estafana Bent, 241
Hicklin, Thomas, 241
Hicklin, Zan, 112, 143, 145, 223, 241
Hickok, James "Wild Bill", 409, 457
Hidalgo, 276
Hidalgo de Parral, Mexico, 465
Hill, James, 133
Hill, Nathaniel P., 450
Hitler, Adolf, 470
Hobbs, Jim, 5
Hockaday & Liggett, 126
Hoe, Richard, 416
Holdsworth, R. B., 195
Hole in the Prairie, 298
Hole in the Rock, 286, 298
Holladay Overland Co., 126, 316, 447
Holladay, Ben, 85, 126, 318
Holland, "Uncle Jack", 247
Holliday, Cyrus, 198, 320
Holliday, Doc, 461, 465, 469
Home Insurance Building (1st U.S. skyscraper), 467
Homestead Act, 293, 439
Honey-Eater band of Comanche, 303
Hoover, Herbert, 456
Horn, Albert M., 329
Horn, John, 160
Horn, Tom, 433
Hough, John, 230
Houghton, Joab, 47, 59, 254
House of Burgesses, iii
Houston, Sam, 28, 400, 407, 408, 413, 414
Howe, Elias, 416, 417, 425
Hudson's Bay Company, 20, 230, 395, 401
Huerfano Creek/River, 89, 147, 217
Huerfano Village, 87-90, 94, 96, 99, 102, 113, 216- 218, 236, 238, 242, 243, 250, 258, 423, 425
Hughes, John T./Colonel, 327
Hulbert, I.H., 461

Humbell, Mr. & Mrs. Henry, 119
Huning Massacre, 309
Hunn, William, 195
Hunning, Franz, 449
Hunt, Alexander, 452
Hunter/Wootton, Leroy Lawrence, 477
Huntington, Collis, 201
Huntley, Dr. & Mrs. E.D., 330
Hurricanes, 475
Hutchins, Rosswell C., 115

I

Immell, Michael, 397
Independence, Missouri, ix, 1, 7, 39, 282, 284, 407, 412, 413, 418, 419, 421, 422
Indian Appropriation Act, 181, 453
Indian George, 69
Indian Mound, 286
Indian Removal Act, 402
Ingalls, Laura (Laura Ingalls Wilder), 448
Inman, Henry, 39, 77, 259
Institute for Infectious Diseases, 473
Interstate Commerce Act, 469
Interstate Commerce Commission, 469
Iron Springs, 164, 286, 298, 332
Irving, Phillip, 334
Isa-tai, 455
Isleta Pueblo, 279

J

Jackson, Andrew/President, ix, 25, 392, 394, 402, 408, 415, 431
Jackson, Captain, 55
Jackson, David, 402, 403
Jackson, George, 125
Jackson, Rachel, 402
Jackson, William Henry, 447
James Gang, 466
James, Dr. Edwin, 276
James, Frank, 413, 442
James, Jesse, 418, 442, 461, 466
James, Robert and Zerelda, 418
James, Thomas, 281
Jamestown, iii, 24, 47, 442
Jaramillo, Francisco and Maria Apolonia, 232
Jaramillo, Ignacia, 223

Jaramillo, Pablo, 35, 50, 52
Jarvis Creek, 158, 285
Jeantet, Jean, 275
Jefferson Barracks, 269
Jefferson, Thomas, 399
Jemez Pueblo, 410
Jenny, Mr., 456
Johnson, Andrew, vi, 167, 172, 176, 444-446, 448, 450, 451
Johnson, Constable Joe, 333
Johnson, James, 13, 261
Johnson Mesa, 464
Johnson, Rattlesnake Bill, 462
Johnson's Ranch, 141
Johnston, Albert S., 110, 136, 231, 245, 266, 429
Johnston, Eliza Griffin, 266
Johnston, Henrietta Preston, 266
Jones, Calvin, 193
Jones, James, 403
Jones, John S., 126
Jones, Martha, 340
Jones, Robert, 397
Jones, Robinson, 439
Jornada (on Santa Fe Trail), 285
Jornada del Muerto, 87, 279, 421, 446
Joseph, Peter, 69
Journal of Commerce, 430
Juarez, Benito, 443
Judson, Whitcomb, 472
Julesburg, 151, 152, 158, 179, 445
Jurnegan, John, 96

K

Kaitsenko—Society of the Ten Bravest, 304
Kansa/Kaw Indians, 106, 263, 294, 301, 304
Kansas City, 38, 99, 227, 284, 298, 412, 415, 425, 426, 434, 435, 440, 452
Kansas City Journal of Commerce, 121
Kansas Pacific Railroad, 164, 172, 452
Kansas Party, 115
Kansas-Nebraska Act, 424
Kaskaskia (Illinois), 246, 275, 393
Kasserman and Co., 127
Kaup, Lillie, 336
Kearney, Frank, 465
Kearney, Nebraska, 151

Kearny Expedition, 276
Kearny, Stephen Watts, 39, 42-44, 46, 47, 49, 101, 140, 221, 224, 225, 233, 240, 253, 256, 259, 266, 276, 312, 314, 327, 415--417, 424
Kearny's Code, 46, 63
Kehler, John, 132, 432
Kelly, Jack, 465
Kelly, Patrick, 133
Kenceleur, William, 34
Kennedy, Burt, 126
Kenner Levee, 391
Kentucky Derby, 456
Kern brothers, 72, 73, 264
Kern, Benjamin, 73, 74, 264, 278, 419
Kern, Edward, 73
Kern, Richard, 73
Ketchum, Black Jack, 443
Khedive's army, 267
Kiker, G.W., 114
King, Ames, 340
King, Rufus, 391
King, Sandy, 465
King's Ferry, 177
Kingman, Lewis, 200, 267
Kinkead, Andres, 242
Kinkead/Kincaid, Mathew, 31, 34, 112, 232, 239, 242
Kiowa, 80, 89, 101, 127, 149, 152, 154, 155, 157, 160, 166, 175, 186, 226, 240, 241, 248, 272, 273, 282, 302-304, 307, 314, 396, 405, 409, 410, 412, 418, 420, 421, 423, 425, 426, 429, 430, 432-436, 442-446, 449, 453, 455, 459
Kiowa Creek, 144, 171
Kirker, James, 61, 69, 408
Kit Carson & Ft. Union Bridge Company, 177
Kit Carson, Colorado, 177
Kitchen, C.H., 447
Klamath Lake, Oregon, 277
Knights of Labor, 470
Koch, Dr. Robert, 473
Koslowski's ranch, 141
Kroenig, Louisa Watrous, 242
Kroenig, Rafaelita Kinkead, 219, 242
Kroenig, William, 78, 87, 89, 90, 109, 165, 193, 219, 238, 242, 243, 261, 423

L

L'Esperance, Joseph and Mary, 246
L'Esperance, Pierre, 246
La Fonda, 472
La Iglesia de Taos, 57
La Junta, Colorado, 2, 177, 198, 199, 235, 321, 322, 324
La Parroquia, 451
La Plazarota, 108
La Verdad (*The Truth*), 415
Lachoné, Luis, 275
Laënnec, Rene, 392
Lafayette, 398
Laforet, François/Francisco, 275
Laforet, Manuel, 59
Laguna Pueblo, 422
Lajeunesse, François, 55
Lake, George B., 267
LaLande, Jean Baptiste, 275
Lamar, Mirabeau B./President, 26, 27, 413
Lambert, Henri, 454
Lamme, Samuel, 402
Lamy, Jean B., 100, 166, 248, 421, 422, 424, 451
Lamy, New Mexico, 201, 298, 324, 451, 474
Land Act of 1820, 394
Lane, William Carr, 422
LaRamee, Jacques, 396
Laramie River, 250, 406
Larié, Anastasio, 275
Larimer Company (See Kansas Party), 115
Larimer, William, 115, 117
Larrazolo, O.A./Governor, 336
Las Animas River, 180, 250
Las Animas, Colorado, 321
Las Cruces, New Mexico, 421, 424
Las Gorras Blancas/the "White Caps", 470
Las Vegas, 27, 44, 139, 140, 149, 164, 201, 219, 243, 246, 267, 280, 286, 299, 313, 322, 324, 325, 337, 406, 416, 443, 447, 460-463, 465, 467, 468, 474, 476, 477
Las Vegas Gazette, 248
Las Vegas Land Grant, 470, 474
Las Vegas Plaza, 27, 44, 139, 474
Las Vegas Vigilance Committee, 461
Latham, Colorado, 151, 153
Laughlin, Richard, 401

Lawrence Party, 114, 429, 430
Lawrence, C.A., 432
Lawrence, Kansas, 113, 114, 442
Lawrence, Richard, ix
Le Bonte, 21
Le Grande, Alexander, 398
Leadville, Colorado, 131, 434, 456, 458
Leal, James, 50, 52
Lean Bear, 437
Leavenworth & Pikes Peak Express Co., 431
LeBlanc, William, 59
Lebrie, Antoine, 426, 434
Ledford, Nannie Wootton, 372
Ledoux, Antoine, 275
Ledoux, Felipe, 249
LeDuc, Elena, 243
LeDuc, Maurice, 21, 33, 101, 243
Lee, Jason, 406
Lee, John D., 110
Lee, Robert E., vi, 136, 164, 319, 433, 437, 445, 452
Lee, Stephen/Steve, 50, 52, 59, 254, 414
Lee, William D., 459
LeFebvre, Augustin and Felicité Vaillancourt, 244
LeFevre, Antonio, 244
LeFevre, Dolores, 62, 244, 329, 419
LeFevre, Francisca Guillerma, 244
LeFevre, Jose Manuel, 244
LeFevre, Manuel, 53, 55, 62
LeFevre, Manuel Carlos, 244
LeFevre, Maria de la Luz, 244
LeFevre, Maria Leonora, 244
LeFevre, Pacifica, 244
LeFevre, Teodora, 62, 244, 329
Leitensdorfer, Eugene, 47
Leroux, Antoine, 59, 63, 71, 74, 76, 78, 245, 264, 312, 419
Leroux, Antoine, siblings of, 244
Leroux, Caroline/Catarina, 245
Leroux, Deluvina, 245
Leroux, Joaquin, 35
Leroux, Jose David, 245
Leroux, Juan de Jesus/Jean, 245
Leroux, Juana Catalina Vigil, 245
LeRoux, Louis and Elena, 244
Leroux, Luis Gonzaga, 245

Leroux, Maria Elena, 245
Leroux, Mariquita Teresa, 245
Leroux, Pablita, 245
Leroux, Ysabel, 245
Leslie, Mrs., 147, 332
L'Esperance, Pedro, 246
L'Esperance, Pierre, 275
Lewis and Clark, 222, 261
Lewis, George, 101
Lewis, William, 141
Lexington (point on Santa Fe Trail), 284
Liliuokalani, Queen, 474
Lincoln County War, 190, 193, 458, 459
Lincoln, Abraham, vi, 133, 134, 142, 148, 154, 164, 227, 430, 435, 437-445, 454
Lincoln, Mary Todd, 466
Lind, Jenny, 410
Lipan Indians, 68
Lisa, Manuel, 276
Lister, Lister, 446
Little Arkansas Crossing, 285
Little Blue River Crossing, 284
Little Cow Creek, 4, 29, 151, 285, 414
Livingstone, David, 412
Lloyd, A.T., 114
Lobato, Buenaventura, 29, 51
Lockett, Susannah, 340
Lockett, Thomas, 340
Lone Bear, 179
Lone Wolf, 21
Long Expedition, 266, 276
Long, David, 276
Long, Guadalupe, 223
Long, Serafina, 257
Long, Stephen, vi, 276, 394
Longabaugh, Harry/Sundance Kid, 447
Longfellow, Henry W., vi
Longwell, Robert, 193
Lopes, Francisco, 443
Lopez, Francisco, 406
Lopez, Jose Ramon and Luz, 62, 238, 239, 244
Loretto Academy, 223
Loring, William, 108, 437
Los Angeles, 86, 87, 268, 279, 325, 326
Los Piños Agency, 189
Lost Spring, 285
Louisiana Purchase, viii, 9, 66, 275, 291, 306

Loving, Joe, 449
Loving, Oliver, 133, 164, 280, 447, 449
Lower Cimarron Springs, 152, 285
Lower Crossing, 285
Lowman, Mary, 470
Lucero, Manuel "Trujeque", 98
Lucero, Pedro, 60
Lujan, Federico, 332
Lujan, Guadalupe, 181, 183
Lujan, Jesus Maria, 333, 336, 374
Lujan, Jose Guadalupe and Luz, 334
Lujan, Jose Ignacio, 470
Lujan, Luz Dillette, 183, 335, 356, 381
Lujan, Mary Pauline, 183, 335, 346, 348, 352, 453
Lujan, Prudencio, 183
Lujan, Will, 335
Luna, Antonia, 33, 258
Luna, Estanislado, 96, 98
Lupton, Lancaster, 11, 411
Lynde, Isaac, 135
Lyon, Nathaniel, 227, 266

M

MacArthur, Douglas, 446
Mackenzie, Ronald/Colonel, 303, 455
Madison, Dolley, 408, 420
Madison, James, 391, 392, 408, 419
Magnes, Peter, 456
Magoffin, James, 44-46
Magoffin, Samuel, 44
Magoffin, Susan, 44
Majors, Alexander, 126, 317
Making-out-Road, 232
Mallet brothers, Paul and Pierre, 274, 275
Ma-na-sa-te (Big Mouth), 437
Manco de Burro Pass, 69, 247, 260
Manifest Destiny, 41, 176, 253, 291, 321
Manitou Springs, 143, 249
Manning, Mary Ann, 100, 332, 425
Mansbach, A., 473
Mantz, Joseph, 31, 239, 242
Manuelito, 312, 313, 314
Marcy, Randolph, 77, 144, 218, 308, 428
Marcy, William L., 46, 67
Marcy-Loring party, 245
Maricopa, 87

Marmaduke, Colonel, 401
Marshall, E.G., 428
Marshall, James W., 419
Marshall, John, 393, 407
Marshall, Joseph, 54
Martin, Juan Blas, 98
Martinez, Antonio Jose, 58, 100, 221, 224, 233, 237, 254, 407, 412, 421, 424
Martinez, Magdalena, 34
Martinez, Mariano, 33
Marty, John, 335
Mary Had a Little Lamb, 391, 458
Mason, John L., 430
Masterson, Bat, 298, 423, 465, 468
Masterson, Bill, 298
Mather, Dave, 460
Mather, Thomas, 293
Matzelinger, Jan Ernst, 466
Maunder Minimum, 391
Maximillian/Emperor of Mexico, 443
Maxwell Land Grant, 161, 190-194, 242, 248, 256, 452, 458, 464, 467
Maxwell Land Grant Case, 466
Maxwell Land Grant Company, 191-196, 242, 248, 256, 267, 452, 458, 462, 464, 467, 469
Maxwell, Hugh H. and Marie Odile, 246
Maxwell, Lucien, 53, 55, 59, 69, 70, 74, 86, 113, 143, 161, 165, 170, 190-192, 197, 220, 234, 243, 246, 257, 260, 277, 305, 450, 452, 456
Maxwell, Luz/Mrs. Lucien, 191, 246
Maxwell, Maria Leonar, 246
Maxwell, Odile Berenisa, 246
Maxwell, Paulita, 246
Maxwell, Peter Menard, 246
Maxwell, Sofia, 246
Maxwell, Virginia, 246
Mayberry, James, 108, 330
McAfee, H., 433
McBride, Amelia, Eliza, and Jennie, 376
McBride, George, 163, 166, 167, 177, 181
McBride, Piedad Dillette/Mrs. George, 376
McCall, Jack, 457
McCandless, James, 439
McCarty, Charles, 468
McClellan, George, 137, 444
McClure, W. P., 128

McComas, H.C. and son Charles, 466
McCook, Edward, 452
McCormick, Cyrus, vi, 404, 412
McCoy, Joseph M., 449
McCready, Albert, 461
McCullouch v. Maryland, 393
McDaniel, John, 29, 413, 414
McDougal, Lloyd and Nancy Lamorie, 333
McDougall, 92, 93
McDougall, Mary Elizabeth, 333
McElroy, Mary Arthur, 204
McFerran, John, 163
McGaa, Denver, 118
McGaa, Mrs. and Mrs. William, 118
McGaa, William, 430
McGee, Robert, 151
McGehee, Micajah, 264, 278
McGregor Western Railway, 268
McHendrie, A.W., 475
McIntyre, James B., 227
McKinley Tariff Act, 471
McKinley, William, 414
McKnight, John, 281
McKnight, Robert, 233, 276, 281, 395, 397, 408
McLaughlin, Red, 467
McLaury, Frank, 465
McLaury, Tom, 465
McLean, Sam, 433
McLeod, Hugh, 26
McLoughlin, Dr. John, 401
McMains, Oscar Patrick, 192-196
McMurtie, J.A., 199, 200, 323
McNair, Alexander, 290
McNees Creek, 286
McNess, Mr., 401
McSween, Alexander, 458
Means, John, 401
Mecklenburg County, iii, vi, ix, 393, 403
Medicine Lodge Treaty, 176, 449
Medina, Carmel, 217
Medina, Juan Rafael, 95, 98
Medina, Louisa, 217
Meeker Massacre, 188, 189, 305, 459
Meeker, Josephine, 188
Meeker, Mrs. Nathan, 188, 189
Meeker, Nathan, 188, 452

Meiklejohn, Alexander /Alec, 336, 362, 365
Meiklejohn, Alexander "Sandy," Jr., 336
Meiklejohn, Lucy Wootton, 336, 362, 363, 381
Meiklejohn, Robert "Bobby" H., 336, 363, 381
Melgares, Facundo, 281, 396
Meline, Colonel, 165
Menard, Pierre, 246
Mercer, Asa, 446
Meriwether, David, 423
Merrick, John L., 123
Merritt, General., 189
Merrival, Joseph, 119
Mesilla (New Mexico), 135, 311, 315, 317, 438, 446, 456
Mestas, Matias, 414
Mestes, Francisco, 98
Metcalf, Archibald, 34, 53, 59, 248, 256
Metcalf, Luz Trujillo, 34, 43, 248
Mexican Central Railroad, 268
Mexican Decree of 1836, 408
Mexican-American War, 54, 61, 65, 66, 68, 105, 110, 225, 226, 233, 234, 240, 241, 245, 264-267, 278, 295, 297, 306, 307, 330, 408, 416, 418, 419, 427, 436
Mexico City, 26, 28, 46, 274, 279, 321, 395, 411, 418, 443
Middle Crossing, 285
Middle Park, 38, 189
Miera, Chipeta, 95, 98, 414
Milam, Benjamin, 407
Miles, Nelson, 455
Military Department of New Mexico, 154
Miller, Robert C., 429
Mills, Melvin, 193
Mills, Ogden M., 342
Mine, Holy Moses!", 470
Mines, Colorado--some by name:, 135
Mine, Minnie 131
Minnnesota Massacre, 440, 441
Minter, E.S., 403
Miranda, Guadalupe, 35, 98, 193, 221, 247, 412
Miranda, Pedro, 35
Mississippi River, 251, 262, 393, 403, 436
Missouri Compromise, vii, 394
Missouri Democrat, 433

Missouri Fur Company, 223
Missouri Intelligencer, 232, 394, 396, 405
Missouri Pacific Railroad,298, 325
Missouri River, 38, 39, 82, 154, 216, 217, 223, 233, 235, 245, 246, 274, 276, 284, 304, 319, 325, 396, 398, 424
Missouri Volunteers, 42, 225, 327, 416, 418
Mitchell, Robert B., 451
Mitchell, General, 158
Mitchell, Levin/Colorado, 33, 40, 55, 87, 89, 94, 96, 99, 242, 423
Modeno, Mariano, 429
Modoc Indians, 265, 454
Mogollon Range, 315
Mojave, 87
Mojave Indians, 400
Monarch Indians, 21
Monfylde, Mary, 340
Monitor and *Merrimack*, 438
Monroe Doctrine, 397
Monroe, James, vi, 293, 392, 395, 398, 404
Montezuma Hot Springs, 324
Montgomery Ward & Co., 454
Montoya, Pablo, 52, 58
Monument Creek, 172
Mooers, John, 173
Moore, Annie, 473
Moore, C.H., 447
Moore, E.M., 447
Moore, Elizabeth Catherine, 243
Moore, George, 447
Moore, James, 321
Moore, John C., 131
Moore, Mary Bent, 228
Moore, R.M., 225, 227
Moore, Scott and Minnie, 461
Moore, William, 165, 243
Mora (New Mexico), 29, 31, 55, 95, 100, 151, 181, 206, 220, 237, 242, 244, 246, 252, 254, 257, 258, 334, 417, 443, 453
Mora Land Grant, 242, 407
Mora River/Valley, 74, 101, 261, 286
Morehead, C.R., 331
Moreno Valley, 165, 191, 450
Moreno Water and Mining Company, 450
Morgan, Captain, 153
Morgan, John Pierpont, 342

Morley, Ada McPherson, 267
Morley, William Raymond, 198-200, 323, 324
Mormon War, 218, 231, 265, 266, 428, 429
Morning News, 41
Morris, Edwin, 134
Morrison, William, 275
Morrow, Albert/Major, 311, 315
Morse, Samuel F.B., 38, 414
Morton, Reverend, 453
Mosby, John Singleton, 319
Motto, Rocco and Eliza, 377
Mountain Branch, 5, 160, 278, 282, 284-286, 320, 322, 328, 427, 435
Mountain Fever, 127
Mountain Meadows, 110, 428
Mt. Baldy, 243
Mt. Blanca, 421
Mt. Robledo, 446
Mt. Tabora, 391
Mt. Vernon Barracks, Alabama, 469
Munnecom, Peter, 166, 167, 205
Munroe, Daniel, 401
Murat, Henri, 118
Murat, Katrina/ Mrs. Henri, 116, 118
Murphy, Joseph, 296
Murphy, Lawrence G., 458
Murray, Lucas, 91
Mussolini, Benito, 467
Mystic Copper Mine, 243
Mystic Lode, 165

N

Naismith, James, 473
Nana, 204, 316, 463, 468
Napoleon III, 443, 453
Napoleonic Wars, 290, 391
Narbona, Antonio/Governor, 23, 399
Nash, Simon, 411
National Day of Fasting and Prayer and Humiliation, 203, 444, 446, 464
Navajo, 7, 11, 44, 47, 63, 64, 87, 97, 148, 149, 165, 176, 216, 234, 306, 307, 311-314, 397, 408, 415, 417-419, 425, 443
Needles, California, 325
Neiland, Albert, 153
Nelson, Jesse, 229, 232, 236, 251
Neosho River, 262, 284, 293

Neosho River Crossing, 3
Neva, 153
New Mexico & Southern Pacific Railway Co. (a name used by the A.T. & S.F.), 322
New York, iii-vi, viii, 14, 38, 234, 254, 290, 326, 342, 397, 399, 404, 411, 426, 427, 430, 433, 442, 454, 459, 471, 473, 475
New York Evening Post, 106
New York Stock Exchange, 454
New York Tribune, 126, 188, 452
New, Bill, 40, 112, 249
New, Mary, 249
Newby, Colonel, 63, 64, 245, 312, 419
Nez Percé, 20, 249
Nez Percé Indian War, 458
Nichols, Captain, 152
Nichols, Charles, 115
Niehans, Fred, 337
Niles Register, 290
Nine Mile Bottom, 236, 251
Nobel, Alfred Bernhard, 449
Norment, Mary, 341
Norment, William, 341
North West Fur Company, 395
Northern Pacific Railway, 321
Northfield, Minnesota, 457
Notre Dame, 336
Nullification Act, 404
Nunn, L.L., 473
Nut, Colonel, 322

O

O'Neil, Jack, 119
O'Neil, Thomas J., 195
O'Neill, B.J., 220
O'Wells, Charles, 338
Oakes & Street, 119
Oakes, D.C., 119, 431
Ocate Creek, 286
Odell, John, 433
Ojo del Oso/Bear Spring, 417
OK Corral, 465
Oklahoma Land Rush, 209, 470
Old Gardiner Mine (Blossburg No. 4), 463
Olin, Dr., 205
Onate, Juan de, 279
O'Neill, Pat, 151

O'Neil's Ranch, 119
Opium War, 413
Oregon Trail, 218, 230, 234, 277, 284, 291, 423
Oregon Treaty, 20, 416
Orem, F.C. "Con", 117
Ortiz Mountains, 401, 405
Ortiz, Jose Francisco, 405
Ortiz, Tomas, 48
Osage Indians, 262, 263, 294, 301, 304, 405
Osborne, Margaret, 340
Osborne, Thomas, 340
Otero, Antonio Manuel, 160
Otero, Miguel A., 171, 184, 199, 200, 322, 458, 466
Outlaws (some of) in Las Vegas, list, 461, 465
Overland Telegraph Company, 438
Owenby, James, 342
Owens, Dick, 36, 73, 234, 249, 250
Owl Creek, 285

P

Pacheco, Joaquin, 96, 98
Pacific Fur Company, 395
Pacific Railway Acts, 319
Pacific Telegraph Company, 438
Packard, Oscar, 153
Packer, Alfred, 183
Padilla, Dolores, 96
Page, Frank, 462
Pah-Ute (Paiute), 21, 278, 423, 437
Pais, Juan (Guerro), 89, 94
Palace of the Governors, 23, 45-47, 140, 287, 396, 452, 456, 460
Palmer, Nathaniel/Captain, 394
Palmer, William, 198, 199, 200, 324, 447, 453
Palmyra Well, 284
Palo Duro Canyon (Texas), 303, 455
Panama Canal, 448
Panic of 1837, 408, 409
Panic of 1857, 428
Panic of 1873, 183, 199
Panic of 1893, 209, 325, 474, 475
Papagos Indians, 400
Parker, Cynthia Ann, 303, 407, 411, 434
Parker, Isaac, 434
Parker, Robert L./ Butch Cassidy, 447

Parker, Samuel, 406
Parker, Topasannah, 434
Parkman, Francis, 416
Pasteur, Louis, 444
Patent Pool Agreement, 425
Patterson, J.D., 331
Pattie, James Ohio, 398-401
Pattie, Sylvester, 398, 399, 401
Pawnee, 39, 48, 107, 158, 179, 218, 227, 229, 285, 302, 304, 307, 409, 417, 418, 426, 431
Pawnee Fork/Crossing, 4, 38
Pawnee River, 285, 444
Pawnee Rock, 105, 285, 422
Payne, Captain, 189
Peace Commission 1866, 314
Pease/Peace River, Texas, 434
Pecos (on Santa Fe Trail), 287
Pecos Pueblo, 27, 410
Pecos River, 148, 280, 304, 313, 314, 398, 440
Pels, M.P, 195
Pena Blanca, 23
Pendleton, George, 444
Penrose, Captain, 176, 451
Peoria Party, 411
Peralta, Pedro de, 287
Perez, Albino/Governor, 7, 32, 406, 408, 409
Perry, Matthew C., 423
Peters, T. J., 320
Pfeiffer, A.H., 446
Philadelphia, iii, 68, 290, 397, 410, 454, 456
Philadelphia Centennial Exposition, 190, 456
Philibert, Joseph, 392
Phillips, Wendell, 308
Pickett, Tom, 463
Picketwire, 18
Pierce, A.E., 433
Pierce, Franklin, 85, 423, 424, 436, 451
Pierce, James H., 143
Pierce, Jane, 443
Pigeon's Ranch, 141, 142, 287
Pike, Albert, 404
Pike Expedition, 275
Pike, Zebulon, 275
Pike's Peak, 114, 121, 124, 126, 133, 134, 275
Pile of Bones, 179
Pile, William, 451
Pilgrims, 443

Pima, 87
Pine River, 462
Pinkerton agents, 195, 470, 473
Piños Altos, 446
Pinto, Father, 270
Pitkin, Frederick, 322, 460
Placerville, 152
Platte, 11, 14, 35, 113, 114, 127, 132, 152, 215, 219, 221, 223, 227, 240, 272, 277, 304, 394, 400, 406, 408, 409, 420, 425, 427, 429, 430, 432
Platte Bridge, 34
Plum Buttes, 285, 449
Plum Creek, 119, 175
Poe, Edgar Allen, vi
Point of Rocks, 285, 286
Poisal, John, 132, 240
Polk, James/President, 42, 66, 224, 415, 416, 419
Polk, Sarah, 473
Pollock, Thomas, 118, 119
Pond Creek, Kansas, 177, 450
Pony Express, 34, 149, 178, 317, 318, 434, 437
Pope, John, 427
Pope, William, 215, 401
Pope's route, 427
Populist Party, 474
Post of Santa Fe, 46, 101
Potato Famine, 415
Powder Face, 179
Powder River Expedition, 231
Powers, Bill, 473
Pratte, Bernard, 220, 252, 398
Pratte, Sylvestre, 23, 398, 400
Price, Martha Head, 266
Price, Sterling, 47, 48, 53, 54, 56-60, 254, 259, 266, 327, 416, 417, 444
Price, William R, 455
Promontory Point, 178, 451
Provost, Etienne, 392
Prowers, John, 230
Pryor, Nathaniel, 401
Pueblo (Colorado), 114, 133, 138, 144, 153, 199, 203, 208, 238, 269, 286, 322, 434, 459, 465, 470
Pueblo Chieftain, 175, 176, 228, 235, 270

Pueblo County courthouse, 144
Pueblo Indians, 26, 29, 33, 50, 302, 304, 306, 311, 314, 420, 424
Pueblo Revolt 1680, 301, 451
Puertecito, 95
Purgatoire (Purgatory) River, 166, 169, 236, 286, 395, 456
Pyle, William, 181

Q

Quahadi Comanche, 455
Quantrill, William, 151, 438, 440, 442
Quantrill's Raiders, 438, 440, 442
Quebec, 274
Quinlan, Tom/Tex, 465
Quinn, Joseph H., 69
Quitman Canyon, 316

R

Rabbit Ears Creek Camp, 286
Ralls, John, 418
Ralston Creek, 113, 114, 420
Ralston, Louis, 113
Randolf, E. J. and family, 195
Randolph, John, 399
Rankin, Violet, 337
Raton Coal & Coking Co., 464
Raton Creek, 162, 164, 328
Raton (New Mexico), 201, 338, 339, 459, 464, 468, 471, 476, 477
Raton Gap, 18
Raton Mountains, 5, 18, 35, 43, 161-163, 184, 186, 193, 198, 284, 476
Raton Pass, 5, 30, 37, 44, 73, 113, 160, 161, 163-167, 177, 181, 183, 185, 191, 198-201, 203, 205, 206, 238, 248, 267, 280, 281, 283, 284, 286, 287, 298, 322, 323, 325, 327-330, 333, 342, 435, 438, 447, 458, 459, 476, 477
Raton Pass road, 161-165, 180, 283, 445, 476
Rattlesnake Springs, 316
Rawhide, 11
Rawlins (Wyoming), 188
Rayado, 35, 234, 239, 246, 247, 249, 257, 286
Rayado Post, 247, 420
Read, Hiram W., 420
Rebellion of 1837, 33, 50, 409, 410

Reconstruction Acts, 448
Red River, 18, 161, 163, 216, 239, 273, 286, 303, 304, 455
Red River War, 186, 304, 455
Reeder, A.H., 424
Reeves, Benjamin, 293
Reitze Henry, 118
Rencher, Abraham, 438
Republic of Texas, 25-27, 29, 41, 266, 408
Republican Party, 133, 426
Republican River, 158, 172
Republican-Democrat Party, 391
Revels, Hiram, 452
Revere, Paul, 392
Reynolds, Major, 63, 64, 73, 264
Reynolds, William V., 231
Rice and Heffner, 118
Rice, Bob, 92
Rice, Elial J., 330
Rice, J. D., 127
Richard, John Baptiste, 34
Richard, Joseph, 128
Richard, Peter, 34
Richard/Rashaw, Joe, 34
Richardson,, Albert D., 126
Richeau, Joseph, 132
Richens, John, iii
Richest Square Mile on Earth, 431
Richmond, Virginia, 230, 231, 311, 329, 437
Rict, Charles, 230
Riddleburger, Matt, 145
Riley, Bennett, 223, 295, 402
Ring, Miss, 132
Ringo, Johnny, 466
Rio Abajo, 288
Rio Arriba, 288
Rio Chama, 279
Rio Colorado, 55, 74
Rio de los Piños, 188
Rio del Almagre, 95
Rio Grande, 15, 26, 39, 42, 45, 46, 55, 62-64, 66, 69, 81, 83, 87, 139, 245, 279, 303, 311, 315, 317, 322, 399, 415, 426, 438
Rio Grande Railroad/D. & R.G., 198-200, 321, 322, 324, 462
Rio Lucero, 245
Rio Pueblo, 245

Rio Sacramento, 61
Ripley, Edward Payson, 325
Robb, Alexander W., 330
Robert, Marshall, 429
Robert, Peter, 54
Roberts, Ben, 139, 438
Robidoux, Antoine, 244, 275, 399, 410, 412
Robidoux, Charles, 59
Robidoux, François/Francisco, 275, 399
Robidoux, Isidore, 275, 399
Robidoux, Joseph, II, 399
Robidoux, Joseph, III, 275, 399
Robidoux, Louis, 275, 399
Robidoux, Michel, 275, 399, 400
Robinson, A.A., 198, 199, 267, 268, 320-323
Rock Corral, 287
Rock Crossing of the Canadian, 286
Rock Island Railroad, 325
Rocky Mountain Fur Company, 230, 240, 402
Rocky Mountain News, 123, 127, 129, 132, 142, 150, 180, 270, 431, 439
Rocky Mountains, 15, 19, 23, 35, 101, 113, 114, 123-125, 127, 135, 155, 215, 218, 222, 230, 231, 236, 244, 245, 251, 252, 263, 270, 277, 325, 393, 394, 398, 415, 431, 447
Roff, Harry, 434
Rogers, Dick, 468
Rogers, Hickory, 433
Rolfe, R.M., 292
Romero, Manuel Antonio, 60
Romero, Miguel, 406
Romero, Tomasito, 51, 58, 59
Romero, Ysidro Antonio, 60
Rooker, Johnnie, 119
Rooker, Rebecca/Mrs. Samuel, 116, 118
Rooker, Samuel, 115
Roosevelt, Franklin D., 465
Roosevelt, Theodore, 430
Ross, Edmund G., 194, 320, 470
Ross, John, 410
Ross, Lewis W., 158
Round Grove, 223, 284, 402
Round Mound, 286
Routt, John, 457, 472
Royal Gorge, 322-324
Rudabaugh, David, 465
Runnels, Jim, 147

Rush-Bagot Agreement, 392
Rusk, Thomas J., 407
Russell, Charles Marion, 222
Russell, Dr. L.J., 429
Russell, Edmund, 401
Russell, Green/William Greeneberry, 113, 114, 142, 143, 241, 420, 429
Russell, John, 114
Russell, Majors, and Waddell, 318
Russell, Marian, 104, 194, 447
Russell, Oliver, 114
Russell, Richard D., 194, 195, 447
Russell, William Hepburn, 126, 317
Russian Mennonites, 321
Ruxton, G.F., 43
Ryder, Ben, 90, 99, 236, 250, 468
Ryder, Children of Ben and Chipeta: Robert, Ben, Willie, Catarina, James, Polly, Lorenza, Anna, 250
Ryder, Chipeta, 90, 99, 250
Rynerson, William, 450

S

Sabille, John, 251, 275
Sacramento (California), 242, 434
Sacramento River Pass, 61
Sacramento Valley, 83, 85, 86, 113, 278, 418, 422
Sacs and Foxes, 251
Saguinet, Charles, 276
Salazar, Damasio, 27, 28
Salazar, Hipolito "Polo", 60
Salazar, Maria del Reyes, 333
Salmon River, 20, 249
Salmon River Mines, 439
Salt Lake, 42, 85, 110, 111, 126, 133, 183, 230, 238, 277, 318, 398, 428, 430, 438
Salt Lake Trail, 111
San Antonio, 26, 28, 267, 307, 407, 411
San Bernardino, California, 86, 231, 260
San Carlos Reservation, 316, 468
San Felipe, New Mexico, 28, 63
San Francisco, 86, 152, 278, 317, 318, 430, 451
San Geronimo, New Mexico, 243
San Jose del Bado, 286
San Juan County War, 463

San Juan Mountains, 71, 74, 133, 183, 264, 434
San Juan River, 15, 64
San Luis Valley, 71, 81, 125, 278, 421, 431
San Miguel del Bado/Vado, 27, 28, 282, 286, 406
Sand Creek, also Sand Creek Massacre:, 154-158, 176, 217, 228, 285, 445
Sandburn, William, 428
Sanders, James, 431
Sanderson, Jared/Colonel, 272, 298
Sandia Mountains, 80
Sandoval, Benito, 40, 94, 95, 98
Sandoval, Choteau, 217
Sandoval, Felix, 95, 97
Sandoval, Gabriel, 474
Sandoval, Juan Ignacio, 97
Sandoval, Juan Isidro, 95
Sandoval, Luisa, 221, 231
Sandoval, Telesfora, 474
Sangre de Cristo Land Grant, 254, 414
Sangre de Cristo Mountains, 54, 71, 141, 275, 287
Sangre de Cristo Pass, 18, 80, 429
Sanserman, Bautista Brison, 275
Santa Ana/President, 28, 30, 49, 406, 407, 414, 423
Santa Clara Springs, 286
Santa Cruz de la Cañada, 62, 409
Santa Fe, vii, 1, 2, 7, 23, 25-27, 43- 50, 53, 60-63, 70, 96, 139, 140, 142, 162, 178, 199, 201, 223, 224, 232, 249, 252, 254, 263, 265, 272, 274, 275, 279, 282, 286, 287, 291, 294, 298, 299, 312, 314, 320, 322, 324, 396, 397, 399, 400, 403, 406, 411, 416-418, 420, 422, 424, 438, 439, 450, 459, 462, 463, 465, 468, 473, 476
Santa Fe/A.T. & S.F. Engine, #2403, "Uncle Dick.", 201, 278, 323, 378
Santa Fe Gazette, 254
Santa Fe *New Mexican*, 209, 420
Santa Fe Pioneers, 26, 27
Santa Fe Plaza, 45, 46, 101
Santa Fe Railroad/A.T. & S.F., 197-203, 206, 242, 261, 267, 268, 291, 298, 320-326, 337, 338, 342, 454, 459, 460, 462-464
Santa Fe Railroad Tunnel, 200, 202

Santa Fe Republican, 229
Santa Fe Ring, 181, 192, 193, 267, 458
Santa Fe Trail, vii, viii, ix, 1, 3, 5, 6, 18, 26-30, 38-40, 42, 44, 76, 80, 88, 99, 101, 103, 104, 107-109, 141, 149, 154, 158, 160-162, 165, 175, 197, 198, 201, 202, 223, 232, 233, 238, 240, 241, 247, 252, 253, 264, 275, 276, 278-302, 304, 309, 320, 322, 325, 327, 328, 397-406, 409- 419, 421, 422, 424-428, 430, 432, 434, 435, 438, 440, 443, 446, 447, 457
Santa Rita copper mine, 13, 233, 399, 408, 411, 442
Santistevan, Juan Delos Reyes, 79
Santo Domingo, 28
Sapello (New Mexico), 101, 298
Sapello River, 101
Savannah (steamship), 393
Sawyer, Mary, 391
Saxon, Walter, 333
Scheurich, Aloys, 223, 235
Schneider, Phil, 185
Schroeder, S., 465
Schurz, Carl, 459
Scolly Grant, 101, 261
Scorch the Earth Policy, 313
Scott, George B., 336
Scott, John, 71, 278, 293
Scott, Winfield, 49, 110, 418
Scudder, Edwin, 125
Scurry, William, 140-142
Sea Islands Hurricane, 475
Sedgwick, John, 427, 434, 435
Segale, Blandina, 168, 175
Selden, Henry, 446
Seminole Indians, 392, 470
Seminole War, 265, 267, 427
Sena, Cristobal, 98
Sequoya, 394, 401, 414
Seven Days' Battle, 427
Seward, William, 443, 448
Seward's Folly/Seward's Icebox, 448
Sharon, Kansas, 164
Shaw, Alston, 153
Shawnee, 19, 408
Sheldon, Lionel A., 463, 464
Sheridan, Philip H., 137, 172, 188, 444, 460
Sherman Antitrust Act, 471

Sherman, Philo, 167
Sherman, William T., 137, 154, 175, 267, 309, 314, 444, 446, 450
Shoshone, 218, 230, 240, 272, 301, 421
Shumate, Charles, 477
Shunk. Dr., 126
Sibley, Dr. John, 266
Sibley, George, 263, 293, 294
Sibley, Henry H., 139-142, 232, 262, 267, 287, 311, 438, 439
Sibley, Samuel Hopkins and Margaret, 266
Sierra de Oro mine, 405
Sierra Nevada Mountains, 85, 222, 318, 417
Silva, Jesus, 35, 193, 194, 256
Silva, Vincente Silva and his Forty Thieves/La Sociedad de Bandidos de Nuevo Mexico, 474
Silva/ Vicente Silva's Thieves by name:, 474
Silver City, 442, 446
Silverton, 133
Simonds, Louey, 55, 56, 59, 234
Simpson, Dr. Robert and Brecia Smith, 257
Simpson, George, 31, 33, 35, 83, 100, 101, 166, 167, 193, 220, 239, 242, 257, 410, 468
Simpson, George and Juanita, children of:, 257
Simpson, Juanita, 33, 220, 257
Simpson's Rest, 257, 258
Singleton, Benjamin, 460
Sioux, 11, 12, 24, 148, 152, 153, 157, 186, 221, 240, 243, 251, 277, 302, 308, 408, 409, 412, 421, 424, 426, 427, 429, 432, 439-441, 443, 447, 456-458
Sivyer, Louise (Mrs.Frank) and children, 375
Six Mile Creek Crossing, 285
Skeratt, Richard, 330
Slaughter, M., 126
Slidell, John, 42, 415
Slough, John P., 140-142, 438, 450
Slover, Isaac, 401
Smith, Alfred N., 339
Smith, Billy, 431
Smith, Dolan B., 329
Smith, Emma, 190
Smith, Henry, 283
Smith, Jack, 156
Smith, Jedediah, 160, 240, 400-403
Smith, John, 89, 115, 156, 430

Smith, John Simpson, 437
Smith, Tom, 400
Smoke, David, 118
Smoke, Mrs. David, 116
Smoky Hills, 451
Smoky Hill area/Route, 149, 176, 448
Snake Indians, 15, 18, 19, 236
Snake River, 20, 38, 219, 277, 458
Snively, Jacob, 28-30, 414
Sobrero, Ascanio, 417
Solomon, H.Z., 132
Solomon River, 426
Solomon's Fork, Kansas, 427
Sonora, Mexico, 86, 253, 400, 404
Sopris, Miss, 132
Sopris, Richard, 120
South Park, 15, 35, 151, 171
South Platte, 11, 13, 151, 217, 427
Spalding, H.H. and Eliza, 408
Spanish Archives of New Mexico, 452
Spanish Commercial Exploration Co., 274
Spanish fever, 111
Spanish Fork, 84
Spanish Lake (Missouri), 251, 252, 255
Spanish Peaks, 215
Spanish Trail/Old Spanish Trail, 279
Sparks, Jack, 151
Spaulding, David, 239
Specie Circular, 408
Speyers, Albert, 38
Spotsylvania, 149, 427
Springer, Frank, 193, 194, 197, 267, 458, 469
St. Charles/San Carlos, 39, 90, 94, 96, 115, 217
St. Charles Town Association/Co., 114, 115, 430
St. Francis Cathedral, 451
St. James Hotel, 192, 454, 466
St. James, L.B., 132
St. Joseph (Missouri), 126, 268, 318, 419, 434, 466
St. Joseph and Denver City Railroad, 268
St. Louis, 8, 24, 31, 39, 80, 82, 86, 113, 121, 122, 127, 128, 215, 219-230, 233, 234, 237, 244, 249, 251-255, 257, 269, 274, 276, 284, 290, 326, 392, 397, 412-414, 421, 430
St. Mars, 275

St. Vrain Cemetery, 216
St. Vrain Creek, 14, 272
St. Vrain, Ceran, vi, 1, 2, 7, 11, 13, 32, 34, 35, 43, 53, 56-59, 87, 97, 125, 143, 151, 176, 181, 220, 222-226, 229, 230, 234, 244, 246, 251-256, 272, 398, 400, 401, 404, 406, 409, 414, 453
St. Vrain, Charles, 256
St. Vrain, Charles Auguste, 251
St. Vrain, Dolores Luna, 252
St. Vrain, Elizabeth Jane Murphy, 255
St. Vrain, Felicitas/Felicité, 252
St. Vrain, Felix, 253
St. Vrain, Felix (Ceran's brother), 404
St. Vrain, Felix (Marcellin's son), 255
St. Vrain, Ignacia Trujillo, 252, 253
St. Vrain, Jacques, 251, 255
St. Vrain, Jacques de Lassus, children of:, 251
St. Vrain, Joseph Felix, 252
St. Vrain, Luisa Branch, 252
St. Vrain, Marcellin, 44, 112, 222, 249, 251, 255, 256, 272, 409, 453
St. Vrain, Marcellin and Elizabeth Jane, children of:, 255
St. Vrain, Marie Felicité, 251, 252, 255
St. Vrain, Mary, 256
St. Vrain, Mary Jane Cope, 256
St. Vrain, Rel, See Bransford, Rel St. Vrain
St. Vrain, Tall Pawnee Woman, 255
St. Vrain, Vicente, 252
Stalwart Republican, 203, 204
Standard Time Act, 467
Stanford, Leland, 201
Stanton, Edwin, 228, 450
Statue of Liberty, 209, 467, 469
Steele, Robert W., 129, 433
Stephenson, George, 319
Steptoe, Edward, 110
Sterling, Colorado, 179, 451
Stilwell, Jack, 173
Stinking Springs, 463, 465
Stinson, A.J. (Jim), 466
Stinson Trail, 466
Stockton & Darlington Railway, 319
Stockton Gang, 464
Stockton, Ike, 463, 464
Stockton, Porter "Port", 463

515

Stockton, Robert F., 49, 278
Stone Fort (Big Timbers), 89, 114, 127, 153, 154, 156, 176, 226, 228, 282, 286, 423, 427, 433
Stone, Dr. J.S., 131
Stonewall, 189, 195, 196, 442
Storrs, Augustus, 293, 398
Stowe, Harriet Beecher, vi, 421
Street, William, 119
Strong, William B., 198, 199, 268, 322, 325
Stuart, James J.E.B., 136, 427, 433, 444
Suaso, Manuel Antonio, 237
Suaso, Teresita, 34, 219, 237, 238, 241, 242, 257
Suaso, Tom, 100, 101, 160
Sublette, Andrew, 11, 221
Sublette, Milton, 23, 240, 400-402, 404
Sublette, Pickney, 404
Sublette, William, 402, 403, 406
Sugarite Creek, 37
Sumner, Edwin V., 101, 421, 427, 434
Sutter, John, 418, 419
Swords, Major, 254

T

Tabasco, Colorado, 339
Tabo Creek Crossing, 284
Tabor, Horace, 465, 475
Tafoya, Frank E., 335
Tafoya, Jesus, 53, 56
Tafoya, Jesus de, 58
Taft, William H., 428
Tall Bear, 437
Tall Bull, 179
Tamme (Duncan) Opera House, 468
Tamme, Charles, 468
Taos, 1, 2, 7, 13, 18, 19, 21, 23, 29, 31, 32, 34-37, 43, 44, 50-60, 62, 64, 65, 69-73, 76, 78-80, 82, 83, 85, 86, 88, 193, 206, 215-217, 220, 222-225, 229, 232, 234, 237, 239, 242, 244-247, 249, 250, 252-254, 256, 262, 263, 272, 279, 294, 303, 304, 332, 398, 400, 401, 409, 411, 418, 420, 422, 423, 443, 456
Taos Massacre and Revolt, 52, 60, 224, 239, 241, 245, 254, 259, 260, 265, 266, 418
Taos Pueblo, 52, 56, 57
Taos Trail, 88

Tappan, Lewis N., 129
Tappan, Samuel (S.F.), 314, 450
Tariff of 1816, 391
Tariff of 1828, ix, 404
Tariff of 1832, 404
Tariff of 1833, ix, 405
Tariff of Abominations, viii, 401
Taylor, Alex, 196
Taylor, Moses, 429
Taylor, Zachary, 42, 49, 419, 420, 436
Tecolote, 246, 286, 447
Telegraph, 134, 438, 451, 458
Telephone, 190, 204, 457, 459, 461, 465, 474
Telfrin, "Russian Bill", 465
Templeton, Jack, 129
Teotihuacan (Mexico), 279
Terrazas, Joaquin/Colonel, 316
Texas Pacific Railway, 248
Texas Panhandle, 37, 79, 155, 186, 273, 404
Texas Rangers, 434
Texas Volunteers, 140, 141, 438
Texas-(Santa Fe) New Mexico Expedition, 25, 140, 413
Thanksgiving, 443
Tharp, Edward, 33, 259, 261
Tharp, Louis, 259
Tharp, William/Bill, 33, 35, 40, 258
Thatcher Brothers, 331
The Caches, 4
The Lantern, 452
The Liberator, 403
The Long Walk, 313
The Quincy (1st American railroad), 319
Thing, Joseph, 249
Thomas, W.R., 180
Thoreau, Henry David, 392
Thornburg, Thomas, 188
Tillotson Academy (Trinidad, Colorado), 338
Tilton, Dr. Henry, 235
Timpas, 286, 298
Tobin, Bartholomew and Sarah, 259
Tobin, Narciso, 259
Tobin, Pasquala Maria Bernal, 259
Tobin, Pasqualita, 259
Tobin, Rosita Quintana, 259
Tobin, Thomas, Jr., 259
Tobin, Tom, 33, 54, 74, 76, 207, 216, 235

Todd, L.L., 131
Tokyo Bay, 423
Tolby, Franklin, 192, 193, 456
Tolque, Louis, 54
Topeka, Kansas, 326
Torres, Juan Cruz, 164
Totten, Oscar, 433
Towne, Charley, 53, 59, 69, 112, 260
Towne, Maria Antonia Montano, 260
Townsite Act of 1844, 38, 415, 448
Townsite Act of 1867, 449
Trader/traders, vii, ix, 2, 5, 7, 8, 10-12, 21, 23, 29, 31, 32, 36, 38-40, 42-44, 53, 79, 89, 93, 108, 113, 154, 155, 165, 176, 223, 225, 226, 229, 233, 235, 240, 244, 252, 254, 255, 258, 270, 272, 274, 275, 279, 281-283, 288-291, 295, 296, 301, 303, 308, 327, 391, 395-398, 401- 404, 406, 408,-410, 412, 414, 415, 417, 418, 449, 472
Trail of Tears, 20, 410
Trammell, Colonel, 233
Trapani, Lena May Wootton, 333
Trapani, Settimo, 333
Trappers' rendezvous, 399
Trapping, 13, 15-19, 21-23, 32, 35, 37-39, 62, 216, 218, 221, 225, 230, 236, 239, 240, 243, 244, 249, 259, 263, 264, 274, 276, 281, 290, 392, 398-400, 404, 409, 410
Travis, Joseph, ix
Treaty of Bosque Redondo, 450
Treaty of Cordoba, 395
Treaty of Ghent, vi
Treaty of Guadalupe Hidalgo, 66, 68, 419
Treaty of Nanking, 413
Treaty of Wanghia, 415
Tres Castillos, Mexico, 316
Trevithick, Richard, 319
Trias, Angel/Governor, 61
Trinchera Pass, 280
Trinidad, 161, 163-167, 169, 170, 183, 185, 195, 196, 198, 200, 203-206, 208-210, 220, 236, 240, 243, 250, 256-258, 269, 270, 280, 286, 298, 322, 323, 329, 330-333, 335-337, 339, 441, 457, 458, 462, 465, 467,469, 471, 473, 475
Trinidad and Ratoon [sic] Mountain Wagon Road Company, 445

Trinidad War, 169, 170
Trudeau, Pierre, 173
Trujillo, Anastasia, 217
Trujillo, Antonio Maria, 60
Trujillo, Jose Francisco and Natividad , 248
Trujillo, Juan Chiquito, 90, 95, 217
Trujillo, Juan Ramon, 60
Trujillo, Paula, 183
Trujillo, Pedro, 414
Trujillo, Vicente, 248
Truman, Harry, 467
Tuecto, New Mexico, 411
Tunstall, John H., 458
Turbush, Albert, 54
Turcotte, François, 275
Turkey Creek, 158, 286, 294, 466
Turley, Jesse, 260
Turley, Simeon, 53, 215, 216, 239, 259
Turley's Mill, 53, 54, 215, 216, 275
Turner, Frederick Jackson, 210, 475
Turner, Nat, ix, 404
Twiss, Thomas, 426, 429, 431, 432
Tyler, C. M., 152
Tyler, John, 24, 412, 414, 415, 438
Tyler, Letitia, 413

U

U. S. Army's Topographical Engineers, 233
U. S. Camel Corps, 425
U. S. Department of Agriculture, 441
U. S. Government, 30, 154, 186, 265, 275, 276, 412, 424, 456, 470
U. S. Military Academy, 436
U. S. Naval Academy, 415
U. S. Peace Commission, 449
U. S. Post Office Department, 420
U. S. Supreme Court, 193, 194, 197, 393, 407, 458, 469
Uinta River, 410
Uintah Reservation, 469
Una de Gato, 18
Uncompahgre River, 83, 84, 183, 412, 462
Union, vi, ix, 99, 110, 133-135, 137-142, 144, 146, 154, 161, 218, 227, 254, 256, 261, 265-267, 269, 271, 282, 311, 317, 319, 339, 435, 437-440, 442- 446, 448, 454, 469
Union Colony, 188

Union Day School, 128, 129, 132
Union Pacific Railroad, 178, 231, 235, 317, 319, 451
United Mine Workers of America, 471
United States Government, 18, 29, 34, 38, 39, 41, 42, 47, 55, 66, 99, 101, 158, 164, 172, 181, 189, 226, 227, 231, 234, 240, 248, 276, 277, 305, 309, 314, 319, 409, 419, 421, 424, 426, 437, 442, 446, 455
University of Colorado begins, 458
Upper (Flag) Creek, 283
Upper (Flag) Spring, 286
Upper Crossing, 285
Ursuline College (Tiffin, Ohio), 206, 336, 337
Ute, 21, 23, 31, 36-40, 62, 69, 70, 73, 74, 76-78, 81, 83-85, 93-98, 101, 126, 148, 165, 166, 169, 170, 171, 186-189, 216, 218, 230, 234, 243, 247, 248, 251, 262-264, 272, 302, 305, 307, 313, 405, 409, 412, 414, 415, 418-420, 422, 424, 441, 458
Ute Creek, 421
Ute Pass, 171

V

Vaillant, Jean, 275
Valdez, Jose Maria, 35
Valdez, Pedro, 245
Valdez-Lobato, Mrs. Juana Catalina, 52
Valencia, Jose Ignacio, 95, 98
Vallé, Alexander, 141
Valley Station, 152
Valverde Mesa, 421
Van Buren, Martin, 408, 439
Vancouver, 20
Vanderwalker, George, 6, 158
Vasquez, Louis, 11, 125, 221, 230, 410
Vasquez, Pike, 132
Vega, Cruz, 192
Vera Cruz, Mexico, 279, 418
Vialpando, Jesus, 96
Vicksburg, 149, 255, 442
Victor Cole and Coke Co., 333
Victor Emmanuel II, 438
Victoria, Princess/Queen, 394, 409, 411
Vidal, Lame, 275
Vigil, Cornelio, 35, 50, 52, 193, 253, 257
Vigil, Donaciano, 47, 48, 415

Vigil, Guadalupe, 95, 98
Vijil Montes, Juan de Jesus and Juana Catarina Valdez de Vijil, 245
Vigil-St. Vrain Land Grant, 87, 253, 414, 435
Villard, Henry, 126
Villasur, Pedro, 327
Virginia City, 165, 191, 431
Virginia Dale, 443
Viscarra, Jose Antonio, 397

W

W.G. Rifenburg Hose Co. (Trinidad), 331
Waddell, William, 317
Wagon master, 99, 103, 104, 223, 287, 294, 304, 444
Wagon Mound, 30, 76, 241, 286, 322, 420
Waite, Davis, 474
Waldo, David, 43, 55, 223, 402
Waldo, Lawrence, 55
Waldo, William, 55, 402
Walker, Eliza Wootton, 164, 180, 183, 205, 208, 342, 465
Walker, Frances Virginia "Jennie", 329
Walker, Mary Eliza "Lizzie", 329
Walker, Olive Agnes "Ollie", 329
Walker Tariff, 416
Walker, Thomas, 168
Walker, William/Judge, 161, 164, 166-168, 180, 183, 205, 208, 298, 329, 330
Wallace, H., 434
Wallace, Lew, 193, 458-464
Walnut Creek, 38, 158, 258, 285, 432, 444
Walsenburg (CO), 215, 236, 250, 251, 468
War of 1812, vi, 242, 262, 276, 290, 392, 393, 407
Ward, Aaron Montgomery, 453
Ward, George M., 468
Warfield, Charles, 29, 413
Warren, Thomas, 118
Wasatch Mountains, 15, 84
Washington, D. C, 38, 120, 148, 167, 227, 391-393, 395, 397, 398, 400-405, 412, 414-416, 419, 420, 427, 437, 441, 444-448, 450, 453, 454, 464, 469
Washington, George, iii, 32, 435
Washington, Lt. Col. John M., 312
Washington Treaty of 1880, 305

Washita River, 176, 451
Waters, Candelaria, 33
Waters, James, 18, 33, 112, 259, 261
Waters, Patrick, 435
Watrous, Belina, 261
Watrous, Emeteria, 261
Watrous, Erastus and Nancy (Bowman), 261
Watrous, Joe, 261, 283
Watrous, Josephine Chapin, 261
Watrous, Louisa, 261
Watrous, Maria/Mary A., 261
Watrous, Rose/Rosa, 261
Watrous, Rose Chapin, 261
Watrous, Samuel, 146, 261, 429
Watrous, Tomacita/Tomasita, 261
Watson, Thomas, 190
Watts, Ella, 336
Webb, J.J., 460, 465
Webster, Daniel, viii, 24, 27, 32, 66, 67, 110, 413, 422
Webster, Noah, 401
Webster-Hayne Debate, 402
Weichell, Maria, 179
Weightman, Richard Hanson, 424
Wells, Dr. Horace, 38
Wells Fargo, 318, 447
Wentworth, John, 41
West Point, 266, 267, 415, 427
Westinghouse Electric Co., 473
Westinghouse, George, 473
Westmore, Alphonso, 293
Westport, 18, 24, 25, 35, 80, 82, 106, 121, 205, 220, 225-227, 273, 282, 284, 287, 290, 410, 445
Whealington, Tom "Red River", 468
Wheaton, Frank, 454
Whetstone Creek, 286
Whetstone Springs, 76, 77
Whigham, Harry, 256
Whigs, 24, 42
Whipple, A.W., 245
White Antelope, 153
White Indians, 15, 58
White Massacre, 76-78, 239, 242, 245, 259, 420
White Mountain reservation, 457
White Oaks, 461

White River Agency, 188, 189
White Rock, 179
White Singing Bird/Chipeta (wife of Ouray; also see pages with Ouray), 462
White, Chandler, 429
Whiterock River, 410
Whitman, Marcus, vi, 35, 230, 406, 413, 414, 418
Whitman, Narcissa, 418
Whitman, Walt, 394
Whitney, Eli, vi
Whitsitt, Richard, 115, 128
Whittlesey, George, 249
Whittlesey, J. H., 73
Whittlesey, Lt., 265
Whittlesey, Maria, 89
Whittlesey, Tom, 89
Wichita Indians, 449
Wild Bunch, 448
Wild West Show, 466
Wildenstein, Carl, 261
Wilder, Edward, 321
Wildman, Augustus, 121, 138
William's Fort, 225
Williams, Andrew J., 115, 125, 126
Williams, Antonia Baca, 262
Williams, B.D., 120, 432
Williams, William/Bill, 18, 34, 69-74, 79, 106, 112, 222, 239, 257, 277, 278, 293, 305, 400, 410, 419
Williams, Captain Charles, 97
Williams, Charles D., 79, 83, 193, 244, 420
Williams, Jose, 262
Williams, Joseph and Sarah Musick, 261
Williams, Mary, 262
Williams, Sarah, 262
Williams, Walter Charles, 334
Williamson, Ad, 153
Williamson, James, 194
Willock, Lieutenant Colonel, 56
Willoughby and Avery, 125
Willow Bar, 38, 285
Willow Springs, 286
Wilson, Woodrow, 426
Wind River, 38
Winter the stars fell, 405
Winternitz, David, 447

Wittman. Joseph, 419
Wolf Creek, 286, 410
Wolf Fire, 425
Wolf Mountain, 286
Wolfskill, William, 279, 397
Womack, Robert, 472
Wood Lake, 440
Wool, General, 61
Wootton (Colorado), 201, 323, 335-338, 342, 445, 454, 466, 468, 471, 475
Wootton (on Santa Fe Trail), 286
Wootton, Alexander James, vii, 206, 373, 399, 475
Wootton, Alfred Adolph, 333
Wootton, Alice Phillips, 332
Wootton, Arthur Jay, 333
Wootton, Bessie Fuss, 337, 363-365
Wootton, Charlotte Fredricka Deckard, 338
Wootton, Children of R.L., Jr, 330
Wootton, Cora C., 333
Wootton, David and Frances/Fannie, iii, viii, 371, 403; their faith, 371
Wootton, David Christopher, iii, vi, 147, 340,
Wootton, David C., Jr., vii, 206, 372, 397
Wootton, Dolores, 71, 73, 80, 82, 83, 87-89, 100, 112, 181, 183, 239, 250, 425
Wootton, Dorothy Marguerite, 337
Wootton, Dorothy May, 338
Wootton, Eileen Wilson, 337
Wootton, Eliza Ann (Dick's daughter), 73, 80, 89, 100, 108, 128, 131, 147, 161, 329, 354, 379
Wootton, Eliza Ann (Dick's sister), ix, 404
Wootton, Ethel Lucille Owen, 339
Wootton, Eva E., 332
Wootton, Evelyn Bailey, 337
Wootton, Evelyn Louise, 337
Wootton, Fannie Brown, 147, 160, 238, 334, 443
Wootton, Fanny (William's daughter), 203
Wootton, Fanny F., 333
Wootton, Fidelis, 183, 184, 190, 201, 203, 329, 334, 335, 357, 359, 365, 381, 454, 477
Wootton, Florence Walker, 183, 330
Wootton, Frances (Dick's sister), ix, 18
Wootton, Frances Dolores, 82, 89, 100, 128, 147, 164, 329, 332, 421
Wootton, Frances E., 409
Wootton, Frances Loraine, 337
Wootton, Frances Virginia (Dick's daughter), 160, 183, 205, 334, 444
Wootton, Frances Virginia Brame, vi, 206, 370, 371
Wootton, Frank, 131, 147, 160, 183, 332, 434
Wootton, Frank Christopher, 205, 208, 210, 335, 338, 359, 360, 366, 468
Wootton, Frank Christopher, Jr., 338, 368
Wootton, Freddie E, 333
Wootton, George, 89, 100, 147, 150, 160, 183, 329, 424
Wootton, Gerardus, 205, 334, 466
Wootton, Glenda Scott, 337
Wootton Hall, 120
Wootton, Helen Jenette, 338
Wootton, Ida Dillon, 184, 186, 190, 206, 210, 334-336, 360, 454
Wootton, James, 333
Wootton, Jennie Catharine Cavaleto, 339
Wootton, Jesse, 205, 210, 335, 339, 359, 360
Wootton, Jesse Owen ("Jr."), 339 , 381
Wootton, John (Dick's grandfather), 340
Wootton, John Christopher, vi, 392
Wootton, John Peter, Jr./Johnnie, 337
Wootton, John Peter, Sr., 203, 205, 206, 208, 210, 334, 335, 358-360, 368, 369, 381, 456
Wootton, John Peter/Johnie, 190, 203, 334, 337, 458
Wootton, Jose Manuel, 100, 329, 425
Wootton, Joseph, (Dick's son), 108, 147, 160, 183, 186, 190, 205, 330, 332
Wootton, Joseph Edward, ix, 113, 119, 406
Wootton, Joseph Gerald, 337, 338
Wootton, Lena May, 333
Wootton, Lillie Mae, 205, 333
Wootton, Lorett, 87, 89, 100, 128, 147, 329, 422
Wootton, Lucy Anne, 190, 206, 210, 334, 358
Wootton, Lucy May Huntley, 205, 330
Wootton, Marjorie, 339
Wootton, Mary (Dick's daughter), 205, 338, 358, 463, 469
Wootton, Mary Ann Manning, 112, 113, 116, 117, 118, 129, 131, 144
Wootton, Mary Catherine, vi, 393

Wootton, Mary Fannie, 205, 335, 467, 468
Wootton, Mary Pauline (John, Sr.'s daughter), 337
Wootton, Mary Pauline Lujan, 184, 201, 203, 205, 206, 208, 239, 352, 346, 348, 356, 365, 381, 476
Wootton, May Tynes, 338, 339, 366, 368
Wootton, Nellie, 333
Wootton, Olive Johnson, 338
Wootton, Oliver, 333
Wootton Place, 208
Wootton, Powell, viii, 130, 206, 402, 475
Wootton, R. L., Jr., 80, 89, 100, 108, 119, 147, 160, 164, 180, 183, 193, 205-207, 210, 329, 355, 357, 420, 447, 457, 458, 465, 467, 471
Wootton Ranch, 162, 183, 207, 329, 334, 349, 350, 453, 454
Wootton, Richens Lacy (Frank C.'s son), 338, 368
Wootton, Richens Lacy (John, Sr.'s son), 337
Wootton, Richens Lacy/Dick/Uncle Dick, i, iii, vii, ix, 1-4, 6-24, 31-36, 39, 52-59, 61-64, 69, 71-73, 75-100, 102-121, 123-125, 127-135, 138, 142-151, 153, 155, 157, 158, 160-166, 169, 171, 175, 177, 180,-184, 186-188, 190, 192-194, 197, 199-210, 215-219, 221, 223, 225, 228, 236, 241, 243-245, 248, 250, 251, 254, 256-259, 262, 265-267, 271, 280, 283-285, 287, 298, 305, 306, 323, 327-329, 332, 335, 337-340, 342, 345-347, 351, 353, 356, 378, 391, 406-410, 412-416, 418-425, 430- 434, 437, 443, 445, 450, 452, 453, 458, 461, 463, 465, 466, 469-476
Wootton, Robert Milton, 337
Wootton, Samuel, iii, 340
Wootton, Samuel F. (Dick's brother), 160, 401
Wootton Station, 208
Wootton, Stella Fram, 337
Wootton, Thomas, vii, 82, 394, 421
Wootton, William (Dick's brother), vii, 18, 398, 410
Wootton, William (Dick's son), 112, 147, 160, 183, 186, 203, 205, 430
Wootton, William Leslie, 337
Wootton, William R., 333
Wootton/Hunter, Chrystella Pauline, 339
Wootton/Hunter, Leroy Lawrence, 339

Workman, David, 232
Workman, William, 242, 260
World's Columbian Exposition, 209, 210, 473
Wyatt, N.S., 119
Wynkoop, Major, 153, 154

Y

Yara, Francis, 96
Year with No Summer, vi
Yellow Tavern, Virginia, 444
Yellowstone, 20, 230, 231, 397, 447, 453, 457
Young Men's' Christian Association, 473
Young, Albert, 331
Young, Brigham, 85, 110, 111
Young, Ewing, 23, 233, 400, 401
Young, Frances D. Wootton, 183, 332, 357
Young, George, 332
Young, Henry, 332
Young, John, 332
Young, L. (Lottie or Lily), 332
Young, Minerva, 332, 353, 357
Young, R.L. "Dick", 332
Young, Thomas, 164, 298, 331, 332
Young, William R., 332
Younger and James Gang, 457
Yuma, 86, 87, 146

Z

Zacatecas, Mexico, 279
Zamora, Felipe, 331
Zubria, Bishop, 404
Zuni Indians, 312

www.ingramcontent.com/pod-product-compliance
Lightning Source LLC
Chambersburg PA
CBHW080720300426
44114CB00019B/2433